JESUS CHRIST
His Life and Teaching

VOLUME ONE
The Beginning of the Gospel

D0875106

Metropolitan
HILARION ALFEYEV

JESUS CHRIST

His Life and Teaching

In Six Volumes

VOLUME ONE

THE BEGINNING
OF THE GOSPEL

ST VLADIMIR'S SEMINARY PRESS
YONKERS, NEW YORK
2018

Library of Congress Cataloging-in-Publication Data

Names: Ilarion, Metropolitan of Volokolamsk, 1966– author.
Title: The beginning of the Gospel / Metropolitan Hilarion Alfeyev.
Other titles: Nachalo Evangeliiã. English
Description: Yonkers, New York : St Vladimir's Seminary Press, 2018. | Series: Jesus
    Christ : his life and teaching ; volume one | In English; translated from Russian. |
    Includes bibliographical references.
Identifiers: LCCN 2017049722 (print) | LCCN 2017050284 (ebook) | ISBN
    9780881416084 | ISBN 9780881416060
Subjects: LCSH: Jesus Christ—Person and offices. | Bible. Gospels.
Classification: LCC BT203 (ebook) | LCC BT203 .I427 2018 (print) | DDC 232—dc23
LC record available at https://lccn.loc.gov/2017049722

ST VLADIMIR'S SEMINARY PRESS
575 Scarsdale Road, Yonkers, NY 10707
1-800-204-2665
www.svspress.com

ISBN 978–088141–608–4 (paper)
ISBN 978–088141–606–0 (electronic)

Unless noted otherwise, scriptural quotations are taken from the King James Version, with some modifications for accuracy or ease of comprehension. Psalms are cited according to the Septuagint (LXX) numbering, which differs from the Hebrew numbering (used by most English translations) in Pss 9–147: LXX Ps 9 = Heb. Pss 9–10; LXX Pss 10–112 = Heb. 11–113; LXX 113 = Heb. 114–115; LXX 114 = Heb. 16.1–9; LXX 115 = Heb. 116.10–19; LXX 116–145 = Heb. 117–146; LXX 146 = Heb. 147.1–11; LXX 147 = Heb. 147.12–20.

TABLE OF CONTENTS

Chapter 7

JESUS AND HIS OPPONENTS:
THE BEGINNING OF THE CONFLICT   465

FOREWORD

Jesus Christ—throughout history there has never been a person about whom so much has been written. The bibliography on him includes the Gospels; the Epistles of the apostles; the works of the Church Fathers; the liturgical texts of the Eastern and Western Churches; the numerous christological treatises of various epochs; the works of Orthodox, Catholic, and Protestant theologians; the reflections on the "historical Jesus" of recent authors; and fictional and scholarly literature. This bibliography consists of hundreds of thousands of volumes, millions of pages; to become acquainted with them is beyond the capabilities of not only a single person, but also an entire research institute. Two thousand years after Jesus Christ came into the world we sense the prophetic power of the words that conclude the Gospel of John: "And there are also many other things which Jesus did, which, if they should be written every one, I suppose that even the world itself could not contain the books that should be written" (Jn 21.25).

Throughout history there has been no other person to whom such a quantity of works of art has been dedicated. The person of Jesus and the events of his life have been documented for us in numerous portraits, beginning with the frescoes of the Roman catacombs from the second to the fourth centuries, the mosaics of Ravenna in the fifth and sixth centuries, the vast number of Byzantine and Russian icons, the Western medieval pictures and statues, the works of the artists of the age of the Renaissance, and ending with works that have appeared in recent history and that continue to appear before our eyes.

Musical works have been dedicated to Jesus Christ, beginning with early Christian liturgical music, including the numerous cantatas and magnificent *Passions* by Bach, right up to the rock opera *Jesus Christ Superstar* and the works of modern-day composers in both the classical and popular genres.

Among the vast list of artistic works devoted to Jesus we must include the twentieth-century screen versions of his life and its various episodes, as well as the huge number of documentary films on the story of Jesus and his disciples, on the locations where his life took place, on the various aspects of his ministry and teaching, and on the beginning and growth of the Church that he founded.

Of no single person has so much been spoken as has been said and continues to be said of Jesus Christ. In the decades after his death and resurrection information on him was disseminated mainly orally, and it was only at a later stage of her development that the Church began to document the oral traditions in written form. But even after the Gospels were written, Christian worship was necessarily accompanied by the oral preaching of a bishop or priest. Thus it has continued for almost two thousand years. And now in hundreds of thousands of Christian churches throughout all parts of the globe, at each service Jesus is preached, and each time an Orthodox or Catholic priest, or a Protestant pastor, endeavors to say something about this Man.

No other figure in human history has been the subject of so much scholarly research. A whole division of Christian theological scholarship—Christology—is devoted to a rational analysis of the phenomenon of Jesus Christ. Thousands of professors from their university chairs lecture on Jesus, on the various characteristics of his personality and the aspects of his teaching, on the episodes of his life, and hundreds of thousands of students write theses and dissertations on these topics. In many countries the life and teaching of Jesus is studied as part of the school curriculum, and millions of children listen to their teachers narrating to them the story of Jesus of Nazareth.

By now so much has been written and said on Jesus that it would appear that there is nothing more to be added to that which has long been said. And yet, each new age generates new attempts to understand his personality, and in each new generation religious ministers, theologians, writers, poets, artists, and composers turn towards this figure, not to mention the

The Savior,
icon, 14th c.

millions of simple people, believers and non believers, each of whom tries
to find his or her own Jesus and his or her own answer to the question of
who he is.

This series of books, offered to the reader's attention under the general
title *Jesus Christ: His Life and Teaching*, is not a retelling of the life of Jesus;
it is not a "biography" in the conventional sense of the word. Many facts
of his life remain unknown to us. In Jesus' biography there are important
lacunae that cannot be filled in. It is enough to say that, with the exception
of one episode (Lk 2.41–52), we know nothing of his childhood and youth:
we do not know what he was doing until he reached thirty years of age.

And, nevertheless, the entire series has a biographical character, since
its central theme is the *human* story of Christ. The task of the present
series of books is not to expound Orthodox Christology—the teaching on
Jesus as God and Man with a description of the heresies that have arisen

and the Church's refutation of them. This description was given in our book series *Orthodox Christianity*, where a large section was devoted to Christology.[1] Here we are setting a different task: to reproduce the living image of Jesus on the basis of the sources available and to present his teaching as it is reflected in the Gospels.

Attention will be concentrated upon the features of his character and perception of the world, as well as the peculiarities of his means of communicating with people. However, Jesus was not a conventional person: he was God incarnate. And all the details of his human story have a direct bearing on the revelation that God gave to people through his only begotten Son. Showing through his human features are the features of the divine countenance; his human word is the word of God addressed to people. It is this that gives his person and teaching a completely special and exclusive significance.

The basic source for us has been the four canonical Gospels, the material from which is examined using a broad range of additional sources, including the Old Testament, the works of ancient historians, the commentaries on the Gospels by the Church Fathers, and contemporary scholarly literature.

Scholarly and critical study of the New Testament has been carried out for more than two centuries; in this time a huge amount of material has accumulated. However, all the existing mass of material, which is truly boundless, in itself requires a critical approach. From the vast heritage of scholars who have researched the New Testament, it is necessary to select that which enables a better understanding of the text, while at the same time casting aside those hypotheses and conclusions that give rise to additional and unnecessary complications.

This series of books on Jesus is not so much for those Christians who are rooted in holy tradition as it is for non-believers, those who doubt and who are hesitant. In the first instance, it may give some answers to those who believe that Jesus never even existed. Secondly, it is for those who admit that Jesus existed, but do not believe that he is God. Thirdly, it

---

[1]See Vol. 1, pp. 47–54 for the historical context and Vol. 2, pp. 287–299 for doctrinal analysis. *Orthodox Christianity* is a five-volume series, published by St Vladimir's Seminary Press.

is for those who perhaps consider themselves Christians, but relate to the Gospel narratives skeptically or view the Gospels through the prism of the criticism to which it was subjected in the works of Western specialists on the New Testament in the nineteenth and twentieth centuries.

We do not intend to sift consistently through the ideas of these specialists, although we will turn to them, at times agreeing with them, at times critiquing and refuting them. Our main task in relation to these ideas is to attempt to separate the wheat from the chaff, and the conscientious analysis of texts from the speculations and hasty conclusions that proceed from certain ideological presuppositions.

The general title of the series points towards its main hero—Jesus Christ. In the Gospel narratives and other sources we will use for our research we will seek out, first of all, that which relates directly to his person, character, biography, and teaching. Other persons of the Gospel story will be touched upon only in as far as they are essential for reconstructing the image of Jesus.

Ultimately, we would like to answer the main question of what Jesus has brought to people and why he is necessary for people today. Two thousand years have passed since he lived and taught: why are his image and preaching as relevant as before? What can Jesus give us, who live in the twenty-first century with all of its complications, challenges, problems, and tragedies?

The Gospel story of Jesus Christ from the perspective of interpretation may be compared to a collection of treasures amassed over two thousand years in a safe with two locks. In order to touch this treasure, we have first of all to open the safe, and in order to open it, two keys are required. One key is the belief that Jesus was fully man with all the attributes of a real flesh-and-blood person. However, we need a second key also—belief that Jesus was God incarnate. Without this key the safe will not open, and the treasures will not glisten with their original brilliance: the Gospel image of Christ will not come to the reader in all its resplendent beauty.

Both keys will be used in our investigation. We will unpack and examine each of the treasures contained in the safe together with the reader.

The Four
Evangelists,
icon, 16th c.

The Orthodox reader may be surprised that in this and in further books of the series we will call our hero by the name that was given to him at birth, and not substitute for this name the titles more usual in Church tradition: the Lord, the Savior, the Son of God. We do this consciously for a number of reasons. Firstly, all four evangelists call him by the name of "Jesus." Secondly, our books are aimed not only at those who "by default" believe Jesus to be Lord, Savior, and the Son of God: it is important to us to *prove* to the reader that Jesus was precisely the One whom the Church accepts him to be. Thirdly, as has already been said, we are interested primarily in the human history of the Son of God, his earthly biography, which begins with his birth and the bestowing of the name of Jesus upon him (Mt 1.25).

In one of the concluding episodes of this story, as set forth in the Gospel of John, the Apostle Thomas, who was absent at the first appearance of the risen Christ, refuses to believe in his resurrection. Eight days later Jesus again appears to a group of apostles. This time Thomas is among them. Jesus shows him the wounds on his body and says, "Be not faithless, but believing" (Jn 20.27). Thomas exclaims, "My Lord and my God!" (Jn 20.28).

Doubting Thomas, panel from Duccio's Maestá Altarpiece of Siena, 1311.

Jesus becomes Lord and God for those who turn from faithlessness to belief. It is our burning desire that each one who reads the Gospels should close that book with the very words pronounced by Thomas. Our journey along the pages of the Gospel text, which we begin in this book, is ultimately driven by this goal.

As the first book in a six-volume series, this book covers the material contained in the opening chapters of the four Gospels: the book examines the narratives about the birth of Jesus and the events connected with it; about the baptism of Jesus and his relationship with John the Baptist; and about the temptation by the devil in the wilderness. Separate thematic chapters are devoted to the prophetic ministry of Jesus, the relationship between Jesus and his disciples, and the beginning of the conflict between him and his opponents. At the end of the book we shall attempt to draw a portrait of Jesus as he is depicted in the Gospels, and examine his way of life and the basic features of his character.

The examination of the Gospel texts is preceded by a short history and analysis of the modern-day state of New Testament scholarship, as well as

Christ the Redeemer, icon, St Andrei Rublev, 1420s.

a description of the sources that we will work with in this and later books in the series.

The second book in the series will be devoted to the Sermon on the Mount (Mt 5–7). The third and fourth books will be devoted, respectively, to the miracles and parables of Jesus. In the fifth book we will turn to those elements of the Gospel of John which do not have parallels in the Synoptic Gospels. The sixth book will examine the narratives about the last days of Jesus' life, his suffering, death, and resurrection. It is in the light of these narratives, which comprise the culminating point of each of the four Gospels, that we find the full meaning of the person and deeds of Jesus Christ—the Son of God and the Son of Man.

Chapter 1

IN SEARCH OF THE "HISTORICAL JESUS"

F or centuries people have tried to solve the enigma of Jesus. No other historical person has drawn so much attention to himself, yet at the same time no other person has evoked such heated debate and contradictory opinions about himself, or so much love and hatred simultaneously.

These arguments began during his lifetime, and they are clearly reflected in the pages of the Gospels. After his death, the arguments did not abate; they have not died down to this day. People have radically different attitudes towards Jesus and differ in their evaluation of his ministry and influence, in their perception of who he was and what he taught.

Ardent love for Jesus has for almost two millennia now coexisted with a fierce hatred towards him. Thousands and millions of people throughout this time have endured great sufferings and death simply for the fact that they believed in Jesus as God and Savior. And to this day the persecution of his followers continues. Some, from love of Jesus, are ready to be deprived of their homes, families, health, and their very life; others, out of hatred for Jesus, are prepared to commit the most terrible crimes, including the mass murder of Christians.

"Think not that I am come to send peace on earth: I came not to send peace, but a sword" (Mt 10.34). These strange words of the One who taught meekness and humility, non-resistance to evil, and love towards enemies again and again remind us of the antinomical character of Christianity, which would appear to have been made for another planet, another world.

Christ with a sword,
fresco, 15th c.

And nevertheless, historical Christianity developed here, on our planet. And it is on this earth, in the very thick of our human community that there appeared the One who was to be become "a sign which shall be spoken against" (Lk 2.34) for all following epochs. Today there are those who believe in him as God incarnate; there are those who recognize him only as a prophet and teacher of morality; there are those who fiercely hate him and his followers; and there are those who altogether deny his historicity. Finally, there are many people in the world who know very little about Jesus: these are the inhabitants of the vast and densely populated regions where the preaching of Christianity has yet to unfold in full measure.

In the present chapter we will at first dwell on the question of whether Jesus was a real historical person. Then we will speak of the authority of those witnesses on whose evidence the facts about Jesus and his teaching rest. Further, we will bring to bear evidence of his divine nature, gathered and systematized by Church tradition. The chapter will conclude with a short overview of the search for the "historical Jesus," which has been undertaken by scholars in the past two centuries.

1. Did Jesus Exist?

The answer to the question of whether Jesus existed in reality and whether he is not an invented literary figure may not seem so evident. One of the elements of the campaign of atheism that unfolded and continued in Russia and several East European countries in the twentieth century was the debunking of the "myth" of Jesus, the aim of which was to prove that he never existed and that he had simply been invented.

A similar type of campaign was carried out in the 1920s and 1930s in Nazi Germany. Among its active proponents was Christian Heinrich Arthur Drews, the author of a book entitled *The Myth of Jesus*, which created quite a storm in its day. In it he tried to prove that Jesus never existed and that the narratives about him were merely parodies of ancient Egyptian and Greek myths of Osiris, Adonis, and other gods and heroes who had died and risen. Drews's services were employed by the ideologues of the Third Reich when they were faced with the task of creating a new "Aryan religion" based on man's belief in himself. In the Soviet Union Drews's book was translated and published in the 1920s, but his ideas lived on for much longer: several generations of those who fought against religion were brought up on them.

These ideas were reflected in Mikhail Bulgakov's famous novel *The Master and Margarita*. The novel's action begins in Moscow at the end of the 1920s. Two atheist writers—the poet Ivan Bezdomny and the editor Mikhail Berlioz—are talking to each other on a humid summer's day. The former has received a commission for a large anti-religious poem on Jesus Christ:

> And now he [Berlioz] was reading Bezdomny a lecture on Jesus in order to stress the poet's fundamental error. It was hard to say exactly what had made Bezdomny write as he had—whether it was his great talent for graphic description or complete ignorance of the subject he was writing on, but his Jesus had come out, well, completely alive, a Jesus who had really existed, although admittedly a Jesus who had every possible fault. Berlioz however wanted to prove to the poet that the main object was not who Jesus was, whether he was bad or good, but that as a person Jesus had never existed at all and that all the stories about him were mere invention, pure myth. The editor was a well-read man and able to make skilful reference to the ancient historians, such as the famous Philo of Alexandria and the brilliantly educated Josephus Flavius, neither of whom mentioned a word of Jesus' existence.[1] With

---

[1]Bulgakov's character is incorrect: while Philo did not mention Jesus, Josephus did. See below, pp. 10–11.—*Ed.*

a display of solid erudition, Mikhail Alexandrovich informed the poet that incidentally, the passage in Chapter 44 of the fifteenth book of Tacitus' Annals, where he describes the execution of Jesus, was nothing but a later forgery. The poet, for whom everything the editor was saying was a novelty, listened attentively to Mikhail Alexandrovich, fixing him with his bold green eyes, occasionally hiccuping and cursing the apricot juice under his breath. "There is not one oriental religion," said Berlioz, "in which an immaculate virgin does not bring a god into the world. And the Christians, lacking any originality, invented their Jesus in exactly the same way. In fact he never lived at all. That's where the stress has got to lie."[2]

It is a fact that when working on the novel Bulgakov made special notebooks in which he kept excerpts from, in particular, Ernest Renan's *Vie de Jésus* and the similarly titled book by David Strauss, as well as from Drews's *The Myth of Christ*.[3] The views of the theorists of the mythological school were extensively reflected in Bulgakov's novel, as the quotation above demonstrates.

The mythological theory of the origin of Christianity, used in its time for ideological purposes, has died along with the ideologies that it was created to support.

Nonetheless, in our time there are authors who stubbornly deny the historicity of Jesus. And the main argument is, as before, a supposed absence of evidence that Jesus lived on the earth. I will limit myself to the famous quotation from the book by the American author Robert Price, a former Baptist minister and now atheist theologian: "There might have been an historical Jesus, but unless someone discovers his diary or his skeleton, we'll never know."[4]

---

[2]Mikhail Bulgakov, *The Master and Margarita*, trans. Michael Glenny (New York, NY: Harper & Row, 1967), 13.

[3]Lidiya Yanovskaya, *Tvorcheskiy put' Mikhaila Bulgakova* [The creative career of Mikhail Bulgakov] (Moscow: Sov. Pisatel', 1983), 249–250.

[4]Robert M. Price, *The Incredible Shrinking Son of Man: How Reliable is the Gospel Tradition?* (Amherst, NY: Prometheus Books, 2003), 351.

We do not ask ourselves whether the handwritten diaries of Homer, Plato, Aristotle, Alexander the Great, and many other historical figures have come down to us, of whom we know from literary works and whose existence nobody has ever doubted. Why should these criteria, then, be applied to Jesus? For those who seek evidence of the real existence of Jesus on this level, it is not possible to find it. The remains of Jesus cannot be found because he is risen, and a diary cannot be found because, as far as we know, he did not leave behind any writings in his own hand.

And here we once more encounter the paradoxical nature of Christianity. We will not here speak of Jesus' resurrection—an event that did not have any direct witnesses and about which even his closest disciples had their doubts at first (Mt 28.17). But why could Jesus not have left behind at least a written document that affirms that he actually existed? Throughout the years that he lived among people, could he not have found a few days or even hours to write something down to be passed on to those who came afterwards as material evidence of his sojourn on earth? We can only imagine the incredible reverence with which his followers would have venerated any fragment of papyrus upon which at least a few words had been inscribed with his own hand.

And yet, he left no such fragment behind. Was he unable or unwilling to do so? Clearly, he was unwilling, as he much preferred to use only one means of communication—oral preaching. He obviously decided to entrust the transmission of his preaching to his disciples, whom he had chosen at the very start of his ministry. It is to them that he addresses his most important words, not intended for the crowd; it is with them that he spoke directly, whereas with others he spoke in parables (Mk 4.11; Lk 8.10). Jesus' disciples passed on to us both that which they heard from him when they were alone with him, and also the exhortations and parables that he addressed to the simple people.

Oral preaching contains certain risks: the preacher's words can easily be forgotten, or may be incorrectly transmitted or mistakenly understood.[5] Did Jesus manage to avoid these risks? How completely did his

---

[5]Werner H. Kelber, *The Oral and the Written Gospel: The Hermeneutics of Speaking and Writing in the Synoptic Tradition, Mark, Paul, and Q* (Philadelphia, PA: Fortress, 1983), 19.

St John the Theologian and Prochorus, miniature, 1401.

disciples convey to us that which they heard from him? And how reliable are the narratives about his deeds?

If we are to speak of evidence for Jesus' historicity, then the main objective proof is nonetheless the written sources that belong, if not to Jesus himself, then at least to his closest disciples. Of course, not a single handwritten document by him, and much less by his disciples—the authors of the Gospels— has come down to us. But even in those instances when it seems evident that the author of the Gospel wrote the text (as, for example, in the instance of the Gospel of Luke, which begins with a written appeal to its readership), the probability of the original autograph [i.e., the original copy of the text, written by the hand of the author himself—*Ed.*] having survived over such a lengthy time is almost nil.

It is quite probable that at least some of the apostles did not write on the papyrus themselves, but dictated the text to their disciples. Thus, for example, Peter concludes his first epistle with the words: "By Silvanus, a faithful brother unto you, as I suppose, I have written briefly" (1 Pet 5.12). Clearly, Silvanus wrote down the epistle from Peter's words. "Many ancient authors did not themselves wield the pen when they composed their writings, for writing was a craft better left to those who had been trained to do it well," notes one researcher, at the same time indicating that even with an amanuensis [i.e., a scribe who takes dictation—*Ed.*] the author did not cease to be the author and considered himself to be such.[6]

The tradition of the Church has documented this method of creating a written text in the icon of the evangelist John: on it the apostle is depicted with his disciple Prochorus, to whom he is dictating the text of the Apocalypse.

---

[6]Richard Bauckham, *Jesus and the Eyewitnesses: The Gospels as Eyewitness Testimony* (Grand Rapids, MI: Eerdmans, 2006), 359.

At the same time, John was one of the New Testament authors who apparently wrote his texts with his own hand. This is affirmed by the endings of two of his epistles: "Having many things to write unto you, I do not want to write with paper and ink, but I trust to come unto you, and speak face to face" (2 Jn 12); "I had many things to write, but I will not with ink and pen write unto thee. But I trust I shall shortly see thee, and we shall speak face to face" (3 Jn 13–14).

As for the apostle Paul, some of his epistles conclude with the following words: "The salutation of Paul with mine own hand" (1 Cor 16.21; 2 Thess 3.17). Inasmuch as this could mean that Paul wrote the entire text with his own hand, it could just as well mean that in this manner he "approved" the text written at his dictation to an amanuensis.

The Apostle Paul, icon, St Andrei Rublev, *c.* 1410.

It is well known that the sole means of reproducing written texts up until the invention of the printing press was copying them out by hand. It was through this method that for centuries the poems of Homer and the works of Plato, Aristotle, and other ancient Greek philosophers were disseminated, as well as historical books and literary works; in this same manner the books of the Old Testament survived and multiplied. Not a single autograph by the hand of Homer, Socrates, Plato, Aristotle, the prophet Isaiah, or any of the ancient authors in general has come down to us. Does this give us reason to believe that they never existed?

Moreover, we know of some of them solely because their image was documented for us by a particular author. Socrates, for example, did not leave any writings, and all of his sayings have come down to us in Plato's retelling. Nonetheless, few doubt the historicity of Socrates, and even fewer would claim that Plato himself was an invented figure.

At the same time, if the quantity of manuscripts of Homer that have come down to us numbers no more than a few hundred, and the earliest of them dates back to a period of ten centuries after the poet supposedly lived, the Greek manuscripts of the New Testament that scholars know

Plato, Roman copy of a bust by Silanion, *c.* 370 BC

about at present number more than 5,600.[7] Moreover, the earliest of them can be dated back to the beginning of the second century. Thus, for example, papyrus P52, which contains a fragment of the Gospel of John, was made around AD 125. By the third century there are already dozens of papyri containing the Gospel texts, while the codices containing the complete text of the New Testament date back to the fourth century.

With regard to the quantity of preserved manuscripts, as well as the proximity of their creation to the time of the events described in them, the Gospels and other books of the New Testaments cannot be compared to any other ancient literary work. The number of extant manuscripts alone should be sufficient testimony to the historicity of the persons and events depicted in their pages.

Proof of Jesus' historicity can be deduced from the fact that the Gospels place his life quite precisely in a particular time. The Gospel of Luke, for example, includes mentions of all the famous rulers under whom the events described took place, in particular Herod, king of the Jews (Lk 1.5), Augustus Caesar, and the governor of Syria, Quirinius (Lk 2.1–2). The beginning of John the Baptist's preaching is quite clearly dated by the evangelist Luke: "In the fifteenth year of the reign of Tiberius Caesar, Pontius Pilate being governor of Judaea, and Herod being tetrarch of Galilee, and his brother Philip tetrarch of Ituraea and of the region of Trachonitis, and Lysanias the tetrarch of Abilene, Annas and Caiaphas being the high priests" (Lk 3.1–2).

The high priests Annas and Caiaphas, King Herod, and the prefect of Judaea Pontius Pilate are also mentioned in the other Gospels. If Jesus Christ never actually existed, it would have been very difficult to fit an invented person into such a clearly defined historical context without this hoax being quickly uncovered by contemporaries or their closest descendants.

---

[7]See Kurt Aland, *Kurzgefasste Liste der griechischen Handschriften des Neuen Testaments,* Arbeiten zur neutestamentlichen Textforschung Bd. 1 (Berlin: Walter de Gruyter, 1994).

Jerusalem

The geography of the Gospel narrative is quite specific: on the pages of the Gospels many towns and villages are described that have survived to this day, such as Jerusalem, Nazareth, Bethlehem, and so on. These geographical references allow us to easily trace Jesus' and his disciples' movements throughout the territory of Palestine. If the Gospels had been produced significantly later than the events that are described in them, and their heroes were a literary fiction, then how could the evangelists place these events so precisely in their locations?

In addition to the numerous internal testimonies to the veracity of the events described in the Gospels, a number of well-known external testimonies ought to be considered, in particular the references to Jesus Christ by the Roman historians Tacitus, Suetonius, and Pliny the Younger, as well as Celsus (as reported by Origen). Tacitus' testimony, which goes back to the beginning of the second century, is worth quoting here:

> Therefore, to scotch the rumor, Nero substituted as culprits, and punished with the utmost refinements of cruelty, a class of men . . . whom the crowd styled Christians. Christus, the founder of the name, had undergone the death penalty in the reign of Tiberius, by sentence of the procurator Pontius Pilatus, and the pernicious superstition was checked for a moment, only to break out once more, not merely in Judea, the home of the disease, but in the capital [Rome] itself. . . . And derision accompanied their end: they were covered with wild

Flavius Josephus

beasts' skins and torn to death by dogs; or they were fastened on crosses, and, when daylight failed were burned to serve as lamps by night. Nero had offered his Gardens for the spectacle.[8]

Here we are dealing with the same Tiberius of whom the evangelist Luke spoke and the same Pontius Pilate who is mentioned by all four evangelists. That Christ, who was executed upon Pilate's orders, was a real person and not an invented one, is not doubted in the least by the Roman historian, who lived several decades after the events described by him.

Jesus is also mentioned by the Jewish historian Flavius Josephus, who wrote in Greek. In his book *Jewish Antiquities*, written in Rome around AD 93, Josephus says that at the time of the high priest Ananus, the Sanhedrin decided to execute several people, among whom was "James, the brother of Jesus, called the Christ."[9] Josephus writes when narrating earlier events that happened under Pontius Pilate:

> About this time there lived Jesus, a wise man, if indeed one ought to call him a man. For he was one who wrought surprising feats and was a teacher of such people as accept the truth gladly. He won over many Jews and many of the Greeks. He was the Messiah. When Pilate, upon hearing him accused by men of the highest standing amongst us, had condemned him to be crucified, those who had in the first place come to love him did not give up their affection for him. On the third day he appeared to them restored to life, for the prophets of God had prophesied these and countless other marvelous things about him. And the tribe of the Christians, so called after him, has still to this day not disappeared.[10]

[8]Tacitus, *Annals* 15.44 (Jackson, LCL).
[9]Flavius Josephus, *Jewish Antiquities*, 20.200.
[10]Ibid., 18.63–64 (Feldman, LCL).

This text was preserved in all the manuscripts of *Jewish Antiquities* and is quoted by Eusebius of Caeserea (fourth century). However, Origen (third century), who repeatedly refers to Josephus, is unaware of this text. Moreover, Origen claimed that Josephus did recognize Jesus to be the Christ.[11] The openly Christian nature of the text has obliged researchers since the sixteenth century to doubt its authenticity. At the present time the majority of scholars is inclined towards the thought that the mention of Jesus in the corresponding place in Josephus' *Jewish Antiquities* is genuine, while the text itself was subjected to Christian revision when it was copied.[12]

What is Truth? (Christ and Pilate), Nikolai Ge, 1890.

Jesus is also mentioned by the pagan Syrian author Mara bar Serapion in his letter to his son, which is dated at the end of the first century. The letter mentions the wise king whom the Jews executed:

> For what advantage did the Athenians gain by the murder of Socrates, the recompense of which they received in famine and pestilence? Or the people of Samos by the burning of Pythagoras, because in one hour their country was entirely covered in sand? Or the Jews by the death of their wise king, because from that same time their kingdom was taken away? For with justice did God make recompense to the wisdom of these three: for the Athenians died of famine; and the Samians were

[11]Origen, *Contra Celsum* 1.47 (SC 132:198); *Commentary on the Gospel of Matthew* 10.17 (SC 162:218).

[12]We note that in the tenth-century book by the Arab Christian historian Agapius of Hierapolis, *Universal History*, the quotation from Josephus is in a slightly different version: "At this time there was a wise man who was called Jesus. And his conduct was good, and [he] was known to be virtuous. And many people from among the Jews and the other nations became his disciples. Pilate condemned him to be crucified and to die. And those who had become his disciples did not abandon his discipleship. They reported that he had appeared to them three days after his crucifixion and that he was alive; accordingly, he was perhaps the Messiah concerning whom the prophets have recounted wonders." (Trans. Shlomo Pines, in Shlomo Pines, *An Arabic Version of the Testimonium Flavianum and its Implications* [Jerusalem: The Israel Academy of Sciences and Humanities, 1971], 16.)

The Madaba Map: the place of Christ's baptism, mosaic, 6th c.

overwhelmed by the sea without remedy; and the Jews, desolate and driven from their own kingdom, are scattered through every country. Socrates is not dead, because of Plato; neither Pythagoras, because of the statue of Juno; nor the Wise King, because of the laws which he promulgated.[13]

The sum total of internal and external testimonies clearly proves the fact that Jesus Christ was an actual historical person, living in a specific period of history at a specific place. And although some researchers have compared the story of Christ's resurrection to the ancient Egyptian myth of Osiris, and see the roots of the Gospel narratives in other ancient myths, the difference between Christ and mythological persons is sufficiently evident. Indeed, testimonies about him have survived in a far greater number than about any other figure in the ancient world.

---

[13]William Cureton, trans. and ed., *Spicilegium Syriacum: Containing Remains of Bardeson, Meliton, Ambrose and Mara bar Serapion* (London: Francis and John Rivington, 1855), 73–74.

2. The Authority of the Witnesses

W e ought to consider as convincing proof of the historicity of Jesus the presence of supposed contradictions or variances between the evangelists who, it would appear, are describing one and the same event but vary in the details. Thus, for example, the Gospel of Matthew (20.30–34) speaks of Jesus' healing of two blind men, while the parallel excerpt in Mark (10.46–52) speaks of only one blind man. In Matthew (8.28–34) Jesus heals two demoniacs, while in Mark (5.1–16) and Luke (8.26–36) he heals only one.

The presence of discrepancies in details between the evangelists in light of the essential similarity of the accounts speaks not against but, on the contrary, *for* the reality of the events described. If we were dealing with a hoax, then the authors would certainly have made sure to check their information with each other. The differences bear witness to the fact that there was no collusion between the evangelists.

"In order to picture to oneself better the mechanism of how such differences arose in the narratives of the evangelists," said Metropolitan—now Patriarch—Kirill,

> let us imagine, for example, a road accident with several people as witnesses. There will, of course, inevitably be differences in the evidence they give—not in essence, but in the particulars, simply by virtue of the fact that each will have his own perception and vision of the event. While being united as to documenting the fact as such, witnesses will always bring into their story an individual understanding of what happened. This variation in eyewitness testimony does not in any way call into question the reality of the event, but, on the contrary, enables an objective reconstruction of the true picture. The same can also be said in relation to the testimony of the evangelists . . . The rare differences we encounter in their narratives merely testify to the authenticity of the texts: indeed, if they had been fabricated, then the falsifiers would

in the first instance be concerned with removing all possible inconsistencies.[14]

The key word in this quotation is "witness."[15] Many researchers define
the Gospel genre as the testimony of eyewitnesses. Richard Bauckham,
author of the book *Jesus and the Eyewitnesses*, notes that eyewitness testimony differs from conventional historical narratives: "[T]he kind of historiography they are is testimony. An irreducible feature of testimony as
a form of human utterance is that it asks to be trusted."[16] We may trust or
not trust the witness, but the mistake of some researchers has been the
tendency to view trust in testimony as an obstacle on the path of a free
search for the truth, which the historian ought to establish and verify inde-
pendently of someone's words. In fact, it is testimony that is for a historian
"a unique and uniquely valuable means of access to historical reality."[17] In
the context of studying the Gospels, testimony becomes a category that
allows us not only to document the life of Jesus, but also to see "the dis-
closure of God in the history of Jesus. . . . Testimony is the category that
enables us to read the Gospels in a properly historical way and a properly
theological way."[18]

A witness differs from a regular historian, chronographer, or chronicler
in that the witness does not set himself the task of objectively, consistently, and exhaustively describing particular events in a detached manner. He speaks of what he has seen, and his story, colored by his personal
relationship towards what has happened, does not carry the systematic
or consistent nature that we would expect from historians and chroni-
clers. There is no such thing as a dispassionate witness: as a rule, witnesses
either sympathize with their hero, or do the opposite. Witnesses are never

---

[14]Metropolitan Kirill (Gundyaev), *Slovo pastyrya. Bog i chelovek. Istoriya spaseniya* [The
pastor's word. God and man. The history of salvation] (Moscow: Izdatel'skiy sovet Russkoy pravoslavnoy tserkvi, 2004), 102.

[15]The Greek word *martyria* can be translated either as "witness" or "testimony," and the verb
form *martyreō* can be translated as "I bear witness" or "I testify." All these English words refer to
the same concept in this section.—*Ed.*

[16]Bauckham, *Jesus and the Eyewitnesses*, 5.

[17]Ibid.

[18]Ibid., 5–6.

entirely third-party observers: they think of themselves as participants in the event, even if they did not take part in it directly; in recalling the event, the witness relives it and, voluntarily or involuntarily, interprets it.

As scholars have noted, "In the Judeo-Christian tradition, testimony fulfills a theological function: certain events are viewed as divine revelations." The witness to these events can refer to his own existential experience, to the shock he has gone through, but the truth of his testimony, from his perspective, "cannot be verified, and there is no other guarantee than that of the testimony itself." It is in this way that "Christians discovered the character of God in the story of Jesus, as he always was and as he will become accessible to all people in the future (Rev 1.8; 21.6; 22.13). The force of historical uniqueness . . . gives the testimony its special power." At the same time, there is the possibility of verifying the testimony, in particular by means of comparing it with other testimonies.[19]

From the Christian perspective the one who testifies is not merely an eyewitness. He does not simply retell events: he bears responsibility for the truth of this testimony. It is no coincidence that the Greek word *martys*, which literally means "witness," has become firmly established in the Christian tradition as meaning someone who endures martyrdom. Bearing witness to Jesus Christ throughout the ages has meant the willingness not only to speak about him and live according to his commandments, but also to suffer and die for him. It is no coincidence either that most of the apostles, including those whose testimonies formed the basis of the Gospel narratives, ended their lives as martyrs.

Bearing witness is similar not so much to a photograph, as to a portrait that reflects not only the model, but also the personality of the artist. The Gospel is the model by which the Church determines the authenticity of other portraits of Jesus written in subsequent centuries; some of these portraits are true to the original, while others are not.[20]

[19]Petr Pokorný and Ulrich Heckel, *Einleitung in das Neue Testament: seine Literatur und Theologie im Überblick* (Tübingen: Mohr Siebeck, 2007), 22–23. Quotes translated from the German by the present translator.

[20]Gerald L. Borchert, *Jesus of Nazareth: Background, Witnesses, and Significance* (Macon, GA: Mercer University Press, 2011), 74–75.

Irenaeus of Lyons,
fresco, 16th c.

Where in the Gospels is the dividing line between historical facts and their interpretation? According to what criteria can we distinguish real historical events from their interpretation by a particular witness? One may argue that if Jesus had wanted to provide his followers with absolutely verifiable, incontrovertible, and scientifically proven facts concerning his life, then he would have found a way of doing so. Since from the very first days of his public ministry he chose his disciples so that they could recall what he said and did, in order that later they could transmit this to their successors, then this means that he had a specific intent in doing so. This means that Jesus entrusted to them, and no one else, the task of passing on what he wanted to say.

St Irenaeus of Lyons spoke of this in the second century in his oft-quoted famous saying on holy tradition:

> It is not necessary to seek the truth among others which it is easy to obtain from the Church; since the apostles, like a rich man depositing his money in a bank, lodged in her hands most copiously all things pertaining to the truth: so that every man, whosoever will, can draw from her the water of life. For she is the entrance to life; all others are thieves and robbers. On this account are we bound to avoid them, but to make choice of the thing pertaining to the Church with the utmost diligence, and to lay hold of the tradition of the truth. For how stands the case? Suppose there arise a dispute relative to some important question among us, should we not have recourse to the most ancient Churches with which the apostles held constant intercourse, and learn from them what is certain and clear in regard to the present question? For how should it be if the apostles themselves had not left us writings? Would it not be necessary, in that case, to follow the course of the tradition which they handed down to those to whom they did commit the Churches?[21]

---

[21]Irenaeus of Lyons, *Against Heresies* 3.4.1 (*ANF* 1:416–417).

These words contain an answer to the heretics of antiquity, who disputed the Church's monopoly on interpreting Jesus' teaching by demonstrating that this teaching was accessible to a wide circle of people, including those who were beyond his immediate circle of followers. Irenaeus opposed the Gnostics in emphasizing that Christ chose his apostles in order to entrust to them the transmission of his message; Christ established the Church so that she could continue his cause and preserve his teaching by transmitting it from generation to generation. If he had entrusted the furtherance of his cause to a concrete group of people, then why should another group have the right to transmit and interpret his teaching?

Irenaeus' words also testify to the importance of the initial oral tradition that formed the basis of the written sources. In our time people are, as a rule, unable to reproduce precisely what they have heard: at best one can retell what one has heard, close to the text. Most of us have gotten used to written text, and, in order to remember what we hear, we have to write it down in a notebook, or on a laptop or smartphone. In the ancient world there was a completely different culture of receiving the spoken word. The majority of people were unable to read, and all books, including Scripture, were received by hearing. The recital of sacred texts by heart was widely practiced. The Jews whom Jesus addressed in the synagogues after the reading of an excerpt from Scripture were in the main illiterate. At the same time, they were able to know by heart significant excerpts of the texts or even whole books of the Bible.

At first, Jesus' sayings and the stories of his life, which later formed the basis of the written text of the Gospels, were spread in oral form. But we can assume that at least in relation to the sayings these were in a verbally fixed form, which was reproduced more or less word for word when being transmitted. Jesus' sayings and the stories of his life were related by the apostles to their disciples, and they repeated them by heart to the next generation of disciples. At a certain point, the time came to put all of these various oral traditions down on paper (or, rather, papyrus or parchment) and give them the form of finished narratives.

But when the narratives of two or three evangelists coincide not only in meaning but also textually this does not mean that we should attribute this to the use of a single written source. The single source could be oral too, and the insignificant differences in the texts, in light of the almost word-for-word similarity of many fragments, merely support this idea.

The Gospels are not a historical narrative in the purest sense. In the Gospels narrative and interpretation are found side by side. Thus, for example, the story according to the evangelist Matthew about the birth of Jesus from the Virgin Mary in Bethlehem constitutes a narrative, whereas the quotations from the Old Testament that the evangelist uses to affirm that Jesus' birth was foretold by the prophets are an interpretation of this narrative. The phrase "in the beginning was the Word" (Jn 1.1), which opens the Gospel of John, is a theological axiom that the evangelist makes the foundation of his book, whereas the following narrative is an illustration and development of this axiom. In the Gospel of John, theological interpretation precedes the narrative more often than it comes after it. Separating the narrative from the interpretation is sometimes very difficult: the one develops into the other, and often does not exist without the other.

It is even more difficult to separate a hypothetical story of the "historical Jesus" from the narrative that belongs to his disciples and that was created within the Church that he founded. Indeed, it is in the Church that the work of compiling the stories of the life and teaching of Jesus, the selection of the Gospels and the attribution of canonical status to them took place, along with the parallel rejection of non-canonical and heretical texts. It is the Church that was the laboratory within which from the very beginning—at first in the form of oral tradition and then in the form of written text—the Gospel story found its existence. And yet, the interpretation of events from the life of Jesus and of his teachings arose practically at the same time as they were being described.

In the Gospels and other books of the New Testament, we find several layers that are not identical in significance from the perspective of the goal of our research. Part of the Gospel text belongs to the eyewitnesses of the events—the twelve apostles. Part of it belongs to their disciples, who either wrote under dictation, or more likely reproduced from memory, but very close to the text, that which they had heard from the apostles. Yet another part consists of the interpretation of events and of the sayings of Jesus. This interpretation, begun by the evangelists and authors of the apostolic letters, was continued by subsequent Church writers.

For example, a significant part of the Gospel of John that reproduces Jesus' polemic with the Jews, his discourses with the disciples, certain events from his life, and his last days, hours, and minutes, appears to be the direct testimony of an eyewitness to and participant in these events. The same can be said with a great deal of probability about the part of Matthew's Gospel that concerns events that

The Tribute Money,
Titian, ca. 1516.

the evangelist could have witnessed and words that the evangelist himself could have heard: these events and words he could have reproduced from memory even many years later.

We also cannot exclude the possibility that one of the disciples may have tried to document Jesus' words directly at the time they were uttered, although the means we have already mentioned were more likely: memorization and recitation by heart.

The Gospel of Mark and a substantial part of the Gospel of Luke we can attribute to the testimonies of eyewitnesses, primarily of Peter, but also perhaps another of the apostles, as recorded by their disciples. They have equal value to the supposed testimonies of the eyewitnesses themselves.

Yet another layer of Gospel narrative is the interpretation of the events by eyewitnesses. Apart from the Prologue of John's Gospel and the prophecies from the Old Testament in the Gospel of Matthew, certain other places and separate phrases from the Gospels belong to the category of interpretation, as well as the greater part of the general epistles that belong to eyewitnesses—apostles from among the Twelve. The interpretative layer is a part of the New Testament that is no less important for an understanding of the "historical Jesus" than the narrative layers.

Finally, there is yet one more layer—the narrative of events that had no eyewitnesses who could have documented them. To this layer belong the first two chapters of the Gospel of Matthew and the first three chapters of the Gospel of Luke. None of Jesus' disciples could have been a witness to the narratives that form the opening chapters of these two Gospels. We can only suggest that the source for the opening chapters of Luke's Gospel is Jesus' mother, Mary, while the information contained in the opening chapters of Matthew's Gospel can be attributed to Joseph and was transmitted through "Jesus' brothers." We shall return to this question later.

The New Testament was written in a definite historical period at a definite stage of the Church's development. This was the stage of the first emergence of holy tradition, which continued to live on in the following generations of Christians. The uniqueness of the stage, reflected in the pages of the New Testament writings, consists in that the apostles were still alive, "which from the beginning were eyewitnesses, and ministers of the Word" (Lk 1.2). It is to them that we can attribute the greater part of the testimonies to Jesus and their original interpretations. It is here that we find the enduring significance of the New Testament and especially the four Gospels as the fundamental source of information on the life and teaching of Jesus.

This source possesses an inner integrity that does not allow us to separate the original Christian *kērygma* (preaching, teaching) from the subsequent layers by means of simply casting aside those parts of the text that may seem unreliable or incompatible with common sense to a particular researcher. The task that many nineteenth- and twentieth-century scholars set themselves was to tear the Gospel text away from its church interpretation, which in itself is a mistake in methodology. It is the same as trying to reproduce the events of a road accident by ignoring the evidence of first-hand witnesses and even those involved in the accident as knowingly false and as hindering the investigation. The presumption of distrust towards the testimonies of witnesses, which characterizes many classic works from the latter half of the nineteenth century and the twentieth century, renders these works dubious, tendentious, and biased, both from the perspective of methodology and in relation to the selection of the material, the exposition of facts, and their interpretation.

3. Was Jesus God?

Both the New Testament and the subsequent Church tradition speak of Jesus Christ as God and Man in one person. The Church has always understood her teaching that Jesus is fully and truly both God and man as a consistent revelation of those truths that are contained in the Gospels and apostolic epistles.

Nonetheless, we cannot ignore the arguments of those who claim that Jesus was not who the Church said he was and that the notion that Jesus was God was not the original belief of the Church. There have been those who have suggested in many ways that the Church gradually, throughout the centuries, created an image of the Son of God from the simple person of Jesus, albeit endowed with special gifts and a peculiar wisdom. To this day many scholars sincerely believe it was only after a number of centuries of argument on whether Jesus was God or a simple person that belief in the divine nature of Jesus held sway among the ecclesiastical hierarchy and was then imposed upon the entire Church.

Christ Pantocrator, icon, 13th c.

What do the canonical Gospels tell us of Jesus' divinity? Can we claim that belief in Jesus as God incarnate was the original belief of the Church? During the course of our investigation we will return repeatedly to the answer to this question. However, we must already, before the narrative about the life of Jesus begins, stop to consider the key titles that the New Testament authors applied to him: the "Son of Man" and the "Son of God." To a large extent, our perception of the image of Jesus and the entire Gospel story rests upon the interpretation of these notions. We should also examine the context within which the terms "God" and "Lord" were used in relation to Jesus.

When speaking of himself in the third person, Jesus would most often call himself the Son of Man: this phrase is encountered in the four canonical Gospels eighty-five times in total. "Son of Man" is an idiom that in Hebrew means nothing else but "man" (Num 23.19; Job 16.21, 23.6; Ps 8.5, 143.3, 145.3; Is 15.12, 56.2, Jer 49.18).[22] In the book of Ezekiel, God often addresses the prophet as the son of man (Ezek 2.1 *et passim*). At the same time, in the book of Daniel, the Son of Man appears as a prefiguration of the Messiah, the eternal King:

> I saw in the night visions, and, behold, one like the Son of man came with the clouds of heaven, and came to the Ancient of Days, and they brought him near before him. And there was given him dominion, and glory, and a kingdom, that all people, nations, and languages, should serve him; his dominion is an everlasting dominion, which shall not pass away, and his kingdom that which shall not be destroyed. (Dan 7.13–14)

One may suppose that in calling himself the Son of Man, Jesus intentionally emphasizes his human, and not divine, origin. At the same time the connection with the image of the Son of Man in the book of Daniel should not be ignored. The Son of Man of whom Jesus speaks is far from a conventional person: he is in heaven (Jn 3.13), God the Father has placed his seal upon him (Jn 6.27), the angels of God ascend and descend upon him (Jn 1.51). The Son of Man came down from the heavens (Jn 3.13) in order to save peoples' souls (Lk 9.26). He has the power on earth to forgive sins (Mt 9.6). The faithful are to partake of his flesh and blood in order to have life within themselves (Jn 6.53). He will rise from the dead (Mk 9.9) and ascend into heaven (Jn 3.13)—to the place where he was before (Jn 6.62). His second coming will be unexpected (Mt 24.44; 25.13), like lightning flashing from one side of the sky and illumining it to the other extreme (Lk 17.24). He will come in the glory of his Father with the holy angels (Mk 8.38), sit on the throne of his glory and seat the apostles on the twelve thrones to judge the twelve tribes of Israel (Mt 19.28), and before

[22]See Maurice Casey, *The Solution to the 'Son of Man' Problem*, The Library of New Testament Studies 343 (London: T&T Clark, 2007), 61–67.

The Ancient
of Days, icon,
16th c.

him all nations will be gathered, and he will separate among them the sheep from the goats (Mt 25.31–33).

Jesus is often called the Son of God (Mt 14.33), the Son of the living God (Mt 16.16; Jn 6.69), and he accepts these appellations (Lk 22.70). To the high priest's question, "Tell us whether thou be the Christ, the Son of God," Jesus replies in the affirmative, but then adds: "Hereafter shall ye see the Son of man sitting on the right hand of power, and coming in the clouds of heaven" (Mt 26.63–64). In relation to himself, Jesus in turn uses the names "Son of Man" and "Son of God" as synonyms:

> And no man hath ascended up to heaven, but he that came down from heaven, even the *Son of Man* which is in heaven. And as Moses lifted up the serpent in the wilderness, even so must the *Son of Man* be lifted up, that whosoever believeth in him should not perish, but have eternal life. For God so loved the world, that he gave his *only begotten Son*, that whosoever believeth in him should not perish, but have everlasting life. For God sent not *his Son* into the world to condemn the world, but that the world through him might be saved. He that believeth on him is not

condemned, but he that believeth not is condemned already, because
he hath not believed in the name of the *only begotten Son of God*. (Jn
3.13–18, emphasis added)

Truly, truly, I say unto you, The hour is coming, and now is, when the
dead shall hear the voice of the *Son of God*: and they that hear shall live.
For as the Father hath life in himself, so hath he given to the Son to have
life in himself. And hath given him authority to execute judgment also,
because he is the *Son of Man*. (Jn 5.25–27, emphasis added)

The biblical appellation "Son of God" does not necessarily mean that
its bearer is God (at least when used in the plural).[23] However, in the New
Testament the expression "Son of God" acquires a special meaning in relation to Jesus Christ. Jesus is the only begotten Son of God (Jn 3.16; 3.18; 1
Jn 4.9), only begotten of the Father (Jn 1.14), who "is in the bosom of the
Father" (Jn 1.18). In his conversations with the disciples and the Jews as
documented by the evangelist John, Jesus repeatedly testifies to his oneness with the Father:

He that honoureth not the Son honoureth not the Father which hath
sent him. (Jn 5.23)

For I came down from heaven, not to do mine own will, but the will of
him that sent me. (Jn 6.38)

As the Father knoweth me, even so know I the Father. (Jn 10.15)

The works that I do in my Father's name, they bear witness of me. . . .
I and my Father are one. (Jn 10.25, 30)

I am in the Father, and the Father in me. (Jn 14.11)

Although Jesus calls himself the Son of God and testifies to his oneness
with the Father, almost nowhere in the Gospels does he call himself God.
The exception is the instance when, in reply to the words of the devil, he

---

[23]In the Old Testament the plural "sons of God" usually refers to angels (Job 1.6; 38.7), and in
the New Testament it can refer to saved human beings in the eschaton (Rom 8.19).—*Ed.*

says: "Thou shalt not tempt the Lord thy God" (Mt 4.7; Lk 4.12). Here he refers to himself using two divine titles: "Lord" and "God." In reply to other words of the devil he says, referring to his Father, "Thou shalt worship the Lord thy God, and him only shalt thou serve" (Lk 4.8).

When somebody calls him "good teacher," Jesus replies: "Why callest thou me good? There is none good but one, that is, God" (Mt 19.17; Mk 10.18; Lk 18.18). It is possible to understand Jesus' reply as a denial of his divine nature, contrasting himself to God. However, his words can be understood in a different sense: in calling me good, you recognize my divine nature.

In the Gospels and the epistles the name "God" (*theos*) is used mainly in relation to the Father, whereas in relation to Jesus the name "Lord" (*kyrios*) is consistently used.[24] In the Acts of the Apostles it is said that God "hath made that same Jesus, whom ye have crucified, both Lord and Christ" (Acts 2.36). "God hath raised up the Lord" (1 Cor 6.14). In the apostolic epistles one often encounters the expressions "God and Father of our Lord Jesus Christ" (1 Pet 1.3; Rom 15.6; 2 Cor 1.3; 11.31; Heb 1.3, 17; Col 1.3), "God our Father, and the Lord Jesus Christ" (Rom 1.7), and other similar formulas.

At the same time, in the epistles of the apostle Paul, Jesus Christ is repeatedly called God: "As concerning the flesh Christ came, who is over all, God blessed for ever. Amen" (Rom 9.5); "Looking for that blessed hope, and the glorious appearing of our great God and Saviour Jesus Christ" (Titus 2.13); "For in him dwelleth all the fulness of the Godhead bodily" (Col 2.9). In his First Epistle, John the Theologian says of Jesus Christ: "This is the true God, and eternal life" (1 Jn 5.20).

In itself the word "Lord" (Greek *kyrios*) does not necessarily point towards the divine nature of its bearer: it simply means "master." It is in this sense that we can understand the repeated use of the word "Lord" (Greek *kyrie*, vocative) when applied to Jesus in the direct speech of the apostles and other figures in the Gospels.

---

[24]See Raymond E. Brown, *Jesus, God and Man: Modern Biblical Reflections* (Milwaukee, WI: Bruce, 1967), 1–18.

King David the Psalmist, fresco, 16th c.

However, already in the Septuagint this word was used to convey the names of God—*Yahweh* (Jehovah, Lord, God) and *Adonai* (my Lord), while in the New Testament the name "Lord" (*kyrios*) is often used in relation to God the Father alongside the name "God" (*theos*).

Meanwhile, in the Psalms the name "Lord" refers to both God and the promised Messiah: "The Lord said unto my Lord, 'Sit thou at my right hand, until I make thine enemies thy footstool'" (Ps 109.1). Citing the words of the psalmist, Jesus asks the Jews: "David therefore himself calleth him Lord; and whence is he then his son?" (Mk 12.37; cf. Lk 20.42–44). Here the name "Lord" is interpreted as indicating the divine nature of its bearer and is used by Jesus in relation to himself.

In the early Christian community, the use of the name "Lord" for Jesus undoubtedly meant the recognition of his divinity. The Apostle Thomas uses the words "Lord" and "God" as synonyms when he addresses the risen Jesus with the words, "My Lord and my God" (Jn 20.28). According to the apostle Paul, "No man is able to say Jesus is the Lord, but by the Holy Spirit" (1 Cor 12.3). In the epistles of Paul, the names "God," "Lord" and "Christ" are often used as synonyms: Paul speaks of the Church of God and the Church of Christ, the kingdom of God and the kingdom of Christ, the grace of God and Christ's grace, the Spirit of God and the Spirit of Christ. According to John Chrysostom, "the name 'God' is not greater than the name 'Lord,' nor is the name 'Lord' inferior to the name 'God,'" for "[t]hroughout the whole Old Testament, the Father is constantly called Lord."[25]

The Gospel of Luke is characteristic in this regard: in it the name "Lord" is repeatedly used in relation to God, but is no less often applied

---

[25]John Chrysostom, *On the Incomprehensible Nature of God* 5.13 (PG 48:738). In John Chrysostom, *On the Incomprehensible Nature of God*, trans. Paul W. Harkins, The Fathers of the Church 72 (Washington, DC: Catholic University of America Press, 1982), 142.

consistently to Jesus.[26] Already in the first chapter of the Gospel the name "Lord" is used sixteen times in relation to God (Lk 1.6, 9, 10, 15–17, 25, 28, 32, 38, 45, 46, 58, 66, 68, 76) and one time in relation to Jesus—when Elisabeth called the Virgin Mary "the mother of my Lord" (Lk 1.43). In the following chapters we see the constant use of the name "Lord," first for God and then for his Son. Jesus is simultaneously "Christ the Lord" (Lk 2.11) and "the Lord's Christ" (Lk 2.26).

John the Baptist was sent to prepare the way of the Lord, that is, Jesus Christ (Lk 3.4; also in Mt 3.3 and Mk 1.3). If in the first six chapters Luke calls Jesus only by his name,[27] as the other evangelists do, then beginning with the seventh chapter the name of Jesus in the narrative is regularly substituted with the name "Lord" (Lk 7.13, 31; 10.1; 11.39; 12.42; 13.15; 17.5, 6; 18.6; 19.8; 22.31, 61; 24.3, 34). This use of the word is encountered in the narrative part only in John (Jn 11.2; 20.18, 20).

The clearest affirmation of the early Church's belief in Jesus Christ's divinity is the Prologue of the Gospel of John, in which Jesus is identified with the eternal Word of God:

> In the beginning was the Word, and the Word was with God, and the Word was God. The same was in the beginning with God. All things were made by him; and without him was not any thing made that was made. In him was life, and the life was the light of men. And the light shineth in darkness; and the darkness comprehended it not. . . . And the Word was made flesh, and dwelt among us, and we beheld his glory, the glory as of the only begotten of the Father, full of grace and truth. (Jn 1.1–5, 14)

It is these words of the Fourth Gospel that are a manifesto of the belief of the ancient Church in the divine nature of Jesus. The Prologue of the Gospel of John contains an explicit recognition of the fact that the Word

[26]See C. Kavin Rowe, *Early Narrative Christology: The Lord in the Gospel of Luke* (Grand Rapids, MI: Baker Academic, 2006), 197–218.

[27]In total the name "Jesus" in the Gospel of Luke is encountered eighty-three times, and of these, seventy-seven times in the narrative part. See David Lee, *Luke's Stories of Jesus: Theological Reading of Gospel Narrative and the Legacy of Hans Frei*, Journal for the Study of the New Testament Supplement Series 185 (Sheffield: Sheffield Academic Press, 1999), 214.

Basil the Great and Gregory of Nyssa, mosaic, 11th c.

of God, the only begotten Son of God, *is* God. The Word became flesh, was made incarnate, became man, and lived among people. It is in the fact that God became man that the good news is contained, which the evangelists and Jesus' apostles brought to the world. And it is in this message that we find the origin of Christianity as a new covenant between God and people.

It is no coincidence that the Gospel of John, which begins with the solemn affirmation of the eternity and divinity of the Word of God, contains in its concluding section Thomas' confession: "My Lord and my God" (Jn 20.28). The entire Fourth Gospel is a consistent revelation of the belief in the divinity of Jesus Christ, and it concludes with a no less solemn affirmation of the belief with which it began.

The Prologue of the Gospel of John ends with the words: "No man hath seen God at any time; the only begotten Son, which is in the bosom of the Father, he hath declared him" (Jn 1.18). Modern-day critical editions of the New Testament quote this text in a slightly different redaction: instead of the "only begotten Son" (*monogenēs huios*), there is in their place "only begotten God" (*monogenēs theos*). This reading is based on more ancient manuscripts, whereas the reading "only begotten Son" is encountered only in some manuscripts beginning with the fourth century. The authenticity of the version quoted in the critical edition is attested by the use of the

The Trinity, icon, St Andrei Rublev, 1420s.

expression "only begotten God" in fourth-century authors such as Basil the Great,[28] Amphilochius of Iconium,[29] and Gregory of Nyssa.[30] The expression "only begotten God" is yet one more confirmation of the faith of the early Church in Christ's divinity and in the fact that his coming to earth was nothing other than the incarnation of God.

Belief in the divine origin of Jesus was the initial faith of the Church, which is reflected in the pages of the New Testament. Names are used in relation to Jesus that are usually used to refer to God. Along with this,

[28]Basil the Great, *Letters* 38.4 (*NPNF²* 8:138).

[29]Amphilochius of Iconium, *De recta fide* [On the true faith], in *Amphilochii Iconiensis Opera*, Corpus Christianorum Series Graeca 3 (Turnhout: Brepols, 1978), 315. This work is preserved in Syriac.

[30]Gregory of Nyssa, *The Great Catechism* 39 (*NPNF²* 5:504–505).

The Trinity, icon,
Simon Ushakov, 1671.

qualities are attributed to Jesus that God possesses, and deeds that God accomplishes; worship is rendered to him that is rendered to God. A detailed examination of the New Testament texts devoted to these topics has led contemporary researchers to the following conclusion:

> The case for the deity of Christ does not rest on a few proof-texts. The popular notion that some fourth-century Christians decided to impose on the church a belief in Jesus as God and wrenched isolated Bible verses from their contexts to support their agenda is a gross misrepresentation of the facts. The framers of the orthodox doctrines of the Incarnation and the Trinity did have an agenda, but it was not to replace a merely human Jesus with a divine Christ. Their agenda was to safeguard the New Testament's clear teaching of the deity of the Lord Jesus Christ in a way that did equal justice to three other clear teachings of the Bible: there is only one God; Jesus is the Son and not the Father; Jesus is also a human being.[31]

Belief in Jesus' divine nature did not immediately acquire a clear dogmatic basis expressed in concrete christological terminology. This terminology was developed over several centuries in response to heresies that arose.

In chronological order, the first to deny the divine origin of Jesus were his contemporaries, the Jews. Some of them were willing to see in him a teacher and prophet, but they were disturbed by his insistent wish to proclaim God his Father and himself God's Son. The more vivid descriptions of these clashes between the Jews and Jesus are contained in the Gospel of John: chapters five to eight of this Gospel are almost wholly devoted to Jesus' polemic with the Jews. When reading these chapters it is difficult to avoid the feeling that Jesus is intentionally provoking the Jews, telling

[31] Robert M. Bowman and J. Ed Komoszewski, *Putting Jesus in His Place: The Case for the Deity of Christ* (Grand Rapids, MI: Kregel Publications, 2007), 267.

The Trinity,
fresco,
1176–1180s.

them things that he knows they cannot accept. His conflict with the Jews looks nothing like an accident and misunderstanding: Jesus consistently and consciously entered into this conflict—both when he denounced the Pharisees as hypocrites and exposed their sanctimoniousness, and when he spoke of himself as the Son of God.

After Jesus' death and resurrection, doubts about his divine nature arose not only among those to whom the apostles' preaching was addressed, but also in the Christian milieu. However, the Church consistently rejected all those who in one way or another disputed Jesus' divine nature, declaring them to be heretics and rejecting their teachings at the councils.

We will not list here the numerous heretical teachings that arose in the early Church and which to one degree or another cast doubt upon Jesus' divine nature. We will mention only one, a teaching that rocked the Church throughout almost the entire fourth century: Arianism. It arose from the notion of one absolutely transcendent God the Father, who cannot be immanent to anyone. The author of this teaching, the Alexandrian presbyter Arius, believed that the Son of God was not equal to and not like the Father: he had a different nature and essence. He was also not co-eternal with the Father, for he had his beginning in time: "There was a time when he was not." The Son is one of God's creatures. He was created by the Father "from non-being" as an intermediary in order to create the world through his hands. He is superior to created beings; however, he is not God, in being changeable by his nature: only the Father is unchanging and only the Father is the one true God, while the Son and the Holy Spirit are subject to him as creatures of God.

This teaching was countered by the Council of Nicaea in AD 325 with the Creed, in which the basic postulates of Arianism were condemned:

> We believe in one God, the Father Almighty, maker of all things vis-
> ible and invisible; and in one Lord Jesus Christ, the Son of God, the
> only-begotten of his Father, of the substance of the Father, God of God,
> Light of Light, very God of very God, begotten (γεννηθέντα) not made,
> being of one substance (ὁμοούσιον, *consubstantialem*) with the Father.
> By whom all things were made, both which be in heaven and in earth.
> Who for us men and for our salvation came down [from heaven] and
> was incarnate and was made man. He suffered and the third day he
> rose again, and ascended into heaven. And he shall come again to judge
> both the quick and the dead. And [we believe] in the Holy Spirit. And
> whosoever shall say that there was a time when the Son of God was not
> (ἦν ποτε ὅτε οὐκ ἦν) or that before he was begotten he was not, or that
> he was made of things that were not, or that he is of a different sub-
> stance or essence [from the Father] or that he is a creature, or subject
> to change or conversion—all that so say, the Catholic and Apostolic
> Church anathematizes them.[32]

Arius' main opponent was Athanasius of Alexandria, according to whose teaching all of the Trinity is the One God—Father, Son, and Holy Spirit, equal in divinity and in essence. The birth of the Son from the Father is pre-eternal: the Father at no time began to be the Father, but was always the Father, and therefore the Son is co-eternal with the Father. The consubstantiality of the Persons of the Holy Trinity is not merely that of equality or likeness: it is an integral oneness of being, an indestructible and unchangeable identity, an unmerged indivisibility of one Person from the Other. The teaching of the Council of Nicaea, which became known as the

---

[32] *The Nicene Creed* (*NPNF²* 14:3).

Sts Athanasius and Cyril of Alexandria, miniature from the Menologion of Basil II, 10th c.

First Ecumenical Council, was later affirmed at the Second Ecumenical Council, convoked in Constantinople in 381.

The subsequent christological heresies, which arose in the Christian East and were condemned by the Ecumenical Councils, to one degree or another touched upon the subject of the correlation of the divine and human natures in Christ, but not a single heretic theologian condemned by the Councils ever denied that Jesus Christ was God incarnate, the Son of God, equal to and of one essence with the Father. In particular, in the fifth century Nestorius was condemned for making a sharp division between God the Word and the man Jesus. In opposition to his teaching, the fathers of the Third Ecumenical Council (431) insisted that God the Word, of whom the Gospel of John speaks, and the man Jesus are one and the same Person. Nestorius, however, never denied that the Son of God was consubstantial with God the Father: he merely stated that the Word of God abided in the man Jesus. In other words, he did not deny Jesus' divine nature, but merely interpreted it in a way that was unacceptable to the Church.

Was the teaching of the First and Second Ecumenical Councils an innovation compared to what Jesus said in the Gospels, or did it merely affirm and clarify the New Testament good news about Jesus as God incarnate? The Church has always insisted that she has never introduced and could not have introduced any innovations with regard to the original

The Venerable John
Damascene, fresco, 16th c.

faith. We have seen that already in the Gospels the name "Lord" was consistently used for Jesus, and in some instances the name "God." Jesus' divine nature was never doubted by the apostle Paul, nor the other apostles, nor the subsequent generations of Church authors, nor even the heretics after Arius. The terminology continued to be refined, but the faith remained the same as that which the apostles received from Jesus himself.

The teaching that categorically denied Jesus' divinity and issued a serious challenge to Christianity was Islam. It arose in the seventh century, began to spread quickly, and at first was understood by Christians as one more heresy. John Damascene, an eighth-century Christian writer, included Islam in the list of heresies as number 101.[33] Damascene linked the appearance of Islam to Arianism, which denied Jesus' divine nature (there are also accounts indicating that Muhammad's teacher was a Nestorian monk). Be that as it may, for Damascene the arrival of Islam appeared to be yet one more departure from the purity of Christian doctrine, and only later did it become clear that Islam was a new religion, and not a heretical current within Christianity.

In the Qur'an "Jesus, the son of Mary" (Isa son of Marium) is mentioned on many occasions. Crucial to an understanding of the role of Jesus in the Qur'an is the following text:

> O followers of the Book! do not exceed the limits in your religion, and
> do not speak (lies) against Allah, but (speak) the truth; the Messiah,
> Isa son of Marium is only an apostle of Allah and His Word which He
> communicated to Marium and a spirit from Him; believe therefore in
> Allah and His apostles, and say not, Three. Desist, it is better for you;

[33]John of Damascus, *De Haeresibus* [On Heresies], in *Die Schriften des Johannes von Damaskos*, vol. 4, *Liber de Haeresibus. Opera Polemica*, ed. Bonifatius Kotter, Patristische Texte und Studien 22 (Berlin: Walter de Gruyter, 1981), 60–67. English translation in John of Damascus, *Writings*, trans. Frederic H. Chase, Jr., The Fathers of the Church 37 (Washington, DC: The Catholic University of America Press, 1958), 153–160.

Allah is only one God; far be It from His glory that He should have a son.[34]

Islam proceeds from the belief that God is one and that he cannot have a son. The Christian teaching on the Trinity is declared to be false, as is the notion that Jesus has a divine origin. As in Christian theology, Islam draws a clear distinction between the Creator and the created. Jesus is understood to be the Word of God; however, unlike the Gospel of John, where it is stated that the "Word was God" (Jn 1.1), in Islam the Word of God has a created origin. This brings the Islamic perception of Jesus closer to Arianism.

Salvator Mundi, Leonardo da Vinci, 1506–1513.

Over the centuries the Church has contended with teachings denying the divine nature of Jesus. When in the fourth century Arius refused to recognize Jesus as the Son of God, consubstantial with the Father, the Church held the First Ecumenical Council, at which Arianism was condemned. Many centuries later, at the beginning of the twentieth century, the Orthodox Church declared the writer Leo Tolstoy to have fallen away from her, as he had attempted to replace the Gospels with his own teaching on Jesus as a moral authority deprived of all divine dignity.

Reacting to these challenges to the notion of Jesus as God and Savior, the Church developed and refined her own theology, which was aimed at refuting them. The terminology used to expound the Church's teaching on Christ was also accordingly clarified. At the same time, Christians believed that the appearance of new theological formulations was aimed not at creating a fundamentally new understanding of the role and significance of Jesus Christ, but merely at a more precise exposition of the original belief in his divinity, which was characteristic of the Church from her very foundation.

---

[34]Qur'an 4.171. Translation from *Al-Qur'ān Al-hakīm* [Holy Qur'an], trans. M. H. Shakir, 2nd U.S. ed. (Elmhurst, NY: Tahrike Tarsile Qur'an, 1983).

It is in this sense that we can say that the Church's teaching on the divine nature of Jesus Christ has been consistent throughout the entire history of Christianity. And even in our day, when Christianity exists in the form of various confessions, denominations, and communities with a broad spectrum of mutual disagreements, all Christians—Catholics, Orthodox, and Protestants—recognize Jesus Christ as God and Savior, of one essence with the Father in his divinity, and of one essence with us according to his humanity.

4. The Search for the "Historical Jesus" and His *Kērygma*

After the appearance of Islam, for many centuries no other new teaching challenged Christianity on the notion of Jesus as God and Savior. In the Christian East and West, art and literature were dominated by the canonical image of Christ, which was depicted in numerous icons, frescoes, stained glass windows, theological treatises, and Church hymns.

Adjustments to this image were introduced at the time of the Renaissance, when artists began to portray Christ in a realistic manner. If in the work of El Greco a genetic dependence on the iconographic canon was still preserved, then in many other masters of the Renaissance period this dependence disappeared, and Jesus appears before us as a simple person, without a halo, and his sufferings are portrayed with exaggerated realism.

The next step on the path of moving away from Church tradition was the period of the Reformation in the West. The Protestants began with rejecting the authority of holy tradition and the Bible was declared to be the sole source of authority. However, in refuting the tradition of the Church, they at the same time very quickly lost the understanding of Scripture as an integral source and began gradually to deconstruct it. Already Luther had cast doubt upon the validity of a number of books in the New Testament, in particular the Epistle of James, since certain of its positions—for example, the teaching that "faith without works is dead" (Jas 2.20)—contradict the Lutheran understanding of salvation.

In the preface to his translation of the New Testament, Luther wrote:

> . . . St. John's Gospel and his first epistle, St. Paul's epistles, especially Romans, Galatians and Ephesians, and St. Peter's first epistle are the books that show you Christ and teach you all that it is necessary and salvatory for you to know, even if you were never to see or hear any other book or doctrine.

Martin Luther, Lucas Cranach the Elder, 1543.

Therefore St. James' epistle is really an epistle of straw, compared to these others, for it has nothing of the nature of the Gospel about it.[35]

Subsequently, Protestants began to cast doubt on the authenticity and meaning of a number of other books of Holy Scripture.

It was on Protestant soil in the latter half of the eighteenth century that the idea arose of reconstructing the image of the "historical Jesus" by liberating him from later layers of church interpretation. Unlike the representatives of the "mythological school" that appeared at the same time, the representatives of the movement to "demythologize the Gospels" did not deny that Jesus was a real person. However, they refused to see in him anything supernatural, and declared the Gospel narratives about his miracles to be the creative work of early Christian writers who had decided to attribute a divine image to the man Jesus.

The founder of this approach is considered to be Hermann Samuel Reimarus (1694–1768), who suggested that Jesus was a revolutionary who twice had failed in attempts to organize an uprising; after he was executed, his disciples invented the story of his resurrection. Reimarus believed Jesus to be a Hebrew rabbi who did not teach any lofty mysteries but merely

[35] Martin Luther, *Preface to the German Translation of the New Testament (1522)*, in Hans J. Hillerbrand, ed., *The Protestant Reformation*, Harper Torchbooks TB 1342 (New York, NY: Harper & Row, 1968), 42.

Head of Christ,
El Greco, 1580–1585.

simple instructions on life's obligations: it was the apostles who gave theological authority to this supposed teaching of Jesus. Reimarus's work was published in 1774 by Gotthold Ephraim Lessing, and since then the search for the "historical Jesus" has acquired a systematic character.

This search developed, in particular, in the works of the representatives of the Tübingen School of New Testament isagogics,[36] headed by Ferdinand Christian Baur (1792–1860), who advanced the theory of the existence of two mutually contending currents in the early Church: Petrine Christianity and Pauline Christianity (that is, the struggle between the followers of the apostle Peter and the followers of the Apostle Paul). The New Testament, which he believed was written in the second century, was supposed to reconcile these two tendencies.

The other representative of the Tübingen School, David Friedrich Strauss (1808–1874), the author of the book *The Life of Jesus*, wanted to prove that within the first generation of Jesus' disciples his life became overgrown with various incredible myths and stories of miracles that never actually happened. A positivist and extreme rationalist, Strauss denied the very possibility of miracles, although he admitted the existence of God.

Strauss's ideas were popularized in France by Ernest Renan (1823–1892), who also assumed a strictly rationalistic position and proceeded from the idea that there is and cannot be anything supernatural in life.

Another rationalist, Leo Tolstoy (1828–1910), also proceeded from analogous presuppositions. He popularized the ideas of Strauss and Renan on Russian soil. A famous writer, he decided to engage in the demythologization of the Gospels; however, he approached his task not as a scholar, which he was not, but as a teacher of morality, which he thought himself to be. Tolstoy made the idea of juxtaposing the Gospel text against the

---

[36]Isagogics (ultimately from Gk. *eisagōgē*, "introduction") refers to introductory study of the Bible preliminary to interpreting it.

Church's teaching the basis of his "commentary and translation" of the Gospels. As a result, the "translation" he made is more reminiscent of a caricature of the Gospel text than a translation or even a retelling.

While Tolstoy's works, which were aimed at discrediting the Church, are today perceived as a sad historical curiosity, we cannot say the same of the works of those Protestant scholars who, at the turn of the twentieth century, furthered the work of the demythologization of the Gospels. Their works to this day continue to exert a considerable influence on research in the field of the New Testament.

A substantial contribution to the development of the school of demythologization was made by a professor of the University of Berlin, Adolf von Harnack (1851–1930). He rejected the conclusions of the Tübingen School that the New Testament was compiled in the second century; however, like the other German rationalist theologians, he could not see a vertical dimension in religion, believing that religion was a mixture of ethics and inner experiences. He treated Jesus as a great teacher of morality who was not the Son of God, but an ordinary person. Harnack interpreted Jesus' resurrection symbolically, seeing in it the expression of the early Christian idea of the triumph of life over death, and not an actual historical fact.

A key figure in Protestant theology in the twentieth century was Rudolf Bultmann (1884–1976). Unlike his predecessors at the University of Tübingen, Bultmann rejected attempts at the reconstruction of the "historical Jesus." Instead, he concentrated upon the search for the original Christian *kērygma*, which, he believed, ought to be demythologized, that is, cleansed of its mythological shell, as well as from its later editorial corrections, the influence of Hellenism, Judaism, and Gnosticism. If for the representatives of the Tübingen School in the nineteenth century Jesus appears as a historical person, "cleansed" of later theological layers, then for Bultmann, on the contrary, the theological *kērygma*, understood in a rationalist spirit, is disassociated from the "historical Jesus" and becomes an independent object of research.

Following researchers in the field of the Old Testament, Bultmann applied to the New Testament a method of interpreting the texts that has since been called the method of form criticism (*die formgeschichtliche*

The Appearance of Christ before the People, Alexander Ivanov, 1837–1857.

Methode), according to which each New Testament narrative has its own *Sitz im Leben*–its "setting in life." According to this method, for an understanding of any given text, the place and time of its appearance and its connection with a concrete historical Christian community are of crucial importance.

Bultmann and other researchers who used this method proceeded from the assumption that each Gospel passage existed for a long time in oral tradition and only later was written down, while this writing down was done with a definite aim and in a definite context, that is, in accordance with the needs of a particular community. In other words, what is primary is not the person of Jesus or his teaching, but the church community, in which one or several authors molded the image of Christ by taking into account the requirements of the community members. In order to restore the historical image of Jesus, it was essential, according to this method, to bring to light those "pure" forms that constituted the original nucleus of the Gospel tradition before it became overgrown with all sorts of additions.[37]

[37]Joel B. Green, Scot McKnight, and I. Howard Marshall, eds., *Dictionary of Jesus and the Gospels: A Compendium of Contemporary Biblical Scholarship* (Downers Grove, IL: InterVarsity, 1992), 243–250.

To Bultmann also belongs the development of the "law of increasing distinctness," which was taken up by many New Testament researchers in the twentieth century. According to this "law,"[38] behind every text that existed in the oral tradition, there is an original kernel that, as the tradition develops, becomes overgrown with ever newer additions: by the time the text is written down, these additions have become a part of the text, although they were absent in the beginning. This view, however, has been disputed by many scholars, who have shown that in the history of oral tradition things often turned out in exactly the opposite way: details were erased or lost over time, while the basic kernel of meaning was preserved.[39] For this reason Bultmann's "law," like many of his other methodological approaches, is today extremely susceptible to criticism.

Apart from the method of form criticism, researchers in the field of the New Testament have used other methods, in particular the method of tradition criticism (*Traditionsgeschichte*). This method involves identifying and investigating the forms in which various traditions about Jesus could have circulated before they were fixed in the text of the canonical Gospels. In light of this, the following criteria for the authenticity of a given tradition were used: repeated instances of testimonies (the tradition is reflected in more than one source); coherence (the tradition accords with other traditions on Jesus); non-convergence with other analogues (for example, the various rabbinical texts of the Jewish tradition or the traditions of the early Church); and brevity (the shorter version of a tradition was considered to be more authentic than its longer version).[40]

The method of redaction criticism (*Redaktionsgeschichte*) is yet another means of restoring the hypothetical authentic Gospel tradition by trimming it of material that had supposedly been added later. The adherents of this method saw the authors of the New Testament writings primarily as compilers who had brought together various oral and written traditions

[38]For more details, see Rudolf Bultmann, *Existence and Faith: Shorter Writings of Rudolf Bultmann*, trans. and ed. Schubert M. Ogden (New York, NY: Meridian Books, 1960), 41–42.

[39]Graham N. Stanton, *Jesus of Nazareth in New Testament Preaching*, Society for New Testament Studies Monograph Series 27 (London: Cambridge University Press, 1974), 178.

[40]See *Dictionary of Jesus and the Gospels*, 831–834.

and edited them in accordance with their theology and the needs of their communities. To the criteria of authenticity listed in our description of the method of tradition criticism, the adherents of this method have also added the following: involuntary evidence of reliability (the narrative details reveal the authorship of an eyewitness); the use of constructions characteristic of the Aramaic language; the use of terms that show Palestinian origin of a given redaction; and the mention of customs characteristic of Palestine in Jesus' time.[41]

All of these aforementioned methods arose from the demand to classify the Gospel material according to a definite form, for example: separate *logia* or a saying (a short utterance by Jesus in the form of a commandment or aphorism); a story with oral speech (narrative material ending with a saying of Jesus); a story of a miracle (an episode describing a healing, the expelling of demons or any other miracle accomplished by Jesus); a parable (a short imaginary story or saying with the use of comparison or likening); a speech (the sayings of Jesus collected into a long speech, for example, the Sermon on the Mount); a historical narrative (the story of a particular event that is, from the researcher's perspective, "legendary" by virtue of the supernatural phenomena described in it); an episode from the passion (the story of the passion is usually highlighted as a separate group of "forms").

We have not set ourselves the task of examining the theories of numerous researchers in the nineteenth and twentieth centuries who have sought out the "historical Jesus" or his *kērygma* beyond the confines of Church tradition or who have set Jesus and his teaching in opposition to holy tradition. The works of these authors, for all their differences in approach, are united by one thing: striving to denounce the Church's perception of Jesus and "show by what right the Christian Churches refer to this Jesus Christ who never existed, to doctrines that he did not teach, to powers that he did not grant, and to divine sonship, which he himself considered impossible and to which he did not pretend."[42]

---

[41]Ibid., 662–669.

[42]Rudolf Augstein, *Jesus Menschensohn* (Munich: C. Bertelsmann, 1972), 7. Translation by present translator.

The Passion of
Christ, mosaic,
530s.

Each of these researchers examined the life and teaching of Jesus by proceeding from a certain philosophical standpoint or ideological presupposition: in the beginning the initial principle would be established, and then this principle would be applied to the text in order to attain the required result. If a particular New Testament text did not fit into the framework of the given principle, it could simply be cast aside and declared to be historically unreliable or unworthy of attention.

Thus, for example, in the 1980s and 1990s in America, the Jesus Seminar was held, which brought together around 150 people, including scholars who represented the extreme liberal wing in the community of New Testament researchers, as well as simple amateurs. These people set themselves the task of recreating the image of the historical Jesus by determining which materials in the Gospels were, from their perspective, historically reliable. In the period between 1991 and 1996, they analyzed 387 excerpts concerning 176 Gospel events. Decisions on the degree of reliability of a particular excerpt were arrived at by a vote, and the excerpt would be assigned a particular color: red (meaning that the fellows of the Seminar "had a relatively high level of confidence that the event actually took place"), pink ("the event probably occurred"), gray ("the event is unlikely"), and black ("the story about the event is a fiction"). Of 176 events only 10 were flagged as red and 19 as pink.[43]

The Jesus Seminar is more of a curiosity in the history of research in the field of the New Testament than an event having any significance for the development of New Testament scholarship. It is difficult to imagine a seminar on medicine that would bring people together who were known to be distrustful of medicine, and in which there would be all sorts of amateurs alongside qualified physicians, and they would pronounce a verdict regarding certain medical drugs or therapeutic methods by means of a vote. Scholarship should not be turned into charlatanism. Nevertheless, the views of charlatans in the field of New Testament studies continue to exert their corrupting influence on a wider public by undermining trust in the Gospels as a historical source.

The result of the work of numerous scholars and pseudo-scholars united by the idea of extracting a historical kernel from mainly unreliable Gospel narratives has been that they have "fabricated a 'historical' Jesus reflecting (and thus justifying) their own theological and philosophical views; they fashioned a Jesus in their own image and likeness. The quest for the historical Jesus had reached an impasse, and many were skeptical about the possibility of writing a biography of Jesus at all."[44]

All of the authors who undertook the search for the "historical Jesus" in the nineteenth and twentieth centuries proceeding from the aforementioned presuppositions are united in their presumption of distrust towards the Gospels as a historical source. In this they have radically departed from traditional Christianity, whether Orthodox, Catholic, or Protestant:

> Christian faith has trusted that in these texts we encounter the real Jesus. . . . Yet everything changes when historians suspect that these texts may be hiding the real Jesus from us, at best because they give us the historical Jesus filtered through the spectacles of early Christian faith, at worst because much of what they tell us is a Jesus constructed

---

[43]Robert W. Funk, ed., *The Acts of Jesus: The Search for the Authentic Deeds of Jesus* (San Francisco, CA: HarperSanFrancisco, 1998), 1.

[44]David E. Aune, *The New Testament in Its Literary Environment*, Library of Early Christianity 8 (Philadelphia, PA: The Westminster Press, 1987), 20.

Statue of Christ
the Redeemer,
Corcovado
mountain, Rio de
Janeiro, Brazil,
1922–1931.

by the needs and interests of various groups in the early church. Then
that phrase "the historical Jesus" comes to mean, not the Jesus of the
Gospels, but the allegedly real Jesus behind the Gospels, the Jesus the
historian must reconstruct by subjecting the Gospels to ruthlessly
objective (so it is claimed) scrutiny. . . . The result of such work is inevitably not one historical Jesus, but many.[45]

Towards the end of the twentieth century, it became evident that the
search for the "historical Jesus," which had lasted for more than two hundred years, had become a fiasco. Nevertheless, there are ever-new attempts
at reviving this process. Each year new "revolutionary biographies" of Jesus
appear on the shelves of bookshops, and the authors of these books make
fantastic discoveries based not so much on new scientific data as on their
personal interests, tastes, sympathies, or antipathies.

The striving to find new, original approaches to the old problem of
the "historical Jesus" has led in recent decades to the appearance of theories, according to which Jesus was an itinerant Jewish rabbi,[46] a Cynic

---

[45]Bauckham, *Jesus and the Eyewitnesses*, 2–3.

[46]He is presented as such in the works of the British scholar of Jewish Hungarian origin
Géza Vermes, who enjoys great popularity and has been repeatedly published in the West. See
Géza Vermes, *The Changing Faces of Jesus* (London: Penguin, 2001), 222–262; Géza Vermes, *The
Authentic Gospel of Jesus* (London: Penguin, 2004), 398–417.

philosopher and revolutionary,[47] or an apocalyptic prophet.[48] Every such theory is based either on a tendentious reading of the canonical sources or on an excessive interest in non-canonical sources, or on other erroneous methodological presuppositions that lead the reader further away from the real Jesus as he is revealed on the pages of the Gospels:

> Modern scholars and writers, in their never-ending quest to find something new and to advance daring theories that run beyond the evidence, have either distorted or neglected the New Testament Gospels, resulting in the fabrication of an array of "pseudo-Jesuses." A variety of influences have led to these results, whether (1) misplaced faith and misguided suspicions, (2) cramped starting points and overly strict critical methods, (3) questionable texts from later centuries, (4) appeals to contexts alien to Jesus' actual environment, (5) skeletal sayings devoid of context altogether, (6) failure to take into account Jesus' mighty deeds, (7) dubious use of Josephus and other resources of late antiquity, (8) anachronisms and exaggerated claims, or (9) hokum history and bogus findings. In short, just about every error imaginable has been made. A few writers have made almost all of them.[49]

At present, practically all rationalist theories of the origin of Christianity have receded into the past. However, attempts at fabricating new Jesuses in accordance with the sympathies and tastes of scholars continue and, evidently, will continue. In a certain sense Jesus has shared the fate of many renowned historical persons, the interest in whom is so great that various generations and groups of scholars consider it their duty to advance new sensational hypotheses concerning their personality, biography, and heritage (suffice it to mention the recent hypothesis that

---

[47]This is how Jesus is presented by the influential American researcher John Dominic Crossan in his book, *The Historical Jesus: The Life of a Mediterranean Jewish Peasant* (San Francisco, CA: HarperSanFrancisco, 1991), 421–422.

[48]Jesus is presented as such by the influential Bible scholar but convinced agnostic Bart Ehrman. See Bart D. Ehrman, *Jesus: Apocalyptic Prophet of the New Millenium* (Oxford: Oxford University Press, 1999), 125–139.

[49]Craig A. Evans, *Fabricating Jesus: How Modern Scholars Distort the Gospels* (Downers Grove, IL: IVP Books, 2006), 16.

Shakespeare was a woman[50]). At the same time, not a single historical person can come close to Jesus in the number of theories that have been advanced about him.

Science fiction, the genre in which we may include a significant number of contemporary "revolutionary biographies" of Jesus, ought to be distinguished from a conscientious historical-critical method of studying the New Testament, which is based on the comparison of manuscripts, the study of the historical context of the Gospels, the comparison of Gospel narratives between themselves, and their examination in the light of new historical and archeological data now accessible to science. This method has become a sound part of scholarship and maintains its position to the present. It cannot be ignored when studying the sources on the life of Jesus, since in itself, independent of the ideological paradigms upon which it was originally based, it has made a valuable contribution to the study of the text of the New Testament.

In the twentieth century this has been demonstrated in particular by the works of some Catholic and Orthodox specialists in the field of New Testament studies who have managed to combine a traditional ecclesiastical approach with attention to the findings of contemporary biblical criticism. At the same time, in the works of a whole series of Protestant theologians, we can observe not only a retreat from the extremes of rationalism, but also a turning towards the tradition of the Church as an important source from the perspective of scholarship for the interpretation of the life and teaching of Jesus. Some of them today are making an important contribution to debunking rationalist theories that contrast the "historical Jesus" with the "Jesus of the faithful."

As Richard Bauckham notes, "All history—meaning all that historians write, all historiography—is an inextricable combination of fact and interpretation, the empirically observable and the intuited or constructed meaning."[51] Since the Gospels contain precisely such a combination, the motivation behind searches for the "historical Jesus" flows from this—the

---

[50]The theory belongs to the American literary critic Robin P. Williams, who declared in 2004 that Mary Sidney, the Countess of Pembroke, wrote under the name of Shakespeare.

[51]Bauckham, *Jesus and the Eyewitnesses*, 3.

Manuscript Greek Gospel,
10th to 11th c.

desire to find the "bare facts," cleansed from all interpretation, which is imparted to these facts by the Gospels themselves and later Church tradition. But not a single historian can, in principle, reject the interpretation of facts: if he rejects one interpretation, he must create another. Consequently, "[a different interpretation] comes not merely from deconstructing the Gospels but also from reconstructing a Jesus who, as a portrayal of who Jesus really was, can rival the Jesus of the Gospels."[52]

Bauckham asks "whether the enterprise of reconstructing a historical Jesus behind the Gospels . . . can ever substitute for the Gospels themselves as a way of access to the reality of Jesus."[53] His answer after reflecting on this issue is:

It cannot be said that historical study of Jesus and the Gospels is illegitimate or that it cannot assist our understanding of Jesus. . . . What is in question is whether the reconstruction of a Jesus other than the Jesus of the Gospels . . . can ever provide the kind of access to the reality of Jesus that Christian faith and theology have always trusted we have in the Gospels. By comparison with the Gospels, any Jesus reconstructed by the quest cannot fail to be reductionist from the perspective of Christian faith and theology.

Here, then, is the dilemma that has always faced Christian theology in the light of the quest of the historical Jesus. Must history and theology part company at this point where Christian faith's investment in history is at its most vital? Must we settle for trusting the Gospels for our access to the Jesus in whom Christians believe, while leaving the historians to construct a historical Jesus based only on what they can verify for themselves by critical historical methods? I think there is a better way forward, a way in which theology and history may meet in the historical Jesus instead of parting company there.[54]

[52]Ibid., 4.
[53]Ibid.
[54]Ibid., 4–5.

The present book, the first of a six-volume series, consists in precisely this attempt—to extend a hand to secular researchers while at the same time standing firmly on the soil of the Gospel text as the fundamental source of reliable information on Jesus. In this book and the subsequent volumes the results of contemporary research will be presented quite broadly. At the same time, the foundation of our investigation will always remain the text of the Gospels, which we will read attentively, investigating it both in its historical context and from a theological perspective. The most important element of this investigation will be the study of parallels—the comparison of different versions of one and the same saying or narrative contained in various Gospels. We will also pay attention to the Old Testament prehistory of the Gospel texts and events. Finally, we will take into account (selectively) the commentaries to which the text has been subjected in Church tradition and with which it has become overgrown in contemporary scholarly literature.

Chapter 2

THE SOURCES

---

1. The Study of the Gospels

The Phenomenon of the Four Gospels

Let us turn to the main source of our knowledge of Jesus—the Gospels. Each person who takes the New Testament into his hands for the first time is immediately struck by the fact that the story of Jesus is expounded in it four times by four different authors, who in many instances repeat each other almost word for word. Why did this happen? And why was it necessary to set forth the same events in one and the same book two, three, or four times?

In order to understand this phenomenon, we must consider the period in which the Gospels were composed. According to the generally accepted opinion of contemporary biblical scholarship, all the Gospels were written in the latter half of the first century. This was the time when the Christian Church was coming into being, when she was beginning to spread quite rapidly.

The first written memorials to be composed that would become part of the New Testament were, as scholars suggest, not the Gospels, but the epistles of the apostle Paul, which were written on various occasions and addressed to various church communities or individuals. It is characteristic

---

The Apostle Paul,
Andrea Vanni, 1390s.

that Paul never quotes the Gospels as a literary source, whereas the Old Testament is quoted in his letters quite abundantly. This may be linked to the fact that the Gospels, at the time when Paul's letters appeared, did not exist in a definite written form, or that they were not yet in universal circulation within the Church.

The dissemination of the good news began practically straight away in the Greek language—the basic language of the *oikoumenē* (the inhabited world) within which Christianity spread. As is known, Jesus and his disciples spoke in Aramaic, whereas all the written sources concerning his life and ministry have come down to us in Greek.

This phenomenon is linked to the fact that the purpose of the creation of the written body of narratives on Jesus Christ was the dissemination of Christianity not in a Jewish, but pagan, and mainly Greek-speaking, environment. The conflict that arose between Jesus and the Jews in his lifetime did not end after his death. The disciples quickly felt that preaching Christianity among the Jews would not have much success, and, to a significant degree under Paul's influence, they took the decision to concentrate upon preaching among the Gentiles (Acts 15.1–34). It was then that the need arose to document in written form all of the narratives on Jesus, which until then had existed only in oral tradition.

The Greek term *euangelion* literally means "good news" and is used in relation to the message that Jesus brought and that was documented by his disciples. Yet each Gospel is headed by the name of a concrete author. In the Greek original, these headings are: "according to Matthew," "according to Mark," "according to Luke," and "according to John."[1] In other words, this is not the good news of each of the four authors, but the good news of Jesus Christ *according to the version* or *exposition* of one of the four evangelists.

[1] The Greek *kata* means not so much "of" as "according to," "in accordance with."

The four Gospels are often compared to four portraits of the same person painted by various artists. Each of them sees their subject's features in their own way. One artist will paint him in profile, another *en face*, one will give a head-and-shoulders portrait, while another will depict him half-length, while the third will paint his subject full-length. The background, clothing, surroundings, and even the facial features may differ. Yet the subject remains the same.

The Miroslav Gospel, Peć, 7th c.

Proceeding from the generally accepted account in modern scholarship that the Gospel of Mark appeared before the other Gospels (more on this will be written below), the important German New Testament scholar Rudolf Schnackenburg notes that it contains a portrait of Jesus that was known to the other two synoptic evangelists, Matthew and Luke. Each of them added to the portrait in accordance with the aim of his narrative, taking into account the interests of the supposed reader. Finally, John raises the Gospel narrative to another, loftier theological level. And yet, all four narratives remain the "one Gospel in four forms,"[2] and the portrait of Jesus is not transformed into portraits of four different persons.

In developing this topic, the contemporary British scholar Richard Burridge states that the early Church deliberately spurned attempts to unite the four Gospel narratives into a single whole, since she "wanted to preserve four different Gospels, each with their own literary and theological purposes in their different portraits of Jesus." Yet, all four evangelists "tell essentially the same story." We have before us "four Gospels, with four pictures, telling four versions of the one story of Jesus."[3]

---

[2]Rudolf Schnackenburg, *Jesus in the Gospels: A Biblical Christology*, trans. O. C. Dean (Louisville, KY: Westminster John Knox Press, 1995), 295–298. Cf. Irenaeus: "the Gospel is quadriform"; *Against Heresies* 3.11.8 (*ANF* 1:429).

[3]Richard A. Burridge, *Four Gospels, One Jesus?: A Symbolic Reading*, 2nd ed. (Grand Rapids, MI: Eerdmans, 2005), 168.

The Evangelist Matthew,
miniature in a Gospel book,
13th c.

The Origin of the Gospels

What do we know of the evangelists, of the time when the Gospels were created, of the order in which they appeared? The earliest information regarding this is contained in the second-century author Irenaeus of Lyons:

> Matthew also issued a written Gospel among the Hebrews in their own dialect, while Peter and Paul were preaching at Rome, and laying the foundations of the Church. After their departure, Mark, the disciple and interpreter of Peter, did also hand down to us in writing what had been preached by Peter. Luke also, the companion of Paul, recorded in a book the Gospel preached by him. Afterwards, John, the disciple of the Lord, who also had leaned upon His breast, did himself publish a Gospel during his residence at Ephesus in Asia.[4]

These are the words of someone who took upon himself the task of setting forth Church tradition as a counter to the numerous heresies that had arisen at that time. The excerpt shows that in the second century a clear idea already existed of how the four Gospels were created, and of their authors. The first, Matthew's Gospel, according to Irenaeus, was written in Hebrew during the lifetimes of Peter and Paul. After their deaths, Mark, the disciple and "translator" and "interpreter"[5] of Peter, and Luke, the disciple of Paul, complied their Gospels. The last Gospel to appear was that of John.

A somewhat different, yet very similar version of the origin of the Gospels is given by Clement of Alexandria (late second century), whose opinion is cited by the fourth-century church historian Eusebius of Caesarea. According to Clement, "those Gospels were first written which include

---

[4]Irenaeus of Lyons, *Against Heresies* 3.1.1 (*ANF* 1:414).

[5]It is noteworthy that the Aramaic equivalent for the term "translator" (*mṯargmānā/mṯurgmānā*) also means "interpreter."

the genealogies,"[6] that is, Matthew and Luke. Like Irenaeus, Clement believes the Gospel of John was the last to have appeared: "John, last of all, conscious that the outward facts had been set forth in the Gospels, was urged on by his disciples, and, divinely moved by the Spirit, composed a spiritual Gospel."[7] Regarding the Gospel of Mark, Clement states:

When Peter had publicly preached the word at Rome, and by the Spirit had proclaimed the Gospel, that those present, who were many, exhorted Mark, as one who had followed him for a long time

St Jerome, Jacques Blanchard, 1632.

and remembered what had been spoken, to make a record of what was said; and that he did this, and distributed the Gospel among those that asked him. And ... when the matter came to Peter's knowledge he neither strongly forbade it nor urged it forward.[8]

By the fourth century, both in the East and in the West, the notion that the Gospels were compiled in the order in which they are placed in the manuscript tradition became universal. At the end of the fourth century, St Jerome wrote of the four evangelists:

The first evangelist is Matthew, the publican, who was surnamed Levi. He published his Gospel in Judaea in the Hebrew language, chiefly for the sake of Jewish believers in Christ, who adhered in vain to the shadow of the law, although the substance of the Gospel had come. The second is Mark, the amanuensis [or *interpres*] of the Apostle Peter, and first bishop of the Church of Alexandria. He did not himself see our Lord and Saviour, but he related the matter of his Master's preaching with more regard to minute detail than to historical sequence. The third is Luke, the physician, by birth a native of Antioch, in Syria, whose praise is in the Gospel [2 Cor 8.18]. He was himself a disciple of the

[6]Eusebius of Caesarea, *Ecclesiastical History* 6.14.6 (Oulton, LCL).
[7]Eusebius, *Ecclesiastical History* 6.14.7 (Oulton, LCL).
[8]Eusebius, *Ecclesiastical History* 6.14.6–7 (Oulton, LCL).

Symbols of the Evangelists, icon, 16th c.

apostle Paul, and composed his book in Achaia and Boeotia. He thoroughly investigates certain particulars and, as he himself confesses in the preface, describes what he had heard rather than what he had seen. The last is John, the Apostle and Evangelist, whom Jesus loved most, who, reclining on the Lord's bosom, drank the purest streams of doctrine, and was the only one thought worthy of the words from the cross, "Behold! thy mother." . . . By all of these things it is plainly shown that only the four Gospels ought to be received, and all the lamentations of the Apocrypha should be sung by heretics, who, in fact, are dead, rather than by living members of the Church.[9]

In the tradition of the Church, Matthew and John are considered to be among the twelve apostles, while Mark and Luke are from among the seventy apostles. The fact that Jesus, apart from the Twelve, chose another seventy apostles is mentioned in the Gospel of Luke (Lk 10.1), and this very fact can testify in favor of Luke belonging to the Seventy. If Mark and Luke were from among the seventy apostles, this means that they could have been eyewitnesses at least to some of the events they describe, and did not only reproduce the stories of Peter or the other apostles. At the same time, Luke's reference to those who "from the beginning were eyewitnesses, and ministers of the Word" (Lk 1.2) being the basic source of information that he used, compels us to conclude that he was not among their number, or at least that he was not an eyewitness to Jesus' life and ministry from the very beginning.

Over the centuries the Gospels were an object of great reverence in the Church, and even the number of evangelists was considered to be sacred.

[9]Jerome, *Commentary on the Gospel of Matthew*, Preface (PL 26:18–20). English translation from *NPNF*[2] 6:495 (up until ellipsis); Saint Jerome, *Commentary on Matthew*, trans. Thomas P. Scheck, The Fathers of the Church 117 (Washington, DC: The Catholic University of America Press, 2008), 56.

The four evangelists were compared to the four corners of the earth; their portrayals were found on the pendentives of crossed-dome churches, each wall of which was situated toward one of the four parts of the world—the east, the west, the north, and the south. The writings of the four evangelists have been interpreted many times over by the Church Fathers. For at least the 11 centuries of the Byzantine empire (from the fourth to the fifteenth centuries), for more than 1,500 years in the West (from the fourth to the nineteenth centuries), for more than 900 years in Russia (from the tenth to the nineteenth centuries), the Gospels were the most quoted sources, and the number of citations from them could not be compared to any other work of literature.

Origen, engraving, 16th c.

The question of how the narratives of the four Gospels were interconnected, and whether there was a mutual dependence between them, occupied Christian writers as far back as the second century. Attempts at a critical analysis of the Gospel text (not in the sense of criticism of the claims contained within them, but in the sense of a comparative analysis of the narratives of the various evangelists) were undertaken in antiquity, in particular in the works of Origen (third century) and John Chrysostom (fourth century). St Augustine (fourth to fifth century) undertook the systematic labor of juxtaposing the narratives of the four evangelists, highlighting and explaining the variant readings between them. His treatise *The Harmony of the Gospels* has not lost its importance to this day.[10]

The blossoming of biblical criticism as a science concentrating on the study of the text of the Bible and the context in which the separate books of the Bible appeared, dates back to the nineteenth and twentieth centuries, when all of the Bible, including the four Gospels, became the object of scrupulous study. This study, as we have already said, was carried out under the influence of various factors, often based on prejudiced ideological standpoints, but in its totality it has given us a great wealth of material

[10]English translation: *NPNF*[1] 6:65–236.—*Ed.*

Blessed Augustine,
mosaic, 7th c.

for a profound and well-rounded understanding of the sources. In addition, the findings of biblical criticism have not only not disproved, but, on the contrary, in many cases have convincingly affirmed the ideas of the individual books of the Bible and their authors, which for many centuries have been preserved in Church tradition.

The Synoptic Problem

Of the four Gospels, three—Matthew, Mark, and Luke—are called "synoptic" in biblical scholarship since they contain much similar material. The term "synoptic" means, in translation from the Greek, "seeing together": this word indicates the significant similarity of the three Gospels and the presence of common material in them.

In many instances, such a degree of textual closeness can be observed between the three Gospel writers (or between two of the three) that it has compelled scholars to think of either the existence of a common literary source, or that they borrowed excerpts of the text from one another. For example, if we compare the stories of the calling of the two disciples in Matthew (Mt 4.18) and in Mark (Mk 1.16), then it is easy to note that the phrase "for they were fishers" is present in both Gospels: therefore, either one of the authors borrowed the text from the other, or both were relying upon a common written or oral source.

There are places where all three evangelists make one and the same syntactical error, that is, in all three cases the construction of the phrase does not correspond to the rules of the Greek language—for example: "But that ye may know that the Son of man hath power on earth to forgive sins, (then saith he to him who wad sick of the palsy)" (Mt 9.6; Mk 2.10; Lk 5.24).

Often the so-called *hapax legomena* (literally, "once spoken")—words or expressions that in the New Testament, or even throughout the whole Bible, are used only once, in one specific place—are identical. These

The Prophet
Malachi, fresco,
14th c.

include, for example, the phrase "and they laughed him to scorn" (Mt 9.24; Mk 5.40; Lk 8.53).

Quotations from the Old Testament are often subjected to similar changes in all three Synoptics. For example, the prophecy of Malachi reads thus in the original: "Behold, I will send my messenger, and he shall prepare the way before me" (Mal 3.1). In the two Synoptic Gospels this text is cited in the following redaction: "Behold, I send my messenger before thy face, which shall prepare thy way before thee" (Mk 1.2; Lk 7.27).

At the same time, between the three Synoptic Gospels there are quite a lot of differences. For example, the text of the Sermon on the Mount in the Gospel of Matthew (chapters five to seven) substantially differs from the so-called Sermon on the Plain in the Gospel of Luke (chapter six). The Beatitudes in Luke are approximately half the length of those in Matthew. The Lord's Prayer in Luke was also originally shorter. Over the centuries, as a result of correcting the text in the manuscripts, the Lord's Prayer in Luke has acquired the same form as it has in Matthew, that is, the phrases that were not found in Luke were gradually added from the Gospel of Matthew. But originally the difference was more substantial.

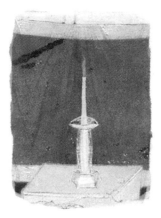

Detail from icon of the
Dormition, Theophanes the
Greek, 15th c.

In many places the sayings of Jesus are given by the same Gospel writer in more detail than by another. For example, in Matthew Jesus says: "Neither do men light a candle, and put it under a bushel, but on a candlestick; and it giveth light unto all that are in the house" (Mt 5.15). The parallel text in Luke goes thus: "No man, when he hath lighted a candle, covereth it with a vessel, or putteth *it* under a bed; but setteth *it* on a candlestick, that they which enter in may see the light" (Lk 8.16).

Thus, on the one hand, in the texts of the Synoptic Gospels there is room for a certain lack of agreement, as a result of either the fact that the evangelists were writing from memory, or as a result of using different sources. On the other hand, a remarkable similarity exists between the Synoptics, including textual similarity, which testifies, according to scholars, to the existence of a literary dependence between them.

There is a great deal of literature containing many hypotheses on how the Gospel text was composed and on the mutual dependence of the Synoptic Gospel writers. For a long time, right up until the mid-nineteenth century, it was believed that the earliest Gospel to appear was that of Matthew. In the twentieth century, however, the majority of scholars were inclined to believe that the Gospel of Mark was the first to appear, and that Matthew and Luke used it as a source.[11]

This is demonstrated, in particular, by the fact that Matthew and Luke agree in chronology concerning the Gospel events that they have in common with Mark, but differ in those places where they are absent in Mark.[12] In order to support this theory scholars refer also to the brevity of this Gospel, which contains 661 verses, whereas the Gospel of Matthew contains

[11]See, in particular, Burnett Hillman Streeter, *The Four Gospels: A Study in Origins: Treating of the Manuscript Tradition, Sources, Authorship, and Dates* (London: Macmillan, 1964), 157–169, which briefly outlines the arguments in favor of the primacy of Mark.

[12]See the chapter "To kata Markon evangelio [The Gospel according to Mark]" in Iōannēs Karavidopoulos, *Eisagōgē stēn Kainē Diathēkē* [Introduction to the New Testament] (Thessaloniki: Ekdoseis P. Pournara, 2007).

1068 verses, and the Gospel of Luke 1149 verses. It is with the Gospel of Mark, supposedly the first to be compiled, that they associate the key moment of the transition from oral to written tradition.[13]

Further evidence of Mark's primacy is based on a comparative analysis of the parallel places in Mark and Matthew. This analysis shows that in a number of instances Matthew omits the references in Mark to the human properties of Jesus that could be seen as not appropriate to his divine dignity.[14] From this the conclusion is reached that Matthew was writing later than Mark and redacted his text so that it would correspond more closely to church teaching. This conclusion, however, can be sustained only if we take Mark's primacy as axiomatic.[15] With the same success, if we proceed from the primacy of Matthew, we can say that Mark was writing after him and, for whatever considerations of his own, he added to the narrative those references of the human properties of Jesus that are absent in Matthew.

Throughout the twentieth century the most widespread theory of the interdependence of the three Synoptic Gospels was the "two-source hypothesis," according to which the text of the two Synoptic Gospels was based on the Gospel of Mark and upon one hypothetical common primary source, known as the Q source.[16] The hypothesis of the existence of this source arose in German Protestant circles on the basis of the words of Papias of Hierapolis (second century), which have survived in the writings of the fourth-century church historian Eusebius of Caesarea, according to whom "Matthew collected the oracles [*logia*] in the Hebrew language, and each interpreted as best he could."[17] From these words the conclusion was made that the proto-Gospel was a collection including the sayings of Jesus

[13]Michael L. Cook, *Christology as Narrative Quest* (Collegeville, MN: Liturgical Press, 1997), 68.

[14]Peter M. Head, *Christology and the Synoptic Problem: An Argument for Markan Priority*, Society for New Testament Studies Monograph Series 94 (Cambridge: Cambridge University Press, 1997), 111–120.

[15]Ibid., 259–260.

[16]From the German *Quelle*, meaning "source." In 1861 Heinrich Julius Holtzmann suggested the existence of this common source, and in 1890 Christian Hermann Weisse introduced the abbreviation Q, which came into common usage.

[17]Eusebius of Caesarea, *Ecclesiastical History* 3.39.16 (Lake, LCL).

Eusebius of Caesarea

without any narrative on his life, death, and resurrection. Over time this hypothesis gained recognition in the German- and English-speaking world, including among many Catholic theologians.[18]

Q is understood as the common primary source that, as has been proposed, included about 230 sayings of Jesus that are present in Matthew and Luke, but absent in Mark. Some scholars believe that the Q source originally was oral in character and was only later documented in written form. Various guesses have been made—and continue to be made—regarding the language and composition of Q, the location and time of its writing, and its literary genre.[19] It has been suggested, following Papias, that it could have been compiled in the Hebrew language, and then translated into Greek. In order to "restore" Q, sayings from the apocryphal *Gospel of Thomas* have also been used.

The appearance of the Q hypothesis, which has been accepted as an axiom by the majority of New Testament scholars in the twentieth century, was not simply the result of a comparative analysis of the texts of the three Synoptic Gospels. To a great degree, it was also linked to the notion that only part of the Gospel material goes back to the "historical Jesus," whereas the remaining part is the fruit of the activities of later redactors. Significant efforts were accordingly directed at uncovering which sayings in the Gospels could be attributed to Jesus. With this aim, scholars deconstructed the Gospel text by dismembering it into parts in order to distinguish the supposed authentic kernel from later added layers and commentaries.

We will not go into the details of the scholarly discussion regarding the Q source, as well as regarding what in the Gospels goes back to the "historical Jesus" and what is the result of later interpretations. The entire discussion is based on nothing more than guesses and presuppositions. At

[18]Benedict T. Viviano, *What Are They Saying About Q?* (New York, NY: Paulist Press, 2013), 10–85.

[19]See, for example, Christopher M. Tuckett, *Q and the History of Early Christianity: Studies on Q* (Edinburgh, T&T Clark, 1996), 83–106.

present, within the scholarly community voices are growing ever louder in asserting that the Q source is nothing more than a phantom invented by scholars who decided to prove to themselves and to the world that Jesus was a conventional teacher of morality who left a collection of moral *sententiae*; only many decades later did people begin to deify him, and his death was given a redemptive meaning.[20] The Q source was necessary for proving that these scholars were right; the desperate search for it did not yield any results, and then it was simply constructed by means of selecting individual sayings from the canonical and non-canonical Gospels.

Contemporary scholarship generally accepts the following data concerning the correlation of textual material between the Synoptics: ninety percent of the material of the Gospel according to Mark is present in the Gospel according to Matthew and more than fifty percent is present in the Gospel according to Luke. At the same time, verbatim matches make up about fifty-one percent of the material shared between the Gospels according to Mark and to Matthew and about fifty-three percent between the Gospels according to Mark and to Luke.[21] These figures, so it would appear to twentieth-century scholars, inevitably ought to lead one to the conclusion that the three Gospel writers are interdependent or at least have a common primary source.

---

[20]The hypothesis of Farrer and his follower Michael Goulder relies on the primacy of the Gospel according to Mark, but sees no need for the Q source to explain the interdependence of the three Synoptic Gospels. See, in particular: Austin M. Farrer, "On Dispensing with Q," in *Studies in the Gospels: Essays in Memory of R. H. Lightfoot*, ed. D. E. Nineham (Oxford: Blackwell, 1955), 55–88; Austin M. Farrer, *A Study in St. Mark* (Westminster: Dacre, 1951); Austin M. Farrer, *St. Matthew and St. Mark* (Westminster: Dacre, 1954); Michael D. Goulder, *Luke, A New Paradigm*, 2 vols. (Sheffield: JSOT, 1989). See also: Eta Linnemann, *Biblical Criticism on Trial: How Scientific is "Scientific Theology"?*, trans. Robert Yarbrough (Grand Rapids, MI: Kregel, 1998), 18–41 (in examining the question of whether Q is a fact or a fantasy, the author comes to the unambiguous conclusion that it is a fantasy); James R. Edwards, *The Hebrew Gospel and the Development of the Synoptic Tradition* (Grand Rapids, MI: Eerdmans, 2009), 209–241 (the author comes to the conclusion that it is time to part with the concept of Q).

[21]A. A. Tkachenko, "Evangelie. Strukturno-tematicheskaya kompozitsiya Evangeliy. Zhanr i literaturnye formy. Proiskhozhdenie i istochniki Evangeliy" [The Gospels. The structural and thematic composition of the Gospels. Genre and literary forms. Origin and sources of the Gospels], in *Pravoslavnaya entsiklopediya* [The Orthodox Encyclopedia], vol. 16 (Moscow: Tserkovno-nauchnyy tsentr "Pravoslavnaya Entsiklopediya," 2007), 670.

However, a contemporary statistical analysis of the correlation of the texts of the three synoptic evangelists corrects this notion. The renowned German New Testament researcher Eta Linnemann produces the following figures.[22] The Gospel according to Mark comprises 116 pericopes (excerpts).[23] Of them, 40 pericopes consisting of 3,635 words do not have parallels in the Gospels according to Matthew and Luke: this is 32.28 percent of the entire Gospel according to Mark. The remaining 76 pericopes, comprising 7,625 words, with parallels in Matthew and Luke, make up 67.72 percent of the Gospel according to Mark. However, from these 7,625 words in the three Synoptics, 1,539 words (20.19 percent) are completely identical, 1,640 words (21.51 percent) in Matthew and Mark, 877 words (11.5 percent) in Mark and Luke, and 381 words (5 percent) in Matthew and Luke. Of the 1,539 words identical between all three Synoptics, only 970 can be considered terms identical in meaning: this is 12.72 per cent of the total number of words making up the parallel material of all three Synoptics. The remainder are prepositions, articles and other auxiliary words, the presence of which in the three texts do not indicate any coincidence in meaning.

On the basis of a simple calculation, Linnemann comes to the conclusion that there is no longer any sufficient foundation to speak of a literary interdependence between the three Synoptic Gospels.[24] In order to be

[22]Linnemann, *Biblical Criticism on Trial*, 71–72. Linnemann is a clear example of a scholar who for a long time worked within the paradigms set down by Bultmann and other founders of the critical approach to the text of the New Testament. But something happened to her that scientific research does not take into account: she converted to Christ and believed in him as God and Savior. This compelled her to completely review the stereotypical concepts of biblical studies and look at them critically. After her conversion she devoted her whole life to debunking the myths created by scholars regarding the Gospels and the early history of the Church.

[23]The word "pericope" (from the Greek *perikopē*, meaning "excerpt") corresponds to the ancient division of the Gospel text preceding its division into chapters in the thirteenth century by Archbishop Stephen Langton. More on the division of the Gospel text will be said on pp. 146–147.

[24]Linnemann's statistical analysis has been subject to criticism in the scholarly community. Alternative statistical research has given different results. See, in particular, Joseph B. Tyson and Thomas R. W. Longstaff, *Synoptic Abstract*, The Computer Bible 15 (Wooster, OH: Biblical Research Associates, 1978). Nonetheless, the general conclusion reached by Linnemann is confirmed by a greater number of scholars in recent research: the presence of similar thematic material and a similar vocabulary among the three evangelists does not necessarily indicate a literary interdependence.

convinced of this, we can conduct a simple experiment: ask three people who do not know each other to describe an event which they witnessed—for example, a road accident—write down their stories, and then compare the three written texts.[25] There will undoubtedly be many differences, as each will describe the event in his own way. However, there will be material that has much in common: a similar subject, identical terminology ("road," "car," "driver," "crash," etc.) and similar word combinations. All this common "synoptic" material may make up thirty, forty, or fifty percent of the whole, and maybe even more. At the same time, in view of the conditions of the experiment, the literary interdependence of the three witnesses has been excluded, as would be the fact that they could be acquainted.

The Role of Oral Tradition

Similar conclusions are reached by another major contemporary specialist in the field of New Testament studies, James Dunn, on the basis of research on the peculiarities of oral tradition. He points out an essential methodological error that has significantly defined a huge amount of work done by scholars in the field of New Testament studies over the past two hundred years or so. This error is linked to the "literary paradigm,"[26] based on the notion that in the early Church there was an intensive process of creating various types of written sources on Jesus. Later on, these written sources were supposedly used by redactors and compilers such as Matthew, Mark, Luke, and John, who composed their narratives from extant fragments, but subjected the original material to intensive reworking for the purposes of their own interests and the interests of the local church communities that they represented.

This approach does not take into account the fact that at the early stage the tradition about Jesus was mainly, if not exclusively, spread in oral form, and this was characteristic of the culture in which the process of forming the Gospels took place. For this culture the most natural means of

[25]Cf. Metropolitan Kirill (Gundyaev), *Slovo pastyra. Bog i chelovek. Isroriya spaseniya* [The pastor's word. God and man. The history of salvation] (Moscow: Izdatel'skiy sovet Russkoy pravoslavnoy tserkvi, 2004), 102. Quoted on pp. 13–14.

[26]James Dunn, *A New Perspective on Jesus: What the Quest for the Historical Jesus Missed* (Grand Rapids, MI: Baker Academic, 2005), 36–39.

spreading information was by oral transmission: stories and traditions were conveyed "from mouth to mouth." An important role in all of this was played by memory, since in order to transmit a particular tradition it was necessary to commit it to memory.

Our generation has been witness to the rapid transition from the epoch of the printed word to the epoch of electronic information and communication. At the same time, the paradigms of transmitting information have substantially changed. Thirty or forty years ago the average person could retain in his memory what is now stored in a computer or mobile phone. For example, each could recall dozens of important phone numbers as they had to be constantly dialed manually. Today we do not have to remember the phone numbers of even those closest to us because they can be crammed into the memory of a mobile phone, which is always at hand, and the number can be brought up with one tap on the name of the person being dialed. This has its advantages and disadvantages. So, for example, if we lose our mobile phone, then we cannot remember a single number through which we could reach a relative.

Even over a span of a few decades, we can see a substantial difference in the way information is transmitted. The difference is far more substantive if we compare our time with the time of two thousand years ago, when the majority of people not only did not have written sources at their disposal, but also were unable to read, and all basic information was received by ear.

In an oral culture the role of memory plays a far greater role. A person who has gotten accustomed to writing down everything that he needs to know does not always concern himself with fixing it in his memory: paper or a computer seem to be far more reliable aids. This is why the person of today distrusts the oral tradition and its main transmitter, the memory. The generally accepted stereotype is that what is stored in the memory cannot be verified or be objective, since, firstly, a person's memory is fickle (over the years a particular episode may acquire various details or, on the contrary, many details may be erased from the memory), and, secondly, a person's memory may embellish any event of the past subjectively (what is important is not the event, but how it is perceived by the person and how it is transformed in his consciousness).

And yet, even in our time many people can recall texts word for word. For example, verses or whole poems are learned by heart and are retained in a person's memory in the form in which he learned them from the original. And the original source may be either written or spoken. Children often learn from hearing, and verses learned in childhood often stay in the memory for the rest of people's life.

Moreover, there are the concepts of professional memory and collective memory. Professional memory is the ability of a person of a particular profession to retain in his memory a huge volume of material that may seem unrealistic to a person of a different profession. For example, a chess master holding a session of thirty-six games must simultaneously retain in his memory the order of movements on each board and the position of the figures on it at each concrete moment. A professional pianist or conductor retains in his memory a huge amount of musical notation.

Collective memory also has a specific nature. If the participants of an event or series of events are a group of people, then when one person reproduces these events, the other participants can easily correct errors that could become a part of the narrative. If these people are not simply a group of incidental witnesses, but a circle of like-minded people united by common interests and a common type of thinking, the probability of erroneous transmission of information about events is almost nil when the other members of the group were participants in the events.

We can project these observations onto the situation as it was two thousand years ago. The traditions about Jesus were preserved within the single group of his disciples and followers. These traditions were fixed both in the memory of separate witnesses and the memory of the entire community. At the same time, as we noted earlier, many traditions had a verbally fixed element: this relates in the first place to the speeches of Jesus, which were transmitted from mouth to mouth and word for word in the same way as today's person conveys verse to other people. The parables of Jesus, his teachings, even the long ones such as the Sermon on the Mount, for a time could only exist in the form of oral traditions, but this in no way had any effect on the way they were conveyed or reproduced. Memory,

Jesus and the Disciples, engraving, Julius Schnorr von Carolsfeld, 19th c.

even more so collective memory, was in its own way no less a reliable means of retaining information as modern-day electronic means.

Did the apostles possess a "professional" memory? As we know, many of them were fishermen. However, by being continually alongside Jesus, the opportunity to see what he did, and to hear many times what he said, made them "professionals" in the cause for which he had chosen them. In his lifetime they knew that they were to convey to the world the word they had heard from him, and after his death and resurrection, this word acquired for them a completely special meaning and significance.

By virtue of these circumstances, we have, on the one hand, not only the opportunity, but also the obligation not to cast doubt on the reliability of the information contained in the Gospels, while, on the other hand, there are no grounds to believe that the process of making the Gospels was solely a process of redacting written texts. Therefore, the hypotheses and theories such as the "two-source hypothesis" recede into the background and lose their meaning. Whether the Q source existed or not does not have any decisive meaning. All attempts to restore or "excavate" it[27] from among the scrapheap of existing literary material are hypothetical and devoid of

---

[27]John S. Kloppenborg, *Excavating Q: The History and Setting of the Sayings Gospel* (Minneapolis, MN: Fortress, 2000).

interest for an understanding of the extant texts of the Gospels in the form in which they have come down to us.

In examining the problems of the correlation between the oral and written traditions, James Dunn makes the following observations:

> Most recognize that there must have been a period in which the memories and accounts of Jesus' mission circulated in oral form, perhaps for a period of twenty years or so before substantial written versions of these traditions began to appear. But they can conceptualize the process of transmission only as written tradition, as the process of copying and editing earlier written material. If then we have to acknowledge a gap of about twenty years before we can begin to understand that process, then we have *a gap between Jesus and the written tradition that we cannot hope to bridge.* And if we regard only written tradition as reliable and cannot conceive of oral transmission through time and space as anything other than unreliable, then *we have to despair of ever bridging that gap.*[28]

Continuing his deliberations, Dunn speaks of the methodological error that lies at the basis of the majority of research in recent times in the field of New Testament studies:

> No wonder, then, that such attempts as have been made to venture behind the earliest written sources have been so contested. . . . For all such attempts are fated to fall into the gulf of the oral tradition period; or to use an alternative metaphor, they have been caught in the bottomless swamp of disputed claims regarding this saying and that story. And all this because our onboard computer has a literary default setting, so that we can only conceptualize the Jesus tradition in terms of a literary process.[29]

An important element of oral tradition is variation, that is, the presence of different variants in transmitting one and the same text. Identical

---

[28]Dunn, *A New Perspective on Jesus*, 41. Italics in original.
[29]Ibid., 41–42.

meaning may be conveyed with the aid of different terms, expressions, and idioms. Semantic emphases can be placed in different ways.

All of the Gospel accounts may be provisionally separated into two types: the narrative, that is, the story of the events from the life of Jesus, and the sayings of Jesus: his teachings, parables and aphorisms. What has been said earlier about the verbally fixed form in which the traditions were conveyed concerns foremost the second type of text, that is, the direct speech of Jesus. In this type, variation is present to a lesser degree. When it is present, it is often linked to the fact that Jesus expounds one and the same thoughts in different situations; therefore, variation was a peculiarity of his own speech.

If we are to speak of the narrative block, then here variation is explained first of all by the fact that stories from the life of Jesus have come down to us in the retelling of several witnesses (two, three, or four), which could differ in detail. For this reason we occasionally have several variants of one and the same story, which has been conveyed by each of the Gospel writers in his own way.

At the same time, practically in all instances the most important principle has been preserved, which has allowed the Church to not merge four witnesses into one narrative, thereby eliminating possible misunderstandings in connection with the presence of differences, but to preserve the four Gospels in the form in which they were written. This principle is very simple: while differing between themselves in detail, the evangelists were never at variance in the essence.

So, for example, in telling the story of the feeding of the five thousand with five loaves and two fishes (Mt 14.13–21; Mk 6.32–44; Lk 9:10–17; Jn 6:1–13), the evangelists differ between themselves in the identification of the location of where this happened; the dialogues between Jesus and the disciples occurr in differing variants; details present in one evangelist are absent in another. But all the basic elements of the miracle in the four evangelists coincide: the miracle occurs in the evening; the number of loaves, fishes, and people are the same in all four evangelists (five, two, and about five thousand respectively); the sequence of events is also the same. Before us is a typical instance of one and the same story told by four

The feeding of the five thousand with five loaves and two fishes, fresco, 16th c.

people, of whom two were probably witnesses of the miracle, and the other two wrote down the story from the words of witnesses: while differing in the details, all four narrators come together in the essence of what actually happened.

The Demythologization of New Testament Scholarship

At present, the scholarly community faces the urgent task of demythologizing New Testament scholarship. The successful completion of this task depends in many ways upon the future direction of New Testament research. What do we mean by this?

For more than two hundred years, New Testament scholarship has developed under the influence of myths created by scholars. A particular myth would appear in the mind of a researcher or group of researchers, and then other scholars would take it up and begin to analyze, add to, develop, and dispute it. As a result, the myth became the subject of scientific inquiry, and not the Gospel text, which was used merely as an aid to prove that the inventors of the myth were correct.

Among such myths are, for example, the concept of the "divine man" (*theios anēr*, or *theios anthrōpos*) by which many scholars have tried to explain Jesus' miracles. This concept was founded on the assertion that the image of Jesus as a miracle worker was modeled by the authors of the New Testament writings on the "divine men" of Greek literature. In particular, in scholarly literature it is considered good taste to compare Jesus with another miracle worker of antiquity, Apollonius of Tyana (AD 1–98), a Neopythagorean philosopher born at the same time as Jesus, but who long outlived him. Supposedly, in the creation of the image of this philosopher and those similar to him, a typology was used that formed the basis of the New Testament notion of Jesus as miracle worker.[30]

This concept, applied mainly to the Gospel according to Mark, is completely far-fetched. The so-called "divine men" were either contemporaries of Jesus or lived after him. All the literary sources that mention them were created much later than the Gospels. The phrase itself— "divine men"—is nowhere used in the New Testament and is the fruit of scholars' imagination. It has proved impossible to highlight a consistent literary connection between the Gospels and Greek literature, in spite of repeated attempts. Even the proposal that the concept of the "divine man," which supposedly influenced the development of early Christology, had an indirect influence on the evangelists via Hellenistic Judaism (mainly through Philo of Alexandria)[31] has not lent scholarly credibility to the hypothesis.

The concept of the "divine man" came about due to the rejection of the divine nature of Jesus and his miracles. It was this starting point that led to the creation of a myth that has been joyfully seized upon as supposedly allowing for the possibility of explaining the appearance of the miracle

---

[30]See, in particular: Otto Weinreich, "Antikes Gottmenschentum," *Neue Jahrbuücher für Wissenschaft und Jugendbildung* 2 (1926): 633–651; Hans Leisegang, "Der Gottmensch als Archetypus," in *Aus der Welt der Urbilder: Sonderband für C. G. Jung zum fünfundsiebzigsten Geburtstag, 26 Juli 1950*, ed. Olga Fröbe-Kapteyn, Eranos Jahrbuch 18 (Zürich: Rhein-Verlag, 1950), 9–45; Ludwig Bieler, *Theios anēr, das Bild des "göttlichen Menschen" in Spätantike und Frühchristentum*, 2 vols. (Vienna: O. Höfels, 1935–1936); Martin Dibelius, *From Tradition to Gospel*, trans. Bertram Lee Woolf (New York, NY: Scribner, 1935), 70–97; Rudolf Bultmann, *The History of the Synoptic Tradition*, trans. John Marsh (Oxford: Blackwell, 1963), 218–231. See the following for a factual recapitulation of this framework: Bart D. Ehrman, *How Jesus Became God: The Exaltation of a Jewish Preacher from Galilee* (New York, NY: HarperCollins, 2014), 11–45.

[31]Ferdinand Hahn, T*he Titles of Jesus in Christology: Their History in Early Christianity*, trans. Harold Knight and George Ogg (London: Lutterworth, 1969), 11–13, 288–299.

stories of Jesus. Of course, the concept has found its critics,[32] and at present many scholars look upon it skeptically[33] or negatively.[34] Nonetheless, it continues to exert an influence upon research into the miracles of Jesus.

One other scholarly myth is connected to the notion that the Gospels were created for a specific narrow audience, that is, for the church communities to which the evangelists belonged. The essence of this theory is that at the end of the first century there were isolated Judeo-Christian communities, which were persecuted by the Gentiles and experienced various inner crises linked to the conflicts between those newly converted from paganism and Judaism. Within these communities Gospels supposedly appeared that had the aim of strengthening the faith of the members of these communities, consoling them in times of persecution from "external enemies" and lowering the internal potential for conflict.[35] Each community, according to this point of view, "projected its own problems and answers back into the reports of the life of Jesus":[36] it is in the light of these problems and issues that we ought to understand the Gospel text.

How is this concept applied in practice? At first, on the basis of the text of a particular Gospel, conclusions are drawn regarding the fundamental characteristics of the hypothetical communities in which they were created, and then the same text is examined in the light of the conclusions made. Thus, for example, the "Matthean community" (or

[32]See, in particular: Vincent Taylor, *The Formation of the Gospel Tradition: Eight Lectures*, 2nd ed. (London: Macmillan, 1935), 119–141; Alan Richardson, *The Miracle-Stories of the Gospels* (London: SCM Press, 1941); William Manson, *Jesus the Messiah* (London: Hodder and Stoughton, 1943), 33–50.

[33]Barry Blackburn, Theios Anēr *and the Marcan Miracle Traditions: A Critique of the* Theios Anēr *Concept as an Interpretative Background of the Miracle Traditions Used by Mark*, WUNT II 40 (Tübingen, J. C. B. Mohr, 1991), 1–12, 263–266.

[34]John P. Meier, *A Marginal Jew: Rethinking the Historical Jesus*, vol. 2, *Mentor, Message, and Miracles* (New York, NY: Doubleday, 1994), 595–601.

[35]For a substantive criticism of this theory as exemplified by the so-called "Marcan community," see Dwight N. Peterson, *The Origins of Mark: The Markan Community in Current Debate* (Leiden: Brill, 2000), 151–202.

[36]Hans Conzelmann, *The Theology of St. Luke*, trans. Geoffrey Buswell (New York, NY: Harper & Row, 1961), 13.

[37]See for example: Krister Stendahl, *The School of St. Matthew and Its Use of the Old Testament* (Uppsala: C. W. K. Gleerup, 1954), 20–29 (the author presents the Gospel according to Matthew as a "textbook" for the "Matthean school").

"school")[37] is presented as divided and torn by inner contradictions and scandals: a hypothetical author (someone denoted by the name of "Matthew") writes a series of moral exhortations for it, putting them in the mouth of Jesus.[38] Originally Judeo-Christian, the Matthean community only recently separated from the synagogue.[39] In time this messianic Jewish community[40] became more open to the Gentiles. This supposedly explains the presence in the Gospel according to Matthew of such seemingly mutually exclusive sayings as the commandment of Jesus not to go the way of the Gentiles (Mt 10.5) and his commandment to baptize "all nations" (Mt 28.19).[41]

We believe this approach to be erroneous and unsound for a whole range of reasons.

First, it undermines trust in the Gospels as historical sources containing reliable information on what Jesus did and taught, as it turns Jesus into a literary character created by a particular author for concrete pastoral needs.

Second, it underestimates the role of inter-church communication. In the period when the Gospels were created, the church communities were in constant and close contact.[42] Between the churches in the first century there already existed what one scholar has wittily called the "holy internet"[43]—a broad communication network which allowed for all sorts

[38]William G. Thompson, *Matthew's Advice to a Divided Community: Mt. 17:22–18:35* (Rome: Biblical Institute Press, 1970), 258–264.

[39]Warren Carter, *Matthew: Storyteller, Interpreter, Evangelist* (Peabody, MA: Hendrickson, 2004), 71.

[40]Celia Deutsch, *Hidden Wisdom and the Easy Yoke: Wisdom, Torah and Discipleship in Matthew 11.25–30* (Sheffield: JSOT Press, 1987), 17.

[41]John P. Meier, *The Vision of Matthew: Christ, Church, and Morality in the First Gospel* (Eugene, OR: Wipf & Stock, 2004), 6–15; John P. Meier, *Matthew* (Collegeville, MN: Liturgical Press, 1980), xi–xii. A similar picture is given by Ulrich Luz, who believes that "[t]he Gospel of Matthew originated in a Jewish Christian community which was becoming more open to the Gentile Christian Church in the period after A.D. 70." See Ulrich Luz, *Studies in Matthew*, trans. Rosemary Selle (Grand Rapids, MI: Eerdmans, 2005), 7–13.

[42]Richard Bauckham, "For Whom Were the Gospels Written?," in *The Gospels for All Christians: Rethinking the Gospel Audiences*, ed. Richard Bauckham (Grand Rapids, MI: Eerdmans, 1998), 45–46.

[43]Michael B. Thompson, "The Holy Internet: Communication Between Churches in the First Christian Generation," in *The Gospels for All Christians*, ed. Bauckham, 49.

of information to be exchanged quickly and regularly. In this situation it is difficult to imagine an author who would write a text of such caliber as any one of the four Gospels proceeding from the narrow needs of his community and not bearing in mind the potential reader from other communities (not to mention future generations of readers). The Gospel according to Matthew cannot be compared to the epistles of the apostle Paul addressed to concrete communities (the Romans, Corinthians, Galatians, Ephesians, and so on): it undoubtedly presupposes a far wider circle of readers.[44]

Thirdly, this approach is based on the aforementioned paradigm of "literary thinking," according to which the whole process of creating the Gospels happened in a study and was reduced to the writing of texts and their redaction. This paradigm does not take into account the peculiarities of the oral tradition within which the Gospels or their prototypes—separate topics from the life of Jesus and his separate sayings—existed for what would appear to have been quite a long time.

As regards the sayings that seem to be mutually exclusive in the Gospel according to Matthew, a more detailed analysis shows that they can be understood as complementing each other: their presence in the direct speech of Jesus does not at all mean that one of them is authentic while the other is not.

Myths often live side by side with dogmas, and the uncritical use of mythology leads to dogmatism. This very word elicits disapproval from secular scholars who work in the field of New Testament studies because one of the goals of their labors is precisely to liberate the New Testament from the layers of Church dogma. However, striving to attain this goal leads to another form of dogmatism—when a particular assertion of scholars begins to be perceived as an indisputable dogma or axiom.

According to one researcher, "an amazing example of uncritical dogmatism in New Testament studies is the belief that the Synoptic Gospels should be dated after the Jewish War of AD 66–70 because they contain prophecies *ex eventu* of the destruction of Jerusalem by the Romans in

---

[44]Graham N. Stanton, *A Gospel for a New People: Studies in Matthew* (Edinburgh: T&T Clark, 1992), 50–51.

The Destruction of the Temple of Jerusalem, Francesco Hayez, 19th c.

the year 70."[45] The expression "prophecy *ex eventu*"[46] in literary studies and historiography denotes a description of an event made already after this event has taken place, but dated to an earlier period with the aim of giving it the appearance of a prediction or prophecy. The fact that all the Synoptic Gospels contain prophecies of the destruction of Jerusalem (Mt 24.2; Mk 13.2; Lk 21.6) compels scholars who adhere to this approach to date the Gospels to the end of the first century.

The notion that the Synoptics could not record Jesus' prophecy of the destruction of the Jerusalem Temple before the event happened in reality is founded either on distrust towards the evangelists as authors of the narrative or on a prejudice against the possibility of Jesus having the gift of prophecy. If we were simply to admit this possibility, it would then undermine the hypothesis of the later origin of the Synoptic Gospels, making it vulnerable, dubious, and ultimately unnecessary. As one contemporary scholar notes, "NT critical scholarship has a curious capacity to identify as 'genuine' prophecy that which failed to be fulfilled and, all too often, to insist that fulfilled prophecy is only after-the-event description dressed up as prophecy."[47]

[45]Bo Reicke, "Synoptic Prophecies on the Destruction of Jerusalem," in *Studies in the New Testament and Early Christian Literature: Essays in Honor of Allen P. Wikgren*, ed. David Edward Aune (Leiden: Brill, 1972), 121.

[46]*Ex eventu* (Latin)—literally, "from the event" or "on the basis of the event."

[47]John Nolland, *The Gospel of Matthew: A Commentary on the Greek Text*, The New

Among the hypotheses that have become dogma, we can include the priority of Mark, from which Matthew supposedly borrowed his themes. The primacy of Mark is first accepted as dogma, then, on the basis of this, doubt is cast on the authorship of the Gospel of Matthew. "[W]hy should one [i.e., the apostle Matthew] who presumably had been an eyewitness of much that he records depend so slavishly upon the account given by Mark, who had not been an eyewitness?"[48] And yet the hypotheses that do not fit the dogma that Mark could follow the text of Matthew or that the two evangelists worked with independent sources (oral or written) continues to be considered marginal.

The Q source, which to this day is referred to as lost, remains as before a dogma for many scholars. Here is a typical example:

> Once upon a time, before there were Gospels of the kind familiar to readers of the New Testament, the first followers of Jesus wrote another kind of book. Instead of telling a dramatic story about Jesus' life, their book contained only his teachings. They lived with these teachings ringing in their ears and thought of Jesus as the founder of their movement. But their focus was not on the person of Jesus or his life and destiny. They were engrossed with the social program that was called for by his teachings. Thus their book was not a Gospel of the Christian kind, namely a narrative of the life of Jesus as the Christ. Rather it was a Gospel of Jesus' sayings, a "sayings Gospel". . . . Then the book was lost. Perhaps the circumstances changed, or the people changed, or their memories and imagination of Jesus changed. In any case, the book was lost to history somewhere in the course of the late first century when stories of Jesus' life began to be written and became the more popular form of charter document for early Christian circles.[49]

International Greek Testament Commentary (Grand Rapids, MI: Eerdmans, 2005), 14.

[48]Bruce Metzger, *The New Testament: Its Background, Growth, and Content*, 2nd ed. (Nashville, TN: Abingdon Press, 1983), 97. See also David L. Turner, *Matthew*, Baker Exegetical Commentary on the New Testament (Grand Rapids, MI: Baker Academic, 2008), 7.

[49]Burton L. Mack, *The Lost Gospel: The Book of Q and Christian Origins*, (San Francisco, CA: HarperSanFrancisco, 1993), 1.

There is a difference, the author continues, whether the founder of a particular movement is remembered for his teaching or for his life and fate. For the early followers of Christ, the main things were the collections of teachings circulating under his name which touched upon various ideas, attitudes towards life, and conduct. And only later, when the movement began to fall apart, did the groups of his adherents in various places and in changed circumstances begin to meditate upon the life which Jesus was to live. It was then that his life began to be covered over with various myths, the main one being the story of his resurrection from the dead, modeled on the myths of the classical world. This story was reflected in the Epistles of Paul, and then in the Gospels that appeared—of Mark in the 70s, of Matthew in the 80s, of John in the 90s, and of Luke at the beginning of the second century. The Gospel narratives took over the original Q source, which appeared when there were no Christians, but only the "people of Jesus" who did not believe in Christ as God and in his resurrection. This is why the discovery of this source by means of dismembering the canonical Gospels and extracting it from them has such importance, even though it offends the followers of traditional Christianity.[50]

Even the manner of the exposition of this fantastic story, wholly and completely the fruit of the imagination of scholars, reminds one of a myth or fairy tale. The problem, however, is not that the fairy tale was created and that it was believed in, but that it gives a false picture of the appearance of Christianity and its development at the beginning. All of the ancient church literature testifies that it is the person of Jesus, his life, death, and resurrection (and not his social or moral teaching) that have stood at the center of Christian faith since the very beginning. To present things as though the early Christians were only interested in Jesus' teaching and that only later, towards the end of the first century, did they begin to make up stories of his life and think up the myth of his resurrection, would mean to turn the history of the appearance of Christianity on its head and propose a distorted and erroneous picture.

[50]Ibid., 1–2.

The ruins of Corinth

The apostle Paul, in the middle of the first century, laid out the essence of the Gospels in the following concise memorandum addressed to the Christians of Corinth:

> Moreover, brethren, I declare unto you the Gospel which I preached unto you, which also ye have received, and wherein ye stand, by which also ye are saved. . . . For I delivered unto you first of all that which I also received, how Christ died for our sins according to the scriptures; and that he was buried, and that he rose again the third day according to the scriptures: and that he was seen by Cephas, then by the twelve. After that, he was seen by above five hundred brethren at once; of whom the greater part remain unto this present, but some are fallen asleep. After that, he was seen by James; then by all the apostles. . . . Now if Christ be preached that he rose from the dead, how say some among you that there is no resurrection of the dead? But if there be no resurrection of the dead, then is Christ not risen. And if Christ be not risen, then is our preaching vain, and your faith is also vain. Yea, and we are found false witnesses of God; because we have testified of God that he raised up Christ, whom he raised not up . . . And if Christ be not raised, your faith is vain; ye are yet in your sins. (1 Cor 15.1–7, 12–15, 17)

The Apostle Paul, icon,
Dionisius, late 15th c.
to early 16th c.

From these words it follows that the central event that lay at the foundation of Christian preaching was Christ's resurrection, and the main evidence of this event consisted in the many appearances of the risen Christ to the various groups of apostles. Christ died for people's sins, was buried, and rose on the third day—these are the three fundamental truths upon which, as Paul says, the Gospel rests. It is the fact of God's entrance into history, his appearance to people in the person of Jesus Christ, that forms the beginnings of Christianity, and not any particular moral or social teaching. The person of Jesus, his life, death, and resurrection are primary; all the rest is secondary. That is why, in setting forth the version of the Gospel that the apostles preached, Paul does not have a single word to say on Christ's teachings or his sayings. He does not say, "If there is no collection of Jesus' sayings, your faith is vain."

"What happened to Q? Why did it disappear?" asks one of the ardent supporters of the existence of this work, who spent many years on its "reconstruction" and popularization.[51] We must answer directly: nothing has happened to it; it has not disappeared—it simply never existed. There never was a "discovery" of Q. There have only ever been more or less clumsy attempts to invent it on the basis of the fragments remaining after the deconstruction of the Gospel text.[52] It is quite plausible that the evangelists used some sources; it cannot be excluded that collections of the sayings of Jesus existed not only in an oral, but also in a written tradition; but in the form in which the Q source has been "reconstructed," "discovered," and "excavated" throughout

[51]John S. Kloppenborg, *Q, The Earliest Gospel: An Introduction to the Original Stories and Sayings of Jesus* (Louisville, KY: Westminster John Knox, 2008), 98.
[52]On the methods by which a reconstruction of Q has been made, see, for example: Shawn Carruth and Albrecht Garsky, *Q 11:2b–4*, Documenta Q (Leuven: Peeters, 1996), v–viii.

the twentieth century, it is a typical scholarly myth raised to the status of dogma.

The creation of this myth was determined by a concrete ideological stance: the negation of the divine nature of Jesus, his resurrection from the dead, and the meaning of his redemptive sacrifice. Scholars who did not believe in Jesus as God incarnate were desperate to create a theory according to which Christianity was born not from the person of its Founder, but from a moral and social teaching that was ascribed to him by a group of followers at the end of the first century.[53] In this sense, by extracting the supposed sayings of Jesus from all that was brought into it by later Church tradition, the so-called "Q reconstruction" very much reminds one of the Sisyphean task of the "demythologization of the Gospels" undertaken in the second half of the nineteenth and beginning of the twentieth centuries.

We could adduce many examples of other dogmas and myths that stray from one piece of scholarship to another. These myths were generated throughout the process of scholarly research, but as the search was to a significant degree motivated by earlier formulated ideological considerations, it has been unable to produce stable and convincing results. Having refused to believe in Jesus, in how he is presented in the Gospels and how he has been preached through the centuries by the Church, many scholars prefer to believe in the myths that they and their colleagues have created, having turned them into dogma.

The pressing task of contemporary biblical studies is to be liberated from these types of myths and dogmas. Today scholars openly discuss the "myth of the historical Jesus,"[54] which has led to an innumerable number of Jesuses created in the image and likeness of the myth-makers. More and more scholars are coming to realize that the search for the "historical Jesus" beyond the confines of the Gospel text is fruitless and counterproductive. The concept of the "historical Jesus," like many other concepts that

---

[53]Over time, even scholars belonging to traditional Christian confessions, and unconnected to ideology presupposing the rejection of Jesus' divinity or resurrection, began to believe in this myth (or felt obliged to accommodate themselves to it).

[54]See Hal Childs, *The Myth of the Historical Jesus and the Evolution of Consciousness* (Atlanta, GA: Society of Biblical Literature, 2000), 223–261.

seemed unshakeable in twentieth-century New Testament scholarship, is today being re-evaluated.[55]

This re-evaluation has influenced, particularly, a change in thinking in the scholarly community on the question of when the New Testament writings appeared.

The Time of the Writing of the Gospels

When were the Gospels written? In scholarly criticism of the nineteenth century, which aimed to present the Gospels as the product of already formed Christian communities, the time when they were compiled was considered to be the first half of the second century. At the same time, the authorship of the eyewitnesses, the apostles, was excluded as patently impossible. Twentieth-century researchers moved the time of the writing of the Gospels towards the end of the first century; however, even in this instance the probability of firsthand testimonies is practically excluded.

What do the Gospels themselves tell us of the time when they appeared?

Our starting point should be the beginning of the Gospel of Luke: "Forasmuch as many have taken in hand to set forth in order a declaration of those things which are most surely believed among us . . ." (Lk 1.1). From these words it follows that Luke was far from being the first Gospel writer.

Luke was also the author of the book of the Acts of the Apostles, which is a direct continuation of his Gospel and written after his Gospel. Thus, to the pen of Luke belongs a two-part work comprising a book on the life and teaching of Jesus and a book on the early years of the Church, including the missionary work of the apostle Paul. The book of Acts ends with the words: "And Paul dwelt two whole years in his own hired house, and

---

[55]We turn the reader's attention, in particular, to one of the latest monographs on the topic: Craig S. Keener, *The Historical Jesus of the Gospels* (Grand Rapids, MI: Eerdmans, 2009), 1–67 (a thorough critical analysis of the conceptions generated in the search for the "historical Jesus"), 177–348 (a reconstruction of the image of the "historical Jesus" on the basis of the Gospel text). The author reaches the conclusion (p. 349) that the portrait of Jesus drawn on the basis of the canonical Gospels is more convincing than any alternative conceptions proposed by scholars.

received all that came in unto him, preaching the kingdom of God, and teaching those things which concern the Lord Jesus Christ, with all confidence, no man forbidding him" (Acts 28.30–31). These words are clear testimony that at the end of the two books by Luke the apostle Paul was still alive and in good health.

The Apostle Luke,
El Greco, 1602–1606.

Moreover, nowhere in Acts is there mentioned—neither directly nor indirectly—the destruction of Jerusalem in AD 70. The author of Acts mentions the killing of Stephen (Acts 7.58–70) and Herod's persecution of "certain of the church" (Acts 12.1–2), but mentions nothing of the murder of James, the Lord's brother—an event that ought to have been noted in the chronicles of the Church's life if they had been compiled before it.

If we bear in mind that James, the brother of the Lord, was executed in AD 62 or 63, and Paul between AD 64 and 68, we should take the most plausible time when the Gospel of Luke was compiled to be some time in the fifth decade of the first century or the beginning of the sixth decade. At the same time, Luke's reference that many others at the same time had already "taken in hand to set forth" (Lk 1.1) analogous narratives can be interpreted in the sense that the process of writing the Gospels had not been finished by then, but had undoubtedly been started, while the Gospel writers, or at least some of them, knew of each other's works. The Gospels may have acquired their definitive shape somewhat later, but it is clear that the basic kernel of the Synoptic Gospels was formed no later than the 60s, that is, no later than twenty or thirty years after the events described in them.

2. The Gospel
of Matthew

First among the four Gospels in both the manuscript tradition and modern editions of the New Testament is the Gospel of Matthew. It is often referred to as the Gospel of the Church, first of all because in the early Church it enjoyed significantly greater renown than the Gospels of Mark and Luke. It was already referred to at the beginning of the second century by Ignatius of Antioch, while in the first half of the third century Origen wrote a full commentary on it. In the fourth century a full commentary on this Gospel was compiled by John Chrysostom.[56] Compared to the Gospel of Mark, the Gospel of Matthew is significantly longer, first of all because of the inclusion of a great deal of material that is absent in Mark (in particular, the genealogy and narratives on the birth of Jesus in the first two chapters and the Sermon on the Mount in chapters five to seven).

The author of this Gospel is a Jew who is well acquainted with the Jewish milieu and the interpretation of the Old Testament traditional for this milieu.[57] The abundance of quotations from the Old Testament is characteristic for the other evangelists too; however, Matthew stands out among them in that he is the most consistent in advancing the idea of the fulfillment of the Old Testament prophecies in the life of Jesus as the promised Messiah.[58]

Some hypothesize that the Gospel of Matthew was written in Hebrew. This is based on the above-quoted words of Papias of Hierapolis ("Matthew collected the oracles in the Hebrew language, and each interpreted as best he could"),[59] as well as on a number of other ancient sources, including the works of St Jerome.[60] What these sayings were remains a mystery.

[56]See Luke Timothy Johnson, *The Writings of the New Testament: An Interpretation*, 3rd ed. (Minneapolis, MN: Fortress, 2010), 165–166.

[57]Craig S. Keener, *The Gospel of Matthew: A Socio-Rhetorical Commentary* (Grand Rapids, MI: Eerdmans, 2009), 40.

[58]R. T. France, *The Gospel of Matthew* (Grand Rapids, MI: Eerdmans, 2007), 11.

[59]Eusebius of Caesarea, *Ecclesiastical History* 3.39.16 (Lake, LCL).

[60]For an overview of these sources, see James R. Edwards, *The Hebrew Gospel and the Development of the Synoptic Tradition* (Grand Rapids, MI: Eerdmans, 2009), 1–96.

There are some apocryphal "gospels" (such as the *Gospel of Thomas*) that were written in the form of Jesus' sayings. However, the content of these *logia* differ greatly from those that became part of the canonical Gospels.

St Matthew,
Frans Hals, 1625.

Are we able to identify these sayings with the Sermon on the Mount and other teachings of Jesus that have become part of the Gospel of Matthew? Contemporary scholarship does not give us a straight answer to this question, although the Sermon on the Mount undoubtedly is a single piece of material containing Jesus' direct speech and woven into the narrative fabric of the Gospel. We cannot exclude the fact that this text existed separately, perhaps in Hebrew. However, it has proved impossible to this day to locate any traces of the existence of a Hebrew text of the Gospel of Matthew. The Greek text of this Gospel does not contain any indication that it was translated from another language.

The composition of the Gospel of Matthew differs from the two other Synoptic Gospels. An important place is allocated to the spoken discourses of Jesus. There are five such discourses: the Sermon on the Mount (Mt 5.3–7.27); the instructions to the disciples (Mt 10.5–42); the teachings in parables (Mt 13.3–52); yet further instructions to the disciples (Mt 18.3–35); and the prophecies and parables on the last times (Mt 24.3–25.46). Each of these discourses is connected to the ensuing narrative by the formula "when Jesus had ended these sayings" (Mt 7.28; 19.1) or something similar (Mt 11.1; 13.53; 19.1). The Gospel author follows the fifth teaching with the words: "when Jesus had finished all these sayings" (Mt 26.1). Thus, Matthew places special emphasis on Jesus' teaching ministry[61] by inserting lengthy discourses into the fabric of the narrative.

To a greater degree than the other evangelists, Matthew accentuates the kingly dignity of Jesus. It is no coincidence that in the very first verse he calls him the son of David, emphasizing his origin from a royal genealogy:

[61]Meier, *The Vision of Matthew*, 45–47.

Christ, the King of Kings, icon, 17th c.

Matthew presents the Messiah King who is *revealed*, the King who is *rejected*, and the King who will *return*. Jesus is painted in royal colors in this Gospel as in none of the others. His ancestry is traced from the royal line of Israel; his birth is dreaded by a jealous earthly king; the magi bring the infant Jesus royal gifts from the east; and John the Baptist heralds the King and proclaims that His kingdom is at hand. Even the temptations in the wilderness climax with Satan offering Jesus the kingdoms of this world. The Sermon on the Mount is the manifesto of the King, the miracles are His royal credentials, and many of the parables portray the mysteries of His kingdom. Jesus identifies Himself with the king's son in a parable and makes a royal entry into Jerusalem. While facing the cross He predicts His future reign, and He claims dominion over the angels in heaven. His last words are that all authority has been given to Him in both heaven and earth [Mt 28.18].[62]

The text of the Gospel of Matthew bears witness to the fact that it was addressed in the main to readers from among the Jews. This is confirmed by numerous examples. In particular, Matthew calls Jerusalem the "holy city" (Mt 4.5). Mark and Luke would probably explain which city is meant; for Matthew and his readers it is obvious that the holy city is Jerusalem, as for the Jews there was no other holy city in the world, as there was no other temple than the Temple of Jerusalem.

The Gospel of Matthew contains many Aramaic words that are left without translation, for example: "Whosoever shall say to his brother, Raca ... shall be in danger of hell fire" (Mt 5.22); "Ye cannot serve God and mammon" (Mt 6.24). Borrowings from Hebrew or Aramaic are seen in Mark also; however, Mark, as a rule, translates them (see, for example,

[62]John F. MacArthur, *Matthew 1–7*, The MacArthur New Testament Commentary (Chicago, IL: Moody Bible Institute, 1985), xii.

Mk 5.41), while Matthew in a number of instances does not consider it necessary as, evidently, his readers, unlike those of Mark, would know the meaning of these words.

Many events from the life of Jesus are presented in Matthew as the fulfillment of the Old Testament prophecies. We encounter allusions to and quotations from the Old Testament in the other evangelists too; however, the number of such quotations in Matthew outweigh them greatly: in his Gospel we find about sixty such quotations and allusions, whereas, for example, in Mark there are only a third as much.[63]

In the Gospel of Matthew there are parallels that are typical of Semitic literature. For example, "He that findeth his life shall lose it, and he that loseth his life for my sake shall find it" (Mt 10.39). Parallels in particular are characteristic of Hebrew poetry: thus, in many of the Psalms the verses are divided into two parts parallel to each other (for example, in Psalm 50). It is clear that these parallels reflect one of the cherished characteristics of Jesus' oral discourses preserved by Matthew.

The use of a particular phrase as a refrain is a characteristic device of Hebrew poetry. In one discourse in Matthew, Jesus repeats multiple times such formulae as, for example, "Ye shall know them by their fruits" (Mt 7.16, 22), "There shall be weeping and gnashing of teeth" (Mt 8.12; 13.42; 22.13), "Woe unto you, scribes and Pharisees, hypocrites!" (Mt 23.13–15, 23, 25, 27), and "Ye fools and blind" (Mt 23.17, 19). These refrains also reflect one of the characteristics of Jesus' speech.

An example affirming that the Gospel of Matthew was addressed primarily to a Jewish audience are Jesus' words: "But pray ye that your flight be not in the winter, neither on the sabbath day" (Mt 24.20). The mention of the Sabbath would have meaning only for the Jews, for whom flight on the Sabbath day meant the violation of the commandment to rest on the Sabbath.

The Gospel of Matthew begins where the Old Testament finishes. The last book of the section of the *Nevi'im* (the Prophets)—the book of

---

[63]On the Old Testament quotations in Matthew, see Stendahl, *The School of Matthew*, 39–142.

Moses Breaking the Tablets
of the Law, Rembrandt, 1659.

Malachi[64]—ends with a prophecy that is interpreted in the Christian tradition as pertaining to John the Baptist. Matthew begins his narrative with the birth of Christ and the preaching of John the Baptist. Perhaps this, as well as the general direction of the Gospel of Matthew (whose audience was mainly Jewish Christians), was the reason why it was given first place in the canon of the New Testament, as though uniting the Old Testament with the New.

The theme of the mutual link between the two Testaments is central to Matthew. It is in his narrative that Jesus builds his main teaching—the Sermon on the Mount—on the contrast of the moral postulates that he puts forth with the commandments of the Mosaic Law: "Ye have heard that it was said by them of old. . . . But I say unto you" (Mt 5.21–22; 5.27; 5.33; 5.38; 5.43). At the same time, it is only in Matthew that Jesus says: "Think not that I am come to destroy the law, or the prophets: I am not come to destroy, but to fulfil. . . . Till heaven and earth pass, one jot or one tittle shall in no wise pass from the law, till all be fulfilled" (Mt 5.17–18). It is only in Matthew that Jesus emphasizes the importance of the Old Testament Law, whereas in the other two Synoptics this motif is virtually absent.

Moreover, in Matthew, Jesus, although he criticizes the Pharisees, nonetheless speaks of how they are also be listened to: "The scribes and the Pharisees sit in Moses' seat. All therefore whatsoever they bid you observe, observe and do; but do not act in accordance with their works: for they say, and do not" (Mt 23.2–3). In no other Gospel do we find such advice.

Jesus' disputes with the Pharisees, documented in the Gospel of Matthew, often concern the topic of the interpretation of the Old Testament Law. These disputes were held by representatives of various schools of

[64]If we take into account the fact that the Old Testament in the Gospels is mainly the "Law and the Prophets" (Mt 11.13; 22.40), the book of the prophet Malachi can to a certain extent be called the culmination of Scripture. By the time of the Gospel events the division of the *Ketuvim* ("Writings") had not yet taken shape.

rabbinical thought of that time, and are reflected in Jesus' words regarding swearing an oath by the Temple or the gold of the Temple, the altar or the gift placed upon it; on the tithe of mint, anise, and cummin; and on the outside and inside of the cup or dish (Mt 23.16–26). For Mark's and Luke's readers, these problems had no significance, whereas the prospective reader of Matthew ought to know the context in which Jesus was expounding his thoughts.

The author of the Gospel of Matthew is identified in Church tradition as the apostle of the Twelve known as Matthew or Levi, the son of Alphaeus (Mt 9.9; Mk 2.14). From the Gospel, nothing is known of his life, apart from the fact that, before being called by Jesus, he was a collector of taxes (Lk 5.27–29). Irenaeus of Lyons dates the Gospel of Matthew to the time when Peter and Paul founded the Church in Rome,[65] that is, to the period between AD 45 and 65. Eusebius of Caesarea, by referring to Origen, maintains that the Gospel of Matthew was written in Hebrew and was intended for Jewish Christians.[66] The occasion for writing the Gospel was, according to Eusebius, Matthew's leaving Palestine.[67]

In spite of the testimonies of these ancient authors, the majority of contemporary scholars is inclined to believe that the Gospel of Matthew appeared after the Gospel of Mark and after the destruction of Jerusalem in AD 70. Burnett Hillman Streeter's theory that the Gospel of Matthew was written around AD 85 in Antioch has found a lively response.[68] The main argument put forward in favor of this dating is that Jesus' words, as quoted by Matthew, contain a clear reference to the destruction of the Temple of Jerusalem (Mt 24.1–2). However, as we have demonstrated above, the presence of prophecies on the destruction of Jerusalem in the Gospel texts in no way signifies that they were written after this event.

Among the locations with which we can link the origin of the Gospel, apart from Antioch, scholars have pointed to Tyre and Sidon in Phoenicia;[69]

---

[65]Irenaeus of Lyons, *Against Heresies* 3.1.1 (*ANF* 1:411).

[66]Eusebius of Caesarea, *Ecclesiastical History* 6.25.4.

[67]Ibid., 3.24.6.

[68]Streeter, *The Four Gospels*, 500–504, 523–524.

[69]George Dunbar Kilpatrick, *The Origins of the Gospel According to St. Matthew* (Oxford: Clarendon, 1946), 134.

Phoenicia

Caesarea in Palestine;[70] and a whole variety of cities, regions, and centers of learning. A theory has been proposed regarding a connection between the Gospel of Matthew and Jamnia—a Jewish city not far from the border with Syria, where a major center of Pharisee learning was located: it has been suggested that a polemic with this center dominates the first Gospel.[71]

There is a widespread view that Matthew redacted the Gospel of Mark in accordance with the needs of the church community to which he belonged. A possible location for the writing of the Gospel in this case would be Syria, where Jewish traditions were strong, and the time of writing would have been the ninth or tenth decades of the first century. According to this view, the author of the Gospel could not be Matthew, the apostle from the Twelve.[72] However, counterarguments can be found to practically any argument in favor of this theory.

Recently, scholars have been more inclined to date the Gospel of Matthew to the period preceding AD 70.[73] This re-examination of a view that

[70]Benedict T. Viviano, *Matthew and His World: The Gospel of the Open Jewish Christians* (Fribourg: Academic Press, 2007), 16–22.

[71]W. D. Davies, *The Setting of the Sermon on the Mount* (Cambridge: Cambridge University Press, 1964), 256–315.

[72]Meier, *The Vision of Matthew*, 6–15; Meier, *Matthew*, xi–xii.

[73]See, for example, Robert H. Gundry, *Matthew: A Commentary on His Handbook for a Mixed Church under Persecution*, 2nd ed. (Grand Rapids, MI: Eerdmans, 1994), 599–609.

has been dominant throughout the entire twentieth century is in many ways linked to a more attentive attitude towards the internal details of the Gospel text itself. More and more questions are being asked as to why Matthew, if he were actually writing his Gospel after AD 70, would mention customs and rites that became obsolete after the destruction of Jerusalem, such as the bringing of a gift to the altar (Mt 5.23–24), the tribute money for the Temple (Mt 17.24–27), the swearing by the Temple and the altar (Mt 23.16–22).[74] The fact that the Gospel of Matthew mentions the Sadducees seven times, of whom nothing more was heard after AD 70, also testifies in favor of an earlier origin of this Gospel.[75]

The notion—axiomatically accepted throughout the twentieth century—that Mark is the primary source for Matthew has been repeatedly and convincingly disputed.[76] If we proceed from the fact that the early Christian Church gradually freed herself from her dependence on Judaism and became more open to the Gentiles (and it is this tendency that is confirmed by the Acts of the Apostles, where the life of the first generation of the Church is described in quite a lot of detail), then why would a Gospel addressed to Jewish Christians be created later than a Gospel addressed to Christians from among the Gentiles? Why should we not suppose that Matthew, who was writing for the first generation of Christians, placed a special emphasis on the link between the Jewish tradition and the teaching of Jesus, whereas Mark, who was writing later for a community that had freed itself from Jewish influences, omitted that which was incomprehensible to Christians from among the Gentiles?

---

[74]Craig L. Blomberg, *Jesus and the Gospels: An Introduction and Survey*, 2nd ed. (Nashville, TN: B&H Academic, 2009), 153.

[75]Leon Morris, *The Gospel According to Matthew*, The Pillar New Testament Commentary (Grand Rapids, MI: Eerdmans; Leicester: Inter-Varsity Press, 1992), 10–11.

[76]See, in particular: William R. Farmer, *The Synoptic Problem: A Critical Analysis* (Dillsboro, NC: Western North Carolina Press, 1976), 1–196 (a detailed overview of the criticism of scholars who insist on the primacy of Mark), 199–232 (alternative suggestions on the solution of the synoptic problem); John Wenham, *Redating Matthew, Mark and Luke: A Fresh Assault on the Synoptic Problem* (Downers Grove, IL: InterVarsity, 1992); David B. Peabody, Lamar Cope, and Allan J. McNicol, eds., *One Gospel from Two: Mark's Use of Matthew and Luke: A Demonstration by the Research Team of the International Institute for Renewal of Gospel Studies* (Harrisburg, PA: Trinity Press International, 2002). See also Linnemann, *Biblical Criticism on Trial*, 42–47.

The miracle of the healing of
the woman with the flow of
blood, fresco, 4th c.

We also ought to pay attention to the fact that
the majority of stories that are common to both
Mark and Matthew, are set forth in Matthew in a
far shorter form (on average by a third). Thus, for
example, the story of the healing of the leper in Mark
includes details absent in Matthew (Mk 1.40–45; Mt
8.1–4). Matthew devotes three verses to the miracle
of the healing of the woman with the issue of blood
(Mt 9.20–22), while Mark devotes ten verses (Mk
5.25–34). We could quote more such examples. In
itself, this fact does not speak in favor of the primacy
of either Mark or Matthew. Rather, it points towards
the independent labor of both evangelists, whose
separate narratives were not welded into one.

The Gospel of Matthew is the only one of the four Gospels that twice
mentions the Church (Mt 16.18; 18.17). It is the only Gospel that uses the
baptismal formula: "in the name of the Father, and of the Son, and of the
Holy Spirit" (Mt 28.19). Some scholars have seen in this proof of the dating of the Gospel of Matthew toward the end of the first century, when
they believe that the Church had already produced a sufficiently developed liturgical tradition, including the baptismal and eucharistic formulae.
According to this view, Matthew adapted the Gospel of Mark in light of
the later liturgical tradition of the Church.

However, this view too has been disputed. The term "Church" is
encountered many times in the epistles of the apostle Paul, written in the
sixth and first half of the seventh decades of the first century. The appearance of this term in the Gospel of Matthew, consequently, does not at all
mean that it was written later than the other Gospels.

Concerning the baptismal formula, then, according to Matthew, it
belongs to Jesus and ought to have been in use in the Church from the
very beginning. From the Acts of the Apostles, we know that baptism and
the Eucharist were the original foundational element on which the life of
the Church was built in the first months and years after Jesus' resurrection (Acts 1.41–42). At baptism, the formula going back to Jesus should

have been used, while in the celebration of the Eucharist the words that he uttered at the Last Supper should have been heard; they are conveyed to us by the three synoptic evangelists (Mt 26.26–28; Mk 14.22–24; Lk 22.17–20).

We have reason to believe that both baptism and the Eucharist were primary in relation to the fixed written text of all of the four Gospels. Therefore, the presence of the baptismal formula in the Gospel of Matthew in no way speaks in favor of the Gospel's later origin in relation to the Gospel of Mark.

We consider secondary the issue of whether the Gospel of Matthew appeared earlier or later than the Gospel of Mark. There is a logic in the presupposition that the Gospel of Mark was elaborated by Matthew and adapted for the Jewish reader. But there is weighty evidence in favor of an earlier origin of the Gospel of Matthew, which occupies the first place in all the ancient codices of the four Gospels, and which in the early Christian period was viewed as the document that most fully demonstrated the Church's rootedness in the teaching of Jesus.[77] It is quite plausible that the Gospel for the Jews, as the most archaic, was also the first to appear. When taking into account Luke's reference to many others who had begun to compose their narratives, we can propose that among these many others was Matthew. Therefore, his Gospel too (even if not in its final version) ought to have appeared no later than the middle of the AD 60s.

3. The Gospel of Mark

C hurch tradition identifies the author of the second Gospel as John Mark, who is mentioned many times in Acts (12.12, 25; 13.13; 15.37–38). According to tradition, Mark was the disciple of the apostle Peter—which is attested by the expression "Mark my son" (1 Pet 5.13)—and retold

---

[77]Raymond E. Brown, *An Introduction to the New Testament* (New Haven, CT: Yale University Press, 1997), 171.

The Apostle Mark,
miniature, 13th c.

that which he had heard from Peter. This tradition, which goes back to Papias of Hierapolis, was preserved by Eusebius of Caesarea.[78] But Mark was close to Paul too, which is testified to by the three mentions of him in Paul's letters: "Aristarchus my fellowprisoner saluteth you, and Mark, the nephew of Barnabas" (Col 4.10); "Take Mark, and bring him with thee: for he is profitable to me for the ministry" (2 Tim 4.11); "Mark, Aristarchus, Demas, Lucas, my fellow labourers" (Philem 24).

In being a disciple of both of those chief among the apostles, of whom only one, Peter, was a close disciple of Jesus and an eyewitness to his deeds, Mark may have based his narrative of events on the stories of Peter. As a result, it is quite plausible that the Gospel of Mark, or rather, according to Mark, is the version of the good news that came from the apostle Peter. Eusebius writes:

> Mark became Peter's interpreter and wrote accurately all that he remembered, not, indeed, in order, of the things said or done by the Lord. For he had not heard the Lord, nor had he followed him, but later on, as I said, followed Peter, who used to give teaching as necessity demanded but not making, as it were, an arrangement of the Lord's oracles, so that Mark did nothing wrong in thus writing down single points as he remembered them. For to one thing he gave attention, to leave out nothing of what he had heard and to make no false statements in them.[79]

Irenaeus of Lyons (second century) believed that the Gospel of Mark was written after Peter's death,[80] which occurred between AD 64 and 67. Clement of Alexandria, by contrast, dated this Gospel to the time of Peter's

---

[78]See Eusebius of Caesarea, *Ecclesiastical History*, 3.39.15. On Mark as the disciple of Peter, see Martin Hengel, *Saint Peter: The Underestimated Apostle*, trans. Thomas Trapp (Grand Rapids, MI: Eerdmans, 2010).

[79]Eusebius of Caesarea, *Ecclesiastical History* 3.39.15 (Lake, LCL).

[80]Irenaeus of Lyons, *Against Heresies* 3.1.1. (*ANF* 1:411)

stay in Rome (around AD 45–66).[81] At present,
many scholars date the compilation of the Gospel
of Mark to around AD 65.[82] The internal indications are that it was written before the destruction
of Jerusalem in AD 70.[83] And yet, some scholars
continue to insist on a later dating, pointing to the
period between AD 70 and 85 as the most plausible
time of the writing of the Gospel.[84]

That the Gospel of Mark transmits Peter's story
of events is borne out, first, by the many references
to Peter in the Gospel text: Peter is seen as the representative of the group of disciples; it is to him
that Jesus often addresses his words that are meant
for all the disciples; Peter often speaks on behalf of
the whole group (Mk 8.29–33). In some cases Peter

The Apostle Peter,
icon, 6th c.

addresses Jesus, but Jesus' reply is addressed to the
whole group (Mk 10.28–30; 11.20–33). In the garden of Gethsemane, Jesus,
according to Mark, turns first to Peter, then to all of the disciples: "And he
cometh, and findeth them sleeping, and saith unto Peter, 'Simon, sleepest
thou? Couldest not thou watch one hour? Watch ye and pray, lest ye enter
into temptation. The spirit truly is ready, but the flesh is weak'" (Mk 14.37–
38). In the parallel narratives of the other Gospel writers, Jesus' words are
addressed to all three disciples.

Secondly, Mark sometimes speaks not only of Peter's actions, but also
of his inner experiences, singling him out from among the other participants of the event. At the same time, "Peter said to Jesus: 'Master, it is good
for us to be here. And let us make three tabernacles: one for thee, and one
for Moses, and one for Elias.' For he knew not what to say; for they were

---

[81]Eusebius of Caesarea, *Ecclesiastical History* 6.14.5–7.

[82]See, in particular, W. R. Telford, *The Theology of the Gospel of Mark*, New Testament Theology (Cambridge: Cambridge University Press, 1999), 12–13.

[83]See Joel Marcus, *Mark 1–8: A New Translation with Introduction and Commentary* (New
York, NY: Doubleday, 1999), 38.

[84]See, in particular, H. N. Roskam, *The Purpose of the Gospel of Mark in Its Historical and
Social Context* (Leiden: Brill, 2004), 81–94.

The Transfiguration of the Lord, icon, Theophanes the Greek, 1403.

sore afraid" (Mk 9.5–6). Here Peter becomes the one who expresses the common mood; however, if all three disciples mentioned in the story are united by fear, then it is only in Peter that this fear is combined with joy ("it is good for us to be here") and bewilderment ("For he knew not what to say").

All these and many other factors, so scholars believe, confirm that Peter was the main source of information for Mark. At the same time, a comparison of the Gospel of Mark with the other Gospels compels us to admit that Peter's role in them is fairly clearly highlighted. Moreover, Mark's story of how Jesus came to the disciples across the water during a storm (Mk 6.47–50) contains no mention of Peter, whereas Matthew adds an expressive scene in which Peter goes to meet Jesus and begins to drown (Mt 14.25–32).

There are also reasons to suggest that Mark himself was a witness to at least some of the events in the life of Jesus. In particular, Mark is identified by some commentators as the man who brings the pitcher of water and shows to Jesus' disciples the location where the Last Supper is to take place (Mk 14.13–15). In Mark there is an episode absent in the other evangelists: he mentions that at the moment of Jesus' arrest there was a young man with him whose naked body was covered in a linen cloth; when he was seized, "the young men laid hold on him. And he left the linen cloth, and fled from them naked" (Mk 14.51–52). The young man's name is not given; however, many interpreters have suggested that it was Mark speaking about himself in the third person.

Summarizing the information on the presupposed sources of the Gospel of Mark, Richard Bauckham writes:

[T]he evidence is at the very least consistent with, at most highly supportive of, the hypothesis that Mark's main source was the body of traditions first formulated in Jerusalem by the Twelve, but that he knew this body of traditions in the form in which Peter related them. We can hardly expect to be able to distinguish features peculiar to Peter's version of these traditions, since he was doubtless already prominent in the traditions as the Twelve told them. . . . Furthermore, we must not neglect the role of Mark's own composition. Judging from the wide range of Jesus traditions attested in the other canonical Gospels, not to mention noncanonical Gospel traditions, it is clear that Mark has been quite selective in choosing material for his very short Gospel. It is, for example, hardly conceivable that Mark knew no traditions of the sayings of Jesus other than those he includes in his Gospel, which are surprisingly few. . . . We cannot tell what interesting memories of Peter Mark has left aside in a narrative that is so strongly focused on certain definite concerns.[85]

The Gospel of Mark is the shortest of the four Gospels. It is distinguished by the special dynamism of its narration. Often at the beginning of a story the present tense is used: "And immediately the Spirit driveth him into the wilderness" (Mk 1.12); "And they come into Capernaum" (Mk 1.21); "And there cometh a leper to him" (Mk 1.40); "And they come and they say unto him" (Mk 2.18); "And the multitude cometh together again" (Mk 3.20); "And he cometh to Bethsaida; and they bring a blind man unto him, and besought him to touch him" (Mk 8.22). As the story continues, the present tense gives way to the past tense.

However, the opposite also occurs, where the narrative changes from the past tense to the present; for example: "But Simon's wife's mother lay sick of a fever, and anon they tell him of her" (Mk 1.30). This device is used 150 times in total: it adds a liveliness and directness to the narrative, making the reader feel that he is a participant in the event being described.

A new subject is introduced by the phrase *kai euthys* ("and immediately"). This expression serves many purposes in Mark: in this instance it does not have any chronological weight, sometimes indicating an event that happens much later than the one mentioned in the previous story. It can be used also within a single narrative, to indicate the result of a particular

---

[85]Richard Bauckham, *Jesus and the Eyewitnesses: The Gospels as Eyewitness Testimony* (Grand Rapids, MI: Eerdmans, 2006), 172.

The healing of Peter's mother-in-law, fresco, 16th c.

action: "And he came and took her by the hand, and lifted her up. And immediately the fever left her, and she ministered unto them" (Mk 1.31). In the first chapter alone, the phrase *kai euthys* is encountered eleven times (in verses 10, 12, 18, 20, 21, 23, 28, 29, 30, 42, 43). In total the word *euthys* is encountered in the Gospel of Mark more than forty times—as many times as in the rest of the text of the New Testament.[86] It is translated in various ways as "immediately," "straightway," "forthwith," and "as soon as."

The dominant element in the Gospel of Mark is the narrative. The didactic element (Jesus' teachings) occupies less space than in the other Gospels. In Mark one does not find the long teachings of Jesus on moral themes, which are so characteristic for Matthew (the material from the Sermon on the Mount has almost no parallels in Mark). Also absent in Mark are the lengthy dialogues with the Jews that are a feature of John: only in some instances does Jesus enter into a polemic with the Jews, and each time not on his own initiative, but in response to their questions, bewilderment, and accusations (Mk 2.15–28; 3.22–30; 7.1–23). The parables do not occupy such an important place in Mark as in Matthew and Luke: the Gospel of Mark contains only five parables. The emphasis is primarily placed on the miracles, to which a significant part of the narrative is devoted right up until the story of the passion.

[86]Burridge, *Four Gospels, One Jesus?*, 37.

There is the widespread view that the main audience of the Gospel of Mark consisted of Christians who had converted from paganism. This is supported, in particular, by the fact that the question of the mutual relationship between the Old and New Testaments, which is quite fully developed in Matthew, is touched upon in Mark only from time to time. Nevertheless, the Gospel of Mark, like the other Gospels, contains numerous references to the Old Testament.[87]

The Greek language of Mark is simpler than the language of the other evangelists. He prefers short phrases and often omits auxiliary particles, as a result of which one and the same phrase can be understood as either a statement or a question. The words of the angel serve as an example: "Ye seek Jesus of Nazareth, who was crucified" (Mk 16.6)—they can be translated both ways. In Matthew these words correspond to a statement: "Fear not ye: for I know that ye seek Jesus, which was crucified" (Mt 28.5). In Luke, by contrast, in the parallel place the sentence is formulated as a question: "Why seek ye the living among the dead?" (Lk 24.5).[88] The particles characteristic of the Greek language *nai* ("yes"), *oun* ("thus"), and *idou* ("behold"), which are used to add to the narrative greater smoothness, liveliness, and expressiveness, in Mark are, as a rule, absent in those instances where Matthew and Luke would have used them.[89]

Numerous Aramaisms are encountered in the Gospel of Mark. It is only in Mark that Jesus calls his disciples James and John by the Aramaic phrase Boanerges, that is, "sons of thunder" (Mk 3.17).[90] Jesus' words addressed to the twelve-year-old girl are quoted in Aramaic: "Talitha cumi" (Mk 5.41).[91] However, the Aramaic words in Mark are always accompanied by a translation. Thus, for example, the words to the girl are additionally translated ("Little girl . . . arise"), and next to the word "Corban" (*qorbān*)

---

[87]See Joel Marcus, *The Way of the Lord: Christological Exegesis of the Old Testament in the Gospel of Mark* (Louisville, KY: Westminster / John Knox Press, 1992), 1–5.

[88]C. H. Turner, "Markan Usage: Notes, Critical and Exegetical on the Second Gospel," in *The Language and Style of the Gospel of Mark: An Edition of C. H. Turner's "Notes on Markan Usage" Together with Other Comparable Studies*, ed. J. K. Elliott (Leiden: Brill, 1993), 23.

[89]Ibid., 78–81.

[90]The reconstructed pronunciation is *banē rageš*.

[91]The econstructed pronunciation is *talīta qūmī*.

The Raising of Jairus' Daughter, Ilya Repin, 1871.

an explanation is given: "that is to say, a gift" (Mk 7.11). This explanation demonstrates that the Gospel was written for people who were not familiar with the word "Corban."[92] In the same chapter (Mk 7.34) the Aramaic word "Ephphatha"[93] is used and translated as "Be opened," while in Mark 14.36 we encounter the expression "Abba, Father" (the Aramaic word *'abbā* with its Greek translation). The fact that the Aramaic words found in Mark are supplied with a translation is considered to be indirect confirmation that his Gospel was addressed to readers who were poorly acquainted with the Jewish tradition.

For what purpose does the Gospel writer insert the Aramaic words in the Greek text intended for readers not familiar with this language? Most probably he does so not only to add a greater liveliness to the narrative. It is possible that he was an eyewitness of some of the events described and the kernel of what occurred had impressed itself on his memory: he recalled the voice of Jesus, his words, the original way they sounded, and wanted to preserve them precisely in the form in which they were uttered. For us these details are precious: we hear the voice of Jesus speaking in his own native tongue. It is even more probable that the individual Aramaic

[92]Josephus mentions that Pontius Pilate used a "sacred donation known as Corban" for the construction of a water canal. See Josephus, *Wars of the Jews*, 29.4.

[93]Reconstructed pronunciation corresponding to the Gospel's "*ephphatha*": *'eppatah*. This form most likely goes back to *'etpatah*.

words and expressions uttered by Jesus resounded in such a lively manner in Peter's stories that Mark, in documenting these stories, decided to preserve these words as he had heard them from his teacher.

In this sense, certain grammatical and syntactical errors that are found in Mark, in which we hear the living voice of Jesus, are also valuable. For example, "And he called the twelve, and began to send them forth by two and two . . . and commanded them that they should take nothing for their journey . . . and not put on two coats" (Mk 6.7–9). In the Greek original the phrase is "and do ye not put on two coats," that is, there is an obvious violation of syntax ("that they should take nothing" in the third person and "do ye not put on" in the second person in the same phrase). The unexpected appearance of the imperative mood suggests that the author of the story (Peter or Mark), in describing Jesus' conversation with his disciples, recalled his voice so vividly that, while transmitting his other words in the form of indirect speech, included elements of direct speech in the text.

Apart from Aramaisms, Latinisms are encountered in Mark. On these grounds some scholars have suggested that his Gospel was written for the inhabitants of Rome (in the first century the vernacular language in Rome was Latin, whereas the main written language was Greek). The evangelist sometimes explains the Aramaic terms using Latin terms. Here are some examples of the Latinisms: "quadrans" and "Praetorium."[94]

---

[94]For an overview of scholarly opinion on the issue of the possible link between the Gospel of Mark and Rome, see Brian J. Incigneri, *The Gospel to the Romans: The Setting and Rhetoric of Mark's Gospel* (Leiden: Brill, 2003), 96–105.

4. The Gospel of Luke

T he Gospel that occupies third place in the corpus of the books of the New Testament bears the name of Luke in the earliest surviving manuscript of this Gospel—Bodmer Papyrus 14, dated to the turn of the third century. This is the only Gospel that has a concrete addressee—a certain "most excellent Theophilus," who is mentioned in the prologue to this Gospel (Lk 1.3), and then in the prologue to the Acts of the Apostles (Acts 1.1). It is not known who he was.[95] Judging by his name, he was a Greek, and not a Roman or a Jew.[96] It was possible that he was the one who commissioned (that is, the "literary patron" of) both books, written by Luke not only for him, but also for the group of educated Hellenes to which he belonged.[97]

In Church tradition Luke is considered to be an apostle of the Seventy, a disciple of the apostle Paul. That Luke accompanied Paul on several of his journeys is borne out by excerpts from the book of Acts, where the author refers to himself as "we" when with Paul (Acts 16.10–17; 20.5–15; 21.1–18; 27.1–28.16). For his part, Paul mentions Luke three times. In the Epistle to the Colossians, Paul writes: "Luke, the beloved physician . . . greets you" (Col 4.14). In the Second Epistle to Timothy, Paul complains that his fellow workers have been scattered among various countries, noting that "only Luke is with me" (2 Tim 4.11). In his Epistle to Philemon, he includes Luke alongside Mark in the list of his four coworkers (Philem 24).

The Gospel of Luke is the longest of the Gospels. And it is the only one of the four that begins with a classic Greek prologue-preface:

---

[95]Joel B. Green, *The Gospel of Luke*, The New International Commentary on the New Testament (Grand Rapids, MI: Eerdmans, 1997), 44.

[96]Robert C. Tannehill, *Luke* (Nashville, TN: Abingdon, 1996), 35.

[97]Patrick E. Spencer, *Rhetorical Texture and Narrative Trajectories of the Lukan Galilean Ministry Speeches: Hermeneutical Appropriation by Authorial Readers of Luke-Acts* (London: T&T Clark, 2007), 31–33.

Forasmuch as many have taken in hand to set forth in order a declaration of those things which are most surely believed among us, even as they delivered them unto us, which from the beginning were eyewitnesses, and ministers of the Word; it seemed good to me also, having had perfect understanding of all things from the very first, to write unto thee in order, most excellent Theophilus, that thou mightest know the certainty of those things, wherein thou hast been instructed. (Lk 1.1–4)

St Luke, Frans Hals, 1625.

There were many treatises, including philosophical and medical ones, that began in this fashion.[97] In particular, the treatise of Pedanius Dioscorides (first century), *De Materia Medica* (Greek *Peri hulēs iatrikēs*), begins with the words: "As so many of the ancients and the moderns have begun to compile narratives on curative means, so too have I thought to do the same, most excellent Arius, in order to examine the subject most thoroughly."[98] In its shape the prologue of Luke's Gospel is similar to this text. The literary dependence of the one work upon the other is highly unlikely,[99] although Luke, like Dioscorides, was a physician and therefore could have been interested in medical tracts.[100]

That Luke had a connection with medicine we know from Paul's Epistle to the Colossians and the tradition based upon it. The internal evidence

[98]For a list of parallel texts, see Loveday Alexander, *The Preface to Luke's Gospel: Literary Convention and Social Context in Luke 1.1–4 and Acts 1.1*, Society for New Testament Studies Monograph Series 78 (Cambridge: Cambridge University Press, 2005), 102–142 (in particular, pp. 107, 116, 125, 136–137). On pages 67–101 of this monograph, there is a detailed analysis of the structure and content of prefaces to works on the natural sciences of the Hellenistic and Roman periods.

[99]Pedanius Dioscorides of Anazarbos, *Pedanii Dioscuridis Anazarbei de materia medica libri quinque*, ed. Max Wellmann (Berlin: Weidmann, 1906–1914), 1:1.

[100]Dioscorides, who lived approximately from AD 40 to 90, was a military physician and took part in many of Nero's campaigns. The treatise is considered to have appeared around AD 77–78.

[101]See also Loveday Alexander, "Luke's Preface in the Context of Greek Preface-Writing," in *The Composition of Luke's Gospel: Selected Studies from* Novum Testamentum, ed. David E. Orton (Leiden: Brill, 1999), 99–113.

The Evangelist Luke, miniature from the Ostromir Gospel, 1056–1057.

of the Gospel of Luke, according to some scholars, confirms his acquaintance with medicine. If we compare the parallel places in the Synoptics where disease is mentioned, we discover that Luke uses more precise medical terms than Mark or Matthew. For example, in both of the latter Gospels it is stated that the mother of Peter's wife lay sick of a fever (Mt 8.14; Mk 1.30), while in Luke she was "taken by a great fever" (Lk 4.38).[102] When mentioning a needle, Matthew and Mark use the term *raphis*, which refers to a sewing needle (Mt 19.24; Mk 10.25), while Luke prefers to use the term *belonē*, which denotes a surgical needle (Lk 18.25). Matthew and Mark call the weakened man a *paralytikos* (paralytic), while Luke (Lk 5.18) uses the more precise medical term, which is close in meaning: *paralelymenos* (paralyzed). The description in Luke of the disease of the woman who was bent over also compels us to see him as someone familiar with medical terminology and practice.[103]

In beginning his Gospel, Luke refers, firstly, to many others who have begun to compile narratives on Jesus; secondly, to eyewitnesses and ministers of the Word, from whose words he intends to set forth the basics of the faith in which his audience was instructed; thirdly, to his own thorough investigation of the material under consideration. Thus, Luke has no claims to be an eyewitness: he performs rather the role of investigator, the gatherer of material that has already been in circulation in the form of a multitude of oral and written traditions.

Luke was the first church chronicler. His narrative is not limited to the story of the life, death, and resurrection of Jesus: the direct continuation

[102] At that time there was a distinction between a usual fever and a strong fever that would be accompanied by loss of consciousness. On this, see William Kirk Hobart, *The Medical Language of St. Luke* (Dublin, 1882), 3–5.

[103] Hobart, *The Medical Language of St. Luke*, 20–22. Hobart's conclusions have been supported by many scholars, in spite of the attempt by H. J. Cadbury to refute them and show that Luke's style does not betray any more evidence of a medical education and interest in medicine than the language of the other authors who were not physicians (Henry J. Cadbury, *The Style and Literary Method of Luke* [Cambridge, MA: Harvard University Press, 1920], 50–51).

Christ at the Sea of Tiberias, Vasily Polenov, 1888.

of his Gospel is the book of the Acts of the Apostles, which summed up the history of the Church practically up to the very time when it was written.[104]

Researchers have noted that the Greek language of the Gospel of Luke is distinguished by its grammatical superiority compared to the language of the other Gospel writers. In the Gospel of Luke one finds rare grammatical forms that are peculiar to the literary Greek language and absent in the other evangelists. Luke is the only one of the evangelists who constantly uses in his narrative the auxiliary particles *de* and *te*, which indicates a devotion to Greek literary style. More often than the other evangelists, Luke uses verbs in their infinitive form.[105]

Unlike the other Gospel authors, who characteristically often use parallelism and repetition, Luke is not inclined towards repetition, which betrays his non-Semitic way of thinking. When telling the story of the feeding of the five thousand with five loaves (Lk 9.10–17), he does not mention the feeding of the four thousand with seven loaves: it is clear that he does not need to speak of the second miracle by virtue of the fact that it has the same format and conveys the same lesson as the first one.

[104]Green, *The Gospel of Luke*, 6–10.

[105]Martin M. Culy, Mikeal C. Parsons, and Joshua J. Stigall, *Luke: A Handbook on the Greek Text* (Waco, TX: Baylor University Press, 2010), xxi.

The Righteous
Zacharias
and Elisabeth,
miniature from
the Menologion
of Basil II, 10th c.

Luke often includes more precise details, which supports the idea that he is addressing the reader who is not so familiar with the geography of Palestine: thus, he makes clear that Capernaum is "a city of Galilee" (Lk 4.31), something which Matthew would never do because his imagined reader would know where Capernaum was located. Luke calls the sea of Galilee the "lake of Gennesaret" (Lk 5.1), as this was the name by which it was known, not by the Jews and Galileans, but by outsiders.

Who were the eyewitnesses and ministers of the Word whom Luke refers to? They were most likely the apostles. It is not clear from his Gospel with whom Luke communicated. According to the testimony of Eusebius of Caesarea, Luke was a disciple of the apostle Paul.[106] When Paul was under arrest in Rome, all of his disciples abandoned him apart from Luke, who remained with him. The closeness of Luke to Paul gives us reason to believe that the Gospel of Luke is also the "Gospel of Paul"—in the sense that Paul's theology exerted an important influence on Luke. However, Paul was not an eyewitness to the events described in Luke's Gospel, whereas Luke, being one of the Seventy, could have been a witness to these events.

The main feature that distinguishes the third Gospel from the first and second is the presence of original material in it that we do not find in the

[106]See Eusebius of Caesarea, *Ecclesiastical History* 5.8.3; 3.4.6–7.

The
Annunciation
of the Most
Holy Theotokos,
miniature, 11th c.

other evangelists: this original material makes up some forty-three percent of the text.

This is primarily the background story of the birth of Jesus, including a narrative on the birth of John the Baptist to Zacharias and Elisabeth, the story of the annunciation to the Mother of God, Elisabeth's visit to her, and the story of Jesus' childhood years. This material stands out from the other texts in the Gospel of Luke by their great dependence on the Greek translation of the Bible (the Septuagint), which has led scholars to put forward a hypothesis of a separate Greek source which Luke used when preparing this material.[107]

[107] See, in particular, Chang-Wook Jung, *The Original Language of the Lukan Infancy Narrative* (London: T&T Clark International, 2004), 208–215.

Some of Jesus' teachings quoted by Luke (particularly the five parables) are absent in the other Gospels. Some details of the narrative on Christ's Passion differ from the parallel narratives of the other evangelists. For example, in Matthew and Mark both the thieves crucified to the left and to the right of Jesus reviled him (Mt 27.44; Mk 15.32), whereas in Luke one of them turns to Jesus in supplication (Lk 23.39–42).

The center of the entire narrative in the Gospel of Luke is Jerusalem, and all of Jesus' earthly ministry is presented not as a wandering from city to city, but as a deliberate journey towards Jerusalem as the final destination. Jerusalem is mentioned in the Gospel of Luke thirty-three times— almost as often as in the other three Gospels taken together. The Gospel of Luke begins in Jerusalem (Lk 1.5) and culminates also in Jerusalem. The fundamental part of the Gospel (Lk 9.51–19.27) describes Jesus' journey to Jerusalem; at the same time, Luke ignores the names of the cities and villages that have no direct connection to Jerusalem. Thus, for example, he states that Jesus "set his face to go to Jerusalem, and sent messengers before his face" (Lk 9.51–52). Then it is stated that on the way to Jerusalem in one of the Samaritan villages he was not received "because his face was as though he would go to Jerusalem" (Lk 9.53); the name of the village is not mentioned, but the goal of the journey—Jerusalem—is. Then it is said that Jesus came to Bethany—the name of the village is given as it is located on the outskirts of Jerusalem (Lk 19.29).

Further, as he went "through the cities and villages, teaching, and journeying toward Jerusalem" (Lk 13.22), Jesus says: "Nevertheless I must walk today, and tomorrow, and the day following; for it cannot be that a prophet perish out of Jerusalem. O Jerusalem, Jerusalem, which killest the prophets, and stonest them that are sent unto thee" (Lk 13.33–34). On the way to the holy city, Jesus turns to his disciples and says: "Behold, we go up to Jerusalem, and all things that are written by the prophets concerning the Son of Man shall be accomplished" (Lk 18.31).

In retelling Christ's parable of the ten pounds, Luke emphasizes that Jesus "was nigh to Jerusalem, and . . . they thought that the kingdom of God should immediately appear" (Lk 19.11). There is one further remark characteristic of the evangelist: "And when he had thus spoken, he went before,

The Mount of Olives and the garden of Gethsemane, photograph, ca. 1890–1900.

ascending up to Jerusalem" (Lk 19.28). A little later on, Luke speaks of how Jesus was "even now at the descent of the mount of Olives" (Lk 19.37): as he drew closer to Jerusalem, the geographical details became more and more precise. As he stood on the descent of the mount, Jesus wept for Jerusalem (Lk 19.41). Luke is the only one of the Gospel writers who mentions this event, demonstrating the importance Jerusalem had for Jesus. Finally, Jesus entered the Temple of Jerusalem (Lk 19.45), after which the final events of his life began, leading to his crucifixion and resurrection

The Gospel of Luke is imbued with an atmosphere of praise, thanksgiving, and glorifying God. It begins by narrating the annunciation to the Virgin Mary and the birth of John the Baptist. From the description it is evident that Zacharias and Elisabeth and Mary lived in an atmosphere of praising God and prayerful thanksgiving. Thus, Mary's sense of thanksgiving is expressed in the song "My soul doth magnify the Lord . . ." (Lk 1.46–55). The same chapter (Lk 1.68–79) contains Zacharias' song of praise and thanksgiving. In speaking of the birth of Jesus Christ, Luke quotes the angels' hymn of praise: "Glory to God in the highest, and on earth peace, good will toward men" (Lk 2.14), and then tells of how the shepherds, having heard about Jesus' birth, returned "glorifying and praising God" (Lk 2.20). When telling the story of the meeting of the infant Jesus in the

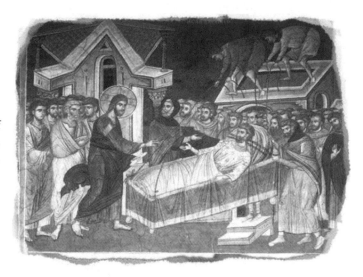

The healing of
the paralytic,
fresco, 16th c.

Temple, Luke quotes Symeon's song of thanksgiving: "Lord, now lettest thou thy servant depart in peace . . ." (Lk 2.29–32).

Further, we may note how the paralytic glorified God after he was healed (Lk 5.25); how the people glorified God after Jesus raised the son of the widow of Nain from the dead (Lk 7.16); how the woman who was bent over glorified God after she was healed (Lk 13.13); the healing of the ten lepers and the gratitude of the Samaritan (Lk 17.15) (this is an instance that Luke especially marks out); how the blind man glorifies God after being healed (Lk 18.43); the joyful glorification of God by the disciples as Jesus enters Jerusalem (Lk 19.37); how the centurion glorifies God after witnessing Jesus' death on the cross (Lk 23.47); and how the disciples glorified God when Jesus ascended into heaven (Lk 24.53).

Scholars have noted the atmosphere of joy that permeates the Gospel of Luke: it speaks of joy at John the Baptist's birth (Lk 1.14), at the moment of the annunciation (Lk 1.28), and at the appearance of the angel to the shepherds (Lk 2.10). Luke narrates how Jesus' disciples, when they returned from preaching, said to him "with joy" that even the devils are subject to them (Lk 10.17); in reply Jesus says: "Notwithstanding in this rejoice not, that the spirits are subject unto you; but rather rejoice, because your names are written in heaven" (Lk 10.20). "In that hour Jesus rejoiced in spirit," writes the evangelist (Lk 10.21). Let us also note the references to the joy of the people when they spoke of the miracles that Jesus performed (Lk 13.17), to the joy with which Zacchaeus was ready to receive Christ in his house (Lk 9.6), and to the joy of the disciples who, when they met Jesus on the road to Emmaus after his resurrection, recognized him in the breaking of bread and asked each other: "Did not our heart burn within us, while he talked with us by the way?" (Lk 24.32).

The raising of the son of the widow of Nain, mosaic, 12th c.

Scholars have also noted the atmosphere of prayer present in the Gospel of Luke. Prayer is mentioned also by the other evangelists, but only in Luke is it noted, for example, that Jesus prayed after being baptized (Lk 3.21), and that he prayed throughout the entire night before choosing the twelve apostles.

Taking the concrete needs of the reader as a starting point, Luke omits those parts in the Gospels that are directly connected to the Jewish tradition: for example, he does not mention the second coming of Elijah before the coming of Jesus. If the leitmotif of the Sermon on the Mount in Matthew is the juxtaposition of the New Testament with the Old Testament ("You have heard it said by men of old . . . But I say unto you"), in the parallel text in Luke this juxtaposition is absent.

Like Mark, Luke omits Jesus' commandment that is found in Matthew: "Go not into the way of the Gentiles, and into any city of the Samaritans enter ye not" (Mt 10.5). On the contrary, Jesus is spoken of as "a light to enlighten the Gentiles" (Lk 2.32), while it is said that the Gospel is to be preached "among all nations" (Lk 24.47). Examples are often given of people who do not belong to the Jewish nation: we may mention the parable of the Good Samaritan (Lk 10.15), the story of the healing of the ten lepers, where the only one who gave thanks was also a Samaritan (Lk 17.11), and Jesus' praise of the centurion, who was a Roman and of whom Jesus said, "I have not found such great faith, no, not in Israel" (Lk 7.9).

The
Annunciation,
mosaic, St
Sophia Cathedral
in Kiev, ca. 1040.

In the Gospel of Luke. women are given a more prominent place than in the other Gospels. This applies primarily to the Virgin Mary, of whom we know mainly from the third Gospel. In Luke we also read of Elisabeth, of the widow of Nain, of the sinful woman, of Martha and Mary. Such close attention to women on the part of the evangelist is all the more remarkable, since in the New Testament era the attitude towards women was quite different from that towards men—women were almost completely not taken into account. It is no coincidence that when enumerating those whom Jesus had fed with the loaves, the Gospel of Matthew states: "And they that had eaten were about five thousand men, beside women and children" (Mt 14.21). In Luke in the corresponding place (Lk 9.4) this comment is absent.

5. The Gospel of John

The Gospel of John differs substantially from the three Synoptic Gospels.

Eusebius of Caesarea provides us with detailed information on the reasons for the writing of the Fourth Gospel and its differences from the other three:

> Mark and Luke had already published the Gospels according to them, but John, it is said, used all the time a message which was not written down, and at last took to writing for the following cause. The three Gospels which had been written down before were distributed to all including himself; it is said that he welcomed them and testified to their truth but said that there was only lacking to the narrative the account of what was done by Christ at first and at the beginning of the preaching. The story is surely true. It is at least possible to see that the three evangelists related only what the Saviour did during one year after John the Baptist had been put in prison and that they stated this at the beginning of their narrative. . . . They say accordingly that for this reason the apostle John was asked to relate in his own Gospel the period passed over in silence by the former evangelists and the things done during it by the Saviour (that is to say, the events before the imprisonment of the Baptist). . . . If this be understood the Gospels no longer appear to disagree, because that according to John contains the first of the acts of Christ and the others the narrative of what he did at the end of the period, and it will seem probable that John passed over the genealogy of our Saviour according to the flesh, because it had been already written out by Matthew and Luke, and began with the description of his divinity since this had been reserved for him by the Divine Spirit as for one greater than they.[108]

---

[108]Eusebius of Caesarea, *Ecclesiastical History* 3.23.7–13 (Lake, LCL).

The Holy
Apostle and
Evangelist John
the Theologian,
icon, 14th c.

As Clement of Alexandria wrote, the Gospel of John complements the
other four Gospels, which reflected the human side of Jesus' ministry—his
miracles and sayings—but did not reveal with sufficient fullness his divine
nature.[109] St Augustine echoes Clement:

> These three evangelists, however, were for the most part engaged with
> those things which Christ did through the vehicle of the flesh of man,
> and after the temporal fashion. But John, on the other hand, had in
> view that true divinity of the Lord in which He is the Father's equal, and
> directed his efforts above all to the setting forth of the divine nature in

[109]Clement's testimony is quoted in Eusebius of Caesarea, *Ecclesiastical History* 6.14.7
(*NPNF*² 1:261).

his Gospel in such a way as he believed to be adequate to men's needs and notions. Therefore he is borne to loftier heights, in which he leaves the other three far behind him; so that, while in them you see men who have their conversation in a certain manner with the man Christ on earth, in him you perceive one who has passed beyond the cloud in which the whole earth is wrapped, and who has reached the liquid heaven from which, with clearest and steadiest mental eye, he is able to look upon God the Word, who was in the beginning with God, and by whom all things were made. And there, too, he can recognize Him who was made flesh in order that He might dwell among us [Jn 1.13–14]; that He assumed the flesh, not that He was changed into the flesh. . . . And whatever other statements there may be to the same effect, calculated to betoken, to those who are possessed of right understanding, that divinity of Christ in which He is the Father's equal, of all these we might almost say that we are indebted for their introduction into the Gospel narrative to John alone. For he is like one who has drunk in the secret of His divinity more richly and somehow more familiarly than others, as if he drew it from the very bosom of his Lord on which it was his wont to recline when He sat at meat [Jn 13.23].[110]

Indeed, the very first words of the Gospel of John show that his fundamental theme will be the presentation of Jesus as God incarnate: "In the beginning was Word, and the Word was with God, and the Word was God. The same was in the beginning with God" (Jn 1.1–2). These words set the tone for the whole Gospel. And in the concluding chapters of John's Gospel we hear Thomas' confession: "My Lord and my God" (Jn 20.28). The idea of Jesus' divinity is expressed in none of the Gospels with such consistency as in John.

That the Gospel of John belongs to one of the closest disciples of Jesus is testified to not only by Church tradition, but also by a multitude of internal factors. The author of the Gospel is an eyewitness to many, if not all the events described in the Gospel. In his narrative John often gives such details that could hardly be known from a retelling by a third person: "It

[110]Augustine, *The Harmony of the Gospels* 1.4.7 (*NPNF*[1] 6:79–80).

The
Transfiguration
and the Raising
of Lazarus, icon
fragment, 12th c.

was about the tenth hour" (Jn 1.39); "It was about the sixth hour" (Jn 4.6);
"It was night" (Jn 13.30).

The author of the Fourth Gospel was not only familiar with the details
of the life of Jesus and his disciples, but also retained a recollection of
the person of Jesus, the features of his human personality and his experiences. In particular, when narrating how Jesus came into a city in Samaria,
John says: "Jesus therefore, being wearied with his journey, sat thus on the
well" (Jn 4.6). When narrating the story of the raising of Lazarus, John
repeatedly conveys the mood and inner state of the Teacher: "When Jesus
therefore saw her weeping, and the Jews also weeping which came with
her, he groaned in the spirit, and was troubled" (Jn 11.33); upon hearing the
Jews' response, "Jesus wept" (Jn 11.35); he approaches the tomb of Lazarus
"groaning in himself" (Jn 11.38). It would be difficult to record these details
from somebody else's words.

The author of the Gospel of John is one of its protagonists. He is invis-
ibly present in this Gospel: sometimes he is out of the picture, sometimes
in the picture—in the shape of the disciple who is not given a name. This
anonymous person in the Gospel of John appears for the first time in the
story of the two disciples of John the Baptist who followed Jesus: here there
is the figure of a nameless disciple (Jn 1.35–39). Then, at the Last Supper, the
disciple "whom Jesus loved" appears: he leans on the bosom of the Teacher
(Jn 13.23). In the story of Jesus' arrest, the evangelist writes: "And Simon
Peter followed Jesus, and so did another disciple: that disciple was known

Crucifixion with the Virgin Mary, St John and St Mary Magdalene, Anthony van Dyck, 1617–1619.

to the high priest" (Jn 18.15). The disciple "whom he loved" stands at Jesus' cross: Jesus entrusts the care of his Mother to him (Jn 19.26–27).

It is the same anonymous disciple who is mentioned in the account of how blood and water flowed from Jesus' body as he died on the cross: "And he that saw it bare record, and his record is true, and he knoweth that he speaketh the truth, that ye might believe" (Jn 19.35). These words might serve as the epigraph to the entire Gospel. Here we have not only the author mentioning himself in the third person, but also a direct appeal to the reader in the second person plural, which we do not find in any other place of the Gospel.

Further, the "disciple whom Jesus loved" appears in the narrative about the empty tomb (Jn 20.2), and then in the story of Jesus' appearance to the

Jerusalem

disciples by the sea of Galilee (Jn 21.7). The Fourth Gospel culminates in the story of how Jesus was followed by Peter and the disciple "whom Jesus loved, who also leaned on his breast at supper, and said, 'Lord, who is he that betrayeth thee?'" (Jn 21.20–21). And only at the end of the book does the author finally reveal himself: "This is the disciple who testifieth of these things, and wrote these things" (Jn 21.24).

Thus, in the very text of the Gospel the anonymous disciple, the same disciple "whom Jesus loved," is unambiguously identified as the author of the Gospel.

In the tradition of the Church, this disciple is believed to be John, the son of Zebedee, the brother of James, who is repeatedly mentioned in the Synoptic Gospels. That it is he who was the author of the Fourth Gospel is testified by Irenaeus of Lyons: "Then John, the disciple of the Lord, who also had leaned upon His breast, did himself publish a Gospel during his residence at Ephesus in Asia."[111] In all the ancient manuscripts the Fourth Gospel is titled as having been written by John, although the manuscript tradition does not clarify which one.

---

[111]Irenaeus of Lyons, *Against Heresies* 3.1.1 (*ANF* 1:415).

The Last Supper,
Leonardo da
Vinci, 1495–1498.

On more than one occasion the suggestion has been made that the author of the Fourth Gospel is not John, the son of Zebedee, but another John, the beloved disciple of Jesus not of the Twelve, who did not travel with Jesus, but lived in Jerusalem and saw him only when Jesus went to Jerusalem. In support of this theory, the following arguments have been put forward: (a) the Gospel of John does not mention many of the key episodes of the Synoptic Gospels in which John, the son of Zebedee, figures; (b) many episodes from the Gospel of John in which the beloved disciple is present are not at all reflected in the Synoptic Gospels; (c) in the Fourth Gospel its author does not identify himself as John, the son of Zebedee, in spite of the fact that the sons of Zebedee are mentioned more than once in this Gospel (Jn 21.2); (d) the Gospel of John is concentrated almost exclusively on events that occurred in Jerusalem or its environs. The fullest and best argued version of this theory is expounded in Richard Bauckham's book *Jesus and the Eyewitnesses*, which is in many other ways an impeccable piece of research into the New Testament texts from the perspective of church orthodoxy.[112]

And yet, the tradition of the Church can present a number of arguments in favor of the author of the Fourth Gospel being one of the twelve apostles and being the same John, the son of Zebedee, who figures in the Synoptic Gospels. The most important argument is that the Fourth Gospel bears the name of John, which was borne by only one of the known disciples of Jesus. Moreover, in what manner could one of the disciples,

---

[112]Bauckham, *Jesus and the Eyewitnesses*, 412–470.

The Last Supper,
fresco, 14th c.

who was not one of the Twelve, be alongside Jesus at the Last Supper, even more so in such a privileged position, leaning on his bosom? It would be strange to the utmost if at the farewell discourse of Jesus with his disciples, a discourse that had exceptional meaning for the subsequent history of the apostolic community, the place closest to the Teacher was occupied by some person who did not take part in the life of the community, but spent his time in Jerusalem awaiting the arrival of Jesus, a secret disciple similar to Joseph of Arimathea (Jn 19.38) or Nicodemus (Jn 3.1; 19.39).

The fact that in the Synoptic Gospels John, the son of Zebedee, is mentioned several times, while in the Fourth Gospel only once, may be interpreted in favor of the Church's tradition. In the Fourth Gospel, the absence of one of the key figures of the apostolic community, while an oft-mentioned anonymous disciple was present, is explained precisely by the fact that the anonymous disciple is John—the very same John of whom the Synoptics speak.

Indeed, in the Gospel of John many important episodes are absent in which, according to the Synoptics, John, the son of Zebedee, participated. But this can be explained by the fact that, according to Church tradition and as confirmed by modern research, the Gospel of John was written later than the other Gospels and also that the author accentuates mainly the events that the Synoptics ignored. It is quite possible that John was familiar with one, two, or three of the Gospels, or their earlier prototypes, and wrote his own Gospel, hoping to add to the existing narratives.

Luke, too, was familiar with the other Gospels or their prototypes. However, we can observe a difference in approach between Luke and John. Luke was not simply acquainted with the other testimonies: to a significant degree he relies upon them and presents himself as a compiler. By contrast, John, for the most part, avoids repeating that which has already been said by the other Gospel writers, with the exception of those instances when

The wedding in Cana of Galilee; the miracle of the transformation of water into wine, fresco, 14th c.

this repetition is essential for the development of the plot line or theological thought.

This could explain the absence in the Gospel of John of the majority of the miracles described by the Synoptics; it contains no parables from the Synoptic Gospels; absent are such important episodes as, for example, John's baptism of Jesus or the communion of the disciples at the Last Supper. At the same time, it is only the Gospel of John that contains Jesus' discourse on the bread of life (Jn 6.22–71) and many other disputes with the Jews not mentioned in the other evangelists. It is only in John that we find such episodes as the miracle of changing water into wine at the wedding feast in Cana of Galilee (Jn 2.13–25), Jesus' conversations with Nicodemus (Jn 3.1–36) and the Samaritan woman (Jn 4.7–43), the healing of the man blind from birth (Jn 9.1–41), the washing of the disciples' feet (Jn 13.1–11), and the lengthy farewell discourse of Jesus with his disciples at the Last Supper (Jn 13.11–16.33).

Regarding the sole mention of the sons of Zebedee (Jn 21.2) in the Gospel of John, alongside Simon Peter, Thomas, Nathaniel, and another two of Jesus' disciples, it is not at all obligatory to include the author of the Fourth Gospel among the last two disciples whose names are not mentioned. By the same token he could be numbered among the sons of Zebedee, whose names are also not mentioned.

And so, the Gospel of John is a series of testimonies to events that he witnessed with his own eyes. Although some of the topics in the Gospel of John resonate with those described in the Synoptics, the textual similarity can be seen only sporadically. Unlike the three other evangelists, John does not strive to give a consistent description of events: his Gospel is addressed to the reader already familiar with the general canvas of the earthly life of Jesus according to the other Gospels.

Nonetheless, it is precisely the Gospel of John that allows us to construct the material given by the Synoptics in a chronologically consistent order, since all of Jesus' ministry in it is divided into several periods, the boundaries between which are formed by the recurring feast of the Passover. The first Passover was heralded by the visit to the Temple and the driving out of the moneylenders (Jn 2.13.23), the second by the healing of the paralytic at the pool by the sheep market (Jn 5.2), the third by the miracle of the multiplication of the loaves (Jn 6.4), and the last, the fourth, by the crucifixion and death of Jesus.[113]

Scholars have noted that the Gospel of John describes fewer events than each of the three Synoptic Gospels; however, each of the events described is developed over the course of a significantly longer narrative than the stories of the Synoptics. In this manner, the reader is invited to a more contemplative and unhurried participation in the story, the form of which contains indications of its meaning.[114] The treatment of one subject in the Gospel of John may be several times longer than the average length of the same subject in the Synoptic Gospels. Thus, for example, the story of the healing of the man blind from birth takes up thirty-eight verses (Jn 9.1–38), while the raising of Lazarus takes up forty-six verses (Jn 11.1–46). In comparison, the story of the healing of blind Bartimaeus in the Synoptic Gospels takes up seven to nine verses (Mk 10:46–52; Lk 18:35–43), and

---

[113]In the second instance, however, John uses the expression "the feast of the Jews," which does not necessarily mean the Passover, but could mean also Pentecost or *Sukkot*—the Feast of Tabernacles (cf. the use of this expression in Jn 7.2, where it indicates the Feast of Tabernacles). However, the tradition of the Church has firmly established that Passover is meant by the phrase "the feast of the Jews" in Jn 5.1.

[114]Richard Bauckham, *The Testimony of the Beloved Disciple: Narrative, History, and Theology in the Gospel of John* (Grand Rapids, MI: Baker Academic, 2007), 197.

The encounter with the Samaritan woman, fresco, 14th c.

the raising of the widow's son of Nain in the Gospel of Luke takes up six verses (Lk 7.11–16).

The Gospel of John is a theological treatise where the events of Jesus' life illustrate certain theological propositions. Thus, for example, the idea that the teaching of Jesus is "living water" is illustrated with the aid of the story of Jesus' encounter with the Samaritan woman (Jn 4.4–42), which is absent in the other Gospels: it gives the images of water, the well, and the tired traveler who has nothing to draw water with and who asks the Samaritan woman to give him a drink.

The idea that Jesus is the "light of the world" (Jn 9.5) is illustrated with the aid of the story of the healing of the blind man at the pool of Siloam (Jn 9.6–38). He who lives without God is blind, and he who believes in God becomes seeing, for faith in Jesus as the Son of God gives sight to a person—this is the basic message of this story.

The narrative on the feeding of the five thousand with five loaves (Jn 6.6–13) is given in order to prepare us for Jesus' words, "I am the bread of life" (Jn 6.35). If the other Gospel writers are attracted by the miracle itself, John focuses attention on the theological meaning of this event: he interprets the miracle as a prototype of the Eucharist.

The Savior,
mosaic, 12th c.

Finally, the story of the raising of Lazarus (Jn 11.1–44), which is absent in the other Gospels, is a prelude to the story of Christ's own resurrection from the dead and an illustration of Jesus' words, "I am the resurrection, and the life" (Jn 11.25).

The entire Fourth Gospel is constructed according to one and the same principle: each theological standpoint finds its place in a plot that has meaning insofar as it illustrates this standpoint. It is possible that this is one of the reasons why John focuses his attention upon the details that have bypassed the other Gospel writers, at the same time ignoring the many events and words of Jesus that are known from their narratives.

One of the characteristic peculiarities of the Gospel of John is the use of a more limited vocabulary than the other evangelists. John's vocabulary is half that of Luke and is substantially smaller than the vocabularies of Matthew and Mark. To a significant degree this is linked to the use of key words that are repeated many times over.[115] As an example, we may quote the first five verses of the first chapter of the Gospel (Jn 1.1–5). Here the terms "Word," "God," and "was in the beginning" are used three times, and twice the phrase "in the beginning" and the terms "life" and "light." It is by using this type of repetition that the author achieves a special effect: the

[115]Repetition is one of the characteristic features of the style of John's Gospel. See Craig S. Keener, *The Gospel of John: A Commentary*, vol. 1 (Peabody, MA: Hendrickson, 2010), 48–49.

Christ
Pantocrator,
icon, 13th c.

theological standpoint advanced by the evangelist is not only assimilated better by the reader, but also, each time the reader returns to it, it acquires additional overtones of meaning.

The author of the Fourth Gospel emphasizes the universal character of the preaching and ministry of Jesus. He is the Savior not only of the people of Israel, but also of the whole world. According to John, Jesus is the "true light, who enlighteneth every man that cometh into the world" (Jn 1.9); Jesus accepts death so that the world may be saved (Jn 3.17); Jesus has

The Good Shepherd, Philippe de Champaigne, 17th c.

"other sheep . . . which are not of this fold," that is, not of the people of Israel, and whom he is to bring to himself so that they may be "one flock"—a saved humanity, and "one shepherd"—Christ (Jn 10.16).

The term "truth" is not used in any of the other Gospels as often as in John: it is repeated in his Gospel twenty five times.[116] At the very beginning of the Gospel he states that "the law was given by Moses, but grace and truth came by Jesus Christ" (Jn 1.17). John constantly accentuates the true nature of Jesus' words. For John, Truth is not an abstract concept: Truth is Jesus himself (Jn 14.6). In the Fourth Gospel we encounter twenty times the expression "Truly, truly, I say unto you. . . ." In the Synoptics this expression, characteristic of Jesus' speech, is transmitted without repetition: "Truly I say unto you. . . ."

One of the fundamental themes of John is the teaching that "God is Light, and in him is there no darkness" (1 Jn 1.5). The juxtaposition of darkness and light is one of the constantly repeated motifs of the corpus of John's writings (Jn 1.5; 3.19, and so on).

One other central theme in John, which is not fully revealed by the other Gospel writers, is that of love. The other Gospels speak of love also, but the true originality of Jesus' teaching on love is revealed only by John. It is only in his Gospel that Jesus says: "A new commandment I give unto you, that ye love one another." The novelty of this commandment is that the human person is called to love his neighbor not merely with a natural human love, but with a special, sacrificial love: "As I have loved you, that ye also love one another" (Jn 13.34). And in his first epistle, John writes that "God is love" (1 Jn 4.8): "truth," "love," and "light" are the names of the incarnate Word. The entire Gospel of John may be seen as an expanded commentary on the various names of Jesus, the Son of God.

[116]In defining this number we have used an electronic search of the Greek text of the New Testament.

Christ the Good
Shepherd,
mosaic, 5th c.

The absence of Jesus' parables in the Gospel of John, which occupy an important place in the narratives of the other evangelists, is linked to the peculiar nature of John's theological thought: in each real event he sees a parable, an image, a symbol, and therefore he has no need of parables to manifest Jesus' theological teaching. For him, it would seem, it is far more important to see the symbolic meaning in the real events of Jesus' life than to retell his parables, which have already been presented by the other Gospel writers.

The Synoptics left out of the picture many of Jesus' words and sayings that bore a clearly expressed theological nature. The basic canvas of the Synoptic Gospels is the story of the life and miracles of Jesus and the reproduction of his moral exhortations; less attention is paid to his theological teaching. It is John who fills this gap. His Gospel for the most part consists of the discourses of Jesus; it contains many dialogues with the Jews, often of a polemical nature. John places a special emphasis on the uniqueness and unprecedented nature of Christ's preaching, noting the reaction of the audience to his words: "No man ever spoke like this man" (Jn 7.46).

In the Gospel of John we notice a certain kind of deliberate evasion. Often the discourse is constructed on this principle: the interlocutor poses a question to Jesus, and Jesus, as though not noticing the question, continues to develop his thought. For example, in the discourse with Nicodemus, Jesus says that the human person is to be born again. Nicodemus asks: "How can a man be born when he is old? Can he enter the second time into his mother's womb, and be born?" Instead of giving an answer, Jesus continues his speech: "Except a man be born of water and of the Spirit, he cannot enter into the kingdom of God" (Jn 3.4–5).

Sometimes the interlocutor's question is simply the starting point for Jesus, who, in his response, often goes further than his interlocutor might expect. It is on this principle that the entire conversation with the Samaritan woman is constructed.

Yet one more example is the story of how Philip and Andrew tried to bring the Greeks to Jesus. In response to the disciples' request for a meeting with them, Jesus foretells his death and the subsequent widespread dissemination of his teaching (Jn 12.23–24). Then nothing more is said of the Greeks, and it remains unknown whether they saw Jesus or not. John is primarily interested in the thought, the theological idea, and not the details of the historical narrative.

In the latter half of the nineteenth century, the attention of scholars was drawn to the so-called chiasmus of the Old Testament and New Testament authors. In John chiastic constructions are encountered more often than with the other Gospel writers. Chiasmus is understood to be those conceptual and phraseological constructions in which statements are placed with more or less symmetry along the pattern of a-b-a, a-b-c-b-a, and so on, while one statement in such an instance is invariably perceived as being central. For example,

(a) "In the beginning was the Word,"
   (b) "and the Word was with God,"
(a) "and the Word was God."

Or,

(a) "The same was in the beginning with God,"
   (b) "All things were made by him; and without him was not any thing made that was made,"
      (c) "In him was life; and the life was the light of men,"
   (b) "And the light shineth in darkness,"
(a) "and the darkness comprehended it not."

Ephesus

Chiasmus can be seen also in larger constructions: separate excerpts, chapters and even in the Gospel as a whole.[117] For all of the formality, arbitrariness, and at times artificiality of such a division of the Gospel, this division can nonetheless help us to understand how the chain of thought of the evangelists developed in certain instances. As a rule, they thought cyclically, that is, their consciousness rotated around a particular theological reference and often returned to it. This is to the utmost degree apparent in John.

The location for the writing of the Gospel of John, according to Irenaeus of Lyons, was Ephesus.[118] Among other possible locations, contemporary scholars have listed Alexandria, Antioch, and the northern Transjordan; however, the majority of scholars hold to the traditional locale that goes back to Irenaeus.[119]

Regarding the time when the Gospel of John appeared, various theories exist. Both the ancient tradition of the Church and contemporary scholarship basically agree that this Gospel was written later than the others. Many scholars date the final redaction of the Gospel of John to the end of the

[117]For more detail, see John Breck, *The Shape of Biblical Language: Chiasmus in the Scriptures and Beyond* (Crestwood, NY: St Vladimir's Seminary Press, 1994).

[118]Irenaeus of Lyons, *Against Heresies* 3.1.1 (*ANF* 1:411).

[119]Raymond E. Brown, *An Introduction to the Gospel of John* (New Haven, CT: Yale University Press, 2003), 202–206.

first century; however, voices can be heard in favor of a significantly earlier dating. Thus, for example, John A. T. Robinson believes that John's Gospel appeared before the destruction of the Temple of Jerusalem in AD 70.[120]

The major New Testament specialist who devoted decades to a study of the Fourth Gospel, Raymond E. Brown (1928–1998), delineated five stages during which, he believes, the text of this Gospel was formed: 1) the existence in the oral tradition of material concerning the life and teaching of Jesus, different from that which formed the basis of the Synoptic Gospels; 2) the selection, exposition, and reworking of this material by the author in oral form; 3) the first written version of the Gospel; 4) the second version made by the same author; 5) the final version made by a redactor. Brown particularly attributes Jesus' discourse with the disciples at the Last Supper (Jn 15–17) to the hand of this hypothetical redactor, as well as a whole series of other passages that he believes are not the work of the evangelist. However, the author of this theory calls it a working hypothesis and admits there may be inconsistencies in it.[121]

Brown's theory helps us to explain why, for example, at the Last Supper after Jesus' words "Arise, let us go hence" (Jn 14.31), nobody arises; on the contrary, Jesus continues to speak and utters the longest of the teachings in the Fourth Gospel.

In our view, however, the attribution to a later redactor of the first three chapters of the Gospel, which have key theological meaning, substantially lessens their importance. Far more plausible is the suggestion that these inconsistencies could have arisen as a result of the work of the author with his text (for example, while preparing the second version) or of the work of the redactor, which presupposed not the writing of new texts, but merely the regrouping of material, written by the evangelist John.

Moreover, if we check these inconsistencies, they may turn out to be illusory. According to one theory, after Jesus' words "Arise, let us go hence," the disciples actually did arise and go, while Jesus continued the discourse on the way to the garden of Gethsemane.

[120]John A. T. Robinson, *The Priority of John*, ed. J. F. Coakley (London: SCM Press, 1985).
[121]Raymond E. Brown, *The Gospel according to John (I–XII)*, Anchor Bible 29 (Garden City, NY: Doubleday, 1966), xxxiv–xxxix.

*The Apostle
John on the
Isle of Patmos,*
by a master of
Lourinhã, 16th c.

Apart from the Fourth Gospel, the authorship of three epistles and the book of Revelation, which have become part of the New Testament, has been attributed to John. The body of John's writings occupies an independent place in the New Testament. Alongside the apostle Paul, John is the founder of Christian theology, as he put Gospel history in the framework of a precise theological vision. It is not by chance that the title of "Theologian" was given to the apostle John in the Church's tradition.

John begins his first epistle with the remarkable words:

> That which was from the beginning, which we have heard, which we have seen with our eyes, which we have looked upon, and our hands have handled, of the Word of life—for the life was manifested, and we have seen it, and bear witness, and show unto you that eternal life, which was with the Father, and was manifested unto us—that which we have seen and heard declare we unto you, that ye also may have fellowship with us; and truly our fellowship is with the Father, and with his Son Jesus Christ. (1 Jn 1.1–3)

These words reflect in full measure the motivation of the author of the Fourth Gospel, who decided to put down on paper that which he had seen with his own eyes, which he examined and touched with his own hands. He is a genuine witness who saw and participated in the events of which he speaks, and the text of the Fourth Gospel contains many affirmations of this.

6. The Letters of Paul

The apostle Paul stands out among the disciples of Jesus. He was not a follower of Jesus in the latter's lifetime, and in the first years after his death he was an active persecutor of the Church that Jesus founded. Saul's miraculous conversion (Acts 9.1–19) changed his life completely: he received baptism and immediately joined the cause of preaching the Gospel.

At first, the other apostles treated him with distrust (Acts 9.26); however, in time they accepted him into their ranks. Nevertheless, Paul had to prove constantly that he belonged to the apostolic community. In addressing the Corinthians, he writes: "Am I not an apostle? Am I not free? Have I not seen Jesus Christ our Lord? Are not ye my work in the Lord? If I be not an apostle unto others, yet doubtless I am to you: for you are the seal of mine apostleship in the Lord" (1 Cor 9.1–2).

Paul saw his mission primarily in preaching the Gospel to the Gentiles. And yet, he emphasized that he had been called by God himself to this cause, and that he did this not at the instruction of the other apostles, but by direct order from God:

But when it pleased God, who separated me from my mother's womb, and called me by his grace, to reveal his Son in me, that I might preach him among the Gentiles, immediately I conferred not with flesh and blood, neither went I up to Jerusalem to them which were apostles

The Conversion of Saul, Michelangelo, 1542–1545.

before me; but I went into Arabia, and returned again unto Damascus. Then after three years I went up to Jerusalem to see Peter, and abode with him fifteen days. But I saw none of the other apostles, save James the Lord's brother. (Gal 1.15–19)

In spite of the fact that Paul was not an eyewitness to the events of Jesus' earthly life, his writings are an important testimony to how Jesus' mission was perceived among the first generation of Christians.

Paul, alongside John, is often called the author of Christian theology. If the synoptic evangelists are concerned primarily with a description of what they saw and heard, and John, who was familiar with these descriptions, concentrates on the theological ideas that issue from them, then Paul sets himself a different task. He was not a participant in the Gospel story, so he interprets this story and creates the theological basis upon which the Church's teaching about Jesus as God incarnate is constructed for all subsequent generations.

It is difficult to overestimate the significance of Paul for the development of Christian theology. There is even the opinion that it was Paul who

The Conversion of Saul,
engraving, Julius Schnorr
von Carolsfeld, 19th c.

made Christianity a religion, taking Jesus' teaching as its basis and grafting onto the man Jesus the identity of the Son of God: this opinion has been expressed by many New Testament researchers in the nineteenth and twentieth centuries.[122] But the early Church also recognized the key role of Paul in the formation of Christian doctrine, comparing him to Christ himself in significance. In the fourth century John Chrysostom even claimed that through Paul, Christ said more to people than he could have said himself during his earthly ministry.[123]

The importance of Paul's epistles, which make up almost a third of the total volume of the New Testament, is determined not only by the fact that they develop the fundamental themes of Christian theology. According to the majority of scholars, Paul's epistles are the earliest memorials of Christian literature, which appeared even before the Gospels were put together as finished literary sources. The earliest of Paul's epistles, to the Galatians, was possibly written around AD 48–49, that is, before the Apostolic Council in Jerusalem. Most of the other epistles are dated to the AD 50s and the beginning of the 60s. As has already been stated, nowhere in his epistles does Paul quote the Gospels as written sources.

Moreover, even in those cases when it would appear that he could have known about the events described from eyewitnesses, he does not refer to these eyewitnesses, but refers rather to revelation from God:

For I have received from the Lord that which also I delivered unto you, that the Lord Jesus the same night in which he was betrayed took bread, and when he had given thanks, he broke it, and said, "Take, eat: this is my body, which is broken for you: this do in remembrance of me." After the same manner also he took the cup, when he had supped, saying, "This cup is the new testament in my blood: this do ye, as oft as ye drink it, in remembrance of me. For as often as ye eat this bread,

[122]For more on this, see N. T. Wright, *What Saint Paul Really Said: Was Paul of Tarsus the Real Founder of Christianity?* (Grand Rapids, MI: Eerdmans, 1997).
[123]John Chrysostom, *Homilies on Romans* 32.3 (PG 60:679).

and drink this cup, ye do show the Lord's death till he come." (1 Cor 11.23–26)

At the same time, Paul emphasizes his complete oneness of mind with the other apostles. The Gospel that he preaches is the Gospel of Christ, identical to the one preached by the other apostles: "Therefore whether it was I or they, so we preach, and so ye believed" (1 Cor 15.11).

How authoritative can Paul's epistles be for a reconstruction of the image of the "historical Jesus," if Paul was not a witness to his life and miracles? The answer to this question depends in many ways upon how we understand the term "historical Jesus." For

The Conversion of Saul, engraving, Gustave Doré, 1864–1866.

those scholars who have set themselves the task of freeing the "historical Jesus" from later church accretions, it is Paul who has become the main object of criticism. From their perspective, it is he who transformed the man Jesus into the Son of God, creating God incarnate out of a simple Galilean carpenter.[124]

However, if we look at this viewpoint more closely, it is superficial and groundless, since anyone who approaches the text of the New Testament in an unbiased way cannot but discover a profound inner unity between what Paul says about Jesus and what the four Gospel writers say about him as well. In spite of the differences in emphases and audience, the image of Jesus in the writings of the evangelists and Paul is not torn asunder. It is the totality of the New Testament writings that give the most complete picture of Jesus as a person, and of his life and teaching.

Had Paul's teaching been at radical variance with the teaching of the other apostles, they would have driven him out from among themselves, as happened with many heretics who tried to feed off the image of Jesus. Nothing of the sort happened with Paul. In spite of an initial distrust, the apostles quickly got used to the idea that there had appeared among them one who had been called to apostolic ministry later than them, but who

---

[124]See, for example, Ehrman, *How Jesus Became God*, 251–269.

The Conversion of Saul, Paolo Veronese, 1580s.

was destined to labor more greatly than all of them in preaching the Gospel (1 Cor 15.10).

The value of Paul's epistles for a reconstruction of the image of Jesus is determined by the fact that, although they are not in full measure a primary source of information on his life, nonetheless they present very rich material for an understanding of how this information was refracted in the minds of the first generation of Christians. The Gospels themselves contain not only information on the life and words of Jesus, but also their interpretation: this is particularly true of the Gospel of John. Paul's epistles give a quite full picture of how Jesus' mission was viewed only twenty or thirty years after his death and resurrection.

7. The Canon of the New Testament and the Apocryphal Gospels

Assembling the New Testament canon was a process that lasted for more than three centuries. The result of this process was that out of the great variety of literature devoted to Jesus and his teaching, by the end of the fourth century the Church had selected those books that were recognized as canonical and made up a single book called the New Testament. At the same time, the four Gospels had in fact already been canonized by the Church much earlier—as far back as in the second century. This is testified to by St Irenaeus of Lyons, who writes:

> For, since there are four zones of the world in which we live, and four principal winds, while the Church is scattered throughout all the world, and the "pillar and ground" [1 Tim 3.15] of the Church is the Gospel and the spirit of life; it is fitting that she should have four pillars, breathing out immortality on every side, and vivifying men afresh. From which fact, it is evident that the Word, the Artificer of all, He that sitteth upon the cherubim, and contains all things, He who was manifested to men, has given us the Gospel under four aspects, but bound together by one Spirit.[125]

The need to select the Gospels and give them canonical status was determined mainly by the appearance of heresies that undermined their authority. The Gnostic Marcion, in particular, recognized only the Gospel of Luke, whereas Montanus constructed his own teaching on the Gospel of John, thereby compromising this Gospel in the eyes of some members of the Church. It is in the context of the polemic with Montanus that the notion of the New Testament as a collection of books approved by the Church became part of Church custom.[126]

---

[125]Irenaeus, *Against Heresies*, 3.11.8 (*ANF* 1:428). On the formation of the canon of the New Testament in the first and second centuries, see Bruce M. Metzger, *The Canon of the New Testament: Its Origin, Development, and Significance* (Oxford: Clarendon, 1987).

[126]Eusebius of Caesarea, *Ecclesiastical History* 5.16.2–14.

At the turn of the third century, Christian authors in both the East and the West were agreed that the four Gospels should be recognized as having unconditional authority. In the concept of the New Testament Origen united a corpus of writings consisting of two parts: the Gospels and the writings of the apostles. He emphasizes: "[W]e approve of nothing but what the Church approves of, namely only four canonical Gospels."[127]

Alongside the canonical texts, in the early Church there were many compositions that have become known as "apocryphal" in scholarly literature. They include a number of gospels, for example the *Gospel of Thomas*, the *Gospel of Philip*, the *Gospel of Peter* and the *Gospel of Nicodemus*.

Some of the apocryphal gospels were condemned by the Church, and their texts were removed from use and destroyed. Among those that were singled out for particular condemnation were the apocryphal gospels of Gnostic origin. By "Gnosticism" we mean the sum of religious currents that developed parallel to Christianity, but which were profoundly unlike it on the doctrinal level. The Gnostic systems of Valentinus, Basilides, and Marcion differed significantly from each other, but they all had in common the combination of separate elements of Christianity with elements from Eastern religions, occultism, magic, and astrology. Characteristic for the majority of the Gnostic systems was the notion of two equally powerful forces that controlled the history of the universe—the power of good and the power of evil. For example, Valentinus juxtaposed the good God, who was made manifest in Christ and who was lord of the spiritual world, against the evil God of the Old Testament, whose power extended to the material world. In the Gnostic systems there was no notion of the human person as a being endowed with free will: the human person was instead viewed as a toy in the hands of good and evil powers.

The person of Christ did not occupy a central place in any of the Gnostic systems. Only a few elements of his spiritual and moral teaching were woven into the phantasmagorical constructions of the Gnostics. Therefore, the Gnostics were dissatisfied with the Gospels used by the Church,

---

[127]Origen, *Homilies on Luke* 1.2. Translation from Origen, *Homilies on Luke; Fragments on Luke*, trans. Joseph T. Lienhard, The Fathers of the Church 94 (Washington, DC: Catholic University of America Press, 1996), 6.

The Arrest of Christ (Kiss of Judas), fresco, Giotto, ca. 1304–1306.

and created their own, alternative versions. One such gospel was the *Gospel of Judas*, which is mentioned by Irenaeus of Lyons[127] and has survived in a Coptic translation. For a long time this Gnostic gospel was thought to have been lost, but in 2006 its text was published. In it Judas is presented as Jesus' closest disciple, to whom Jesus reveals the "mysteries of the kingdom"; he betrays Jesus, it would appear, at Jesus' direct command. Contemporary scholars believe that the *Gospel of Judas* was written by a Gnostic sect hostile to Christianity."[128]

Some of the apocryphal gospels were written with the aim of filling in the gaps in Jesus' biography in the four Gospels. Thus, for example, the *Infancy Gospel*, allegedly written by the apostle Thomas, contains episodes that have a consciously invented character and that relate to Jesus' childhood, of which nothing is said in the canonical Gospels. The Church rejected this pseudo-gospel.

---

[128]Irenaeus of Lyons, *Against Heresies* 1.31.1 (*ANF* 1:358).

[129]For a discussion of the *Gospel of Judas* in relation to second-century Gnosticism, see N. T. Wright, *Judas and the Gospel of Jesus: Have We Missed the Truth about Christianity?* (Grand Rapids, MI: Baker Books, 2006).

The Capture of Christ, fresco, Fra Angelico, ca. 1440.

Apart from the heretical apocryphal gospels, other apocryphal works exist that were not rejected by the Church, even though they did not become a part of the New Testament canon. Some of them have been preserved in the Church's tradition in an indirect way: their ideas entered into the liturgical texts, as well as into hagiographical literature. Among these apocryphal gospels are the *Protevangelium of James*, which narrates the birth, infancy, and youth of the Virgin Mary, and the *Gospel of Nicodemus*, which narrates Christ's descent into hell. The former of these works formed the basis of two church feast days: the Nativity of the Mother of God and her Entrance in the Temple, while the latter work forms the basis of worship for Great and Holy Saturday.

Although some of the apocryphal gospels had an influence on the formation of Christian theology and worship, none of them, including those that were accepted by Church tradition, can be seen as a source for the reconstruction of the image of Jesus. All of these writings appeared no earlier than the second century (some of them later), and they are all secondary in relation to the canonical Gospels.

The appeal to the apocryphal gospels as a source of information on Jesus is one of the most widespread methodological errors of the liberal wing of New Testament studies. This error has been pointed out by the major contemporary specialist in the field of New Testament studies, John P. Meier, who has compared the selection of the trusted material on Jesus to the parable of the dragnet (Mt 13.47–48) by means of separating the good fish from the bad. If we take the body of material on Jesus to be all that was once written about him, then we may include in this body the apocryphal gospels, the Gnostic works, and even the rabbinical literature. However, it is essential to have a process separating the reliable sources from the unreliable in order to conduct serious scholarly inquiry. A lack of discernment in relation to the sources is, so this scholar believes, the direct consequence of distrust towards the canonical Gospels as the sole indisputable testimony regarding the "historical Jesus":

> It is only natural for scholars—to say nothing of popularizers—to want more, to want other access roads to the historical Jesus. This understandable but not always critical desire is, I think, what has recently led to the high evaluation, in some quarters, of the apocryphal Gospels and the Nag Hammadi codices as sources for the quest. It is a case of the wish being father to the thought, but the wish is a pipe dream. For better or for worse, in our quest for the historical Jesus, we are largely confined to the canonical Gospels. . . . For the historian it is a galling limitation. But to call upon the *Gospel of Peter* or the *Gospel of Thomas* to supplement our Four Gospels is to broaden out our pool of sources from the difficult to the incredible.[130]

---

[130]John P. Meier, *A Marginal Jew: Rethinking the Historical Jesus*, vol. 1, *The Roots of the Problem and the Person* (New York, NY: Doubleday, 1991), 140–141.

8. The Texts of the Gospels in the Manuscript Tradition

Before examining the text of the Gospels, it is necessary to pause briefly on the form in which the New Testament text originally existed, what changes it was subjected to over time and for what reasons. It is important to have a grasp of this general knowledge in order to understand the peculiarities of these sources, which have become familiar to all who study the life and teaching of Jesus.

The Prophet Isaiah, icon, 15th c.

All of the ancient manuscripts that have come down to us are either in the form of scrolls or codices. In the New Testament era the Jews only had scrolls—long sheets of papyrus (between seven and ten meters long), which were rolled up and wound around one or two handles: the text would be read as the scroll was unfolded. When Jesus entered the synagogue in Nazareth, "there was delivered unto him the book of the prophet Isaiah. And when he had opened the book," he began to read from it. Then, "he closed the book, and he gave it again to the minister," and Jesus sat down and began to preach (Lk 4.17, 20). As we read this, we imagine to ourselves a book sewn from separate sheets which can be opened and closed on a particular page. And yet, the book that Jesus held was a scroll that he first unrolled to the right place, and then rolled back up.

It was only later, in the Christian era, that codices came into general use—books containing separate pages sewn into them. At the same time, in the Jewish tradition the use of scrolls has been preserved up until our day. Codices were borrowed by the Christian Church from antiquity (books in the form of codices existed in Greece and Rome). Of the five and a half

A scroll of the
Old Testament

thousand manuscripts of the New Testament that have come down to us, only about one hundred are scrolls, while the others are codices. In the third and fourth centuries, scrolls were for all intents and purposes completely replaced by codices.

The gradual replacement of scrolls by codices may be explained by reasons of a practical nature. Codices are easier to use, are better preserved, and are less inclined to decay. However, there is also a theological meaning in this. Scrolls were one of the attributes of the Old Testament religion that were considered in the Jewish tradition to be sacred and inviolate, yet rejected by Christians. Then again, this did not happen immediately. The first Gospels, we may suppose, were written on scrolls. Let us note that the Gospel writers were sometimes depicted on ancient icons as holding scrolls and not codices; in Byzantine iconography, however, they are always portrayed as holding codices, while the prophets are depicted with scrolls in their hands. When dealing with Jesus Christ, on all of the icons known to us where he is portrayed as holding the Gospels, in his hands there is a codex and not a scroll. In this way the scroll symbolizes the Old Testament, while the codex the New Testament.

When books were made in antiquity, two types of material were used—papyrus and parchment. As a rule, scrolls were made from papyrus, while codices were made from parchment. Papyrus was produced from the plant *Cyperus papyrus* (hence the name for the material); parchment, on the other hand, which is firmer, was made from the treated hides of animals.

Among the codices of the New Testament that have come down to us, some of them are so-called palimpsests—parchment manuscripts in which the original text had been scratched out or erased, and another text

An aprakos
Gospel
(containing
daily readings
beginning from
Pascha), 8th c.

written over it. Among these we can count, for example, the famous fifth-century Codex Ephraemi Rescriptus: in it, works by St Ephrem the Syrian were written over the original Greek text. With the aid of infrared rays scientists have been able to restore the original text in some cases.

All of the manuscripts of the New Testament that have come down to us were written in the Greek language, whose writing style is divided into uncials and minuscules. Uncial script contains only capital letters (it received its name from the *uncia*—a small coin, the size of which roughly corresponds to a letter), and minuscule script consists only of small letters. All ancient manuscripts of the New Testament are in uncial script. From the tenth century minuscule manuscripts began to predominate.

When writing both types, whether uncial or minuscule, the many auxiliary devices of organizing a text that we use today were not used. Thus there was no distinction between capital and small letters; all letters were either capitals (in the uncial script) or lower case (in the minuscule script). There was no division of the text into paragraphs. Punctuation was almost completely absent: no full stops were placed between sentences, and no commas were put between parts of a sentence; there were no question or exclamation marks, brackets, and other means that we use for organizing a text.

Moreover, the text was written without spaces between the words. An ancient manuscript is one long thread of words, in either uppercase or lowercase. There were no rules governing syllabification. Many sacred names and some of the more frequently used words were written in a shortened form. All of this made the text difficult to understand and became the reason for the many variants in interpreting selected places in Scripture, as well as the appearance of variant readings when copying the text.

Scholars have linked the origin and dissemination of minuscule manuscripts to the gradual development of the culture of reading to oneself in the Byzantine tradition. It is noteworthy that in both Christian and classical antiquity it was not the done thing to read to oneself: books were only read aloud. Even when alone, one would read using one's lips and not only one's eyes. We recall the story from the Acts of the Apostles: "A man of Ethiopia, a eunuch . . . was returning, and sitting in his chariot read Isaiah the prophet. Then the Spirit said unto Philip, 'Go near, and join thyself to this chariot.' And Philip ran thither to him, and heard him read the prophet Isaiah, and said, 'Understandest thou what thou readest?'" (Acts 8.27–30). If the eunuch, as he sat in his chariot, had been reading to himself silently, Philip would not have been able to hear what he was reading.

We may also recall the story from Augustine's *Confessions* (fourth to fifth century) of how, as he approached Ambrose of Milan, found the latter reading to himself: this fact greatly surprised Augustine, as it was contrary to contemporary practice.[131]

In general, the book culture of antiquity was radically different from what we are used to. In antiquity, there was a reverential, awed attitude towards the written word. Today, as we pick up a newspaper, we look through it, scanning thousands and tens of thousands of words, often not even taking in their meaning. However, at the time when Holy Scripture was being made, the written word was very highly valued—and not only because writing material was expensive and the labor of scribes was voluminous: it was in general unacceptable to write solely in order to express oneself. If one were to sit down at the table and take the stylus in one's hand, then it was assumed that one had something of importance to write, something significant. This is why the attitude towards books was different;

---

[131] Augustine, *Confessions* 6.3 (PL 32:720–721).

Eusebian canon tables (a system of dividing the Four gospels), showing the end of Canon I. From a Latin manuscript of the Gospels, 5th c.

and for this reason books were not read to oneself, but only aloud—unhurriedly, thoughtfully, reverently.

Scripture was an integral part of early Christian worship. Special copies of the Gospels were made for liturgical use—the so-called *aprakoses*, or lectionaries: they contained the text not in its usual order, but in the order in which it would be read in worship.

The liturgical use of the manuscripts of the Old and New Testaments became the reason for the appearance of various auxiliary signs that made reading aloud easier. These signs—*neumata*—were placed in the text above the line and indicated with what intonation a certain word or phrase was to be read. Later, with the help of neumes, the melodies of liturgical hymns would be written down: this is how neumatic notation developed in Byzantium and in Rus' (in Rus' it received the name of "hook notation").

Many New Testament manuscripts contain miniatures—illustrations that make the text easier to understand. We can use the miniatures to judge how a particular sacred text was understood at the time when a particular manuscript was made.

At a fairly early stage the complete Gospel text began to be divided into thematic excerpts. The first time this division was made was by the second-century Syrian writer Tatian. He compiled a single Gospel from the four Gospels—the *Diatessaron* (literally, "according to four [evangelists]"). Tatian's *Diatessaron* was in widespread use in the Syrian Church: in the fourth century St Ephrem the Syrian wrote a commentary on it. However, in the Byzantine tradition the *Diatessaron* was not widely used. Moreover, some Byzantine church figures used all means possible to combat the spread of the *Diatessaron*: St Epiphanius of Cyprus, particularly, systematically sought out manuscripts of this work and burned them.

More enduring was the work of the third-century Alexandrian deacon Ammonius, who, although he did not merge all four Gospels into one, divided the Gospel text into so-called pericopes—excerpts of various length (the shortest pericopes would often only contain one phrase). The modern-day division of the Gospel text into chapters goes back to the Archbishop of Canterbury Stephen Langton (d. 1228). The division of chapters into verses was first done by the Parisian book publisher Robert Estienne (Stephanus) in 1551.

Only in nineteenth century editions of the Bible did references appear to the so-called parallel passages: they are printed in almost all modern editions of the New and Old Testaments, in the margins. The parallel passages help us to compare the exposition of one and the same event in different Gospels, and to find the primary sources of the Old Testament

Archbishop of Canterbury
Stephen Langton

quotations in the New Testament. From the third to the sixth centuries there was no need to do so, as people knew the Bible far better than they do now. When we read the Church Fathers, we cannot but be struck by the virtuosity with which they handled the biblical texts as they drew parallels from the most disparate parts of the Bible, using manuscripts that contained no references to parallel passages. But for the modern reader the parallel passages have become a great help.

In speaking of the fate of the Gospels, we cannot pass over in silence the issue of the corruption that the supposed original text has been subjected to throughout the centuries in the manuscript tradition. Numerous errors appeared in the manuscripts as a result of copyists' mistakes. Some of them would be corrected later by other copyists, while some would remain uncorrected and begin to be perceived as the norm. The differences concern not only separate words and sentences, but also whole fragments that are present in some manuscripts while absent in others. Thus, for example, the second half of the sixteenth chapter of the Gospel of Mark (Mk 16.9–20) is missing in two of the most authoritative ancient codices, Sinaiticus and Vaticanus. In the majority of manuscripts, the Gospel of John does not contain the story of the woman caught in adultery (Jn 8.1–11).

Errors in the manuscripts could be either accidental or intentional. Among the former we can count so-called mistakes of the eye, mistakes of the memory, and judgmental errors.[132]

Visual errors appeared as a result of imperfect writing and the inconvenience of reading a long text, in which many words were shortened and some could be mistakenly placed elsewhere or erased, and certain individual words might look similar to others; sometimes the text was so small that the copyist was unable to make it out.

Mistakes caused by memory arose in particular because the copyist, having glanced at a phrase, would not remember it exactly, and having copied it down, did not check it against the original.

Errors of judgment occurred when the poorer of two variants would be chosen when there was a distorted reading. So, if the copyist were looking at two codices, one of which contained the correct reading, and the other the incorrect reading, he might choose the latter, since for whatever reason he might think it was correct.

Deliberate corruption of the text includes those distortions made by heretics in order to justify their false teachings. Thus, for example, Marcion, when copying the Gospel of Luke, consciously changed or excluded from the text those passages that did not accord with his Gnostic system. However, we should note that the texts corrupted by heretics would quickly be identified by the Church and taken out of use.

More complex is the issue of an intentional alteration of the text tied to a linguistic or rhetorical correction: the copyist might have thought that the text was badly written, or concluded that an error had entered the text, and he would take the risk of changing a phrase, word, or letter.[133]

Finally, we should point to the type of intentional corruption of the text that modern scholarship calls "harmonic correction"—when the text of one Gospel was altered so that it would correspond to the text of another Gospel. As an example, we can use the aforementioned difference between the version of the Lord's Prayer in the Gospels of Matthew and Luke. In the

---

[132]For more detail on this, see Bruce Metzger, *The Text of the New Testament: Its Transmission, Corruption, and Restoration* (Oxford: Oxford University Press, 2005), 251–58.

[133]See Metzger, *The Text of the New Testament*, 259–61.

King James and New King James Version, the text is almost identical, whereas in the critical edition, based on the most ancient manuscripts, the Lord's Prayer in Luke is shorter than in Matthew. If we proceed from the idea that the original text chosen for the KJV and NKJV reflects the development that the Gospel text underwent for many centuries, and the critical edition restores the text as close as possible to the original, then it becomes evident that in the original version in the Gospel of Luke the Lord's Prayer was given in a shortened version; however, subsequent copyists added to it from the Gospel of Matthew, with the result that the differences have been eradicated and the text is identical.

Title page of the first volume of the Complutensian Polyglot Bible

Before the sixteenth century the New Testament existed only in manuscript form. The first printed edition—the so-called *Complutensian Polyglot Bible*—appeared in 1514: in it the Greek and Latin texts of the New Testament were printed in parallel columns. Then five editions were printed by Erasmus of Rotterdam in Basel (1516–1535). In 1624 the Greek text was printed by the Elzevir brothers. In one of the later editions, the brothers inform the reader that the text they have published is the best and most authoritative: they called it *textus ab omnibus receptus*, literally, "the text that everyone accepts," that is, the text that received universal recognition. This text indeed became accepted as the most authoritative and came to be called the *Textus Receptus* (the "received text," i.e., the standard text).

However, in the nineteenth century greater attention was beginning to be paid to the ancient manuscripts of the New Testament that contained numerous variant readings differing from the *Textus Receptus*. In the mid-nineteenth century the German biblical scholar Constantin von Tischendorf published several such manuscripts, among the most famous of which was the fifth-century Codex Sinaiticus, which he had found in the library of St Catherine's Monastery on Sinai.

The Codex
Sinaiticus,
opened to show
two pages

Gradually the number of manuscripts known to scholarship grew, and at the end of the nineteenth century critical editions began to appear in which the Greek text of the New Testament, restored on the basis of the manuscript tradition, was printed with interlinear notes containing variant readings. These editions became known as the Nestle-Aland New Testament.[134]

From the mid-twentieth century, the United Bible Societies joined the work of editing the critical text of the New Testament. Among them were Catholic, Protestant, and Orthodox scholars. As a result of these joint endeavors, the Greek text of the New Testament was prepared, "which was the logical outcome of using an ever greater circle of manuscript traditions, the development of methods of research in textual criticism, and the perfecting of the tools of philological and theological criticism."[135]

The text contained in the third edition of the Greek New Testament prepared by the United Bible Societies is identical to the text contained in the twenty-sixth edition of Nestle-Aland (the differences between the

[134]Work on compiling the critical text of the New Testament was begun by the major German specialist on biblical textual criticism Eberhard Nestle (1851–1913). After his death the work was continued by his son Erwin Nestle (1883–1972), who was helped from the mid-twentieth century onwards by the renowned expert in New Testament textual criticism Kurt Aland (1915–1994). The twenty-sixth edition of the critical text of the New Testament, which came out in 1979, is known as the Nestle-Aland text. The most recent edition (the twenty-eighth), was published in 2012. In it, "The Catholic Letters were revised according to a fundamentally new concept which in the long run will be adopted for the entire edition." *Novum Testamentum Graece*, 28th rev. ed. (Stuttgart: Deutsche Bibelgesellschaft, 2012), 48.

[135]A. A. Alekseyev, *Tekstologiya Novogo Zaveta i izdanie Nestle-Alanda* [Textual Criticism of the New Testament and the Nestle-Aland edition] (St Petersburg: Dmitriy Bulanin, 2012), 81.

St Catherine's
Monastery on
Sinai

two editions concern only the critical apparatus, not the text itself). This testifies to a definite consensus achieved by scholars around the world regarding the basic variant readings in the New Testament text.

Nevertheless, the work of perfecting a critical text of the New Testament that is as close to the supposed original as possible should not be considered finished. It is still in progress, approaches to the text are changing, and the opinions of researchers that had been taken as axioms (including those that give preference to particular variants of the text) are being re-examined.

Work on the critical edition of the New Testament has highlighted its uniqueness as a literary record, to which there is no equal in the history of humanity in the number of manuscripts. At the same time, taking into account the unprecedented number of manuscripts, it is not surprising that there are a great number of variations between them too. Of more than the five thousand manuscripts known to scholarship, no two are completely identical.[136] The general number of variant readings known to scholarship and reflected in the Nestle-Aland edition surpasses ten thousand; between the *Textus Receptus* and the Nestle-Aland edition, there are several hundred substantial variant readings that may influence the understanding of the meaning of the text.[137]

---

[136]Bruce Metzger, *A Textual Commentary on the Greek New Testament: A Companion Volume to the United Bible Societies' Greek New Testament*, 3rd ed. (Stuttgart: Deutsche Bibelgesellschaft, 1971), xxiv.

[137]Alekseyev, *Tekstologiya Novogo Zaveta*, 88, 98.

9. The Interpretation
of the Sources

In order to understand the meaning of the Gospel narratives, their separate episodes, and the sayings of Jesus, it is very important to be able to interpret the Gospel text correctly. There is no other book in the world that has had such a historic wealth of interpretation, and which has been explained in so many different ways in different eras, by different authors, and in different contexts.

The history of the interpretation of the Gospel story may be divided into several periods.[138]

The first period is the first century, when the Gospel story was written down by various authors. As we have already said, the Gospel text contains not only a narrative, but also an interpretation of the events described. The letters of the apostle Paul have made a decisive contribution to the Church's interpretation of the Gospel story by laying the foundations for its subsequent theological exegesis.

The second period is the era of the Apostolic Fathers (Clement of Rome, Ignatius of Antioch, Papias of Hierapolis, Irenaeus of Lyons) and other early Christian authors, both from the East and from the West (Clement of Alexandria, Tertullian, Origen), who were engaged in the research and exegesis of the Gospel narratives. This epoch stretches over both the second and third centuries. In this period the Gospels came to be seen as the authoritative source of information on Jesus Christ, they began to be taken as Scripture for all Christians, they were actively commented on, and quotations from them were used by writers in their own texts.

One of the Apostolic Fathers, Ignatius of Antioch, when speaking of the interpretation of the Gospels, says: "I flee to the gospel as to the flesh of Jesus and the apostles as to the presbytery of the church. And we should

---

[138]For more on the Orthodox understanding of Scripture, see Met. Hilarion Alfeyev, *Orthodox Christianity, vol. 2, Doctrine and Teachiing of the Orthodox Church*, trans. Andrew Smith (Yonkers, NY: St Vladimir's Seminary Press, 2012), 23–41.

The Hieromartyr Ignatius of Antioch, miniature in the Menologion of Basil II, 10th c.

also love the prophets, since their proclamation was of the gospel; they hoped for it and awaited it, and by believing in it they were saved."[139]

The teaching of the Gospel as the "flesh of Jesus," his incarnation in the word, was developed by Origen. Throughout all of Scripture he sees the *kenōsis* (emptying) of God the Word, embodied in the imperfect forms of human words: "For we are told of what was said there and considered to be the Word of God, the Word made flesh, and who, as regards being God with God [Jn 1.2], emptied Himself [Phil 2.7]. Wherefore we see the Word of God on earth, for that He became man, in human guise; for even in the Scriptures the Word became flesh that He might tabernacle among us [Jn 1.14]."[140]

Origen was one of the founders of the so-called allegorical, or spiritual, method of interpreting Scripture,[141] based on the notion that Scripture contains not only literal meaning, "but also another, which escapes the notices of most. For those (words) which are written are the forms of certain mysteries, and the images of divine things." The spiritual meaning of Scripture "is not known to all, but to those only on whom the grace of the

---

[139]Ignatius of Antioch, *Epistle to the Philadelphians* 5.1–2. Translation from *Ignatius of Antioch, The Letters*, trans. Alistair Stewart, Popular Patristics Series 49 (Yonkers, NY: St Vladimir's Seminary Press, 2013), 81.

[140]Origen, *Philokalia [of Origen]*, 15.19.26–31 (SC 302:438). Translation from Origen, *The Philocalia of Origen*, trans. George Lewis (Edinburgh: T&T Clark, 1911), 76.

[141]See Henri Crouzel, *Origen*, trans. A. S. Worrall (Edinburgh: T&T Clark, 1989), 64–84.

The Descent of the
Holy Spirit, icon, 16th c.

Holy Spirit is bestowed in the word of wisdom and knowledge."[142]

The allegorical method of interpreting Scripture became widespread in the Christian tradition thanks to the Old Testament commentaries of Philo of Alexandria (c. 25 BC to c. AD 50). Written in Greek, these commentaries were forgotten in late Judaism, but exerted a decisive influence on the formation of the allegorical method in Christian authors, and have come down to us precisely thanks to the Christian copyists of his works. Origen was undoubtedly influenced by Philo of Alexandria when he compiled his commentaries.

Like Philo, Origen took as his starting point the idea of the presence of two levels in Scripture—literal and spiritual—and of the need to see in each word of Scripture an allegorical, spiritual meaning. With the help of this method, which the modern reader may think unfruitful and pointless,[143] but which was appropriate for the cultural tradition of educated Hellenes of his time, Origen made commentaries on many books of Scripture.

The third period in the history of interpreting the Gospel text encompasses the whole epoch of the Ecumenical Councils from the fourth to eighth centuries. This gives us an enormous wealth of material for the interpretation of the Gospel story. Theological disputes, including those relating to the person of Jesus Christ as God and man, brought forth the need to turn to the Gospels constantly, as well as to the other books of the New Testament, in order to refute mistaken and heretical opinions. Apart from the polemical literature containing a detailed analysis of some of the New Testament episodes and sayings of Jesus, it was in this period that whole commentaries were composed on entire Gospels and even on the entire corpus of the four Gospels.

---

[142]Origen, *On First Principles*, Preface, 8 (*ANF* 4:241)

[143]John Meyendorff, *Vvedenie v svyatootecheskoye bogoslovie: konspekty lektsiy* [Introduction to patristic theology: lecture notes], trans. Larissa Volokhonskaya (Klin: Khristianskaya zhizn', 2001), 109–110.

The allegorical tradition of interpreting the Gospels in this period was reflected in the works of the representatives of the Alexandrian school, in particular Cyril of Alexandria. This type of commentary was actively used by Gregory of Nyssa and Maximus the Confessor. The latter spoke of the two forms in which Scripture reveals itself to people: the first was in a "common and very public appearance and not for the few," while the second was "more hidden and attainable to the few, to those who much like Peter, James, and John have become apostles, before whom the Lord was transfigured into a glory prevailing over sensory perception."[144] In the manner of Origen, Maximus the Confessor divides Scripture into body and spirit:

The Prophet Moses receiving the Tables of the Law, icon, 12th c.

[T]he Old Testament [is taken] as body and the New Testament as spirit and mind. Moreover . . . the historical letter of the entire holy Scripture, Old Testament and New, is a body while the meaning of the letter and the purpose to which it is directed is the soul. . . . For as man who is ourselves is mortal in what is visible and immortal in the invisible, so also does holy Scripture, which contains a visible letter which is passing and a hidden spirit underneath the letter which never ceases to exist, organize the true meaning of contemplation.[145]

Maximus the Confessor spoke of the exegesis of Scripture as the ascent from the letter to the spirit.[146] The anagogical method of interpreting Scripture (from the Greek *anagōgē*, meaning "ascent") as an allegorical method proceeds from the idea that the mystery of the biblical text is

[144]Maximus the Confessor, *Chapters on Theology and the Incarnate Economy of the Son of God* 1.97 (PG 90:1121). Translation from St Maximus the Confessor, *Two Hundred Chapters on Theology and the Incarnate Economy of the Son of God*, trans. Luis Joshua Salés, Popular Patristics Series 53 (Yonkers, NY: St Vladimir's Seminary Press, 2015), 101.

[145]Idem, *Mystagogy* 6 (PG 91:684). Translation from Maximus the Confessor, *Maximus Confessor: Selected Writings*, trans. George C. Berthold, Classics of Western Spirituality (New York, NY: Paulist Press, 1985), 195.

[146]Idem, *Chapters on Theology* 2.18 (PG 90:1133; PPS 53:119).

St Jerome as Scholar,
El Greco, ca. 1610.

inexhaustible: only the external canvas of Scripture is limited by the narrative framework, while its "contemplation" (*theōria*) or mystical inner meaning can know no bounds. Everything in Scripture is linked to the inner spiritual life of the human person, and the letter of Scripture elevates us to this spiritual meaning:

When the word of God becomes altogether radiant and brught in us, his face, too, will radiate just like the sun; then even his garments will appear white; that is, the words of the holy Scripture of the Gospels, clear and distinct, having nothing hidden. But also Moses and Elijah are present with him; that is, the more spiritual principles of the Law and the Prophets.[147]

Alongside the allegorical interpretations in the period of the Ecumenical Councils, the tradition of the literal interpretation of the Gospel text also developed, particularly in the works of the representatives of the Antiochian school such as Ephrem the Syrian, John Chrysostom, and Theodore of Mopsuestia. These authors were primarily interested in the literal meaning of the story from Jesus' life and his sayings, which were viewed through the prism of Old Testament prophecies, as well as in the general context of human history.

Chrysostom in his commentaries on the Gospels accentuates the moral lessons that must be taken from them by constantly projecting situations from the life of Jesus and his disciples onto the life of his contemporaries. This means of interpreting the Gospels has become the most widespread one in church preaching right up until the present time.

The tradition of the literal and allegorical interpretation of the Gospels developed in this period in the West too. An important contribution to the understanding of the Gospel text was made by two of the greatest Latin theologians, who enjoy the status of doctors in the Catholic tradition: Augustine of Hippo and Jerome of Stridon. The former was the author of

[147]Idem, *Chapters on Theology* 2.14 (PG 90:1132; PPS 53:115).

The Savior,
icon, 15th c.

many commentaries on the Gospel texts, based on a combination of literal and allegorical approaches. The latter was the author of a large number of biblical commentaries and studies in textual criticism. It is Jerome, in particular, who is the author of the complete Latin translation of the Old Testament and a new redaction of the Latin translation of the New Testament. Moreover, he is the author of a four-volume commentary on the Gospel of Matthew and a number of commentaries on other books of the Bible. In his commentaries, Jerome in the main adheres to the literal method with elements of literary criticism (he comments on separate words and expressions and their translation).

Christ Mocked (The Crowning with Thorns), Hieronymus Bosch, ca. 1510.

In the period of the Ecumenical Councils, an approach to the texts of the Old Testament was definitively formed, by which these texts were viewed as prototypes of New Testament realities and seen through the prism of the New Testament. This type of commentary became known in scholarship as "typological." Its beginning goes back to Jesus, who said of the Old Testament: "Search the Scriptures; for in them ye think ye have eternal life; it is they that testify of me" (Jn 5.39). Following this exhortation, many of the events from the life of Jesus in the Gospels (especially in the Gospel of Matthew) have been interpreted as the fulfillment of the Old Testament prophecies.

In the Christian tradition, the Old Testament, the Gospels, and the corpus of the apostles' writings are viewed as three parts of an indivisible whole. At the same time, the Gospels are given unconditional preference as the source that transmits to Christians the living voice of Jesus, while the apostolic letters are seen as an authoritative interpretation of the Gospels coming from the disciples closest to Christ.

It was in the period of the Ecumenical Councils that the tradition developed of the daily reading of the Gospels in worship. This tradition is preserved in most Christian churches, including the Orthodox Church, to this day. The four Gospels are read in their entirety at Orthodox worship throughout the year, while there is a special Gospel reading set for every day of the church calendar (outside Great Lent), which the faithful listen to while standing. On Great Friday, when the Church recalls Jesus' sufferings and the death on the cross, a special service is celebrated with twelve Gospel readings containing the passages on Christ's Passion.

The yearly cycle of Gospel readings begins on Pascha night when the Prologue of the Gospel of John is read. After the Gospel of John, which is read during the Paschal period, the Gospels of Matthew, Mark, and Luke are read. The Acts of the Apostles, the Catholic Epistles, and the Epistles of the apostle Paul are also read in church daily and also in their entirety

The Agony in the Garden, El Greco, 1600–1605.

throughout the whole year: the reading of Acts begins on Pascha night and continues throughout the Paschal period, after which the Catholic Epistles and the Epistles of the apostle Paul follow.

In the period of the Ecumenical Councils, the idea emerged that in Scripture on the whole, and in the Gospels in particular, all the basic dogmatic truths are set forth: one needed only to be capable of discerning them. Gregory the Theologian suggests a method of reading Scripture that we may called retrospective: it consists of looking at the scriptural texts from the starting point of subsequent Church tradition and identifying in them the dogmas that are more fully formulated in the later period. This approach to Scripture is fundamental to the patristic period. In particular, Gregory believed that not only the New Testament, but also the Old Testament texts contain the teaching on the Holy Trinity:

> With David be enlightened, who said to the Light, "In Your Light shall we see Light" [Ps 35.10], that is, in the Spirit[148] we shall see the Son; and what can be of further reaching ray? With John thunder, sounding forth nothing that is low or earthly concerning God, but what is high

[148]Cf. Basil the Great, *On the Holy Spirit* 18.47; 26.64 (PPS 42:83).

St Gregory the Theologian,
mosaic, 11th c.

and heavenly, Who is in the beginning, and is with God, and is God the Word [Jn 1.1], and true God of the true Father. . . . And when you read, I and the Father are One [Jn 10.30], keep before your eyes the unity of substance; but when you see, "We will come to him, and make Our abode with him" [Jn 14.23], remember the distinction of Persons; and when you see the Names, Father, Son, and Holy Spirit [Mt 28.19], think of the Three Personalities. With Luke be inspired as you study the Acts of the Apostles. Why do you range yourself with Ananias and Sapphira . . . stealing the Godhead Itself, and lying, not to men but to God, as you have heard[?][149]

In this manner, according to Gregory, Scripture ought to be read in the light of the dogmatic tradition of the Church. In the fourth century both orthodox Christians and heretics had recourse to scriptural texts in order to affirm their theological standpoints. Depending on these standpoints, various criteria were applied to one and the same texts and were interpreted in different ways. For Gregory the Theologian, as for the other Church Fathers, particularly Irenaeus of Lyons, there is only one criterion for the correct approach to Scripture—faithfulness to the Church's tradition. The only interpretation of the biblical texts that is legitimate, these authors believe, is the one based on Church tradition; all other interpretation is false as it "robs" the Godhead. Out of the context of tradition, the biblical texts lose their dogmatic significance. And, by contrast, within tradition even the texts that do not express dogmatic truths directly are understood anew. Christians see in scriptural texts that which non-Christians cannot see: to those who believe rightly is revealed that which remains hidden to the heretics. The mystery of the Trinity for those who find themselves outside of the Church remains hidden by a veil that is removed only by Christ and only for those who abide within his Church.

[149]Gregory the Theologian (Gregory of Nazianzus), *Orations* 34.13–14 (*NPNF*[2] 7:337).

Lamentation over the Dead Christ, Sandro Botticelli, ca. 1495.

The typological, allegorical, and anagogical interpretations of Scripture, which were formed in the period of the Ecumenical Councils and which to a significant degree have lost their relevance for the modern researcher of the Gospel text, have been preserved in the worship of the Orthodox Church. The main goal of reading Scripture at worship is to help the faithful to become participants in the events described—to partake of the experience of biblical persons and to make it their own experience.

Thus, for example, in the liturgical texts of Holy Week, we encounter many examples of the interpretation of Scripture with reference to the inner, spiritual life of the Christian. In following Christ day after day, the believer becomes a participant in the events described in the Gospels. For example, the episode of the fig tree that bore no fruit (Mt 21.19) is explained thus: "O brethren, let us fear the punishment of the fig tree, withered because it was unfruitful; and let us bring worthy fruits of repentance unto Christ."[150] The story of Judas' betrayal inspires the author of the liturgical texts, together with their listener, to enter into a direct dialogue with Judas: "What reason led thee, Judas, to betray the Saviour? Did He expel thee from the company of the apostles? Did He deprive thee of the gift of healing? When thou wast at supper with the others, did He drive

---

[150]Lenten Triodion. Great and Holy Monday, Matins, Aposticha, Tone 8. Translation from *The Lenten Triodion*, trans. Mother Mary and Kallistos Ware (South Canaan, PA: St. Tikhon's Seminary Press, 2002), 516.

"Do not lament me, O Mother," icon, 16th c.

thee from the table? When He washed the others' feet, did He pass thee by? How many are the blessings that thou hast forgotten! Thou art condemned for thine ingratitude."[151] In a hymn on the crucifixion, the author speaks on behalf of the Virgin Mary, while in a hymn on Jesus' burial he speaks on behalf of Joseph of Arimathea.

At the Matins of Good Friday, the following words are sung at this service: "O Life, how canst thou die? How canst Thou dwell in a tomb? ... O Jesus, my sweetness and light of salvation, how art Thou hidden in a dark tomb? . . . O thrice-blessed Joseph, bury the body of Christ, the Giver of Life."[152] The believer is so deeply drawn into the liturgical drama of Holy Week that he enters into a dialogue with all of its protagonists. Jesus' sufferings are relived by Orthodox Christians and become part of their own personal experience.

In the period of the Ecumenical Councils, the monastic tradition occupied a special place in the history of the interpretation of the Gospels. It was within the monastic environment that the view of Scripture as the source of religious inspiration was formed: monks not only read and interpreted it, but also learned it by heart.[153] The monastic tradition knows of a special method of using Scripture—the so-called *meletē* ("reflection," "applied study"), which presupposed the constant repetition, aloud or in a whisper, of separate verses and excerpts from the Bible. In the West an analogous practice arose, known as *lectio divina* ("divine reading").

Monks, as a rule, were not interested in the scholarly exegesis of Scripture: they viewed Scripture as a guide to daily life and strove to understand it by means of carrying out what was written in it. In their works the ascetic fathers insist that all that is stated in Scripture ought to be applied

[151]Lenten Triodion. Great and Holy Friday. The Service of the Twelve Gospel Readings. Sessional Hymn. Translation from *The Lenten Triodion*, 577.

[152]Lenten Triodion. Great and Holy Saturday. Matins. The Praises. Translation from *The Lenten Triodion*, 623, 624, 640.

[153]In fourth-century Egyptian monasteries, learning scriptural texts by heart was an obligatory daily occupation for each monk.

Left: St Gregory Palamas, fresco, 15th c.
Right: St Symeon the New Theologian, pen and ink drawing by Mikhail Boskin, based on an ancient fresco of the Pantokrator Monastery on Mt Athos.

to one's own life: then the hidden meaning of Scripture will become clear. This approach to Scripture was especially characteristic in the *Sayings of the Desert Fathers*: "It is good to do what is written," says Abba Gerontius (fourth century).[154] This simple formula encapsulates the entire experience of interpreting and understanding Scripture in early monasticism. Noteworthy, too, is the saying of Anthony the Great (fourth century): "Always have God before your eyes wherever you go. Whatever you are doing, have the testimony from Holy Scripture to hand."[155]

We may consider the fourth period in the history of the interpretation of the Gospels to be the ten centuries that came after the Seventh Ecumenical Council in AD 787 up until the latter half of the eighteenth century. In this period in the Orthodox East, no new original commentaries on the Gospel text were produced and no new methods of interpretation were worked out. The Gospel commentaries that appeared in this period were of the composite and imitative sort. Thus, for example, the *Commentary on the Gospels* by Theophylact of Ohrid (mid-eleventh century to the beginning of the twelfth century) was to a significant degree based on the commentaries of earlier authors, primarily John Chrysostom.

---

[154]*Sayings of the Desert Fathers*, Gerontius 1 (PG 65:153AB). Translation from *Give Me a Word: The Alphabetical Sayings of the Desert Fathers*, trans. John Wortley, Popular Patristics Series 52 (Yonkers, NY: St Vladimir's Seminary Press, 2014), 88.

[155]*Sayings of the Desert Fathers*, Anthony 3 (PG 65:76C; PPS 52:32). Translation from *Give Me a Word*, 32.

Martin Luther, Lucas
Cranach the Elder, 1543.

At the same time, the Gospels continued to remain a source of inspiration for church writers, many of whom interpreted the Gospel texts through the prism of their own spiritual experience. We find extremely interesting commentaries on selected Gospel passages in the works of Symeon the New Theologian (eleventh century), Gregory Palamas (fourteenth century), and a whole range of other authors.

In the same period in the Christian West the text of Scripture, both the Old and New Testaments, attained the status of being an indisputable authority in questions of faith and morality. Simultaneously, Scripture was viewed exclusively through the prism of the Church's interpretation. Any interpretation of the biblical text that contradicted the teaching of the Catholic Church was declared to be heretical, with all of the consequences that would flow from this, including the fires of the Inquisition.

Moreover, right up until the Reformation, the text of the Bible was read in Western Europe in Latin, which few people could understand. This limited the possibility for simple people to have access to the biblical text. People learned about it most often from the sermons of bishops and priests, as well as from various written commentaries in the vernacular language. One of the main tasks of the ideologues of the Reformation, which began in 1517, was to translate the Bible into the various languages of the nations: the founder of the Reformation, Martin Luther, translated the Bible into German with his own hand.

The issue of the importance of the biblical texts arose during the polemics between the Reformation and the Counter-Reformation in the sixteenth and seventeenth centuries. The leaders of the Reformation (Luther, Calvin) put forward the principle that Scripture was itself enough to be counted as authoritative and should be used in the church as the sole authority. Regarding the later documents on the teaching of the faith, whether the decisions of the councils or the works of the Church Fathers,

they were regarded as authoritative only insofar as
they were in agreement with scriptural teaching (the
more radical reformers rejected the authority of the
Church Fathers altogether). The dogmatic formulations, and the liturgical and ritual traditions that
were not based on the authority of Scripture, could
not be (so the leaders of the Reformation believed)
recognized to be legitimate, and therefore had to
be abolished.

John Calvin

As a counterpoint to the Protestant principle of
sola scriptura (Latin for "by Scripture alone"), the
theologians of the Counter-Reformation underlined
the importance of holy tradition, without which, in their opinion, Scripture would have not authority. Luther's opponent at the Leipzig Disputa-
tion of 1519 claimed that "Scripture is not authentic without the authority
of the church."[156] The opponents of the Reformation referred back to the
words of St Augustine: "I should not believe the Gospel except as moved
by the authority of the Catholic Church."[157] They pointed in particular to
the fact that the canon of Scripture was formed by Church tradition, which
determined which books ought to be part of it and which ones not. At the
Council of Trent in 1546, the theory was formulated that Scripture cannot
be seen as the sole source of divine revelation: a no less important source
is Tradition, which is a vitally important addition to Scripture.

It was the Lutheran tradition, with its heightened interest in the Bible
as the sole source of divine revelation, which became the moving force in
the study of the New Testament and which in the middle of the eighteenth
century led to the appearance of so-called biblical criticism. It is from this
time that we can reckon the fifth period in the history of the interpretation
of the Gospels.

At the basis of biblical criticism lies the historical-philological approach
to the biblical text. This approach presupposes, first, a textual criticism

---

[156]Quoted in Alister E. McGrath, *Reformation Thought: An Introduction*, 4th ed. (Oxford:
Wiley-Blackwell, 2012), 100.

[157]Augustine, *Against the Epistle of Manichæus* 5.6 (*NPNF*[1] 4:131).

analysis (the restoration of the oldest form of the text through the comparison of manuscripts), second, a philological analysis (using other written records of the Ancient East and antiquity), and third, a historical and cultural analysis (by taking into account our knowledge of the history and realities of the ancient world, of the life, customs, and worldview of people of that time). The distinguishing feature of European biblical studies is that the same methods of analysis used with other ancient texts are applied to the biblical text.

The most characteristic peculiarity of this period in the history of research on the Gospel text is the search for the "historical Jesus," which we attempted to describe in the previous chapter. This search continues to this day. At a certain stage of the development of contemporary criticism of the New Testament text a distinct tendency was observed, linked to the desire of scholars to go as far away as possible from the Church's interpretation of the text. This tendency dominated in New Testament studies from the latter half of the nineteenth century to the mid-twentieth century, and has led to the creation, *inter alia*, of an entire school for the demythologization of the Gospels, and to the appearance of the notion that Jesus was an invented person.

However, in the latter half of the twentieth century, and especially in the beginning of the twenty-first century, the reverse tendency has become more noticeable—scholars working in the field of New Testament research have more and more frequently had recourse to the traditional Church interpretation of the Gospel texts as one of the important sources for their understanding of Scripture. We may say that in modern New Testament studies a second discovery is taking place in the approach to the Bible as a whole, and to the Gospels in particular, in which they are thought of as part of a tradition going back to the origins of Christianity: outside of this tradition they lose their meaning to a significant degree.

Contemporary scholars are becoming more aware of a simple truth: that it is in the Church that the Gospel text continues its life, not as some lifeless museum exhibit, but as the living source of faith and morality. Therefore, it is the Church's interpretation of the Gospel text that in many

St Philaret of
Moscow

ways provides the key to its correct understanding, which to the highest degree corresponds to that which the author put in this text.

Within the Church environment there is in parallel a growing interest in biblical criticism, especially in those aspects that do not contradict the Church's interpretation of the Bible, but, on the contrary, confirm that this interpretation is correct. Among the Orthodox, particularly, the understanding is growing ever wider that a reverential attitude towards the Bible in no way excludes an analysis of its text—a critical analysis not in the sense of negating or disputing the divinely revealed truth that it contains, but in the sense of a thoughtful comparative examination of its various versions.

Anton Kartashov

The comparison of ancient manuscripts, the restoration of variant readings, and the highlighting of the most authoritative text in no way contradicts an Orthodox understanding of Scripture. Critical editions of the biblical texts are no less valuable for the Orthodox Christian than for the Catholic, Protestant, or secular scholar.

It is a completely different issue altogether if we approach the biblical text critically and selectively, throwing out various hasty conclusions and speculations based exclusively on certain ideological presumptions. In the nineteenth century St Philaret of Moscow believed it necessary to approach the text of Holy Scripture critically, and the translation of the Bible that was done under his direction took into account the achievements of the biblical criticism of the time. However, St Philaret certainly did not view biblical criticism uncritically: he actively worked with sources, and he would use secondary literature only insofar as it was needed for his work on the texts.

The modern-day reader of the Gospel also needs to be familiar with the results of biblical studies so that he does not get confused by the huge variety of interpretations, including those that are deliberately mistaken, sectarian, and heretical. The renowned historian and one of the leading professors of the St Sergius Theological Institute in Paris, Anton Kartashov, spoke about this in 1944:

> The revolution brought about in this instance by biblical criticism is one of the major events in the history of the spiritual life of humanity. . . . In the inevitable forthcoming missionary campaign of the Russian Church throughout our vast homeland, we cannot be content with applying obsolete means from the arsenal of our scholarly theological backwardness. In order to defeat the enemy on all of his leading and scientific positions, we have to be in possession of the weapons of modern scholarly techniques. But for this we have first to perceive it

The St Sergius
Theological
Institute in Paris

creatively, master it, and transform it within the bosom of the Church's theology and the Church's truth.[158]

We can consider these words to be prophetic. In 1944 it was difficult to imagine the scale of this "missionary campaign," which is now being carried out by the Russian Orthodox Church.

But we should not forget that others, too, are laboring in the missionary field, including representatives of various sectarian communities. Some of them (for example, the Jehovah's Witnesses) use their own translations and commentaries of the same Gospel texts that are used by Orthodox Christians, but at the same time interpreting them in a completely different way. Sectarian literature is distributed parallel to Church literature, and very often people who are not acquainted with the history of interpreting the Bible in the Church and scholarly traditions are unable to distinguish truth from falsehood in this literature.

The works of those engaged in modern biblical studies are becoming more and more accessible to the Church reader, to whom the historical-critical approach to the Bible may seem shocking and blasphemous. Today there is a boundless sea of scholarly literature devoted to Jesus and his

[158]Anton V. Kartashev, *Vetkhozavetnaya bibleyskaya kritika* [Old Testament biblical criticism] (Paris, 1947), 96.

teaching. It is this literature that fills the shelves of religious bookshops, whether in Oxford, Tübingen, Paris, or Harvard. The Church's traditional interpretations of the Gospels are very rarely found on the shelves of such bookshops.

The contemporary Orthodox student of the New Testament can no longer ignore the results of biblical criticism, and as we study the life and teaching of Jesus, we will have constant recourse to them. However, we will approach them critically, disputing that which we believe does not correspond to the image of Jesus that emerges from an unprejudiced view of the Gospel story. Moreover, in many instances we will turn to the tradition of the Church's interpretation of the Gospels by using, when necessary, the vast body of patristic works beginning from the second century. This will allow us to obtain a well-rounded view of the many-sided image of Jesus and the multi-layered interpretation of his teaching.

Chapter 3

THE SON OF MAN

---

1. People, Country, and Language

People and Country

Jesus belonged to a people originating from the biblical patriarch Abraham. According to the Bible, Abraham originally lived in Ur of the Chaldees, located in south Babylonia[1] not far from the coast of the Persian Gulf. Receiving the command from God (Gen 12.3; Acts 7.2), he set off from there to the land of Canaan, arriving first in Haran,[2] and then in Schechem, where God had promised him this land (Gen 12.7). It is from this time that the settlement of the land of Canaan by Abraham and his descendants began, who received the name of the people of Israel, from the name of Abraham's grandson Jacob, to whom God gave the new name Israel (Gen 32.28). For the people of Israel this was the holy land belonging to God himself: they looked upon it as his inheritance and estate (1 Sam 26.19; 2 Sam 14.16; Jer 16.18; 50.11). The Bible reproduces the words of God addressed to the people of Israel: "For the land is mine; for ye are strangers and sojourners with me" (Lev 25.23).

All of Old Testament history, beginning with Abraham, is the story of the struggle of the Hebrews for the right of ownership of the Promised

---

[1]Now in Iraq.
[2]Now in Turkey near the border with Syria.

171

Abram going
to the land of
Canaan, mosaic,
13th c.

Land. By the time Abraham arrived there, it was densely populated. The twelve sons of Jacob settled in Canaan, but as a result of prolonged famine, they were forced to resettle in Egypt. The book of Genesis ends with this. The book of Exodus is dedicated to the return of the people of Israel from Egypt; the main hero of Exodus is Moses, who led the people of Israel out their bondage in Egypt.

The second time Abraham's descendants entered the Promised Land after their exodus from Egypt, around the fifteenth century BC,[3] was accompanied by numerous wars. The people of Israel originally had no government. For a time they were ruled by judges, that is, clan leaders: the book of Judges is dedicated to this period. Then, around 1030 BC, the Prophet Samuel anointed Saul as king, and from this time the story reflected in the two books of Samuel, the two books of Kingds, and the two books of Chronicles begins.

The second king of the Israelites was David, who, shortly after being anointed as king (this happened around 1002–1001 BC), took Jerusalem,

[3]Conservative scholars give a date in the fifteenth century BC, following the chronological data found in Scripture (e.g., Gen 15.16; Ex 13.40; 1 Kg 6.1) in addition to archaeological findings. Other scholars tend to give a later date for the Exodus (often in the thirteenth century BC). In the popular consciousness, Exodus is most often envisaged in the reign of Ramses II (reigned c. 1279–1213 BC), likely because Exodus 1.11 tells of a store-city called "Ramses." But there is no consensus in tradition or in contemporary scholarship about which city this was, including where it was or when it existed, which makes it useless as evidence for the date of the exodus.—Ed.

making it the capital of the united kingdom of Israel. David entered the history of the Jewish nation as its most successful ruler: the political and cultural flowering of Israel is associated with his name. David, moreover, is known as a prophet and poet and the author of most of the psalms that make up the Psalter. David's son, Solomon, built the First Temple of Jerusalem.

David, sculpture, Michelangelo, 1501–1504.

After the death of Solomon, the kingdom of Israel was divided in two: the kingdoms of Israel and Judah. As a result of many wars, the territorial borders of these two kingdoms constantly changed. After the soldiers of Nebuchadnezzar, the king of Babylonia, destroyed the first Temple in 586 BC, the Babylonians led most of the Jews away into captivity. In 539 BC, when Babylonia was conquered by King Cyrus of Persia, the Jews were allowed to return to their land and restore the Temple. The construction of the Second Temple was completed in 516 BC. Meanwhile, the territory of the former kingdoms of Israel and Judah became part of the Persian empire, within which Judah and Samaria were two separate provinces.

In the period after the Babylonian captivity many synagogues (assembly houses) were built throughout the territory of Judah, Galilee, and Samaria. Unlike the Temple, the synagogue was not treated as a place of worship: it was primarily a house for teaching, where pious Jews read the Torah (the Pentateuch) and the books of the prophets, and discussed the books that they read. At the same time, common prayer, bearing the nature of public worship, was offered up in the synagogues. The Jews gathered in the synagogues on the Sabbath. The Gospels describe many instances of Jesus visiting the synagogues (Mt 3.23; 9.35; 12.9; 13.54; Mk 1.21; 3.1; 6.2; Lk 4.15–16; 6.6; 13.10; Jn 6.59).

And yet, the main spiritual center for the Jews remained the Temple of Jerusalem. The head of the spiritual hierarchy of the Jewish nation—the high priest—conducted his ministry in the Temple. The ministry of the high priest was hereditary; it was transmitted, as a rule, from father to son. The first person in the history of the Jewish people to receive this ministry was

Scale model of
the Temple of
Jerusalem

Moses' brother Aaron, from whom it was passed on to his descendants.
During the period of the Babylonian captivity, the Jewish people had no high
priest, but the high priestly ministry was restored after the captivity. Apart
from the many liturgical privileges that the high priest enjoyed, he also had
judicial power: it was he who was the head of the Sanhedrin—the highest
judicial organ, modeled after the council of seventy elders that Moses had
gathered at the Lord's command (Num 11.16). Both the high priest and the
members of the Sanhedrin belonged to the Jewish aristocracy.

In 332 BC Alexander the Great took Judah and Samaria. It was in this
period that the conflict between the Jews and the Samaritans, which began
after the Jews returned from Babylonian captivity, reached its apogee.
Alexander permitted the Samaritans to build their own temple on Mount
Gerizim as opposed to the Temple of Jerusalem, which remained the center of the Jews' liturgical life.

Thanks to Alexander's policy of tolerance, the Jews were dispersed
throughout the various cities of the empire he headed, in which the pre-
dominant language was Greek. Thus the vast diaspora of Jews arose, for
whom Greek was the main language of communication. It was for these
Jews that the Greek translation of the Bible was produced in Alexandria
during the reign of the Egyptian king Ptolemy II Philadelphus (282–246
BC). This translation became known as the Septuagint, since it was translated by seventy interpreters.

In the history of the Israelites, the mid-second century BC was marked by the attempt to restore their political independence, an attempt associated with the name of Judah Maccabee, who in 166 BC headed the revolt against the Seleucid dynasty. For the next one hundred years, the Jews' struggle against the Seleucids was accompanied by inner strife generated by various family clans' struggle for power. In 63 BC the Roman emperor Pompey entered Jerusalem at the request of the two warring clans. From that moment onwards, Israel became politically depen dent on Rome as one of its provinces.

The most ancient manuscript of the Septuagint

In 37 BC Herod the Great became the sole ruler of the kingdom of Israel.[4] It was during his rule that the events described in the Gospels of Matthew and Luke began to unfold. Although the Gospels call Herod a king, his power was not absolute: in reality he ruled Israel on behalf of the Romans, who had put him in this position.

In the period of internecine strife that preceded Herod's rule, the Temple of Jerusalem fell into a state of decay, and Herod undertook its reconstruction on a monumental scale. Many elements of Greek classical architecture were used—colonnades, balustrades, galleries, and porticoes. The scale of Herod's Temple was significantly greater than that of the original Temple of Solomon. The building and restoration work continued after Herod's death. By the time Jesus began his ministry, the Temple of Jerusalem was a gigantic ensemble of buildings that drew the admiration of contemporaries with its beauty and splendor: "Now the outward face of the temple in its front wanted nothing that was likely to surprise either men's minds or their eyes; for it was covered all over with plates of gold of great weight, and, at the first rising of the sun, reflected back a very fiery splendor, and made those who forced themselves to look upon it to turn

[4]Antipater, the father of Herod the Great, became a Roman citizen in 47 BC, and he is also named by Caesar as "procurator of Judea." In 46 BC, Antipater installed his two sons, Phasael and Herod, as military commanders of Jerusalem and Galilee. In 40 BC, Antipater's son Herod received the support of Octavian and Antony and was appointed king of Judea by the Roman Senate. But it was not until 37 BC, after a power struggle with Antigonus, that Herod gained full control.

*The Massacre of
the Innocents,*
Matteo di
Giovanni, 1488.

their eyes away, just as they would have done at the sun's own rays," wrote
Josephus.[5]

After the death of Herod in 4 BC, the emperor Augustus divided
Herod's dominion between his sons: Herod Archelaus was given jurisdic-
tion over Judah, Idumea, and Samaria; Herod Antipas over Galilee and
Perea; Philip the Tetrarch over a number of other regions; and part of the
lands went to Herod's sister Salome. In AD 6 Herod Archelaus was sent
into exile, and direct rule by the emperor was introduced in Judah through
the Roman prefects, the fifth of which was Pontius Pilate. Herod Antipas,
meanwhile, retained his territory, which he ruled over until AD 39. It is this
Herod who is mentioned in the Gospel narratives about the death of John
the Baptist (Mt 14.1–2; Mk 6.14–29; Lk 3.19–20) and Jesus' interrogation
in Jerusalem (Lk 23.6–12).

The main events of the Gospel story took place at a time when Palestine
was divided between several rulers. The action unfolds in Galilee, Samaria,
and Judah; Jesus also visits Syrian Palestine (the lands of Caesarea Philippi)
and Decapolis (most of these ten cities were situated on the opposite bank

[5]Flavius Josephus, *Wars of the Jews* 5.5.6 (trans. Whiston).

of the Jordan). Thus, Jesus' activity embraces practically all of the regions of the former kingdoms
of Israel and Judah, and all of the Promised Land,
which was then fully part of the Roman empire.

One of the characteristic features of the Jewish
people was their acute sense of history and their
place within it. Today, many people are content to
live without knowing the history of their people, or
knowing it only in the most general outline from
their studies in school, which they have happily
forgotten. With rare exceptions, the events of history—"the lore of ages long gone by, in hoary antiquity compounded"[6]—are not viewed as something
that should influence a person's life, his present and
future. People, as a rule, remember the events of
the recent past that took place over the past two or
three generations. As for events from which they
are far more removed, these are gradually erased
from the collective memory.

Augustus Caesar,
sculpture, 1st c.

In view of this, it is difficult for people today to understand why the Jews
were so attached to their history. This attachment is explained first of all by
the fact that the Jews knew the history of their people not so much through
school textbooks as through their Scripture, that is, the books of the Old
Testament. In the Torah, the history of the people of Israel is presented
interspersed with the divine commandments; in the books of the Prophets,
the voice of God is heard against the historical background; the Old Testament in its sum is simultaneously a textbook of history and a collection
of spiritual and moral exhortations underpinned by the authority of God
himself. All of the religious feasts of the Jews are connected with the history
of the Israelites: Passover (*Pesach*) is the remembrance of the exodus of the
Jews from Egypt; the Feast of Tabernacles (*Sukkot*) is the remembrance of

---

[6]This is a citation from Pushkin's famous poem, *Ruslan and Liudmila*. Quoted translation
from Alexander Pushkin, *Ruslan and Liudmila*, trans. Walter Arndt (Ann Arbor, MI: Ardis,
1974), 7.

how the Jews wandered through the wilderness; the feast of the Rededication of the Holy Temple (*Hanukkah*) was established in memory of the renewal of worship in the Second Temple after it was desecrated by the Persians; and the feast of Pentecost (*Shavuot*) was established in remembrance of how the people of Israel were given the Torah through Moses.

Language

Hebrew is part of the Semitic language family and has a history stretching back over many thousands of years. In Jesus' time in Palestine, two related languages coexisted—Hebrew and Aramaic. Hebrew was the language of the Old Testament: Scripture was written in it, and learned Jews would apparently conduct philosophical debates in it. A variant of literary Hebrew was the spoken Hebrew that survived in Judah and Jerusalem. Another spoken language was Aramaic, which was divided into several dialects, including Galilean and Samaritan. Since Jesus and his disciples were from Galilee, it is most probable that they spoke in the Galilean dialect among themselves.[7] This is partially confirmed by the following story from Matthew:

> Now Peter sat without in the palace, and a young woman came unto him, saying, "Thou also wast with Jesus of Galilee." But he denied before them all, saying, "I know not what thou sayest." And when he was gone out into the porch, another young woman saw him, and said unto them that were there, "This man was also with Jesus of Nazareth." And again he denied with an oath, "I do not know the man." And after a while came unto him they that stood by, and said to Peter, "Surely thou also art one of them; for thy speech bewrayeth thee." (Mt 26.69–73)

From this story, where Jesus is called a Galilean, it is evident that Jesus and his disciples are identified with Galilee and the dialect in which they spoke betrayed their Galilean origin. It is noteworthy that this theme is also present in the parallel passages of the two other Synoptic Gospels. In

[7]For more details about the language of Jesus, see John P. Meier, *A Marginal Jew: Rethinking the Historical Jesus*, vol. 1, *The Roots of the Problem and the Person* (New York, NY: Doubleday, 1991), 255–268.

Christ foretells
Peter's denial,
mosaic, 6th c.

Mark, those who stand around Peter say to him: "Surely thou art one of them, for thou art a Galilaean, and thy speech is like [the Galilaean dialect]" (Mk 14.70). In Luke, Peter is also called a Galilean (Lk 22.59).

We also know from the Gospel of John that the Judeans had a skeptical and derisive attitude towards the Galileans. The evangelist describes three episodes confirming this. In one of them, Philip announces to Nathaniel: "We have found him, of whom Moses in the law, and the prophets, did write, Jesus of Nazareth, the son of Joseph." But Nathaniel replies to him in a dismissive manner: "Can any good thing come out of Nazareth?" (Jn 1.45–46). In another instance the Judeans who listened to Jesus ask each other: "Shall Christ come out of Galilee?" (Jn 7.41). Finally, in Nicodemus' dialogue with the Pharisees, the latter contemptuously say: "Art thou also of Galilee? Search, and look: for out of Galilee ariseth no prophet" (Jn 7.52).

From the same Gospel we learn that "the Jews have no dealings with the Samaritans" (Jn 4.9). Apart from the differences in their manner of worshiping God, there were also linguistic differences between the Jews and Samaritans. It is quite possible that, when conversing with the Samaritan woman, Jesus used the Samaritan dialect of the Aramaic language. At the same time, when conversing with the Jews on serious theological topics (there are many such discourses in the Gospel of John), as well as when addressing his audience in the synagogue, Jesus could have used literary Hebrew. In one such instance described, Jesus, when in the synagogue, begins at first to read an excerpt from Scripture in Hebrew, and then, when closing the book (or rather, having rolled up the scroll), he gives his commentary on what has been read (Lk 4.15–30). It is possible that he would then have spoken in classical Hebrew.

As we have already remarked, in the Gospels, which were written in Greek, some words have been preserved in their original pronunciation, transcribed by Greek letters. Among such transliterations we find both Aramaic and Hebrew words. The evangelists Matthew and Mark transcribe Jesus' exclamation on the cross differently (this difference is evident even in the English translation): *"Eli, Eli, lama sabachthani?"* (Mt 27.46) or *"Eloi, Eloi, lama sabachthani?"* (Mk 15.34). In this instance Matthew describes Jesus' cry to God in Hebrew (*ēlī*—see Ps 21.2), and Mark in Aramaic (reconstructed pronunciation *'ilāhī*, cf. the biblical Aramaic *'ēlāhī*).[8] In which language was it originally said? It is possible that it was Aramaic, the spoken language of Jesus and his disciples. At least, the words of Jesus that Mark keeps in their original sound have an Aramaic origin: "Talitha cumi" (Mk 5.41), "Ephphatha" (Mk 7.34), and "Abba" (Mk 14.36). In the parallel narratives of the other evangelists these words are absent.

Apart from the different variants of Hebrew and Aramaic that Jesus could have used, in Palestine of his time Greek was widely used as the language of international communication in the Roman empire. The inhabitants of Galilee were more or less proficient in Greek.[9] Latin was much less significant. Did Jesus know these languages, and if so, to what degree? We can only surmise that his discourse with Pontius Pilate was conducted not in Aramaic and not in Hebrew, which the Roman prefect would hardly have spoken. It is most likely that the conversation was conducted in Greek.[10]

---

[8] Ludwig Koehler and Walter Baumgartner, *Hebräisches und Aramäisches Lexikon zum Alten Testament*, Lfg. 5 (Leiden: Brill, 1996), 1666.

[9] Mark A. Chancey, *The Myth of a Gentile Galilee*, Society for New Testament Studies Monograph Series 118 (Cambridge: Cambridge University Press, 2004), 180.

[10] Armand Puig i Tàrrech, *Jesus: A Biography* (Waco, TX: Baylor University Press, 2011), 180.

We also know from the Gospel of John of the desire of the Hellenes (Greeks) to meet with Jesus (Jn 12.20–22). Did Jesus speak with them, and if so, in what language? The Gospel writer does not give an answer to this question, as he does not give an explanation to the puzzled question of the Jews regarding Jesus: "Will he go unto the dispersed among the Gentiles, and teach the Gentiles?" (Jn 7.35). No matter what the case, it is more than plausible that Jesus was acquainted with the Greek language and used it in certain situations.

2. The Years of His Life

The Gospels contain definite indications of the time in which the events they describe took place. Thus, for example, Luke begins his narrative on the birth of John the Baptist with the words: "There was in the days of Herod, the king of Judaea . . ." (Lk 1.5). Here he is referring to Herod the Great, who ruled the kingdom of Israel from 37 to 4 BC.

The main source of information on Herod are the writings of Flavius Josephus, although he is also mentioned in a number of other sources as well. The father of Herod Antipas became a Roman citizen and in 47–48 BC became the governor of Judah. He appointed his twenty-five-year-old son, also Herod, ruler of Galilee. In 40 BC Herod was granted the right to the throne of Israel by the Romans, but was able to exercise this right only in 37 BC. Herod's rule was marked by many cruelties, vividly described by Josephus. Herod's death is dated, as a rule, at 4 BC, although some scholars dispute this date.

The evangelist Luke begins his narrative on the birth of Jesus with the words: "In those days, that there went out a decree from Caesar Augustus, that all the world should be taxed. (This taxing was first made when Quirinius was governor of Syria.)" (Lk 2.1–2). Quirinius is mentioned in a whole array of historical sources, including Tacitus, Florus, and Josephus.

The Nativity
of Christ, icon,
15th c.

The latter speaks of the census organized by Quirinius at the command
of the emperor:

> Quirinius, a Roman senator, and one who had gone through other
> magistracies, and had passed through them till he had been consul,
> and one who, on other accounts, was of great dignity, came at this
> time into Syria, with a few others, being sent by Caesar to be a judge of
> that nation, and to take an account of their substance. Coponius also,
> a man of the equestrian order, was sent together with him, to have
> the supreme power over the Jews. Moreover, Quirinius came himself
> into Judea, which was now added to the province of Syria, to take an
> account of their substance, and to dispose of Archelaus's money; but
> the Jews, although at the beginning they took the report of a taxation
> heinously, yet did they leave off any further opposition to it, by the

persuasion of Joazar, who was the son of Beethus, and high priest; so they, being over-persuaded by Joazar's words, gave an account of their estates, without any dispute about it.[11]

Tiberius, sculpture, 1st c.

The dating of the census in question poses significant difficulties. Josephus links it to the removal of Archelaus, which occurred in AD 6. If we believe Josephus, then it was to Judah that Quirinius set off. However, there is a gap of about ten years between this year and the supposed date of Jesus' birth. In order to make the chronologies agree, the theory has been put forward that Quirinius was made proconsul of Syria twice. This theory is confirmed to some degree by the inscription found in the environs of Rome in the latter half of the eighteenth century: it mentions a man who, during the time of Augustus, was twice awarded triumphal honors and was proconsul in Asia and Syrian Phoenicia. It is quite plausible that the reference is to Quirinius and that he was proconsul in Syria at first under Herod the Great, and then once more—ten years later, after Herod's death.[12] In this case, we can understand why Luke makes his account more precise: this census was the first in Quirinius of Syria's reign. It is clear that the census mentioned by Josephus was not the first.

In the Gospel of Luke the story of the beginning of John the Baptist's preaching is dated to the fifteenth year of the reign of Tiberius (Lk 3.1). Tiberius ruled the Roman empire from August 19th, AD 14, to March 16th, AD 37. We can, consequently, date John's emergence as a preacher to the latter half of AD 29 or the first half of AD 30. We do not know how much time passed between the beginning of John's preaching and his baptizing Jesus. Luke mentions that Jesus was thirty years old when he began his ministry (Lk 3.23).

---

[11]Josephus, *Antiquities of the Jews* 18.1.1 (trans. Whiston).

[12]For more details see Raymond E. Brown, *The Birth of the Messiah: A Commentary on the Infancy Narratives in the Gospels of Matthew and Luke* (New Haven, CT: Yale University Press, 1999) 547–556.

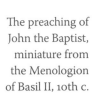

The preaching of
John the Baptist,
miniature from
the Menologion
of Basil II, 10th c.

The reckoning of years from the birth of Christ was introduced in
Europe by the sixth-century Latin monk Dionysius Exiguus in his works.
He selected the 754th year from the foundation of Rome as the year of
Jesus Christ's birth, which corresponded to the evidence given in the third
chapter of Luke's Gospel. In the first chapter of his Gospel, however, when
relating events directly preceding Jesus' birth, Luke dates them to the time
of the reign of "Herod, king of Judaea" (Lk 1.5). Matthew also speaks of the
birth of Jesus "in the days of Herod the king" (Mt 2.1) and of the slaughter
of the children "from two years old and under" at Herod's command (Mt
2.16). All of these events, therefore, should have occurred before Herod's
death, as should have Joseph's and Mary's flight to Egypt with the infant
Christ. It is only upon the death of Herod (Mt 2.19), when Herod's son
Archelaus already reigned in Judah (Mt 2.22), that Joseph and Mary could
have returned to Egypt.

If we proceed from the assumption that Herod the Great died in 4 BC,
Jesus' birth should be dated to 5 or 6 BC. This dating is adhered to by the
majority of contemporary scholars. Yet one more indication that helps us
to reconstruct the chronology of the life and ministry of Jesus is contained
in the Gospel of John. It quotes the words of Jesus uttered at the outset
of his ministry: "Destroy this temple, and in three days I will raise it up."
The Jews, who thought he was referring to the Temple of Jerusalem in the
form in which it was reconstructed by Herod the Great, said in reply to

The Flight into Egypt, Titian, 1508.

this: "This temple was built [*oikodomēthē*] in forty-six years, and wilt thou rear it up in three days?" (Jn 2.19–20).

According to Josephus, the reconstruction of the Temple of Jerusalem began in the eighteenth year of the reign of Herod the Great,[13] that is, in 20–19 BC. If we count forty-six years from this year, we come to the year AD 28.[14] We cannot state with certainty, however, that Jesus' discourse with the Jews happened at Passover in precisely that year, since the construction of the Temple is mentioned as an event that ended in the previous year (the form of the passive aorist is used).[15]

An original (though not uncontroversial) interpretation of Jn 2.19–20 was proposed by Jack Finegan, the author of a foundational study on biblical chronology. The scholar points to the fact that it is only in this place that the evangelist John uses the word *naos* (literally, "sanctuary") to denote the Temple, whereas in other instances (including the story when the

---

[13]Josephus, *Antiquities of the Jews*, 15.11.1. In a different place (*Wars of the Jews* 1.21.1), Josephus dates the beginning of the reconstruction of the Temple at the fifteenth year of Herod's reign; however, the first date is considered to be more reliable (Jack Finegan, *Handbook of Biblical Chronology: Principles of Time Reckoning in the Ancient World and Problems of Chronology in the Bible*, rev. ed. [Peabody, MA: Hendrickson, 1998], 347–348).

[14]See Raymond E. Brown, *The Gospel according to John (I–XII)*, Anchor Bible 29 (Garden City, NY: Doubleday, 1966), 116.

[15]Finegan, *Handbook of Biblical Chronology*, 349.

The Expulsion of the Money-Changers from the Temple, Giotto, 1304–1306.

moneylenders are driven from the Temple, which immediately precedes this text), he uses the term *hieron* (literally, "sacred place," "temple"). The latter refers to the Temple as a whole, including the courtyard of the Jews and the courtyard of the Gentiles, and, indeed, the evangelist uses it every time when he speaks of Jesus' and the people's presence in the Temple (Jn 2.14; 5.14; 7.28; 8.20; 18.20). By contrast, the term *naos* also had a special meaning too—the "inner part of the temple," accessible only to the priests (this meaning, known from classical literature in relation to pagan temples, is found in Josephus). The fact that in Jn 2.19–20 the Gospel writer uses the word *naos* instead of the more usual word *hieron* allows us to suggest that what is being referred to here is not the Temple as a whole, but a shrine, the reconstruction of which is described by Josephus separately.[16] In this instance, however, forty-six years cannot mean the time taken for construction, since work in the shrine lasted only a year and a half.[17] If we take into account the fact that the passive aorist denotes an event in the past, Finegan proposes we should take the words *tesserakonta kai hex etesin oikodomēthē* to mean not "was built over a period of forty-six years,"

[16] Josephus, *Antiquities of the Jews* 15.11.5–6.
[17] Josephus, *Antiquities of the Jews* 15.11.6.

Pilate washing
his hands, fresco,
16th c.

but "was built forty-six years ago." Since the year-and-a-half work should
have been completed in 18 or 17 BC, then Jesus' discourse with the Jews
on the first Passover of his public ministry should have taken place In AD
29 or 30.[18]

Jesus was crucified under Pontius Pilate, who ruled Judah from AD 26
to 36. It is noteworthy that Pontius Pilate is mentioned in all four Gospels
in the narrative on Christ's Passion. His name was also preserved by the
subsequent Christian tradition and was included in the Creed adopted
at the Second Ecumenical Council in 381 ("crucified for us under Pontius
Pilate"). The inclusion of this name in the Creed undoubtedly has the aim
of demonstrating Jesus' historicity by means of synchronizing his death
with the time of the rule of the Roman prefect. The year of the beginning
of Pilate's rule and the year of its end can, correspondingly, be viewed as
the *terminus ante quem* and *terminus post quem*[19] for determining the
year of Jesus' death.

---

[18]Finegan, *Handbook of Biblical Chronology*, 348–349.

[19]The Latin phrase *terminus ante quem* denotes the period of time no earlier than which an
event took place. *Terminus post quem* denotes the period of time no later than which an event
took place.—Ed.

The Crucifixion,
Albrecht
Altdorfer, 1526.

The totality of the data available allows us only to draw approximate conclusions regarding the time of Jesus' birth: he was born no earlier than 7 BC and no later than 4 BC. There is far greater clarity concerning the date of his death. On the basis of the unanimous testimony of the evangelists that Jesus was crucified on a Friday (Mt 27.62; Mk 15.42; Lk 23.54; Jn 19.14, 31), as well as on the basis of the testimony of the evangelist John that the paschal lamb was to have been slaughtered on this day (Jn 18.28), Jack Finegan comes to the conclusion that the crucifixion took place on April 7th, AD 30, or April 3rd, AD 33.[20] The scholar gives preference to the

[20]Finegan, *Handbook of Biblical Chronology*, 359–363. Finegan makes use of the astronomical calculations quoted in articles by Fotheringham and Parker (John Knight Fotheringham, "The Evidence of Astronomy and Technical Chronology for the Date of the Crucifixion," *Journal of Theological Studies* 35 [April 1934]: 146–162; Richard A. Parker and Waldo H. Dibberstein, *Babylonian Chronology 626 B.C.–A.D. 45*, Studies in Ancient Oriental Civilization 24 [Chicago, IL: University of Chicago Press, 1942]). The calculations presented in both publications partially coincide and partially differ from each other because Parker and Dubberstein postulated for certain years the addition of the so-called "second Adar" so that the calendar would not be misaligned. This practice is well known from the rabbinical tradition; however, for the period of the Gospel events it is impossible to ascertain with certainty for which years this addition was used and whether it was used at all. In order to cover all of the possibilities, Finegan takes into account the findings of both publications. He reasons in the following manner. 1. It follows

second date.[21] Other scholars, however, are inclined towards the year 30 as the most probable year of Jesus' crucifixion.[22]

For how many years did Jesus live? In the second century, Irenaeus of Lyons attempted to prove that it was just under fifty. He based his arguments on the words that Jesus addressed to the Jews: "Thou art not yet fifty years old, and hast thou seen Abraham?" (Jn 8.57). According to Irenaeus,

---

from both the Synoptic Gospels and from the Gospel of John that the crucifixion took place on a Friday. 2. At the same time, it follows from the Synoptic Gospels that this Friday is dated as the 15th of the month of Nissan, for the Last Supper took place on the day when the Passover lamb was slaughtered, that is, on the 14th of Nissan. 3. By contrast, according to the Gospel of John, Jesus was crucified not at the Passover, but on the day when the lamb was slaughtered, that is, the 14th of Nissan (according to Jn 19.14, Jesus was crucified on the Friday before the Passover, and on this day, according to Jn 18.28, the Passover lamb was to be consumed). Finegan checks these two dates (the crucifixion on Friday the 15th day of Nissan and the crucifixion on Friday the 14th day of Nissan) against the data from Fotheringham and from Parker and Dubberstein. The 1st of Nissan could only be a Friday in the year 27 (according to both analyses) or the year 34 (according to the analysis by Parker and Dubberstein). These are the possible dates for the crucifixion according to the Synoptic Gospels. The 14th of Nissan was a Friday in the years 30 and 33: these are the possible dates for the crucifixion according to the Gospel of John. Further, Finegan establishes two extreme points within the confines of which the calculations for the date of the crucifixion are possible. The earliest proposed date for Jesus' baptism is the year 26. The shortest period of time proposed for the length of his earthly activity is about one year. The latest possible date for Jesus' baptism is the year 29. The longest period of time for his ministry calculated from the Gospels is three to four years. In this manner, we obtain the extreme points—the years 27 and 34. Now Finegan chooses the most plausible of these dates. The years 27 and 34, obtained on the basis of the chronology of the Synoptic Gospels, correspond to the extreme points of the aforementioned interval and are therefore improbable. The years 30 and 33, obtained from the chronology of John, fit well into this interval: thus, the scholar believes that John's chronology is to be preferred.

[21]Finegan, *Handbook of Biblical Chronology*, 362. In choosing between the years 30 and 33, Finegan reasons in the following manner: in the year 31 the praetor Lucius Ennius was removed from office and executed, who by this time had been the actual ruler of the empire when Tiberius was unable to act. Lucius was noted for his extreme anti-Semitism and exerted a direct influence on Roman policy in Palestine. This influence in many ways determined the brutal policy of the first half of Pilate's reign. Therefore, Finegan believes, it is highly unlikely that Pilate's attempt to avoid Jesus' execution and his fear at the same time of coming into conflict with the religious elite of Judah took place in the year 30, when Lucius was already at the height of his power. Thus, Finegan arrives at the year 33 as the most plausible date of the crucifixion. He refers to a number of specialists who share the same position, including Harold Hoehner (Harold W. Hoehner, *Chronological Aspects of the Life of Christ* [Grand Rapids, MI: Zondervan, 1977], 65–113, 141–142).

[22]See, for example, Gerard S. Sloyan, *The Crucifixion of Jesus: History, Myth, Faith* (Minneapolis, MN: Fortress Press, 1995), 11.

they could have uttered these words to "one who has already passed the age of forty, without having as yet reached his fiftieth year, yet is not far from this latter period." If he had been a little over thirty, so Irenaeus believes, then the Jews would have said to him, "Thou art not yet forty," since "it is altogether unreasonable to suppose that they were mistaken by twenty years, when they wished to prove Him younger than the times of Abraham." Irenaeus also refers to the apostle John the Theologian, who supposedly asserted that Jesus taught at the age of forty to fifty years, "as the Gospel and all the elders testify; those who were conversant in Asia with John, the disciple of the Lord, affirming that John conveyed to them that information. And he remained among them up to the times of Trajan. Some of them, moreover, saw not only John, but the other apostles also, and heard the very same account from them, and bear testimony as to the validity of the statement."[23]

This testimony is not to be ignored, since Irenaeus claims to have received this evidence directly from those who had heard the apostles. Nevertheless, a solid tradition was later formed according to which Jesus lived for about thirty-three years. It is based on a literal understanding of the words of the Gospel of Luke, that Jesus was thirty years old when he began preaching, and the evidence of the evangelist John, who divided Jesus' public ministry into three periods: from the first Passover to the second, from the second Passover to the third, and from the third Passover to the fourth.

The narratives of the Synoptics give us no indication of how long Jesus' ministry lasted. Nevertheless, the totality of the above evidence concerning his birth and death compels us to propose that, no matter how we look at it, he could hardly have lived till the age of forty. Considering that the majority of scholars date his birth around the years 5 or 6 BC and his death to AD 30 or 33, then the length of his earthly life would have been from thirty-five to thirty-eight years.

---

[23]Irenaeus of Lyons, *Against Heresies* 2.22.5–6 (*ANF* 1:391–392).

3. The Problem of
the Two Genealogies

The Gospel of Matthew, which opens the New Testament, begins with the words: "The book of the generation of Jesus Christ, the son of David, the son of Abraham" (Mt 1.1). The Greek expression *biblios geneseōs* (which corresponds to the Hebrew *tôlǝḏôṯ*) literally means "the book of origin," "the book of genealogy," or "the book of being." In the Septuagint (and in English Bibles, which transliterate the Greek), the word *genesis* is used as the title of the first book of the Bible; it is used even in the text of the book of Genesis when referring to the origin of the heavens and the earth (Gen 2.4) and the genealogy of Adam (Gen 5.1).[24] Consciously or otherwise, the evangelist draws a parallel between the creation of the world and the human person on the one hand, and the coming into the world of the God-man Jesus Christ on the other. In relation to Jesus, the term *genesis* points towards the same type of "genealogy" that Adam had: as Adam had no earthly father, since God was his Maker and Father, so too Jesus had no earthly father.

The "book of the generation" of Jesus Christ contains a long list of names—his ancestors in the flesh. The list is given in a form that is unusual for the modern reader: "Abraham begat Isaac; and Isaac begat Jacob; and Jacob begat Judas and his brethren" (Mt 1.2). This list is completed by the following words: "And Jacob begat Joseph the husband of Mary, of whom was born Jesus, who is called Christ. So all the generations from Abraham to David are fourteen generations; and from David until the carrying away into Babylon are fourteen generations; and from the carrying away into Babylon unto Christ are fourteen generations" (Mt 1.16–17).

This text compels the reader to ask a multitude of questions. Why is Jesus called "the son of David, the son of Abraham" (Mt 1.1)? Why does the story of Jesus' life begin with his genealogy? Why is Jesus' genealogy in actual fact the genealogy of Joseph, who, as is evident from the subsequent

[24]Adolf von Schlatter, *Der Evangelist Matthäus: seine Sprache, seine Ziel, seine Selbstständigkeit* (Stuttgart: Calwer Verlag, 1929), 1.

narrative of the same Gospel writer, was not Jesus' biological father? What is the meaning of the division of the genealogy into three parts, each with fourteen generations?

Other questions are added to these when we compare the list of names in Matthew with the names of the genealogy contained in Luke (Lk 3.23–38), as well as with the books of the Old Testament that mention the people listed in both genealogies. Why do Matthew and Luke differ from each other in so many ways? Why is it that in Matthew's genealogical chain a number of links are absent due to the omission of a number of names that could be easily restored from the Old Testament books?

Let us try to answer these questions. First of all, let us note that Matthew calls Jesus the Christ, that is, the Anointed of God, from the very first verses presenting him as the Messiah promised by the prophets. Unlike Mark, who in the first verse of his Gospel speaks of "Jesus Christ, the Son of God" (Mk 1.1), Matthew accentuates not his divine, but his human origin, calling Jesus the son of David and the son of Abraham. At the same time, he, like Mark, emphasizes his messianic role, using the term "Christ" alongside the proper name of "Jesus."

The term "son" is used with the meaning found in the Jewish tradition. In the language of the Old Testament, any male descendant was called a son, including grandsons, great-grandsons, great-great-grandsons, and so on. It should be noted that genealogies—lists of the names of the forefathers of any given person—possess great importance in the Bible.[25] The entire book of Numbers consists mainly of lists of names, which say nothing to the modern reader, but which were undoubtedly important to the authors of the book. The need to include the genealogical lists in the book of Numbers and other parts of the Bible was determined by the notion that a genealogy was viewed not simply as a list of names helping one to establish the origin of a particular person. A genealogy primarily pointed towards the heritage that each person carried within himself; it wove his name into an unbroken chain of names going back to the father of the Jewish nation, Abraham, and through him to the father of all nations, Adam. In giving us the names of Jesus' ancestors, the evangelist wanted to emphasize

[25]Cf. Gen 10.1; 11.10; 11.27; 25.12; 36.1; and others.

the fact that he was a real Person, whose name was woven into the unbroken thread of human names.

The Gospel of Matthew was intended in the first place for Jewish readers, and the author of this Gospel set himself the task of placing Jesus in the context not merely of human history, but the history of a concrete nation, the representatives of which were the author of this Gospel, his protagonists, and his readers. In order that the latter would perceive Jesus as one of their own, it was essential to present him first of all as the descendant of the key figures in the history of the Jewish nation as reflected on the pages of the historical books of the Old Testament.

Jesus' contemporaries called themselves the seed of Abraham, with pride saying of themselves: "Abraham is our father" (Jn 8.39). The name of Abraham enjoyed indisputable authority among the Jewish people: it is with him that God made his covenant, on the basis of which the Jews believed themselves to be the chosen people. This covenant in the Christian perspective is reinterpreted as the Old Covenant, as opposed to the New, which was made through Jesus, the "son" of Abraham.

The interconnection between the Old and New Testaments is the leitmotif of the Gospel of Matthew. Jesus' genealogy in Matthew's Gospel spans almost two thousand years of Old Testament history, of which one thousand falls in the period from David to Jesus. In beginning his Gospel with a genealogy, Matthew thereby emphasizes that Jesus' ministry is the continuation of this history.

It was no less important to immediately demonstrate Jesus' messianic origin. Matthew's readers knew well that the Messiah was to come from the Tribe of Judah, according to the prophecy: "The sceptre shall not depart from Judah, nor a lawgiver from between his feet, until Shiloh come; and unto him shall the gathering of the people be" (Gen 49.10). In Balaam's prophecy, the Messiah is seen to be the descendant of Jacob (Israel): "I shall see him, but not now; I shall behold him, but not nigh. There shall come a Star out of Jacob, and a Sceptre shall rise out of Israel" (Num 24.17). Jacob was the father of Judah, and Abraham was his great-grandfather.

In the book of the prophet Isaiah, the promise of the Messiah is tied to the house of Jacob (Is 2.2–4). In the same book the Messiah is called "a rod

Bethlehem

out of the stem of Jesse" (Is 11.1). Jesse, who came from Bethlehem in Judea, was the father of King David (1 Sam 17.12), whom the Old Testament often mentions as the one from whose generation the Messiah shall appear.

The words of Nathan addressed to David from God have been interpreted in a messianic sense: "And when thy days are fulfilled, and thou shalt sleep with thy fathers, I will set up thy seed after thee, which shall proceed out of thy body, and I will establish his kingdom. He shall build a house for my name, and I will establish the throne of his kingdom forever. I will be his father, and he shall be my son" (2 Sam 7.12–14). The verses from the psalm have been viewed in the same way: "I have made a covenant with my chosen, I have sworn unto David my servant, 'Thy seed will I establish for ever, and build up thy throne to all generations'" (Ps 88.3–4). Finally, no less important is the prophecy of Jeremiah: "'Behold, the days come,' saith the Lord, 'that I will raise unto David a righteous Branch, and a King shall reign and prosper, and shall execute judgment and justice in the earth. In his days Judah shall be saved, and Israel shall dwell safely, and this is his name whereby he shall be called, 'The Lord our righteousness'" (Jer 23.5–6).

Thus, according to the prophecies, the Messiah was to be a direct descendant of David,[26] and this is why the author of the genealogy of Jesus thought it necessary to mention David. The expression "son of David" is

[26]For more details on this, see Sigmund Mowinckel, *He That Cometh: The Messiah Concept in the Old Testament and Later Judaism*, trans. G. W. Anderson (Grand Rapids, MI: Eerdmans, 2005), 165–181.

David and Goliath, Caravaggio, 1599.

often encountered in Matthew and in the parallel narratives of the other Synoptics. Jesus was called the son of David by those who turned to him and besought him to heal them (Mt 9.27; 15.22; 20.30–31). The expression "Christ, the son of David" was applied to Jesus (Mt 12.23); as he entered Jerusalem he was greeted by the words: "Hosanna to the Son of David" (Mt 21.9). The Jewish belief that the Messiah was to come from the line of David is confirmed by the words of the Pharisees: "Hath not the scripture said that Christ cometh from the seed of David?" (Jn 7.42). The Synoptics documented a dispute between Jesus and the Jews on whether the Messiah was the son of David:

While the Pharisees were gathered together, Jesus asked them, saying, "What think ye of Christ? Whose son is he?" They say unto him, "The Son of David." He saith unto them, "How then doth David in Spirit call him Lord, saying, 'The Lord said unto my Lord, "Sit thou on my right hand, till I make thine enemies thy footstool"'? [Ps 109.1] If David then call him Lord, how is he his son?" (Mt 22.41–45; cf. Mk 12.35–37; Lk 20.40–44)

As is evident from this narrative, Jesus did not reject the Jewish belief that the Messiah was to come from the line of David. But he emphasized that in relation to David, the Messiah is Lord: he is not only the direct descendant of David, but also his Lord.

After Jesus' resurrection, this theme was continued by the apostles as they made it central to their endeavors in proving the messianic role of Jesus. The book of Acts gives us Peter's speech, which was uttered on the day of Pentecost and was of a programmatic nature: in it Peter sets forth the essence of the Gospel that he and the other apostles intend to preach. An important place in this exposition is given to David:

For David speaketh concerning him, "I foresaw the Lord always before my face, for he is on my right hand, that I should not be moved" [Ps 15.8]. . . . Men and brethren, let me freely speak unto you of the patriarch David, that he is both dead and buried, and his sepulcher is with us unto this day. Therefore being a prophet, and knowing that God had sworn with an oath to him, that of the fruit of his loins, according to the flesh, he would raise up Christ to sit on his throne; he seeing this before spake of the resurrection of Christ, that his soul was not left in hell, neither his flesh did see corruption. This Jesus hath God raised up, of which we all are witnesses." (Acts 2.25, 29–32)

The topic of David occupies an important place also in the preaching of the apostle Paul. In his epistles he twice appeals to it (Rom 1.3; Tim 2.8), and the book of Acts transmits to us one of his spoken homilies:

And when he had removed him, he raised up unto them David to be their king; to whom also he gave testimony, and said, "I have found

David the son of Jesse, a man after mine own heart, which shall fulfill all my will." [Ps 88.21] Of this man's seed hath God according to his promise raised unto Israel a Saviour, Jesus.... And we declare unto you glad tidings, how that the promise which was made unto the fathers, God hath fulfilled the same unto us their children, in that he hath raised up Jesus again; as it is also written in the second psalm, "Thou art my Son, this day have I begotten thee." [Ps 2.7] And as concerning that he raised him up from the dead, now no more to return to corruption, he said on this wise, "I will give you the sure mercies of David." [Is 55.3] Wherefore he saith also in another place, "Thou shalt not suffer thine Holy One to see corruption." [Ps 15.10] For David, after he had served his own generation by the will of God, fell asleep, and was laid unto his fathers, and saw corruption. But he, whom God raised again, saw no corruption. (Acts 13.22–23, 32–37)

We note that, although the Gospel of Matthew occupies first place in the body of the New Testament, the speeches of the apostles Peter and Paul quoted above obviously precede this Gospel chronologically, as they heralded the inception of the apostolic preaching. The mentions of the origin of Jesus from the line of David in Paul's epistles in all probability also preceded the Gospel of Matthew.

Genealogies were always drawn up according to the male line—from father to son, and so on. Matthew adheres strictly to this order. Both the form in which the genealogy is presented, and the names it contains are borrowed from the books of the Old Testament. Some borrowings are almost identical (for example, Mt 1.3–6 corresponds to 1 Chr 2.10–12 and Ruth 4.18–22).

The four women mentioned in Matthew's genealogy were the wives of those whose direct descendant was, according to Matthew, Jesus. Different opinions exist as to why their names were included in the genealogy. In two instances the women whom Matthew mentions were not the legitimate wives of the men from whom their son was born, who was included in the genealogy: these were Tamar, with whom Judah {her father-in-law) sinned, taking her to be a prostitute (Gen 38.13–30), and Bathsheba, the wife of

Uriah, with whom David sinned (2 Sam 11.2–27). Ruth is mentioned possibly because a whole book of the Bible (Ruth 2.1–4.16) is devoted to her relationship with Boaz.[27]

The greatest enigma among the women mentioned by Matthew is Rahab. Many scholars have identified her as the prostitute Rahab, mentioned in the book of Joshua of Nun (Josh 2.1–24; 6.16). However, nowhere in the Old Testament does it state that Rahab married Salmon. It is possible that Matthew was relying upon other, non-biblical sources and had in mind a Rahab who is not mentioned in the Bible.

Why does Matthew reproduce Joseph's genealogy if, according to this Gospel writer, Joseph was not Jesus' biological father? The answer to this question comes from the custom of the Jews by which a child's father was considered to be the husband of his mother, even if the child was not born from him. In being betrothed to Mary, "being great with child" (Lk 2.5), Joseph took upon himself the responsibility of bringing up her Child. Although not the Infant's natural father, he was his lawful father, which is why even as an adult Jesus was still referred to as the son of Joseph (Lk 4.22; Jn 1.45).

When comparing the genealogy from the Gospel of Matthew with the books of the Bible that narrate the story of the Jewish kings, we are struck by Matthew's omission of three kings between Joram and Ozias—Ahaziah, Joash, and Amaziah. It is clear that this omission was made with the aim of obtaining the number fourteen when counting the generations between David and the Babylonian resettlement. For Matthew, the symbolism of numbers has far greater significance than the historical consistency of the names. It is also possible that the desire to obtain by any means the number fourteen in each chronological section was connected to the fact that the numeric values of the Hebrew letters of the name "David" add up to fourteen.

It is no coincidence that Matthew divides the genealogy into sections from Abraham to David, from David to the relocation to Babylon, and from the resettlement in Babylon to Christ. In this construction, Abraham,

[27]Ruth was a Moabite. The Law excluded Moabites from the religious life of Israel: "An Ammonite or Moabite shall not enter into the congregation of the Lord; even to their tenth generation they shall not enter into the congregation of the Lord forever" (Deut 23.3). Nevertheless, she became the great-grandmother of King David, and thus an ancestor of Christ. The inclusion of a Gentile in Christ's genealogy foreshadows the Gospel's universal scope.—*Ed.*

David, and Christ become the pillars, the symbolic names, upon which the edifice rests.

The greatest mystery for scholars is the fact that the two genealogies of Jesus Christ differ from each other substantially. The genealogies in Matthew and Luke agree only in the part containing the names from Abraham to David. Further, Matthew follows the "royal" line, listing the kings of Judah as they are mentioned in the Old Testament, while Luke reproduces a different line. The difference in the genealogies is sustained from David until Salathiel, in Matthew through sixteen generations, and in Luke twenty generations. The lines come together with Salathiel and Zorobabel, who are present in the lists of both evangelists (Mt 1.12; Lk 3.27), but then the genealogies part again up until Joseph, the husband of Mary. Even the name of Joseph's father differs between the evangelists: in Matthew he is called Jacob, while in Luke he is called Heli.

Scholars have noted that Matthew, in constructing the genealogy of Jesus Christ, mainly follows 1 Chronicles, whereas Luke was not familiar with this book.[28] The genealogy in the Gospel of Luke is based on other biblical sources and on the whole, so scholars believe, more precisely corresponds to historical reality, at least in relation to the period before the Babylonian exile.[29]

The presence of two genealogies attracted the attention of early Christian authors, who attempted to explain the differences between the evangelists by referring to Jewish laws, particularly the law of levirate marriage, whereby if one brother dies childless, then another brother is obliged to marry his widow, and "the firstborn which she beareth shall succeed in the name of his brother which is dead, that his name be not put out of Israel" (Deut 25.5–6). In the Old Testament, including the Septuagint, this was called the raising up of the name of one's brother (Deut 25.7); in the New Testament this law was referred as the raising up of the seed of one's brother (Mt 22.24; Mk 12.19; Lk 20.28). The Old Testament rule in this instance pursued a clear goal: the law is invoked so that the name of the

[28]Joachim Jeremias, *Jerusalem in the Time of Jesus*, trans. F. H. Cave and C. H. Cave (London: SCM Press, 1991), 280, 295.

[29]Ibid., 296. For the differences between the genealogies of Christ in Matthew and Luke, see Brown, *Birth of the Messiah*, 66–94.

childless deceased would not be blotted out in Israel. The name of this man, consequently, was to become part of the genealogy of the one whose biological father he was not, but of his brother.

Sextus Julius Africanus (third century) explained the presence of the two genealogies by this law of levirate marriage. He is quoted by Eusebius of Caesarea:

> The names of the families in Israel were reckoned either by nature or by law; by nature, when there was genuine offspring to succeed; by law, when another man fathered a child in the name of a brother who had died childless. . . . These genealogies therefore comprise some who succeeded their actual fathers, and some who were the children of one father but were registered as children of another. Thus the memory of both was preserved—of the real and nominal fathers. Thus neither of the Gospels is in error, since they take into account of both nature and law. For the two families, descended from Solomon and Nathan respectively, were so interlocked by the re-marriage of childless widows and the "raising up" of offspring, that the same persons could rightly be regarded at different times as the children of different parents—sometimes the reputed fathers, sometimes the real. Thus both accounts are perfectly true, bringing the line down to Joseph in a manner complex perhaps but certainly accurate.[30]

This complex path, or rather two paths, led the two evangelists, so Africanus believes, to two different fathers of Joseph, one of whom was such according to the law, the other according to the flesh. Eusebius of Caesarea was in agreement with Africanus and notes: "In tracing thus the genealogy of Joseph, Africanus has virtually proved that Mary belonged to the same tribe as her husband, in view of the fact that under the Mosaic law intermarriage between different tribes was forbidden, for the rule is that a woman must wed someone from the same town and the same clan, so that the family inheritance may not be moved from tribe to tribe."[31]

[30]Eusebius of Caesarea, *Ecclesiastical History* 1.7.2–4. Translation from Eusebius of Caesarea, *The History of the Church from Christ to Constantine*, trans. G. A. Williamson (Harmondsworth: Penguin Books, 1989), 20.

[31]Eusebius of Caesarea, *Ecclesiastical History* 1.7.17. Translation from Eusebius of Caesarea, *The History of the Church from Christ to Constantine*, 22–23.

This interpretation is followed by John Damascene (eighth century). After Africanus, he speaks of how the two parallel lines of the descendants of David at a certain point come down to Jacob and Heli, who were

> brothers on the mother's side, Jacob being of the tribe of Solomon and Heli of the tribe of Nathan. Then Heli of the tribe of Nathan died childless, and Jacob his brother, of the tribe of Solomon, took his wife and raised up seed to his brother and begat Joseph. Joseph, therefore, is by nature the son of Jacob, of the line of Solomon, but by law he is the son of Heli of the line of Nathan. . . . But that Joseph is descended from the tribe of David is expressly demonstrated by Matthew and Luke, the most holy evangelists. But Matthew derives Joseph from David through Solomon, while Luke does so through Nathan; while over the holy Virgin's origin both pass in silence.[32]

And yet, in recent centuries the theory that Luke reproduced the genealogy of Mary and not Joseph has gained widespread currency. It was first advanced by the humanist Annius of Viterbo (1432–1505) and later accepted by many scholars. According to this theory, Heli, who is mentioned in Luke immediately after Joseph, was not the father of Joseph, but the father of Mary, and all the subsequent names comprise her genealogy and not his. Annius' theory allows one to disentangle oneself from the apparently unsolvable mystery of the two genealogies more elegantly than by reference to the law of levirate marriage.

Indirect confirmation of this theory can be found in the form in which Luke gives his genealogy. The list of names begins with the words: "And Jesus himself began to be about thirty years of age, being (as was supposed) the son of Joseph, who was the son of Heli" (Lk 3.23). In using the phrase "as was supposed," the evangelist appears to be defending himself from possible accusations of imprecision. Moreover, in the Greek text of the Gospel of Luke, the article *tou* is not used for the name of Joseph in the genealogy, whereas all the other names are given with the definite article. This can mean that Joseph, as the putative father of Jesus, is contrasted with the real ancestors of Jesus according to the maternal line. In this case, the text

[32]John of Damascus, *An Exact Exposition of the Orthodox Faith* 4.14 (*NPNF*[2] 9:84b).

ought to be understood in the sense that Jesus was, "as was supposed," Joseph's son, while being in fact the son (descendant) of Heli and the other persons mentioned—the ancestors of Mary.

A substantial difference between Luke's genealogy and Matthew's genealogy is that Luke traces the line back not to Abraham, but to Adam. In this way, Luke, who addressed his Gospel not to former Jews, but to former Gentiles, accentuates the universal nature of Jesus' mission: he is the son not only of Abraham and David, but foremost "of Adam" and "of God" (Lk 3.38). The expression "son of Adam" is practically identical to the expression "son of man," which Jesus repeatedly uses, since Adam in the Old Testament tradition is seen as the first person and symbol of all humanity [in Hebrew *adam* can also mean "man" or "mankind"—*Ed.*]. And the expression "son of God" emphasizes the point that, while being included in a specific human genealogy, and therefore being fully man, Jesus was at the same time God.

We will not go further into the details of the discussion on the difference between the two genealogies, nor the study of the hypothesis of their supposed sources.[33] We shall only say that the genealogies in both Gospels have not only historical, but also theological significance. The early Christian authors saw in Jesus' genealogy a direct link with the teaching on the redemption of the human race by Jesus as God and Savior. John Chrysostom stated in the fourth century:

> Being Son of the Unoriginate God, and His true Son, He suffered Himself to be called also Son of David, that He might make thee Son of God. He suffered a slave to be father to Him, that He might make the Lord Father to thee a slave. Seest thou at once from the beginning of what nature are the Gospels? If thou doubt concerning the things that pertain to thee, from what belongs to him believe these also. For it is

---

[33]Thus, for example, some scholars believe that Matthew used two sources: one of them dealing with the birth of Jesus from the Virgin without a father, and the other with him as the son of Joseph and descendant of David. Matthew supposedly combined these two mutually exclusive sources, while Luke used Matthew's data, making it broader and more precise. See William Hinsdale Scheide, *The Virgin Birth: A Proposal as to the Source of a Gospel Tradition* (Princeton, NJ: Princeton Theological Seminary, 1995), 139–141. The artificiality of this theory is obvious.

Adam and Eve,
mosaic, 13th c.

far more difficult, judging by human reason, for God to become man, than for a man to be declared a Son of God. When therefore thou art told that the Son of God is Son of David and of Abraham, doubt not any more that thou too, the son of Adam, shall be.[34]

In these words we find an answer to those readers of the New Testament who ask themselves for what purpose the two evangelists included Jesus' genealogy in their narratives. Every person has his genealogy that can be traced back to distant ancestors and through them to the forefather of the human race, Adam. In this sense, all people are related to each other and all of humanity is one family. This is how humanity is viewed in Christianity. By including himself in the human genealogy, God incarnate became a fully-fledged member of the human race, while human beings, as St Symeon the New Theologian says, became his "brothers and kin according to the flesh."[35]

[34]John Chrysostom, *Homilies on the Gospel of Matthew* 2.3 (*NPNF*[1] 10:9–10).
[35]Symeon the New Theologian, *Ethical Discourses* 13.152–155 (SC 129:410). Translation from

If Matthew first of all accentuates Jesus' affinity with his brothers in the flesh—the Jewish nation—then in Luke we find a more universal approach. At the same time, both evangelists, for all their differences in emphases, unambiguously perceive Jesus to be the Son of Man and the Son of God simultaneously, and his coming into the world is considered an event having a bearing on both the chosen nation of the Jews and on humanity as a whole.

---

4. The Events Preceding Jesus' Birth

L et us now examine the Gospel texts concerning the events leading up to the birth of Jesus. These events are described in the Gospel of Luke. They are a sort of prologue to the main part of the text and have practically no parallels in the other Gospels. Some scholars have suggested the existence of a special source originating from a sect of followers of John the Baptist, which Luke supposedly used.[36]

Luke informs us that Jesus and John were related, and that their fates were linked by divine providence even before birth. The news of the birth of John the Baptist was transmitted by the archangel Gabriel to his father Zacharias, an aged, childless priest who was fulfilling his priestly office in the Temple of Jerusalem:

> There was in the days of Herod, the king of Judaea, a certain priest named Zacharias, of the course of Abia, and his wife was of the daughters of Aaron, and her name was Elisabeth. And they were both righteous before God, walking in all the commandments and ordinances

Symeon the New Theologian, *On the Mystical Life: The Ethical Discourses*, vol. 2, *On Virtue and Christian Life*, trans. Alexander Golitzin (Crestwood, NY: St. Vladimir's Seminary Press, 1996), 168.

[36]For an overview and criticism of this theory, see Walter Wink, *John the Baptist in the Gospel Tradition*, Society for New Testament Studies Monograph Series 7 (London: Cambridge University Press, 1968), 60–82.

The Archangel Gabriel Strikes Zacharias Dumb, Alexander Ivanov, 1850s.

of the Lord blameless. And they had no child, because Elisabeth was barren, and they both were well stricken in years. And it came to pass, that while he executed the priest's office before God in the order of his course, according to the custom of the priest's office, his lot was to burn incense when he went into the temple of the Lord. And the whole multitude of the people were praying outside at the time of incense. And there appeared unto him an angel of the Lord standing on the right side of the altar of incense. And when Zacharias saw him, he was troubled, and fear fell upon him. But the angel said unto him, "Fear not, Zacharias, for thy prayer is heard, and thy wife Elisabeth shall bear thee a son, and thou shalt call his name John." (Lk 1.5–13)

The priesthood in ancient Israel was hereditary, and the general population of priests numbered several thousand.[37] However, they were never in the Temple together at the same time: as a rule, the participation of each priest in Temple worship was limited to two weeks of the year. This time was now Zacharias' turn. The priest could also come to the Temple for great feast days, if the distance between the Temple and home allowed it.

---

[37]Using calculations based on historical data, Joachim Jeremias concludes that in the time of Jesus there were 7,200 priests and 9,600 Levites. Jeremias, *Jerusalem in the Time of Jesus*, 203–204.

"Angel with Golden Hair"
(the Archangel Gabriel),
icon, 12th c.

The archangel continues to predict to Zacharias the fate of his son:

> And thou shalt have joy and gladness; and many shall rejoice at his birth. For he shall be great in the sight of the Lord, and shall drink neither wine nor strong drink; and he shall be filled with the Holy Spirit, even from his mother's womb. And many of the children of Israel shall he turn to the Lord their God. And he shall go before him in the spirit and power of Elias, to turn the hearts of the fathers to the children, and the disobedient to the wisdom of the just; to make ready a people prepared for the Lord. (Lk 1.14–17)

Here John is described as a prophet sent to the people of Israel: his mission will not extend to the Gentiles. The image of John drawn by the angel reminds one of the Old Testament images of the Nazarites—people who made (as a rule, for a limited period) a vow to lead an ascetic way of life, in particular, not to drink wine or any other drink made from the grape, not to cut their hair, and not to touch a dead body (Num 6.1–7).

The story of the appearance of the angel to Zacharias reminds us of the biblical stories of how God appeared to the ninety-nine-year-old Abraham and announced to him the birth of his heir. At first, Abraham laughed in reply to this news, not believing the prophecy, and exclaimed: "Shall a child be born unto him that is an hundred years old? And shall Sarah, that is ninety years old, bear?" (Gen 17.17). The second time this prediction was made, Sarah inwardly laughed and said: "After I have grown old shall I have pleasure, my lord being old also?" (Gen 18.12).

In this instance the priest Zacharias does not laugh, but shows the same disbelief:

> And Zacharias said unto the angel, "Whereby shall I know this? For I am an old man, and my wife well stricken in years." And the angel answering said unto him, "I am Gabriel, that stand in the presence

of God; and I am sent to speak unto thee, and to show thee these glad tidings. And, behold, thou shalt be dumb, and not able to speak, until the day that these things shall be performed, because thou believest not my words, which shall be fulfilled in their season." And the people waited for Zacharias, and marveled that he tarried so long in the temple. And when he came out, he could not speak unto them; and they perceived that he had seen a vision in the temple, for he beckoned unto them, and remained speechless. And it came to pass, that, as soon as the days of his ministration were accomplished, he departed to his own house. And after those days his wife Elisabeth conceived, and hid herself five months, saying, "Thus hath the Lord dealt with me in the days wherein he looked on me, to take away my reproach among men." (Lk 1.18–25)

The Annunciation, icon, 12th c.

The words regarding Elisabeth's reproach serve as a reminder that childlessness in ancient Israel was viewed as a curse imposed by God: the childless were looked upon as sinners to whom God had not granted posterity, as a punishment for their sins.

Six months after the angel's appearance to Zacharias, Gabriel announces to the Virgin Mary the coming birth of the Divine Infant, blessing her with the angelic greeting:

And in the sixth month the angel Gabriel was sent from God unto a city of Galilee, named Nazareth, to a virgin betrothed to a man whose name was Joseph, of the house of David; and the virgin's name was Mary. And the angel came in unto her, and said, "Hail, thou that art highly favoured, the Lord is with thee: blessed art thou among women." And when she saw him, she was troubled at his saying, and cast in her mind what manner of salutation this should be. And the angel said unto her, "Fear not, Mary, for thou hast found favour with God. And, behold, thou shalt conceive in thy womb, and bring forth a son, and

shalt call his name Jesus. He shall be great, and shall be called the Son
of the Highest, and the Lord God shall give unto him the throne of
his father David. And he shall reign over the house of Jacob forever,
and of his kingdom there shall be no end." Then said Mary unto the
angel, "How shall this be, seeing I know not a man?" And the angel
answered and said unto her, "The Holy Spirit shall come upon thee,
and the power of the Highest shall overshadow thee. Therefore also
that holy thing which shall be born of thee shall be called the Son of
God." (Lk 1.26–35)

A specific angel—Gabriel—acts, both in the story of the appearance
of the angel to Zacharias and in the story of the annunciation.[38] In the
latter story, Mary is twice referred to as a virgin (*parthenos*). All of her
discourse with the angel is constructed around the topic of the seedless
conception.

From what source could the evangelist Luke have obtained his information on the events described in the opening chapters of his Gospel,
particularly on the annunciation? An answer suggests itself: the Virgin
Mary herself could have imparted the contents of her conversation with
the angel many years later to the disciples. This theory does not seem so
unlikely if we take into account the fact that after Jesus' resurrection, the
apostles "all continued with one accord in prayer and supplication, with
the women, and Mary the mother of Jesus" (Acts 1.14). Shaken by the death
of Jesus and still astonished by his resurrection, they could have asked
Mary about his birth and early years of his life. Some of these stories later
(or perhaps at the time they were told) were written down.

The story of the birth of John is preceded by the story of the encounter
between the two kinswomen, Elisabeth and Mary:

And Mary arose in those days, and went into the hill country with
haste, into a city of Juda, and entered into the house of Zacharias, and
saluted Elisabeth. And it came to pass, that, when Elisabeth heard the
salutation of Mary, the babe leaped in her womb; and Elisabeth was

[38]The veneration of the archangel Gabriel in the Christian Church is based primarily on
this story.

Visitation,
Domenico
Ghirlandaio,
1491.

filled with the Holy Sprit, and she spake out with a loud voice, and said, "Blessed art thou among women, and blessed is the fruit of thy womb. And whence is this to me, that the mother of my Lord should come to me? For, lo, as soon as the voice of thy salutation sounded in mine ears, the babe leaped in my womb for joy. And blessed is she that believed, for there shall be a performance of those things which were told her from the Lord." (Lk 1.39–45)

The leaping of the infant John in the womb has been called by commentators the first prophecy of John the Baptist, who prepared people for the coming of the Messiah. In reply to Elisabeth's blessing, the Virgin Mary praises God, who grants to people his ineffable gifts of grace:

And Mary said, "My soul doth magnify the Lord, and my spirit hath rejoiced in God my Saviour. For he hath regarded the low estate of his handmaiden; for, behold, from henceforth all generations shall call me blessed. For he that is mighty hath done to me great things; and holy is his name. And his mercy is on them that fear him from generation to generation. He hath shown strength with his arm; he hath scattered the proud in the imagination of their hearts. He hath put down the mighty from their seats, and exalted them of low degree. He hath filled the hungry with good things; and the rich he hath sent empty away. He hath helped his servant Israel, in remembrance of his mercy, as he spake to our fathers, to Abraham, and to his seed forever." (Lk 1.46–55)

This hymn of praise, called the Hymn of the Mother of God (the Magnificat), has been a part of church worship since the first centuries. The Hymn of the Mother of God is similar in form to many Old Testament hymns, in particular those that praise God for his aid to the chosen people (Ex 15; Judg 5; 1 Sam 2; Hab 3). It proclaims the fulfillment of the messianic hopes of Israel and all humanity. In the patristic tradition, the Hymn of the Mother of God is sometimes understood as a prophecy about the Church.[39] For the faithful, it is especially precious as one of the few sayings of the Mother of God that are recorded in the Gospels.

The story of the evangelist Luke about the encounter between Elisabeth and the Virgin Mary is one of the most often heard excerpts from the Gospels in Orthodox worship: it is read at matins on feasts of the Mother of God.

Having spent three months with Elisabeth, Mary "returned to her own house" (Lk 1.56). Elisabeth then gives birth to her child, and this birth is accompanied by a miracle:

Now Elisabeth's full time came that she should be delivered; and she brought forth a son. And her neighbors and her cousins heard how the Lord had shown great mercy upon her; and they rejoiced with her. And it came to pass, that on the eighth day they came to circumcise the child; and they called him Zacharias, after the name of his father. And his mother answered and said, "Not so, but he shall be called John." And they said unto her, "There is none of thy kindred that is called by this name." And they made signs to his father, how he would have him called. And he asked for a writing tablet, and wrote, saying,

[39]Irenaeus of Lyons, *Against Heresies* 3.10.2 (*ANF* 1:424).

"His name is John." And they marveled all. And his mouth was opened immediately, and his tongue was loosed, and he spake, and praised God. And fear came on all that dwelt round about them; and all these sayings were noised abroad throughout all the hill country of Judaea. And all they that heard them laid them up in their hearts, saying, "What manner of child shall this be!" And the hand of the Lord was with him. (Lk 1.57–66)

In ancient Israel there was a tradition of passing on names: a newly born infant was named in honor of his father or one of his ancestors. This tradition was broken with the birth of John, because the name of the future prophet was given by God and announced to his parents through an angel.

After this, Zacharias regains his ability to speak, and he utters a prophecy about the fate of his son:

And his father Zacharias was filled with the Holy Spirit, and prophesied, saying, "Blessed be the Lord God of Israel, for he hath visited and redeemed his people, and hath raised up a horn of salvation for us in the house of his servant David, as he spake by the mouth of his holy prophets, which have been since the world began, that we should be saved from our enemies, and from the hand of all that hate us, to perform the mercy promised to our fathers, and to remember his holy covenant, the oath which he sware to our father Abraham, that he would grant unto us, that we being delivered out of the hand of our enemies might serve him without fear, in holiness and righteousness before him, all the days of our life. And thou, child, shalt be called the prophet of the Highest, for thou shalt go before the face of the Lord to prepare his ways, to give knowledge of salvation unto his people by the remission of their sins, through the tender mercy of our God, whereby the dayspring from on high hath visited us, to give light to them that sit in darkness and in the shadow of death, to guide our feet into the way of peace." (Lk 1.67–79)

*Madonna and Child with
the Infant Saint John*, Vittore
Carpaccio, 16th c.

The first part of this prophetic hymn is dedicated to the coming Messiah, in whose person the priest Zacharias sees the special benevolence of God towards the people of Israel and the house of David. The expression "horn of salvation" is borrowed from the Old Testament, where it is one of the names of God: "The Lord is my rock, and my fortress, and my deliverer, the God of my rock, in him will I trust. He is my shield, and the horn of my salvation, my high tower, and my refuge, my saviour. Thou savest me from violence" (2 Sam 22.2–3; cf. Ps 17.2–3). Here this name probably refers to the Messiah, since the "horn of salvation" is not identified as God, but is described as being raised up by God.[40]

The second part of the hymn is devoted to John the Baptist: it foretells his mission "to prepare the way" for the promised Savior. Zacharias' words echo those that he had earlier heard from the angel (Lk 1.14–17). But the Forerunner will always remain in the shadow of the One whom Zacharias calls the "dayspring on high": this expression reminds us of the messianic prophecies about the light that shined on "those that dwell in the land of the shadow of death" (Is 9.2).

The further life of John is conveyed only in brief: "And the child grew, and waxed strong in spirit, and was in the deserts till the day of his showing unto Israel" (Lk 1.80).

---

[40]See Leonard J. Maluf, "Zechariah's 'Benedictus' (Luke 1:68–79): A New Look at a Familiar Text," in *New Perspectives on the Nativity*, ed. Jeremy Corley (New York, NY: T&T Clark, 2009), 53–56.

5. The Virgin Birth

The story of the birth of Jesus is reported by two of the evangelists, Matthew and Luke. The Gospel of Luke gives us the following account of this event:

> And it came to pass in those days, that there went out a decree from Caesar Augustus, that all the world should be taxed. (This taxing was first made when Quirinius was governor of Syria.) And all went to be taxed, every one into his own city. And Joseph also went up from Galilee, out of the city of Nazareth, into Judaea, unto the city of David, which is called Bethlehem (because he was of the house and lineage of David), to be taxed with Mary his betrothed wife, being great with child. And so it was, that, while they were there, the days were accomplished that she should be delivered. And she brought forth her firstborn son, and wrapped him in swaddling clothes, and laid him in a manger; because there was no room for them in the inn. And there were in the same country shepherds abiding in the field, keeping watch over their flock by night. And, lo, the angel of the Lord came upon them, and the glory of the Lord shone round about them: and they were sore afraid. And the angel said unto them, "Fear not, for behold, I bring you good tidings of great joy, which shall be to all people. For unto you is born this day in the city of David a Savior, which is Christ the Lord. And this shall be a sign unto you: ye shall find the babe wrapped in swaddling clothes, lying in a manger." And suddenly there was with the angel a multitude of the heavenly host praising God, and saying, "Glory to God in the highest, and on earth peace, good will toward men." And it came to pass, as the angels were gone away from them into heaven, the shepherds said one to another, "Let us now go even unto Bethlehem, and see this thing which is come to pass, which the Lord hath made known unto us." And they came with haste, and found Mary, and Joseph, and the babe lying in a manger. And when they had seen it, they made

The Nativity, fresco, Giotto, 1305–1313.

known abroad the saying which was told them concerning this child. And all they that heard it wondered at those things which were told them by the shepherds. But Mary kept all these things, and pondered them in her heart. And the shepherds returned, glorifying and praising God for all the things that they had heard and seen, as it was told unto them. (Lk 2.1–20)

In the Gospel of Matthew we have another version of the same story, which is substantially different from Luke's version:

Now the birth of Jesus Christ was on this wise: when as his mother Mary was betrothed to Joseph, before they came together, she was found with child of the Holy Spirit. Then Joseph her husband, being a just man, and not willing to make her a public example, was minded to put her away privately. But while he thought on these things, behold, the angel of the Lord appeared unto him in a dream, saying, "Joseph, thou son of David, fear not to take unto thee Mary thy wife, for that which is conceived in her is of the Holy Spirit. And she shall bring forth a son, and thou shalt call his name Jesus, for he shall save his people from their sins." Now all this was done, that it might be fulfilled which was spoken of the Lord by the prophet, saying, "Behold, a virgin shall be with child, and shall bring forth a son, and they shall call his name Emmanuel," [Is 7.14] which being interpreted is, "God with us." Then Joseph being raised from sleep did as the angel of the Lord had bidden him, and took unto him his wife, and knew her not till she had brought forth her firstborn son, and he called his name Jesus. (Mt 1.18–25)

We note that while the appearances of the angel in Luke—to Zacharias (Lk 1.11–20) and Mary (Lk 1.26–38)—occurred in broad daylight, in Matthew Joseph four times receives a revelation in his dreams (Mt 1.20–23; 2.13; 2.19; 2.22). The wise men (Mt 2.12) and Pilate's wife (Mt 27.19) also received revelations in their sleep. In Matthew there are six

instances of revelations in dreams,[41] which makes
Matthew different from the three other evangelists, who mention no such revelations. Scholars
have seen in this the influence of the Old Testament tradition, in which dreams are accorded
great meaning.[42]

The familiar Greek term *genesis* ("birth," "origin"),
encountered in the very first verse of the Gospel of
Matthew, is translated by the word "nativity." Further, Matthew contains the story of the adoration of
the Magi, which is absent in Luke:

> Now when Jesus was born in Bethlehem of Judaea
> in the days of Herod the king, behold, there came
> wise men from the east to Jerusalem, saying,
> "Where is he that is born King of the Jews? For
> we have seen his star in the east, and are come

*The Appearance of the
Angel to St Joseph*, Giovanni
Baglione, ca. 1599.

> to worship him." When Herod the king had heard
> these things, he was troubled, and all Jerusalem with him. And when
> he had gathered all the chief priests and scribes of the people together,
> he demanded of them where Christ should be born. And they said
> unto him, "In Bethlehem of Judaea, for thus it is written by the prophet,
> 'And thou Bethlehem, in the land of Juda, art not the least among the
> princes of Juda. For out of thee shall come a Governor, that shall rule
> my people Israel.' [Mic 5.2]" Then Herod, when he had privately called
> the wise men, inquired of them diligently what time the star appeared.
> And he sent them to Bethlehem, and said, "Go and search diligently for
> the young child, and when ye have found him, bring me word again,
> that I may come and worship him also." When they had heard the
> king, they departed. And, lo, the star, which they saw in the east, went

---

[41]Derek S. Dodson, *Reading Dreams: An Audience-Critical Approach to the Dreams in the
Gospel of Matthew*, The Library of New Testament Studies Series (New York, NY: T&T Clark
International, 2009), 134.

[42]George M. Soares Prabhu, *The Formula Quotations in the Infancy Narrative of Matthew*,
Analecta Biblica 63 (Rome: Biblical Institute Press, 1976), 185–187, 223–225.

The Marriage of the Virgin,
Raphael, 1504.

before them, till it came and stood over where the young child was. When they saw the star, they rejoiced with exceeding great joy. And when they were come into the house, they saw the young child with Mary his mother, and fell down, and worshipped him. And when they had opened their treasures, they presented unto him gifts: gold, and frankincense, and myrrh. And being warned by God in a dream that they should not return to Herod, they departed into their own country another way. (Mt 2.1–12)

Both evangelists agree that Jesus was born of a virgin without a husband, and in both instances the Holy Spirit is mentioned. How are we to understand the action of the Holy Spirit in the birth of Jesus, and what is the meaning of Jesus' birth from a virgin without the participation of a husband? For the evangelists who wrote about this, the meaning is obvious: Jesus was born by supernatural means because he was not only the Son of David and the Son of Abraham, not only the Son of Man, but also the Son of God. As the Son of Man, he is born from Mary—the representative of the whole human race. But as the Son of God, he is born of God himself through the action of the Holy Spirit.

Meanwhile, in the New Testament Jesus is never called the Son of the Holy Spirit: he is the Son of God the Father; the Holy Spirit merely participates in his birth by descending upon Mary, but is not his parent. St Maximus the Confessor refers to the opinion of "some among the saints," according to whom Jesus received a soul from the Holy Spirit "in the manner of the man's seed," while his "flesh is formed from the virginal blood."[43] Modern-day commentators interpret the birth from the Virgin in more generalized terms: "The virgin birth is not to be understood as a

---

[43]Maximus the Confessor, *Questions and Doubts* 50 (PG 90:797). Translation from Maximus the Confessor, *St. Maximus the Confessor's Questions and Doubts*, trans. Despina D. Prassas (DeKalb, IL: Northern Illinois University Press, 2010), 72.

The Adoration
of the Magi,
mosaic, 12th c.

comment on the biological process of conception: it points towards the essence of the person of Jesus in his unique relationship to God as the Son of God."[44]

In the subsequent Church tradition the strong conviction arose that Jesus was born of the Virgin without a husband because the act of conception was linked to sin, whereas the Son of God was free from sin. This is not evident from the Gospel narrative: here it is said that the Son of the Virgin will come to save his people from their sins, but it is not said that the act of a man and woman conceiving a child is itself sinful. At the same time, the notion of the act of conception being harnessed to sin is present already in the Old Testament; it is expressed particularly in the familiar words of the psalm: "Behold, I was conceived in iniquities, and in sins did my mother bear me" (Ps 50.5). Here we are dealing not with the sinfulness of sexual relations between a man and a woman: such an idea contradicts the Bible and does not originate from it. We are dealing here with the

---

[44]Pokorný and Heckel, *Einleitung in das Neue Testament*, 448–449.

*The Adoration
of the Magi,*
Leonardo da
Vinci, 1480s.

ancestral sin that is transmitted, through the act of conception, from one
person to another, from father to son.

This theme is to be found in the New Testament in the apostle Paul,
who draws a parallel between Adam and Christ: "For as in Adam all die,
even so in Christ shall all be made alive. . . . The first man Adam was made
a living soul; the last Adam was made a life-giving spirit. . . . The first man
is of the earth, earthly; the second man is the Lord from heaven" (1 Cor
15.22, 45, 47). It is Paul who develops the teaching that "as by one man sin
entered into the world, and death by sin; and so death passed upon all men,
for all have sinned" (Rom 5.12). It is more than plausible that the evangelist
Luke, Paul's traveling companion, was familiar with the Pauline epistles or
with their ideas, which Paul could have expressed orally. It is possible that
the decision to extend the genealogy of Jesus from Adam to God was made
by Luke under the influence of Paul's teaching on the parallel between the
first Adam and the second Adam, Christ.

The prophecy of Isaiah, which is quoted in the Gospel of Matthew,
is taken from the Greek translation of the Septuagint, where the word
actually used is "virgin" (*parthenos*). In the Hebrew text of the Bible that

has come down to us, in this place we have the word *'almā*, which means "young woman." As early as the second century, church writers already noted this discrepancy: in his polemical dispute with Trypho the Jew, who believed the prophecy of Isaiah was about the king Hezekiah and not Jesus, Justin insists that the reading of the Septuagint regarding the birth of Jesus from the Virgin is correct.[45] Justin even puts forward the theory that the Jews had consciously distorted the original text of Scripture. The theory, however, that the text of the Septuagint in this instance contains the original reading, whereas the Jews after Christ deliberately distorted the text in order to remove it as far as possible from a Christian understanding by substituting the word *bətulā* (virgin) with the word *'almā*, has no textual confirmation.

No matter what the original reading of the prophecy of Isaiah was, it is clear to us that the teaching about the birth of Jesus from the Virgin was an integral part of the Christian *kērygma* (preaching) from the very beginning—at least, from the appearance of the New Testament writings. Matthew and Luke imparted to this teaching a literary form, while John and Paul placed it in a theological framework. It is true that neither in John's writings nor in Paul's epistles is Jesus' birth from the Virgin directly mentioned. However, both apostles—Matthew and Luke—believe that Jesus is the Son of God and that his coming into the world possessed an unusual, supernatural quality. The idea of the virgin birth of Jesus fits perfectly into this theological vision.

The name "Jesus" (*yēsua'*, shortened from *yēhosua'*) in translation from the Hebrew literally means "the Lord is salvation."[46] Moreover, it sounds like the Hebrew word *yəsuā*, "salvation":[47] in Matthew the words "he shall save his people from their sins" are a direct interpretation of the meaning of this name. For both Gospel writers, the name "Jesus" is understood to

---

[45]Justin Martyr, *Dialogue with Trypho* 43 (PG 6:568–569).

[46]Ludwig Koehler and Walter Baumgartner, *Hebräisches und Aramäisches Lexikon zum Alten Testament*, Lfg. 2 (Leiden: Brill, 1974), 379. The name *yəhosua'* is a combination of the theophoric element *yəho* with a formation from the root *šw'* ("to help," "to save") (ibid., Lfg. 4 [Leiden: Brill, 1990], 1339–1340). See also ibid., Lfg. 2, 425–426.

[47]Koehler and Baumgartner, *Hebräisches und Aramäisches Lexikon zum Alten Testament*, Lfg. 2, 426.

Savior
Emmanuel,
fresco, 14th c.

be the name given to him by the angel before his conception in the womb
(Lk 2.21). In Matthew, however, the angel announces this name to Joseph
in a dream, whereas in Luke the angel announces it to Mary when she is
awake. We note that in the Gospel of Matthew the name Jesus is encountered around 150 times—around the same as in the Gospels of Mark and
Luke taken together.[48]

It is not clear to every modern-day reader why the prophecy of the
giving of the name Emmanuel is fulfilled in the giving of the name Jesus. It
becomes evident in the context of the biblical understanding of the name.
In the Old Testament, a name was taken to be not merely a conventional
designation for a particular person or object, or as a combination of sounds
and letters, allowing one to distinguish one person from another. In the
language of the Bible, a name indicates the fundamental characteristics of
its bearer, it reveals his innermost essence.[49] God in the Old Testament is
given many names, while one name, *Yahwē* (Yahweh, Jehovah, the Lord),

[48]Richard A. Burridge, *Four Gospels, One Jesus?: A Symbolic Reading*, 2nd ed. (Grand Rapids,
MI: Eerdmans, 2005), 70.
[49]Oscar Cullman, *Prayer in the New Testament: With Answers from the New Testament to
Today's Questions* (London: SCM Press, 1994), 44.

is perceived to be his personal name.⁵⁰ It is practically identified with God himself and is surrounded with special reverence. In the post-exilic period, the Jews even ceased to pronounce this name aloud as a sign of their special awe before it.

The Old Testament theology of the name is fully reflected in the New Testament. The appearances of the angel to Zacharias, Mary, and Joseph, described in the Gospels of Matthew and Luke, bear a direct relation to the theology of the name. In all three instances the Good News consists of two parts: the angel at first speaks of the birth of a son, and then of the name that he will be given. The angel says to Zacharias: "Fear not, Zacharias: for thy prayer is heard; and thy wife Elisabeth shall bear thee a son, and thou shalt call his name John" (Lk 1.13). The angel comes to Mary six months later with analogous news: "Fear not, Mary; for thou hast found favour with God. And, behold, thou shalt conceive in thy womb, and bring forth a son, and shalt call his name Jesus" (Lk 1.30–31). Finally, the angel appears to Joseph in a dream with the words: "And she shall bring forth a son, and thou shalt call his name Jesus" (Mt 1.21).

The angel's naming of Jesus has a special significance. The sacred name of Yahweh (the Lord) is present in the name of Jesus, which now acquires an additional overtone: it is not the majesty, nor the power, nor the glory of Yahweh that is glorified, but his saving strength. We can say that the good news of the New Testament begins with the appearance of a new name of God, which is genetically linked to the sacred name Yahweh, but which, nevertheless, points towards the inception of a new era in the mutual relationship between God and humanity. Henceforth God was for people not "a jealous God, visiting the iniquity of the fathers upon the children unto the third and fourth generation" (Ex 20.5), but the One who "shall save his people from their sins" (Mt 1.21).

---

⁵⁰For more details see Metropolitan Hilarion Alfeyev, *Orthodox Christianity*, vol. 2, *Doctrine and Teaching of the Orthodox Church*, trans. Andrew Smith (Yonkers, NY: St Vladimir's Seminary Press, 2012), 63–74.

Savior
Emmanuel with
archangels, icon,
17th c.

The name Emmanuel, which literally means "God is with us," does not sound like the name Jesus, but is semantically linked with it: in both names the mention of God is present. We may say that the two names are different in form, but similar in content. It is for this reason that the presence of both names in one and the same narrative did not puzzle either the evangelist Matthew, writing for those who were still familiar with the Hebrew language, or his first readers.

To the above we ought to add that in Jesus' time many Jews had two names, the second of which was more of a nickname than a personal name. The second such name in the Gospels for Jesus was the name Christ ("the Anointed One"), with which he has entered history.

The name Emmanuel, however, has also been preserved in Church tradition, in particular in certain liturgical hymns, as well as in iconography. The iconographic type in which Christ is depicted as a youth with curly hair is called the "Savior Emmanuel." This type, which we find in the frescoes of the catacombs in Rome and the mosaics in Ravenna, became widespread throughout Byzantium and Rus'.

6. The Circumstances of Jesus' Birth

As we have seen, the evangelists Matthew and Luke describe the events accompanying the birth of Jesus in a fair amount of detail: the adoration of the Magi (Mt 2.1–12) and shepherds (Lk 2.8–20), the circumcision of Jesus (Lk 2.21), and his presentation in the Temple of Jerusalem (Lk 2.22–38). Events that took place approximately two years after Jesus' birth are described in Matthew: these are the flight of Joseph and Mary with the Infant to Egypt (Mt 2.13–15) and the slaughter of the innocents by an enraged King Herod (Mt 2.16–18).

Of these stories, only one has a parallel in the historical literature beyond the Christian tradition: the slaughter of the innocents. This episode is mentioned in the work of the pagan author Macrobius, the *Saturnalia*, which says of the emperor Augustus: "On hearing that the son of Herod, king of the Jews, had been slain when Herod ordered that all boys in Syria under the age of two be killed, Augustus said, 'It's better to be Herod's pig than his son.'"[51] Of course, we may surmise that Macrobius, a Neoplatonist living in the fifth century, knew of Herod's slaughter of the innocents from Christian sources, and that the story of the emperor Augustus' reaction was no more than an anecdote. Nonetheless, the presence of this reference in Macrobius serves as indirect confirmation of the historicity of Matthew's narrative on the slaughter of the innocents. Of Herod's unbelievable cruelty and that he executed three of his sons (although it is true that none of them were children at the time they were executed) we know from other sources.[52]

The stories of the circumstances connected to Jesus' birth are interesting not so much from the historical as from the theological perspective. Each of these stories accentuates the special nature of Jesus' birth from the Virgin as an event that transcends the boundaries of normal human history. The genealogy of Jesus, the appearance of the angels, Joseph's

---

[51]Macrobius, *Saturnalia* 2.4.11 (Kaster, LCL).
[52]Josephus, *Wars of the Jews* 1.27.6; 1.33.6.

*The Massacre of
the Innocents,*
fresco, Giotto,
1305–1313.

dreams, and other details of the story illustrate the fundamental message
that God has intervened in human history by sending his Messiah to earth,
whose coming fulfilled the hopes and expectations of the chosen people
of God.[53]

In the account of the arrival of wise men from the east we notice the
evangelist's lack of concrete detail when describing their origin and occupation. The term "wise men" (in Greek, *magoi*) in classical literature was
used quite widely and could in a narrow sense denote priests of the Zoro-
astrian religion or the Babylonian astrologer priests, or in a broader sense
denote astrologers in general or diviners (magicians). Since the story is
about wise men "from the east," we may surmise, taking into account the
geographical location of Bethlehem and Palestine, that they came from
Persia or Babylon. Justin Martyr (second century) believes that the wise
men came from "Arabia";[54] however, in his time this geographic term was
used in a general sense and referred to the so-called Arabia Petraea.[55]

[53]Cf. Margaret Hannan, *The Nature and Demands of the Sovereign Rule of God in the Gospel
of Matthew* (London: T&T Clark, 2006), 21.
[54]Justin Martyr, *Dialogue with Trypho* 88 (PG 6:685).
[55]The region whose capital was in Petra (modern Jordan).

The silver star in the Grotto of the Nativity in Bethlehem

Very different theories exist regarding the star that the wise men "saw in the east." As early as 1614 the German astronomer Johannes Kepler proposed that the Gospel of Matthew was speaking of the "star" that had appeared as a result of the conjunction of the planets Jupiter and Saturn in the constellation Pisces in 7 BC. Other theories have also been put forward, among which is that of the light of a supernova in the year of Jesus' birth. However, considering the fact that the star led the wise men in a definite direction, we can surmise that the wise men saw a bright comet, the tail of which was directed in such a manner that it would have shown them the way. Chinese sources note three comets in the years 12, 5, and 4 BC. The comet in 5 BC appeared in the period between March 6 and April 9 and was observed for seventy days in the constellation Capricorn.[56] It is possible that this is what the wise men also saw.[57]

[56]Konradin Ferrari d'Occhieppo, *Der Stern von Bethlehem: in astronomischer Sicht: Legende oder Tatsache?* (Giessen: Brunnen, 1991).

[57]St John interpreted the "star" not as an astronomical phenomenon, but as an angelic manifestation for several reasons: (1) it moved from north to south, not from east to west (presuming the magi came from Persia to Palestine); (2) the star appeared in daylight; (3) it disappeared for a time (the reason the magi ask Herod about the Child [Mt 2.2]), which Chrysostom compares to the pillar of fire in the wilderness; (4) when the star reappears, it leads the wise men to a particular house, which is not possible for a star or comet. Chrysostom, *Homilies on Matthew* 6.3 (*NPNF*[1] 10:37–38).

*The
Circumcision,*
Rembrandt, 1661.

The appearance of the star that heralded the birth of Jesus and the adoration of the wise men before Jesus was already being interpreted in the early Church as a symbol of how Christianity was to subdue paganism and magic:

> A star shone in heaven brighter than all the stars, and its light was indescribable and its newness brought amazement. All the other stars, with the sun and the moon, formed a chorus to the star, whose light surpassed all other. There was agitation regarding its origin, as it was new, and unlike any other. So was all sorcery undone, and every bond of evil brought to nothing. Ignorance was destroyed and the ancient realm brought down as God appeared in a human manner for the renewal of eternal life. What had been prepared by God received its beginning.[58]

In the opening chapters of the Gospels of Matthew and Luke, which describe the events linked to Jesus' birth, the angels play a great role. There are many stories in the Old Testament about the appearance of angels to men. Angels were perceived not only as messengers from God, the heralds of the divine will, but also as participants in human history. Angels serve

---

[58]Ignatius of Antioch, *Epistle to the Ephesians* 19.2–3 (PPS 49:41).

The Meeting
of the Lord,
miniature from
the Menologion
of Basil II, 10th c.

as the connecting link between the world of men and the celestial world
in which God abides. The participation of the angels in the events linked
to Jesus' birth accentuates his divine origin. From the very first chapters
of the two Gospel narratives, Jesus is portrayed as the promised Messiah,
the birth of whom is heralded by a host of angels.

Like all male Jewish infants, Jesus was circumcised. In Luke's account,
we note numerous references to the Mosaic Law, which the evangelist calls
the law of the Lord:

> And when eight days were accomplished for the circumcising of the
> child, his name was called Jesus, who was so named by the angel before
> he was conceived in the womb. And when the days of her purification
> according to the law of Moses were accomplished, they brought him to
> Jerusalem, to present him to the Lord (as it is written in the law of the
> Lord, "Every male that openeth the womb shall be called holy to the
> Lord" [Ex 13.2, 12]) and to offer a sacrifice according to that which is
> said in the law of the Lord, "a pair of turtledoves, or two young pigeons."
> [cf. Lev 12.2–8] And, behold, there was a man in Jerusalem, whose
> name was Simeon. And the same man was just and devout, waiting
> for the consolation of Israel, and the Holy Spirit was upon him. And it
> was revealed unto him by the Holy Spirit, that he should not see death,
> before he had seen the Lord's Christ. And he came by the Spirit into the

temple, and when the parents brought in the child Jesus, to do for him according to the custom of the law, then took he him up in his arms, and blessed God, and said, "Lord, now lettest thou thy servant depart in peace, according to thy word. For mine eyes have seen thy salvation, which thou hast prepared before the face of all people, a light to enlighten the Gentiles, and the glory of thy people Israel." And Joseph and his mother marveled at those things which were spoken of him. And Simeon blessed them, and said unto Mary his mother, "Behold, this child is set for the fall and rising again of many in Israel; and for a sign which shall be spoken against (yea, a sword shall pierce through thy own soul also) that the thoughts of many hearts may be revealed." And there was one Anna, a prophetess, the daughter of Phanuel, of the tribe of Asher; she was of a great age, and had lived with a husband seven years from her virginity, and she was a widow of about eighty-four years, who departed not from the temple, but served God with fasting and prayers night and day. And she coming in that instant gave thanks likewise unto the Lord, and spake of him to all them that looked for redemption in Jerusalem. And when they had performed all things according to the law of the Lord, they returned into Galilee, to their own city Nazareth. (Lk 2.21–39)

The custom of circumcising male infants goes back to God's covenant with Abraham, whom God commanded: "And he that is eight days old shall be circumcised among you, every male child in your generations, he that is born in the house, or bought with money of any stranger, who is not of thy seed. He that is born in thy house, and he that is bought with thy money, must be circumcised; and my covenant shall be in your flesh for an everlasting covenant" (Gen 17.12–13). The Christian Church abolished this custom at an early stage as a result of the decision to open up the Church to the "uncircumcised," that is, the Gentiles (Acts 11.3). The apostle Paul developed the teaching of the Church as the New Israel, where "there is neither Greek nor Jew, circumcision nor uncircumcision" (Col 3.11).

Nonetheless, Luke, undoubtedly familiar with Paul's theology and writing for the Gentiles, is the only one of the Gospel writers who believes it necessary to mention that Jesus was circumcised as a sign of his belonging to the chosen people of God—the Jews. Luke is also the only one who tells how the infant Jesus was brought into the Temple of Jerusalem in order to "present him to the Lord."

Both stories—the circumcision of Jesus and his presentation in the Temple—demonstrate Joseph's and Mary's fidelity to the Mosaic Law:

> If a woman has conceived seed, and given birth to a male child, then she shall be unclean seven days; according to the days of the separation for her infirmity shall she be unclean. And in the eighth day the flesh of his foreskin shall be circumcised. And she shall then continue in the blood of her purifying thirty-three days; she shall touch no hallowed thing, nor come into the sanctuary, until the days of her purifying are fulfilled. ... And when the days of her purifying are fulfilled, for a son, or for a daughter, she shall bring a lamb of the first year for a burnt offering, and a young pigeon, or a turtledove, for a sin offering, unto the door of the tabernacle of the congregation, unto the priest, who shall offer it before the Lord, and make an atonement for her. And she shall be cleansed from the issue of her blood. This is the law for her that hath given birth to a male or a female. And if she is not able to bring a lamb, then she shall bring two turtledoves, or two young pigeons: the one for the burnt offering, and the other for a sin offering, and the priest shall make an atonement for her, and she shall be clean. (Lev 12.2–4, 6–8)

The sacrifice of purification, or the sacrifice for sin, had a redemptive and purifying effect. It was offered after voluntary or involuntary sins had been committed, as well as at the end of a woman's period of physical impurity. The rite of purification was performed on the fortieth day after the birth of a male infant. Two turtledoves or two young pigeons were brought by the woman who did not have sufficient means to bring a lamb: this confirms that Joseph was a man of modest means, in spite of

The Meeting of
the Lord, fresco,
16th c.

his coming from the line of David. The fact that no place could be found
for Joseph and Mary at the inn at Bethlehem is also indirect testimony to
Joseph's limited means.

The words uttered by Simeon when he took the Infant in his arms (Lk
2.29–32) emphasize the significance of the Messiah not only for the people
of Israel, but also for "all peoples," that is, for the Gentiles. A scholar who
wished to isolate the image of the "historical Simeon" from the Gospel
story would no doubt stumble upon these words and declare them to be
devoid of all veracity, since the elder, brought up in strict Jewish traditions,
"a man who was just and devout, waiting for the consolation of Israel"
(Lk 2.25), could in no way foretell that Jesus would become the Savior not
only of the people of Israel, but also of "all peoples" and the Gentiles. And
yet, the notion of the universality of the mission of Jesus who was born
in Bethlehem became a part of the Church's teaching at a very early stage
of her historical existence, and this idea is reflected in full measure in the
opening chapters of the Gospel of Luke.

Simeon addresses these words to Mary: "Yea, a sword shall pierce
through thy own soul also" (Lk 2.35). This is the first prophecy in the Gospels of Christ's sufferings and the sufferings of his Mother connected to
them. In Church tradition, the teaching arose that at Jesus' birth, Mary did
not experience the usual pains of birth. According to John Damascene, the

The Meeting of
the Lord, mosaic,
13th c.

Most Holy Virgin "brought him into the world without suffering the pains
that adhere to our nature,"[59] yet she experienced this pain when she stood
by the cross of Jesus "when she beheld Him, Whom she knew to be God
by the manner of His generation, killed as a malefactor."[60]

The accounts of the evangelists Matthew and Luke form the basis of
the feast of the Nativity of Christ—the second most important feast in the
Christian calendar after Pascha. A fixed date—December 25—was chosen
for this feast. Originally there was only one feast in the church calendar—
Epiphany on January 6, instituted no later than the second century. At the
same time, Epiphany was taken to be a whole series of events tied to the
incarnation of the Son of God, including the birth of Jesus from the Virgin
and his baptism in the Jordan.

The feast of the Nativity of Christ, celebrated separately from Epiphany
on the December 25, appeared in the west no later than in the third century.[61] The beginning of a separate celebration of the Nativity of Christ in
the east can be dated to the last quarter of the fourth century. In his homily
on the Nativity, delivered between 386 and 388 in Antioch, John Chrysostom says: "Although ten years have not yet elapsed since we have come to
know this day, as it seems that it was given to us so long and so many years

---

[59]John of Damascus, *Second Homily on the Dormition* 3 (Daley, PPS).
[60]John of Damascus, *An Exact Exposition of the Orthodox Faith* 4.14 (*NPNF*[2] 9:86b).
[61]Gregory Dix, *The Shape of the Liturgy*, new ed. (London: Continuum, 2005), 357.

ago, so too has it been glorified by your zeal."[62] The expression "ten years have not yet lapsed" may, correspondingly, point to the years 377–388 as the time when the feast of the Nativity was instituted in Antioch.

In Jerusalem, in contrast, for a very long time, most likely up until the sixth century, the Nativity was celebrated along with Epiphany on January 6.[63] Also for quite a long time the same common feast day survived in the calendar of the Church of Alexandria.[64] The tradition of the joint celebration of the birth of Jesus from the Virgin and his baptism in the Jordan has survived in the Oriental (the non-Chalcedonian) Churches.

The narratives from the Gospel of Luke also form the basis of three other Church feasts: of the Annunciation, the Circumcision of the Lord, and the Presentation in the Temple. The Nativity was used as the point from which the dates of these feasts were established: the Annunciation is celebrated on March 25, nine months before the Nativity; the Circumcision on the eighth day after the Nativity; and the Presentation in the Temple on the fortieth day. The liturgical texts for these feasts contain theological commentary on the excerpts read from Luke's Gospel.

7. The Place of Jesus' Birth

B oth the evangelists who tell the story of Jesus' birth name the town of Bethlehem as the place of his birth. Different explanations, however, are given for this.

Matthew does not mention where Mary and Joseph come from according to their lineage. He asserts that "Jesus was born in Bethlehem of Judaea in the days of Herod the king" (Mt 2.1). It is in Bethlehem that the wise men

---

[62]John Chrysostom, *Homily on the Nativity of Our Savior* (PG 49:351). [Trans. present translator.]

[63]Archbishop Sergiy (Spasskiy), *Polny mesyatseslov Vostoka* [The complete Menaion of the East], vol. 3, *Svyatoy Vostok. Chasti vtoraya i tret'ya* [The holy East. Parts two and three] (Moscow: Pravoslavnyy palomnik, 1997), 522.

[64]Dix, *The Shape of the Liturgy*, 358.

Nazareth
(excavations of
the ancient city)

from the east (Mt 2.11) find Mary with the Infant as they enter the house, and it is Bethlehem and its environs that become the location of the bloody drama of the slaughter of the innocents at the command of Herod (Mt 2.16). Then follows the story of the flight of Joseph and Mary into Egypt and their return to Judea, after which Joseph, "being warned by God in a dream, he turned aside into the parts of Galilee, and he came and dwelt in a city called Nazareth, that it might be fulfilled which was spoken by the prophets, 'He shall be called a Nazarene'" (Mt 2.22–23).

All of this, we may surmise, took place over a period of no less than three years, considering the age of the infants murdered by Herod, to which we should add the time of the journey of the Holy Family to Egypt and back. From the story it follows that Matthew believed Bethlehem to be Joseph's native town, since his "house" was located there. The relocation to Nazareth is depicted as a forced move.

Luke draws a different picture. He begins his account with the story of the parents of John the Baptist: Zacharias, a priest, "of the course of Abia," and his wife Elisabeth "of the daughters of Aaron" (Lk 1.5). Their house was located in hill country "in a city of Juda" (Lk 1.39). It was to this place that the Virgin Mary came to greet Elisabeth. "A city of Juda" could be taken to mean any city that historically belonged to the tribe of Judah. However, it was no later than the sixth century that the tradition was established of identifying the city of Juda with the village of Ain Karem, situated to the southwest of Jerusalem (now within the city's limits).[65]

Meanwhile, Mary, according to Luke, lived in "a city of Galilee, named Nazareth" (Lk 1.26). Joseph is also mentioned as coming "from Galilee, out of the city of Nazareth" (Lk 2.4). Both Joseph and Mary were in Bethlehem as a result of the census: "Joseph came unto the city of David, which is called Bethlehem; (because he was of the house and lineage of David)." The birth of the Infant took place in Bethlehem, yet not in a house but in a stable. This is indicated by the words "she wrapped him in swaddling clothes, and laid him in a manger, because there was no room for them in the inn" (Lk 2.4, 7). The word "manger" (*phatnē*) does not mean a child's cradle, but a trough for feeding cattle, into which the newly born Infant was laid for lack of a more worthy place. In the story of the shepherds' adoration of the Infant, the "babe . . . lying in a manger" (Lk 2.12, 16) is mentioned twice. Thus, according to Luke, Joseph had no house in Bethlehem.

Then there are the accounts of the circumcision and naming of Jesus, and then his being brought into the Temple. The accounts are concluded with the words: "And when they had performed all things according to the law of the Lord, they returned into Galilee, to their own city Nazareth" (Lk 2.39). Thus, in Luke the gap between Jesus' birth and the return of the Holy Family to their native city of Nazareth was a little more than forty days (it could hardly have been possible to have lived in a stable much longer).

Whose account accords with reality to a greater degree and who imparts the more exact information on where Joseph's own home was located: Matthew or Luke? Scholars have answered this question in different ways. We cannot exclude the possibility that Luke in this case is more precise, as the geographical locations of the events he describes in connection with Jesus' birth are elaborated in more detail.

Commenting on the differences between Matthew and Luke in describing the events linked to the story of Jesus' birth, St Augustine writes:

---

[65]See, for example, Sloyan, *The Crucifixion of Jesus*, 11.

With respect to the city of Bethlehem, Matthew and Luke are at one. But Luke explains in what way and for what reason Joseph and Mary came to it; whereas Matthew gives no such explanation. . . . The evangelist constructs his own particular narrative on a kind of plan which gives it the appearance of being the complete and orderly record of the events in their succession. For, preserving a simple silence on the subject of those incidents of which he intends to give no account, he then connects those which he does wish to relate with what he has been immediately recounting, in such a manner as to make the recital seem continuous. At the same time, when one of them mentions facts of which the other has given no notice, the order of narrative, if carefully considered, will be found to indicate the point at which the writer by whom the omissions are made has taken the leap in his account, and thus has attached the facts, which it was his purpose to introduce, in such a manner to the preceding context as to give the appearance of a connected series, in which the one incident follows immediately on the other, without the interposition of anything else. On this principle, therefore, we understand that where he tells us how the wise men were warned in a dream not to return to Herod, and how they went back to their own country by another way, Matthew has simply omitted all that Luke has related respecting all that happened to the Lord in the temple, and all that was said by Simeon and Anna; while, on the other hand, Luke has omitted in the same place all notice of the journey into Egypt, which is given by Matthew, and has introduced the return to the city of Nazareth as if it were immediately consecutive.[66]

In this way, Augustine considers the two accounts of Christ's Nativity to be complementary. He believes that Matthew merely omits the story of Mary's and Joseph's arrival in Bethlehem that Luke tells, while Luke, for his part, omits an entire series of events described by Matthew. Nevertheless, we have seen how it is impossible, no matter how we wish, to completely harmonize the accounts of the two evangelists.

---

[66] Augustine, *The Harmony of the Gospels* 2.5.15–16 (*NPNF*[1] 6:108–109).

Tikhvin icon of the Mother of
God with miracle scenes.

What is the cause of the divergences between
them? It would appear that it is primarily in how
each of the evangelists understands the events
from the theological perspective. We ought not
to forget that the Gospels are not merely biographies or historical chronicles. Each Gospel is
first of all a theological treatise in which the life
of Jesus is inserted into a definite theological
context.

The Gospels are a sort of verbal icon, in
some ways similar to Byzantine and Old Russian icons with marginal scenes. The defining
feature of these icons is that the main image is in the center, while on
the edges within frames there are numerous windows (marginal scenes)
with various side subjects. If two icons of the Nativity of Christ were to
be produced on the basis of the two Gospel narratives, then the central
composition would be identical, while the marginal scenes would differ
substantially in both content and quantity.

Luke, it appears, knows far more details concerning the story of Jesus'
birth. He inserts this story into another story, that of the circumstances of
the birth of John the Baptist. The two stories not only develop in parallel, but
also contain a multitude of similar elements. The same angel—Gabriel—
appears to Zacharias, the father of John, and then to Mary, the Mother of
Jesus. Zacharias, seeing the angel, "was troubled" (Lk 1.12); Mary, seeing
the angel, also "was troubled" (Lk 1.29). In both cases the angel speaks not
only of the birth of a child, but also of the manner in which he is to be
named (Lk 1.13, 31). Of John the angel says: "He shall be great in the sight
of the Lord" (Lk 1.15), while of Jesus he says: "He shall be great, and shall
be called the Son of the Highest" (Lk 1.32). Zacharias asks the angel: "By
what shall I know this? For I am an old man, and my wife well stricken in
years" (Lk 1.18). Mary puts the question to the angel: "How shall this be,
seeing I know not a man?" (Lk 1.34). The time comes for Elisabeth to give
birth to a son, and on the eighth day he is circumcised and is given a name
(Lk 1.57–65). The time comes for Mary to give birth, and she gives birth

to her firstborn son (Lk 2.21), who is circumcised on the eighth day and is given a name (Lk 2.21). Of John, the evangelist says: "And the child grew, and waxed strong in spirit, and was in the deserts till the day of his show-ing unto Israel" (Lk 1.80), while the story of Jesus' birth concludes with the words: "And Jesus increased in wisdom and stature, and in favour with God and man" (Lk 2.52).

Alongside the obvious and deliberate parallels between the two sto-ries,[67] the idea that Jesus is greater than John can be traced in many details of Luke's narrative. John is miraculously born of two barren parents, but Jesus is born in a supernatural manner from the Virgin and the Holy Spirit. Elisabeth, the mother of John, greets Mary, the Mother of Jesus, as her elder, although Mary is significantly younger than her relative in age. She also calls Mary the "mother of [her] Lord" (Lk 1.43).

The birth of John becomes a family celebration, and his father Zacha-rias addresses the newborn child with words of blessing: "And thou, child, shalt be called the prophet of the Highest. For thou shalt go before the face of the Lord to prepare his ways, to give knowledge of salvation unto his people by the remission of their sins" (Lk 1.76–77). On the fortieth day after his birth Jesus is blessed by the prophet and elder Simeon, who says: "Lord, now lettest thou thy servant depart in peace, according to thy word. For mine eyes have seen thy salvation, which thou hast prepared before the face of all people, a light to enlighten the Gentiles, and the glory of thy people Israel" (Lk 2.29–32). If in the first case all of the action takes place in the house of Zacharias, before the eyes of the relatives and friends of the family, then in the second case the event occurs in the Temple of Jerusa-lem, most likely before the eyes of a multitude of bystanders. If Zacharias' blessing refers to the people of Israel, then Simeon's blessing refers not only to the Jews, but also to the Gentiles and all peoples. Simeon is then joined by Anna, who "gave thanks likewise unto the Lord, and spake of him to all them that looked for redemption in Jerusalem" (Lk 2.38). The terms "salvation" and "redemption," which in Christian theology have a special meaning, are applied only to Jesus, but not to John.

[67]See Ian Boxall, "Luke's Nativity Story: A Narrative Reading," in *New Perspectives on the Nativity*, ed. Jeremy Corley (London: T&T Clark, 2009), 30–31.

Madonna Litta, Leonardo da Vinci, 1490–1491.

For Luke, the story of the birth of John the Baptist is the framework into which the account of the birth of Jesus is inserted. Matthew sets the same story in another framework, that of the Old Testament prophecies concerning the fate of the people of Israel. Quotations from the Old Testament accompany and conclude all of the main episodes in the story of Jesus' birth. The following formulas are used: "That it might be fulfilled which was spoken of the Lord by the prophet" (Mt 1.22); "For thus it is written by the prophet" (Mt 2.5); "That it might be fulfilled which was spoken of the Lord by the prophet" (Mt 2.15); "Then was fulfilled that which was spoken by Jeremiah the prophet" (Mt 2.17); "That it might be fulfilled which was spoken by the prophets" (Mt 2.23). With the aid of these oft-repeated formulas, which have no direct analogy in the Old Testament or in post-biblical Hebrew literature,[68] Matthew emphasizes that Jesus came to fulfill the prophecies: particular events of his life occur so that what was spoken of in the Old Testament "might be fulfilled". The entire story of the birth of Jesus is presented by Matthew in such a way as to emphasize that the events developed according to a script that had already been written.

Bethlehem, correspondingly, became the location of the birth of the Messiah not because Mary and Joseph went there to participate in the census, but in fulfillment of the prophecy: "And thou Bethlehem, in the land of Juda, art not the least among the princes of Juda; for out of thee shall come a Governor, that shall rule my people Israel" (Mt 2.6). Matthew quotes only the beginning of the text, which should have been familiar to his readers. The complete text runs thus:

> But thou, Bethlehem Ephratah, though thou be little among the thousands of Judah, yet out of thee shall he come forth unto me that is to be ruler in Israel, whose goings forth have been from of old, from

[68]See Soares Prabhu, *The Formula Quotations in the Infancy Narrative of Matthew*, 46.

everlasting. Therefore will he give them up, until the time that she who is in labor hath brought forth. . . . And he shall stand and feed in the strength of the Lord, in the majesty of the name of the Lord his God; and they shall abide; for now shall he be great unto the ends of the earth. (Mic 5.2–4)

Joseph and Mary set off for Egypt not only from fear for the Child's fate, but also "that it might be fulfilled which was spoken of the Lord by the prophet, saying, 'Out of Egypt have I called my son'" (Mt 2.15). In other words, it was necessary for the Son of God to visit Egypt and return from there so that what had been said by the prophet might be fulfilled. Here Matthew is quoting the book of Hosea, in which God says: "When Israel was a child, then I loved him, and called my son out of Egypt" (Hos 11.1). The exodus from Egypt was the most important event in the life of the people of Israel, and it is to this event that the most important sacred remembrance is dedicated—Passover. Matthew draws a link between this event and the return of the Holy Family to Judea. Like the prophet Moses who led the people of Israel out of Egyptian bondage, the infant Jesus returns to the land of Israel after a forced sojourn in Egypt.

Joseph and Mary settle in Nazareth, Matthew states, not because Joseph's house was located there, but in order to fulfill that which had been spoken through the prophets, that "he shall be called a Nazarene" (Mt 2.23). Nowhere in the Old Testament do we find a prophecy that the Messiah will be a Nazarene. It is unlikely, however, that the evangelist is referring to a source unknown to us, as some scholars believe.[69] Rather, we see here how the link is drawn between the destiny of Jesus and the story of the birth of Samson to Manoah and his barren wife, to whom an angel appeared with the words: "Behold now, thou art barren, and bearest not; but thou shalt conceive, and bear a son. . . . The child shall be a Nazarite unto God from the womb" (Judg 13.3–5).

The term "Nazarite" in the Old Testament was used to denote people who had made (as a rule, for a limited period of time) a vow to lead

---

[69]See Edwin D. Freed, *The Stories of Jesus' Birth: A Critical Introduction*, Biblical Seminar 72 (Sheffield: Sheffield Academic Press, 2001), 82.

*Distant View
of Nazareth,*
William Holman
Hunt, 1860–1861.

an ascetic way of life, in particular, not to drink wine, cut their hair, or touch a dead body (Num 6.1–7). In the Greek text of the Gospel of Matthew the name of the Galilean town of Nazareth (*Nazaret*) resembles the word "Nazarene" (*nazōraios*). Between the corresponding Hebrew words (*Nasrat* and *nāzîr*) there is no exact resemblance.[70] It is even more evident that at the level of the Greek text the evangelist Matthew intended to link the location where Joseph, Mary, and the Infant settled after returning from Egypt to the Old Testament custom of the vow of a Nazarite.[71]

Attempts have been made to find a connection between the name of the town of Nazareth and the term "Nazarene" in the Gospel of Matthew at the level of the Hebrew text: the word *Nasrat* (Nazareth) resembles the famous Messianic title from the prophecy of Isaiah—"branch" (*nēser*), from the root of Jesse (Is 11.1).[72] St Jerome has also indicated the possibility of such an understanding.[73]

The theory has been advanced that Nazareth was the place where a group of Nazarites settled in the second century BC, in whose honor the

[70]Ulrich Luz, *Das Evangelium nach Matthaus*, Bd. 1 (Zurich: Benziger, 1985), 187.
[71]For more detail, see Soares Prabhu, *The Formula Quotations in the Infancy Narrative of Matthew*, 201–207, 215.
[72]Luz, *Das Evangelium nach Matthäus*, Bd. 1, 188.
[73]Jerome, *Letters* 57.7 (PL 22:574).

town was named.[74] This theory, however, is not confirmed by historical sources.

Why did Matthew find it necessary to indicate a connection between the vow of a Nazarite and Jesus? At first glance, the image of Jesus little resembles the description of a Nazarite; the image of John the Baptist would resemble this description far better. It appears that for the evangelist it is important here to show the continuity of the legacy of holiness from the Old Testament to the New. The way of life of a Nazarite was unambiguously associated with holiness (Num 6.8). In the Gospel of Matthew, the account of John the Baptist, who "had his raiment of camel's hair, and a leathern girdle about his loins; and his meat was locusts[75] and wild honey" (Mt 3.4) immediately follows after the reference to the prophecy that "he shall be called a Nazarene" (Mt 2.23). Clearly, Matthew wants to draw a direct link between holiness, in the form in which it existed in the Old Testament, and John the Baptist, and, through him, Jesus.

From the subsequent accounts by the evangelists regarding Jesus' earthly ministry, it is clear that among the people he was known as a "prophet of Nazareth of Galilee" (Mt 21.11). It seems Jesus' birth in Bethlehem was not known to those who doubted that he was the Messiah on the basis of the prophecy that "out of Galilee ariseth no prophet" (Jn 7.52). Of Jesus' birth in Bethlehem in Judea (and not in Galilee) we know from both Gospels, but nowhere in the Gospels is it said that Jesus or his disciples mentioned this fact in their polemics with the Jews. John gives us the Jews' question: "Hath not the scripture said that Christ cometh of the seed of David, and out of the town of Bethlehem, where David was?" (Jn 7.42). But he does not note any reply from either Jesus or his disciples. The Galilean origin of Jesus was one of the factors that caused the Jews to not recognize him as the Messiah: they could not believe that a "Gali-

---

[74]Adrian Leske, "Jesus as a Ναζωραῖος," in *Resourcing New Testament Studies: Literary, Historical, and Theological Essays in Honor of David L. Dungan*, eds. Allan J. McNicol, David B. Peabody, and J. Samuel Subramanian (New York, NY: T&T Clark International, 2009), 80.

[75]Locusts are types of grasshoppers that, according to the Mosaic Law, could be used as food (see Lev 11.22). They were also eaten fried or boiled in the Qumran community. See R. T. France, *The Gospel of Mark: A Commentary on the Greek Text* (Grand Rapids, MI: Paternoster Press, 2002), 69.

laean" (Mt 26.69; Lk 23.6) could be the Messiah whom the prophets had foretold and who, of course, was to have been born within Judea in the city of David.[76]

Matthew set himself the task of answering these puzzles and of presenting Jesus primarily as the One of whom the prophets wrote and spoke. That is why for him it was important to show from the outset that Bethlehem was not only the place where he was born as a result of circumstances coming together, but the city in which the house of Joseph, his father according to law, was to be found.

The prototypes of the life of Jesus for Matthew are an entire series of Old Testament subjects and images, including Moses and Samson. Luke, on the other hand, presents a different version of Jesus' birth, the nearest prototype of which is the life of John the Baptist. Both evangelists, however, agree that Jesus was born in Bethlehem of Judea, but was brought up in Nazareth in Galilee. This is confirmed by the numerous episodes quoted above in which Jesus and his disciples are linked with Galilee, and not Judea, by their origin, upbringing, and accent.

8. "Parents," "Brothers and Sisters"

The evangelist Luke calls Joseph and Mary the "parents" of Jesus (Lk 2.41). Mark and Matthew also quote the words of the inhabitants of Nazareth, Jesus' contemporaries, on his family: "Is not this the carpenter, the son of Mary, the brother of James, and Joses, and of Juda, and Simon? And are not his sisters here with us?" (Mk 6.3; cf. Mt. 13.55–56).

Jesus' brothers are repeatedly mentioned on the pages of the New Testament writings. Jesus came to Capernaum accompanied by his Mother and brothers (Jn 2.12). In Galilee, when Jesus was preaching to the people,

---

[76]On how the Galilean origin of Jesus fitted in with the messianic expectations current at that time, see, in particular, Sean Freyne, *Galilee and Gospel: Collected Essays* (Boston, MA: Brill, 2000), 230–270.

his Mother and brothers stood outside the house, wanting to speak with him (Mt 12.46–49; Mk 3.31–35; Lk 8.19–21). John notes that Jesus' brothers did not believe in him (Jn 7.5), while Mark relates how they tried to take him home, thinking that he had gone mad (Mk 3.21). After the resurrection of Jesus, we find his brothers and Mary together with the disciples (Acts 1.14). The apostle Paul also mentions the brothers of the Lord (1 Cor 9.5; Gal 1.19).

St Joseph, Guido Reni, *c.* 1635.

On the basis of these references, critics of the Church's interpretation of the Gospels have cast doubt on the teaching of the perpetual virginity of the Mother of God. The author of a modern-day biography of Jesus, who claims to be an independent historian, writes:

> This report assumes that Jesus, being called son of Mary and having named brothers and unnamed sisters, was the brother of other children of Mary. Other ideas are due to later Christian belief in the perpetual virginity of the Blessed Virgin Mary, a piece of imaginative doctrine which has no place in historical research, and no connection with the historical Miriam. We must prefer the evidence of Mark: Miriam had several children.[77]

We have to object: Mark does not produce any evidence that Mary had several children; he, along with the other evangelists, simply mentions that Jesus had brothers. But neither he nor the other evangelists say who these brothers were—siblings or cousins, or that the word "brothers" was used in a broad context, indicating relatives in general. According to the way words are used in the Bible, a cousin, nephew, and any close male relative could be called a brother. In the Greek translation of the Bible, the word *adelphos* means not only brothers, but also close relatives (Gen 13.8; 14.14; 29.12, 15; 31.32; Lev 10.4; 2 Kg 10.13; 1 Chr 23.22).

---

[77]Maurice Casey, *Jesus of Nazareth: An Independent Historian's Account of His Life and Teaching* (London: T&T Clark, 2010), 144.

In the opinion of this type of independent historian, Matthew also testifies against the perpetual virginity of the Mother of God in what he says about Joseph: "Then Joseph being raised from sleep did as the angel of the Lord had bidden him, and took unto him his wife, and knew her not till she had brought forth her firstborn son" (Mt 1.24–25). From these words they draw the conclusion that after Mary gave birth to her firstborn, Joseph "knew" her, and she then gave birth to other children, Jesus' brothers.

And yet, only at a first superficial glance does the Gospel text allow for such an interpretation. The word "firstborn" does not presuppose the existence of other children: it refers to any child "that openeth the womb" (Lk 2.23). The word *heōs*, translated as "till," "in its biblical usage may denote not a temporal limitation, but a direct simultaneity of events. . . . The evangelist's thought may be conveyed thus: Joseph did not know Mary. And meanwhile she gave birth to her firstborn."[78]

Belief in the seedless conception of Jesus by Mary, as we have shown above, was the Church's teaching from the very beginning, and in no way a later invention. At the beginning of the second century, Ignatius of Antioch writes of Mary's virginity as one of the mysteries hidden from the devil: "For our God, Jesus the Christ, was conceived by Mary, in accordance with God's plan, of the seed of David and the Holy Spirit. . . . The virginity of Mary and her giving birth, and likewise the death of the Lord, elude the ruler of this world. Three mysteries of crying out were performed in the quietness of God."[79]

If we are to speak of Mary's perpetual virginity (the preservation of her virginity after Jesus' birth), then the Gospels contain no direct indications of this. However, there are no direct refutations either. The Church's teaching from the earliest times has asserted that the Most Holy Mother of God is a "Virgin before and after the Nativity."[80]

---

[78]See A. S. Nebol'sin, "Brat'ya Gospodni [The Brothers of the Lord]," in *Pravoslavnaya entsiklopediya* [The Orthodox Encyclopedia], vol. 6 (Moscow: Tserkovno-nauchnyy tsentr "Pravoslavnaya Entsiklopediya," 2003), 214.

[79]Ignatius of Antioch, *Epistle to the Ephesians* 18.2–19.1 (Stewart, PPS).

[80]This is the name of one of the miraculous icons of the Mother of God. In the hymnography for the feast of the Dormition of the Mother of God, the following are sung: "In giving birth, O

Research into the Church's teaching on the perpetual virginity of the Mother of God is not part
of the task of the present book: we have devoted a
section of another book to this dogma, to which we
refer the reader.[81] We cannot pass over the topic of
the "brothers and sisters" in silence, however, insofar as it has a direct bearing not only on the dogma
of the perpetual virginity of the Mother of God, but
also on the main subject of our study.

In the Gospel of Matthew, the family into which
Jesus was born and in which he was brought up,
consists of three people: Joseph, Mary, and Jesus.

"A Virgin before and after
the Nativity," icon, 19th c.

It is as such that the family travel to Egypt, return to Judea, and settle in
Galilee. There is not a single mention here of either brothers or sisters. So
where do they come from in the accounts of Jesus' public ministry?

Church tradition gives us two versions of the answer to the question
of who Jesus' brothers were. The earliest source on this topic is the *Protevangelium of James*, in which Joseph is presented as an elderly widower
with sons: he is chosen "to take into [his] keeping the virgin of the Lord."[82]
Together with Joseph and Mary, Joseph's sons from his first marriage
travel to Bethlehem to take part in the census.[83] The opinion that Jesus'
brothers were Joseph's sons from a first marriage held sway in the eastern
Christian tradition.[84] Epiphanius of Salamis presents Joseph as an eighty-
year-old widower, with six children from his first marriage, at the time
he married Mary.[85]

Theotokos, thou hast retained thy virginity, and in falling asleep thou hast not forsaken the world
. . ." (troparion of the feast); ". . . Virgin after bearing child and alive after death . . ." (ninth irmos of
the first canon). Translations from *The Festal Menaion*, trans. Mother Mary and Kallistos Ware
(South Canaan, PA: St. Tikhon's Seminary Press, 1998), pages 511 and 523 respectively.

[81]See Metropolitan Hilarion Alfeyev, *Orthodox Christianity*, vol. 2, *Doctrine and Teaching of
the Orthodox Church*, trans. Andrew Smith (Yonkers, NY: St Vladimir's Seminary Press, 2012),
473–488, esp. pp. 474–477.

[82]*Protevangelium of James* 9 (*ANF* 8:363).

[83]Ibid., 17 (*ANF* 8:365).

[84]See, in particular, Origen, *Commentary on the Gospel of Matthew* 10.17 (SC 162:216).

[85]Epiphanius of Salamis, *Panarion* 51.10.

St Jerome gives us another version of the answer. He believes that the brothers of the Lord are Jesus' cousins, the sons of Mary, the wife of Cleopas (Lk 24.18), whom he identifies as Mary, the mother of James and Joses (Mt 27.56; Mk 15.40). As we have seen, James and Joses are mentioned in the same Gospels as being among Jesus' brothers, and it would be strange if in the account of the crucifixion the Mother of Jesus was mentioned only as the "mother of James and Joses" and not a single word was said of her being the Mother of the One crucified on the cross. It is evident that here we are dealing with a different Mary. This Mary could have been Mary of Cleopas, named in the Gospel of John as the sister of the Mother of Jesus (Jn 19.25). If she was the sister of the Virgin Mary, then her sons would be the cousins of Jesus.[86]

The weightiest evidence in favor of Mary having no other children is that Jesus, while on the cross, entrusts her to his disciple, after which the disciple takes her to his home (Jn 19.27). There would be no need of this if Mary was part of a large family and if she had other sons who could take care of her after Jesus' death. This argument is put forward, in particular, by John Chrysostom in his commentary on Matthew's words on how Joseph "knew her not till she had brought forth her firstborn son" (Mt 1.25):

> He hath here used the word "till," not that thou shouldest suspect that afterwards he did know her, but to inform thee that before the birth the Virgin was wholly untouched by man. . . . So then here likewise, it uses

[86]There is one weak link in this theory—the notion that Mary, the wife of Cleopas was the sister of the Mother of Jesus. This notion, firstly, contradicts the holy tradition on the birth of Mary from Joachim and Anna as a late and only child. Secondly, it is difficult to imagine that two sisters had the same name. Professor A. P. Lebedev (1845–1908) of the Moscow Theological Academy defended a somewhat different perspective. He believed that Mary of Cleopas was not the Virgin Mary's sister, but the wife of Cleopas, the brother of Joseph: ". . . in other words, Mary of Cleopas and Mary the Mother of Jesus were considered to be the legitimate wives of two brothers and were sister-in-laws to each other." The name of the "sister of the Mother of Jesus" applied to Mary of Cleopas is understood by this scholar in a broad context, as is the name of the "brothers of Jesus," by which he understands the children of Cleopas and his wife Mary "who were the cousins of Christ (from the judicial and popular perspective)." See A. P. Lebedev, *Brat'ya Gospodni: Issledovaniya po istorii drevney Tserkvi* [The Brothers of the Lord: Studies in the history of the early Church], 2nd ed. (St. Petersburg: Izdatel'stvo Olega Abyshko, 2010), 80–87. On Mary of Cleopas, see also Richard Bauckham, *Gospel Women: Studies of the Named Women in the Gospels* (Grand Rapids, MI: Eerdmans, 2002), 204–212.

the word "till," to make certain what was before the birth, but as to what follows, it leaves thee to make the inference. Thus, what it was necessary for thee to learn of Him, this He Himself has said; that the Virgin was untouched by man until the birth; but that which both was seen to be a consequence of the former statement, and was acknowledged, this in its turn he leaves for thee to perceive; namely, that not even after this, she having so become a mother, and having been counted worthy of a new sort of travail, and a child-bearing so strange, could that righteous man ever have endured to know her. For if he had known her, and had kept her in the place of a wife, how is it that our Lord commits her, as unprotected, and having no one, to His disciple, and commands him to take her to his own home?[87]

We know very little of Jesus' parents from the New Testament. With the exception of the accounts of Matthew and Luke regarding his birth and early years, the Virgin Mary only episodically appears on the pages of the Gospels. We see her with Jesus at the marriage feast in Cana in Galilee (Jn 2.3–5), and then in Capernaum (Jn 2.12). We hear of how she appears with the brothers of Jesus at the doors of the house in which he was preaching. We see her by the cross of Jesus (Jn 19.25–27). With the exception of this last episode and the story of the marriage in Cana of Galilee, in the other instances the Mother of Jesus is mentioned together with his brothers, including in the Acts of the Apostles, where we encounter a later mention of her (Acts 1.14). The epistles of the apostles are silent about Mary, the Mother of Jesus.

As for Joseph, he appears for the last time in Luke's story of the visit of Jesus' parents to the Temple of Jerusalem (Lk 2.41–51). Joseph does not figure at all in the account of Jesus' public ministry. This, it appears, testifies to the notion that by the time Jesus had ventured out to preach, Joseph was no longer alive. The same circumstance would be indirect proof of Joseph's old age at the time he was betrothed to Mary. In any case, Joseph was certainly no longer alive when Jesus, dying on the cross, entrusted his Mother to the disciple.

---

[87]John Chrysostom, *Homilies on the Gospel of Matthew* 5.5 (*NPNF*[1] 10:33).

St James, the
Brother of the
Lord, icon,
16th c.

What was the fate of the "brothers and sisters" of Jesus after his death and resurrection? Christian sources are completely silent on the fate of the sisters, and of the brothers, only one is mentioned: James, the brother of the Lord.[88] He is repeatedly mentioned in the Acts of the Apostles. After being freed from prison, Peter says: "Go show these things unto James, and to the brethren" (Acts 12.17), which testifies to the special role of James within the group of Jesus' disciples. In the account of the apostolic council, James addresses the apostles (Acts 15.13). There is also an account of the meeting between the apostle Paul and James, to whom Paul speaks about the conversion of the Gentiles (Acts 21.18–19). Paul himself mentions this meeting, calling James the brother of the Lord (Gal 2.19).

All of these references point towards the special role that James played in the community of Jesus' disciples after his death and resurrection.

[88]See John Painter, *Just James: The Brother of Jesus in History and Tradition* (Edinburgh: T&T Clark, 1997), 42–156.

Unconditional primacy in the community belonged to Peter, but James had his own place. Holy tradition considers him to be the first bishop of Jerusalem, and it is with this title that his name has entered the diptychs of the saints. It is believed that he was one of the Seventy Apostles and met a martyr's death. This is confirmed by the testimony of Josephus, who mentions the execution of James, the brother of Jesus, called the Christ, by order of the Sanhedrin in 62–63.[89]

9. Childhood and Youth: Upbringing and Education

The childhood years of Jesus were spent in Nazareth. We know very little about these years. Matthew does not say a single word about them, while Luke summarizes the entire period of Jesus' life up until the age of twelve in a single sentence: "And the child grew, and waxed strong in spirit, filled with wisdom; and the grace of God was upon him" (Lk 2.40). What lies behind this sentence?

In order to understand how Jesus the Son of Man was brought up, we have to picture to ourselves the life of a pious family with average means from the humble region of Galilee. If we believe the suggestion that Joseph had six children from his first marriage, then it is extremely likely that they all lived in the same house and that Jesus was brought up among his adopted brothers and sisters, who were significantly older than him.

It has been suggested that no more than five hundred people lived in Nazareth at that time.[90] Everybody knew each other, and relatives knew each other, which is convincingly confirmed by the story of the visit of Jesus of Nazareth when he was already a mature adult: "And when he was come into his own country, he taught them in their synagogue, insomuch that they were astonished, and said, 'Whence hath this man this wisdom, and these mighty works? Is not this the carpenter's son? Is not his mother

[89]Josephus, *Antiquities of the Jews* 20.9.1.
[90]Puig i Tàrrech, *Jesus: A Biography*, 180.

St Joseph from the *Merode
Altarpiece*, Robert Campin,
ca. 1427–1432.

called Mary? And his brethren, James, and Joses, and Simon, and Judas? And his sisters, are they not all with us? Whence then hath this man all these things?'" (Mt 13.54–56).

In this story, Jesus is called a carpenter's son. In the parallel account of Mark, which we quoted earlier, Jesus is called a "carpenter" (Mk 6.3). This indicates Joseph's profession, which, we can surmise, Jesus also learned. The majority of the city's inhabitants worked in the fields, and it is extremely probable that Joseph made their work tools for them. This is what Justin Martyr surmised in the second century: "He was considered to be the son of Joseph the carpenter . . . and He was deemed a carpenter (for He was in the habit of working as a carpenter when among men, making ploughs and yokes)."[91] The use by Jesus of the term "yoke" in Matthew 11.30 may serve as an indirect confirmation of this presupposition.

At the same time, we ought to note that the Greek word *tektōn*, used to denote Joseph's profession, means not only "carpenter," but also "builder": the term was applied not only to those who worked with wood, but also to those who built from wood or stone. Construction metaphors are common in Jesus' speech, and we can infer that he was familiar with the art of building. His parable of the house built on stone and the house built on sand may be considered an example (Mt 7.24–27).

The profession of carpenter or builder would presuppose economic activity, since carpenters would sell their wares, and builders would receive payment for their work. Jesus was familiar with the laws of commerce, with the system of agreements between sellers and buyers, lenders and borrowers. In his teachings he many times used images from this realm, in particular, in the parables on the two debtors (Mt 18.23–35) and the talents (Mt 25.14–30; Lk 19.12–27), and in many others.

---

[91]Justin Martyr, *Dialogue with Trypho* 88 (*ANF* 1:244).

Agricultural images, often encountered in the parables of Jesus, testify to the notion that he was well acquainted with the work of his fellow countrymen: here we meet sowers, reapers, and husbandmen. Jesus could have become acquainted with certain trades when he was a boy as he observed how his compatriots would work.

What sort of education did Jesus receive? His older contemporary, Philo of Alexandria, tells us the subjects studied in his time in the curriculum of a general education:

> For grammar, by teaching you the histories which are to be found in the works of poets and historians, will give you intelligence and abundant learning; and, moreover, will teach you to look with contempt on all the vain fables which erroneous opinions invent. . . . And music will teach what is harmonious in the way of rhythm, and what is ill arranged in harmony, and, rejecting all that is out of tune and all that is inconsistent with melody, will guide what was previously discordant to concord. And geometry, sowing the seeds of equality and just proportion in the soul, which is fond of learning, will, by means of the beauty of continued contemplation, implant in you an admiration of justice. And rhetoric, having sharpened the mind for contemplation in general, and having exercised and trained the faculties of speech in interpretations and explanations, will make man really rational. . . . And dialectic science, which is the sister, the twin sister of rhetoric, as some persons have called it, separating true from false arguments, and refuting the plausibilities of sophistical arguments, will cure the great disease of the soul, deceit. It is profitable, therefore, to aide among these and other sciences resembling them, and to devote one's especial attention to them.[92]

The curriculum here described comprised an average education in the Hellenic school of Jesus' time, but had nothing in common with the education that Jesus could have received in his own town. Here neither

[92]Philo of Alexandria, *On Mating with the Preliminary Studies* 15–18. In *The Works of Philo: Complete and Unabridged*, trans. C. D. Yonge, updated ed. (Peabody, MA: Hendrickson, 1993), 305.

Christ preaching
in the synagogue
in Nazareth,
fresco, 14th c.

grammar, nor music, nor rhetoric, nor dialectic were taught. From what we know of Galilee in the time of Jesus, we cannot state with certainty that there was a school in the town where he was brought up. In any case, we can have no doubt that Jesus' first teachers were Joseph and Mary, to whom "he was subject" (Lk 2.51). It is possible that Jesus' brothers, if they were older than him, could have also taken part in his upbringing and education.

What did study consist of in a Galilean family of Jesus' time? Primarily the study of the Torah—the Pentateuch of Moses, which was Scripture for all Jews and which had indisputable authority. The Torah was not merely an anthology of narratives on the history of the people of Israel: it included the laws by which the Jewish people were to live and the moral rules that were regarded as immutable and that all people were to observe. Every child brought up in a Jewish family was expected to know the Torah.

In what manner was Scripture studied? It was not usually studied from the written text. The majority of Jesus' peers did not know how to read, and biblical texts were received by listening and learning them by heart. From the Gospels we know that he preached in the synagogue at Nazareth. This story is to be found in all the Synoptics, but only Luke makes it clear that, when he entered the synagogue, Jesus began to read from a book:

And he came to Nazareth, where he had been brought up; and, as his custom was, he went into the synagogue on the sabbath day, and stood up to read. And there was delivered unto him the book of the prophet Isaiah. And when he had opened the book, he found the place where it was written, "The Spirit of the Lord is upon me, because he hath anointed me to preach the Gospel to the poor; he hath sent me to heal the brokenhearted, to preach deliverance to the captives, and recovering of sight to the blind, to set at liberty them that are bruised, to preach the acceptable year of the Lord." [Is 61.1–2] And he closed the book, and he gave it again to the minister, and sat down. And the eyes of all them that were in the synagogue were fastened on him. And he began to say unto them, "This day is this scripture fulfilled in your ears." And all bare him witness, and wondered at the gracious words which proceeded out of his mouth. And they said, "Is not this Joseph's son?" And he said unto them, "Ye will surely say unto me this proverb, 'Physician, heal thyself': whatsoever we have heard done in Capernaum, do also here in thy country." And he said, "Truly I say unto you, no prophet is accepted in his own country." (Lk 4.16–24)

Luke's story confirms that Jesus knew how to read Hebrew. But why does the fact that he took the book (or, rather, scroll) and, having opened it, began to read, cause his kinsmen to be so amazed that they fixed their gaze on him until, having closed the book (that is, having rolled up the scroll), he began to interpret that which has been read? And why, having listened to his teaching, did they ask: is this the son of Joseph? Clearly because they believed that in Joseph's house Jesus could not have received such an education that would have allowed him to read fluently in Hebrew and interpret the words of the prophets.[93] His listeners would have known well the conditions in which he was brought up, and they could not imagine that the son of a carpenter could turn into a teacher capable of reading the Scriptures and interpreting them.

[93]Other interpreters read this differently: it was Jesus' "custom" *both* to go "into the synagogue" *and* "to read" (v. 16). This would explain why he was handed the scroll of Isaiah (v. 17): they expected him to read it. In this interpretation of the passage, the hearers' astonishment does not come from Jesus' ability to read, but from the fact that he proclaimed the prophecy was "fulfilled in [their] ears" (v. 21).—*Ed.*

Christ in the
Synagogue,
Nikolai Ge, 1868.

The possibility cannot be excluded that, apart from being educated by his family, Jesus received an education at a rudimentary school (if there was such a school in Nazareth) and then at the local synagogue. According to later Jewish sources, boys would complete their rudimentary schooling at the age of twelve or thirteen, after which the more gifted of them would begin studying at a *bēt ha-miḏraš* (house of study), where they studied the Torah under the guidance of an experienced teacher. This instruction, however, was available only to a few boys. There was no established system of secondary and higher education in the Israel of Jesus' time.[94]

We know that Jesus was very well acquainted with the Old Testament, and we cannot doubt that he got to know the books of the Bible at a very early age. In his youth the main center for study, apart from his house, would have been the local synagogue—the very same synagogue that he would visit many years later as a grown man. It is here, in participating in the Sabbath prayer gatherings together with his parents, that the young Jesus could hear the words of the Scriptures, be present when they were discussed by the adults, and imbibe the sacred texts, the words of the psalms, prayers, and hymns. Philo of Alexandria describes how the prayer gatherings would take place in the synagogues of Jesus' time:

[94]Meier, *A Marginal Jew*, vol. 1, 272.

Accordingly, on the seventh day there are spread before the people in every city innumerable lessons [or schools] of prudence, and temperance, and courage, and justice, and all other virtues; during the giving of which the common people sit down, keeping silence and pricking up their ears, with all possible attention, from their thirst for wholesome instruction; but some of those who are very learned explain to them what is of great importance and use, lessons by which the whole of their lives may be improved.[95]

It is not by chance that Philo calls the synagogue a school: the reading of the Scriptures and their interpretation by an experienced teacher made up the main part of the prayer gathering on the Sabbath. All things considered, Jesus did not visit any other school in his youth apart from the synagogue in Nazareth. There is no evidence of him having ever studied under a famous rabbi, or in a philosophical school, or in the Temple of Jerusalem. The Jews who heard him in the Temple in Jerusalem were puzzled: "How knoweth this man letters, having never learned?" (Jn 7.15). The words "having never learned" indicate the absence of a formal education of the sort that the scribes and Pharisees had in his time. In contemporary language, Jesus was self-taught, and when he spoke as a teacher, this caused bewilderment not only in his native town, where everyone knew about his lack of education, but also in Jerusalem, where he was considered to be a newcomer and stranger who had intruded into the closed association of teachers and scribes without any apparent right to do so.

The lack of a formal education does not exclude the possibility that Jesus had periodic contact with teachers as a youth. One such episode has been preserved for us in the Gospel of Luke. Here it is stated that every year the parents of Jesus went to Jerusalem for the feast of the Passover (Lk 2.41). The custom of visiting Jerusalem at the Passover was widespread, and many pious Jews observed it religiously. Jesus himself kept this custom up until the end of his life. The Gospel tells us:

---

[95]Philo of Alexandria, *The Special Laws* 2.62. In *The Works of Philo*, trans. Yonge, 574.

Jesus in the Temple with the Learned Men, engraving, Gustave Doré, 19th c.

And when he was twelve years old, they went up to Jerusalem after the custom of the feast. And when they had fulfilled the days, as they returned, the child Jesus tarried behind in Jerusalem; and Joseph and his mother knew not of it. But they, supposing him to have been in the company, went a day's journey; and they sought him among their kinsfolk and acquaintance. And when they found him not, they turned back again to Jerusalem, seeking him. And it came to pass, that after three days they found him in the temple, sitting in the midst of the doctors, both hearing them, and asking them questions. And all that heard him were astonished at his understanding and answers. And when they saw him, they were amazed; and his mother said unto him, "Son, why hast thou thus dealt with us? Behold, thy father and I have sought thee sorrowing." And he said unto them, "How is it that ye sought me? Know ye not that I must be about my Father's business?" And they understood not the saying which he spake unto them. And he went down with them, and came to Nazareth, and was subject unto them; but his mother kept all these sayings in her heart. And Jesus increased in wisdom and stature, and in favour with God and man. (Lk 2.42–52)

How could the evangelist have known about this episode? The only possible source is the Virgin Mary, who related it to Luke or to one of the apostles (Peter?), from whose words Luke wrote it down. Many details of the narrative speak of how the entire scene was rendered from the words of Jesus' Mother: we seem to view this scene through her eyes. In the evangelists' words, "all that heard him were astonished at his understanding and answers," we hear the loving maternal voice retelling this episode many years later. The same voice is heard in the emotional words of the Mother: "Son, why hast thou thus dealt with us?" The concluding phrase of the narrative ("but his mother kept all these sayings in her heart") also conclusively point towards the source: nobody but the Mother could have kept in her heart this episode and the words that at that moment she found incomprehensible, but that she understood after the "sword" pierced her heart (Lk 2.35).

When he attained maturity and ventured out to preach, Jesus would speak much about his heavenly Father. And yet already at the age of twelve he knew that his Father was God, and that the Temple of Jerusalem belonged to his Father. We find it hard to believe that Mary could tell a twelve-year-old boy that Joseph was not his father. It was even less likely that Joseph might have said something like this. The words of the twelve-year-old Jesus, addressed to his parents and not understood by them, but preserved in the heart of his Mother, testify that at an early age he knew he was the Son of God.

The moving episode related by Luke is the only one in the Gospels that concerns Jesus' adolescent years. The next time Jesus appears in the Gospel of Luke is when he is around the age of thirty. Between this episode and the appearance of Jesus on the banks of Jordan there is a gap of about twenty years, which Luke covers with the single sentence: "And Jesus increased in wisdom and stature, and in favour with God and man" (Lk 2.52). Of these years in the life of Jesus, we know nothing and can merely guess that outwardly his life was in no way different from the life of most people, his peers and his compatriots. To all appearances, until the age of thirty he continued to live in obedience to his parents, worked as a carpenter, and studied the Scriptures.

Could Jesus in his youth have received an education somewhere beyond the confines of Israel? The possibility cannot be excluded that before the age of thirty he traveled through various countries. If this was the case, however, why then do the evangelists all remain silent about it? If Jesus had a rounded philosophic education, why was this not reflected in his speech or the accounts about him? Not one of the Gospels gives even a hint that Jesus could have received an education outside of his own country.

His only journey beyond Israel mentioned in the Gospels is the short stay in Egypt when he was still an infant. Could this stay have in some way had an impact on the formation of Jesus' personality? According to Matthew, the Holy Family returned to Judea at the time when Herod's son, Archelaus, reigned. His reign began after the death of Herod the Great in 4 BC, and ended in AD 6 when the emperor Augustus sent him into exile. The return of Mary and Joseph from Egypt thus could not have occurred later than AD 6; however, it is more than likely that this happened closer to the beginning of Archelaus' reign than to the end. This is indicated by the words "when Herod was dead" (Mt 2.19) and "when he heard that Archelaus did reign in Judaea in the room of his father Herod" (Mt 2.22): both remarks suggest that the death of Herod and the beginning of Archelaus' reign were events that had happened comparatively recently. Thus, by the time of the Holy Family's return from Egypt, Jesus could hardly have been older than three or four. The stay in Egypt, consequently, could hardly have exerted a substantial influence on his upbringing and education.

10. Two Traditions— Two Witnesses?

W e have looked at the two accounts of the birth of Jesus. Before proceeding to the next chapter, we must attempt to answer the following questions: what is the historical value of these accounts? What do they contribute to our understanding of Jesus and his mission? And why is there so much dissimilar material in them?

Most contemporary New Testament scholars agree among themselves that the first two chapters of Matthew and the first three chapters of Luke are quite late material added to an already extant earlier tradition on the life of Jesus that was in circulation. This earlier tradition is documented in the Gospel of Mark, which remains silent about the birth of Jesus and begins its narrative with the preaching of John the Baptist. The material of the Gospels of Matthew and Luke that do not correspond to Mark are later additions, which possess significantly less veracity than the narratives beginning with John the Baptist.

This is the opinion of the majority of scholars, in a summarized and toned-down form. The most radical critics speak openly of the mythological and legendary nature of all the evidence contained in Matthew and Luke concerning the birth, childhood, and adolescence of Jesus. Some scholars propose examining the Gospel accounts of the Nativity not as testimonies to events that took place in reality, but as parables: Jesus' followers, so these scholars believe, learned from Jesus himself how to compose parables, and on the basis of a few scarce facts composed two different story-parables on his birth and childhood.[96]

If we view the first chapters of the Gospels of Matthew and Luke as a historical document, then neither of them meets the strict criteria applicable to a historical account. It is practically impossible to sew them into a single narrative fabric, although attempts to do so have been made often

---

[96]Marcus J. Borg and John Dominic Crossan, *The First Christmas: What the Gospels Really Teach About Jesus's Birth* (New York, NY: HarperOne, 2007), 25–54.

*The Adoration
of the Shepherds,*
Giovanni
Domenico
Tiepolo,
1751–1753.

enough (it suffices to recall St Augustine). In approaching these texts as historical documents, we have to admit that we are dealing with two different stories, which intersect with each other only at certain points, rather like how the two genealogies of Jesus come into contact only at certain points.

If, on the other hand, we approach both accounts as the testimonies of eyewitnesses, then a different picture unfolds before us. Here the synchronization of the two accounts with the aim of achieving maximum historical credibility recedes into the background, while a credibility of a different type comes into the foreground, one based on trust in the witnesses. It is this method that we have decided to apply to the Gospel account, and in this instance it cannot be more appropriate.

Who are the witnesses that Matthew and Luke rely upon? It is evident that the evangelists themselves cannot be witnesses. We have already stated that some episodes of the first chapters of the Gospel of Luke limit the circle of witnesses to one person—Mary, the Mother of Jesus. Only she could know how the angel appeared to her and announced the birth of the Messiah. Only she could relate Elisabeth's visit to her. She is the most credible source for the narratives of the adoration of the shepherds, the meeting of Jesus in the Temple with Simeon and Anna, and, finally, the behavior of the twelve-year-old Jesus in Jerusalem. All of these accounts are contained in the Gospel of Luke, and Mary is actually shown by the author of the Gospel as the fundamental source of these accounts: "But Mary kept all these things, and pondered them in her heart" (Lk 2.19); "but his mother kept all these sayings in her heart" (Lk 2.51). To keep something in one's heart means to retain it in the memory. It is from the memory of the Virgin Mary that all of these stories were later drawn.

We observe a different picture in the narrative of Matthew. Here the central figure is not Mary, but Joseph. We learn from this Gospel not only of the deeds, but also the thoughts of Joseph (Mt 1.20), of how he received a vision in his dreams (Mt 1.22) and of how three times an angel appeared to him (Mt 1.20; 2.13; 2.19). Joseph is presented as the source of decisions: it is he who after the appearance of the angel takes Mary and the Infant and sets off with them to Egypt; he makes the decision at first to return to the land of Israel, and then to settle in Galilee. All of this testifies that the most credible source of information for Matthew is Joseph.

In what manner was this information received by Matthew? By the time Jesus embarked on his preaching, Joseph was no longer alive, and so direct contact between him and Matthew can be practically excluded. But Jesus' brothers were still alive, who after his death and resurrection played a notable role in the life of the Christian community. Could not, for example, James, the brother of Lord, have conveyed to Matthew and the other disciples that which he had once heard from Joseph regarding the birth of Jesus? We cannot exclude this version, moreover as it is to James that holy tradition links the appearance of a literary work that relates the birth and childhood years of Mary, and Jesus' birth from her. A significant part of the Protevangelium of James thematically echoes the first chapters of the Gospels of Luke and Matthew.[97]

The *Protevangelium of James* is part of the apocryphal literature that did not enter the canon of the New Testament. It appeared, as is supposed, around the middle of the second century, and the apostle James, so scholars believe, could not have been its author. Nevertheless, the tradition

---

[97]See Willem S. Vorster, *Speaking of Jesus: Essays on Biblical Language, Gospel Narrative and the Historical Jesus*, ed. J. Eugene Botha, Supplements to Novum testamentum 92 (Leiden: Brill, 1999), 243–264.

laid out in it could in some parts go back to the brother of the Lord, and through him to Joseph. In spite of its openly apocryphal character, the work is valuable in that it is the first attempt at synchronizing the two divergent Gospel accounts of Jesus' birth. The work, meanwhile, in many places adds to the accounts of Matthew and Luke with various details. For example, this is how Joseph's reaction is described when he saw that Mary was pregnant:

> And she was in her sixth month; and, behold, Joseph came back from his building, and, entering into his house, he discovered that she was big with child. And he smote his face, and threw himself on the ground upon the sackcloth, and wept bitterly, saying, "With what face shall I look upon the Lord my God? And what prayer shall I make about this maiden? Because I received her a virgin out of the temple of the Lord, and I have not watched over her. Who is it that has hunted me down? Who has done this evil thing in my house, and defiled the virgin? Has not the history of Adam been repeated in me? For just as Adam was in the hour of his singing praise, and the serpent came, and found Eve alone, and completely deceived her, so it has happened to me also." And Joseph stood up from the sackcloth, and called Mary, and said to her: "O thou who hast been cared for by God, why hast thou done this and forgotten the Lord thy God? Why hast thou brought low thy soul, thou that wast brought up in the holy of holies, and that didst receive food from the hand of an angel?" And she wept bitterly, saying, "I am innocent, and have known no man." And Joseph said to her, "Whence then is that which is in thy womb?" And she said, "As the Lord my God liveth, I do not know whence it is to me."[98]

This story, while not being part of the New Testament canon, but it has actually become a part of the Church's tradition through liturgical worship. In Orthodox worship on the eve of the Nativity we find this text compiled as though by Joseph:

---

[98]*Protevangelium of James* 13 (*ANF* 8:364).

Joseph and Mary in detail from *The Adoration of the Shepherds*, Giorgione, 1505–1510.

What is this doing, O Mary, that I see in thee? I fail to understand and am amazed, and my mind is struck with dismay. Go from my sight, therefore, with all speed. What is this doing, O Mary, that I see in thee? Instead of honour, thou hast brought me shame; instead of gladness, sorrow; instead of praise, reproof. No further shall I bear the reproach of men. I received thee from the priests of the temple, as one blameless before the Lord. And what is this that I now see?[99]

In another place[100] we have stated that the liturgical texts of the Orthodox Church are not simply a commentary on the Gospels: they often narrate that which the Gospels are silent about. In Matthew's story of Jesus' birth from a Virgin, much remains behind the scenes. The evangelist is

---

[99]Festal Menaion, the Eve of the Nativity of Christ, first hour, troparion. Translation from *Festal Menaion*, trans. Mother Mary and Kallistos Ware, 225.

[100]See Metropolitan Hilarion Alfeyev, *Orthodox Christianity*, vol. 4, *The Worship and Liturgical Life of the Orthodox Church*, trans. Andrei Tepper (Yonkers, NY: St Vladimir's Seminary Press, 2016), 64.

silent, in particular, regarding Joseph's personal drama: we can only guess at his apprehension and doubts, at what he could say to his Bride when he discovered that she was "with child." The Protevangelium of James, and the subsequent liturgical texts, attempt to restore in poetic form the dialogue between Joseph and Mary. We may treat texts of this sort as poetic license and church rhetoric, or we can see something greater within them—the endeavor to gain an insight into the feelings and emotions of the people through whose hands sacred history was made.

* * *

Let us, then, draw some conclusions regarding the two Gospel accounts of the birth of Jesus. They agree in the following key details:[101]

1. At the moment of the conception of the Infant by Mary, Joseph and Mary were betrothed, but had not begun to live together as man and wife (Mt 1.18; Lk 1.24).
2. Joseph was from the line of David (Mt 1.16; Lk 1.27; 2.4).
3. The angels announced the birth of the Infant (Mt 1.20–23; Lk 1.30–35).
4. Mary conceived not by Joseph, but by the Holy Spirit (Mt 1.18–20; Lk 1.34–35).
5. It was an angel that named the Infant (Mt 1.21; Lk 1.31).
6. The angel announced that the Infant would be the Savior (Mt 1.21; Lk 2.11).
7. Jesus was born in Bethlehem (Mt 2.1; Lk 2.4–6).
8. Jesus was born in the reign of King Herod the Great (Mt 2.1; Lk 1.5).
9. Jesus was brought up in Nazareth (Mt 2.23; Lk 2.39).

These general points make up a historical outline that goes directly back to the biography of Jesus. The divergences testify to the presence of two witnesses, upon whose evidence the two parallel stories are based. The theory of the two witnesses presents us with the key to understanding why

---

[101]Raymond E. Brown, *The Birth of the Messiah*, 34–35.

these narratives diverged so significantly in their details. This theory also helps us to understand the difference between the two genealogies of Jesus.

The evangelist Luke painting an icon of the Mother of God, icon, early 15th c.

We have already spoken of how, in the opinion of some scholars, the Gospel of Luke gives us the genealogy of Mary, and the Gospel of Matthew the genealogy of Joseph. Without at all insisting that this opinion is true, we nonetheless ought to note the greater proximity of the Gospel of Luke to Mary than to Joseph. Perhaps it is no coincidence that the apostle Luke is seen in holy tradition as the apostle who knew the Mother of God closely and even painted her first portrait (icon).

Further on, we shall have occasion to compare time and again the testimony of two or several witnesses, and we will observe far more similarities than differences between them. But we will be referring to testimonies of a different type, belonging directly to the eyewitnesses of events—the apostles. As for the accounts of Jesus' birth, in them we are dealing with materials that, although they go back to specific witnesses, have gone through various stages of editing.

The accounts of Matthew and Luke about the birth of Jesus contain foremost a theological meaning. Each of them is in its own way a prologue to the story of Jesus' public ministry. In both accounts, Jesus is presented as the Son of God and the Son of Man simultaneously, even if Matthew places greater emphasis on the human origin of Jesus as the son of Abraham and the son of David, while Luke accentuates the notion that he is the Son of God. It appears that this initial theological standpoint is the main connecting link between the two accounts, and it is this that makes these accounts an integral part of the original Christian teaching reflected on the pages of the New Testament.

Chapter 4

THE SON OF GOD

---

1. "In the beginning
was the Word"

I f the Gospels of Matthew and Luke begin with accounts of the birth of Jesus, the Gospels of Mark and John open with the account of the preaching of John the Baptist. It is from the preaching of John the Baptist that the thematic material that is common to the three synoptic evangelists, and which is partially echoed by the fourth evangelist, begins. In Mark this material is prefaced by the words: "The beginning of the Gospel of Jesus Christ, the Son of God" (Mk 1.1). In John, on the other hand, the account of John the Forerunner is woven into the general context of the Prologue, which has its own independent theological significance.

In the first verse of the Gospel of Mark, the term "Gospel" is used not in relation to the specific literary genre denoting an evangelist's account of events, but in relation to the good news itself of Jesus Christ, the Son of God. Here we are dealing with the earliest and most authentic use of the term "Gospel," which refers to the message of Jesus, and, in a wider sense, to his life and teaching.

The term "Gospel" is found multiple times in the New Testament: eight times in Mark, four times in Matthew, two times in Acts, and sixty times in the epistles of the apostle Paul. The term belongs to Jesus himself (Mt 24.14; 26.13; Mk 1.15; 13.10; 14.9; 16.15) and is one of the keys to understanding the importance that the early Church attached to his mission

---

and preaching. The term "Gospel" is first and foremost connected to Jesus' teaching concerning the kingdom of heaven, which is why the evangelists use the expressions "the Gospel of the kingdom of God" (Mk 1.14) or, simply, "the Gospel of the kingdom" (Mt 4.23; 9.35; 24.14). For the apostle Paul, the word "Gospel" signifies the entirety of the apostolic tradition regarding the life, death, and resurrection of Jesus Christ (1 Cor 15.1–5).

As he begins his narrative, Mark speaks of the Gospel of the Son of God, emphasizing Jesus' divine origin. Unlike Matthew, Mark is not interested in Jesus' birth or his genealogy, including his descent from the house of David, or in his earthly life before he went out to preach. The Gospel of Mark begins with the theological affirmation that Jesus is the Son of God, and all of the subsequent narrative is aimed at revealing this theological axiom.

John begins his Gospel from this same axiom, but here it is given in a much more detailed and theologically elaborated form. The Prologue to the Gospel of John is of key significance for understanding how Jesus' mission was understood in the early Church:

> In the beginning was the Word, and the Word was with God, and the Word was God. The same was in the beginning with God. All things were made by him; and without him was not any thing made that was made. In him was life; and the life was the light of men. And the light shineth in darkness; and the darkness comprehended it not. . . . *That* was the true Light, which lighteth every man that cometh into the world. He was in the world, and the world was made by him, and the world knew him not. He came unto his own, and his own received him not. But as many as received him, to them gave he power to become the sons of God, *even* to them that believe on his name: Which were born, not of blood, nor of the will of the flesh, nor of the will of man, but of God. And the Word was made flesh, and dwelt among us, and we beheld his glory, the glory as of the only begotten of the Father, full of grace and truth. (Jn 1.1–5, 9–14)

The key themes of the Gospel of John are laid out in the Prologue. First of all, John begins not with Jesus' birth on earth, but with the existence of the Word of God from the beginning "with God." This divine Word (*logos*), as the subsequent narrative makes clear, is none other than the Son of God, Jesus Christ. The first words of the Prologue tell us that the coming of Jesus Christ into the world is connected to a new revelation about God. The Old Testament proclaimed the oneness of God and excluded any thought of the possibility that in God there might exist someone other than God himself; John speaks of the Word of God's existence "with God" from the beginning:

> Since in Jesus Christ God himself has definitively, unreservedly and unsurpassably revealed and communicated himself, Jesus is part of the definition of God's eternal nature. . . . Jesus is the Son of God from eternity and God from eternity is the "Father of our Lord Jesus Christ." The history and fate of Jesus are thus rooted in the nature of God: God's nature proves to be an event. Thus the New Testament pre-existence statements lead to a new, comprehensive interpretation of the term God.[1]

The central point of the Prologue of the Gospel of John is the doctrine of the incarnation. It is most succinctly expressed in the words: "And the Word was made flesh, and dwelt among us . . . full of grace and truth" (Jn 1.14). In these words lies the very heart of the good news that the evangelists brought to the world.

According to the understanding of the Old Testament, an insuperable divide exists between God and the created world: God absolutely transcends the world, matter, and flesh, since he is bodiless Spirit. The concept of flesh is encountered in the Bible as early as the story of the creation of man. When God brings Adam's wife to him, Adam says, "This is now bone of my bones, and flesh of my flesh: she shall be called Woman, because she was taken out of Man" (Gen 2.23). Further on in the narrative, the concept of "flesh" is applied chiefly to collective humanity (Gen 6.3; Ps 77.39), while the expression "all flesh" is an umbrella term, signifying all people or all that live on earth (including animals). For the prophet Isaiah, the flesh is in direct contrast with the spirit (Is 31.3). Typical in this respect are the words

[1] Walter Kasper, *Jesus the Christ*, trans. V. Green (New York, NY: Paulist Press, 1976), 175.

of the prophets, in which corruptible human flesh is contrasted with the eternal word of God: "All flesh is grass, and all the goodliness thereof is as the flower of the field. . . . The grass withereth, the flower fadeth, but the word of our God shall stand for ever" (Is 40.6, 8).

In the New Testament, the ontological divide between God and flesh, between the divine and the human, is overcome by the Word of God becoming flesh. If, earlier, God participated in the life of the nation of Israel from above, from heaven, now the Son of God comes to earth and becomes part of human history. At the same time, he remains who he has been: the pre-eternal Word of God, inseparable from God. All four Gospels, each in its own way, are dedicated to revealing the mystery of the entrance of God into human history, and all the evangelists believe in Jesus as the Son of God. But of the four evangelists only John gives genuinely theological support for this faith, beginning his narrative not from the moment of God's entrance into history, but with the backstory: from the pre-eternal existence of God the Word, who at a specific moment in history became a human being.

The Prologue of the Gospel of John concludes in a striking manner, with its simplicity and with the paradoxical statement: "No man hath seen God at any time; the only begotten Son, which is in the bosom of the Father, he hath declared him" (Jn 1.18). The first part of this sentence could belong to an atheist. Its meaning, however, becomes clear only in the context of the whole sentence, the whole Prologue, the whole Gospel of John, and the whole New Testament. What is being discussed here is a new revelation of God, a revelation brought to earth by Jesus.

In the Old Testament, God dwelled in absolute inaccessibility. Being invisible by nature, he never appeared to people in a visible form. When Moses said to God, "I beseech thee, show me thy glory," God answered him: "Thou canst not see my face: for there shall no man see me, and live." But God promised to show himself to Moses from behind: "And it shall come to pass, while my glory passeth by, that I will put thee in a clift of the rock, and will cover thee with my hand while I pass by. And I will take away mine hand, and thou shalt see my back parts, but my face shall not be seen" (Ex 33.18, 20–23). God's revelation to Moses consisted in God appearing to Moses in the cloud of his glory and proclaiming his holy name (Ex 34.5).

The evangelist John undoubtedly had this biblical story in mind when he wrote that "no man hath seen God at any time." The use of the term "glory" in the Prologue of the Gospel of John also emphasizes the connection to the account of God's appearance to Moses. Here John is speaking directly of how the coming of the only begotten Son of God into the world was a new revelation to mankind about God. If, earlier, no one had seen God, and even Moses could only see God from behind, now, the only

The Only-Begotten Son, icon, 1668.

begotten Son of God has revealed the countenance of the invisible God to men. The matter at hand is precisely a new revelation, a new degree of knowledge of God compared to the monotheism of the Old Testament:

> Believing in God as a Christian signifies something different, something new compared with Jewish monotheism: one can no longer talk about God without talking about Christ. God and Christ are one in such a way that Christ can, and must, be referred to as God, without thereby producing a rivalry for the divinity of God. The meaning of this unity, which completely reshapes our understanding of God, is only unlocked, of course, in the concrete life, death, and Resurrection of Jesus.[2]

In this sense it is possible to say that the Prologue of the Gospel of John is a key not only to understanding the rest of the text of this Gospel, but also to understanding the narratives of the other evangelists, and also all of the New Testament teaching about Jesus—the Son of God and the Son of Man. The Prologue of the Gospel of John is a magnificent theological overture to the action that plays out on the pages of the Gospels.

The story of Jesus described in them, his words, and the events of his life cannot be understood outside of the context of the theology presented

[2]Christoph Schönborn, *God Sent His Son: A Contemporary Christology,* trans. Henry Taylor (San Francisco, CA: Ignatius Press, 2010), 77.

in the Prologue of John's Gospel. In our day, the conscious refusal to anchor oneself to these theological tenets, which give the key to understanding the events in the Gospels, has brought into total collapse the more than two-century-long campaign for the search for the "historical Jesus." One can try to learn the historical fabric of the story of Jesus' life from the general context of New Testament theology; one can declare the Prologue of the Gospel of John a theological invention that arose after the Gospel narrative itself; but one cannot separate the "historical Jesus" from God the Word, "who is in the bosom of the Father," without having the integral Gospel image of Jesus fall apart into tiny pieces.

It is precisely in this that we find the supreme mystery of the person of Jesus. He is not simply a man, a prophet, or a moral teacher: he is God himself in his revelation to the world. And the Gospels are not simply a story about the earthly acts, miracles, and words of Jesus: they are the revelation of God become man. Only in the light of this tenet, so vividly presented by John in the Prologue of his Gospel, does the Gospel story about Jesus acquire its meaning. And only belief in the divinity of Jesus makes the eyewitness testimonies that lie at the foundation of the Gospel accounts trustworthy in the absolute sense of the word.

2. "John came baptizing in the wilderness"

The paradox of all four Gospels consists in the fact that the "Gospel of Jesus Christ, the Son of God" begins not with the preaching of Jesus Christ, but with the preaching of another figure. And the formula with which Jesus began his mission—"Repent, for the kingdom of heaven is at hand" (Mt 4.17)—does not belong to Jesus. Its originator is John the Baptist (Mt 3.2), or the Forerunner—the title with which he entered the history of the Church.

John is one of the few protagonists of the New Testament about whom we have "a good testimony among those who are outside" (1 Tim 3.7, NKJV), which serves as additional confirmation of his historicity. Josephus writes about him in the *Antiquities of the Jews*:

> Herod slew him, who was a good man, and commanded the Jews to exercise virtue, both as to righteousness towards one another, and piety towards God, and so to come to baptism; for that the washing [with water] would be acceptable to him, if they made use of it, not in order to the putting away [or the remission] of some sins [only], but for the purification of the body; supposing still that the soul was thoroughly purified beforehand by righteousness. Now when [many] others came in crowds about him, for they were very greatly moved [or pleased] by hearing his words, Herod, who feared lest the great influence John had over the people might put it into his power and inclination to raise a rebellion, (for they seemed ready to do any thing he should advise,) thought it best, by putting him to death, to prevent any mischief he might cause, and not bring himself into difficulties, by sparing a man who might make him repent of it when it would be too late. Accordingly he was sent a prisoner, out of Herod's suspicious temper, to Macherus, the castle I before mentioned, and was there put to death. Now the Jews had an opinion that the destruction of this army was sent as a punishment upon Herod, and a mark of God's displeasure to him.[3]

The story of John the Forerunner is presented in a fair amount of detail in the Gospels. Luke tells of his birth to the priest Zacharias and his wife, Elisabeth (Lk 1.5–25). The three synoptic evangelists tell of his imprisonment and execution by the order of Herod (Mt 14.1–12; Mk 6.14–29; Lk 3.19–20; 9.9). Their accounts agree on the whole with the aforementioned words of Josephus, and provide certain additional details.

A biography of John the Forerunner is not our present task. However, we cannot overlook his preaching, which not only preceded the beginning of Jesus' preaching, but also undoubtedly exerted a definite influence on it. This influence can be seen, if nothing else, from the fact that Jesus began his own preaching with the very same words that were a leitmotif of John

[3] Josephus, *Antiquities of the Jews* 18.5.2 (trans. Whiston). Square brackets in original.

The Preaching of John the Baptist, Jan Brueghel the Elder, 1598.

the Baptist's preaching, and consciously emphasized with those words the continuity of his teaching with the teaching of the Forerunner.

We find the shortest and most succinct description of the Forerunner's preaching in the Gospel of Mark:

> John did baptize in the wilderness, and preach the baptism of repentance for the remission of sins. And there went out unto him all the land of Judaea, and they of Jerusalem, and were all baptized by him in the river of Jordan, confessing their sins. And John was clothed with camel's hair, and with a girdle of a skin about his loins; and he did eat locusts and wild honey. And preached, saying, "There cometh one mightier than I after me, the latchet of whose shoes I am not worthy to stoop down and unloose. I indeed have baptized you with water, but he shall baptize you with the Holy Spirit." (Mk 1.4–8)

We learn from this description that John was an ascetic, lived in the wilderness, preached to the people, and accompanied his preaching with a special ritual—ablution in the waters of the Jordan. The testimony of Matthew is almost identical (Mt 3.1–6); however, he adds to the words documented by Mark a separate exhortation of John, addressed to the Pharisees and Sadducees:

O generation of vipers, who hath warned you to flee from the wrath to come? Bring forth therefore fruits meet for repentance. And think not to say within yourselves, "We have Abraham to our father." For I say unto you, that God is able of these stones to raise up children unto Abraham. And now also the axe is laid unto the root of the trees; therefore every tree which bringeth not forth good fruit is hewn down, and cast into the fire. (Mt 3.7–10)

John the Forerunner as the angel of the wilderness, icon, mid-17th c.

From this account we see that John's preaching took on the character of a harsh rebuke when it had to do with the Pharisees and Sadducees. Jesus adopts this manner of addressing the Pharisees from John, even down to verbal correspondences, such as the insult "generation of vipers" (Mt 12.34; 23.33) and the words "Every tree that bringeth not forth good fruit is hewn down, and cast into the fire" (Mt 7.19).

Luke's account almost entirely agrees with the stories of Matthew and Mark, although it does add some extra touches. First and foremost, Luke presents John as a new prophet: "Now in the fifteenth year of the reign of Tiberius Caesar . . . the word of God came unto John the son of Zacharias in the wilderness" (Lk 3.1–2). The books of the Prophets begin in an analogous way, with the formula "the word of the Lord came to":

The words of Jeremiah the son of Hilkiah . . . to whom the word of the Lord came in the days of Josiah the son of Amon king of Judah, in the thirteenth year of his reign. (Jer 1.1–2)

In the fifth day of the month, which was the fifth year of king Jehoiachin's captivity, the word of the Lord came expressly unto Ezekiel the priest, the son of Buzi, in the land of the Chaldeans by the river Chebar. (Ezek 1.2–3)

The word of the Lord that came unto Hosea, the son of Beeri, in the days of Uzziah, Jotham, Ahaz, and Hezekiah, kings of Judah. (Hos 1.1)

John the Baptist, icon, 13th c.

Now the word of the Lord came unto Jonah the son of Amittai. (Jon 1.1)

The word of the Lord that came to Micah the Morasthite in the days of Jotham, Ahaz, and Hezekiah, kings of Judah, which he saw concerning Samaria and Jerusalem. (Mic 1.1)

Luke is the only one of the evangelists who records John's conversations with the different groups of people who come to him:

Then came also publicans to be baptized, and said unto him, "Master, what shall we do?" And he said unto them, "Exact no more than that which is appointed you." And the soldiers likewise demanded of him, saying, "And what shall we do?" And he said unto them, "Do violence to no man, neither accuse any falsely; and be content with your wages." (Lk 3.12–14)

As we can see, John's attitude towards the publicans and soldiers was much more tolerant than it was towards the Pharisees and Sadducees.

In the Gospel of John, we read the story of how the priests and Levites from Jerusalem came to John in order to find out who he was and why he was baptizing in the waters of the Jordan:

And this is the record of John, when the Jews sent priests and Levites from Jerusalem to ask him, "Who art thou?" And he confessed, and denied not, but confessed, "I am not the Christ." And they asked him, "What then? Art thou Elias?" And he saith, "I am not." "Art thou that prophet?" And he answered, "No." Then said they unto him, "Who art thou? that we may give an answer to them that sent us. What sayest thou of thyself?" He said, "I am the voice of one crying in the wilderness, 'Make straight the way of the Lord,' as said the prophet Isaiah."

[Is 40.3] And they which were sent were of the Pharisees. And they asked him, and said unto him, "Why baptizest thou then, if thou be not that Christ, nor Elias, neither that prophet?" John answered them, saying, "I baptize with water, but there standeth one among you, whom ye know not. He it is, who coming after me is preferred before me, whose shoe's latchet I am not worthy to unloose." (Jn 1.19–29)

John the Forerunner, icon, 16th c.

The collective witness of the four evangelists gives us a fairly full picture of what was happening on the banks of the Jordan before Jesus appeared there. The activity of John the Baptist elicited great interest from the Jews, while his severe, ascetic image attracted crowds of people to him. As far as one can judge, John's preaching was primarily of a moral nature. John addressed each class of people with specific advice. He treated certain groups (particularly the Pharisees and Sadducees) with marked severity. John's activity was not to the liking of the Pharisees, who responded to him with mutual antipathy. Nevertheless, John answered their questions—directly, and in brief. He understood that he was not the Messiah or Elijah the prophet. He saw the main aim of his mission as preparing the way for the One who was greater than him and whose shoes he was not worthy to untie. As to who this person was, John did not know, until the person himself appeared on the banks of the Jordan (Jn 1.21).

In what did John's baptism consist? In its form, it recalled little of the ritual ablutions known in Old Testament practice (a detailed description of such washing is contained in Leviticus 13–17). The closest parallel is found in the practice of the community of the Essenes, known to us through the writings of Josephus and the Qumran manuscripts (also known as the Dead Sea Scrolls). Josephus mentions the reception of new members into the community through ritual ablution.[4] In the Qumran manuscripts,

---

[4]Flavius Josephus, *Wars of the Jews* 2.8.7.

washing is associated with repentance, cleansing from sins, observance of moral purity, and entrance into a covenant with God.[5]

Notwithstanding certain possible parallels, John's baptism possessed strongly pronounced individual features that made it a unique event in the life of the people of Israel.

3. The Baptism of Jesus

Among those baptized by John was Jesus. We find the shortest account of this in Mark:

> And it came to pass in those days, that Jesus came from Nazareth of Galilee, and was baptized by John in Jordan. And straightway coming up out of the water, he saw the heavens opened, and the Spirit like a dove descending upon him. And there came a voice from heaven, saying, "Thou art my beloved Son, in whom I am well pleased." (Mk 1.9–11)

Matthew points out that Jesus came to the Jordan "from Galilee," and fills out the scene with the dialogue between Jesus and John that took place before the baptism: "But John forbad him, saying, 'I have need to be baptized by thee, and comest thou to me?' And Jesus answering said unto him, 'Allow it to be so now, for thus it becometh us to fulfil all righteousness.' Then he suffered him." The voice of the Father is rendered in a somewhat different way: "This is my beloved Son, in whom I am well pleased" (Mt 3.14–15, 17).

Luke does not describe the baptism of Jesus separately, but mentions that he was baptized together with the people: "Now when all the people were baptized, it came to pass, that Jesus also being baptized, and

[5]For a more detailed comparison between the Qumram practice of ritual washing and John's baptism, see John P. Meier, *A Marginal Jew: Rethinking the Historical Jesus, vol. 1, The Roots of the Problem and the Person*, Anchor Bible Reference Library (New York: Doubleday, 1991), 49–56.

praying, the heaven was opened, and the Holy Spirit descended in a bodily shape like a dove upon him, and a voice came from heaven, which said, 'Thou art my beloved Son; in thee I am well pleased'" (Lk 3.21–22). In this way, Luke places Jesus in the crowd of people being baptized by John, not distinguishing the baptism of Jesus as an event carried out apart from the others who were baptized.

We have before us three almost identical testimonies, differing from each other only in minor details. From all three testimonies it is clear that the baptism in the Jordan was a boundary event in Jesus' biography that divided his life into a "before" and "after."

The Baptism of the Lord, fresco from the catacombs of Rome, 3rd c.

Before his baptism, no one knew of him: the unknown Son of a carpenter, he came to John as one among many, one of the multitude. After his baptism, Jesus ceased to be an inconspicuous figure, one of the multitude: the people recognized him due to the testimony of John, the descent of the Holy Spirit on him, and the voice of the Father, which the people heard. Immediately after his baptism, Jesus withdrew to the wilderness, and then returned to the people no longer as some unknown "Jesus . . . from Nazareth of Galilee" (Mk 1.9), but as "a prophet mighty in deed and word before God and all the people" (Lk 2.19), whom even his relatives ceased to recognize.

The main event that divided these two radically different periods in Jesus' life was his baptism.[6] It turned out to be the "bridge-burning event" between the previous thirty years and the new period in the life of Jesus.[7] The baptism from John became a "prelude . . . to Jesus' [subsequent] activity."[8] From this moment his journey to Golgotha began.

---

[6]John P. Meier, *A Marginal Jew*, 108–111.

[7]Kilian McDonnell, *The Baptism of Jesus in the Jordan: The Trinitarian and Cosmic Order of Salvation* (Collegeville, MN: Liturgical Press, 1996), 4–5.

[8]Rudolf Schnackenburg, *The Gospel of Matthew*, trans. Robert R. Barr (Grand Rapids, MI: Eerdmans, 2002), 34.

The Baptism
of the Lord,
mosaic, 5th c.

Why was baptism necessary for beginning this journey? If one is speaking of Jesus as the Son of Man, then perhaps he came to John because he was in need of a kind of starting point for his mission, in need—as a human being—of the blessing of the one who was already carrying out a similar mission, in anticipation of his own mission. As a human being, he received a blessing from the greater, but in the kingdom of heaven that opened up with his coming, he, the lesser, turned out to be greater than John (Mt 11.11; Lk 7.28).

That is the whole point of Jesus' answer to John's question: "I have need to be baptized of thee, and comest thou to me?" In answering, "Allow it to be so; for thus it becometh us to fulfil all righteousness" (Mt 3.14–15), Jesus emphasized with the word "now" (*arti*) the temporary, transitional nature of the situation in which the two of them found themselves—John, who was aware of Jesus' superiority and therefore attempting to prevent his baptism, and Jesus, who was receiving baptism from John, because he saw in this the fulfillment of the will of the Father.

Saint John Baptizing in the River Jordan, Nicolas Poussin, *c.* 1630s.

This situation reminds us of another moment in the same story of the self-emptying of the Son of God, also connected with water: the washing of the disciples' feet at the Last Supper. Here, in a role analogous to that of the Baptist, we find Peter, who attempted to prevent Jesus from washing his feet, saying, "Lord, dost thou wash my feet?" But Jesus answered him, "What I do thou knowest not now; but thou shalt know hereafter" (Jn 13.6–7). The parallelism between the two stories is noted by Gregory the Theologian (fourth century), who gives the following theological commentary on the event:

> The baptizer does not accept it; Jesus debates [with him]. "I need to be baptized by you," [Mt 3.14] the lamp [Jn 5.35] says to the sun [Mal 4.2], the voice [Mt 3.3; Is 40.3] to the Word, the friend to the bridegroom [Jn 3.29], the one above all born of women [Mt 11.11] to the first born of all creation [Col 1.15]. . . . For he knew that he would be baptized by martyrdom or, like Peter, would not have only his feet cleansed. [Jn 13.9] "And you come to me?" This is also prophetic. For he knew that after the madness of Herod would come that of Pilate, so as he himself departed beforehand, Christ would follow. But what does Jesus say? "Let it be so now"; for this is the divine plan. For he knew that shortly he himself would baptize the baptizer.[9]

[9]Gregory of Nazianzus, *Orations* 39.15 (Harrison, PPS).

The Baptism of
the Lord,
mosaic, 11th c.

The evangelists depict Jesus as a Man who clearly knows what he is doing as he goes along the path foreordained for him by the Father. This awareness does not come to him at some specific moment: it is with him from the very beginning. Already as a twelve-year-old youth he was confidently speaking of God as his Father, and of the Temple as a place belonging to his Father (Lk 2.49). His unshakeable dedication to fulfilling the will of the Father leads him to the Jordan. The same dedication will lead him to the cross.

It is no coincidence that already in the early Church, Jesus' baptism was understood as a prefiguration of his death on the cross. Jesus himself uses the term "baptism" in relation to his passion and death: "But I have a baptism to be baptized with; and how constrained I am till it be accomplished!" (Lk 12.50). He asks the disciples who wish to sit at his right and left: "Are ye able to drink of the cup that I shall drink of, and to be baptized with the baptism that I am baptized with?" (Mt 20.22).

The baptism administered by Jesus' disciples according to his commandment is also understood as an image of his death. The apostle Paul writes: "Know ye not, that so many of us as were baptized into Jesus Christ were baptized into his death? Therefore we are buried with him by baptism into death" (Rom 6.3–4). Addressing the newly baptized, Cyril of Jerusalem (fourth century) says:

The Baptism of Christ, Annibale Carracci, 1584.

You professed this saving confession and you descended three times into the water and ascended again, thereby also re-enacting through symbol the three-day burial of Christ. For just as our Savior spent "three days and three nights in the heart of the earth" (Mt 12.40), so also you in your first ascent imitated the first day of Christ in the earth. . . . And in this same time you died and were reborn, and that saving water become both grave and mother for you. . . . And one time brought about both of these, and your birth was brought together with your death.[10]

If the baptism from John was a "baptism of repentance for the remission of sins" (Mk 1.4), what effect did it have on Jesus? The evangelists present Jesus entirely unequivocally as the one who, being the Son of Man and the Son of God, possesses the power to remit sins (Mt 9.6; Mk 2.10; Lk 5.24 and others). The New Testament authors emphasize many times and in many ways that "in him is no sin" (1 Jn 3.5); on the contrary, he is the source of the forgiveness of sins. In the words of the apostle Peter, the Son

---

[10]Cyril of Jerusalem, *On the Mysteries* 2.4 (Johnson, PPS).

The Baptism of the Lord,
Mikhail Nesterov, 1891.

of God "did no sin . . . [he] bare our sins in his own body on the tree, that we, being dead to sins, should live unto righteousness" (1 Pet 2.22, 24).

In light of this teaching, the descent of the Son of God into the waters of the Jordan can be understood in only one way: it was necessary to deliver mankind from sin. In the Second Epistle to the Corinthians, the apostle Paul says, "For he hath made him to be sin for us, who knew no sin, that we might be made the righteousness of God in him" (2 Cor 5.21). Being without sin, Jesus wholeheartedly identifies himself with sinful mankind, and therefore receives the baptism that others received for the cleansing of their personal sins: he receives it for no other reason than that he "taketh away the sin of the world" (Jn 1.29).

The baptism in the Jordan was for Jesus an important step on the path of diminishment, self-emptying, and self-effacement (*kenōsis*), the path that he would walk to the end—"unto death, even the death of the cross" (Phil 2.8). This path began when the Son of God became the Son of Man. As the Son of Man, he merged into the crowd of people seeking absolution for their sins, becoming as though one of them in order to, as the Son of God, take the burden of their sins upon himself. Justin Martyr speaks of this in his *Dialogue with Trypho*, insisting that baptism was necessary not for Jesus, but for the people whom he would redeem from death:

> And then, when Jesus had gone to the river Jordan, where John was baptizing, and when He had stepped into the water, a fire was kindled in the Jordan; and when He came out of the water, the Holy Spirit lighted on Him like a dove. . . . Now, we know that he did not go to the river because He stood in need of baptism, or of the descent of the Spirit like a dove; even as He submitted to be born and to be crucified, not because He needed such things, but because of the human race, which from Adam had fallen under the power of death. . . . And when Jesus came to the Jordan . . . the Holy Spirit . . . for man's sake . . .

lighted on Him in the form of a dove, and there came at the same instant from the heavens a voice, which was uttered also by David when he spoke, personating Christ, what the Father would say to Him: "Thou art My Son: this day have I begotten Thee" [Ps 2.7].[11]

The Baptism of Christ,
Piero della Francesca,
ca. 1448–1450.

John Chrysostom emphasizes that Jesus was not in need of baptism—neither that of John, nor of some other sort. On the contrary, "baptism needed the power of Christ."[12] In Church tradition the opinion has become firmly established that Jesus sanctified the waters of the Jordan as he descended into them. In the words of Ignatius of Antioch, Jesus "was born and was baptized, so that he might purify the water through his submission."[13] He is echoed by Gregory the Theologian, who asserts that Jesus was baptized "to hallow water."[14] Cyril of Alexandria emphasizes that Jesus "was not baptized as one repenting but as one cleansing sins and sanctifying the waters."[15]

One modern Orthodox theologian uncovers the meaning of the Church's view of Jesus' descent into the waters of the Jordan in the following way:

People repenting in response to the preaching of John the Forerunner came to wash themselves in these waters; how heavy these waters were with the sin of the people who washed in them! . . . And it was in these waters that Jesus came to immerse himself at the beginning of the labor of his preaching and gradual ascent to the cross, to submerge himself in these waters, carrying the whole burden of human sin—he, the sinless one. . . . The Lord now full grown in his manhood, the Man

[11]Justin Martyr, *Dialogue with Trypho* 88 (*ANF* 1:243–244).
[12]John Chrysostom, *Homilies on the Gospel of John* 17.2 (*NPNF*[1] 14:60).
[13]Ignatius of Antioch, *Epistle to the Ephesians* 18.2 (Stewart, PPS).
[14]Gregory of Nazianzus, *Orations* 29.20 (Wickham, PPS).
[15]Cyril of Alexandria, *Commentary on the Gospel of Matthew* 29 [=Fragment 29] (ACCS NT 1a:53).

*The Baptism
of Christ,*
Joachim Patinir,
1475–1480.

Jesus Christ, who has reached the full measure of his maturity, who
has united perfect love and perfect obedience to the will of the Father,
comes of his own free will, in order to voluntarily fulfill that which
the Pre-Eternal Counsel foreordained. Now the Man Jesus Christ
brings this flesh as a sacrifice and offering not only to God, but to all of
mankind; he takes upon his shoulders all the horror of human sin and
human fallenness, and immerses himself in these waters, which are
now the waters of death, an image of perdition, carrying in themselves
all evil, all poison, and all of sinful death.[16]

Special attention should be paid to the evangelists' references to the
voice of the Father that was heard when Jesus came out of the waters.
This was a landmark moment for the revelation of God that received the
name of the New Testament. This moment is directly related to the last
words of Jesus addressed to his disciples: "Go ye therefore, and teach all
nations, baptizing them in the name of the Father, and of the Son, and of
the Holy Spirit" (Mt 28.19). It was precisely at this moment, when Jesus

[16]Metropolitan Anthony (Bloom), *Vo imya Ottsa i Syna i Svyatogo Dukha: Propovedi* [In
the name of the Father and the Son and the Holy Spirit: Sermons] (Klin: Khristianskaya zhizn,'
2001), 37–38.

was coming out of the waters of the Jordan, that the Father, Son, and Holy Spirit were revealed to the people in undivided unity: the Father bore witness about the Son by a voice from heaven; the Son, having emerged from the baptismal waters, prayed to the Father; and the Spirit descended on the Son in the form of a dove. "Here then we have the Trinity in a certain sort distinguished. The Father in the Voice,—the Son in the Man,—the Holy Spirit in the Dove," said the blessed Augustine.[17]

The Baptism of the Lord, icon, 15th c.

The appearance of God the Father as described by the evangelists is in line with the revelations of God that we are told about in the Old Testament. In many cases it was through a voice that God revealed himself to men (Gen 3.8, 10). On Sinai "Moses spake, and God answered him by a voice" (Ex 19.19). Moses heard the voice of God from above the mercy seat of the ark of the covenant (Num 7.89). Of the prophet Elijah it is said that "there came a voice unto him" (1 Kg 19.13). Some of those who heard the voice of God did not recognize him straight away, such as, for example, the boy Samuel, who did not understand who was speaking with him, because he "did not yet know [the voice of] the Lord" (1 Sam 3.4–7).

Here we may recall once again the words from the Prologue of the Gospel of John: "No man hath seen God at any time" (Jn 1.18). These words concern God the Father, who has never appeared to anyone in a visible form. However, regarding God the Father one cannot say that no one has ever heard him, since his voice was heard at the moment when the Son of God was revealed to the people of Israel. On the Mount of Transfiguration, three of the disciples again heard the very same voice pronouncing the very same words: "This is my beloved Son, in whom I am well pleased" (Mt 17.5; cf. Mk 9.7; Lk 9.35).

However, while on the mountain the Father bears witness about the Son in the third person (that is, the witness is addressed to Jesus' companions, and not to him directly), in the account of Jesus' baptism in Mark and

[17]Augustine of Hippo, *Sermons* 52.1 (PL 38:356)=*Sermons* 2 (*NPNF¹* 6:259).

The Baptism of the Lord, miniature from the Echmiadzin Gospels, 6th c.

Luke the voice of the Father is addressed directly to Jesus: "Thou art my beloved Son" (Mk 1.11, Lk 3.22). Is it possible to interpret this address as some sort of event in the history of the relationship between the Father and the Son—as the moment when the Father, speaking to the Son whom he sent into the world, publicly testifies of his love for him in order to strengthen him for his upcoming ministry?

The theme of the relationship between the Father and the Son is developed on the pages of the Gospels in a series of episodes and in the speeches of Jesus. The evangelists speak many times of Jesus addressing the Father. But only twice do we hear how the Father addresses the Son. The first time is at the moment of Jesus' baptism, according to Mark and Luke. The second instance is mentioned by John. When before his last Passover Jesus exclaims, "Father, glorify thy name," a voice from heaven answers him: "I have both glorified it, and will glorify it again" (Jn 12.28). Both episodes occur in relation to turning points in Jesus' life: the first is connected with his embarkation on public ministry, and the second with his approach towards Jerusalem, where arrest, judgment, and execution awaited him.

In the first case, Jesus does not answer the voice of the Father in any way and does not comment on his words. In the second case, Jesus gives this explanation: "This voice came not because of me, but for your sakes" (Jn 12.30). From this we can conclude that, at the moment of baptism also, the witness of the Father, even if it was addressed to the Son, was necessary not so much for the Son as for the people who stood round about. At the same time we cannot exclude the possibility that Jesus himself, as a man, was in need of the fortifying witness of the Father at the moment when it was time for him to begin the labor of his ministry to the people—the labor that would be crowned by his death.

What does the descent of the Holy Spirit on Jesus after his emergence from the waters of the Jordan mean? In the life of Jesus, the Holy Spirit acts in a special way. By the Holy Spirit, without the participation of a husband,

The Baptism of Christ, Pietro Perugino and Pinturicchio, 1482.

the Virgin Mary conceived the divine Infant. John prophesies that Jesus would baptize with the Holy Spirit and with fire. Immediately after his baptism, the Spirit leads Jesus into the wilderness (Mt 4.1; Mk 1.12; Lk 4.1). By the Spirit of God, Jesus would drive out demons (Mt 12.28). Of the Holy Spirit, Jesus would say that "whosoever speaketh against the Holy Spirit, it shall not be forgiven him, neither in this world, neither in the world to come" (Mt 12.32; Mk 3.29; Lk 12.10). The promise of the Holy Spirit would be one of the main themes of Jesus' farewell discourse with the disciples (Jn 14.16–17.26; 15.26; 16.7–15). After the resurrection, Jesus would breathe on the disciples and say to them, "Receive ye the Holy Spirit" (Jn 20.22). And on the day of Pentecost the Holy Spirit would descend on the disciples in the form of tongues of flame (Acts 2.4).

We have seen that the evangelists present the baptism of Jesus as a turning point in his human destiny. One may suggest that at this important moment in his life Jesus, as a man, was in need not only of strengthening from the Father before beginning his preaching, but also of a special manifestation of the Holy Spirit. Inasmuch as his ministry would be akin to that of the prophets, as a human being he needed the same inspiration possessed by the prophets, who received it from the Spirit of God. Later on he would send the Holy Spirit to his disciples, inspiring them for the apostolic ministry, but now he himself was in need of this inspiration.

At the same time, it would be mistaken to imagine that Jesus' baptism in the Jordan was for him an event of a psychological character—that it

The Baptism of Christ,
El Greco, 1596–1600.

was accompanied by a "dissociative psychological transformation" of his personality, which caused him to become aware of his messianic calling and made him a "spirit-possessed man whose new social role resulted from that specific status."[18] Excessive psychologizing of this event is fraught with conjectures and speculations regarding the new role that Jesus supposedly was earlier not aware of and took upon himself only under the influence of the Holy Spirit.

As we have said, Jesus had been aware of his status as the Son of God and of his special mission from the time of his childhood (Lk 2.43–52). And although we know very little about Jesus' life before his baptism, we have no grounds to suppose that it did not consist in gradual development and progressive preparation towards the goal that Jesus came into the world to achieve. The Holy Spirit's descent on Jesus, for all the importance of this event, does not mean that the Holy Spirit was hitherto absent from his life. The accounts of his nativity by the evangelists Matthew and Luke testify the opposite.

In the story itself of Jesus' baptism, the descent of the Holy Spirit is a key moment. From this moment, his messianic ministry begins. The Holy Spirit acts as the creative power of God that establishes the beginning of the messianic era.[19] In the Acts of the Apostles, we read Peter's speech, which includes these words: "That word ye know, which was published throughout all Judaea, and began from Galilee, after the baptism which John preached, how God anointed Jesus of Nazareth with the Holy Spirit and with power, who went about doing good, and healing all that were oppressed by the devil, for God was with him" (Acts 10.37–38). The simultaneous mention of baptism, anointing, and the Holy Spirit may indicate

---

[18]Stevan L. Davies, *Jesus the Healer: Possession, Trance, and the Origins of Christianity* (New York, NY: Continuum, 1995), 65.

[19]C. K. Barrett, *The Holy Spirit and the Gospel Tradition* (London: S.P.C.K., 1947), 44–45.

that it was at the moment of baptism that, due to the descent of the Holy Spirit on him, Jesus was revealed to the world as God's Anointed, the promised Messiah.[20]

The descent of the Holy Spirit on Jesus is also mentioned in the Gospel of John, in which an account of his baptism is absent. Here the words of John the Baptist regarding Jesus are quoted: "I saw the Spirit descending from heaven like a dove, and it abode upon him." The Baptist emphasizes: "And I knew him not, but he that sent me to baptize with water, the same said unto me, 'Upon whom thou shalt see the Spirit descending, and remaining on him, the same is he which baptizeth with the Holy

The Baptism of the Lord, icon, 12th c.

Spirit" (Jn 1.32–33). The repeated verb "abide," or "remain," indicates that from the moment of Jesus' baptism, the Holy Spirit stays with him and perpetually abides with him.

The dove as a symbol of peace and humility, but at the same time also a symbol of salvation (Gen 8.8–12), was the form in which the Holy Spirit was revealed to the people. His descent on Jesus, which took place at the moment when the voice of the Father was heard bearing witness about the Son, constituted a visible confirmation of the unity of the three Persons of the Trinity, who are spoken of at the end of the Gospel of Matthew (Mt 28.19).

The story of Jesus' baptism at the hands of John received its continuation in the tradition of the Church. This is expressed foremost in the feast of Theophany, which, as we have already said, encompassed at first the remembrance of the nativity of Jesus from the Virgin and his baptism from John, but which by the fourth century was separated out into the independent celebration of the baptism of the Lord. The liturgical texts of this feast contain an interpretation of the event of the baptism itself, the role of John the Baptist, the descent of the Holy Spirit on Jesus, and other aspects of the story of Jesus' baptism. Multiple references to this story are contained also

[20]McDonnell, *The Baptism of Jesus*, 11.

in the order of service (service text) for the sacrament of baptism, which is administered to each person who wishes to join the Church.[21]

The baptism of Jesus in the Jordan is reflected in the iconographic tradition as well. In ancient icons, mosaics, and frescoes, Jesus, having descended into the waters of the Jordan, is depicted fully unclothed. This has a deep theological significance, linking Jesus with the first human beings, Adam and Eve, who before the fall "were naked . . . and were not ashamed" (Gen 2.25). The perception of nakedness as something shameful was Adam's first discovery after he ate from the tree of the knowledge of good and evil (Gen 3.10). From that time nakedness became a symbol of the defenselessness of the human being before the devil, and a symbol of his shame, which was the consequence of a sinful life. Through baptism, Jesus raises the human being up to his original dignity; Jesus' nakedness symbolizes the original purity of the human body undefiled by sin.

It is no coincidence that from the time of the apostle Paul, the image of garments has been used to illustrate the change that takes place in the believer after receiving baptism: "For as many of you as have been baptized into Christ have put on Christ" (Gal 3.27). Christ himself becomes the garment in which those baptized into him are clothed, having been set free from uncleanness and nakedness. In the words of Gregory of Nyssa, God banished man from paradise in the beginning, but through Christ he has again called him back, taken from him the "unseemly covering"—the leaves of the fig tree—and clothed him in a "costly garment." Therefore it was no longer necessary for Adam to be ashamed and hide among the trees of paradise.[22] "[I]n the Baptism of Jesus," Gregory writes, "all we, putting off our sins like some poor and patched garment, are clothed in the holy and most fair garment of regeneration."[23]

---

[21]For more details, see Metropolitan Hilarion Alfeyev, *Orthodox Christianity*, vol. 4, *The Worship and Liturgical Life of the Orthodox Church*, trans. Andrei Tepper (Yonkers, NY: St Vladimir's Seminary Press, 2016), 285–292; *Orthodox Christianity*, vol. 5, trans. Nathan Williams (Yonkers, NY: St Vladimir's Seminary Press, forthcoming) will contain a treatment of the sacrament of baptism.

[22]Gregory of Nyssa, *On the Baptism of Christ* (*NPNF*[2] 5:524).

[23]Ibid. (*NPNF*[2] 5:522–523).

4. Temptation by the Devil

According to the Synoptics, after Jesus' baptism, he was led by the Spirit into the wilderness. Mark uses the word "immediately" (Mk 1.12), Matthew uses the less specific word "then" (Mt 4.1), and Luke says that Jesus "returned from Jordan, and was led by the Spirit into the wilderness" (Lk 4.1). In this story the Synoptics introduce a new character into the narrative: Satan, or the devil.

In the Old Testament this character figures in the story of the fall of the first human beings (Gen 3.1–15). There he is called a serpent, but Old Testament tradition already identified him as the devil. In particular, in the book of the Wisdom of Solomon, it is said that "through envy of the devil came death into the world" (Wis 2.24): what is in view here is the story of the serpent's temptation of Adam and Eve in the book of Genesis.

The same character appears, with the name Satan, in the book of Job as one of the sons of God [i.e., angels—*Ed.*] who regularly present themselves before the Lord (Job 1.6; 2.1). God enters into a dialogue with him and asks whether he has taken note of the righteousness of Job. Satan answers that Job is righteous because God has "made an hedge about him, and about

Jesus Tempted in the Wilderness, James Tissot, 1886–1894.

*The Temptation
of Adam,*
Tintoretto, 1551.

his house, and about all that he hath on every side" (Job 1.10). God puts
into Satan's hands all of Job's possessions and children, who perish one
after another, and then also his body, which becomes covered with sores
(Job 1.8–2.7).

In 1 Samuel there are multiple mentions of an "evil spirit from God," or
"evil spirit from the Lord" (1 Sam 16.14–16, 23; 18.10; 19.9), which falls upon
Saul and drives him into a rage. In 1 Kings the Lord puts a "lying spirit"
in the mouths of the prophets of Ahab (1 Kg 22.21–23). Finally, in one of
the psalms, David turns to God with a request to punish the wrongdoer:
"Set thou a wicked man over him, and let Satan stand at his right hand"
(Ps 108.6).

In the book of Job and also the books of Samuel and Kings, Satan, or
the evil spirit, acts as though at the direct command or with the permission of God. The Old Testament did not attempt to answer the questions of
the origin of Satan and his relationship with God. However, the beginning
of the book of Job shows that, in the understanding of the Old Testament
author, Satan was one of the sons of God, who was in personal contact with
God. Satan acts within the limits placed by God, and outside these limits he
cannot act. He visits harm upon humankind, and this is allowed by God.

In the book of the prophet Zechariah, Satan antagonizes the high priest
Joshua, who is clad in stained garments (Zech 3.1–3). This prophecy was

understood in the early Christian Church as a reference to Jesus Christ, whose garments are stained with human sins.[24] Blessed Theodoret (fifth century) writes:

> [J]ust as the avenging and wicked devil was very opposed to Joshua for being high priest and making intercession to God on behalf of the people, so in turn this same enemy was an opponent of Jesus the great high priest in the order of Melchizedek [Heb 7.21] for taking away the sin of the world [Jn 1.29]. . . . [W]hen [the devil] approached Jesus the savior of the world, he was rebuked by him, as by his God and Lord, and hears, "Get behind me, Satan" [Mt 4.10].[25]

The Messengers Bring to Job Evil Tidings, engraving, Gustave Doré, 1860s.

In the Gospels the devil and demons are mentioned many times. The Synoptic Gospels contain multiple accounts of Jesus driving out a demon or demons from the possessed. Jesus gave his disciples the power to drive out demons (Mt 10.8; Mk 3.15, 6.13). In the Gospel of Luke, Jesus says to Peter: "Simon, Simon, behold, Satan hath desired to have you, that he may sift you as wheat. But I have prayed for thee, that thy faith fail not" (Lk 22.31–32).

Jesus mentions the devil in his parables and in his discourses with the Jews. In one of the parables the devil is compared to a sower who sows tares (Mt 13.39). In another passage Jesus speaks of how the devil takes away the word of God that is sown in a person's heart (Lk 8.12). To the Jews Jesus says: "Ye are of your father the devil, and the lusts of your father ye will do. He was a murderer from the beginning, and abode not in the truth, because there is no truth in him. When he speaketh a lie, he speaketh of

---

[24]Jerome, *Homilies on the Psalms, Alternate Series* 61. In *The Homilies of Saint Jerome,* vol. 2, *Homilies 60–96,* trans. Marie Liguori Ewald, The Fathers of the Church 57 (Washington, DC: The Catholic University of America Press, 1966), 31.

[25]Theodoret of Cyrus, *Commentary on the Prophet Zechariah* 3 (PG 81:1892). Translation from Theodoret of Cyrus, *Commentaries on the Prophets,* vol. 3, *Commentary on the Twelve Prophets,* trans. Robert Charles Hill (Brookline, MA: Holy Cross Orthodox Press, 2006), 239–240.

The Temptations of Christ (fresco in the Sistine Chapel), Sandro Botticelli, 1481–1482.

his own. For he is a liar, and the father of it" (Jn 8.44). Referring to the Last Judgment, Jesus mentions the "everlasting fire, prepared for the devil and his angels" (Mt 25.41).

We will not expound here the Christian teaching about the devil. We will say only that in the accounts of Jesus' temptation in the wilderness in the Synoptics, the devil is presented as a being who has direct access to Jesus and who enters into a dialogue with him, similar to how Satan in the book of Job enters into a dialogue with God. As in the book of Job, Satan acts first of all as a tempter.[26]

The shortest version of the account of the temptation in the wilderness is contained in Mark: "And immediately the Spirit driveth him into the wilderness. And he was there in the wilderness forty days, tempted of Satan; and was with the wild beasts; and the angels ministered unto him" (Mk 1.12–13). Here the Spirit, angels, Satan, and wild beasts are all present. However, we do not know any details about what the temptation consisted of, and whether it took place over the span of forty days, or at the conclusion of this period.

Mark's version is full of enigmas.[27] The subject is mentioned, but practically undeveloped. In the meantime, the scholar will take note of the

---

[26]See Susan R. Garrett, *The Temptations of Jesus in Mark's Gospel* (Grand Rapids, MI: 1998), 33.

[27]See Jeffrey B. Gibson, *The Temptations of Jesus in Early Christianity* (London: T&T Clark International, 1995), 42–82.

Christ in the Wilderness, Ivan Kramskoy, 1872.

symbolism of the images contained in this version, and of a certain parallelism between Mark's account of the temptation in the wilderness and Jesus' words addressed to his disciples: "I beheld Satan as lightning fall from heaven" (Lk 10.18). When and where could Jesus have seen Satan fall from heaven? Could it have been in the wilderness, when Satan was tempting him? In that case, not only the theological, but also the historical import of the synoptic accounts of the temptation in the wilderness would become clear: in both accounts "an event [is being described] which cannot adequately be expressed in everyday language: the conquest of evil and the dawning of God's new world. Reverence for the ultimate mysteries demands that they shall be spoken of in veiled terms. But this veiled language is no more than a hint at the mystery; its use is in no way an argument against the presence of a historical nucleus of a narrative or a logion."[28]

Jesus is led into the wilderness by the Holy Spirit, but he is led for no other reason than to meet a different spirit—the father of evil spirits, and a battle with him awaits Jesus: "The devil, as a spirit contrary to God, confronts the (Holy) Spirit as an opponent."[29]

[28]Joachim Jeremias, *New Testament Theology: The Proclamation of Jesus* (New York, NY: Scribner, 1971), 70–71.
[29]Schnackenburg, *The Gospel of Matthew*, 37.

"Get thee hence, Satan" (The Temptation of Christ), Ilya Repin, 1901–1903.

The image of the wilderness, which dominates the first thirteen verses of the Gospel of Mark and makes them a compositional whole,[30] plays an essential role in the Old Testament, especially in the book of Exodus, and also in the Psalms and in some of the Prophets.[31] The reference to the wilderness and the forty-day fast from food cannot but remind one of Moses, who on Mt Sinai in the wilderness "was there . . . forty days and forty nights; he did neither eat bread, nor drink water" (Ex 34.28). Another parallel appears in the story of the prophet Elijah, who was fed with bread in the wilderness by an angel, after which he walked for forty days and forty nights to Mount Horeb (1 Kg 19.5–8). The meaning of the evangelist Mark's short account becomes clearer upon comparison with these Old Testament images.

Matthew and Luke contain a significantly more detailed account about Jesus' sojourn in the wilderness. Their narratives differ from each other

---

[30]William L. Lane, *The Gospel According to Mark: The English Text with Introduction, Exposition, and Notes,* New International Commentary on the New Testament 2 (Grand Rapids, MI: Eerdmans, 1974), 39.

[31]Ulrich Mauser, *Christ in the Wilderness: The Wilderness Theme in the Second Gospel and Its Basis in the Biblical Tradition,* Studies in Biblical Theology First Series 39 (Eugene, OR: Wipf & Stock, 2009), 20–52. First published 1963 by SCM Press.

in the order in which the three temptations occur. Here is Matthew's version:

Then was Jesus led up by the Spirit into the wilderness to be tempted by the devil. And when he had fasted forty days and forty nights, he was afterward hungry. And when the tempter came to him, he said, "If thou art the Son of God, command that these stones be made bread." But he answered and said, "It is written, 'Man shall not live by bread alone, but by every word that proceedeth out of the mouth of God.'" [Deut 8.3] Then the devil taketh him up into the holy city, and setteth him on a pinnacle of the temple, and saith unto him, "If thou art the Son of God, cast thyself down. For it is written, 'He shall give his angels charge concerning thee, and in their hands they shall bear thee up, lest at any time thou dash thy foot against a stone.'" [Ps 90.11–12] Jesus said unto him, "It is written again, 'Thou shalt not tempt the Lord thy God.'" [Deut 6.16] Again, the devil taketh him up into an exceeding high mountain, and showeth him all the kingdoms of the world, and the glory of them, and saith unto him, "All these things will I give thee, if thou wilt fall down and worship me." Then saith Jesus unto him, "Get thee hence, Satan. For it is written, 'Thou shalt worship the Lord thy God, and him only shalt thou serve.'" [Deut 6.13] Then the devil leaveth him, and, behold, angels came and ministered unto him. (Mt 4.1–11)

The Temptation of Christ,
Juan de Flandes, 16th c.

In Luke's version, the devil first asks Jesus to turn stones into bread, and then takes him to a high mountain and shows him all the kingdoms of the world, after which he leads him into Jerusalem and places him on a pinnacle of the Temple (Lk 4.1–13). Luke specifies that throughout the forty days Jesus "ate nothing" (Lk 4.2). He does not mention the angels who came to Jesus at the end of the temptation, but says only that "when the devil had ended all the temptation, he departed from him for a season"

The Temptation of Christ,
icon, 17th c.

(Lk 4.13). In the rest, the account of Luke is almost identical to that of Matthew.

The term *peirasmos*, used by both evangelists (Marks uses the related participle *peirazomenos*, "being tempted"), is encountered in the New Testament twenty-one times, and in most instances denotes not only "temptation," but also "trial," "testing." So, for instance, in the First Epistle of Peter it is written: "Beloved, think it not strange concerning the fiery trial [*pyrōsei*] which is to try you [*pros peirasmon hymin ginomenē*], as though some strange thing happened unto you" (1 Pet 4.12). By going out into the wilderness for forty days, guided by the Holy Spirit, Jesus is testing his strength, so to speak, both physical and spiritual, before going out to preach. And the devil, for his part, is testing Jesus' endurance.

The story described by Matthew and Luke places a multitude of questions before us. How literally should it be understood? Did all the action take place in the wilderness and was it a kind of temptation in the mind for Jesus, or did Jesus and the devil go together to Jerusalem and get up on the pinnacle of the Temple, and go up the mountain together? What is this mountain from which one can see "all the kingdoms of the world"? What is the significance of the biblical quotations in the direct speech of Jesus and the devil, which on the surface resembles a scholarly dispute between two scribes?

The very way in which the material is presented, which recalls in some respects the biblical story of the serpent's temptation of Adam and Eve (Gen 3.1–5), prompts us to perceive this story not as a historical account, but as a portrayal of a singular spiritual experience that Jesus had in the wilderness and which was a consequence of his extended fast. The source for the information here could only be Jesus himself, who related this experience to his disciples. There were no other witnesses. The aforementioned words of Jesus about Satan falling from heaven, as well as other mentions of the devil in the direct speech of Jesus, support the hypothesis that Jesus was the principal source.

Such a view is not shared by those scholars who strive to isolate the figure of the "historical Jesus" from the Gospel narrative by pruning away later church additions. One of these scholars considers the story of the three temptations to be a mythological elaboration of the fact that before going out to preach Jesus prayed and fasted.[32] Others have seen in this story "an imaginative midrash[33] with a large scriptural element, [which] should be attributed to an early Christian storyteller."[34]

This latter view is based to a significant degree on the stance that the devil is an invention and a myth. Yet the existence of the devil is axiomatic in both the Old and New Testaments and in the Christian Church. The very death of Jesus on the cross and his resurrection would be interpreted as a conclusive victory over the devil. His first victory over him consisted in overcoming the three temptations.

The experience of Jesus in the wilderness, which is reported by the three evangelists, lies beyond the reach of historicism, rationalism, and psychologism. That is why this account is so difficult to place within the framework of the search for the "historical Jesus." The Russian philosopher S. N. Trubetskoy writes:

> It is hardly possible to find a notion more repellent to the modern worldview than the notion of Satan or of the kingdom of Satan. It does not follow from this, however, that scholarly or philosophical research into the teaching of Christ can get around this notion, which corresponded to a real moral experience in the life of Christ. The Gospels inform us that at the beginning of his ministry, immediately after his baptism, Jesus withdrew into the wilderness, where he spent forty days in prayer and fasting and was tempted by Satan. Only a short-sighted critic can consider this Gospel account incredible, supported as it is

[32]E. P. Sanders, *The Historical Figure of Jesus* (London: Penguin Press, 1993), 117.

[33]A Hebrew term denoting the study or interpretation of the Torah (the Mosaic Law); in a broader sense, it denotes a subset of the oral tradition: a story on biblical themes.

[34]Maurice Casey, *Jesus of Nazareth*, 177.

by so many analogies in the religious lives of a variety of ascetics from the most diverse periods and peoples.[35]

Judging by the nature of the experience described by the evangelists, the philosopher emphasizes:

> Without abandoning the foundation of indubitable psychological and moral facts, we suggest that even someone who believes in neither God nor Satan can wholeheartedly allow the possibility of visions, especially for a person living a spiritual life—for someone who fasts, who prays, who undertakes spiritual labor. Psychologists or physiologists . . . can explain the highest expressions of human spiritual life in their own way. But if it is absurd to limit oneself to reference to the physiology of the nervous system when explaining the external senses, it is even more absurd, when speaking of a person's spiritual life, to limit oneself to declarations that it has its own physical correlate. It is clear that neither the historian nor the philosopher would be moved in the least by such an assertion. For, if one sees in Christ only a man, or an ascetic like the rest, even then it is important for the historian of Christianity to know: do his visions amount merely to an incidental, morbid stirring of a hallucinating imagination outside of any connection with the spiritual life, or are they, so to speak, the exteriorization of an interior spiritual experience, an expression of actual facts and of the first principles of the spiritual life?[36]

We will not comment on the explanation that Jesus was hallucinating as a result of prolonged fasting, inasmuch as it has no relation at all to the actual fabric of the Gospel account. If the evangelists had been capable of even thinking of the possibility of such an interpretation, they would not have included this account in their narrative. Meanwhile, the fact that this account is present in all three of the Synoptics in itself testifies to the significance that it was accorded—precisely as a witness to an important spiritual experience that Jesus underwent, and to Jesus' victory over the

[35]S. N. Trubetskoy, *Uchenie o Logose v ego istorii* [The doctrine of the Logos in its history] (Moscow: Izdatel'stvo ACT, 2000), 439.
[36]Ibid., 439–440.

Man of Sorrows,
William Dyce,
1860.

devil at the very beginning of his messianic journey, before he went out into public ministry.

This victory, in the versions of Matthew and Luke, is made up of three episodes, each of which must be considered separately. What does the proposal to turn stone into bread mean, and why does Jesus reject it? First of all we must point out that, while Jesus performs various miracles later on, in certain instances he refuses to perform a miracle. In Nazareth the local inhabitants address Jesus with the words, "Whatsoever we have heard done in Capernaum, do also here in thy country" (Lk 4.23). But he does not only refuse his fellow countrymen: the evangelist emphasizes that "he could there do no mighty work" (Mk 6.5). The Pharisees demand a sign from him more than once. But he answers: "An evil and adulterous generation seeketh after a sign, and there shall no sign be given to it, but the sign of the prophet Jonas" (Mt 12.39; 16.4; Lk 11.29). When Jesus is nailed to the cross, the people mock him, saying: "If thou art the Son of God, come down from the cross" (Mt 27.40). But he does not come down from the cross; he does not perform a miracle that could compel someone to believe in him. Jesus consistently refuses to perform miracles to prove his omnipotence or his being the Son of God, whether at the request of the people or the prompting of the devil.

Jesus always performs miracles for the sake of others and not for his own sake. Jesus rejects the temptation to turn stone into bread to satisfy his own hunger, whereas later on, without anyone asking him to do so, he would miraculously multiply a small amount of bread in order to feed thousands of people. This event would take place in the wilderness as well.

We should look for the meaning of the first temptation in the saying cited by Jesus (part of it has turned into a proverb: "not by bread alone"). This saying is taken word for word from the Old Testament, where God addresses the people of Israel before their entrance into the promised land after forty years in the wilderness:

> And thou shalt remember all the way which the Lord thy God led thee these forty years in the wilderness, to humble thee, and to prove thee, to know what was in thine heart, whether thou wouldest keep his commandments, or no. And he humbled thee, and suffered thee to hunger, and fed thee with manna, which thou knewest not, neither did thy fathers know, that he might make thee know that man doth not live by bread only, but by every word that proceedeth out of the mouth of the Lord doth man live. (Deut 8.2–3)

The key to understanding the first temptation lies precisely in these words. The people of Israel's forty years of wandering in the wilderness, where God tormented them with hunger, becomes the prefiguration of Jesus' forty-day sojourn in the wilderness and of the hunger that he experienced. Addressing the people of Israel, God reminds them that the source of life is not material bread, but God himself, and the word that proceeds out of his mouth. Here the subject is not only the superiority of the spiritual over the material, about which Jesus would speak to his disciples more than once, but also the role of God in the life of man. God is the source of all blessing, both material and spiritual. Following his will and obeying his word is more important than material riches and physical satisfaction. Physical hunger can be satisfied by bread, but spiritual hunger can only be satisfied by God alone. The final outcome of forty days without food cannot simply be the end of a physical fast; it is the first victory over the tempter, who seeks to place the material above the spiritual. This victory precedes Jesus' going out to preach, the prefiguration of which was the entrance of the people of Israel into the promised land.

The opinion generally accepted in the subsequent Christian tradition is that the devil tempted Jesus as a man, and not as the Son of God. At the same time, the devil twice (during the first and second temptations in Matthew, and in the second and third in Luke) turns to Jesus with the words, "if thou art the Son of God." John Chrysostom interprets these words as meaning that the devil, seeing Jesus hungry, could not "receive it [i.e., believe] that He was Son of God."[37] On the other hand, Jesus had nowhere yet declared that he was the Son of God, and the devil's question sets the stage, so to speak, for Jesus' declarations about himself, which only lay ahead of him and which would provoke the indignation and bewilderment of the Jews.

In the account of the three temptations, as in other episodes in the Gospels, one cannot separate the man Jesus Christ from the Son of God. The devil tempts Jesus by taking advantage of the weakness of his human flesh and the feeling of hunger that he experiences as a man. At the same time, in answer to the devil, Jesus directly calls himself God: "Thou shalt not tempt the Lord thy God" (Mt 4.7; Lk 4.12). He rejects all the temptations, both as man and as God.

Having received an answer from Jesus to the first temptation in the form of a citation from Holy Scripture, the devil, tempting him a second time, cites Scripture himself. This agrees with the biblical understanding of the devil as a seducer who, when tempting someone, uses images attractive to that person and appeals to that which is sacred to him or her. He tempted Adam and Eve with the fruits of the tree that was pleasing to the eye, with the words "ye shall be as gods, knowing good and evil" (Gen 3.5). He attempts to entice Jesus with a citation from the Scriptures that speaks of him, saying that the angels would bear him up.

In its conceptual content the second temptation is similar to the first: here Jesus is again asked to perform a miracle for the sake of a miracle. However, if in the first case the motivation to yield to the temptation, from the devil's point of view, must be the feeling of physical hunger experienced by Jesus, then in the second case the allurement is connected with the proposal that Jesus acknowledge his omnipotence and reveal himself

[37]John Chrysostom, *Homilies on the Gospel of Matthew* 13.3 (NPNF[1] 10:81).

*The Temptation
of Christ on the
Mount*, panel
from the Maestá
Altarpiece of
Siena, Duccio
di Buoninsegna,
1308–1311.

in glory. We are speaking here of a mental temptation, which Jesus rejects with a citation of the words from Deuteronomy, given here in full: "Ye shall not tempt the Lord your God, as ye tempted him in Massah" (Deut 6.16). This is an allusion to the account in the book of Exodus of how the sons of Israel, tormented by thirst in the desert, tempted the Lord, saying: "Is the Lord among us, or not?" (Ex 17.7). In response to the murmuring of the people, Moses, at the command of God, strikes a stone, and water flows from it.

Veiled biblical allusions make up the context in which the dialogue between Jesus and the devil develops. Events from the history of the people of Israel, which are indicated by citations from the Bible, become the prefigurations of New Testament realities. It is no coincidence that the second part of the dialogue (in Luke, the third) takes place on the pinnacle of the Jerusalem Temple—the central holy place of the people of Israel. Both interlocutors know the history of this people.

Of the three temptations, the third (in Luke, the second) is the most significant in its conceptual content: this is a temptation involving political power and might. The devil shows Jesus "all the kingdoms of the world" and proposes to give him power over them. The condition is that he must worship the devil. Jesus rejects the temptation with the words, "Get thee hence, Satan," adding to it a reference to the Old Testament: "Thou shalt worship the Lord thy God, and him only shalt thou serve" (Mt 4.10; Lk 4.8). This is a slightly altered version of the words given twice in the book of Deuteronomy: "Thou shalt fear the Lord thy God, and serve him alone, and shalt swear by his name" (Deut 6.13; 10.20).

The temptation of earthly power followed Jesus over the entire period of his ministry: it was connected with the idea of the Messiah as a political leader who would come to free Israel from the foreign yoke and become king over Israel.

However, in the given situation, the devil offers Jesus political power not only over Israel, but also over all the kingdoms of the world. It follows that what is being discussed is a broader context of the understanding of power as such—not only on the scale of a single country. It is worthwhile to pay attention to the words of the devil, as given by Luke: "All this power will I give thee, and the glory of them, for that is delivered unto me and to whomsoever I will I give it. If thou therefore wilt worship me, all shall be thine" (Lk 4.6–7). Unlike Matthew, Luke speaks directly of power (*exousian*) as the subject of the dispute, and in Luke's account the devil claims that he not only wields this power, but can give it to whomever he wishes.

What power is under discussion here, and why does Jesus reject it? The idea that the devil has power over the world has never been characteristic of either the Old Testament or Christianity. Being a deceiver, the devil possesses only an illusory power, and if he offers to trade this power, it is not because he possesses it, but because he is being deceptive, passing himself off as God. John Chrysostom writes:

> But marvel thou not, if he in reasoning with Christ oftentimes turn himself about. For as boxers, when they have received deadly blows, reel about, drenched in much blood, and blinded; even so he too, darkened by the first and the second blow, speaks at random what comes uppermost: and proceeds to his third assault. . . . For since he was now come to sinning against the Father, saying, that all that is the Father's

The Temptation
of Christ, icon,
19th c.

was his, and was endeavoring to make himself out to be God, as arti-
ficer of the universe; [Christ] then rebuked him.[38]

The story of the three temptations of Jesus, although commented on
by the Church Fathers, did not receive serious theological interpretation
in the patristic age. Its interpretation mainly amounted to a moral call to
reject the temptations of the devil, in this respect imitating Christ.

Yet in this story there is a deep theological and philosophical meaning,
which is grasped only in light of the centuries-long history of humanity's
existence after Christ. It is not without reason that the story of the three
temptations received completely new exposure in modern times, particularly in Russian religious thought—from Fyodor Dostoyevsky, Vladimir
Solovyov, and Nikolai Berdyaev.

Dostoyevsky discusses this story in "The Legend of the Grand Inquisitor."[39] He places in the mouth of his protagonist the idea that in the three
questions posed by the devil to Jesus, "the whole subsequent history of
mankind is, as it were, brought together into one whole, and foretold, and

---

[38]Ibid. 13.4–5 (*NPNF*[1] 10:82–83).
[39]This story is found in Part 2, Book 5, Chapter 5 of Dostoyevsky's novel *The Brothers
Karamazov.—Trans.*

in them are united all the unsolved historical contradictions of human nature." The Inquisitor says to
Jesus:

> Nothing has ever been more insupportable for a
> man and a human society than freedom. But seest
> Thou these stones in this parched and barren wil-
> derness? Turn them into bread, and mankind will
> run after Thee like a flock of sheep, grateful and
> obedient.... But Thou wouldst not deprive man of
> freedom, and didst reject the offer, thinking what
> is that freedom worth if obedience is bought with
> bread? ... Thou didst promise them the bread of
> Heaven, but, I repeat again, can it compare with
> earthly bread in the eyes of the weak, ever sinful,
> and ignoble race of man? And if for the sake of the
> bread of Heaven thousands and tens of thousands shall follow Thee,
> what is to become of the millions and tens of thousands of millions of
> creatures who will not have the strength to forego the earthly bread
> for the sake of the heavenly? ... There are three powers, three pow-
> ers alone, able to conquer and to hold captive for ever the conscience
> of these impotent rebels for their happiness: those forces are miracle,
> mystery and authority. Thou hast rejected all three.... Thou didst not
> come down from the Cross when they shouted to Thee, mocking and
> reviling Thee, "Come down from the cross and we will believe that
> Thou art He." Thou didst not come down, for again Thou wouldst not
> enslave man by a miracle, and didst crave faith given freely, not based
> on miracle. Thou didst crave free love and not the base raptures of the
> slave before the might that has overawed him forever.[40]

Portrait of Fyodor Dostoyevsky, engraving, Vladimir Favorsky, 1929.

The Grand Inquisitor opposes the religion of peace, brought to earth by
Jesus, to the religion of slavery, founded on miracle, mystery, and authority.

---

[40]Fyodor Dostoyevsky, *The Grand Inquisitor: With Related Chapters from "The Brothers Karamazov,"* trans. Constance Garnett, ed. Charles B. Guignon (Indianapolis, IN: Hackett, 1993), 25–29.

Human beings—Dostoyevsky's protagonist says—are not in need of freedom, but slavish submission; they do not need heavenly bread, but earthly bread. Like a submissive flock, they will follow whoever gives them bread, shows them miracles, and demonstrates authority.

We will leave aside the social message of "The Legend of the Grand Inquisitor" and its anti-Catholic tendency. We will only point out that which relates to the theological and philosophical interpretation of the story of the three temptations. At the basis of the conflict between Jesus and the devil lies a conflict between two value systems. On the one hand, we have the preaching of the Kingdom of God, the teaching of the superiority of the spiritual over the material, and the idea that following God must be the free choice of a person not based on material benefits or adulation in the face of a miracle. On the other hand, we have a set of values belonging exclusively to "this world": material wealth (bread), miracles, and earthly power.

The juxtaposition of these two value systems runs through the entirety of the Gospels. Jesus says to the people: "Now is the judgment of this world: now shall the prince of this world be cast out" (Jn 12.31). By "the prince of this world" he means the devil, the one who tempted him in the wilderness. Jesus came in order to cast him out from the world, to free people from his illusory power, and to remind them that the only ruler of the world is God, and that the only value system that one must follow is that of God's commandments. He would expound on this system in the Sermon on the Mount, especially in its beginning section—the Beatitudes—and also in his numerous parables about the kingdom of heaven.

Instead of power over all earthly kingdoms, Jesus prefers the kingdom of heaven, which does not look for social equality and wellbeing in the understanding of earthly life. Rejecting material wealth, miracles, and earthly power, Jesus sets in opposition to all of these a value system founded on the only absolute value and source of all values, that is, God. In place of all that the devil offers humanity, Jesus offers people God. Instead of earthly prosperity, power, and might, Jesus chooses God, the pursuit of whom presupposes the renunciation of earthly values in favor of spiritual values.

In his book *Jesus of Nazareth*, Pope Benedict XVI poses the question: "What did Jesus actually bring, if not world peace, universal prosperity, and a better world? What has he brought? The answer is very simple: God. He has brought God." This answer derives from the story of the three temptations:

> The earthly kingdoms that Satan was able to put before the Lord at that time have all passed away. Their glory, their *doxa*, has proven to be a mere semblance. But the glory of Christ, the humble, self-sacrificing glory of his love, has not passed away, nor will it ever do so. Jesus has emerged victorious from his battle with Satan. To the tempter's lying divinization of power and prosperity, to his lying promise of a future that offers all things to all men through power and through wealth—he responds with the fact that God is God, that God is man's true Good.[41]

The story of the three temptations lays out the foundational principles on which all the subsequent ministry of Jesus would be built. He would perform miracles, but not for the sake of demonstrating his might. He would place the spiritual above the material. He would reject political power in favor of spiritual power, and reject coercion of any individual in favor of a free confession of faith in him and in his heavenly Father.

Why did Jesus himself have to go through temptation by the devil? Would it not have been sufficient to simply teach people to struggle against the devil and triumph over him? It was necessary for Jesus to be tempted for the same reason he himself was baptized and did not merely command his disciples to baptize people. Jesus wholly identified himself with humanity. The fate of humanity and of each specific human being is linked with the human fate of Jesus, who himself went through trials and temptations in order that he would be able to lead people through them. In the Epistle to the Hebrews this is spoken of: "For in that he himself hath suffered being tempted, he is able to succour them that are tempted" (Heb 2.18).

---

[41]Pope Benedict XVI, *Jesus of Nazareth: From the Baptism in the Jordan to the Transfiguration*, trans. Adrian J. Walker (New York, NY: Doubleday, 2007), 44–45.

The Temptation
of Christ, icon,
13th c.

The key to the story of the three temptations, as with the other stories on the pages of the Gospels, is faith that Jesus is simultaneously both God and man. He overcomes the devil's temptations not only as God, but also as a man, thereby demonstrating that every person whom the devil tempts can overcome temptation and choose in favor of God. In Jesus "we have not a high priest who cannot be touched with the feeling of our infirmities; but was in all points tempted like as we are, yet without sin" (Heb 4.15). He accepted the devil's challenge and did not refuse to go through temptations, but, in responding to the propositions of the devil, he did not sin—not in deed, or in word, or in thought.

5. Jesus and John the Baptist

What happened to Jesus after his victory over the devil in the wilderness? In the Synoptic Gospels, after the story of the three temptations, the account of his going out to preach immediately follows. In the Gospel of Luke it is written: "And Jesus returned in the power of the Spirit into Galilee, and there went out a fame of him through all the region round about" (Lk 4.14). The reader may surmise that Jesus' return to Galilee took place immediately after the temptation by the devil. Matthew and Mark, however, tell of Jesus' return to Galilee only after he finds out that John

Deisis: Christ, the Mother of God, and John the Forerunner, mosaic in Hagia Sophia, 13th c.

has been placed under arrest (Mt 4.12; Mk 1.14). What, then, happened between the conclusion of the temptation in the wilderness and Jesus' return to Galilee?

We find the answer in the Gospel of John. Its author does not mention the temptation in the wilderness at all, but neither does he mention Jesus' baptism. In place of this, he tells in the beginning of how John answers the Jews sent to him: "There standeth one among you, whom ye know not" (Jn 1.26); from this one may conclude that this conversation takes place in the presence of Jesus, who is standing unnoticed in the crowd. The evangelist then describes the meeting of Jesus with John on the banks of the Jordan "the next day" (Jn 1.29) and then again another meeting that takes place "the next day" (Jn 1.35). This meeting concludes with two disciples of John following Jesus. And again on "the following day," Jesus decides to go to Galilee (Jn 1.43); he finds Philip, and Philip finds Nathaniel. Finally, on "the third day," Jesus, together with his Mother and disciples, arrives at the wedding in Cana of Galilee (Jn 2.1). In this way, we have a narrative describing the events of four days in a row.

To harmonize these descriptions with the accounts of the Synoptics is possible in only one way—if we suppose that the events on the banks of the Jordan that are described in the Gospel of John took place after Jesus had already returned from the wilderness. This means that Jesus did not go to Galilee immediately after leaving the wilderness, but returned first to John. In this case it becomes clear why, in the Gospel of John, John the Baptist speaks of Jesus' baptism in the past tense:

> Behold the Lamb of God, who taketh away the sin of the world. This is he of whom I said, "After me cometh a man who is preferred before me, for he was before me." And I knew him not, but that he should be made manifest to Israel. . . . I saw the Spirit descending from heaven like a dove, and it abode upon him. And I knew him not, but he that sent me to baptize with water, the same said unto me, "Upon whom thou shalt see the Spirit descending, and remaining on him, the same is he which baptizeth with the Holy Spirit." And I saw, and bare record that this is the Son of God. (Jn 1.29–34)

The phrase "of whom I said" points to some unspecified moment in the past. John's words "I knew him not," said twice, are evidence that before Jesus' first appearance on the banks of the Jordan they were not acquainted with each other, notwithstanding the fact that, according to Luke, their mothers were relatives (Lk 1.36). The words "I saw the Spirit" also sound like a recollection of an event that took place some time earlier. These words could not be pronounced at the moment of Jesus' baptism: they are already addressed to a new crowd of people—those who were not witnesses of this event. In the Gospel of John, the Baptist does not mention the event of Jesus' baptism itself, but by comparing this account with the story presented by the Synoptics, we can conclude that John saw the Spirit of God descending on Jesus immediately after Jesus, having received baptism, emerged from the waters of the Jordan.

Why does the author of the Fourth Gospel not describe the scene of Jesus' baptism? First, it had already been described in the Synoptic Gospels, with which (or, at least, with one of which) he was apparently already familiar. And, second, he was most likely not present at Jesus' baptism and not an eyewitness of that scene. Instead, he was an eyewitness of the other encounters between Jesus and John the Baptist—at the very least, of the last of the encounters he describes.

Deisis, icon,
17th c.

For what reason did Jesus come again to John after the temptation by the devil, and twice, at that? Certain scholars think that Jesus was initially a disciple of John. In the opinion of the contemporary Catholic scholar Armand Puig i Tàrrech, "Once Jesus had been baptized by John, they established a relationship in which John guided him. Jesus became a follower and collaborator of his in his baptismal mission, which included welcoming those who came to be baptized."[42]

Yet the text of the Gospels gives no grounds for such a hypothesis. We only see that Jesus came to John after his baptism twice, at minimum; but why he came, we do not know. We cannot exclude the possibility that he came in order to select his first disciples from the disciples of John: the

[42]Armand Puig i Tàrrech, *Jesus: A Biography*, 294.

Deisis (Christ
Pantocrator
and John the
Forerunner),
icon, 13th c.

story of the two disciples of John who went to follow Jesus could be indirect
confirmation of this (Jn 1.37–39).

The Gospel of John mentions that for a period of time, before John
was imprisoned, Jesus and the Forerunner were active concurrently: "After
these things came Jesus and his disciples into the land of Judaea; and there
he tarried with them, and baptized. And John also was baptizing in Aenon
near to Salim, because there was much water there. And they came, and
were baptized" (Jn 3.22–23). This story is evidence that in the beginning
Jesus adopted the external form of John's preaching and did what John
was doing, only in another place. However, the given fact can hardly be
interpreted to mean that John "guided" Jesus.

The evangelist continues: "When therefore the Lord knew how the
Pharisees had heard that Jesus made and baptized more disciples than John
(though Jesus himself baptized not, but his disciples), he left Judaea, and
departed again into Galilee" (Jn 4.1–3). The enigmatic mention of Jesus'
unwillingness to share a single missionary territory with John might lead

one to think that between the two groups, of Jesus' disciples and John's disciples, there was—at least in the eyes of outside observers— a definite rivalry.

One more episode from the Fourth Gospel supports the idea that the disciples of John were dissatisfied with the independent activity of Jesus and his disciples:

The Church of St John
the Baptist in Kerch

Then there arose a question between some of John's disciples and the Jews about purifying. And they came unto John, and said unto him, "Rabbi, he that was with thee beyond Jordan, to whom thou barest witness, behold, the same baptizeth, and all men come to him." John answered and said, "A man can receive nothing, except it be given him from heaven. Ye yourselves bear me witness, that I said, 'I am not the Christ,' but that 'I am sent before him.' He that hath the bride is the bridegroom; but the friend of the bridegroom, which standeth and heareth him, rejoiceth greatly because of the bridegroom's voice: this my joy therefore is fulfilled. He must increase, but I must decrease. He that cometh from above is above all; he that is of the earth is earthly, and speaketh of the earth. He that cometh from heaven is above all. And what he hath seen and heard, that he testifieth; and no man receiveth his testimony. He that hath received his testimony hath set to his seal that God is true. For he whom God hath sent speaketh the words of God; for God giveth not the Spirit by measure unto him. The Father loveth the Son, and hath given all things into his hand. He that believeth on the Son hath everlasting life, and he that believeth not the Son shall not see life, but the wrath of God abideth on him." (Jn 3.25–36)

In the words of John's disciples we can hear unconcealed dissatisfaction. Yet, in his answer, John consistently holds to the same line as when Jesus appeared on the banks of the Jordan. He refers to his prior witness about Jesus and confirms it again.

Moreover, if we take the text beginning from the words "He that cometh from above is above all" as a continuation of the direct speech of

Deisis with
St Nicholas,
icon, 11th c.

the Forerunner,[43] then John here demonstrates not just familiarity with what Jesus did and taught. He almost exactly reproduces the main themes of Jesus' teachings as they would be reflected in the subsequent chapters of the Gospel of John. The Forerunner contrasts himself with Jesus, calling himself the one from the earth, but Jesus the one coming from above, or from heaven. He speaks of the testimony of Jesus, which no one accepted: evidently, already in this beginning of Jesus' ministry, his preaching was provoking rejection from the Jews. Finally—and most importantly—the Forerunner presents the teaching of the oneness of the Son with the Father. Here he is already speaking not as an Old Testament prophet, but as a New Testament theologian, proclaiming to people the coming of the Son of God into the world.

After his arrest, while in prison, John continued to pay attention to Jesus' activity. The evangelist Matthew describes the following incident:

[43]In view of the absence of quotation marks or other means of distinguishing direct speech from authorial commentary in the original text of the Gospel, the given excerpt could be understood not as the direct speech of the Forerunner, but as authorial commentary on the speech ending with the words "He must increase, but I must decrease." Certain modern scholars understand the given text in this sense. We, however, do not see any reason to reject the understanding of the text from "He that cometh from above" as being a continuation of the direct speech of John the Baptist, as is accepted in Church tradition (see, for example, John Chrysostom, *Homilies on the Gospel of John* 30.1 [PG 59:172] [*NPNF*[1] 14:103–104]). [Modern English translations differ on this question. E.g., the RSV and ESV mark the end of the speech at v.30, but the New Jerusalem Bible, the NKJV, and the NIV do not mark its end until v.36.—*Ed.*]

Now when John had heard in the prison the works of Christ, he sent two of his disciples, and said unto him, "Art thou he that should come, or do we look for another?" Jesus answered and said unto them, "Go and show John again those things which ye do hear and see: the blind receive their sight, and the lame walk, the lepers are cleansed, and the deaf hear, the dead are raised up, and the poor have the Gospel preached to them. And blessed is he, whosoever shall not be offended in me." (Mt 11.2–6)

What does this story mean? Can we suppose that, while in prison, John doubted Jesus' messiahship? Perhaps at a certain point it appeared to him that he had been mistaken, and that Jesus was not the One for whom he was supposed to prepare the way? The possibility of such a demonstration

Deisis ("Upon thy right and did stand the queen"), icon, 14th c.

of human weakness in a man who was in prison awaiting death cannot be excluded. In that case, Jesus' words, "And blessed is he, whosoever shall not be offended in me," come across as a stern warning to John:

John is in prison, within the four walls of a stone fortress, and the Lord allows him to be tested by the most terrible trials. The faith of the greatest among those born of woman is subject to the attacks of the tempter. The enemy's voice attempts to cloud his soul with doubt: "You see, Jesus is not the Messiah at all. He is not even able to take you out from your prison." John the Forerunner lived in expectation of a conquering Messiah, the Anointed of God, who would deliver Israel from all his enemies: the Son of Man announced by Daniel, coming on the clouds of heaven to bring judgment on the ungodly and slay them with the breath of his lips. This Messiah was the one preached by John to the people in the wilderness: the Judge with axe in hand, who even now would hew down all the trees that bore no fruit, the heavenly Winnower with winnowing fan in hand, who would separate the wheat from the chaff. And it was not so. Could the Christ have deceived him?

Could God have deceived him? . . . Christ does not straightforwardly answer the question posed to him. He does not say, "I am the one who should come." He wants the one who asked to give the answer to his own question.[44]

At the same time there is another interpretation: basically, John himself did not doubt that Jesus was the Messiah, but it was his disciples who doubted, so he sent them to Jesus, that they themselves might receive an answer from him. In the words of Chrysostom, "neither did [John] send as being himself in doubt, nor did he ask in ignorance." However, his disciples "as yet . . . knew not who Christ was, but imagining Jesus to be a mere man, but John greater than after the manner of man, were vexed at seeing the former held in estimation, but the latter, as he had said, now ceasing. And this hindered them from coming unto Him, their jealousy quite blocking up the access." Therefore John sends two of his disciples to Jesus for clarification. Jesus, "knowing the purpose of John," does not answer them straight away, but asks them to draw their own conclusions based on his works.[45]

Continuing the account, Matthew reports Jesus' words about John the Baptist, which he addressed to the people (from which we may conclude that his interaction with John's disciples took place in the presence of the people):

And as they departed, Jesus began to say unto the multitudes concerning John, "What went ye out into the wilderness to see? A reed shaken with the wind? But what went ye out for to see? A man clothed in soft raiment? behold, they that wear soft clothing are in kings' houses. But what went ye out to see? A prophet? Yea, I say unto you, and more than a prophet. For this is he, of whom it is written, 'Behold, I send my messenger before thy face, which shall prepare thy way before thee.' [Mal 3.1] Truly I say unto you, among them that are born of women there hath not risen a greater than John the Baptist; notwithstanding

[44]Aleksandr Shargunov, *Evangelie dnya* [The Gospel of the day], 2nd ed., vol. 1 (Moscow: Izdatel'stvo Sretenskogo monastyrya, 2010), 254–255.

[45]John Chrysostom, *Homilies on the Gospel of Matthew* 36.1–2 (*NPNF*[1] 10:239).

The meeting of Christ and John the Forerunner, miniature, 13th c.

he that is least in the kingdom of heaven is greater than he. And from the days of John the Baptist until now the kingdom of heaven suffereth violence, and the violent take it by force. For all the prophets and the law prophesied until John." (Mt 11.7–13)

In the image of the reed shaken by the wind, certain scholars have seen a hint at the opportunistic politics of the king Herod Antipas (noting at the same time that the Judean coins of the time had the depiction of a reed). In any case, Herod is understood in the image of the man wearing soft clothing and living in kings' houses. In contrast to this king, who imprisoned John and subsequently beheaded him, we have John, whose way of life was totally different from that of a king.[46]

[46]Richard Bauckham, *Gospel Women: Studies of the Named Women in the Gospels* (Grand Rapids, MI: Eerdmans, 2002), 149.

The expression "until John" (*heōs Iōannou*) can be understood in two ways: up to and including John, or up to but not including John.[47] If in the former sense, that would mean that John belongs still to the Old Testament. It seems that in the parallel text in Luke (Lk 16.16) the analogous expression (*mechri Iōannou*) is understood precisely in this way, which is supported by the words of the same author elsewhere (Acts 1.5; 13.24–25; 19.4). However, Matthew places the Forerunner in the context of the New Testament good news, as suggested by the words: "And from the days of John the Baptist until now the kingdom of heaven suffereth violence." John the Baptist is presented here as the initial link in the good news of the kingdom of heaven, which is revealed in its fullness in the preaching of Jesus.

Regardless of our understanding of the words "until John," it is obvious that, by his way of thinking, his mode of action, and the content of his preaching, John the Forerunner still belongs to the Old Testament. He is the last of the Old Testament prophets. At the same time, he stands on the threshold of the New Testament: the account of him occupies an important place in all four Gospels; his preaching thematically echoes the preaching of Jesus; he is the first to announce the coming of the kingdom of heaven. Much of what was only outlined or prophetically foretold in the preaching of the Forerunner receives its substantiation and development in the preaching of Jesus.

Jesus valued John highly. The following words testify to this: "Among them that are born of women there hath not risen a greater than John the Baptist." But what does the continuation of the sentence mean, that "he that is least in the kingdom of heaven is greater than he"? This can be understood in two ways. In one interpretation, what is being spoken of is the kingdom of heaven as a new reality, in which each person acquires a quality of a different kind, and even the greatest person on earth is lesser than the least in the kingdom of heaven. In another interpretation the word "least" applies to Jesus: he is the least, who received baptism from John and bowed his head under his hand, but by his importance he is greater, since the mission of John was only preparatory, while the mission of Jesus is the "kingdom of God [that has] come with power" (Mk 9.1).

[47]See Jeremias, *New Testament Theology*, 46–47.

The Sermon on the Mount, engraving, Gustave Doré, 1860s.

In the external form of his preaching and ministry, Jesus borrowed much from John. Especially in the beginning, his preaching looked like a direct continuation of John's ministry. As we have already noted, John was the first to speak the words that became a leitmotif of Jesus' preaching at the outset: "Repent, for the kingdom of heaven is at hand." John was the first to enter into polemics with the Pharisees, and Jesus adopted the style and manner of his interaction with them. Even the teaching regarding the Father and the Son first came from the lips of the Forerunner (Jn 3.35–36), and only later was it developed by Jesus.

But the most important thing that Jesus and the Christian Church after him adopted from John is the rite of baptism, which Jesus imbued with his own content. The fact that Jesus practiced baptism at an early stage of his preaching is mentioned only in the Fourth Gospel, and further on in the text we hear no more about this (the Synoptics are altogether silent about whether Jesus or his disciples baptized anyone). The practice of baptism

The Beheading
of John the
Forerunner,
fresco, 16th c.

would be reborn in a completely different context—after the resurrection of Jesus, but at his direct command: "Go ye therefore, and teach all nations, baptizing them in the name of the Father, and of the Son, and of the Holy Spirit" (Mt 28.19). This would no longer be the baptism of John, "of repentance," but the baptism "with the Holy Spirit, and with fire" (Mt 3.11), of which John was the herald.

For all the striking similarities between certain external aspects of Jesus' ministry at its outset and the ministry of the Forerunner, there are also very substantial differences, most of all concerning the filling in of the conceptual outlines given by the Forerunner. This relates not so much to baptism as to the content of Jesus' preaching:

> John proclaimed, "*Judgment* is at hand, repent!" Jesus proclaimed, "The *kingly reign of God* is dawning; come, you who are troubled and over-burdened!" John the Baptist remains within the framework of *expectation*; Jesus claims to bring *fulfilment*. John still belongs in the realm of the *law*; with Jesus, the *Gospel* begins. Therefore the smallest in the *basileia* is greater than John.[48]

---

[48]Jeremias, *New Testament Theology*, 49. Italics in original.

Comparing John's ministry with Jesus' mission, Justin Martyr says that "Christ, while [John] still sat by the river Jordan, having come, put an end to his prophesying and baptizing, and preached also Himself, saying that the kingdom of heaven is at hand."[49] In the historical sense this is not entirely accurate, since, as we have seen, for a period of time before John's imprisonment, Jesus and John were preaching concurrently. But in the historical sense, Jesus' preaching truly marks the end of John's mission, albeit not all at once, but gradually. John himself recognized this; otherwise, he would not have said, "He must increase, but I must decrease" (Jn 3.30).

The diminishment of John the Baptist is a distinct storyline in the Gospels. Matthew describes the death of John in detail:

> At that time Herod the tetrarch heard of the fame of Jesus, and said unto his servants, "This is John the Baptist; he is risen from the dead, and therefore mighty works do show forth themselves in him." For Herod had laid hold on John, and bound him, and put him in prison for Herodias' sake, his brother Philip's wife. For John said unto him, "It is not lawful for thee to have her." And when he would have put him to death, he feared the multitude, because they counted him as a prophet. But when Herod's birthday was kept, the daughter of Herodias danced before them, and pleased Herod. Whereupon he promised with an oath to give her whatsoever she would ask. And she, being before instructed by her mother, said, "Give me here John the Baptist's head in a charger." And the king was sorry; nevertheless for the oath's sake, and them which sat with him at meat, he commanded it to be given her. And he sent, and beheaded John in the prison. And his head was brought in a charger, and given to the girl: and she brought it to her mother. (Mt 14.1–11)

Such was the end of a man to whom not too long ago thousands of people were streaming, whose preaching thundered throughout all of Judea.

The fate of John became a prefiguration of the fate of Jesus, the Son of Man. The execution of John preceded the execution of Jesus. The parallelism of the two lives, which began with the meeting of their mothers, Mary

[49]Justin Martyr, *Dialogue with Trypho* 51 (*ANF* 1:221).

The Beheading
of John the
Forerunner,
icon, 18th c.

and Elisabeth (Lk 1.39–56), and continued with their meeting in person on the banks of the Jordan and their parallel mission for a period of time, concluded with each ascending his own cross—first the Forerunner, and then the One whom he foretold. Church tradition says that, after his death, John the Baptist descended to hades to prepare the way there for Jesus, who would descend there after his death on the cross.[50]

It seems that the Gospel of Matthew intentionally and consciously emphasizes the parallelism between the lives of John and Jesus, using the same expressions in relation to both the one and the other. About Herod's desire to kill John, it says: "And when he would have put him to death, he feared the multitude, because they counted him as a prophet" (Mt 14.5). And of Jesus: "But when they sought to lay hands on him, they feared the multitude, because they took him for a prophet" (Mt 21.46). The words

[50]About this, see Metropolitan Hilarion Alfeyev, *Christ the Conqueror of Hell: The Descent into Hades from an Orthodox Perspective* (Crestwood, NY: St Vladimir's Seminary Press, 2009), 158.

"laid hold on" and "bound" are used in relation to both John and Jesus (Mt 14.3; 21.46; 27.2). Herod orders the execution of John seemingly against his will (Mt 14.9), and Pilate sentences Jesus to death against his will (Mt 27.24). The scene of the burial of John (Mt 14.12), in its content and vocabulary, seems to presage the scene of the burial of Jesus (Mt 27.57–60).

Matthew's account of the death of the Forerunner concludes with the words: "And his disciples came, and took up the body, and buried it, and went and told Jesus. When Jesus heard of it, he departed thence by ship into a desert place apart" (Mt 14.12–13). Then follows the story of the feeding of the five thousand with five loaves, after which "Jesus constrained his disciples to get into a ship, and to go before him unto the other side, while he sent the multitudes away. And when he had sent the multitudes away, he went up into a mountain apart to pray; and when the evening was come, he was there alone" (Mt 14.22 23). Why does the evangelist so emphasize the fact that Jesus twice went away from his disciples in order to be alone? And why does this happen immediately after he learns of the death of John the Baptist?

In the Gospels it is mentioned multiple times that Jesus would go away from his disciples to be in complete solitude (Mt 14.23; Mk 6.46; Lk 5.16; 6.12; Jn 6.15; 8.1). The first time this happens is after he learns of the death of John the Forerunner. The last time this happens is in the garden of Gethsemane, immediately before his arrest. Jesus leaves his disciples to be alone when he needs to pray. Sometimes he spends the entire night in prayer (Lk 6.12).

What did Jesus think and pray about after learning of the death of John the Baptist? About the fate of the Baptist? About his own fate? About the death that awaited him? The evangelists are silent on this. But they do not conceal from us that the Son of Man deeply suffered the death of the one who had come into the world to prepare the way for him; who had borne witness about him being the Lamb of God and the Son of God; under whose hand he had bowed his head and from whom he had received baptism.

6. "Galilee of the Gentiles"

W hat happened after Jesus' baptism? Where did his public ministry begin?

In the Gospel of John, as we have seen, after his second visit to John the Baptist, Jesus "wanted to go forth into Galilee" (Jn 1.43). On the third day he was already present at the wedding in Cana of Galilee, where he did his "beginning of miracles" (Jn 2.1–12). From Cana he, together with his Mother, brothers, and disciples, came to Capernaum, and they "continued there not many days" (Jn 2.12). Then Jesus came to the Passover in Jerusalem and drove out the traders from the Temple (Jn 2.13–15). It was in Jerusalem, we must surmise, that he conversed with Nicodemus (Jn 3.1–21). After this "came Jesus and his disciples into the land of Judaea; and there he tarried with them, and baptized" (Jn 3.22). How long this continued, the evangelist does not specify. Jesus returned to Galilee after finding out how "the Pharisees had heard that Jesus made and baptized more disciples than John" (Jn 4.1–3). Along the way to Galilee, he visited Samaria: this visit took two days (Jn 4.4–43). From Samaria, Jesus came to Cana of Galilee, where he performed his second miracle: the healing of the son of the nobleman of Capernaum (Jn 4.46–54).

All the events that took place in this period, when John the Baptist was still free, are not found in the Synoptics. In the Gospel of Mark, Jesus' ministry begins when he leaves his native town of Nazareth and settles in Capernaum (Mt 4.13). It was in Capernaum that, according to Matthew, Jesus "began to preach, and to say, 'Repent, for the kingdom of heaven is at hand'" (Mt 4.17). There he also called Peter and Andrew, and then James and John, the sons of Zebedee (Mt 3.18–22).

In the Gospel of Mark, the place where the beginning of Jesus' public ministry unfolds also turns out to be Capernaum. The first miracle described by Mark—the casting out of a demon from a possessed man—took place in a synagogue in Capernaum (Mk 1.21–28). That there was a

The synagogue
in Capernaum

synagogue in Capernaum is supported by archaeological excavations, in which the ruins of a synagogue from the fourth to fifth centuries AD were found. It was evidently built on the site of the same synagogue where Jesus had been more than once.[51] Jesus' healing of Peter's mother-in-law also took place in Capernaum, since Peter's home was located there. There, too, in all likelihood, the healing of the leper took place (Mk 1.40–44), after which Jesus "could no more openly enter into the city, but was outside in desert places," where people came to him from everywhere (Mk 1.45). "After some days" we again see Jesus in Capernaum, where he heals the paralytic (Mk 2.1–12).

So, according to Matthew and Mark, the place where Jesus' ministry begins is Capernaum, where he comes, "leaving Nazareth" (Mt 4.13). Why did he decide to leave Nazareth and settle in Capernaum? We find the answer in the Gospel of Luke, according to which, after the temptation by the devil, "Jesus returned in the power of the Spirit into Galilee, and there went out a fame of him through all the region round about. And he taught in their synagogues, being glorified by all" (Lk 4.14–15). Here nothing is said about which cities of Galilee Jesus preached in.

[51]Jerome Murphy-O'Connor, *The Holy Land: An Oxford Archaeological Guide from Earliest Times to 1700*, 5th ed. (Oxford: Oxford University Press, 2008), 188–193.

The first episode that Luke describes in detail is connected to Nazareth, where Jesus, "as his custom was . . . went into the synagogue on the
sabbath day, and stood up to read" (Lk 4.16; the beginning of this story is
given above). At first his preaching was received favorably, but very soon,
when he began to say, "No prophet is accepted in his own country" (Lk
4.24), favor was replaced by wrath:

> But I tell you of a truth, many widows were in Israel in the days of
> Elijah, when the heaven was shut up three years and six months, when
> great famine was throughout all the land. But unto none of them was
> Elias sent, save unto Sarepta, a city of Sidon, unto a woman that was
> a widow.52 And many lepers were in Israel in the time of Elisha the
> prophet, and none of them was cleansed, saving Naaman the Syrian.53
> And all they in the synagogue, when they heard these things, were filled
> with wrath, and rose up, and thrust him out of the city, and led him
> unto the brow of the hill whereon their city was built, that they might
> cast him down headlong. But he passing through the midst of them
> went his way. (Lk 4.25–30)

Note that the evangelist does not distinguish a particular group of people who are dissatisfied with Jesus, such as the scribes or Pharisees. He
paints a vivid picture of the change in the mood of the audience as Jesus
continued his speech. In the very beginning, as soon as Jesus finished the
reading and said that the prophecy was fulfilled, "all bore him witness, and
wondered at the gracious words which proceeded out of his mouth" (Lk
4.22). Then, when he began to rebuke them and tell them how God sent
prophets to the Gentiles and foreign peoples, their mood changed to the
other extreme, and all of them were filled with rage. The evangelist Mark
adds, in connection with this episode, that Jesus "could do no mighty work
there. . . . And he marvelled because of their unbelief" (Mk 6.5–6).

This same episode is presented in brief in Matthew, but takes place a
significant amount of time after Jesus went out to preach (Mt 13.53–58). In
Luke, on the other hand, it is with this episode that Jesus' ministry starts,

52See 1 Kg 17.8–10.
53See 2 Kg 5.10–14.

and only after it does Jesus come to Capernaum (Lk 4.31). We can imagine that Jesus' resettlement in Capernaum was done out of necessity: in his native town, people not only did not accept Jesus, but wanted to kill him. Besides this, Jesus' relatives lived in Nazareth, and their relationship with him, as we will see, worsened after he went out to preach.

Describing how Jesus settled in Capernaum, Matthew makes a reference to a prophecy of Isaiah, according to which Galilee was to be enlightened by the light of the true faith:

> Now when Jesus had heard that John was cast into prison, he departed into Galilee, and leaving Nazareth, he came and dwelt in Capernaum, which is upon the sea coast, in the borders of Zabulon and Nephthalim, that it might be fulfilled which was spoken by Isaiah the prophet, saying, "The land of Zabulon, and the land of Nephthalim, by the way of the sea, beyond Jordan, Galilee of the Gentiles, the people which sat in darkness saw great light, and to them which sat in the region and shadow of death light is sprung up." (Mt 4.12–16)

The mention of "Galilee of the Gentiles" has given certain scholars reason to assume that Gentiles very nearly made up the majority of the population in Galilee.[54] However, Matthew is only citing the words from the book of the prophet Isaiah (Is 9.1–2), in whose time there were indeed many Gentiles living in Galilee. By the first century AD, Galilee was populated predominantly by Jews; Gentiles were, by proportion, only an insignificant part of the total number of the inhabitants of the region.[55]

All four Gospels testify that the main site of Jesus' preaching and ministry was Galilee. It was here that he delivered his principal sermons and parables, and performed the most number of miracles. He came to Jerusalem only on feast days, while he lived and preached in the cities and villages of Galilee. This was not only because Galilee was his native land, where

---

[54]E.g., Burton L. Mack, *The Lost Gospel: The Book of Q & Christian Origins* (San Francisco, CA: HarperSanFrancisco, 1993), 51–68.

[55]Mark A. Chancey, *The Myth of a Gentile Galilee*, Society for New Testament Studies Monograph Series 118 (Cambridge: Cambridge University Press, 2002), 169–170.

he was educated and grew up. In other places, his preaching met with less favorable a response than in Galilee.

Thus, for example, on the other bank of the Jordan, in the land of the Gergesenes, the appearance of Jesus and the miracle he performed provoked such alarm that "the whole city came out to meet Jesus. And when they saw him, they besought him that he would depart out of their coasts" (Mt 8.34). In Samaria he was not accepted, "because his face was as though he would go to Jerusalem" (Lk 9.53). And Judea and Jerusalem are connected with the most dramatic episodes of Jesus' life.

In comparison with Judea and Samaria, Galilee was less hostile to Jesus' preaching. Admittedly, in Galilee, too, as we have seen, Jesus was not accepted at all times or in all places. He was driven out of his native town. He evidently stayed away from large cities such as Tiberias and Sepphoris,[56] preferring the smaller cities and villages. As he enumerates the places in which his mighty works were most manifest, Jesus mentions Chorazin, Bethsaida, and Capernaum, but bitterly admonishes them for not repenting in response to his preaching:

> Woe unto thee, Chorazin! Woe unto thee, Bethsaida! For if the mighty works, which were done in you, had been done in Tyre and Sidon, they would have repented long ago in sackcloth and ashes. But I say unto you, it shall be more tolerable for Tyre and Sidon at the day of judgment, than for you. And thou, Capernaum, which art exalted unto heaven, shalt be brought down to hell. For if the mighty works, which have been done in thee, had been done in Sodom, it would have remained until this day. But I say unto you, that it shall be more tolerable for the land of Sodom in the day of judgment, than for thee. (Mt 11.20–24)

Chorazin appears nowhere later on in the Gospels, except in the parallel passage in Luke (Lk 10.13–15), and we know nothing of what mighty works were done there. Bethsaida is mentioned in the Gospels seven times in total: a series of miracles is linked to this town. Capernaum is encountered on the pages of the Gospels more often than the other places: in total,

[56]N. T. Wright, *Jesus and the Victory of God*, Christian Origins and the Question of God 2 (Minneapolis, MN: Fortress, 1996), 168.

we find sixteen mentions of this town; it is arguably
to this place that Jesus returned most often from his
missionary journeys.

The words quoted above show how deeply Jesus'
mission was rooted in biblical history. He compared what happened to him and around him with
what happened in the pages of the Old Testament,
returning again and again to images familiar to his
audience. Tyre and Sidon were Phoenician cities
known as hotbeds of vice; the books of the Prophets contain multiple denunciations addressed to the
inhabitants of these cities (Is 23.1–14; Joel 3.4; Am
1.9–10; Zech 9.2–4). The custom of clothing oneself
in sackcloth[57] and sitting in ashes as a sign of repen-

The Prophet Isaiah,
icon, 15th c.

tance is also noted in the Prophets: thus, for example, in response to the
preaching of the prophet Jonah the Ninevites declared a fast and dressed in
sackcloth, while the king of Nineveh rose from his throne, clothed himself
in sackcloth, and sat down in ashes; even the cattle were covered in sackcloth (Jon 3.5–6, 8). Finally, the story of Sodom—a city that God destroyed
with brimstone and fire as a punishment for the wickedness of its inhabitants (Gen 19.1–29)—was a paradigmatic example of God's judgment on
and punishment for sins.

All these biblical allusions appear in Jesus' speech as he mentions the
cities in which his preaching did not receive the desired response. The
image used in relation to Capernaum reminds one of the words from the
book of the prophet Isaiah:

> How art thou fallen from heaven, O Lucifer, son of the morning! How
> art thou cut down to the ground, who didst weaken the nations! For
> thou hast said in thine heart, "I will ascend into heaven, I will exalt
> my throne above the stars of God. I will sit also upon the mount of

---

[57]"Sackcloth" renders the Hebrew *śaq* (literally, "sack") and the Greek *sakkos* (coarse fabric,
sack; figuratively, a garb of repentance). This word is used to denote clothing made from camel
hair or another coarse fabric that is worn as a sign of repentance or mourning.

The Marriage in Cana,
engraving, Gustave Doré,
1860s.

the congregation, in the sides of the north. I will ascend above the heights of the clouds; I will be like the Most High." Yet thou shalt be brought down to hell, to the sides of the pit. (Is 14.12–15)

These words, which Isaiah addressed to the king of Babylon, are reinterpreted in the Christian tradition as a prophecy of God's conclusive victory over the devil, who falls from heaven (Lk 10.18) and will be cast into a lake of fire and sulfur (Rev 20.10). In this instance the great and wicked Babylon becomes a prefiguration of Capernaum—a modest fishing settlement on the shore of the Sea of Galilee, chosen by Jesus so that he might manifest there his "mighty works" (that is, perform miracles and signs).

From the very beginning, Jesus' preaching meets with an enthusiastic response from some, and opposition, rejection, and indifference from others. Jesus is followed by thousands who long to receive healing, see a miracle, and hear his word, but at the same time tens and hundreds of thousands remain unmoved by his preaching or are indifferent to it. In spite of the miracles that are performed, a mass conversion to the new faith—and it was precisely a new faith, in the final analysis, that Jesus brought to earth—does not occur. This provokes his disappointment and indignation, which are reflected in the words addressed to the cities of Galilee. Later on, similar words would be uttered concerning Jerusalem (Mt 23.37–38; Lk 13.34–35).

7. Jesus and His Relatives

The relationship between Jesus and his relatives is a theme on which all four Gospels touch to some degree.

At the wedding in Cana of Galilee, Jesus was present together with his Mother and disciples (Jn 2.2). From Cana he comes to Capernaum—"he, and his mother, and his brethren, and his disciples. And they continued there not many days" (Jn 2.12). Thus, according to the Fourth Gospel, in the first days after going out to preach, Jesus was surrounded by a mixed group consisting of his relatives according to the flesh and some disciples.

However, the evangelists' subsequent mentions of Jesus' relatives testify that, soon after he went out to preach, a conflict arose between him and his brothers.

In the Gospel of Mark, immediately after the story of the selection of the twelve disciples, we read: "And when his friends heard of it, they went out to lay hold on him, for they said, 'He is beside himself'" (Mk 3.21). The expression *hoi par' autou* (literally, "those with him"), which is translated as "friends," can refer to friends or followers, although in this case it most likely refers to relatives: the latter is how this verse is understood in the majority of existing translations and commentaries. The expression "went out to lay hold on" is evidence of the intention of Jesus' relatives to force Jesus to stop his public activity and return home to the family. The words "they said" could refer to Jesus' relatives or to the surrounding people in general (in the first case, "they went out to lay hold on him, because they thought that he was beside himself"; in the second case, "they went out to lay hold on him, because people were saying of him that he was beside himself"). The term *exestē* ("beside himself") indicates that, at some point, Jesus' relatives thought that he had gone mad. The fact that he had left their family's customary way of life, elected to live as an itinerant preacher, and was surrounded by the demon-possessed and the sick, elicited complete incomprehension on their part.

The Tribute Money, fresco, Masacchio, 1425.

In another episode, which is mentioned only by John, the brothers of Jesus say to him while with him in Galilee: "Depart hence, and go into Judaea, that thy disciples also may see the works that thou doest. For there is no man that doeth any thing in secret, and he himself seeketh to be known openly. If thou do these things, show thyself to the world." Having presented this fairly rude remark, which testifies to the poorly concealed dissatisfaction of Jesus' brothers towards his activity, the evangelist notes: "For neither did his brethren believe in him." Jesus' answer is self-restrained in the same tone; he demonstrates that he is not in need of their unsolicited advice, and sharply contrasts himself to them: "My time is not yet come, but your time is alway ready. The world cannot hate you; but me it hateth, because I testify of it, that the works thereof are evil." At the conclusion of the conversation, Jesus asks his brothers to go to the feast without him. When they arrive at the feast, he arrives as well—"not openly, but as it were in secret" (Jn 7.3–10). In secret—from whom? Implicitly, from his brothers.

The third episode, which is mentioned in all three Synoptics, contains a kind of resolution to the conflict:

> There came then his brethren and his mother, and, standing outside, sent unto him, calling him. And the multitude sat about him, and they said unto him, "Behold, thy mother and thy brethren outside seek for thee." And he answered them, saying, "Who is my mother, or my brethren?" And he looked round about on them which sat about him, and said, "Behold my mother and my brethren! For whosoever shall do the

will of God, the same is my brother, and my sister, and mother." (Mk 3.31–35; cf. Mt 12.46–50; Lk 8.19–21)

From this account it becomes clear that Jesus consciously and even demonstratively (the scene takes place in the presence of tens or even hundreds of people) estranged his relatives from himself, preferring his disciples and listeners instead. John Chrysostom comments on this episode thus:

> To have borne Christ in the womb, and to have brought forth that marvellous birth, hath no profit, if there be not virtue. And this is hence especially manifest. . . . "[W]ho is my mother, and who are my brethren?" And this He said, not as being ashamed of His mother, nor denying her that bare Him; for if He had been ashamed of her, He would not have passed through that womb; but as declaring that she hath no advantage from this, unless she do all that is required to be done. For in fact that which she had essayed to do, was of superfluous vanity; in that she wanted to show the people that she hath power and authority over her Son, imagining not as yet anything great concerning Him; whence also her unseasonable approach. See at all events both her self-confidence and theirs. Since when they ought to have gone in, and listened with the multitude; or if they were not so minded, to have waited for His bringing His discourse to an end, and then to have come near. . . . [T]heir regard for Him was as towards a mere man, and they were vainglorious, He casts out the disease, not insulting, but correcting them. . . . [I]t was not with intent to drive them to perplexity, but to deliver them from the most tyrannical passion and to lead them on by little and little to the right idea concerning Himself, and to convince her that He was not her Son only, but also her Lord.[58]

In connection with this episode, Chrysostom recalls another similar episode that is described in the Gospel of Luke. There a woman from the crowd raises her voice and says: "Blessed is the womb that bare thee, and the breasts which thou hast sucked." And Jesus answers: "Yea rather,

---

[58]John Chrysostom, *Homilies on the Gospel of Matthew* 44.1 (*NPNF*[1] 10:278–279).

Icon of the Mother of God
the "Milkgiver," 15th c.

blessed are they that hear the word of God, and keep it" (Lk 11.27–28). As is evident from these words, Jesus consistently presents one and the same idea in different situations—the superiority of fulfilling the word of God over any form of kinship according to the flesh. Chrysostom comes to the following conclusion: "For if she is nothing profited by being His mother, were it not for that quality in her, hardly will any one else be saved by his kindred."[59]

Chrysostom's commentary contrasts sharply with the language used by the Church to speak of the Mother of Jesus in the fifth century, when disputes surrounding the Nestorian heresy caused the Church to take special pains to develop terminology explaining how in Jesus Christ two natures coexist—the divine and the human. At that time another teaching was formulated—about the Virgin Mary as the Birthgiver of God (*Theotokos*), who gave earthly life to God the Word incarnate. While Nestorius was of the opinion that she should be called the Birthgiver of Christ (*Christotokos*), since she gave life to Jesus Christ as a man, and not God the Word, Cyril of Alexandria, whose teaching prevailed at the Third Ecumenical Council (431), insisted that God the Word and Jesus Christ were one and the same Person. Consequently, the title of the Virgin Mary as the Birthgiver of God permanently entered the liturgical tradition at that time as legitimate and correct.

The Church needed four centuries to fully recognize the role and significance of the Mother of Jesus and her participation in his labor of redemption. At the time of Chrysostom (the end of the fourth century), this teaching was still in its formative stage.

As for the Gospels, the Mother of Jesus occupies an essential position only in the accounts in Matthew and Luke of Jesus' birth, childhood, and youth (Mt 1–3; Lk 1–3). Mark mentions her only once, in the episode we discussed earlier (Mk 3.31–35). John mentions her twice: in the story of the wedding in Cana of Galilee (Jn 2.1–12), and in the account of how she stood before the cross of Jesus (Jn 19.35–37).

[59]Ibid. (*NPNF*[1] 10:279–280).

Synaxis of the
Twelve Apostles,
icon, 14th c.

In this book we will not develop the theme of the relationship between Jesus and his Mother any further. At the current stage of our investigation, which deals with the beginning period of his ministry, we can make only one inference on the basis of the abovementioned episodes from the Gospels: all of them indicate that there was a fairly sharp conflict between Jesus and his relatives, who originally took some part in his public ministry. The reason for this conflict, which concluded in Jesus practically breaking away from them, was their sharply expressed incomprehension of his actions. This conflict was reflected in the words of Jesus: "A prophet is not without honour, but in his own country, and among his own kin, and in his own house" (Mk 6.4; Mt 13.57).[60]

After Jesus called his disciples, it was they who became his new family, the family to which he would tie the remainder of his short life. The very same dynamic can be traced through all four Gospels: at first, Jesus was surrounded by his relatives according to the flesh, but fairly soon they were superseded by his new family, consisting of his relatives according to the spirit.[61]

[60]These same words are cited by Luke and John, but without mention of kin and house (see Lk 4.24; Jn 4.44).

[61]For more detail about the relational dynamics of Jesus and his relatives, see, in particular, Stephen C. Barton, *Discipleship and Family Ties in Mark and Matthew*, Society for New Testament Studies Monograph Series 80 (Cambridge: Cambridge University Press, 1994), 67–96.

8. "Repent, for the kingdom of heaven is at hand"

Jesus' preaching began with a call to repentance. The first words that he uttered in Capernaum, according to Matthew, were: "Repent, for the kingdom of heaven is at hand" (Mt 4.17). Mark, who does not specify the name of the town in which Jesus began his preaching, tells us how "Jesus came into Galilee, preaching the Gospel of the kingdom of God, and saying, 'The time is fulfilled, and the kingdom of God is at hand. Repent ye, and believe the Gospel'" (Mk 1.14–15).

We have already noted that Jesus began his preaching with the words that first issued from the lips of John the Forerunner. In Mark these words are somewhat expanded: in particular, the term "Gospel" is added. But the call to repentance—common to both Jesus and John the Baptist—is found in the versions of both evangelists. What does this call mean?

The literal meaning of the Greek verb *metanoeite*, which is used by the evangelists, is "to change one's mind," "to change one's way of thinking." John the Baptist invested a fairly specific meaning in this term (or, more precisely, in its Aramaic equivalent): people must change their way of thinking before the approach of the Messiah, whose arrival is connected with the coming of the age of the kingdom of heaven. One had to change not only one's way of thinking, but also one's way of life: soldiers should not wrong anyone, and publicans should not collect more than the appointed tax. The baptism of repentance, which John practiced, was a baptism for the remission of sins, and it was performed after the one seeking it confessed his or her sins.

From the lips of Jesus the call to repentance must have had the same meaning: this was also a call to change one's way of thinking and way of life. However, while the theme of judgment and retribution predominates in John's preaching, the leitmotif of Jesus' preaching is the theme of the mercy of God and the salvation of mankind. Repentance, for both these preachers, is connected with the approach of the kingdom of heaven. But

The Sermon of Christ on the Shore of the Lake, Alexander Ivanov, 1850s.

if John is waiting in anticipation, if for him the arrival of the kingdom of heaven is connected with the coming Messiah, then Jesus is that very Messiah, who brings the kingdom of heaven to men.

Therefore, on his lips the words, "Repent, for the kingdom of heaven is at hand" (Mt 4.17), acquire a completely different tone: they turn out to be the proclamation not of something that must be anticipated and for which one must prepare oneself, but of that which had already come. In this sense, on Jesus' lips, the word translated "at hand" (*ēngiken*) also acquires a meaning different from the sense in which John used it. Elsewhere (Mt 12.28; Lk 11.20), Jesus says directly that the kingdom of God has already come (*ephthasen eph' hymas*; "is come unto you").

We note that the expression "kingdom of heaven" is encountered thirty-two times in the Gospel of Matthew, mainly in Jesus' direct speech. This expression is absent from the other Gospels: Mark, Luke, and John use the phrase "kingdom of God." The two expressions are synonymous: the first is a typical Semitism; one can assume that Matthew is reproducing Jesus' words, while the other evangelists give a conceptual translation. One can alternatively assume that Jesus himself used both expressions as synonyms ("kingdom of God" is also found in Matthew).

What meaning does Jesus invest in the idea of the kingdom of heaven? Is this a kingdom of the present or of the future? Does it relate to a person's earthly life or to life beyond the grave?

*The Sermon
of Christ in
the Temple,*
Alexander
Ivanov, 1850s.

In New Testament scholarship of the end of the nineteenth century
to the first half of the twentieth century, the theme of the kingdom of
God received various interpretations.[62] Certain scholars understood the
kingdom of God exclusively as a metaphor that referred to a group of
moral qualities, the central one of which was love. Others emphasized the
supertemporal, eschatological, and apocalyptic character of this concept.
One point of view became widespread, according to which the kingdom
of God was Jesus himself: through him, "[t]he absolute, the 'wholly other'
has entered into time and space," "history had become the vehicle of the
eternal; the absolute was clothed with flesh and blood."[63]

As we might think, each of these points of view has an element of
truth to it. The kingdom of heaven is such a comprehensive concept for
Jesus that it cannot be reduced to the present, nor to the future, nor to an
earthly reality, nor to eternity. The kingdom of God does not have concrete
earthly contours, nor does it have a concrete verbal articulation. It cannot be localized in time or in space. It is oriented not to the here and now
and the external, but to the heavenly, the future, and the internal. It exists

[62]See Norman Perrin, *The Kingdom of God in the Teaching of Jesus* (Philadelphia, PA: Westminster Press, 1963), 13–157.

[63]C. H. Dodd, *The Parables of the Kingdom*, rev. ed. (New York, NY: Scribner, 1961), 82, 159.
[Origen held this view. Commenting on Mt 18.23—"Therefore is the kingdom of heaven likened
unto a certain king . . ."—he wrote: "But if it be likened to such a king . . . who must we say that it
is but the Son of God? For he is the king of the heavens, and as he is wisdom itself and righteousness itself, and truth itself, is he not so also the kingdom itself (*autobasileia*)?" *Commentary on
the Gospel of Matthew* 14.7 (PG 13:1197; *ANF* 9:498 [revised])—*Ed.*]

in parallel with the earthly world, but intersects with it in the destinies of human beings. The kingdom of heaven is eternity superimposed on time but not merging with it.

As he uncovers the meaning of the concept of the "kingdom of heaven," Jesus never gives it an exhaustive definition. He only casts into the minds of his listeners certain ideas or images that can draw them closer to an understanding of the meaning of this concept. He compares the kingdom of heaven to a man sowing seeds in his field; to a mustard seed; to leaven worked into a piece of dough; to a pearl that a merchant sells all his belongings in order to buy; and to a fishing net that is cast into the sea and catches fish of every kind (Mt 13.24, 31, 33, 45–47). To the question of the Pharisees as to "when the kingdom of God should come," Jesus answers: "The kingdom of God cometh not with observation. Neither shall they say, 'Lo here!' or, 'lo there!' For, behold, the kingdom of God is within you" (Lk 17.20–21).

As he proclaims the coming of the kingdom of God, Jesus opens up to human beings a new dimension of life, the focal point of which is God:

> We can put it even more simply: When Jesus speaks of the Kingdom of God, he is quite simply proclaiming God, and proclaiming him to be the living God, who is able to act concretely in the world and in history and is even now so acting. . . . In this sense, Jesus' message is very simple and thoroughly God-centered. The new and totally specific thing about his message is that he is telling us: God is acting now—this is the hour when God is showing himself in history as its Lord, as the living God, in a way that goes beyond anything seen before.[64]

However, Jesus' message about the kingdom of God is not only theocentric: it is also christocentric. Otherwise, it would not differ at its core from the message of the Old Testament prophets. After all, they also spoke of the need to repent and change one's way of thinking and way of life, of God's action in history, and of his presence among human beings. The God of the Old Testament is also a living God, with the difference being that he

---

[64]Pope Benedict XVI, *Jesus of Nazareth*, 56.

Christ on the Sea of Galilee, Eugène Delacroix, 1854.

dwells far from people, in the heavens, beyond the clouds, and reveals his glory in thunder and lightning.

The radical novelty of Jesus' message about the kingdom of heaven consists in the fact that he himself brings down this kingdom from heaven to earth. And not only the kingdom: he brings down God himself from heaven to earth, revealing to people what had hitherto been invisible and unknown, hidden and inaccessible—the countenance of God. The kingdom of heaven becomes not only a reality of the future, but also a new dimension in people's lives here and now, on earth and in time. This is that dimension that the apostle Paul calls "eternal life through Jesus Christ our Lord" (Rom 6.23). It is not simply life in God, but life in Jesus Christ. It is eternal not because it begins for people after death: it already begins here—from the moment a person believes in Jesus and becomes his disciple—and continues into eternity.

In preaching the kingdom of God, Jesus preaches himself. Being God himself and the Son of God, through himself he reveals to mankind the path to God the Father. In the final analysis, the main content of his preaching about the kingdom of heaven consists precisely in this. This kingdom is inseparable from the person of Jesus, from his works, from his preaching, and from his witness.

Chapter 5

THE PROPHET
OF NAZARETH
OF GALILEE

When Jesus embarked on his preaching ministry, it produced a vivid impression on the people. Word of the new Teacher and Wonderworker quickly spread throughout all of Palestine. This is how Matthew describes the initial reaction to Jesus' emergence in the public arena:

> And Jesus went about all Galilee, teaching in their synagogues, and preaching the Gospel of the kingdom, and healing all manner of sickness and all manner of disease among the people. And his fame went throughout all Syria, and they brought unto him all sick people that were taken with diverse diseases and torments, and those which were possessed with devils, and those which were lunatic, and those that had the palsy, and he healed them. And there followed him great multitudes of people from Galilee, and from Decapolis, and from Jerusalem, and from Judaea, and from beyond Jordan. (Mt 4.23–25)

Soon people began to speak of Jesus as a "great prophet" (Lk 7.16). What meaning did Jesus' contemporaries attach to the word "prophet" when they applied it to him? And to what extent can we say that his ministry was prophetic? On the one hand, we see a definite continuity between the ministry of the prophets and that which Jesus said and did: the line of succession passes through John the Baptist, who becomes the link between Jesus and the Old Testament prophets. On the other hand, the essential

Christ Preaching,
etching,
Rembrandt,
ca. 1652.

differences between Jesus' mission and the ministry of the prophets cannot avoid catching our attention.

1. The Old Testament Prophets

The Hebrew term *nābî'*, usually translated as "prophet," literally means "the one who has been called." In ancient Israel, this word was used to refer to people whom God had called in a special way, for a special ministry. The biblical prophets directly communicated with God: they received revelations from God and delivered them to the people. The activity of certain prophets, such as Elijah, Elisha, and Samuel, are described in the historical books of the Bible. Other prophets—Isaiah, Jeremiah, Ezekiel, Daniel, and the twelve so-called "minor prophets"—left books inscribed with their names. It was these books,[1] together with the historical books,[2]

---

[1]With the exception of the book of Daniel, which in the Jewish tradition belongs to the division of the Ketuvim (*kətuḇîm*, "the Writings").

[2]That is, the books of Joshua, Judges, and 1 and 2 Samuel and 1 and 2 Kings. In the Jewish tradition, the books of Ruth and Chronicles belong to the division of the Ketuvim.

that were named the Nevi'im (*nəḇi'îm*, "the Prophets"): together with the Torah (the Law) they were read and interpreted in the synagogues.

The prophets were people inspired by the Spirit of God. An excerpt from the book of Isaiah, which Jesus read in the synagogue in Nazareth (Lk 4.16–20), begins with the words: "The Spirit of the Lord God is upon me, because the Lord hath anointed me to preach good tidings unto the meek. He hath sent me to bind up the brokenhearted, to proclaim liberty to the captives, and the opening of the prison to them that are bound, to proclaim the acceptable year of the Lord" (Is 61.1–2). The king and prophet David testifies concerning himself, "The Spirit of the Lord spake by me, and his word was in my tongue" (2 Sam 23.2). The prophet Micah writes: "Then shall the seers be ashamed, and the diviners confounded. Yea, they shall all cover their lips; for there is no answer of God. But truly I am full of power by the Spirit of the Lord, and of judgment, and of might, to declare unto Jacob his transgression, and to Israel his sin" (Mic 3.7–8). Here the prophet, inspired by the Spirit of God, contrasts himself to the false seers and diviners, who call to God but do not receive an answer, like the prophets of Baal, who called to their god, but he did not listen to them (1 Kg 18.26–29).

The Prophet Micah,
fresco, 14th c.

In the books of the Prophets, the formulas "the word of the Lord came unto me," "thus saith the Lord," "and the Lord said unto me," as well as other similar formulas indicating that God himself was addressing the people of Israel through the prophets, are used many times. The prophets become the conduits of God's will; they pass on the commands of God to the people and interpret them. Moses speaks with God, receives commandments and laws from him, and then reports them to the people (Ex 24.3). God says to Ezekiel, "Son of man, go, get thee unto the house of Israel, and speak with my words unto them" (Ezek 3.4). The Lord commands Jonah, "Arise, go to Nineveh, that great city, and cry against it; for their wickedness is come up before me" (Jon 1.2). In all these and many other instances mentioned in the Old Testament, the prophets act as the intermediary between God and men, whether the latter be the entire people of Israel, the inhabitants of certain cities, specific persons or even a single person, such as a particular king (2 Sam 12.1; Is 45.1).

Revelations from God often came to the prophets in the form of mysterious visions. Isaiah begins his book with the words, "The vision of Isaiah the son of Amoz, which he saw concerning Judah and Jerusalem in the days of Uzziah, Jotham, Ahaz, and Hezekiah, kings of Judah" (Is 1.1). These words serve as a kind of title for the entire book, which consists of a whole series of visions and revelations. The first vision is linked with Isaiah's call to prophetic ministry:

> In the year that king Uzziah died I saw also the Lord sitting upon a throne, high and lifted up, and his train filled the temple. Above it stood the seraphim. Each one had six wings; with two he covered his face, and with two he covered his feet, and with two he did fly. And one cried unto another, and said, "Holy, holy, holy, is the Lord of hosts. The whole earth is full of his glory." And the posts of the door moved at the voice of him that cried, and the house was filled with smoke. Then said I, "Woe is me! for I am undone, because I am a man of unclean lips, and I dwell in the midst of a people of unclean lips. For mine eyes have seen the King, the Lord of hosts." Then flew one of the seraphim unto me, having a live coal in his hand, which he had taken with the tongs from off the altar, and he laid it upon my mouth, and said, "Lo, this hath touched thy lips, and thine iniquity is taken away, and thy sin purged." Also I heard the voice of the Lord, saying, "Whom shall I send, and who will go for us?" Then said I, "Here am I. Send me." And he said, "Go, and tell this people, 'Hear ye indeed, but understand not; and see ye indeed, but perceive not.' Make the heart of this people fat, and make their ears heavy, and shut their eyes; lest they see with their

The Prophet Isaiah, Marc Chagall, 1968.

eyes, and hear with their ears, and understand with their heart, and convert, and be healed." (Is 6.1–10)

The vision described is presented as an event that took place during a specific period in history—in the year of the death of King Uzziah (in view of the absence of a standard calendar, years were usually reckoned by the dates of the reigns and deaths of kings). Before the prophet a mysterious picture of the heavenly world unfolds; he sees and hears angels. The vision overawes him and he becomes aware of his own sinfulness. But God sends him an angel, who, with the help of a symbolic action, proclaims to him the forgiveness of his sins. Then the prophet hears the voice of God calling, and responds to it with readiness. Only after this does God pronounce the message that the prophet is to transmit to the people of Israel.

Jeremiah begins his book with a description of the circumstances in which God called him to his ministry. Again, the timing of the event is precisely indicated: it takes place in the thirteenth year of the reign of Josiah, the son of Amon. God addresses the prophet with these words: "Before I formed thee in the belly I knew thee; and before thou camest forth out of the womb I sanctified thee, and I ordained thee a prophet unto the nations." But the prophet does not immediately respond to the call. He answers, "Ah, Lord God! Behold, I cannot speak, for I am a child." God

The Prophet
Jeremiah on the
Sistine Chapel
ceiling, fresco,
Michelangelo,
1508–1512.

overrules the objection of his chosen one: "Say not, 'I am a child.' For thou shalt go to all that I shall send thee, and whatsoever I command thee thou shalt speak." After this, God stretches out his hand and touches the lips of the prophet with the words, "Behold, I have put my words in thy mouth. See, I have this day set thee over the nations and over the kingdoms, to root out, and to pull down, and to destroy, and to throw down, to build, and to plant" (Jer 1.5–7, 9–10).

The book of Ezekiel opens with a majestic vision of the likeness of the glory of the Lord in the form of four living creatures that had the likeness of a man, each with four wings and four faces—that of a man, a lion, an ox, and an eagle (Ezek 1.4–9). After the prophet falls upon his face in fear, he hears the voice of God: "Son of man, stand upon thy feet, and I will speak unto thee" (Ezek 2.1). The Spirit enters the prophet and stands him on his feet, and God says to him:

> "Son of man, I send thee to the children of Israel, to a rebellious nation that hath rebelled against me. They and their fathers have transgressed against me, unto this very day. For they are impudent children and stiffhearted. I send thee unto them, and thou shalt say unto them, 'Thus saith the Lord God.' And they, whether they will hear, or whether they

will refuse (for they are a rebellious house), yet shall they know that there hath been a prophet among them." (Ezek 2.3–5)

After this the prophet sees a hand extended to him, and in it a scroll of a book with the inscription "lamentations, and mourning, and woe" (Ezek 2.10). God commands the prophet to eat the scroll. He eats it, and in his mouth it is "as honey for sweetness" (Ezek 3.3).

In all the instances described, the initiative of calling the prophet comes from God: the man is only required to carry out that which God commands him to do with precision. The call comes at a specific, clearly dated period in time; it is accom-

The Prophet Ezekiel on the Sistine Chapel ceiling, fresco, Michelangelo, 1508–1512.

panied by a vision possessing a symbolic meaning and by the voice of God, which is addressed directly to the one whom God chooses for this ministry. God's intrusion into the life of the prophet, who possibly hitherto had not suspected that he would have a special mission, is unexpected, overawes the prophet, and elicits different reactions: while Isaiah readily accepts the mission that God has entrusted to him and even seems to volunteer himself to carry it out, Jeremiah, in contrast, hesitates, and only the commanding voice of God compels him to submit to the call.

In the book of Jonah one more variant of the prophet's reaction to being called is described: active resistance. God sends Jonah to Nineveh, but instead of going there, Jonah flees from the face of the Lord (Jon 1.1–3), like Adam, who attempted to hide from God in paradise (Gen 3.8). A series of miraculous events, including Jonah being swallowed by a whale, compels the prophet to return to his starting point. His resistance to God's will does not have any influence on God. As soon as he is again on dry land, the word of the Lord is addressed to him a second time: "Arise, go unto Nineveh, that great city, and preach unto it the preaching that I bid thee" (Jon 3.2). God remains unmoved, his will is unchanged, and the prophet must carry it out, whether he likes it or not.

The Prophet
Jonah, miniature
from the
Menologion of
Basil II, 10th c.

Sometimes God calls the prophet to actions that are not amenable to either logical explanation or, it might seem, justification from the point of view of universally accepted human morality. At first, God commands Hosea: "Go, take unto thee a wife of prostitution and children of prostitution, for the land hath committed great prostitution, departing from the Lord" (Hos 1.2). The prophet takes a prostitute as his wife, and she bears him a son and a daughter. Then God gives the prophet a new command: "Go yet, love a woman beloved of her friend, yet an adulteress, according to the love of the Lord toward the children of Israel, who look to other gods" (Hos 3.1). All these commands and actions are usually interpreted symbolically—as a vision, a parable, or an allegory, pointing to Israel's unfaithfulness towards God.[3]

However, certain ancient commentators accept the historicity of the events described in the book. In particular, Irenaeus of Lyons writes:

> However, it was not by means of visions alone which were seen, and words which were proclaimed, but also in actual works, that He was beheld by the prophets, in order that through them He might prefigure and show forth future events beforehand. For this reason did Hosea the prophet take "a wife of whoredoms," prophesying by means

[3]For more details, see Eugen J. Pentiuc, *Long-Suffering Love: A Commentary on Hosea with Patristic Annotations* (Brookline, MA: Holy Cross Orthodox Press, 2002), 23–27, 47–62, 83–90.

of the action, "that in committing fornication the earth should fornicate from the Lord," that is, the men who are upon the earth; and from men of this stamp it will be God's good pleasure to take out a Church which shall be sanctified by fellowship with His Son, just as that woman was sanctified by intercourse with the prophet.[4]

In the ministry of the prophets, word and deed were tied together. The prophets did not only proclaim the words of God to the people, call them to faith, repentance, and fulfillment of the commandments and laws, and denounce them for idolatry, disobedience to God, and turning away from moral

Saul Meets with Samuel,
James Tissot, 1896–1900.

purity. They also carried out various actions through which the glory of God was revealed to the people. Certain prophets possessed gifts of wonderworking. The miracles of the prophets Elijah and Elisha are described in 1 and 2 Kings.

A special relationship connected the prophets with the rulers of Israel. In Israel, the kingship itself derived from the prophetic charism: the prophet Samuel anointed Saul, who became the first king of Israel (1 Sam 10.1). However, after God declared to Samuel that Saul had turned away from him and had not fulfilled his word, the prophet said to Saul: "Because thou hast rejected the word of the Lord, he hath also rejected thee from being king" (1 Sam 15.23). Saul's attempts to justify himself and show remorse were unsuccessful: God remained unmoved. Then Samuel ceased all relations with Saul (1 Sam 15.35) and, according to God's command, anointed David as king. After this the Spirit of the Lord departed from Saul and rested on David (1 Sam 16.12–14).

The prophet Nathan became the herald of God's will for David (2 Sam 7.5). After David sends one of his military leaders to his death in order to

[4]Irenaeus of Lyons, *Against Heresies* 4.20.12 (*ANF* 1:492). See also Theodoret of Cyrus, *Commentary on the Prophet Hosea*, in *Commentary on the Prophets*, vol. 3, *Commentary on the Twelve Prophets*, trans. Robert Charles Hill (Brookline, MA: Holy Cross Orthodox Press, 2006), 38–81.

The prophet Nathan chastising David, miniature, 9th c.

take his wife (Bathsheba) for himself, Nathan comes to the king and tells him a parable about a rich man who takes a poor man's only ewe lamb (2 Sam 12.1–4). David does not immediately understand that this parable is addressed to him. Then the prophet declares to him the will of God: "'Now therefore the sword shall never depart from thine house, because thou hast despised me, and hast taken the wife of Uriah the Hittite to be thy wife.' Thus saith the Lord, 'Behold, I will raise up evil against thee out of thine own house, and I will take thy wives before thine eyes, and give them unto thy neighbor, and he shall lie with thy wives in the sight of this sun. For thou didst it secretly, but I will do this thing before all Israel, and before the sun'" (2 Sam 12.10–12).

The prophets had disciples and even entire schools: 2 Kings mentions "the sons of the prophets that were at Bethel," "the sons of the prophets that were at Jericho," and "fifty men of the sons of the prophets" (2 Kg 2.3, 5, 7). However, the prophetic charism was not handed down through simple instruction. Between the great prophets there was a clear succession that was assured by the fact that the spirit of one prophet would, after the latter's death or departure, pass on to another prophet. At the same time, one prophet could not give his gift to another like an inheritance: everything depended exclusively on the will of God. This is how the transfer of the prophetic charism from Elijah to Elisha is described in 2 Kings:

> And Elijah took his mantle,[5] and wrapped it together, and smote the waters, and they were divided hither and thither, so that they two went over on dry ground. And it came to pass, when they were gone over, that Elijah said unto Elisha, "Ask what I shall do for thee, before I be taken away from thee." And Elisha said, "I pray thee, let a double portion of thy spirit be upon me." And he said, "Thou hast asked a hard thing; nevertheless, if thou see me when I am taken from thee, it shall be so unto thee; but if not, it shall not be so." And it came to pass, as

[5] A mantle is an item of clothing made from sheep's wool—a cloak or a shawl.

they still went on, and talked, that, behold, there appeared a chariot of fire, and horses of fire, and parted them both asunder; and Elijah went up by a whirlwind into heaven. And Elisha saw it, and he cried, "My father, my father, the chariot of Israel, and its horsemen." And he saw him no more. And he took hold of his own clothes, and rent them in two pieces. He took up also the mantle of Elijah that fell from him, and went back, and stood by the bank of Jordan, and he took the mantle of Elijah that fell from him, and smote the waters, and said, "Where is the Lord God of Elijah?" And when he also had smitten the waters, they parted hither and

The prophet Elijah ascends to heaven on a fiery chariot, icon, 17th c.

thither, and Elisha went over. And when the sons of the prophets which were to view at Jericho saw him, they said, "The spirit of Elijah doth rest on Elisha." And they came to meet him, and bowed themselves to the ground before him. (2 Kg 2.8–15)

One of the fundamental characteristics of the prophets was the ability to foretell the future. The Greek word *prophḗtēs*, used in the Septuagint and the New Testament to translate the Hebrew *nā̲bî*, indicates precisely this aspect of their activity: *prophḗtēs* literally means "one who speaks beforehand," "foreteller." The books of the prophets are full of predictions that concern the fate of the people of Israel, other peoples, and different lands and cities. Dreadful portents, warnings, and indications of afflictions as a consequence of disobeying God and not fulfilling his commandments are interwoven with promises connected to the expectation of the coming of the Messiah. This messianic element is the main feature that attracted the New Testament authors in the books of the prophets.

The era of the prophets encompasses a substantial period in the history of Israel: from the eleventh century BC, when Samuel lived, to the fifth century BC, when Malachi died—the last of the "minor prophets" whose books entered the Old Testament. Over the course of approximately four centuries before the birth of Jesus, there were no prophets in Israel—at least, there were none whose degree of influence could be compared to the ancient prophets. However, the expectation of the return of one of the prophets was widespread.[6]

In particular, it was supposed that Elijah could return to earth, since, according to 2 Kings, he did not die, but was lifted up to heaven. The expectation of the second coming of Elijah was based in particular on the words of the prophet Malachi: "Behold, I will send you Elijah the prophet before the coming of the great and dreadful day of the Lord, and he shall turn the heart of the fathers to the children, and the heart of the children to their fathers, lest I come and smite the earth with a curse" (Mal 4.5–6). These words were well known in the time of Jesus.

The expectation of the "last prophet" was just as widespread as the expectation of the Messiah. Some equated this prophet with the promised Messiah; others equated him with Elijah, supposing that his coming would precede the coming of the Messiah. This is why the appearance of John the Baptist on the banks of the Jordan elicited tremendous excitement among the people, and this is why the name of Elijah was often mentioned in connection with him. Jesus himself said of him, "And if ye will receive it, this is Elijah, who was to come" (Mt 11.14). These words should be understood in the sense that, although John is not Elijah (Jn 1.21), he is carrying out the mission that Elijah was to carry out before the coming of the Messiah (Mt 11.14; cf. Mt 17.11–12). For the same reason, some saw Elijah in Jesus himself.

[6]Oscar Cullman, *The Christology of the New Testament*, trans. Shirley C. Guthrie and Charles A. M. Hall, 2nd Eng. ed. (London: SCM Press, 1963), 16–18.

2. "A prophet mighty in deed and word"

The term "prophet" is encountered multiple times on the pages of all four Gospels—both in the narrative and in Jesus' direct speech. Most often, this term is used when the evangelists are referring to a particular Old Testament prophecy that is fulfilled in Jesus' life and ministry. Time and again, Jesus is called a prophet by those who see his miracles or hear his teachings. Finally, Jesus himself refers more than once to the Old Testament prophets and cites examples from their lives. Besides this, he uses the term "prophet" in relation to John the Baptist (Mt 11.9, 13–14) and to himself (Mt 13.51; Mk 6.4; Lk 4.24; 14.33).

Jesus spoke many times of his mission as a continuation of the mission of the prophets. In the Sermon on the Mount he affirms that he had "not come to destroy [the law or the prophets], but to fulfil" (Mt 5.17), that is, to continue and complete them. In connection with the future persecution of his followers, he says, "So persecuted they the prophets which were before you" (Mt 5.12).

The same theme arises in Jesus' parables. In one of the parables, a rich man in hell turns to Abraham requesting that he send Lazarus to his brothers who are still alive, in order to warn them of the fate that awaits rich people who are indifferent to the misfortune of others. But Abraham answers him, "They have Moses and the prophets; let them hear them." The rich man objects, "Nay, father Abraham, but if one went unto them from the dead, they will repent." By the one risen from the dead, Jesus means himself. However, Abraham says, "If they hear not Moses and the prophets, neither will they be persuaded, though one rose from the dead" (Lk 16.27–31).

In another parable (Mt 21.33–41; Mk 12.1–9; Lk 20.9–16) Jesus tells of how the owner of a vineyard at first sends a servant to the vine dressers there, and then his own son, whom the vine dressers kill: the servants are understood to be the prophets, and the son of the owner of the vineyard is

The parable of the rich man and Lazarus, icon, 17th c.

the Son of God. In this way, there is a direct link between the teaching of the prophets and the teaching of Jesus. This link is realized through John the Baptist (Mt 11.13).

Jesus drew on the imagery of the prophets in his polemics with his fellow Jews. In the synagogue in Nazareth the anger of his hearers was aroused most of all by the fact that Jesus had drawn a direct parallel between his mission and episodes in the lives of Elijah and Elisha in support of the assertion, "No prophet is accepted in his own country" (Lk 4.24).

Jesus rebuked the scribes and Pharisees for building tombs for the prophets, decorating the sepulchers of the righteous, and saying, "If we had been in the days of our fathers, we would not have been partakers with them in the blood of the prophets" (Mt 23.30). Jesus considered his opponents to be the successors of those who persecuted the prophets: "Therefore ye are witnesses unto yourselves, that ye are the children of them which killed the prophets. Fill ye up then the measure of your fathers" (Mt 23.31–32). In contrast, Jesus considered himself and his followers to be the successors of the prophets (Mt 23.33–39).

The Gospels contain many parallels between different aspects of Jesus' ministries and the activity of the prophets.[7] Thus, for example, the prophet Micaiah, the son of Imlah, says of the people of Israel, "I saw all Israel scattered upon the hills, as sheep that have not a shepherd" (1 Kg 22.17). Of Jesus it is said, "Jesus . . . saw much people, and was moved with compassion toward them, because they were as sheep not having a shepherd" (Mk 6.34). He calls himself the "good shepherd," who "giveth his life for the sheep" (Jn 10.11).

[7]See N. T. Wright, *Jesus and the Victory of God*, Christian Origins and the Question of God 2 (Minneapolis, MN: Fortress Press, 1996), 166–168.

Christ Driving the Traders from the Temple, El Greco, ca. 1600.

Jesus' conduct in the Temple, when he drove out those who were buying and selling (Mt 21.12–13; Mk 11.15–17; Lk 19.45–46; Jn 2.15–17), reminded the disciples of the words of the psalm: "The zeal of thine house hath eaten me up" (Ps 68.10). And the words that Jesus addressed to those whom he was driving out were none other than an allusion to the words of the prophets Jeremiah and Isaiah: "Is this house, which is called by my name, become a den of robbers in your eyes?" (Jer 7.11); "my house shall be called a house of prayer for all people" (Is 56.7).

Jesus' prophecy concerning the destruction of the Temple in Jerusalem (Mt 24.2; Mk 13.2; Lk 19.42–44) was a renewal of the analogous prophecy of Jeremiah (Jer 7.12–14), and also of the prophecy of Daniel, which Jesus directly refers to (Mt 24.15; Mk 13.14). In this prophecy the death of the Messiah is foretold, which is to be followed by an invasion by a foreign king, the destruction of the Temple, and the end of the Levitical priesthood (which happened in AD 70):

> Know therefore and understand, that from the going forth of the commandment to restore and to build Jerusalem unto the Messiah the Prince there shall be seven weeks, and sixty-two weeks; the street shall be built again, and the wall, even in troublesome times. And after

John the
Forerunner with
scenes from his
life, icon, 13th c.

sixty-two weeks shall Messiah be cut off, but not for himself. And the people of the prince that shall come shall destroy the city and the sanctuary; and the end thereof shall be with a flood, and unto the end of the war desolations are determined. And he shall confirm the covenant with many for one week; and in the midst of the week he shall cause the sacrifice and the oblation to cease, and for the overspreading of abominations he shall make it desolate. (Dan 9.25–27)

The parallels between the activity of the prophets and the ministry of Jesus were obvious: it was precisely because of this that the term "prophet" was so often applied to Jesus by those who became witnesses of his miracles and listeners of his speeches. After John the Baptist was beheaded, some began to identify Jesus with John. Word of the new prophet reached King

Herod, and having "heard of him (for his name was spread abroad) . . . he said that John the Baptist was risen from the dead, and therefore mighty works do show forth themselves in him. Others said, 'It is Elijah.' And others said, 'It is a prophet, or as one of the prophets.' But when Herod heard of it, he said, 'It is John, whom I beheaded: he is risen from the dead'" (Mk 6.14–16). Luke gives Herod's reply in a somewhat different form: "John have I beheaded. But who is this, of whom I hear such things?" (Lk 9.9).

Jesus Christ Healing the Man Born Blind, Vasily Surikov, 1888

The reputation of being a prophet passed from John to Jesus: more than that, some saw in Jesus a sort of reincarnation of the Baptist. Of course, Jews did not believe in reincarnation. But they believed that the spirit of one prophet could pass on to another prophet, as the spirit of Elijah passed on to Elisha.

Jesus himself, as is clear from the Gospel narratives, was not indifferent to what was being said about him among the people. In Caesarea Philippi he asks the disciples, "Whom do men say that I the Son of Man am?" And he receives the answer, "Some say that thou art John the Baptist; some, Elijah; and others, Jeremiah, or one of the prophets" (Mt 16.13–14; cf. Mk 8.27–28). Many thought that in the person of Jesus "one of the old prophets [was] risen again" (Lk 9.19). This belief was based not so much on his words as on the miracles and signs that he was performing: in the popular memory, these miracles recalled the stories of the great prophets of old.

A whole series of stories attest that Jesus gained a reputation as a prophet because of his miracles. Telling of how Jesus opened the eyes of the man born blind, the evangelist John quotes the dialogue between the man and the Pharisees. They ask him, "What sayest thou of him, that he hath opened thine eyes?" And they receive a perfectly straightforward answer: "He is a prophet" (Jn 9.17).

The Gospel of Luke contains the story of how, having come to the city of Nain, Jesus saw a funeral procession by the city gates: "there was a dead man carried out, the only son of his mother, and she was a widow, and many

The Raising of Lazarus, Giotto, 1304–1306.

people of the city were with her." Jesus had compassion on the mother and said to her, "Weep not." Then, coming up to the bier, he touched it and said, "Young man, I say unto thee, arise." The dead man immediately rose, sat up, and began to speak. The reaction of the witnesses of his miracle is described with the following words: "And there came a fear on all, and they glorified God, saying, 'A great prophet is risen up among us,' and, 'God hath visited his people'" (Lk 7.12–16).

The raising of Lazarus, which took place before Jesus entered Jerusalem for the last time, produced an impression in no way inferior. The evangelist John, who gives an account of this miracle, relates that, when Jesus entered the city, "The people therefore that were with him when he called Lazarus out of his grave, and raised him from the dead, bore record [to the miracle]. For this cause the people also met him, for they heard that he had done this miracle" (Jn 12.17–18). In the words of Matthew, who describes this same scene, "all the city was moved, saying, 'Who is this?' And the multitude said, 'This is Jesus the prophet of Nazareth of Galilee'" (Mt 21.10–11). A little later Matthew points out that the chief priests and Pharisees wanted to arrest Jesus, "But when they sought to lay hands on him, they feared the multitude, because they took him for a prophet" (Mt 21.46).

Jesus' prophetic abilities were disputed by the Pharisees. When Jesus dined with one of them, a sinful woman came, "stood at his feet behind him weeping, and began to wash his feet with tears, and wiped them with the hairs of her head, and kissed his feet, and anointed them with the ointment. Now when the Pharisee which had bidden him saw it, he spake within himself, saying, 'This man, if he were a prophet, would have known who and what manner of woman this is that toucheth him, for she is a sinner.'" (Lk 7.38–39). But Jesus read his thoughts and responded to them. To the woman he said, "Thy sins are forgiven." At that the others who were reclining at table began to say to themselves, "Who is this that forgiveth sins also?" (Lk 7.48–49).

Remembering that the ancient prophets performed signs, and having heard much about the miracles that Jesus performed, the Pharisees time and again demanded that he demonstrate his supernatural abilities. Jesus refused to do this:

> Then certain of the scribes and of the Pharisees answered, saying, "Master, we would see a sign from thee." But he answered and said unto them, "An evil and adulterous generation seeketh after a sign, and there shall no sign be given to it, but the sign of the prophet Jonah: for as Jonah was three days and three nights in the whale's belly, so shall the Son of Man be three days and three nights in the heart of the earth. The men of Nineveh shall rise in judgment with this generation, and shall condemn it, because they repented at the preaching of Jonah. And, behold, one greater than Jonah is here. The queen of the south shall rise up in the judgment with this generation, and shall condemn it, for she came from the uttermost parts of the earth to hear the wisdom of Solomon. And, behold, one greater than Solomon is here." (Mt 12.38–42; cf. Lk 11.29–32)

With these words, Jesus, foretells his death and resurrection, as in the parable about the rich man and Lazarus. In the parable, he clearly said that even his resurrection would not convince those who would not listen to the word of the prophets. Here, he underlines the significance of his own mission in comparison with the mission of the prophets. The word

King Solomon, miniature from the Erznka Bible of 1269 (an Armenian illuminated manuscript).

"greater" (*pleion*, also "more") is used in the same sense as when Jesus spoke of John the Baptist being a prophet and "more than a prophet" (Mt 11.9; cf. Lk 7.26). The story of Jonah, who was swallowed by a whale, is significant only inasmuch as it is a prefiguration of what would happen to the Son of God. And the preaching of Jonah, which led the Ninevites to repentance (Jon 3.5–10), is but a prefiguration of the call to repentance that issues from Jesus' lips. On the one hand, Jesus speaks of himself as a successor to the work of the prophets; on the other hand, he insists that his mission possesses an incomparably greater significance.

The abovementioned story involving the queen of the south is worth quoting here in full:

And when the queen of Sheba heard of the fame of Solomon concerning the name of the Lord, she came to prove him with hard questions. And she came to Jerusalem with a very great train, with camels that bare spices, and very much gold, and precious stones. And when she was come to Solomon, she communed with him of all that was in her heart. And Solomon told her all her questions. Nothing was hid from the king, which he told her not. And when the queen of Sheba had seen all Solomon's wisdom, and the house that he had built, and the food of his table, and the sitting of his servants, and the attendance of his ministers, and their apparel, and his cupbearers, and his ascent by which he went up unto the house of the Lord, there was no more spirit in her. And she said to the king, "It was a true report that I heard in mine own land of thy acts and of thy wisdom." Howbeit I believed not the words, until I came, and mine eyes had seen it. And, behold, the half was not told me. Thy wisdom and prosperity exceedeth the fame which I heard. Happy are thy men, happy are these thy servants, which stand continually before thee, and that hear thy wisdom. (1 Kg 10.1–8)

Solomon entered the history of Israel as a king who possessed not only untold riches, but also exceptional wisdom. In the Gospel of Luke, Jesus' reference to Solomon and the queen of the south follows immediately after Jesus' words, "Blessed are they that hear the word of God, and keep it" (Lk 11.28). We do not know whether Luke meant to draw a parallel between the words of the queen of Sheba about the blessedness of Solomon's servants who heard his wisdom, and the words of Jesus concerning the blessedness of those who hear and keep the word of God; however, we can in no way exclude this possibility. The main idea of the whole passage is this: the wisdom of Jesus transcends the wisdom of Solomon, and his mission is of greater significance that the mission of the prophets.

Solomon and the Queen of Sheba, a panel from the "Gates of Paradise" bronze doors of the Baptistery of the Duomo, Florence. Bronze, Lorenzo Ghiberti, 15th c.

The term "prophet" on the lips of the hearers and interlocutors of Jesus, as well as the witnesses of his miracles, did not necessarily refer to one of the prophets of old. This term could refer also to the Messiah, whom the Jews watched for with trepidation. This use of the term is based on the tradition deriving from the book of Deuteronomy, in which God foretells the following to Moses: "I will raise them up a Prophet from among their brethren, like unto thee, and will put my words in his mouth, and he shall speak unto them all that I shall command him" (Deut 18.18). It was of such a Prophet-Messiah, a new Moses, that people began to speak after the feeding of the five thousand with five loaves of bread: "Then those men, when they had seen the miracle that Jesus did, said, 'This is of a truth that Prophet that should come into the world'" (Jn 6.14).

The disputes over whether Jesus was simply a prophet, or "that Prophet," that is, the Messiah, are reflected in the Gospel of John:

Many of the people therefore, when they heard this saying, said, "Of a truth this is the Prophet." Others said, "This is the Christ." But some said, "Shall Christ come out of Galilee? Hath not the scripture said, that

Christ Pantocrator,
icon, St Catherine's
Monastery, Mt Sinai, 6th c.

Christ cometh of the seed of David, and out of
the town of Bethlehem, where David was?" So
there was a division among the people because
of him. (Jn 7.40–43)

As we can see, Jesus' prophetic charism was not
in doubt. However, his Galilean origin was a conve-
nient reason for the Jews to reject his messiahship.
The Pharisees, in particular, believed that a prophet
could not come from Galilee (Jn 7.50–53). The people were of a different opinion: in Jerusalem, Jesus
was called the "prophet of Nazareth of Galilee" (Mt
21.11). In Galilee itself, people were saying of Jesus,
"'A great prophet is risen up among us'; and . . . 'God
hath visited his people'" (Lk 7.16). At the same time,
as the evangelist notes, "This rumor of him went
forth throughout all Judaea, and throughout all the
region round about" (Lk 7.17).

Thus, in both Judea and in Galilee, people were speaking of Jesus not
only as a prophet or one of the prophets: some were calling him a great
prophet, and others were explicitly stating that he was "that prophet that
should come into the world," that is, the Messiah.

Meanwhile, the Messiah was anticipated not only in Judea and Galilee:
in Samaria, people had their own ideas about the coming Anointed One of
God. This is attested to by the conversation between Jesus and the Samaritan woman. After he tells her that she has no husband, since she has been
married five times, the woman says to him, "Sir, I perceive that thou art a
prophet" (Jn 4.19). And she asks him a question that draws the dividing line
between the Jews and the Samaritans: where was one to worship God—on
Mount Gerizim, or in Jerusalem? Jesus answers that one must worship the
Father "in spirit and in truth." Then the woman speaks of what united the
Jews and the Samaritans—of the coming Messiah: "I know that Messiah
cometh, which is called Christ. When he is come, he will tell us all things"
(Jn 4.25). Jesus says to her, "I that speak unto thee am he" (Jn 4.26). Did

Christ
Pantocrator,
fresco,
Theophanes the
Greek, 15th c.

his answer convince the Samaritan woman? From all appearances, not completely, since she looks to others for confirmation. Returning to the city, she says to the people, "Come, see a man, which told me all things that ever I did. Is not this the Christ?" (Jn 4.29). Only after he stays with them for two days are they convinced that "this is indeed the Christ, the Savior of the world" (Jn 4.42).

Slowly but surely, through the entire story of Jesus' visit to Samaria, the evangelist John leads up to the idea that Jesus is not simply a prophet. The Samaritan woman understood almost immediately that he was a prophet. But she could not immediately believe that he was the Christ.

Just such a gradual realization of the fact that Jesus is "more than a prophet" dawns on his disciples. In Caesarea Philippi, not one of the disciples aside from Peter confesses that Jesus is the Christ (Mt 16.13–16; Mk 8.27–30; Lk 9.18–20). We may, of course, suppose that Peter was responding on behalf of all the others and that the other apostles agreed with him, but the text of the Synoptic Gospels say nothing about this. It is entirely conceivable that, at that moment, there was no consensus among the apostles regarding whether Jesus was a prophet or the Christ.

More than that, the disciples did not possess a clear understanding that Jesus was the Christ even after his death and resurrection. When the risen Jesus approached two disciples on the road to Emmaus, not recognizing him, they began to tell him about Jesus of Nazareth, "who was a prophet mighty in deed and word before God and all the people" (Lk 24.19). After mentioning his crucifixion, the disciples continue: "But we trusted that it had been he who should have redeemed Israel" (Lk 7.21). The disciples' conviction that Jesus was a prophet and their doubt that he was the Christ are plain to see. But Jesus, still unrecognized, turns to none other than the writings of the prophets, demonstrating that they witnessed to him.

The whole episode revolves around the theme of the relationship between Jesus and the prophets. This same theme appears in the speech that the apostle Peter delivered in the Jerusalem Temple soon after Jesus' resurrection. Addressing the Jews, whom Jesus had not too long ago called the sons of those who persecuted the prophets, Peter calls them "the children of the prophets, and of the covenant" (Acts 3.25), who killed the Just One "through ignorance" (Acts 3.17). At the same time, Jesus himself appears in the speech simultaneously as a successor to the mission of the prophets, and as the promised Messiah, the Son of God:

> For Moses truly said unto the fathers, "A Prophet shall the Lord your God raise up unto you of your brethren, like unto me. Him shall ye hear in all things whatsoever he shall say unto you. And it shall come to pass, that every soul, which will not hear that prophet, shall be destroyed from among the people." [Deut 18.18–19] Yea, and all the prophets from Samuel and those that follow after, as many as have spoken, have like-

wise foretold of these days. . . . Unto you first God, having raised up his Son Jesus, sent him to bless you, in turning away every one of you from his iniquities. (Acts 3.22–24, 26)

References to the prophets are extremely abundant in Acts as well as in the apostolic epistles. However, we see that, already in the first generation of Christians, the idea of Jesus as a prophet mighty in deed and word is completely replaced by the teaching of Jesus being the Son of God, whom the prophets foretold. The doubts that racked the disciples in the first days after Jesus' resurrection (Mt 28.17) soon dispersed, and faith in Jesus as Lord and God (Jn 20.28) triumphed in the Christian community. It is this faith that became the main driving force of the apostles' preaching, which was a continuation of the preaching of Jesus, and, through him, also a continuation of the preaching of John the Baptist and the prophets.

The apostle Paul,
icon, 14th c.

The Epistle to the Hebrews, which concludes the corpus of the apostolic epistles and is ascribed to the apostle Paul in the tradition of the Church,[8] has as its basic theme the mutual relationship between the Old and New Testaments. The epistle begins with the following words: "God, who at sundry times and in diverse manners spoke in time past unto the fathers by the prophets, hath in these last days spoken unto us by his Son . . ." (Heb 1.1–2). Here the mission of the Son of God is presented as a continuation of the mission of the Old Testament prophets. However, the Son of God immediately emerges as the one through whom God "also . . . made the worlds" (Heb 1.2). He, "being the brightness of his

---

[8]Here and later in the present book, as well as in the other books in the series *Jesus Christ: His Life and Teaching*, we will refer to the Epistle to the Hebrews as one of the epistles of the apostle Paul, in accordance with the attribution accepted in the tradition of the Church. An analysis of the polemics surrounding the authorship of this epistle is outside the scope of our investigation.

glory, and the express image of his person, and upholding all things by the word of his power, when he had by himself purged our sins, sat down on the right hand of the Majesty on high, being made so much better than the angels, as he hath by inheritance obtained a more excellent name than they" (Heb 1.3–4).

The words concerning how God "made the worlds" through his Son cannot but remind us of the beginning of the Gospel of John: "All things were made by him, and without him was not any thing made that was made" (Jn 1.3). The expression "the brightness of his glory" echoes the words of John about the glory of the Son of God: he "was the true Light, which enlighteneth every man that cometh into the world. . . . and we beheld his glory, the glory as of the only begotten of the Father" (Jn 1.9, 14). Both the Prologue to the Gospel of John and the Epistle to the Hebrews are manifestos of the faith of the ancient Church in Jesus being not simply one of the prophets, similar to Elijah or John the Baptist, and not simply the latest prophet who came to the people of Israel in order to renew the inter-rupted prophetic tradition. He is the Son of God who was with the Father from the beginning and participated together with him in the creation of the world and mankind, and then, "in these last days," himself became a man and came to the people.

Turning to Old Testament history, the author of the Epistle to the Hebrews mentions all its key characters—Abraham, Isaac, Jacob, Joseph, Moses, and other protagonists of the historical books (Heb 11.17–32). The prophets merit a separate reference,

> who through faith subdued kingdoms, wrought righteousness, obtained promises, stopped the mouths of lions, quenched the violence of fire, escaped the edge of the sword, out of weakness were made strong, waxed valiant in fight, turned to flight the armies of the aliens. Women received their dead raised to life again, and others were tortured, not accepting deliverance, that they might obtain a better resurrection; and others had trial of cruel mockings and scourgings, yea, moreover of bonds and imprisonment; they were stoned, they were sawn asun-der, were tempted, were slain with the sword; they wandered about

Christ in
Majesty, icon,
Dionisius, 16th c.

in sheepskins and goatskins, being destitute, afflicted, tormented—of
whom the world was not worthy; they wandered in deserts, and in
mountains, and in dens and caves of the earth. (Heb 11.33–38)

All of them, the epistle continues, although they proved their faith,
"received not the promise, God having provided some better thing for us"
(Heb 11.39–40). This better thing is "Jesus the author and finisher of our
faith" (Heb 12.2). He is above Moses, who was only a servant in his house,
"but Christ [is] as a son over his own house; whose house are we" (Heb 3.6).
He is the "great high priest, that is passed into the heavens" (Heb 4.14), who
became "the author of eternal salvation unto all them that obey him" (Heb

5.9). He is the "great shepherd of the sheep" (Heb 13.20), who sanctified the people "with his own blood" (Heb 13.12).

* * *

The external parameters of Jesus' earthly ministry recalled in many ways the way of life and action of the prophets, and he was therefore taken for a prophet. He himself considered himself to be the successor to the work of the prophets. However, contrary to the prevailing opinion, he was not just one of the prophets: he was the Prophet, with a capital "P," the promised Messiah.

All the prophets, including Moses, were earthly people, although they were also endowed with a special charism and carried out a special mission. But Jesus was not simply a man, but also God incarnate, whom the Father anointed "to preach the Gospel to the poor . . . to heal the broken-hearted, to preach deliverance to the captives, and recovering of sight to the blind, to set at liberty them that are bruised, to preach the acceptable year of the Lord" (Lk 4.18–19). Being God, Jesus said that he was insepa-rable from God the Father to such an extent that he was able to state, "I and my Father are one" (Jn 10.30). Not a single prophet in the history of Israel ever made such a claim not only to intimacy with God, but also to full unity with him.

Chapter 6

JESUS AND THE DISCIPLES

---

1. The Calling of the First Disciples

The beginning of Jesus' ministry was heralded when he gathered a group of disciples around himself. John and the Synoptics give different accounts of how this happened.

John's Account

We have already said that after the temptation in the wilderness Jesus did not immediately go out to preach, but first returned to John the Baptist at the Jordan; this is apparent from the Gospel of John. From the same Gospel we learn that Jesus acquired his first disciples from among the disciples of John the Baptist:

> Again the next day John was standing with two of his disciples. And looking upon Jesus as he walked, he saith, "Behold the Lamb of God!" And the two disciples heard him speak, and they followed Jesus. Then Jesus turned, and saw them following, and saith unto them, "What seek ye?" They said unto him, "Rabbi" (which is to say, being interpreted, "Teacher"), "where dwellest thou?" He saith unto them, "Come and see." They came and saw where he dwelt, and abode with him that day. For it was about the tenth hour. (Jn 1.35–39)

The apostle Andrew the First-Called, icon at the Monastery of Vatopedi on Mount Athos, 15th c.

The evangelist then clarifies: "One of the two who heard John speak, and followed him, was Andrew, Simon Peter's brother" (Jn 1.40). Who was the other disciple, who remains unnamed? We may suppose that this was John himself, the author of the Fourth Gospel. There are several reasons for such a supposition.

First, the story is written with details that suggest the involvement of an eyewitness of the events. The two disciples appear at the very beginning of the story. They hear what the Forerunner says about Jesus. They follow after Jesus and ask him a question that, it would appear, does not contain any theological content. These details in themselves—this question, Jesus' answer, and the mention of two disciples going with him where he was staying—would not warrant inclusion in the Gospel if the entire story were not, for its author, the recounting of the cherished memory of his first encounter with the Teacher. The observation that "it was about the tenth hour" reveals a witness who remembers the entire episode to the smallest detail.

Second, the anonymous disciple appears more than once later on in the Gospel of John. As we have said earlier, Church tradition identifies the unnamed disciple (Jn 1.40; 19.35)—also the "other disciple" (Jn 20.2–4, 8) or the "disciple, whom Jesus loved" (Jn 13.23; 19.26; 20.2; 21.7, 20)—with John the son of Zebedee, the brother of James.

Thus a picture takes shape of a group of four disciples, consisting of two pairs of brothers: Peter and Andrew, John and James. If one supposes that the two disciples of John the Baptist who followed Jesus were Andrew and John (the latter not mentioned by name), then the story later on of how Andrew "first findeth his own brother Simon, and saith unto him, 'We have found the Messiah,' which is, being interpreted, the Christ" (Jn 1.41) becomes completely understandable. The one who would become the

The apostles Peter, Paul, Andrew the First-Called and John the Theologian, icon, 16th c.

head of the apostolic community after Jesus' death and resurrection was indebted to his brother for his first encounter with Jesus.

John continues the story of the calling of the apostles in the following narrative:

The following day Jesus wanted to go forth into Galilee, and findeth Philip, and saith unto him, "Follow me." Now Philip was of Bethsaida, the city of Andrew and Peter. Philip findeth Nathanael, and saith unto him, "We have found him, of whom Moses in the law, and the prophets, did write, Jesus of Nazareth, the son of Joseph." And Nathanael said unto him, "Can any good thing come out of Nazareth?" Philip saith unto him, "Come and see." Jesus saw Nathanael coming to him, and saith of him, "Behold an Israelite indeed, in whom is no guile!" Nathanael saith unto him, "Whence knowest thou me?" Jesus answered and said unto

The apostle Philip,
fresco, 14th c.

him, "Before Philip called thee, when thou wast under the fig tree, I saw thee." Nathanael answered and saith unto him, "Rabbi, thou art the Son of God; thou art the King of Israel." Jesus answered and said unto him, "Because I said unto thee, 'I saw thee under the fig tree,' believest thou? Thou shalt see greater things than these." And he saith unto him, "Truly, truly, I say unto you, hereafter ye shall see heaven open, and the angels of God ascending and descending upon the Son of Man." (Jn 1.43–51)

How and in what circumstances does Jesus find Philip? The evangelist is silent on this. It would be logical to assume that Andrew and Peter acquainted Jesus with Philip, inasmuch as the latter was from the same town as they were. The evangelist does not explain why Philip goes to find Nathanael: one can only assume that they were friends or, at the very least, knew each other well.

A whole chain of encounters is set up: at first, Andrew and "the other disciple" meet Jesus on the bank of the Jordan; the very same day, Andrew finds Simon and brings him to Jesus; the next day, Jesus finds Philip, and the latter finds Nathanael. Over two days, five disciples come to Jesus.

Nathanael's reaction to the news of the discovery of the Messiah reveals the characteristic Judean disdain for Galileans: "Can any good thing come out of Nazareth?" We have already discussed how the obscure Galilean town of Nazareth was in no way understood to be the place from which the Messiah, the Son of David, could come. Philip is clearly unaware of Jesus' birth in Bethlehem of Judea; he only answers, "Come and see."

The dialogue that follows between Nathanael and Jesus can be interpreted in several different ways. Jesus could have noticed Nathanael earlier, when he was sitting somewhere under a fig tree (in this case, the words "when thou wast under the fig tree" relate to what follows them: "I saw thee"). Jesus could have seen Nathanael before Philip found him sitting under the fig tree and told him about Jesus (in this case, the words "when thou wast under the fig tree" relate to what precedes them: "Before Philip called thee"). Finally, Jesus could have not seen Nathanael in the literal sense at all: it is entirely possible to interpret his words as an indication that Jesus knew of Nathanael's thoughts and that the latter doubted the possibility that the Messiah could come from Nazareth. In this case, the words "Behold an Israelite

The apostle Bartholomew (Nathanael), fresco, 16th c.

indeed, in whom is no guile!" find their explanation: by "Israelite" Jesus means an inhabitant of Judea, who does not believe that the Messiah could come from Galilee.

In his commentary on this story, John Chrysostom unites the second and the third of the above interpretations. In his words, Jesus "was present when they were conversing." Nathanael tests Jesus as a man, but Jesus answers him as God: "'I saw thee by the fig-tree'; when there was no one present there but only Philip and Nathanael who said all these things in private." Jesus pronounced the words, "Behold an Israelite indeed," "before Philip came near . . . that the testimony might not be suspected. For this reason also He named the time, the place, and the tree." Thus Jesus, according to Chrysostom, revealed his indisputable foreknowledge.[1]

Thus, according to the Gospel of John, the first group of Jesus' disciples, selected by him over the course of two days, included Peter, Andrew, Philip, Nathanael, and, it would seem, John himself. One can assume that it was this group of five men that was present the next day at the wedding in Cana of Galilee, where "both Jesus was called, and his disciples" (Jn 2.2). These same disciples came with him to Capernaum (Jn 2.12).

We encounter the disciples again in John the Evangelist's story of Jesus' arrival in the land of Judea, where he "tarried with them, and baptized" (Jn 3.22). Then we read that Jesus learned of "how the Pharisees had heard that

---

[1]John Chrysostom, *Homilies on the Gospel of John* 20.2 (*NPNF*¹ 14:71).

Jesus made and baptized more disciples than John (though Jesus himself baptized not, but his disciples)" (Jn 4.1–2). In the story of Jesus' conversation with the Samaritan woman, the disciples are again mentioned, who at first "were gone away unto the city to buy meat" (Jn 4.8), and then returned and "marveled that he talked with the woman" (Jn 4.27). The disciples are not mentioned in the stories of Jesus' visit to Galilee (Jn 4.43–54), the healing of the paralytic in Jerusalem (Jn 5.1–16), and the dialogue that follows between Jesus and the Jews (Jn 5.17–47). The disciples appear again in the narrative together with Jesus when he went up the mountain near Tiberias (Jn 6.1–3). Here he performed the miracle of the multiplication of the loaves, in which the disciples participated, with two of them being mentioned by name: Philip, and Andrew, the brother of Simon Peter (Jn 6.7–8). In the evening of the same day, the disciples, who were in a boat, witnessed Jesus walking to them on the water (Jn 6.16–21).

In none of the abovementioned episodes does John mention the number of the disciples; however, the context of the narrative permits one to assume that their number was gradually increasing. While there were apparently only five disciples with Jesus at the wedding in Cana of Galilee and the same number in Capernaum, already in Judea he "made and baptized more disciples than John." One can imagine that here the reference points to a fairly large circle that believed in Jesus and were following after him.

This assumption is supported by the story of Jesus' preaching in the synagogue in Capernaum in the Fourth Gospel. "Many . . . of his disciples" are mentioned, who, upon hearing his preaching, said: "This is a hard saying; who can hear it?" In answer, Jesus, who "knew in himself that his disciples murmured at it," chastised them for their unbelief, foretelling that one of them would betray him. "From that time many of his disciples went back, and walked no more with him. Then said Jesus unto the twelve, 'Do you also want to go away?'" (Jn 6.60–67). Here is the first instance where John mentions a specific number: twelve.

Thus, according to John, Jesus at first had five disciples, whose number clearly increased considerably; then a significant proportion of his disciples left him and no longer walked with him. Where did the twelve disciples

The Miraculous Draught of Fishes, engraving, Gustave Doré, 1860s.

come from, the number of which John gives in the end? In order to answer this question, we must turn to the accounts of the Synoptics.

The Synoptics' Account

The story of the calling of the first disciples in the Synoptics differs significantly from the story presented by John. Matthew and Mark give the same, textually identical story:

> Now as he walked by the sea of Galilee, he saw Simon and Andrew his brother casting a net into the sea, for they were fishers. And Jesus said unto them, "Come ye after me, and I will make you to become fishers of men." And straightway they forsook their nets, and followed him. And when he had gone a little further thence, he saw James the son of Zebedee, and John his brother, who also were in the ship mending their nets. And straightway he called them: and they left their father Zebedee

The apostle Peter, icon, 6th c.

in the ship with the hired servants, and went after him. (Mk 1.16–20; Mt 4.18–22)

From reading this excerpt, one gets the impression that Jesus calls people unknown to him, and they, leaving their nets, follow after him. Meanwhile, an attempt to harmonize this story with the stories from the Gospel of John gives a completely different picture. Of the four disciples mentioned by Matthew and Mark, John mentions two, and one of them was most likely John himself. At the same time, as we recall, Andrew and John had been disciples of John the Baptist and followed after Jesus, and then Andrew found Peter and led him to the Teacher. All this happened immediately after Jesus' two meetings with John the Baptist, which took place, as we have proposed, after Jesus' return from the wilderness.

In the Synoptics, between the temptation in the desert and Jesus' going out to preach after John's imprisonment, there is a temporal gap that is not filled by anything. This gap is only partially filled by John's stories about Jesus' meeting with John the Baptist, about the two disciples of John who followed after Jesus and spent the day with him, about Jesus' acquaintance with Peter, Philip, and Nathanael, and about the participation of the disciples in the wedding in Cana of Galilee. We can assume that Peter and Andrew, after they met Jesus and spent some days with him, returned to Galilee to their usual occupations. The same was the case for John. Speaking of the two disciples of John the Baptist who followed Jesus, John Chrysostom notes: "Neither was it unnatural for them to follow Him at the beginning, and then leave Him again and return anew to their own craft, when they saw both John thrown into prison, and Himself departing. Accordingly you see that He finds them actually fishing. But He neither forbad them at the first when minded to withdraw, nor having withdrawn themselves, did He let them go altogether; but He gave way when they started aside from Him, and comes again to win them back."[2] Chrysostom

[2]John Chrysostom, *Homilies on the Gospel of Matthew* 14.3 (*NPNF*[1] 10:88).

is echoed by Augustine: "[W]e are to understand that those men did not gain such a view of Jesus on the occasion connected with the vicinity of the Jordan as would lead them to attach themselves to Him for ever, but that they simply came to know who He was, and, after their first wonder at His Person, returned to their former engagements."[3]

In that case, the story in the Synoptics takes on another tone. Of the four persons called by Jesus, at least three were already known to him: these were the brothers Peter and Andrew, and also John, the brother of James (in fact, as we shall see later, all four were known to Jesus). Accordingly, he addresses them not as people unknown to himself, but as people whom he had already met earlier, but is now calling to a new ministry. Their immediate readiness to follow Jesus, therefore, is likewise explained not so much by them somehow being very strongly impressed by a mysterious Stranger, as by the fact that he was not a stranger to them: they had already met him earlier, and were inwardly ready to respond to his call.

These are the four disciples who, according to the Gospel of Mark, come with Jesus to Capernaum, where he drives out the unclean spirit from the possessed man (Mk 1.21–28), and later they are the ones who, called by their names, come with Jesus to Peter's home, where he heals Peter's mother-in-law (Mk 1.29–31). In the morning of the next day, "rising up a great while before day, [Jesus] went out, and departed into a solitary place, and there prayed. And Simon and they that were with him followed after him. And when they had found him, they said unto him, 'Everyone seeketh for thee'" (Mk 1.35–37). Again, "Simon and they that were with him" refers to the four disciples.

In Matthew, between the calling of the four disciples and the healing of Peter's mother-in-law, there is the story of Jesus' visit to Galilee (Mt 4.23–25), the Sermon on the Mount (Mt 5–7), and the stories of the cleansing of the leper (Mt 8.1–4) and the healing of the servant of the centurion in Capernaum (Mt 8.5–13). After the account of the healing of Peter's mother-in-law (Mt 8.14–15), there are several episodes involving the disciples, including the dialogue with the scribe (Mt 8.18–20), the storm on the sea (Mt 8.23–27), the healing of two demon-possessed men in the

---

[3]Augustine of Hippo, *The Harmony of the Gospels* 2.17.37 (*NPNF*[1] 6:122).

country of the Gergesenes (Mt 8.28–34), and the healing of the paralytic in Nazareth (Mt 9.1–8). One can assume that, in all these episodes, there were four disciples present: Peter, Andrew, John, and James.

In the Gospel of Luke, Simon Peter first appears in the story of the miraculous catch of fish:

> And it came to pass, that, as the people pressed upon him to hear the word of God, he stood by the lake of Gennesaret, and saw two ships standing by the lake, but the fishermen were gone out of them, and were washing their nets. And he entered into one of the ships, which was Simon's, and prayed him that he would thrust out a little from the land. And he sat down, and taught the people out of the ship. Now when he had left speaking, he said unto Simon, "Launch out into the deep, and let down your nets for a draught." And Simon answering said unto him, "Master, we have toiled all the night, and have taken nothing; nevertheless at thy word I will let down the net." And when they had this done, they enclosed a great multitude of fishes, and their net brake. And they beckoned unto their partners, which were in the other ship, that they should come and help them. And they came, and filled both the ships, so that they began to sink. When Simon Peter saw it, he fell down at Jesus' knees, saying, "Depart from me, for I am a sinful man, O Lord." For he was astonished, and all that were with him, at the draught of the fishes which they had taken. And so was also James, and John, the sons of Zebedee, which were partners with Simon. And Jesus said unto Simon, "Fear not. From henceforth thou shalt catch men." And when they had brought their ships to land, they forsook all, and followed him. (Lk 5.1–11)

Thus we see yet another story of the calling of the disciples. Here, in contrast to Matthew and Mark, not four, but three disciples are spoken of: Peter, John, and James—the same ones who would be marked in the Synoptics as being the closest disciples of Jesus. In the accounts of all the Synoptics, nets are mentioned: in the first two Gospels, Peter and Andrew let down nets, while James and John, together with their father, mend nets; in Luke, the fishermen are washing nets. All the accounts give Jesus' words

The Miraculous Draught of Fishes, Raphael, 1515–1516.

that he would make his disciples "fishers of men" (Mt 4.19; Mk 1.17); in two Gospels these words are addressed to Peter and Andrew, and in Luke, to Peter alone.

One can reconcile the accounts of Matthew and Mark with the account of Luke in only one way—by granting that there are two different episodes being discussed. This is what Augustine thought, who was of the opinion that the episode described by Luke preceded the episode described by the other two Synoptics:

> What Luke introduces here was what took place first, and that these men were not called by the Lord on this occasion, but only that the prediction was uttered to Peter by himself, that he would be a fisher of men. That saying, moreover, was not intended to convey that they would never thereafter be catchers of fish. For we read that even after the Lord's resurrection they were engaged again in fishing [Jn 21.3]. . . . And in this way we are at perfect liberty to suppose that they returned to the catching of fish, according to their habit; so that those incidents which are related by Matthew and Mark might easily take place at a period subsequent to this. I refer to what occurred at the time when He called the disciples two by two, and Himself gave them the command

The Miraculous Draught of Fishes, Peter Paul Rubens, 1618–1619.

to follow Him, at first addressing Peter and Andrew, and then the others, namely, the two sons of Zebedee. For on that occasion they did not follow Him only after they had drawn up their ships on shore, as with the intention of returning to them, but they went after Him immediately, as after one who summoned and commanded them to follow Him.[4]

A whole series of encounters takes place between Jesus and his future disciples, beginning from the moment when two disciples of John the Baptist followed after Jesus. Of these two disciples, one is Andrew: he finds his brother Peter and leads him to Jesus; then both brothers return to work at fishing. Then follows the story of the miraculous catch of fish, when Jesus says to Peter alone that he would make him a fisher of men. And then the next episode follows: when Jesus finds Andrew and Peter and tells both of them what he had already said once to Peter. They leave their nets and follow him.

Concerning John and James, the following picture emerges. John, the supposed "other disciple" of the Baptist, follows Jesus together with Andrew and spends the whole day with him. Further on, he becomes the likely witness of the first miracles of Jesus, and then, after some interval, appears together with his brother James in the episode of the miraculous

---

[4]Ibid., 2.17.41 (*NPNF*[1] 6:123).

catch of fish. Finally, Jesus calls Peter and Andrew, and after them, James and John also, as four people already known to him from earlier.

The Calling of Matthew (Levi)

The following story on the same theme concerns the calling of one more disciple. In Luke he is called Levi (Lk 5.27), and in Mark he is called Levi the son of Alphaeus: "And as he passed by, he saw Levi the son of Alphaeus sitting at the receipt of custom, and said unto him, 'Follow me.' And he arose and followed him" (Mk 2.14). In the parallel passage in the Gospel of Matthew (Mt 9.9–13), the publican is called Matthew.

Was Matthew Levi familiar to Jesus before his calling, or does Jesus call an unknown person whom he is seeing for the first time in his life? The Synoptic Gospels do not give us a direct answer to this question. However, the identification of Matthew the publican with Matthew the evangelist allows us to suppose that Matthew could have been among the audience of the Sermon on the Mount (Mt 5–7). In that case (as in the case of Peter, Andrew, James, and John), it turns out that Jesus is calling not a person unknown to him, but someone whom he has already met.

Who are these publicans who are mentioned time and again in the Gospels? These were tax collectors in the service of the Roman emperor. In effect, they served the interests of the occupying power, for which they were despised by the Jews. In the view of the latter, they ranked among the other sinners who were openly violating the Jewish people's traditions, and even prostitutes. Hence the expressions used in the Gospels: "publicans and sinners" (Mt 9.11; 11.19; Mk 2.16; Lk 5.30; 7.34), or "the publicans and the harlots" (Mt 21.31). Disregarding the Jews' contempt for publicans, Jesus associated with them multiple times, and even made one of them his disciple.

Why is the publican called by two different names? The Jews of Jesus' time could have two names: one Hebrew, given by their parents at birth, and the other Greek or Latin. The second name could also contain the name of the person's father (for example, "Simon Bar-Jonah" in Mt 16.17), indicate the person's place of origin (Joseph of Arimathea, Mary Magdalene, Philo of

Alexandria), or be a nickname (for example, "Thomas, who is called Didymus [i.e., the twin]" in Jn 11.16, "sons of thunder" in Mk 3.17). However, it would be strange if a single person had two Hebrew names.[5]

Matthew is called a publican in the list of the twelve disciples that is presented in the Gospel of Luke; in the three other lists that are in Mark, Luke, and Acts, Matthew is not called a publican (Mk 3.18; Lk 6.15; Acts 1.13). In the opinion of a range of scholars, all this is evidence that the author of the Gospel of Matthew and the publican Levi the son of Alphaeus are two different people. Church tradition, however, takes Matthew the publican, Levi the son of Alphaeus, and Matthew the Evangelist to be one and the same person.

The verb "to follow" (akoloutheō) is common to the synoptic accounts of the calling of the first disciples (Mt 4.20, 22; Mk 1.18; Lk 5.11), of the calling of Matthew Levi (Mt 9.9; Mk 2.14; Lk 5.28), and of how Peter said to Jesus on behalf of the disciples, "Behold, we have forsaken all, and followed thee" (Mt 19.27; Mk 10.28; Lk 18.28). This verb is found in the Gospels seventy-nine times in total (twenty-five in Matthew, eighteen in Mark, seventeen in Luke, and nineteen in John), of which seventy-three instances refer to following Jesus.[6] The calling of the apostles consists first of all in following the Teacher—both in the literal sense (going after him) and in the metaphorical sense (fulfilling his commandments and following his teaching).

[5]John P. Meier, *The Vision of Matthew: Christ, Church, and Morality in the First Gospel* (Eugene, OR: Wipf & Stock, 2004), 23–24.

[6]Paul S. Pudussery, "Discipleship, A Call to Suffering and Glory: An Exegetico-Theological Study of Mk 8,27–9,1; 13,9–13 and 13,24–27" (Ph.D. diss., Pontifical Urban University, Rome, 1987), 18.

2. The Choosing of the Twelve Apostles

A comparative analysis of the accounts of the four evangelists indicates that the community of disciples formed around Jesus gradually. The total number of disciples varied: if we follow John, there were five in the beginning, and then there were significantly more, and then many went away. The Synoptics do not trace such a dynamic: from their accounts, we can only infer that the number of disciples gradually increased.

It is in the Synoptic Gospels that we find the account of how Jesus chose the Twelve from the total number of disciples. The versions of this account are identical in content in all three Synoptics, though they differ in the details. Matthew says nothing at all of the selection of the Twelve from a larger group: "And when he had called unto him his twelve disciples, he gave them power against unclean spirits, to cast them out, and to heal all manner of sickness and all manner of disease" (Mt 10.1). Mark specifies that the Twelve were chosen from the total number of disciples: "And he goeth up into a mountain, and calleth unto him those whom he wanted; and they came unto him. And he ordained twelve, that they should be with him, and that he might send them forth to preach, and to have power to heal sicknesses, and to cast out devils" (Mk 3.13–15). Luke clarifies that Jesus first "went out into a mountain to pray, and continued all night in prayer to God," and then, "when it was day, he called unto him his disciples: and of them he chose twelve, whom also he named apostles" (Lk 6.12–13).

The following expression of Mark calls attention to itself: "calleth unto him those whom he wanted." This emphasizes that the initiative for the choosing of the Twelve belonged to Jesus alone, and that he himself determined the composition of the members of the group. It was impossible to sign oneself up for this list on one's own initiative; Jesus would straightforwardly speak of this in his farewell discourse with his disciples: "Ye have not chosen me, but I have chosen you" (Jn 15.16).

Of the three Synoptics, Mark is the most specific in his description of the aims for which Jesus chose the Twelve: "that they should be with him,

Synaxis of the
Twelve Apostles,
icon, 16th c.

and that he might send them forth to preach." The apostles were to share
Jesus' labors and his joys and sorrows, be with him in all the circumstances
of his life, and listen to and remember his words. But they were chosen not
only for the period of his earthly life: they were his emissaries, and after his
death and resurrection they would bring his word to the world, preach his
doctrine, and continue his work.

After his resurrection, Jesus would say to his apostles: "As my Father hath
sent me, even so send I you" (Jn 20.21). That he was the Father's emissary, he
said time and again to both his disciples and the wider circle of his listeners:
according to the Gospel of John, this was one of the refrains of his preaching (Jn 5.36–38; 6.57; 7.29; 8.42; 11.42; 17.8, 18–25). In choosing disciples for

himself, Jesus makes them not only his apostles, but also the apostles of God the Father. The connection by which he is united with his Father must also bind the apostles to him, and, through him, to the Father.

We make note of Luke's words: "whom also he named apostles." This indicates that Jesus not only chose specific people for ministry, but also himself invented a unique name for this ministry. The term "apostle" (*apostolos*), which only Luke uses in this episode, literally means "emissary" (one who is sent away; from the verb *apostellō*—"to send away"). In the Septuagint, the term is encountered only once (1 Kg 14.6), but it is found multiple times in the New Testament. Only in rare instances does it refer to some abstract emissary, such as in the following words of Jesus: "The servant is not greater than his lord; neither he that is sent (*apostolos*) greater than he that sent him" (Jn 13.16). In the majority of instances, this term refers to one of the twelve disciples chosen by Jesus for a specific goal at a distinct stage of his ministry.

According to the proposal of Jerome, the Greek term *apostolos* ("apostle") is a translation of the Hebrew *šālîᵃh* ("messenger," "emissary"). Both the Greek term and its proposed Semitic equivalent refer to a person who acts not on his own behalf, but on behalf of another—the one who sent him.

In all three Synoptics, the list of the twelve apostles begins with Simon Peter and ends with Judas Iscariot (Mt 10.2–4; Mk 3.16–19; Lk 6.14–16). After Peter, in Matthew and Luke there follow Andrew, the brother of Peter, and then James the son of Zebedee and John, his brother; in Mark, Andrew follows after James and John. The fifth and sixth places in all three lists are taken by Philip and Bartholomew respectively, and the seventh and eighth by Matthew and Thomas (in this order in Mark and Luke, and the other way in Matthew). In the ninth place in all three lists, there is James the son of Alphaeus, but then the name of the tenth disciple varies between the three lists: in Matthew he is "Lebbaeus, whose surname was Thaddaeus," in Mark "Thaddaeus," and in Luke "Simon called Zelotes [i.e., the Zealot]." The eleventh place in Matthew and Mark is taken by Simon the Canaanite, and in Luke by Judas "of James."

The differences between the lists is explained first of all by the fact that, as we have already said, Jews in the time of Jesus could possess two names, or a name and a nickname. Thus, for example, the Bartholomew present in all three lists is usually identified with Nathanael, whom the evangelist John mentions (in this case, Nathanael is his name, and Bartholomew his nickname, or, more accurately, his patronymic, since it literally means "son of Talmai"). Simon the Zealot and Simon the Canaanite are the same person (the tenth in the list of Luke, and the eleventh in the lists of Matthew and Mark): the nickname "Canaanite" in translation from the Hebrew means "zealot," which is the same as the Greek *zēlōtēs* (Luke simply translates the nickname from the Hebrew to the Greek).

The sole remaining position can be taken by only one apostle, who is known by three names: Judas "of James," also Thaddaeus, also "Lebbaeus, whose surname was Thaddaeus" (Mt 10.3). Clearly, Thaddaeus is a nickname, while "of James" is also a nickname, indicating that this apostle was the brother of James. This same apostle is mentioned in the Gospel of John by the name "Judas . . . not Iscariot" (Jn 14.22). In Church tradition, he is considered to be the author of the Epistle of Jude in the New Testament, where he calls himself the "brother of James" (Jude 1). This same person is identified in Church tradition with Jude (or Judas) the brother of the Lord (Mt 13.55).

We will not enter into a detailed scholarly discussion regarding whether one or more persons are in view under the names Judas of James, Lebbaeus, Thaddaeus, and Jude the brother of the Lord, inasmuch as such a discussion is beyond the limits of our main theme (we are entirely persuaded by the arguments of those who think that there is only person in question[7]). We will only note the obvious fact of the existence among the twelve apostles of two people with the same name of Judas, which was widespread in Jewish circles. This must have created a certain inconvenience during prolonged association in a fairly close group. Already in Jesus' lifetime one of them could have been called more often by his nickname in order to distinguish him from the other. But after Judas Iscariot betrayed Jesus

---

[7]For more details on the identification of Judas the brother of the Lord, with Judas the brother of James and Lebbaeus called Thaddaeus, see O. S. Grinchenko and V. L. O., "Iuda, brat Gospoden'" [Jude, the brother of the Lord], in *Pravoslavnaya Entsiklopediya* [The Orthodox Encyclopedia], vol. 28 (Moscow: Tserkovno-nauchnyy tsentr "Pravoslavnaya Entsiklopediya," 2012), 380–387.

and left the company of the disciples, his name quickly came to have negative associations, and the evangelists, speaking of the other Judas who remained in the number of the apostles, either used different nicknames instead of his personal name (Thaddaeus, Lebbaeus) or added to his name (Judas the brother of James, Judas "not Iscariot") in order to clearly distinguish him from the traitor.

In the Synoptic Gospels, with the exception of the stories about the calling of the first four disciples and Matthew, the twelve apostles appear most often as a single group under the general name "the disciples" or "the Twelve." They are named all together only once, in the complete list. Peter, John, and James merit individual mentions. In connection with the story of the betrayal of Jesus, Judas Iscariot is also separately mentioned.

Why was the number of apostles twelve precisely? The most trivial explanation is that twelve is the optimal number of people with whom one leader can directly work. However, twelve is also a sacred number for the people of Israel, recalling the sons of Jacob and the twelve tribes of Israel that came from them. Jesus himself would draw this parallel when he would say to the apostles: "In the regeneration when the Son of man shall sit in the throne of his glory, ye also shall sit upon twelve thrones, judging the twelve tribes of Israel" (Mt 19.28).

The group of the twelve apostles is thought of as the nucleus of the Church, while the Church is thought of as the New Israel, which unites all who believe in Jesus. And if at the head of the people of Israel stood Jacob with his twelve sons, then at the head of the new people of God stands Jesus with his twelve apostles. The recognition of the importance of preserving the sacred number twelve moved the apostles, after the death and resurrection of Jesus, to first of all choose another person to replace Judas the traitor, who had left their midst (Acts 1.15–26).

How old were the apostles? The Gospels do not speak directly about this. However, we know, for example, that at the time of the calling of James and John, their father was alive and active (Mt 4.21), while Peter's mother-in-law was alive, and also quite active (Mt 8.14–15). According to the surviving testimonies, the apostles outlived Jesus by an average of thirty years, and most of them suffered death at the hands of others. Based

John the Theologian,
mosaic, 9th c.

on this, one may assume that at the moment of their calling all the apostles were close in age to Jesus, and some were younger than him.

In Church tradition the view was established fairly early of John being the youngest of the apostles, having come to Jesus while still a youth. This tradition is indirectly referenced by Irenaeus of Lyons, according to whose testimony John was still alive during the time of the emperor Trajan (98–117).[8] In early Christian frescoes and mosaics, as a rule, John is depicted as a beardless youth.

3. Lack of Understanding

Thus, from the first days of his public ministry, Jesus began to gather around himself a group of young people, who were with him at all times. Over the course of some time he became familiar with them, and they became familiar with and listened to him. Some liked what was going on and some did not; correspondingly, some stayed "on the team," while others left. Eventually, Jesus chose twelve from the general number of his followers, and then, according to Luke, another seventy, who were to continue his work on earth (Lk 10.1).

How did the mutual relationship between Jesus and his disciples develop? The theme of this mutual relationship is one of the central themes in all four Gospels. A significant proportion of Jesus' teachings that are presented in the Gospels is addressed to the disciples. Jesus converses with them in private, addresses them separately before addressing the people, and, at their request, explains to them what they do not understand in his teachings addressed to the people. The Gospels give Jesus' dialogues with one or a few of the disciples, recording the various reactions of the

[8]Irenaeus of Lyons, *Against Heresies* 2.22.5 (*ANF* 1:392).

disciples to the words of Jesus and the given situation: awe, astonishment, surprise, incomprehension, bewilderment, unbelief, fear, and protest.[9] The rich range of the disciples' personal feelings, experiences, and emotions is presented on the pages of the Gospels. At the same time, certain relationships are drawn out as particular themes: Jesus and Peter, Jesus and John, Jesus and the three closest disciples (Peter, John, and James), and Jesus and Judas Iscariot.

All of this vast material would by itself merit a separate book. In the present section, we will note only one extremely characteristic aspect of the relationships between Jesus and his disciples: their lack of understanding of his words and actions. This theme is a refrain throughout the Synoptic Gospels and in the Gospel of John.[10]

The disciples did not understand the meaning of parables in particular. According to Mark, after Jesus tells the parable of the sower, "they that were about him with the twelve" (Mk 4.10) ask him about the meaning of the parable. Jesus answers: "Unto you it is given to know the mystery of the kingdom of God, but unto them that are outside, all these things are done in parables, that 'seeing they may see, and not perceive; and hearing they may hear, and not understand; lest at any time they should be converted, and their sins should be forgiven them.' [Is 6.9–10] . . . Know ye not this parable? And how then will ye know all parables?" (Mk 4.11–13).

In the parallel passage in Matthew, the disciples do not simply not understand the meaning of the parable—they do not understand why Jesus chooses to address the people in such a way: "Why speakest thou unto them in parables?" (Mt 13.10). He answers them with almost the same words that are in Mark, and then says: "But blessed are your eyes, for they

[9]Fear can have a positive overtone as well as a negative overtone. Compare, for example, Mk 4.41 (fear at the greatness of the sign that Jesus performed) and Mt 14.26 (fear at his sudden appearance in the night). About this, see Jeannine K. Brown, *The Disciples in Narrative Perspective: The Portrayal and Function of the Matthean Disciples*, Academia Biblica 9 (Leiden: Brill, 2002), 142–145.

[10]In certain instances, the episodes in which the disciples do not understand the meaning of Jesus' words and actions are linked into a semantic chain. Interesting examples of such semantic chains in the Gospel of Luke are given in Ivan Shing Chung Kwong, *The Word Order of the Gospel of Luke: Its Foregrounded Messages*, Library of New Testament Studies 298 (London: T&T Clark, 2005), 117–127.

see, and your ears, for they hear. For truly I say unto you, that many prophets and righteous men have desired to see those things which ye see, and
have not seen them; and to hear those things which ye hear, and have not
heard them" (Mt 13.16–17).

The parable of the tares in the field again elicit a question from the
disciples (Mt 13.36). The disciples do not understand the meaning of Jesus'
words: "Not that which goeth into the mouth defileth a man; but that
which cometh out of the mouth, this defileth a man" (Mt 15.11). Upon
hearing this, Peter asks on behalf of the entire group, "Explain unto us this
parable" (Mt 15.15). Jesus answers Peter's question with a question: "Are ye
also yet without understanding? Do ye not yet understand, that whatsoever entereth in at the mouth goeth into the belly, and is cast out into the
draught? But those things which proceed out of the mouth come forth
from the heart, and they defile the man" (Mt 15.16–18).

The disciples heard Jesus' answer to the Pharisees about divorce, but
what was said clearly did not satisfy them, and "in the house his disciples
asked him again of the same matter" (Mk 10.10). In Matthew the reaction
of the disciples to Jesus' words on divorce is described differently: "His
disciples say unto him, 'If the case of the man be so with his wife, it is not
good to marry'" (Mt 19.10). In this way, in Matthew's version, the disciples
do not simply ask him a question: they dispute with him and are indignant
at what he said, openly expressing their bewilderment.

Jesus had the custom of addressing his disciples in the presence of the
crowd (this happened, for example, when he delivered the Sermon on the
Mount). In such instances, the disciples did not always understand which
part of the teaching was addressed to them, and which part to the people.
In the Gospel of Luke, we are told of how, "when there were gathered
together an innumerable multitude of people, insomuch that they trod one
upon another, [Jesus] began to say unto his disciples first of all, 'Beware ye
of the leaven of the Pharisees, which is hypocrisy'" (Lk 12.1). The teaching
quickly passes into a series of parables, and, since the people are standing
round about, Peter asks, "Lord, speakest thou this parable unto us, or even
to all?" (Lk 12.41). Jesus does not answer Peter, but, as though ignoring
his question, continues his teaching. Only at the end of the teaching is it

made clear that it was addressed to the disciples, since at its conclusion the evangelist writes: "And he said also to the people . . ." (Lk 12.54).

Jesus often chastises his disciples for having little faith and for lack of faith. In particular, this happens after they wake him as he is sleeping in the boat during the storm at sea. In each of the three Synoptics, the rebuke sounds somewhat different, although the idea remains the same: "Why are ye fearful, O ye of little faith?" (Mt 8.26); "Why are ye so fearful? How is it that ye have no faith?" (Mk 4.40); "Where is your faith?" (Lk 8.25). When the disciples ask why they could not heal the possessed child, Jesus answers, "Because of your unbelief" (Mt 17.20).

After Jesus feeds the five thousand with five loaves and two fishes, the disciples set out on a boat to cross the lake, and Jesus remains alone. In the middle of the night, in the midst of the storm, he comes to them on the water, and, taking him to be a ghost, they cry out from fear. Jesus says to them, "Be of good cheer: it is I; be not afraid" (Mk 6.50). Commenting on this event, Mark notes: "and they were exceedingly amazed in themselves beyond measure, and wondered. For they considered not the miracle of the loaves: for their heart was hardened" (Mk 6.51–52).

The theme of the hardening of the heart, which time and again occurs in Jesus' speech concerning people who do not understand the meaning of his teaching, occurs also in his addresses to the disciples: "Perceive ye not yet, neither understand? Have ye your heart still hardened? Having eyes, see ye not? And having ears, hear ye not? And do ye not remember?" (Mk 8.17–18). These words convey Jesus' emotional reaction to the disciples' discussion about their not having brought bread—a discussion elicited by his words: "Take heed, beware of the leaven of the Pharisees, and of the leaven of Herod" (Mk 8.15). The entire episode shows the level of the disciples' understanding of Jesus' words. He uses images familiar to them (in this case, leaven) in order to lead them to think about spiritual reality, but their perception does not stretch beyond natural physical needs.

We find a similar level of understanding in the Samaritan woman, to whom Jesus speaks about quenching spiritual thirst, while she asks him how he is able to get water if he has nothing to draw it with (Jn 4.10–11). In the encounter with the Samaritan woman, the disciples are surprised

*Christ in
Majesty,* icon,
St Andrei
Rublev, 15th c.

that he is conversing with a woman, but nobody asks him any undue questions. When she leaves, they ask him to eat, but he refuses, saying, "I have
food to eat that ye know not of." Their reaction is puzzlement: "Hath any
man brought him aught to eat?" (Jn 4.32–33). They do not ask him directly,
but in his presence they talk among themselves, trying to understand the
meaning of his words and speaking of him in the third person.

Jesus' multiple hints and express statements that his life would end in
death and resurrection also elicit the incomprehension of the disciples. In
one such episode, Jesus, while in Galilee, says to his disciples (and not for
the first time), "The Son of man is delivered into the hands of men, and
they shall kill him; and after that he is killed, he shall rise the third day." But

the disciples "understood not that saying, and were afraid to ask him" (Mk 9.31–32). Why were they afraid? We do not find a direct answer regarding this. An indirect answer is contained in the parallel passage in Luke, where the reaction of the disciples is given more fully: "But they understood not this saying, and it was hid from them, that they perceived it not; and they feared to ask him of that saying" (Lk 9.45). Apparently they were afraid to ask precisely because they did not understand the meaning of his words. Or perhaps it was because they had a premonition of disaster, and did not want to acknowledge that feeling within themselves.

The Gospels do not conceal from us that conflicts periodically arose between the disciples. They were connected in particular with disputes about primacy, which are mentioned multiple times by the evangelists. Here is one such episode in the version of Mark:

> And he came to Capernaum, and being in the house he asked them, "What was it that ye disputed among yourselves by the way?" But they held their peace, for by the way they had disputed among themselves, who should be the greatest. And he sat down, and called the twelve, and saith unto them, "If any man desire to be first, the same shall be last of all, and servant of all." And he took a child, and set him in the midst of them. And when he had taken him in his arms, he said unto them, "Whosoever shall receive one of such children in my name, receiveth me, and whosoever shall receive me, receiveth not me, but him that sent me." And John answered him, saying, "Master, we saw one casting out devils in thy name, and he followeth not us, and we forbid him, because he followeth not us." But Jesus said, "Forbid him not. For there is no man who shall do a miracle in my name, that can lightly speak evil of me. For he that is not against us is on our side. For whosoever shall give you a cup of water to drink in my name, because ye belong to Christ, truly I say unto you, he shall not lose his reward. And whosoever shall offend one of these little ones that believe in me, it is better for him that a millstone were hanged about his neck, and he were cast into the sea." (Mk 9.33–42)

Mark vividly describes the disciples' reaction to Jesus' question: they are ashamed that they tried to ascertain who was the greatest among them, and they remain silent. Matthew gives a different and somewhat shorter version of the same episode; in Matthew, the disciples do not dispute among themselves about primacy, but ask Jesus who is the greatest in the kingdom of heaven. In answer to their question, Jesus places a child among them and says, "Truly I say unto you, except ye be converted, and become as little children, ye shall not enter into the kingdom of heaven" (Mt 18.3). These words should be understood in the sense that the disciples are being called to wholly change their way of thinking, and to reconsider their ideas about the criteria for the hierarchy of persons in the kingdom of heaven. Here one may recall what Jesus said to the disciples concerning John the Baptist: "He that is least in the kingdom of heaven is greater than he" (Mt 11.11).

Matthew does not record John's question, or Jesus' answer, at all. The words regarding the cup of cold water are, in his Gospel, woven into another of Jesus' discourses—the instruction to the Twelve after their choosing (Mt 10.42). Luke follows Mark on the whole (Lk 9.46–50). However, he omits from this episode the final, stern words of Jesus concerning the person who "shall offend one of these little ones" (Mt 18.6) and the millstone. He cites these words in a different place (Lk 17.1–2).

The given episode—with all the variations that we see in the Synoptics—is evidence that the disciples' disputes about primacy had to do with both the internal hierarchy of the group of the twelve apostles, as well as their possible place in the kingdom that Jesus was constantly telling them about, but of which they, by all appearances, had an extremely hazy conception. The pedagogical method that Jesus uses to deliver them from their disputes about primacy seems somewhat unexpected and not devoid of humor: he places a child in front of them. Taking the child into his arms, Jesus addresses the disciples, but not at all with words about primacy: he does not directly answer the questions that the disciples were discussing among themselves along the way, but diverts the entire conversation into another course.

Christ with Children, Carl Heinrich Bloch, 19th c.

In another instance, we see how the disciples do not wish to allow children to come to Jesus, but he says to them, "Allow the little children, and forbid them not, to come unto me, for of such is the kingdom of heaven" (Mt 19.14). At the same time, he again reminds the disciples that, in the kingdom of heaven, a person's importance is assessed using different criteria than on earth.

The same theme is developed in another episode, which is presented in two parallel passages in Mark and Matthew. Mark tells of how the two brothers, James and John, the sons of Zebedee, come to Jesus with a request: "Grant unto us that we may sit, one on thy right hand, and the other on thy left hand, in thy glory" (Mk 10.37). In Matthew, it is the mother of the sons of Zebedee who comes to Jesus with the same request on their behalf: "Grant that these my two sons may sit, the one on thy right hand, and the other on the left, in thy kingdom" (Mt 20.20–21). The dialogue that follows between Jesus and the two brothers shows how differently the Teacher and his disciples conceived of the coming glory and the future kingdom:

But Jesus answered and said, "Ye know not what ye ask. Are ye able to drink of the cup that I shall drink of, and to be baptized with the baptism that I am baptized with?" They say unto him, "We are able." And he saith unto them, "Ye shall drink indeed of my cup, and be baptized with the baptism that I am baptized with. But to sit on my right hand, and on my left, is not mine to give, but it shall be given to them for whom it is prepared of my Father." (Mt 20.22–23)

By baptism and the cup, Jesus is referring here to the suffering awaiting him and to his death. Regarding this cup, he would ask of his Father in the garden of Gethsemane: "Abba, Father, all things are possible unto thee; take away this cup from me" (Mk 14.36). The meaning of Jesus' words is entirely hidden from the disciples: they do not know of what baptism and of what cup he is speaking, and therefore express unhesitating readiness to be baptized with this baptism and to drink this cup. They remain deaf to his multiple predictions of the suffering awaiting him.

Continuing this same story, the evangelists tell of how the other ten disciples become indignant at the two brothers (Mt 20.24; Mk 10.41). Indignation is the natural reaction to the conduct of the two who, for some reason, decided to reserve for themselves the two chief places in the future glory of the Teacher. Seeing how the ten disciples react to the behavior of James and John (or, in Matthew's version, of their mother), Jesus says:

Ye know that the princes of the Gentiles exercise dominion over them, and they that are great exercise authority upon them. But it shall not be so among you; but whosoever will be great among you, let him be your minister. And whosoever will be chief among you, let him be your servant, even as the Son of Man came not to be ministered unto, but to minister, and to give his life a ransom for many. (Mt 20.25–28)

Disputes about primacy continued among Jesus' disciples right up until his final days on earth. According to Luke, even at the Last Supper, the disciples argued about which of them was to be considered the greatest. In answer, Jesus again gives himself as an example: "He that is greatest among you, let him be as the younger; and he that is chief, as he that doth serve.

For who is greater, he that reclineth [at the table], or he that serveth? Is not he that reclineth [at the table]? But I am among you as he that serveth" (Lk 22.26–27). In both cases—both in the story of Matthew given earlier, and in Luke's account of the Last Supper—Jesus speaks of his mission as serving. He does not expect that others serve him; he himself came in order to "minister" (i.e., serve) and to "give his life a ransom for many."

In the Gospels we encounter practically no instances where the disciples show their Teacher visible support, or even simply express approval of his actions, or joy. One exception is the account of Luke (which we will examine below) of the return of the Seventy and of the joy that they shared with Jesus (Lk 10.17–24). One more exception is the account of the transfiguration, when Peter says to Jesus, "Lord, it is good for us to be here" (Mt 17.4; cf Mk 9.5; Lk 9.33). In all other cases, the disciples only ask questions, and sometimes also express open bewilderment at what the Teacher says or proposes to do. The Teacher's reaction to the disciples' conduct is often emotional: he may answer their question with a question, or he may chastise them for incomprehension or lack of faith. They love him, but are afraid to ask one more question than necessary, lest they incur his wrath on themselves.

This entire situation leads to the crisis of their mutual relationship that would reach its peak in the narrative of the passion, when one of the Twelve would betray the Teacher, another would deny him, and the rest would scatter in fear. And only one disciple would stand by his cross and become an eyewitness to his death (Jn 19.26, 35). Even after Jesus' resurrection, there would be both believers and doubters in their midst (Mt 28.17; Jn 20.25).

The evangelists do not conceal from us the complexities in the relationship between Jesus and his disciples. Nevertheless, as we read the Gospels, we perceive Jesus' disciples as a united and, on the whole, close-knit team. They do not understand much of what he says and does, but continue to stay with him, follow him, and listen to and remember his teachings and parables. Some force keeps them with him, regardless of the perpetual tension that comes from them living on another intellectual and spiritual level compared to their Teacher.

4. Jesus
and Peter

The strength of the spiritual attraction emanating from Jesus comes through in a series of episodes involving Peter—the apostle mentioned the most on the pages of all four Gospels. He is mentioned in the Gospels under various names (Peter, Simon, Cephas) 110 times in total: 75 times in the Synoptics, and 35 times in John.[11]

The arc of the relationship between Jesus and Peter goes through the entire Gospel narrative: from the first accounts of the calling of the disciples to the story of Peter's denial and his being forgiven by the resurrected Jesus.

We recall that Peter was one of the first to be called, and headed the list of the Twelve. The name Peter (Cephas) was given to him by Jesus in place of his original name, Simon. Mark mentions this in connection with the choosing of the Twelve: "And Simon he surnamed Peter" (Mk 3.16). According to John, Jesus named Simon "Peter" at their first encounter (Jn 1.42). Only John gives Simon's Aramaic name, Cephas (*kēpā*), which means both "stone" and "rock." The Greek word *petros*, used to translate the Aramaic Cephas, also has both these meanings. In the New Testament, besides in the above passage in the Gospel of John, the Aramaic name Cephas is mentioned only in the epistles of Paul (1 Cor 1.12; 3.22; 9.5; 15.5; Gal 2.9).

In the biblical tradition, a change of name always bears a special significance. When God changes a person's name, this is a sign that this person has become a servant of God and has entered into a new and more intimate relationship with him. God changes the names of his chosen ones—those in whom he has shown trust, to whom he has entrusted some mission, with whom he has made a covenant. Thus, for example, after God made a covenant with Abram that he would become the father of many nations,

---

[11]Martin Hengel, *Saint Peter: The Underestimated Apostle*, trans. Thomas Trapp (Grand Rapids, MI: Eerdmans, 2010), 10.

The Calling of the Apostles Peter and Andrew, Duccio, 1308–1313.

Abram became Abraham (Gen 17.1–5), and his wife Sarai became Sarah (Gen 17.15). Jacob received the name of Israel ("he who struggles with God," or, in another interpretation, "he who sees God") after he struggled with God and God blessed him (Gen 32.27–28).

By giving Peter a new name, Jesus singles him out from among the disciples. The other disciples do not receive this honor, with the exception of John and James, to whom Jesus gives the nickname of "the sons of thunder" (Mt 3.17). Why does Jesus give new names to three of his disciples? "To show," answers John Chrysostom, "that it was He who gave the old covenant, that it was He who altered names, who called Abram 'Abraham,' and Sarai 'Sarah,' and Jacob 'Israel.' "[12] It was these three disciples, who received new names from Jesus—Peter, James, and John—who were the closest to him over the course of his life.

However, Peter is singled out not only from among the Twelve, but also from among this group of three. All three Synoptic Gospels contain the account of how Peter confessed Jesus to be the Christ:

[12]John Chrysostom, *Homilies on the Gospel of John* 19.2 (*NPNF*[1] 14:68).

The apostle Peter,
fresco, 14th c.

And Jesus went out, and his disciples, into the towns of Caesarea Philippi. And by the way he asked his disciples, saying unto them, "Whom do men say that I am?" And they answered, "John the Baptist, but some say, Elijah, and others, one of the prophets." And he saith unto them, "But whom say ye that I am?" And Peter answereth and saith unto him, "Thou art the Christ." (Mk 8.27–29)

In Luke's version, Peter answers, "The Christ of God" (Lk 9.20). Matthew gives the fullest version of Peter's answer: "Thou art the Christ, the Son of the living God" (Mt 16.16).

Why did Peter alone answer Jesus? Was it because he was quicker to respond than the others? Or because he was answering on behalf of all? Or was he the only disciple at the time who was able to confidently recognize Jesus as the Christ? The narratives of Mark and Luke do not give an answer. In Matthew, we find the continuation of the story. According to Matthew, after Peter confesses Jesus to be the Christ, Jesus singles him out from among the disciples and responds not to all, but to him alone:

> Blessed art thou, Simon Bar-Jonah, for flesh and blood hath not revealed it unto thee, but my Father which is in heaven. And I say also unto thee, that thou art Peter, and upon this rock I will build my Church, and the gates of hell shall not prevail against it. And I will give unto thee the keys of the kingdom of heaven; and whatsoever thou shalt bind on earth shall be bound in heaven; and whatsoever thou shalt loose on earth shall be loosed in heaven. (Mt 16.17–19)

This story can be understood as meaning that Jesus is giving Peter a new name in response to his confession. But if we consider the fact that, according to Mark and John, this change of name had already happened earlier, the story of Matthew can be understood as a reminder to Peter of this change: at first, Jesus calls him by his former name (Simon Bar-Jonah), and then by his new name (Peter).

St Peter's Basilica
in the Vatican

This story is one of two places within the entirety of the four Gospels where the word "Church" is used (the other instance is in Mt 18.17). Later on, beginning with Acts and the apostolic Epistles, this word (Gk. *ekklēsia*) would become the main term for the community of Jesus' followers—on a universal scale,[13] as well as on a local level,[14] and even on the level of a single family.[15] The fact that Jesus' promise regarding the foundation of the Church is connected with Peter's confession, and that Peter is the rock on which the Church would be built, gives this apostle a special importance that cannot be compared with the significance of the other apostles.

The given text from the Gospel of Matthew played a vital role in the formation of the Christian teaching about the Church; however, this text has received different interpretations in the East and in the West. In the West, the role of Peter as the head of the apostolic community is emphasized, who passed on his primacy to the bishops of Rome. Over the centuries

[13]For example: "Therefore as the church is subject unto Christ, so let the wives be to their own husbands in every thing. Husbands, love your wives, even as Christ also loved the Church" (Eph 5.24–25); "And he is the head of the body, the Church" (Col 1.18).

[14]For example: "the church which was at Jerusalem" (Acts 8.1), "[t]he *church that is* at Babylon" (1 Pet 5.13), and the churches in Ephesus, in Smyrna, in Pergamos, in Thyatira, in Sardis, in Philadelphia, and of the Laodiceans (Rev 2.1–3.22).

[15]The expression "the church in [*name's*] house" (1 Cor 16.19; Col 4.15; Philem 2) refers to a house church.

Christ Giving Peter the Keys of Paradise, Jean-Auguste-Dominique Ingres, 1820.

this tradition led to the formation of the dogma of the pope of Rome being the successor of the apostle Peter and the vicar of Christ on earth, in possession of absolute and universal authority in the Church. In the East, another interpretation gained currency, according to which the Church is built not on Peter, but on belief in the divinity of Jesus Christ, of which Peter's words were a confession.[16]

The Peter himself insisted that the cornerstone of the Church is Christ:

To whom coming, as unto a living stone, rejected indeed of men, but chosen of God, and precious, ye also, as living stones, are built up a spiritual house, an holy priesthood, to offer up spiritual sacrifices, acceptable to God by Jesus Christ. Therefore also it is contained in the scripture, "Behold, I lay in Sion a chief corner stone, elect, precious. And he that believeth on him shall not be confounded." [Is 28.16] Unto you therefore which believe he is precious, but unto them which be disobedient, "the stone which the builders rejected, the same is made the head of the corner," [Ps 117.22] and "a stone of stumbling, and a rock of offence," [Is 8.14–15] even unto them which stumble at the word, being disobedient: unto which also they were appointed. (1 Pet 2.4–8)

These words of Peter are his own interpretation of Jesus' words, which were sometime addressed to him.[17] He emphasizes that the cornerstone placed at the foundation of the Church is not he, Peter, but Christ. Moreover, Peter cites the same words from the Old Testament (Ps 117.22–23) that Jesus cited as he concluded his parable on the laborers in the vineyard (Mt 21.42).

---

[16]John Chrysostom, *Homilies on the Gospel of Matthew* 54.3: "'And I say unto thee, Thou art Peter, and upon this rock will I build my Church;' that is, on the faith of his confession" (*NPNF*[1] 10:333).

[17]We do not share the point of view of certain scholars who consider the two epistles of Peter, which are in the corpus of the New Testament, to be pseudepigrapha that appeared at the turn of the second century (see, for example, Hengel, *Saint Peter*, 12).

The Gospel of John presents an episode that is distinctly similar to the episode presented in the Synoptics. Here, also, Peter confesses Jesus to be the Christ, the Son of God. However, the action takes place not in Caesarea Philippi, but in Capernaum, and there is every reason to believe that these are two different episodes. As he narrates how many of Jesus' disciples left him after he set before them the teaching about the bread from heaven, the evangelist continues: "Then said Jesus unto the twelve, 'Do you also want to go away?' Then Simon Peter answered him, 'Lord, to whom shall we go? Thou hast the words of eternal life. And we believe and are sure that thou art the Christ, the Son of the living God'"[18] (Jn 6.67–69).

St Peter Throws Himself into the Waters, Lluís Borrassà, 15th c.

Peter responds more quickly than the other disciples to Jesus' words and actions. We have only just seen how he was the first of the disciples to call Jesus the Christ. Peter is the only disciple who, seeing Jesus walk on the sea, went out to meet him, while the others waited for Jesus in the boat (Mt 14.28). Similarly, after Jesus' resurrection, seeing him standing on the shore, Peter swims out to him, while the others get to shore by boat (Jn 21.7–8). Peter's fervor and his readiness to go out immediately to meet the Teacher contrast with the behavior of the other disciples. One gets the impression that he makes big decisions and important discoveries earlier than the others.

The evangelist Mark tells of how Jesus, on his way to the towns of Caesarea Philippi, "began to teach them, that the Son of Man must suffer many things, and be rejected of the elders, and of the chief priests,

[18]This is Peter's answer as given in the in the King James Version, which is based on the Textus Receptus. However, in the critical Nestle-Aland edition, which is based on the most ancient manuscripts, we find a somewhat different version of Peter's answer: "and we believe and are sure that thou art the holy one God [*ho hagios tou theou*]." In this case the appearance in later manuscripts of the words "thou art that Christ, the Son of the living God" could be a consequence of a harmonizing correction to the text of the Gospel of John in order to make it correspond better to the text of Matthew.

The Denial of Peter,
Carl Heinrich Bloch, 19th c.

and scribes, and be killed, and after three days rise again. And he spoke that saying openly." Peter, taking him aside, "began to rebuke him." Jesus, "when he had turned about and looked on his disciples, he rebuked Peter, saying, 'Get thee behind me, Satan. For thou dost not set thy mind on the things of God, but the things that be of men.' And when he had called the people unto him with his disciples also, he said unto them, 'Whosoever will come after me, let him deny himself, and take up his cross, and follow me'" (Mk 8.31–34). We see that Peter begins to dispute with Jesus after taking him aside, but Jesus answers him so that the other disciples would hear. It is likely that Peter was expressing the general bewilderment of the whole group, which is why all of them had to hear Jesus' sharp response.

At the Last Supper, Jesus turns to Peter with the words: "Simon, Simon, behold, Satan hath desired to have you, that he may sift you as wheat. But I have prayed for thee, that thy faith fail not; and when thou art converted, strengthen thy brethren" (Lk 22.31–32). These words would turn out to be prophetic. By them, on the one hand, Jesus foretells Peter's denial; on the other, he speaks of Peter's subsequent destiny, specifically that Peter would head the community of the Twelve after Jesus' death.

We will return to the theme of the mutual relationship between Jesus and Peter in the sixth book in this series, *Jesus Christ: His Life and Teaching*, where we will discuss Peter's denial, and then the different episodes involving Peter that are connected with the story of Jesus' resurrection. Here it only remains for us to add that, already in Jesus' lifetime, Peter was understood to be the most senior of the apostles, which is apparent in all four Gospels. Sometimes the evangelists call a group consisting of some of the disciples of Jesus "Peter and they that were with him" (Lk 8.45; 9.32) or "Simon and they that were with him" (Mk 1.36).

5. Other Apostles of the Twelve

James and John

In the Synoptic Gospels, alongside Peter, the brothers James and John, the sons of Zebedee, merit special mention. Of them it is said that Jesus called them "Boanerges, which is, the sons of thunder" (Mk 3.17). In this instance, this name, which is given to both disciples simultaneously, should be understood as a nickname that both brothers received, supposedly for their emotional intensity and abundant religious zeal.[19]

In Church tradition we find a different, allegorical interpretation of this nickname. Basil the Great, in particular, says that it is possible "according to ecclesiastical diction to call by the name of thunder the doctrine which after baptism is in the souls of those already perfect by the eloquence of the Gospel." Jesus' bestowing of a new name on the two disciples, in Basil's opinion, shows that "the Gospel is thunder (*brontē to Euangelion*)."[20]

As has already been said, Peter, James, and John are presented in the Synoptic Gospels as the three closest disciples of Jesus. They alone are present at one of his major miracles—the raising of the daughter of Jairus, concerning which the evangelists note that Jesus "allowed no man to follow him, save Peter, and James, and John the brother of James" (Mk 5.37) and did not allow any of the disciples, except for these three, to come into the house (Lk 8.51). Jesus takes these same three disciples to the mount where he is transfigured in front of them (Mt 17.1; Mk 9.2; Lk 9.28). The same group, with the addition of Andrew, asks Jesus in private about the signs of his second coming (Mk 13.3). Finally, these same three are present

---

[19]Joachim Gnilka, *Das Evangelium nach Markus*, vol. 1, *Mk 1–8,26*, EKK II/1 (Zürich: Benziger; Neukirchen-Vluyn: Neukirchener, 1978), 141.

[20]Basil the Great, *Homily on Psalm 28* 3 (PG 29:292). Translation from Basil the Great, *Saint Basil: Exegetic Homilies*, trans. Agnes Clare Way, The Fathers of the Church 46 (Washington, DC: Catholic University of America Press, 1963), 201.

The apostle James,
icon, 16th c.

at one of the most dramatic moments in the gospel story—Jesus' prayer in the garden of Gethsemane (Mt 26.37; Mk 14.33).

It is possible that this privileged position became the reason that the two brothers, James and John, decided (or that their mother decided) to go to Jesus with the bold request to sit at Jesus' right and left. In making this request, they not only set themselves against the other disciples, but also encroached on the first place of Peter in the apostolic community. Jesus had to quench the fervor of the two brothers, and this was not the only instance.

Another incident is recorded by Luke, who tells of how John and James, indignant that a Samaritan town did not want to receive Jesus, asked him, "Lord, doest thou will that we command fire to come down from heaven, and consume them, even as Elijah did?" (Lk 9.54). The story being referred to here is that of how, at the word of Elijah, fire consumed two detachments of fifty soldiers that were sent to him by the king (2 Kgs 1.10, 12). But Jesus answered them, "Ye know not what manner of spirit ye are of" (Lk 9.55). In some versions of the Gospel of Luke, this answer is absent; in others, it is present; in yet others, there is an addition to it: "For the Son of Man is not come to destroy men's lives, but to save" (Lk 9.56).[21] It is possible that this episode was one of the reasons that the two brothers received from Jesus the nickname of "the sons of thunder."

As we have already mentioned in chapter two, Church tradition identifies John the son of Zebedee, the brother of James, with the unnamed disciple who is present in the Fourth Gospel and is styled as its author. If we follow this tradition, then John, in addition to several stories in which he figures in the Synoptics, is also present in an entire series of episodes in the Fourth Gospel. The absence of these episodes from the Synoptic Gospels, just like the absence in the Fourth Gospel of the accounts in which John the son of Zebedee figures in the Synoptics, is explained, as we have

[21]See *Novum Testamentum Graece*, 28th rev. ed. (Stuttgart: Deutsche Bibelgesellschaft, 2012).

said, by John writing his Gospel after the others: he adds the material that is absent from the Synoptics, including that which directly concerns himself.

Thomas and Philip

The Gospel of John contains a whole range of episodes featuring individual disciples called by name.

Thomas, who is mentioned in the Synoptics only in the complete list of the Twelve, appears in the Gospel of John in three episodes, where he plays a fairly independent role.

The apostle John the Theologian, icon, 16th c.

The first episode describes Jesus' intention to go to Judea and the protests of the disciples, who say to him, "Master, the Jews of late sought to stone thee; and goest thou thither again?" (Jn 11.8). Jesus nevertheless reaffirms his intention, and then Thomas, addressing the disciples, says, "Let us also go, that we may die with him" (Jn 11.16). By this time, the foreboding that the end would come soon has apparently become fairly palpable in the community of the disciples, but only Thomas turns out to be capable of expressing this with such clarity.

The second episode takes place at the Last Supper. Here Thomas reacts to Jesus' words: "And whither I go ye know, and the way ye know." Interrupting the Teacher's speech, Thomas asks, "Lord, we know not whither thou goest; and how can we know the way?" Jesus answers, "I am the way, the truth, and the life. No man cometh unto the Father, but by me" (Jn 14.4–6).

Finally, the third episode relates to the period after Jesus' resurrection. The Gospel of John is the only one that contains a detailed account of how Thomas doubted that Jesus had risen from the dead, and how Jesus, appearing to the disciples, addressed him. The account concludes with words that contain the only confession, of its own kind, of faith in Jesus as God, coming from the lips of the apostle: "My Lord and my God" (Jn 20.28).

*The Incredulity
of Saint Thomas,*
Caravaggio,
1601–1602.

Of course, three episodes are not enough to establish an idea of the character of Thomas and his spiritual quests. Nonetheless, they demonstrate several of the apostle's distinguishing features. We see that Thomas sincerely loves Jesus and expresses his readiness to share the fate of the Teacher and die together with him. This aligns Thomas with Peter, who said, "Though I should die with thee, yet will I not deny thee" (Mt 26.35; cf. Mk 14.31), or in Luke's version, "Lord, I am ready to go with thee, both into prison, and to death" (Lk 22.33). Hearing about the path that awaited Jesus, Thomas tries to ascertain the nature of this path. Finally, after Jesus' resurrection, he is among those who doubt, but when Jesus convinces him of the truth of the resurrection, it is he—the only one of all the disciples—who calls Jesus not only Christ or the Son of God, but Lord and God.

Philip is mentioned in the Gospel of John four times. The first time is in the story of the calling of the apostles and of the conversation between Jesus and Nathanael (discussed earlier).

The second time, Philip appears in the story of Jesus feeding the five thousand with five loaves and two fishes. This episode is present in all four Gospels, but only John gives the dialogue between Jesus and Philip:

> When Jesus then lifted up his eyes, and saw a great company come unto him, he saith unto Philip, "Whence shall we buy bread, that these may

eat?" And this he said to test him, for he himself knew what he would do. Philip answered him, "Two hundred pennyworth [Gk. *denarii*] of bread is not sufficient for them, that every one of them may take a little." (Jn 6.5–7)

The third time, Philip, "which was of Bethsaida of Galilee" (Jn 12.21), is mentioned in connection with the desire of the Greeks to see Jesus. Philip does not go to the Teacher directly: he first speaks about this with Andrew, and then, with Andrew, brings the request to Jesus (Jn 12.20–22). The evangelist does not explain why Philip does not immediately tell Jesus about the request but first finds it necessary to obtain Andrew's support. This detail is simply additional evidence that within the community of Jesus' disciples, the apostles who came from the same town (Jn 1.44) continued to preserve close relations with each other. We ought not forget that the small Galilean towns mentioned in the Gospels each consisted of several hundred inhabitants, each of whom personally knew all the rest (especially when this concerned members of the same profession, or people close in age).

The fourth time, Philip appears in the account of the Last Supper. Here, right after Thomas, Philip interrupts Jesus' speech with the request: "Lord, show us the Father, and it sufficeth us." Jesus answers, "Have I been so long with you, and yet hast thou not known me, Philip? He that hath seen me hath seen the Father. And how sayest thou, 'Show us the Father?' Believest thou not that I am in the Father, and the Father in me?" (Jn 14.8–10).

The third person who interrupts the Teacher's speech at the Last Supper is Judas "not Iscariot" (and this is the only individual mention of this apostle in the entire corpus of the Gospels, not counting the mention of him in the complete list of the Twelve). He asks Jesus the question: "Lord, how is it that thou wilt manifest thyself unto us, and not unto the world?" (Jn 14.22).

In three of these four episodes from the Gospel of John where Philip is present, Jesus enters into a dialogue with him: in the first and third instances on his own initiative, and in the fourth instance, on Philip's. It is hardly possible, on the basis of these episodes, to speak of some special relationship between Jesus and Philip, or to say that Jesus somehow singled him out from within the group of disciples.

If anything, these episodes illustrate the fact that Jesus not only associated with his disciples as a single group, but often also entered into conversation with one of the representatives of this group. And while, according to the accounts of the Synoptics, this representative almost always turns out to be Peter, in the Fourth Gospel a more diverse picture is presented. And while the Synoptics (especially Matthew and Mark) emphasize that the disciples do not understand Jesus, are afraid to ask him questions, and receive his rebukes and chastisement, in John the mutual relationship between the disciples with the Teacher seems more harmonious: they do not fear him, are not afraid to ask him questions, and, when necessary, even interrupt his speech in order to ask them.

6. The Instruction to the Twelve Apostles

It is not our aim to give a biography of each of the twelve apostles. Some of them we will meet more than once over the course of the story of the Gospels, while others will not be mentioned again by the evangelists.[22]

Inasmuch as our goal is to obtain, as far as possible, a maximally complete reconstruction of the figure of Jesus, the story of the choosing of twelve apostles leaves us with a key question: why did Jesus need them, what did he expect from them, for what purpose did he choose them, and with what aim did he give them the power to drive out demons and heal diseases? In order to answer this question, we must turn to Jesus' discourse addressed to his disciples, which is given in the Gospel of Matthew immediately after the account of the choosing of the Twelve.

---

[22]A list of all of them, with the exception of Judas the traitor, will be reproduced again in Acts 1.13.

In the opinion of many scholars, the instruction to the Twelve that is contained in the Gospel of Matthew is a collection of Jesus' sayings that were said at a different time.[23] This possibility cannot be ignored, all the more so as in Mark we find only a small fragment of it (Mk 6.7–13). We find the same fragment in Luke (Lk 9.1 6); however, another part of the instruction, which Jesus addresses to the Twelve in Matthew, is addressed to the Seventy in Luke (Lk 10.1–16), and yet another part (Lk 21.12–19) is included in Jesus' discourse addressed to his disciples in the Temple in Jerusalem.

These parallels, however, do not at all necessarily indicate that Jesus' discourse addressed to the disciples, as presented in Matthew, is a compilation. One can suppose that Jesus gave similar instructions to different groups of disciples, and that Luke, who was himself an apostle of the Seventy, recorded what he heard from the Teacher when he was speaking to the Seventy, while Matthew recorded the teaching addressed to the Twelve.

Regardless of whether the instruction to the Twelve was given as a whole or in parts, what interests us is its entirety, since in that form it gives us an understanding of the tasks that Jesus set before his apostles. As with the Sermon on the Mount, this sermon possesses an internal integrity, and there are recurrent themes and repetitions in it that are characteristic of Jesus' speech.

"Go not into the way of the Gentiles"

The instruction to the Twelve begins, like Jesus' other sermons (such as the Sermon on the Mount), without introduction or preface:

> Go not into the way of the Gentiles, and into any city of the Samaritans enter ye not. But go rather to the lost sheep of the house of Israel. (Mt 10.5–6)

The term "house of Israel," which is encountered multiple times in the Old Testament, refers here to the entire Hebrew nation, with the exception

---

[23]John P. Meier, *A Marginal Jew: Rethinking the Historical Jesus*, vol. 3, *Companions and Competitors*, Anchor Bible Reference Library (New York, NY: Doubleday, 2001), 543.

Christ and
the Canaanite
Woman, Pieter
Lastman, 17th c.

of the Samaritans. The expression "Go not into the way of the Gentiles" can be understood as meaning that the disciples were not to visit the Gentile settlements located along the seashore.[24] Jesus emphasizes that the main task of the apostles is to preach among the right-believing Jews. At the same time, Jesus does not limit the preaching of the apostles *exclusively* to them: he only says that the disciples should go "rather" (in the sense of "sooner," "especially"; Gk. *mallon*) to the lost sheep of the house of Israel, that is, to pay attention *primarily* to them.

Not only is the Gentile world excluded from the territories where the original mission of the apostles was supposed spread, but Samaria as well. We note that this is the only place in the Gospel of Matthew where Samaria is mentioned: on the basis of the Gospels of Matthew and Mark, one could conceivably infer that Jesus and his disciples were never in Samaria. However, the Gospel of Luke says that, not long before his death, while on the way from Galilee to Jerusalem, Jesus intended to visit Samaria, "and sent messengers before his face, and they went, and entered into a village of the Samaritans, to make ready for him. And they did not receive him, because his face was as though he would go to Jerusalem" (Lk 9.52–53). It also says that, on the way to Jerusalem, Jesus "passed through the midst of Samaria and Galilee" (Lk 17.11). And only from the Gospel

[24]W. F. Albright and C. S. Mann, *Matthew: Introduction, Translation, and Notes*, Anchor Bible 26 (Garden City, NY: Doubleday, 1971), 119.

of John do we find out that on the way from Judea to Galilee Jesus "must go through Samaria" (Jn 4.4), and that he conversed with the woman at the well and then spent two days in her town, thanks to which many Samaritans believed in him (Jn 4.39–41). From the entirety of the witness of the Gospels, it follows that Jesus was in Samaria only on the way from Galilee to Judea or back, but, in contrast to these two regions, Samaria was never a place where he preached or to which his disciples were sent as part of their mission.

The fact that Jesus places an emphasis precisely on preaching among the Jews supports the story from the same Gospel of Matthew about the woman of Canaan who beseeched Jesus to heal her daughter, while he at first "answered her not a word" (Mt 15.23). When the disciples asked him to send her away, he said, "I am not sent but unto the lost sheep of the house of Israel," and added, "It is not right to take the children's bread, and to cast it to dogs." Only after the woman humbly says to him, "Yea, Lord, yet the dogs eat of the crumbs which fall from their masters' table," does he heal her daughter with the words, "O woman, great is thy faith: be it unto thee even as thou wilt" (Mt 15.24, 26–28). This incident is also recounted in Mark; however, in his telling, the words "I am not sent but unto the lost sheep of the house of Israel" are absent, while the woman is called "a Greek [i.e., a Gentile], a Syrophenician by nation" (Mk 7.26).

The words uttered by Jesus in the presence of the woman of Canaan are almost completely identical to the first words from his instruction to the Twelve. In this similarity one cannot help but see an indication that, at least on some level, Jesus' mission was understood by himself and his disciples as directed overwhelmingly towards the "house of Israel." The idea of the universal scope of this mission would come to his disciples much later—after he rose from the dead—and after they recognized, not without Paul's influence, the utter lack of success of their preaching among the Jews against the backdrop of the triumphal success of their preaching among the Gentiles.

In what sense does Jesus call those to whom the apostles were going "lost sheep"? It seems that here there is a reflection of the approach that would be characteristic of Jesus over the course of the entire period of his public ministry. He gives the most attention to the rejected and marginalized: publicans and sinners, lepers and paralytics, the poor and the destitute. Among those with whom he would associate and whom he would allow to approach himself, we find both the woman caught in adultery (Jn 8.10–11) and the sinful woman (Lk 7.37–39). As for the Pharisees and teachers of the law, who considered themselves righteous, to them he said, "Truly I say unto you, that the publicans and the harlots go into the kingdom of God before you" (Mt 21.31). One cannot help but recall here as well the words of Jesus that "the Son of Man is come to save that which was lost" (Mt 18.11), and the parable immediately after these words about the lost sheep, for whose sake the shepherd leaves the ninety-nine that are not lost in order to go out and find it (Mt 18.12–13).

"Freely ye have received, freely give"

Continuing his instruction to the disciples, Jesus repeats the call to repentance that he inherited from John the Baptist. Now this call is to sound from the lips of his disciples also:

> And as ye go, preach, saying, "The kingdom of heaven is at hand." Heal the sick, cleanse the lepers, raise the dead, cast out devils. Freely ye have received, freely give. Provide neither gold, nor silver, nor brass in your purses, nor bag for your journey, neither two coats, neither shoes, nor yet staves. For the workman is worthy of his food. (Mt 10.7–10)

Like Jesus, his disciples would accompany the proclamation of the kingdom of God with miracles. The disciples receive the power to perform miracles from him without cost.

Jesus' words here echo his answer to the disciples of John the Baptist: "The blind receive their sight, and the lame walk, the lepers are cleansed, and the deaf hear, the dead are raised up, and the poor have the gospel preached to them" (Mt 11.5). The Gospels describe multiple instances of healing and the driving out of demons, and also three instances of the raising of the dead, performed by Jesus. However, in the Gospels it does not say that his disciples raised the dead. It is only mentioned that they drove out demons in the name of Jesus (Lk 10.17), and not always successfully, at that (Mt 17.19). Only after his resurrection would the disciples receive from him the ability to not only perform healings, but also to raise the dead, which is described in the Acts of the Apostles (Acts 9.36–41; 20.9–12).

The Dispute with Simon Magus, Filippino Lippi, 15th c.

The expression "freely ye have received, freely give" should be understood to mean that the activity of the apostles was to be carried out free of charge: they were not to preach or perform miracles in exchange for money. At the same time, Jesus adds that "the workman is worthy of his food." This means that, in return for their work, Jesus' disciples could receive food and lodging. Could they have received monetary donations? Obviously, yes. This can be inferred from the fact that in the community of Jesus' disciples there was one (Judas Iscariot) who "had the money box; and he used to take what was put in it" (Jn 12.6, NKJV). Thus, what was forbidden was to preach or perform miracles in exchange for money, but receiving donations was not forbidden.

The Christian Church was organized on the basis of these principles after Jesus' resurrection. The apostles strictly forestalled any attempt to sell the gifts of God; the story of Simon Magus serves as evidence of this (Acts 8.18–20). At the same time, they remembered that "the Lord ordained that those who preach the Gospel should live of the Gospel" (1 Cor 9.14), and actively engaged in the collection of funds, having established a system such that "as many as were possessors of lands or houses sold them, and brought the prices of the things that were sold, and laid them down at the apostles' feet" (Acts 4.34–35).

The command of poverty is given in Luke in the same form as in Matthew (Lk 9.3–4), while in Mark Jesus commands the disciples to "take nothing for their journey, save a staff only; no bag, no bread, no money in their purse, but be shod with sandals; and not put on two coats" (Mk 6.8–9). The variant readings seem insignificant, but, in practice, following the version of Matthew would mean that Jesus expected his disciples to walk barefoot and forbade them to even use a staff. It seems that, here,

Mark is closer to reality: in his version, Jesus forbids the disciples to possess a full "travel kit," including a purse with money, but does not call them to extreme asceticism.

Besides this, Mark's version may contain a veiled allusion to the Old Testament command on how the Passover lamb should be eaten: "And thus shall ye eat it; with your loins girded, your shoes on your feet, and your staff in your hand; and ye shall eat it in haste" (Ex 12.11). In the Jewish tradition, the Passover meal was a remembrance of the exodus of the people of Israel from Egypt: the haste with which it was necessary to eat the lamb, doing so while holding one's staff in hand, led the participants of the meal to think about the temporary nature of earthly blessings, and symbolized the readiness to follow the call of the Lord at any moment. The mission of the apostles was to be imbued with this same attitude: at the call of Jesus, they set out to preach, ready to fulfill that which he had commanded them to do.

"Peace be to this house"

The instruction continues, and Jesus gives the disciples a series of practical counsels. These simple words of advice indicate, first of all, that acceptance of the apostles' preaching about the kingdom of heaven is a voluntary action, and that each person listening to this preaching makes his or her own choice either in favor of the kingdom of heaven, or in favor of this world:

> And into whatsoever city or town ye shall enter, inquire who in it is worthy; and there abide till ye go thence. And when ye come into a house, salute it [saying: "Peace be to this house"].[25] And if the house be worthy, let your peace come upon it; but if it be not worthy, let your peace return to you. And whosoever shall not receive you, nor hear your words, when ye depart out of that house or city, shake off the dust of your feet. Truly I say unto you, It shall be more tolerable

[25]The words in brackets are present in Matthew 10.12 in the Greek Byzantine text form (including the 1904 ed. used liturgically in the Greek Church), the Vulgate, and the Slavonic. Compare with Luke 10.5.—Trans.

Lot and His Daughters Fleeing the Destruction of Sodom and Gomorrah, Raphael, 1496.

for the land of Sodom and Gomorrha in the day of judgment, than for that city. (Mt 10.11–5)

The expression "peace be to this house" was likely the usual greeting in Jesus' time, along the lines of the greeting "peace be unto thee," which we find multiple times on the pages of the Old Testament (Judg 6.23; 1 Sam 20.21; 1 Chr 12.18; Ps 121.8; Dan 10.19). This greeting is addressed to the entire family, and one can assume that the preaching of the apostles was addressed to families (as a rule, a family of several people lived under one roof). St Jerome writes:

> In a concealed way he has expressed a greeting of the Hebrew and Syriac languages. For what is said in Greek by χαῖρε [*chaire*] and in Latin by *ave* is said in Hebrew and Syriac speech as *shalom lach* or *shalama lach*, that is, "peace be with you." He is commanding the following: When you enter a house, you should call down peace upon the host, and as far as it depends on you, settle the wars of discord. But if opposition arises, you will have a reward from the peace offered, and they will possess the war that they wanted to have.[26]

---

[26]Jerome, *Commentary on Matthew* 1.10 (PL 26:64). Translation from Jerome, *Commentary on Matthew*, trans. Thomas P. Scheck, The Fathers of the Church 117 (Washington, DC: Catholic University of America Press, 2008), 119.

*The Last
Judgment,*
fresco in the
Sistine Chapel,
Michelangelo,
1536–1541.

The word *shalom* (*šālôm*—peace) is used to this day as a basic greeting
in the Hebrew language. In the Old Testament, peace is a key concept:

> To appreciate at its full value the reality concealed beneath this word,
> one must sense the earthly flavor which subsists in the Semitic expres-
> sion. . . . We find it this way in the Bible right up through the last book
> of the NT. . . . The Hebrew word *šālôm* is derived from a root which,
> according to its usages, designates the fact of being intact, complete
> [Job 9.4] . . . or the action of reestablishing things to their former state,
> their [integrity]. . . . Biblical peace, then, is not only the "pact" which
> permits a tranquil life, nor the "time of peace" in opposition to "the
> time of war" [Eccl 3.8]. . . . It also indicates the wellbeing of daily exis-
> tence, the state of the man who lives in harmony with nature, with
> himself, with God.[27]

[27] *Dictionary of Biblical Theology*, ed. Xavier Léon-Dufour, trans. under dir. of P. Joseph
Cahill, rev. and trans. E. M. Stewart, 2nd ed. (London: G. Chapman, 1988), 411.

The Last Judgment, Hans Memling, 1467–1471.

Peace, according to the Bible, is a blessing from God: "The Lord will give strength unto his people; the Lord will bless his people with peace" (Ps 28.11). God himself is the source of peace and is even equated with peace (Judg 6.24). The words that Jesus places on the lips of the apostles also carry an element of blessing: entering a house, they not only greet its inhabitants, but also bless the whole family in the name of God. If the apostles are not received in that house, the blessing returns to them; but if the preaching of the apostles is heeded, the blessing remains on the whole family.

Jesus uses the expression "shake off the dust," found once in the Old Testament (Is 52.2), to refer to the practice of visibly expressing disagreement with the behavior or reaction of people living in a specific place. The mention of Sodom and Gomorrah is an allusion to the biblical account of the destruction of these two cities. The disciples' departure from the town in which they are not received is similar to the departure of Lot from Sodom: Lot had to leave in haste without looking back (Gen 19.17–28).

The phrase "day of judgment," which is encountered in the Gospels several times (Mt 11.22, 24; 12.36; Mk 6.11), reflects the Christian understanding of the Last Judgment, with which the history of the world will end. The apostle Peter says of this day: "But the heavens and the earth, which are now, by the same word are kept in store, reserved unto fire against the day of judgment and perdition of ungodly men" (2 Pet 3.7). Jesus presents the teaching regarding the Last Judgment over several exhortations. Here we only need to point out that he conceives of the disciples' preaching as having an immediate bearing on the fate of their listeners in eternity. The deciding factor in determining the posthumous fate of those to whom the Gospel has been preached is the presence or absence of faith in Jesus Christ: "He that believeth on him is not condemned, but he that believeth not is condemned already, because he hath not believed in the name of the only begotten Son of God" (Jn 3.18).

"Be ye therefore wise as serpents, and harmless as doves"

The subsequent instruction is more general and concerns not so much the first missionary journey of the apostles, from which they would soon return, as much as the type of witness on the whole that Jesus expects from his followers. He does not promise them any success; on the contrary, he predicts ever-present conflict between them and the surrounding world:

> Behold, I send you forth as sheep in the midst of wolves. Be ye there-
> fore wise as serpents, and harmless as doves. But beware of men. For
> they will deliver you up to the councils, and they will scourge you in
> their synagogues, and ye shall be brought before governors and kings
> for my sake, for a testimony against them and the Gentiles. But when
> they deliver you up, take no thought how or what ye shall speak; for it
> shall be given you in that same hour what ye shall speak. For it is not
> ye that speak, but the Spirit of your Father which speaketh in you. And
> brother shall deliver up brother to death, and the father the child: and
> children shall rise up against their parents, and cause them to be put
> to death. And ye shall be hated by all men for my name's sake: but he
> that endureth to the end shall be saved. (Mt 10.16–22)

It is distinctive that, while the subject at the beginning of the instruction is exclusively the apostles' mission to the Jews, at this point, Jesus significantly broadens the perspective: now the subject is their witness before rulers, kings, and Gentiles. This means that, according to Matthew, Jesus already foresaw at the very beginning of his ministry that his mission, and the mission of his disciples, would go beyond the borders of the house of Israel and spread among the Gentile peoples.

At the same time, he emphasizes from the start the controversial nature of this mission, which would be fulfilled in spite of the longstanding laws of both the Jewish and Gentile worlds, which would provoke anger, rejection, and malice, and which would be the cause of family strife. He does not behave at all as a Jewish rabbi of his time would, who probably would promise his disciples various blessings, predict success in their undertaking, and teach them how to achieve it. Jesus says nothing of the sort. He does not promise his disciples success, happiness in their personal life, material prosperity, or spiritual comfort. He does not promise them acceptance from their compatriots, the Gentiles, or even their close relatives.

We can only guess what sort of reaction such predictions elicited from the disciples. As John Chrysostom writes:

> For indeed we have great cause to marvel, how they did not straightway dart away from Him on hearing these things, apt as they were to be startled at every sound, and such as had never gone further than that lake, around which they used to fish; and how they did not reflect, and say to themselves, "And whither after all this are we to flee? The courts of justice against us, the kings against us, the governors, the synagogues of the Jews, the nations of the Gentiles, the rulers, and the ruled." (For hereby He not only forewarned them of Palestine, and the ills therein, but discovered also the wars throughout the world, saying, "Ye shall be brought before kings and governors;" signifying that to the Gentiles also He was afterwards to send them as heralds.)[28]

What, then, was to be the primary motivation for Jesus' disciples? The expectation of the second coming of the Son of Man? Jesus says to the disciples:

> But when they persecute you in this city, flee ye into another. For truly I say unto you, ye shall not have gone over the cities of Israel, till the Son of Man is come. (Mt 10.23)

A literal understanding of these words would have to mean that the disciples' mission would continue for only a short time, and that the second

---

[28]John Chrysostom, *Homilies on the Gospel of Matthew* 33.4 (*NPNF*[1] 10:221).

coming of Jesus would find them among the living. To all appearances, this was how the disciples understood his words. It is no coincidence that in Jerusalem on the eve of his death they would ask, "Tell us, when shall these things be? And what shall be the sign of thy coming, and of the end of the world?" (Mt 24.3). They would pose him a similar question immediately after his resurrection: "Lord, wilt thou at this time restore again the kingdom to Israel?" (Acts 1.6).

In the early Christian Church, the opinion prevailed that the coming of Jesus would happen very soon—possibly even during the lifetime of the apostles. This understanding was partly based on a literal interpretation of the abovementioned words, and also of the words that Jesus uttered not long before his death: "This generation shall not pass, till all these things are fulfilled" (Mt 24.34). In the epistles of the apostles, it is written: "The coming of the Lord draweth nigh" (Jas 5.8); "The end of all things is at hand" (1 Pet 4.7). The apostle Paul probably supposed that the coming of Christ would happen within his lifetime: "We shall not all sleep, but we shall all be changed" (1 Cor 15.51); "For yet a little while, and he that shall come will come, and will not tarry" (Heb 10.37). In the First Epistle to the Thessalonians, Paul writes: "We who are alive and remain unto the coming of the Lord shall not precede those who are asleep. . . . The dead in Christ shall rise first. Then we who are alive and remain shall be caught up together with them in the clouds, to meet the Lord in the air; and so shall we ever be with the Lord" (1 Thess 4.15–17).

However, over the course of time, the Christian community came to the understanding that the second coming of Christ could happen at some point in the distant future. In the Second Epistle to the Thessalonians, Paul even dissociates himself to some degree from what he said in his First Epistle: "Now we beseech you, brethren, by the coming of our Lord Jesus Christ, and by our gathering together unto him, that ye be not soon shaken in mind, or be troubled, neither by spirit, nor by word, nor by letter as from us, as that the day of Christ is at hand" (2 Thess 2.1–2).

Meanwhile, in his Second Epistle, the apostle Peter directly answers the question, "Where is the promise of his coming?" (2 Pet 3.4). In the words of the apostle Peter: "The Lord is not slow concerning his promise, as some men count slowness; but is longsuffering toward us, not willing that any should perish, but that all should come to repentance" (2 Pet 3.9). At the same time, Peter refers to the epistles of Paul, "in which are some things hard to be understood, which those that are unlearned and unstable twist, as they do also the other scriptures, unto their own destruction" (2 Pet 3.16). Peter's mention of the epistles of Paul in connection with the theme of the second coming leaves no room for doubt that the he is referring primarily to Paul's two epistles to the Thessalonians, and especially the passages in those epistles that discuss the proximity of the coming of the Lord.

Many of Jesus' exhortations in the Gospels can be interpreted as relating to different time periods. On the one hand, Jesus speaks of what awaits the disciples in the near future. On the other hand, in the events of the near future, the later fate of the Church is also glimpsed. In this sense, the words addressed to the Twelve become Jesus' instruction to all his disciples in all subsequent times, and the reference to the second coming only serves to confirm the extratemporal nature of this instruction and its continued relevance for the ages.

"The disciple is not above his teacher"

Jesus goes on to speak about how imitating the Teacher does not promise the disciples any earthly blessings or honor:

> The disciple is not above his teacher, nor the servant above his lord. It is enough for the disciple that he be as his teacher, and the servant as his lord. If they have called the master of the house Beelzebub, how much more shall they call them of his household? (Mt 10.24–25)

This section of the instruction consists of a series of aphorisms, which are at first sight unrelated to each other. We find a literal parallel to this section in the Gospel of John, where Jesus says similar words at the Last Supper after washing his disciples' feet. The apostles called Jesus "Teacher" (Gk. *didaskalos*), and he accepted it as proper: "Ye call me 'Master' and 'Lord,' and ye say well; for so I am" (Jn 13.13). But he insists that discipleship consists first of all in imitating him: "For I have given you an example, that ye should do as I have done to you." And then he says, "Truly, truly, I say unto you, the servant is not greater than his lord; neither is he that is sent greater than he that sent him" (Jn 13.15–16). A little later in the same speech he again returns to the image of the servant and his lord: "Remember the word that I said unto you, the servant is not greater than his lord. If they have persecuted me, they will also persecute you; if they have kept my saying, they will keep yours also" (Jn 15.20).

Here we see an example of Jesus' multiple repetitions of the same saying, which has the character of a proverb. However, with each repetition, it acquires new shades of meaning. If in one case Jesus cites a proverb in order to emphasize that the disciples ought to imitate him, then in the other case the subject is the anticipated reaction of the people to their mission. The proverb has the same connotation in Matthew: the disciple is not above the teacher, and if people do not listen to the teacher, then they will also not listen to the disciple; if they suspect that demonic forces are at work in the teacher, then the disciple will also elicit the same suspicions.

In order to understand what relevance the theme of Beelzebub[29] has to the theme of teacher and disciples, one must recall how the Pharisees, according to the Synoptic Gospels, accused Jesus more than once, saying, "This man doth not cast out devils, but by Beelzebub the prince of the devils." To this Jesus replied, "Every kingdom divided against itself is brought to desolation, and every city or house divided against itself shall not stand. And if Satan cast out Satan, he is divided against himself. How shall then his kingdom stand? And if I by Beelzebub cast out devils, by whom do your children cast them out? Therefore they shall be your judges" (Mt 12.24–27; Mk 3.22–26). By "children" here he means the apostles: to them Jesus gave the power to heal infirmities and drive out demons, a power that he himself possessed; those who challenged the divine power of Jesus and accused him of making use of demonic forces belonged to the generation of the apostles' parents.

---

[29]The term "Beelzebub" is found six times in the Synoptic Gospels and refers to the devil. The etymology of this term is usually traced back to the Canaanite deity Baal (1 Kg 18.16–40), although there are also other theories regarding the origin of this term. The name "Beelzebub" is found in 2 Kg 1.2, where it is used as the name of the "god of Ekron," that is, one of the pagan idols.

"Fear not"

The following series of exhortations, reinforced by the threefold "fear not," begins with an idea that Jesus has repeated more than once:

> Fear them not therefore. For there is nothing covered, that shall not be revealed, and hid, that shall not be known. What I tell you in darkness, speak ye in light, and what ye hear in the ear, preach ye upon the housetops. (Mt 10.26–27)

We encounter a similar text in Luke in the instruction to the Seventy (Lk 12.2). We also find it in Mark and Luke, in the words that follow the image used in the Sermon on the Mount (Mt 5.15) of the light on the stand (Mk 4.22; Lk 8.17). This saying ought to be understood to mean that Jesus is revealing mysteries to the disciples that they in turn are to reveal to people.

It is no coincidence that in Mark this saying precedes the formula "If any man have ears to hear, let him hear" (Mk 4.23), while in Luke it comes after a similar formula (Lk 8.15). This formula, which is found in the Synoptics ten times in total, was used by Jesus when he wanted to emphasize that what he was saying possessed a concealed meaning, particularly when he was speaking a parable. He revealed the meaning of certain parables to the disciples in private, and addressed many of his sermons to the disciples only. Their task was to make explicit what he taught them in secret.

Continuing his speech, Jesus calls the disciples to place their confidence in the will of God and to fear neither people nor trials:

> And fear not those who kill the body, but are not able to kill the soul; but rather fear him who is able to destroy both soul and body in hell [Gk. *gehenna*, "Gehenna"]. Are not two sparrows sold for a coin [Gk. *assarion*, one-tenth of a drachma]? And one of them shall not fall on the ground without your Father. But the very hairs of your head are all numbered. Fear ye not therefore, ye are of more value than many sparrows. (Mt 10.28–31)

The term "Gehenna," which is found in the Synoptic Gospels ten times (eight time in Matthew and twice in Mark), refers to the Valley of Hinnom located in the southern part of Jerusalem, where human sacrifices were carried out in the time of the kings Ahaz and Manasseh. Consequently, this valley became a place where a fire was maintained and the corpses of people and animals were burned: thus the expression "hell fire" (literally in Gk. "the Gehenna of fire") (Mt 5.22; 18.9). By the time of Jesus, the term was used to mean a place of posthumous punishment, where "their worm dieth not, and the fire is not quenched" (Mk 9.44). The one "who is able to destroy both soul and body in hell" (Mt 10.28) is understood to be God: it is in his power to condemn human beings to eternal torment. It is he whom the disciples must fear, and not earthly rulers and kings, who are able to destroy only a person's body but not the immortal soul.

Concerning the sparrows sold for a coin, we have the following variant reading in the Gospel of Luke: "Are not five sparrows sold for two coins, and not one of them is forgotten before God? But even the very hairs of your head are all numbered. Fear not therefore; ye are of more value than many sparrows" (Lk 12.6–7). Here these words are part of the sermon that Jesus addressed to the disciples "when there were gathered together an innumerable multitude of people, insomuch that they trod one upon another" (Lk 12.1). The idea that without the will of God not one hair of a person's head would fall to the ground is present in the Old Testament (1 Sam 14.45; 2 Sam 14.11; 1 Kg 1.52). Jesus uses these same images in order to encourage the disciples: if God knows the number of hairs on a person's head and cares about the smallest birds, all the more would he care about those who give their lives in service to him.

The Public Confession of Faith

Further on in Jesus' words we hear an idea that he has repeated time and again in various contexts:

> Whosoever therefore shall confess me before men, him will I confess also before my Father who is in heaven. But whosoever shall deny me before men, him will I also deny before my Father which is in heaven. (Mt 10.32–33)

The Apostle Paul Explains the Doctrines of the Faith to Agrippa, Vasily Surikov, 1875.

We encounter similar ideas in the Gospel of Mark: "For what shall it profit a man, if he shall gain the whole world, and lose his own soul? Or what shall a man give in exchange for his soul? Whosoever therefore shall be ashamed of me and of my words in this adulterous and sinful genera tion, of him also shall the Son of man be ashamed, when he cometh in the glory of his Father with the holy angels" (Mk 8.36–38). In Luke we find both the versions of Matthew (Lk 18.8–9) and of Mark (Lk 9.25–26), with the words "Father who is in heaven" in the Matthean variant replaced by the "angels of God."

Why does confession of Jesus have to be public—"before men"? The answer to this question touches the very essence of the Christian faith and concerns the nature of the Church as the community of the followers of Jesus. The Church was created by him in no way as a secret society and not at all for the public sphere. The contemporary conception of religion as a private affair of separate individuals deeply contradicts the very nature of Christianity. All of Jesus' ministry took place in the open, in public. He called his disciples publicly, not secretly. His life, and the life of the community that he created, ran its course before the eyes of multitudes of people, and his sermons were often delivered before thousands of hearers. Even that which he said to his disciples in private, "in the ear"—this they were to preach "upon the housetops" (Mt 10.27).

A public confession of faith is not required of all disciples without exception, and it is not required in all circumstances. As we have said, among the disciples of Jesus, there were ones who remained secret disciples out of fear of the Jews. The phenomenon of secret Christianity is known from the time of Jesus right up to our day: it is especially distinctive of times when the Church was persecuted. But an apostle cannot be secret. An apostle always acts in the public sphere and must be ready to witness to the faith—even at the cost of his very life, if necessary.

"I came not to send peace, but a sword"

The following part of the instruction is about how faith in Jesus can affect a person's relationship with his or her relatives:

> Think not that I am come to send peace on earth. I came not to send peace, but a sword. For I am come to set a man at variance against his father, and the daughter against her mother, and the daughter-in-law against her mother-in-law. And a man's foes shall be those of his own household. (Mt 10.34–36)

In the Gospel of Luke, we find similar words: "Suppose ye that I am come to give peace on earth? I tell you, nay, but rather division. For from henceforth there shall be five in one house divided, three against two, and two against three. The father shall be divided against the son, and the son against the father; the mother against the daughter, and the daughter against the mother; the mother-in-law against her daughter-in-law, and the daughter-in-law against her mother-in-law" (Lk 12.51–53).

One contemporary scholar, the author of one "revolutionary biography" of Jesus, is of the opinion that Jesus is here making a stand against the "patriarchal chauvinism" characteristic of the Mediterranean culture of his time. The standard family consisted of five members: father and mother, their son with his wife, and an unmarried daughter: all of them lived under one roof. The line of separation, the scholar notes, runs between generations: Jesus directs his fire at the patterns of family life that give power to the older generation over the younger generation, to the parents over the children. His ideal is the kingdom of heaven, in which there is no place for abuse of power.[30]

---

[30]John Dominic Crossan, *Jesus: A Revolutionary Biography* (San Francisco, CA: HarperSanFrancisco, 1994), 59–60.

Only one point in this interpretation deserves attention: if one reads the text literally, the line of separation does indeed run between generations. Jesus does not say that he came to divide husband from wife, or brother from sister; he does not say that the man that loves his wife more than him, or the wife that loves her husband more than him, is not worthy of him. But do Jesus' words really mean that the dividing line would run only and exclusively between generations?

First of all, we must point out that these words are a paraphrase of the words of the prophet Micah: "For the son dishonoureth the father, the daughter riseth up against her mother, the daughter-in-law against her mother-in-law; a man's enemies are the men of his own house" (Mic 7.6). In this text, the son is against the father, the daughter against the mother, and the daughter-in-law against the mother-in-law. The absence of any mention of other relations in this excerpt can explain their absence in Jesus' words as well. Aside from this, we may again recall the words of Jesus addressed to his disciples: "And every one that hath forsaken houses, or brethren, or sisters, or father, or mother, or wife, or children, or lands, for my name's sake, shall receive a hundredfold, and shall inherit everlasting life" (Mt 19.29). Here, alongside representatives of the older and younger generations, there are representatives of the same generation (brothers, sisters, wife).

The general context of the instruction, which is addressed to the disciples whom Jesus is sending out for missionary ministry, unambiguously speaks in favor of the central point of these words being faith in Jesus, and the readiness to overcome obstacles in order to preach his doctrines. These obstacles include the possible rejection of the apostles' preaching by their closest relatives. As we have seen, Jesus' relatives, at least in the beginning, reacted extremely negatively to his preaching and chosen way of life. Since "The disciple is not above his master" (Mt 10.24), the apostles, too, can expect a similar reaction to their preaching from their relatives and the members of their household.

The words about how Jesus has brought not peace to the world, but a sword, seem at first glance to contrast sharply with what he said earlier to the apostles about the peace that they were to bring with them into a house.

Considering the enormous significance that the concept of peace possessed in the Semitic tradition, this saying of Jesus could have been understood by his hearers to be provocative. There could have been the impression that he was infringing on one of the core values of human existence, values having their source in God himself. The family was also understood as an absolute value; an intrusion into family life, resulting in intergenerational conflict, could not have been seen as something positive.

Yet, the subject under discussion is something else, and the word "peace" is not being used in its everyday sense. The discussion is not at all about family life or the relationships between relatives. The sword that divides, among other things, family connections, is faith in Jesus and the readiness to follow him. Jesus is speaking of situations where this faith turns out to be not a uniting, but dividing factor, that is, when one member of a family accepts his teaching, while the rest aggressively oppose that person.

The image of the sword would be used in the Epistle to the Hebrews in relation to the word of God: "For the word of God is living, and powerful, and sharper than any two-edged sword, piercing even to the division of soul and spirit, and of the joints and marrow, and is a discerner of the thoughts and intents of the heart" (Heb 4.12). Here the sword of the word of God is presented as something that brings division into the substance of a single person. In Jesus' preaching, the sword of faith divides the members of a single family.

"He that loveth father or mother more than me . . ."

Jesus' next words reflect an idea to which he clearly returned more than once:

> He that loveth father or mother more than me is not worthy of me: and he that loveth son or daughter more than me is not worthy of me. (Mt 10.37)

In the Gospel of Luke, analogous words, in a more forceful form, would be addressed to the multitude: "If any *man* come to me, and hate not his father, and mother, and wife, and children, and brethren, and sisters, yea,

Christ
Pantocrator,
mosaic, late
12th c.

and his own life also, he cannot be my disciple" (Lk 14.26). The difference between the two sayings consists in that, first, in Matthew two generations are once more in view (father, mother, son, daughter), while in Luke the list contains only representatives of a single generation (wife, brother, sister); second, while in Matthew Jesus does not permit one to *love* one's relatives more than him, in Luke he issues the call to *hate* them.

How do these exhortations relate to the fifth Mosaic commandment: "Honour thy father and thy mother" (Ex 20.12; Deut 5.16)? How can they be reconciled with the commandment that Jesus calls one of the two greatest in the law: "Thou shalt love thy neighbour as thyself" (Mt 22.39; cf. Lev 19.18)? Is Jesus here, too, infringing on immutable, universal human values such as the love of children for their parents and of parents for their children? And how far does the call to "hate" (in Luke's version) fit in with the general character of Jesus' preaching, at the center of which stands love?

Jesus is placing spiritual ties based on unity of faith higher than natural family ties. This understanding is fully reflected in the abovementioned words from the instruction to the disciples, and also in the parallel text from the Gospel of Luke. Words cannot be taken out of their context. What is being said is that, in a situation where one has to choose between faithfulness to Jesus and faithfulness to family ties, the disciples of Jesus must choose the first. One contemporary scholar gives the following definition: "In most cases these two are not incompatible; and to hate one's parents *as such* would be monstrous. . . . But Christ's followers must be

*Christ
Pantocrator,*
fresco, Viktor
Vasnetsov,
1885–1896.

ready, if necessary, to act towards what is dearest to them as if it were an object of hatred. . . . Jesus, as often, states a principle in a startling way, and leaves His hearers to find out the qualifications."[31]

In his commentary on the passage from the Gospel of Matthew above, John Chrysostom quotes also the parallel passage from the Gospel of Luke. He gives the general meaning of both sayings in the following manner: "not commanding simply to hate them, since this were even quite contrary to the law; but 'when one desires to be loved more than I am, hate him in this respect.'"[32] Augustine describes an imaginary dialogue in which a believer addresses his parents with the following words: "I do love you, in Christ; I don't love you instead of Christ. Be with me in him; I won't be with you without him."[33] Both passages, each in its own way, reflect the situation

---

[31] Alfred Plummer, *A Critical and Exegetical Commentary on the Gospel According to St. Luke,* International Critical Commentary 28 (New York, NY: Charles Scribner's Sons, 1896), 364.

[32] John Chrysostom, *Homilies on the Gospel of Matthew* 35.3 (*NPNF*[1] 10:233).

[33] Augustine of Hippo, *Sermons* 65a.5. Translation from Augustine of Hippo, *The Works of Saint Augustine: A Translation for the 21st Century,* trans. Edmund Hill, ed. John E. Rotelle, pt. 3, vol. 3, *Sermons on the New Testament, 51–94* (Brooklyn, NY: New City Press, 1991), 200.

that Jesus predicted and which has arisen more than once in the experience of his followers over the centuries—when a person has to make a choice between Jesus and that person's own relatives.

The subject under discussion is also that of a correct ordering of priorities, from Jesus' point of view: the readiness to follow him must be stronger than any earthly attachment, including feelings of kinship. This is spoken of in the episode in which one of those whom Jesus calls to follow him says to him, "Lord, allow me first to go and bury my father" (Mt 8.21). In Luke's version, Jesus answers, "Let the dead bury their dead; but go thou and preach the kingdom of God" (Lk 9.60). Luke also gives Jesus' answer to the man who asks for leave to say goodbye to his household: "No man, having put his hand to the plough, and looking back, is fit for the kingdom of God" (Lk 9.62). It is distinctive that, in both answers, the kingdom of God takes center stage. It is this kingdom that is the reality over which no earthly attachment ought to be preferred.

"And he that taketh not his cross . . ."

In the following section of the instruction to the disciples, for the first time in the Gospel, the cross is mentioned:

> And he that taketh not his cross, and followeth after me, is not worthy of me. He that findeth his life [lit. "soul"] shall lose it; and he that loseth his life [lit. "soul"] for my sake shall find it. (Mt 10.38–39)

Certain scholars have understood this reference to the cross as an editorial addition to the words of Jesus, made by the evangelist in light of the event of the crucifixion, and also under the influence of Paul's theology of the cross. However, there is nothing to prevent us from understanding Jesus' words as a prophecy of his path to the cross: "[I]n the climate of the times it is hard to suppose that Jesus did not foresee a violent end to his ministry. . . . [L]ong before the time of Jesus, impaling or crucifixion had become typical of violent death."[34] That those condemned to death carried their own cross was also a well-known fact.

[34] Albright and Mann, *Matthew*, 132.

*Christ Carrying
the Cross,*
attributed to
a follower of
Hieronymus
Bosch,
1510–1535.

We will add that the expression "take up one's cross" is encountered in Jesus' direct speech more than once (Mt 16.24; Mk 8.34; Lk 9.23; 14.27). Evidently, the image of one condemned to death, carrying his cross on his shoulders, is used by Jesus as a warning of the kinds of risks associated with following him.

Jesus' words about the soul [Gk. *psychē*; English translations render this as "life"—*Ed.*], which a person can either save or lose, is one of his distinctive sayings: we encounter it with minor variations another four times in the Synoptic Gospels (Mt 16.25; Mk 8.35; Lk 9.24; 17.33). According to the universally accepted interpretation, the word "soul" is used here to mean "life." In the Gospel of John, Jesus' saying is quoted in the following form: "He that loveth his life [lit. 'soul'] shall lose it; and he that hateth his life [lit. 'soul'] in this world shall keep it unto life eternal" (Jn 12.25). John's version, it would seem, gives the key to understanding the meaning of Jesus' words: one ought not hold on to earthly life at any cost; the one who sacrifices transient life for Jesus' sake will save it for eternal life.

Reward

Concluding his extended instruction to his disciples, Jesus speaks of the reward awaiting the one who responds to the preaching of the apostles:

He that receiveth you receiveth me, and he that receiveth me receiveth him that sent me. He that receiveth a prophet in the name of a prophet shall receive a prophet's reward; and he that receiveth a righteous man in the name of a righteous man shall receive a righteous man's reward. And whosoever shall give to drink a cup of cold water unto one of these little ones only in the name of a disciple, truly I say unto you, he shall in no wise lose his reward. (Mt 10.40–42)

The first sentence of this passage is encountered in a modified form in the Gospels of Luke and John (Lk 10.16; Jn 13.20); the middle portion is found only in Matthew; and the concluding sentence we find also in Mark (Mk 9.41).

We turned our attention to the fact that Jesus does not promise any reward to his disciples for the missionary labors he is sending them to carry out: instead of a reward, he promises them afflictions, sufferings, persecutions, and death. Here the word "reward" is encountered thrice in relation to the one who receives the prophets and apostles.

We note that in the Sermon on the Mount the term "reward" is used by Jesus mainly in relation to the recompense that a person receives directly from the heavenly Father (Mt 5.12, 46; 6.1, 4–6, 16–18). This recompense he promises not only to the apostles, but to all the subsequent generations of those who believe in him thanks to their preaching.

7. The Disciples Not of the Twelve

Besides the Twelve, Jesus also had other disciples: these included the seventy apostles mentioned in Luke, the women of whom all four evangelists speak, and a series of other figures, called by name or left anonymous.

The Seventy

Luke is the only evangelist who mentions that, besides the Twelve, Jesus later chose another seventy disciples:

> After these things the Lord appointed other seventy also, and sent them two by two before his face into every city and place, where he himself would come. Therefore said he unto them, "The harvest truly is great, but the laborers are few. Pray ye therefore the Lord of the harvest, that he would send forth laborers into his harvest." (Lk 10.1–2)

In a large number of manuscripts, seventy-two disciples are mentioned instead of seventy. On this basis, in the contemporary critical editions of the New Testament, the number "seventy-two" is given in the text (but not in the critical apparatus, as is the case with less authoritative readings); however, the number "two" is enclosed in square brackets.[35] This decision was made by the United Bible Societies under the influence of the foremost authority on New Testament textual criticism, Kurt Aland, who considered "seventy-two" to be the original reading, and "seventy" to be the product of harmonizing correction by copyists who wished to change a number that did not have any symbolic or sacred meaning to one that did.[36] If the number twelve corresponded to the twelve tribes of Israel, then the number seventy corresponds to the seventy elders whom Moses chose from the sons of Israel (Ex 24.1; Num 11.16, 24), or the seventy offspring of Israel (Ex 1.5; Deut 10.22).[37]

Church tradition, however, has preserved the names of seventy, and not seventy-two, apostles. In their ranks are the evangelists Mark and Luke, and also certain persons who are mentioned in the epistles of the apostle Paul, or who were the recipients of these epistles.

The instruction that Jesus addressed to the Seventy corresponds to a significant degree to the instruction he addressed to the Twelve in Matthew (Mt 10.9):

[35] *Novum Testamentum Graece*, 177.

[36] Joseph A. Fitzmyer, *The Gospel According to Luke: Introduction, Translation, and Notes*, vol. 2, *X–XXIV*, Anchor Bible 28a (Garden City, NY: Doubleday, 1985), 845.

[37] According to the reading of certain manuscripts of the Old Testament, Jacob had seventy-five offspring.

Go your ways. Behold, I send you forth as lambs among wolves. Carry neither purse, nor bag, nor shoes; and salute no man by the way. And into whatsoever house ye enter, first say, "Peace be to this house." And if a son of peace be there, your peace shall rest upon it; if not, it shall turn to you again. And in the same house remain, eating and drinking such things as they give. For the laborer is worthy of his hire. Go not from house to house.

Synaxis of the Seventy Apostles, icon detail.

And into whatsoever city ye enter, and they receive you, eat such things as are set before you. And heal the sick that are therein, and say unto them, "The kingdom of God is come nigh unto you." But into whatsoever city ye enter, and they receive you not, go your ways out into the streets of the same, and say, "Even the very dust of your city, which cleaveth on us, we do wipe off against you. Notwithstanding be ye sure of this, that the kingdom of God is come nigh unto you." But I say unto you, that it shall be more tolerable in that day for Sodom, than for that city. (Lk 10.3–12)

The differences between this instruction and the one addressed to the Twelve are the commands not to greet anyone along the way, not to go from one house to another, and to eat anything offered to them. The custom of greeting people one meets on the road is widespread to this day in the Near East. The rejection of this custom ought to be understood in the general context of the call to goal-oriented missionary travel. Not to greet anyone on the road means not to get distracted by extraneous things and not to enter into conversation with people who happen to be passing by: all interaction with people must be subjected to the goal for which Jesus is sending the disciples out into the world. It is appropriate here to recall what Elisha said to his servant Gehazi when the former learned of the death of the widow's son in Shunem: "Gird up thy loins, and take my staff in thine hand, and go thy way. If thou meet any man, salute him not; and if any salute thee, answer him not again" (2 Kg 4.29).

The Fall of the Rebel Angels,
Luca Giordano, 1660–1665.

Luke includes in the instruction to the Seventy the reproaches addressed to the cities that did not believe in Jesus: Chorazin, Bethsaida, and Capernaum (Lk 10.13–15). The instruction concludes with these words: "He that heareth you heareth me; and he that despiseth you despiseth me; and he that despiseth me despiseth him that sent me" (Lk 10.16). Similar words, in different variants, are present in the other Gospels (Mt 10.40; Mk 9.37; Jn 13.20).

Saying nothing of how the mission of the Seventy was carried out, Luke tells of how they return to Jesus with a report of their labors:

And the seventy returned again with joy, saying, "Lord, even the demons are subject unto us through thy name." And he said unto them, "I beheld Satan as lightning fall from heaven. Behold, I give unto you power to tread on serpents and scorpions, and over all the power of the enemy, and nothing shall by any means hurt you. Notwithstanding in this rejoice not, that the spirits are subject unto you. But rather rejoice, because your names are written in heaven." In that hour Jesus rejoiced in spirit, and said, "I thank thee, O Father, Lord of heaven and earth, that thou hast hid these things from the wise and prudent, and hast revealed them unto babes. Even so, Father, for so it seemed good in thy sight. All things are delivered to me by my Father, and no man knoweth who the Son is, but the Father, and who the Father is, but the Son, and he to whom the Son will reveal him." And he turned him unto his disciples, and said privately, "Blessed are the eyes which see the things that ye see. For I tell you, that many prophets and kings have desired to see those things which ye see, and have not seen them; and to hear those things which ye hear, and have not heard them." (Lk 10.17–24)

The words about the fall of Satan from heaven should be examined in the general context of the opposition between Jesus and the devil, which is reflected on the pages of the four Gospels. The verb "have seen" is used in the past tense and may refer to some event in the past; for example, to Jesus' overcoming of the temptation from the devil in the wilderness. We have given such an interpretation of these words earlier. However, what is in view could also be a prophetic vision[38] relating to the final victory over the devil, which would take place thanks to the death and resurrection of Jesus. Taking into consideration the missionary context of the exhortation, we may suppose that Jesus sees his disciples as participating in this victory, inasmuch as they would continue his work on earth.

That Jesus is looking towards the future is also suggested by the words: "Behold, I give unto you power to tread on serpents and scorpions, and over all the power of the enemy." These words are in keeping with Jesus' prediction of the signs that would accompany those who believe in him: "In my name shall they cast out devils; they shall speak with new tongues. They shall take up serpents; and if they drink any deadly thing, it shall not hurt them" (Mk 16.17–18). Evidently, as he converses with the Seventy, Jesus is speaking not only about their mission in the near future, but also about the mission of the coming generations of his disciples over the course of the centuries to come.

The expressions "at that time" or "in that hour," used by Matthew and Luke respectively (Mt 11.25; Lk 10.21), may indicate a change in the circumstance or the addressee: the evangelists use these words to introduce events that relate to the foregoing action and continue its line of thought, but which are not necessarily part of that action. The words that Jesus addresses to the Father are quoted by the two evangelists in different contexts, but in both cases they are separated from the preceding material by the expressions "at that time" or "in that hour."

According to Luke, after Jesus' prayer to the Father, he again addresses the disciples. The words that he addresses to them ("Blessed are the eyes which see the things that ye see") are also found in Matthew (Mt 13.16–17). There they serve to explain why Jesus speaks to the people in parables but clarifies the meaning of the parables to the disciples in private. As for the reproaches addressed to the cities where Jesus was not received, in the

---

[38]Joel B. Green, *The Gospel of Luke*, New International Commentary on the New Testament (Grand Rapids, MI: Eerdmans, 1997), 419.

Gospel of Matthew they are included in the sermon that Jesus delivers in front of the people after the instruction to the Twelve (Mt 11.1, 7–24). In Matthew this sermon concludes with the words that, in Luke, are included in the instruction to the Seventy (Mt 11.25–28).

Harmonizing the material of Matthew and Luke presents a significant difficulty to scholars who assume that Jesus never repeated himself. In this case the presence of one and the same saying in two different stories by two evangelists would be construed in terms of literary dependence: Luke must have taken the saying from Matthew (or vice versa).

However, the accounts involving the twelve apostles and the seventy apostles are plain evidence that Jesus repeated the same words in different circumstances. Such repetition is more than natural in a situation in which the Teacher at first instructs one group of disciples, and then another. If both groups had the same mission, why could they not receive similar or identical instructions? A supporting argument in favor of such an understanding is the presence in one and the same Gospel—that of Luke—of two different instructions analogous in content: one addressed to the Twelve (Lk 9.3–6), and the other to the Seventy (Lk 10.4–11).

What is being spoken of in the words: "I thank thee, O Father, Lord of heaven and earth, that thou hast hid these things from the wise and prudent, and hast revealed them unto babes"? And who are these babes? In the opinion of John Chrysostom, those whom Jesus calls wise and prudent are the scribes and Pharisees, but "in calling them 'wise,' He means not the true and commendable wisdom, but this which they seemed to have through natural shrewdness." By babes, he means the simple and guileless fishermen whom Jesus made his apostles.[39]

The following saying, which is identical almost to the word in Matthew and Luke, possesses many parallels in other passages, including in the Gospel of John:

> All things are delivered to me by my Father: . . . All power is given unto me in heaven and in earth. (Mt 28.18)

---

[39]John Chrysostom, *Homilies on the Gospel of Matthew* 38.1 (*NPNF*[1] 10:251).

The Father loveth the Son, and hath given all things into his hand. (Jn 3.35)

. . . and no man knoweth who the Son is, but the Father; and who the Father is, but the Son, and him to whom the Son will reveal him. (Lk 10.22; cf. Mt 11.27)

As the Father knoweth me, even so know I the Father. (Jn 10.15)

No man hath seen God at any time; the only begotten Son, who is in the bosom of the Father, he hath declared him. (Jn 1.18)

. . . he that hath seen me hath seen the Father. (Jn 14.9)

Here what is being spoken of is not the usual human knowing and seeing, but knowing and seeing of a special kind. The Son knows the Father as God, and the Father knows the Son as God; faith in Jesus as God opens to man the possibility of knowing and seeing the Father. This is the knowledge that God has "hid . . . from the wise and prudent," but "revealed . . . unto babes"—his unschooled disciples.

Secret Disciples

Jesus had secret disciples. One of them appears in all four Gospels in the account of the burial of Jesus. Matthew calls him "a rich man of Arimathaea, named Joseph, who also himself was Jesus' disciple" (Mt 27.57). In Mark, Joseph is "an honorable counselor, who also waited for the kingdom of God" (Mk 15.43), and in Luke he is "a counselor, and he was a good man, and a just (the same had not consented to the counsel and deed of them) . . . who also himself waited for the kingdom of God" (Lk 23.50–51). John calls him "a disciple of Jesus, but secretly for fear of the Jews" (Jn 19.38). Besides this episode, Joseph is mentioned nowhere else in the Gospels.

In John, in the scene of the burial, another figure appears alongside Joseph—"Nicodemus, who at the first came to Jesus by night" (Jn 19.39). The nocturnal conversation between Jesus and Nicodemus is presented in detail in the third chapter of the Gospel of John, beginning from the words: "There was a man of the Pharisees, named Nicodemus, a ruler of the Jews" (Jn 3.1). From this mention and from the subsequent conversation, it is

Joseph of
Arimathea
before Pilate,
fresco, 16th c.

not clear that Nicodemus is a disciple of Jesus: it is more likely that he is here as one of the Pharisees interested in Jesus' teaching. However, unlike the other Pharisees, who disputed with Jesus in the daytime and in public, Nicodemus comes to him at night, which is evidence of his desire to communicate with the Teacher in private, and not in the presence of other Pharisees.

After the abovementioned conversation, Nicodemus appears twice more on the pages of the Fourth Gospel: he unsuccessfully tries to dissuade the Pharisees from passing judgment on Jesus in the latter's absence (Jn 7.50–53), and later participates in the burial of Jesus. These two mentions are evidence that, even if Nicodemus was not a disciple of Jesus in the beginning, then at the very least he remained sympathetic towards him and, perhaps, became his disciple later. That being said, like Joseph of Arimathea, he preferred to keep his acquaintance with Jesus secret.

In Church tradition, both these secret disciples—Joseph and Nicodemus—are reckoned among the saints: they have been given the title of "Righteous."

Zacchaeus

Another one of Jesus' disciples whose name has also entered the Church calendar with the title of "Righteous" is Zacchaeus. We learn of him only in the Gospel of Luke:

> And Jesus entered and passed through Jericho. And, behold, there was a man named Zacchaeus, who was the chief among the publicans, and he was rich. And he sought to see Jesus, who he was; and could not for the press, because he was little of stature. And he ran before, and climbed up into a sycamore tree to see him, for he was to pass that way. And when Jesus came to the place, he looked up, and saw him, and said unto him, "Zacchaeus, make haste, and come down. For today I must abide at thy house." And he made haste, and came down, and received him joyfully. And when they saw it, they all murmured, saying that he was gone to be guest with a man that is a sinner. And Zacchaeus stood, and said unto the Lord, "Behold, Lord, the half of my goods I give to the poor. And if I have taken any thing from any man by false accusation, I restore him fourfold." And Jesus said unto him, "This day is salvation come to this house, forsomuch as he also is a son of Abraham. For the Son of Man is come to seek and to save that which was lost." (Lk 19.1–10)

This story stands out in the corpus of the four Gospels. It does not belong among the miracle accounts, which fill the pages of the Gospels; in this story there is no healing taking place, nor the driving out of a demon, nor any other sign worthy of notice. There were probably many such stories in Jesus' life; after all, he was constantly surrounded by crowds. But the evangelists, with rare exceptions, did not preserve accounts of encounters that were not accompanied by miracles. The story of Zacchaeus is one such exception.

Zacchaeus,
Niels Larsen
Stevns, 1913.

There is a comic element to this story: a short man climbs a tree in order to see Jesus, who is passing by; he understands that if he does not do this, he will not be able to see anything from behind the backs of other people. Moreover, Zacchaeus was not an ordinary tax collector, as Matthew Levi was. He was the chief publican, and that meant that he had under his command people from whom he could expect respect. At the same time, as a publican, he was an accomplice of the occupying power, and consequently was despised by his own people.

For a grown, well-to-do man in such a position to climb a tree like a boy before the eyes of a crowd means that he would attract the curiosity of those around him and become the object of ridicule and gossip. But Zacchaeus pays no attention at all to the inescapable consequences of his action. All his attention is concentrated on Jesus. He climbs up the tree because it is important to him to see Jesus with his own eyes, and not only hear about him from someone else's words.

And his zeal is rewarded in full: he not only sees Jesus passing by, but also draws his attention to himself. Jesus knows why he has climbed up on the tree, and what potential for faith is hidden in this unusual action. And he calls him by name, which neither Zacchaeus himself nor the people around them could have anticipated, and speaks to him about his intention to come to his house.

Jesus' visit to the house of a publican provokes murmuring, because he is visiting a sinful person. Although in this case the evangelist describes this as the reaction of "all," the reader understands that the ones primarily responsible for this murmuring are the Pharisees, who perpetually complain of Jesus that he "eateth and drinketh with publicans and sinners" (Mk 2.16). But neither Jesus nor Zacchaeus pays attention to the murmuring. Cheered by Jesus' visit to him, Zacchaeus promises to change his life: to give the poor half of his possessions, and to pay back fourfold those whom he has defrauded.

Being a rich person, Zacchaeus was capable of counting money. And even in the incident described above, while riding the wave of an emotional lift, he does not promise to distribute all his possessions to the poor, as Jesus asks the rich young man to do (Mt 19.21; Mk 10.21; Lk 18.22). As for the promise to pay back fourfold, here the calculation is based on the order in the Mosaic Law, which prescribes that four sheep should be paid back in return for stealing one (Ex 22.1). But even this turns out to be sufficient for salvation, which Jesus proclaims to Zacchaeus and his "house" (family). The emotional outburst of the chief of the publicans finds a response in Jesus' heart, and Jesus does not demand from him anything beyond what he is able to give.

The Gospel of Luke says nothing of what happens to Zacchaeus later on, and in Acts his name is not mentioned. According to Church tradition, after Jesus' resurrection, Zacchaeus was made the bishop of Caesarea in Palaestina. According to the writings attributed to Clement of Rome, he accompanied the apostle Peter, preached in Rome, and received a martyr's death at the hands of the emperor Nero.[40]

The story of Zacchaeus is read in the Orthodox Church on the Sunday of the fourth week before Great Lent. It begins a series of Gospel readings dedicated to repentance: on the next three Sundays we read the parables

---

[40]Clement of Rome (Pseudo-), *Recognitions* 1.20.73–74; 3.66 (PG 1:1217, 1247–1248, 1311); Rufinus Aquileia, *Introduction to the Translation of Clement of Rome's "Recognitions"* (PG 1:1207–1208).

Zacchaeus on
the sycamore
tree, mosaic,
13th c.

from the Gospel of Luke about the publican and Pharisee (Lk 18.9–14) and about the prodigal son (Lk 15.11–32), and also the teaching about the Last Judgment from the Gospel of Matthew (Mt 25.31–46). In this way, the story of Zacchaeus becomes the first link in a chain of four readings that serve to prepare the faithful for their entrance into Great Lent as a time for profound repentance, reexamining one's orientation in life, prayer, and the active doing of good deeds.

In the teaching of the Church, fasting consists not only in abstaining from food. One of the hymns from the beginning of Great Lent says:

> While fasting with the body, brethren, let us also fast in spirit. Let us loose every bond of iniquity; let us undo the knots of every contract made by violence; let us tear up all unjust agreements; let us give bread to the hungry and welcome to our house the poor who have no roof to cover them, that we may receive great mercy from Christ our God.[41]

That which Zacchaeus promised to do entirely conforms to the tone of this call.

Perhaps it is no coincidence that fasting is mentioned as one of the good deeds of the Pharisee in the parable of the publican and the Pharisee. The connection between the story of Zacchaeus and this parable is discernible not only in the Church calendar, but also in the Gospel of Luke itself. The

---

[41]Stichera at "Lord I call," vespers of Wednesday in the first week of Great Lent. *The Lenten Triodion*, trans. Mother Mary and Kallistos Ware (South Canaan, PA: St. Tikhon's Seminary Press, 2002), 235.

good deeds that the Pharisee lists in his prayer to God includes fasting (full abstinence from food from sunrise to sunset) twice a week, and giving a tenth of all he gets. Zacchaeus does not promise to observe the fast, but promises to renounce half of all he owns for the sake of the poor (and not only half of what he would gain in the future), and to settle accounts with all whom he has taken advantage of. In Jesus' eyes, these professed intentions are more valuable than all the ostentatious righteousness of the Pharisees, who elicit nothing from Jesus but sharp criticism (Mt 5.20; 6.2, 5, 16 and elsewhere).

Women

Time and again in the narratives of all four Gospels, images of the women who followed Jesus emerge. Matthew speaks of how before his cross "many women were there beholding afar off, who followed Jesus from Galilee, ministering unto him" (Mt 27.55). In the parallel passage in Mark, more details are given about the women: "There were also women looking on afar off, among whom was Mary Magdalene, and Mary the mother of James the less and of Joses, and Salome (who also, when he was in Galilee, followed him, and ministered unto him), and many other women which came up with him unto Jerusalem" (Mk 15.40–41). In both cases, the verb used is "minister" (or "serve"; Gk. *diakoneō*), which indicates that the main work of the women was providing various kinds of help to Jesus and his disciples in everyday matters.

The Penitent Magdalene,
Titian, 1565.

In the Gospel of Luke another important role played by the women in Jesus' circle is mentioned. Again the verb "minister" is used:

And it came to pass afterward, that he went throughout every city and village, preaching, and showing the glad tidings of the kingdom of God; and the twelve were with him, and certain women, who had been healed of evil spirits and infirmities, Mary called Magdalene, out

Christ in the House of Martha and Mary, Johannes Vermeer, 1654–1655.

of whom went seven demons, and Joanna the wife of Chuza Herod's steward, and Susanna, and many others, which ministered unto him of their substance. (Lk 8.1–3) [42]

The phrase "ministered . . . of their substance" indicates that some of the women who followed Jesus invested their material resources into his work. At least one of the three women mentioned above, the wife of the steward, must have been fairly well-to-do.[43] It is no coincidence that she turns out to be the only one of the women mentioned in the Gospels whose social status the evangelist finds necessary to point out.

In the two places where the Gospel of John mentions the sister of Lazarus, Martha, the verb "serve" used in relation to her refers to her service at the table, including the preparation of food (Jn 10.30; 12.2). This is exactly what Martha is doing in the episode narrated in Luke:

> Now it came to pass, as they went, that he entered into a certain village, and a certain woman named Martha received him into her house. And she had a sister called Mary, who also sat at Jesus' feet, and heard his word. But Martha was distracted about much serving, and came to him, and said, "Lord, dost thou not care that my sister hath left me to serve alone? Bid her therefore that she help me." And Jesus answered and said unto her, "Martha, Martha, thou art worried and troubled about many things. But one thing is needful, and Mary hath chosen that good part, which shall not be taken away from her." (Lk 10.38–42)

---

[42]On the role of women in the Gospel of Luke, see Rudolf Schnackenburg, *Jesus in the Gospels: A Biblical Christology*, trans. O. C. Dean (Louisville, KY: Westminster John Knox Press, 1995), 198–208.

[43]Richard Bauckham, *Gospel Women: Studies of the Named Women in the Gospels* (Grand Rapids, MI: Eerdmans, 2002), 117.

Christ in the House of Martha and Mary, Mikhail Nesterov, 1908.

This story has attained exceptional significance in the Orthodox Church thanks to its being read at the divine liturgy for every feast of the Mother of God. In the patristic tradition the two sisters are most often interpreted as being images of two types of the Christian life—the active and the contemplative:

> Understand that Martha represents active virtue, while Mary represents divine vision. Action entails distractions and disturbances, but divine vision, having become the ruler of the passions (for *Maria* means *mistress*, she who rules), devotes itself entirely to the contemplation of the divine words and judgments. . . . Therefore, whoever sits at the feet of Jesus, that is, whoever steadfastly follows and imitates Jesus, is established in all active virtue. Then such a man will also come to the listening of the divine words, that is, he will attain to divine vision. Mary first sat, and by doing this she was then able to listen to Jesus' words. Therefore you also, O reader, if you have the strength, ascend to the rank of Mary: become the mistress of your passions, and attain to divine vision. But if you do not have the strength, be Martha, and devote yourself to active virtue, and by this means welcome Christ.[44]

---

[44]Theophylact of Ochrid, *Explanation of the Gospel of Luke* 10.38–42 (PG 123:853). Translation from Theophylact of Ochrid, *The Explanation by Blessed Theophylact of the Holy Gospel According to St. Luke*, trans. Christopher Stade, vol. 3 of *Blessed Theophylact's Explanation of the New Testament* (House Springs, MO: Chrysostom Press, 1997), 121–122.

Christ in the House of Martha and Mary, Henryk Siemiradzki, 1886.

However, in the actual words of Jesus that he addresses to Martha, nothing is said about contemplation. Rather, he is talking about listening to his words, which are the source of life and salvation. Jesus speaks of this in other places as well: "He that heareth my word, and believeth on him that sent me, hath everlasting life, and shall not come into condemnation, but is passed from death unto life" (Jn 5.24). Chiding Martha for being concerned with too many cares, Jesus does not condemn her, but reminds her of what must come first: his personal presence in the life of a person, and the desire of a person to listen to him.

Jesus himself did not choose the path of contemplation, and his moral instruction is dedicated mainly to active love for one's neighbor. Speaking of the Last Judgment, he cites different examples of good deeds: "For I was hungry, and ye gave me food; I was thirsty, and ye gave me drink; I was a stranger, and ye took me in; naked, and ye clothed me; I was sick, and ye visited me; I was in prison, and ye came unto me" (Mt 25.35–36). And he mentions not a single word about contemplation.

Martha and Mary are singled out from among the rest of the women, the female followers of Jesus. The evangelist John notes, "Now Jesus loved Martha, and her sister, and Lazarus" (Jn 11.5). A few days before his death, Jesus was invited to Bethany, where "they made him a supper, and Martha served, but Lazarus was one of them that sat at the table with him. Then Mary took a pound of ointment of spikenard, very costly, and anointed the feet of Jesus, and wiped his feet with her hair" (Jn 12.2–3).

The appearance
of the risen
Christ to Mary
Magdalene, icon,
16th c.

About the other women we learn much less. Over the course of the
entire Gospel narrative (this concerns all four Gospels), women seem to
stay in the background; they come into the foreground only in the concluding chapters of the Gospels—in the accounts of Jesus' death on the cross
and the events that follow. We note Luke's words that among them were
those whom Jesus had healed of evil spirits and diseases.

The word "many" in relation to the women in Jesus' circle is used by
all three synoptic evangelists (Mt 27.55; Mk 15.41; Lk 8.3). However, only a
few of these women were in the intimate circle that Luke denotes with the
word "certain." It was this circle of women who were the female disciples
of Jesus that occupies an essential place in the accounts of the events connected with his death and resurrection.

The complete list of women called by name in Jesus' circle includes the
following: Mary Magdalene (Mt 27.56, 61; 28.1; Mk 15.40, 47; 16.1, 9; Lk 8.2;

Mary Magdalene,
Carlo Crivelli, ca. 1480.

24.10; Jn 19.25; 20.1, 11–18); the sisters Martha and Mary of Bethany (Lk 10.38–42; Jn 11.1–44; 12.1–8); Mary, the mother of James and Joses (Mt 27.56; Mk 15.40, 47; 16.1; Lk 24.10); the other Mary (Mt 27.61; 28.1); Mary of Cleopas (Jn 19.25); Joanna (Lk 8.3; 24.10); Salome (Mk 15.40; 16.1); and Susanna (Lk 8.3). There are nine names in total (or eight, if one considers Mary the mother of James and Joses to also be the "other Mary"), and of them five (or four) are named Mary. As is clear from the list, Mary Magdalene is mentioned more often than the other women who followed Jesus, and she is the only one mentioned in all four Gospels.

In Acts, after listing the names of the eleven apostles, Luke says: "These all continued with one accord in prayer and supplication, with the women, and Mary the mother of Jesus, and with his brethren" (Acts 1.14). The death and resurrection of Jesus united those who had been connected with him in his lifetime into a single community numbering about 120 persons (Acts 1.16). This community included the apostles, the relatives of Jesus according to the flesh, including his Mother, and those same "certain women" who had ministered to him even in Galilee. These women are not mentioned again in the narrative of Acts, and Peter's first speech, though it was delivered in the presence of the women, begins with the words, "Men and brethren [*Andres, adelphoi*]" (Acts 1.16), which are addressed to the male apostles.[45]

[45]Craig Keener comments: "His address, 'Men, brothers' (Ἄνδρες, ἀδελφοί), need not imply that on this occasion the women (Acts 1:14) were absent. . . . [T]he masculine address was common rhetoric for addressing public assemblies . . . and appears even where gender-mixed audiences may be presumed. . . . [T]he phrase used here appears in other speeches, even to clearly gender-mixed groups (e.g., 2:29, 37). Luke . . . simply employs the conventional vocative for such speeches." Craig S. Keener, *Acts: An Exegetical Commentary, Vol 1: Introduction and 1:1–2:47* (Grand Rapids, MI: Baker Academic, 2012), 756–757.

In contemporary scholarship there is a widespread view that there were women among Jesus' apostles. So, for example, Richard Bauckham considers Joanna a female apostle. Based on the similarity between the names, he identifies her with Junia, who is mentioned by the apostle Paul: "Salute Andronicus and Junia, my kinsmen, and my fellow prisoners, who are of note among the apostles, who also were in Christ before me" (Rom 16.7). The reconstruction of the figure of Joanna-Junia, as undertaken by this scholar,[46] is not devoid of cleverness, but all the same it relates more to the realm of scholarly fantasy than to scholarship based on the sources. The information that we have in the Gospels does not allow us to draw the conclusion that the apostolic mission entrusted by Jesus to twelve men also carried over to any of the women.

The Holy Empress Helen, fresco, 14th c.

At the same time, we know from the subsequent history of the Church that certain women were honored with the title of "Equal to the Apostles" and entered as such into the Church calendar. The first of these was the very same Mary Magdalene, "out of whom [Jesus] had cast seven demons" (Mk 16.9). The other women who are equal to the apostles include the holy empress Helen (†327), the mother of Emperor Constantine; St Nina, the Enlightener of Georgia (†335), and St Olga (†969), the grandmother of Prince Vladimir, the Baptizer of Rus'. Not one of these women was a successor to the sacramental ministry that passed from the apostles to the succeeding generation of bishops, and from them to priests: this line of succession exclusively involved men. However, women did also take part in the ministry of preaching and education.

The role of women in Jesus' circle, regardless of what contemporary researchers may say,[47] corresponds on the whole to the role that women played in Israelite society in Jesus' time. Women were in the background:

[46]Bauckham, *Gospel Women*, 109–202.

[47]The tendency to overstate the role of women in Jesus' circle is characteristic of a feminist reading of the Gospels. See, for example, Satoko Yamaguchi, *Mary and Martha: Women in the World of Jesus* (Maryknoll, NY: Orbis Books, 2002), 120–124, 135–138.

they ministered to men while the latter were engaged in important work. The community of apostles was a fellowship consisting solely of men.

However, if we are to speak of the Church as a whole, already at the earliest stage of its existence, both men and women were joining it (Acts 5.14; 8.12; 17.4, 12, 34). And already in the first generation of Christians were the words of Paul, addressed to the entire community of Jesus' disciples, heard: "For as many of you as have been baptized into Christ have put on Christ. There is neither Jew nor Greek, there is neither bond nor free, there is neither male nor female, for ye are all one in Christ Jesus" (Gal 3.27–28).

Failed Disciples

The Gospels contain references not only to the disciples who came to Jesus, but also to those who went away from him. As we recall, John mentions "many of his disciples," who, after Jesus' discourse to the Jews about the bread from heaven, "went back, and walked no more with him" (Jn 6.66).

Matthew and Luke tell of persons who had the intention of joining the community of Jesus' disciples, but we do not know whether their intention was realized. Luke describes three such cases:

> And it came to pass, that, as they went in the way, a certain man said unto him, "Lord, I will follow thee wherever thou goest." And Jesus said unto him, "Foxes have holes, and birds of the air have nests; but the Son of Man hath not where to lay his head."

> And he said unto another, "Follow me." But he said, "Lord, allow me first to go and bury my father." Jesus said unto him, "Let the dead bury their dead; but go thou and preach the kingdom of God."

> And another also said, "Lord, I will follow thee; but let me first go bid them farewell, who are at home at my house." And Jesus said unto him, "No man, having put his hand to the plough, and looking back, is fit for the kingdom of God." (Lk 9.57–62)

The first two cases are mentioned also in Matthew (Mt 8.18–22). Matthew refers to the first petitioner by the term "scribe," and the second with the words "another of his disciples." This most likely means that the second petitioner did join the community of the disciples, and perhaps the first did as well. Nevertheless, we find no other reference in the Gospels to the effect that there were scribes among the disciples of Jesus, not counting such words about how "every scribe who is instructed unto the kingdom of heaven is like unto a man who is an householder, who bringeth forth out of his treasure things new and old" (Mt 13.52).[48]

The words "let the dead bury their dead" have been understood and continue to be understood by many as contradicting the norms of universal human morality. In any case, they contradicted Old Testament moral norms, according to which a son is obligated to bury his father (Tob 4.3; 6.15). First of all, however, these words do not have to be understood as meaning that the father of the petitioner had already died and his dead body was awaiting burial: they can be understood as a request for permission for the petitioner to return home, wait for his father to die, and, after burying him, return to Jesus and become his disciple. Second, Jesus structures his utterance as a proverb, in which the word "dead" most likely possesses a metaphorical meaning: let those who are spiritually dead occupy themselves with worldly affairs.[49]

At the same time, this utterance is entirely consistent with the radicalism that is expressed in Jesus' other calls, for example in the words: "If any man come to me, and hate not his father, and mother, and wife, and children, and brethren, and sisters, yea, and his own life also, he cannot be my disciple" (Lk 14.26).

---

[48]On the term "scribe" in the Gospel of Matthew, see, in particular, Aaron M. Gale, *Redefining Ancient Borders: The Jewish Scribal Framework of Matthew's Gospel* (New York, NY: T&T Clark, 2005), 98–105; David E. Orton, *The Understanding Scribe* (Sheffield: JSOT Press, 1989), 20–38, 137–176.

[49]For more details, see Joseph A. Fitzmyer, *The Gospel According to Luke: Introduction, Translation, and Notes*, vol. 1, *I–IX*, Anchor Bible 28 (Garden City, NY: Doubleday, 1981), 836; Green, *The Gospel of Luke*, 408; Martin Hengel, *The Charismatic Leader and His Followers*, trans. James D. G. Greig, ed. John Riches (Edinburgh: T&T Clark, 1981), 7–8.

Jesus' radicalism frightened away even his own community of the people who had come to him with, what appear to be, pure and serious intentions. The story about the rich young man, which is given by all three Synoptics, testifies to this:

> And, behold, one came and said unto him, "Good Teacher, what good thing shall I do, that I may have eternal life?" And he said unto him, "Why callest thou me good? There is none good but one, God. But if thou wilt enter into life, keep the commandments." He saith unto him, "Which?" Jesus said, "Thou shalt do no murder, thou shalt not commit adultery, thou shalt not steal, thou shalt not bear false witness, honour thy father and thy mother, and, thou shalt love thy neighbour as thyself." The young man saith unto him, "All these things have I kept from my youth up. What lack I yet?" Jesus said unto him, "If thou wilt be perfect, go and sell that thou hast, and give to the poor, and thou shalt have treasure in heaven. And come and follow me." But when the young man heard that saying, he went away sorrowful. For he had great possessions. (Mt 19.16–22)

Neither Mark nor Luke calls the protagonist of this story a young man: Mark calls him by the neutral word "one," and in Luke he is "a certain ruler." In both these Gospels the following words are absent: "If thou wilt be perfect." However, Mark adds three details that allow us to imagine the scene more vividly: "Then Jesus beholding him loved him, and said unto him, 'One thing thou lackest. Go thy way, sell whatsoever thou hast, and give to the poor, and thou shalt have treasure in heaven. And come, take up the cross, and follow me.' And he was sad at that saying, and went away grieved: for he had great possessions" (Mk 10.21–22). In the rest, the two Synoptics (Mk 10.17–22; Lk 18.18–23) agree almost completely with Matthew's version.[50]

---

[50]The abovementioned difference between the versions of Matthew and Mark usually serves as one of the arguments in favor of an earlier dating of the Gospel of Mark, which Matthew supposedly edited, removing the human element in it ("beholding him loved him") in favor of a more "churched" image of Jesus. However, according to an alternative hypothesis, Mark, writing later than Matthew, expanded the version of the latter while in possession of Luke's version. See Peter M. Head, *Christology and the Synoptic Problem: An Argument for Markan Priority*, Society for New Testament Studies Monograph Series 94 (Cambridge: Cambridge University Press, 1997), 49–65.

Christ and the Rich Young Man, Fyodor Chumakov, 1866–1867.

Why is it that Jesus does not demand that Zacchaeus give away all his possessions and follow him, "tak[ing] up the cross," but presents such severe demands to the rich young man that they cause him to leave in sorrow? It seems to us that the answer must be sought in the words "If thou wilt be perfect," which hold key significance for understanding this episode. In answer to the question of what good one must do in order to inherit eternal life, Jesus only lists the basic Old Testament commandments. Only after the young man says that he has kept them does Jesus utter the words that sadden him and scare him away.

We see a sharp distinction between what pertains to the ordinary person who desires to inherit eternal life, and what pertains to the one who wishes to achieve perfection, that is, accept Jesus' teaching in its most radical aspects. Jesus points to the path of spiritual perfection, which involves the full renunciation of all earthly attainments and even family ties. At the same time, he does not impose this path on everyone; he also leaves the possibility of salvation open for those who are not ready for a complete break with the world, including the rich.

About there being some "loophole" for them to enter the kingdom of heaven as well, we can judge by the words that Jesus addressed to his disciples immediately after the departure of the rich young man:

> And Jesus looked round about, and saith unto his disciples, "How difficult shall it be for those that have riches to enter into the kingdom of God!" And the disciples were astonished at his words. But Jesus answereth again, and saith unto them, "Children, how hard is it for them that trust in riches to enter into the kingdom of God! It is easier for a camel to go through the eye of a needle, than for a rich man to enter into the kingdom of God." And they were astonished out of measure, saying among themselves, "Who then can be saved?" And Jesus looking upon them saith, "With men it is impossible, but not with God. For with God all things are possible." (Mk 10.23–27; cf. Mt 19.16–26; Lk 18.24–27)

Here Jesus is not saying that it is *impossible* for the rich to enter the kingdom of God, but he does say that it is *difficult*. Salvation itself is presented as a gift from God, and not as the fruit of human efforts. In another place, Jesus speaks of the strait gate and narrow way that leads to eternal life (Mt 7.13–14), which is consistent with the idea that it is difficult, but not impossible, to attain to the kingdom of heaven.

The saying about the camel and the eye of the needle characterizes Jesus' way of speaking as figurative and metaphorical: the largest of working animals is compared to the smallest known aperture. However, the unusual nature of this juxtaposition has caused even commentators of the ancient Church to look for alternative ways to interpret it. Origen, and Cyril of Alexandria after him, proposed that the word *kamēlos* (camel) refers not to an animal, but to a rope (*schoinion*);[51] Theophylact of Ochrid also mentions this opinion, repeating Cyril's words almost exactly.[52] The phonetic similarity between *kamēlos* (camel) and *kamilos* (rope, thick cable) serves as the basis for this interpretation.[53] In this view, it can seem

---

[51] Origen, *Fragments on Matthew* 390 (GCS 41/1:166); Cyril of Alexandria, *Commentary on the Gospel of Matthew* [=Fragment 219] (TU 61:226).

[52] Theophylact of Ochrid, *Explanation of the Gospel of Matthew* 19 (PG 123:356D; in English: ACCS NT 1b:102).

[53] Certain manuscripts of the Gospel give this spelling. See Kurt Aland, *Synopsis Quattor Evangeliorum: Locis parallelis evangeliorum apocryphorum et partum adhibitis*, 13th rev. ed. (Stuttgart: Deutsche Bibelgesellschaft, 1988), 341.

that there is more logic in the comparison: two images are taken from the same realm.[54]

One more explanation has been proposed in the modern age: supposedly, there was a narrow opening in the wall of Jerusalem that was called "the eye of the needle," through which one could drag a camel only with great difficulty.[55] However, nothing is known about the existence of such an opening or gate with such a name.

The story of the rich young man concludes the evangelists' series of stories about the failed disciples of Jesus. These disciples can be separated into three categories: those who themselves elected to follow him, but, after learning of his proposed requirements, turned back; those whom he invited to follow him, but who were frightened by his requirements; and those who became his disciples, but later fell away. Among the last group is Judas Iscariot.[56]

*   *   *

Summarizing what we have said in the present chapter, we can confirm that the circle of Jesus' disciples and followers was a fairly large one. It included the twelve apostles, who were specially chosen and appointed to ministry, and also the seventy other apostles mentioned by Luke. Jesus also had secret disciples, of which two are known by name. Besides the male disciples, there were women among the followers of Jesus—some called by name, and others who have remained anonymous.

The apostles were necessary for Jesus; their task was to share in his labors, to listen to and to remember his teachings, and later to continue his work. It was they who constituted the nucleus of the Church, which Jesus established for all time.

The creation of the Church was the largest missionary project in the history of the human race. The twelve disciples could hardly have understood this at the time when Jesus chose them, when he instructed them

[54]In other words, rope is similar to thread, but too large to pass through the eye of a needle: an impossibility, but not an absurdity.—*Ed.*

[55]Georg Aicher, *Kamel und Nadelöhr: eine kritisch-exegetische Studie über Mt 19,24 und parallelen*, Neutestamentliche Abhandlungen Bd. 1 heft. 5 (Münster: Aschendorff, 1908), 16–21.

[56]His image and fate will be treated in the sixth volume of this series.

before sending them out to preach, or when he conversed with them, whether as a group all together or with some individual disciple apart. Their consciousness was confined to the patch of land on which Gospel history was unfolding. The idea that the main audience of their preaching was the house of Israel was something that they had heard many times from the Teacher himself.

The fact that his instruction to the disciples, which began with that idea, also contains the notion of the universal scope of the Christian mission, has been attributed by many scholars to the work of later redactors, who supposedly compiled the instruction from various fragments that existed in the oral and written tradition while taking into account the experience of the Christian Church in the second half of the first century. We, however, are of the opinion that the presence of both the one message and the other in the instruction to the disciples is evidence of the multilayered task that Jesus placed before them. Their preaching was to be spread at first within the small area of Judea and Galilee, but, in the long term, to embrace the whole universe.

Chapter 7

JESUS AND HIS OPPONENTS: The Beginning of the Conflict

T he conflict between Jesus and his opponents is a leitmotif of all four Gospels. This conflict arose shortly after Jesus went out to preach and only grew over the course of time. The denouement of the conflict came with the plot of the chief priests and elders against Jesus, his trial, and the pronouncement of his death sentence.

We will examine the core material relating to this conflict in the subsequent books of the series *Jesus Christ: His Life and Teaching*. In the second book, we will talk about Jesus' rebukes of the Pharisees in the Sermon of the Mount. In the third book, we will look at the Pharisees' reaction to the miracles that Jesus performed. In the fourth book, we will examine the passages in Jesus' parables dedicated to the Pharisees, and also their reaction to these parables. A significant part of the fifth book will be dedicated to analyzing the polemics between Jesus and the Jews, as reflected on the pages of the Gospel of John. Finally, in the sixth book, the subject will be the denouement of the conflict.

In the present chapter, we will only trace the general contours of this conflict and demonstrate, using several episodes as examples, how this conflict arose and the directions in which it began to develop.

1. Who
Opposed Jesus?

I n the Gospels we encounter different names for Jesus' opponents: "the scribes and the Pharisees," "the chief priests and the elders," "priests and Levites," "the chief priests and the elders and the scribes," "the Pharisees and the Sadducees," "the Pharisees and lawyers," "the Pharisees . . . with the Herodians." Among his opponents, eight categories of people are mentioned in total. What do we know about them?

The chief priests (*archiereis*). This term is encountered in the Gospels and the Acts of the Apostles forty-six times in the plural, most often paired with other categories ("the chief priests and the scribes," "the chief priests and Pharisees," "the chief priests and elders"). Although the incumbent high priest at the time of Jesus' public ministry was Caiaphas,[1] the latter's predecessor, Annas (who happened to be his father-in-law), was also still alive and actively participated in legal proceedings. The term "chief priests" in the plural, however, did not just refer to these two persons. It is more likely that the evangelists grouped under this term all the leading priests of the Temple, who, like the chief priests, possessed specific civil and legal powers, one of which was membership in the Sanhedrin.[2]

The priests and Levites (*hiereis kai Leuitas*). These are mentioned in the Gospels as two separate categories (Lk 10.31–32; Jn 1.19). While the number of persons that could be designated by the term "chief priests" did not exceed a few dozen, the number of priests and Levites, as has been said earlier, was in the thousands.

Those who were called Levites in Jesus' time were the lesser servers in the Temple, including readers, singers, musicians, acolytes, cleaners, and guards.

[1]Historical accounts about him beyond the New Testament are scarce. They are mainly confined to mentions in the works of Josephus. See Adele Reinhartz, *Caiaphas the High Priest*, Studies on Personalities of the New Testament, ed. Moody D. Smith (Minneapolis, MN: Fortress Press, 2013), 11–23.

[2]Joachim Jeremias, *Jerusalem in the Time of Jesus*, trans. F. H. Cave and C. H. Cave (London: SCM Press, 1991), 179.

In Israel, not only the priesthood itself, but the rank of priesthood, was also hereditary. All who served came from the tribe of Levi. While the high priest descended from Aaron, the other leading priests (or chief priests) descended from Zadok, the high priest during the reigns of the kings David and Solomon (2 Sam 20.25). Other priests and Levites descended from humbler members of the tribe of Levi and consequently could not aspire to higher positions in the hierarchy than those occupied by their own fathers (that is, their ancestors in the paternal line).

The elders, or rulers (archontes). This is a term that, as a rule, refers to members of the Jewish elite, who were influential in society. To this group belonged Nicodemus, "a ruler of the Jews" (*archōn tōn Ioudaiōn*), who came to Jesus by night (Jn 3.1). Rulers could be priests or laymen, could be part of the Sanhedrin, and could belong to the party of the Pharisees.

Aaron the High Priest, fresco, 14th c.

The Herodians (Hērōdianoi). These are mentioned in the Synoptic Gospels thrice, and always paired with the Pharisees (Mk 3.6; 12.13) or with the latter's disciples (Mt 22.16). In all likelihood, this term refers to persons serving in the court of Herod Antipas.[3]

The scribes (grammateis) and lawyers (nomikoi). These played an important role in the life of the people of Israel. These terms do not just refer to people who could read, as opposed to the illiterate majority. Scribes were the copyists and keepers of the holy books, and, in a wider sense, they were experts in the law to whom people would turn for clarification in matters of controversy. The term "lawyer" is often used in the Gospels as a synonym for the term "scribe." In Luke, the expression "Pharisees and

---

[3]John P. Meier, *A Marginal Jew: Rethinking the Historical Jesus*, vol. 3, *Companions and Competitors*, Anchor Bible Reference Library (New York, NY: Doubleday, 2001), 562.

The scribes and
the Pharisees
before Pilate,
miniature, 11th c.

lawyers" (Lk 7.30) is a synonym for the oft-used expression "scribes and
Pharisees" (which acts as a refrain in Mt 23).

In Palestine in Jesus' time there were several sects (parties), two of
which are mentioned in the Gospels: the Pharisees and the Sadducees.

The Pharisees (Pharisaioi). This term is thought to come from the Aramaic *prīšāyē*,[4] which means "set apart."[5] Little is known of the Pharisees

[4]The reconstructed pronunciation of what this might have sounded like during the time of
the gospel events is *parīšāyē*.

[5]Joseph A. Fitzmyer, *The Gospel According to Luke: Introduction, Translation, and Notes*, vol.
1, *I–IX*, Anchor Bible 28 (Garden City, NY: Doubleday, 1981), 581. The term *prīšāyā* ("Pharisee") is
not attested in the rabbinical literature, as demonstrated by reference to the following dictionaries: Marcus Jastrow, *A Dictionary of the Targumim, the Talmud Babli and Yerushalmi, and the
Midrashic Literature* (London: Luzac, 1903); Michael Sokoloff, *A Dictionary of Jewish Palestinian
Aramaic of the Byzantine Period*, Dictionaries of Talmud, Midrash and Targum 2 (Ramat-Gan:
Bar Ilan University Press, 1990); Michael Sokoloff, *A Dictionary of Jewish Babylonian Aramaic of
the Talmudic and Geonic Periods*, Dictionaries of Talmud, Midrash and Targum 3 (Ramat-Gan:
Bar Ilan University Press, 2002); and the Comprehensive Aramaic Lexicon Project at the Hebrew
Union College Jewish Institute of Religion, available online at http://cal1.cn.huc.edu/. The term
is encountered only in Christian texts—in Syrian texts (R. Payne Smith, *Thesaurus Syriacus*,
vol. 2 [Oxford: Clarendon, 1901], 3302) and Palestinian Aramaic texts (Friedrich Schulthess,
Lexicon Syropalaestinum [Berlin: G. Reimer, 1903]), where it is mostly likely a back translation
of *pharisaios* in the Gospels. In the rabbinical literature the Hebrew term *pārûš* is used (Jastrow,
Dictionary, 1222), with the same literal meaning: "set apart."

of Jesus' time.[6] The main source of evidence about this group besides the New Testament writings is in the works of Josephus, who writes, in part, the following:

> Now, for the Pharisees, they live meanly, and despise delicacies in diet; and they follow the conduct of reason; and what that prescribes to them as good for them they do; and they think they ought earnestly to strive to observe reason's dictates for practice. They also pay a respect to such as are in years; nor are they so bold as to contradict them in any thing which they have introduced; and when they determine that all things are done by fate, they do not take away the freedom from men of acting as they think fit; since their notion is, that it hath pleased God to make a temperament, whereby what he wills is done, but so that the will of man can act virtuously or viciously. They also believe that souls have an immortal rigor in them, and that under the earth there will be rewards or punishments, according as they have lived virtuously or viciously in this life; and the latter are to be detained in an everlasting prison, but that the former shall have power to revive and live again; on account of which doctrines they are able greatly to persuade the body of the people; and whatsoever they do about Divine worship, prayers, and sacrifices, they perform them according to their direction.[7]

The Sadducees (Saddoukaioi).[8] This term derives from the Hebrew *səḏûqîm*[9] or from the Aramaic *saḏūqāyē*.[10] This term is possibly linked to the name of the high priest Zadok. According to another account in the rabbinical tradition, the term "Sadducee" is linked to the name of another Zadok, the disciple of Antigonus of Sokho.[11]

---

[6]On the Pharisees, see Emil Schürer, *The History of the Jewish People in the Age of Jesus Christ (175 B.C.–A.D. 135)*, rev. English ed., vol. 2, rev. and ed. Geza Vermes, Fergus Millar, and Matthew Black (Edinburgh: T&T Clark, 1979), 388–403; Meier, *A Marginal Jew*, 3:289–388.

[7]Flavius Josephus, *Antiquities of the Jews* 18.1.3 (trans. Whiston).

[8]On the Sadducees, see Schürer, *The History of the Jewish People*, 2:404–414; Meier, *A Marginal Jew*, 3:389–487.

[9]The reconstructed pronunciation of what this might have sounded like during the time of the Gospel events is *saḏūqîm*.

[10]This is the reconstructed pronunciation (but this form is not attested in the rabbinical corpus).

[11]See Jastrow, *Dictionary*, 1261 (with references to rabbinical sources).

Christ and the Tribute Money, engraving, Gustave Doré, 1860s.

Concerning the Sadducees, Josephus notes that, according to their doctrine, "souls die with the bodies." The Sadducees, in Josephus' words, "do [not] regard the observation of any thing besides what the law enjoins them; for they think it an instance of virtue to dispute with those teachers of philosophy whom they frequent." The historian emphasizes that this doctrine "is received but by a few, yet by those still of the greatest dignity," but their influence is negligible: "when they become magistrates, as they are unwillingly and by force sometimes obliged to be, they addict themselves to the notions of the Pharisees, because the multitude would not otherwise bear them."[12]

[12]Josephus, *Antiquities of the Jews* 18.1.4 (trans. Whiston).

To the two philosophical schools mentioned in the Gospels, Josephus adds a third: that of the Essenes.[13] He describes them as a group consisting of men who lived in isolated communities, had their possessions in common, and did not marry: there were more than four thousand of them in total. The Essenes accepted the immortality of the soul and performed prayers outside of the Jerusalem Temple, since "they [did] not offer sacrifices because they [had] more pure lustrations of their own."[14] The existence of the Essenes was confirmed by the Qumran manuscripts, which were found in caves near the shore of the Dead Sea between 1947 and 1956. In the opinion of many scholars, these manuscripts, which contain excerpts from the Old Testament and original texts, belonged to the community of the Essenes. Certain scholars perceive a link between the Essenes and John the Baptist, but there is no documentary confirmation of this connection.

The teaching of the Essenes is not mentioned in the Gospels. As for the Pharisees and Sadducees, Jesus often entered into debates with them about some aspect or other of their teaching. Sometimes he acted as an arbitrator in disputes between representatives of different movements or schools within the party of the Pharisees. In his time, such disputes would occur particularly between the followers of Hillel and Shammai—two prominent rabbis among the Pharisees, each of whom founded his own school of interpretation of the Torah (the law of Moses).

In their interpretations, both rabbis took into account both written and oral sources, considering the latter no less important than the former, and recognizing the right of teachers of the law to interpret the law. However, both rabbis fundamentally differed over questions concerning how to apply the principles of the Torah in practice. Hillel (who was about sixty-five years older than Jesus) was quite liberal in his interpretation of the law: he allowed much which was not allowed by other teachers, particularly Shammai. The latter (who was younger than Hillel by only one generation) was distinguished by his significantly greater rigor and literalness in interpreting the Torah.

[13]Ibid. 18.1.2.
[14]Ibid. 18.1.5 (trans. Whiston).

Both teachers were still alive at the time of Jesus' birth: Hillel died when Jesus was a youth, while Shammai died around the time Jesus went out to preach. Some of Jesus' instructions on moral themes, especially those given in the Gospel of Matthew, are a direct reflection of the disputes over the interpretation of specific regulations in the law of Moses—disputes that were going on between the representatives of two schools in Jesus' time: the House of Hillel and the House of Shammai.

While one can fairly confidently speak of the Essenes as a religious movement, the groups of the Pharisees and the Sadducees combined the traits of a religious movement, a philosophical school, and a political party. The term "sect" is applied to these groups quite loosely (Gk. *haireseis,* which can be translated as "heresies," "sects," "movements," "schools," "parties" [see Acts 5.17, 15.5, 26.5]), used in relation to them and to the Essenes.[15] The ability of the Pharisees and Sadducees to collaborate with each other is confirmed by Josephus, as well as by the Gospels. The Essenes, on the contrary, were in opposition to both movements.

From the totality of extant sources we obtain the following image of the Pharisees:

> The Pharisees emerge then as an organized party of members committed to a particular understanding of Israel's Law, maintaining its practice themselves and advocating its adoption by others. Where rulers could be influenced, Pharisees lobbied for their views. Moreover, Pharisees were sufficiently schooled in the ways of the world to participate in councils and coalitions with rivals when the situation required it and common goals could be established. . . . In this respect they functioned as a "political interest group". . . . On the other hand, competition with rival groups was fierce and, fueled by the fervor of religious conviction, mutual denunciations were harsh.[16]

---

[15]Josephus calls the Essenes, together with the Pharisees and Sadducees, three different "philosophies." Ibid., 18.1.2.

[16]Joel B. Green, Scot McKnight, and I. Howard Marshall, eds., *Dictionary of Jesus and the Gospels,* 1st ed. (Downers Grove, IL: InterVarsity, 1992), 611.

To paint a faithful portrait of the party of the Sadducees is more difficult, since the opinion of scholars regarding this party's characteristic features is fundamentally divided, while there is too little information from extant sources. It is thought that there were far fewer Sadducees than Pharisees, but those who joined the former party were, by and large, members of the elite. Certain chief priests were Sadducees. In contrast to the Pharisees, the Sadducees did not have much influence on the people.[17]

2. The Beginning of Polemics with the Scribes and Pharisees

At the initial stage of the conflict between Jesus and his opponents, out of all the groups listed above, two groups were predominantly active: the scribes and the Pharisees. The other groups (the chief priests, elders, and Sadducees) would show up later. The scribes and Pharisees acted in tandem, and one can assume that many scribes belonged to the party of the Pharisees.

Can One Eat with Publicans and Sinners?

We do not know how the conflict between Jesus and the scribes and Pharisees began. The first episode in which the latter are active participants is mentioned in all three Synoptic Gospels. Here is the version of Mark:

> And as he passed by, he saw Levi the son of Alphaeus sitting at the receipt of custom, and said unto him, "Follow me." And he arose and followed him. And it came to pass, that, as Jesus sat at dinner in his house, many publicans and sinners sat also together with Jesus and his disciples; for there were many, and they followed him. And when the scribes and Pharisees saw him eat with publicans and sinners, they said

[17]Meier, *A Marginal Jew*, 3:392–399.

unto his disciples, "How is it that he eateth and drinketh with publicans and sinners?" When Jesus heard it, he saith unto them, "They that are whole have no need of the physician, but they that are sick. I came not to call the righteous, but sinners to repentance." (Mk 2.14–17)

As we have said, Matthew's version differs from Mark's in that Levi is called Matthew. Besides this, it does not mention the scribes (the only actors are the Pharisees), and the name of the host is not mentioned (although one could also suppose that the episode took place in Matthew's home). At the conclusion of the episode, Jesus adds: "But go ye and learn what this meaneth, 'I desire mercy, and not sacrifice'" (Mt 9.13; cf. Hos 6.6). Luke, who follows Mark in general, adds that Levi, in response to Jesus' call, "left all, rose up, and followed him." He also mentions that "Levi made him a great feast in his own house: and there was a great company of publicans and of others that sat down with them" (Lk 5.28–29).

This, then, is the Pharisees' first accusation of Jesus: why does he eat with publicans and sinners? In order to understand the meaning of this accusation, it must be said that, in the Old Testament, holiness and purity were understood first of all as being separate from all that is unclean and unholy.[18] The words "ye shall therefore be holy, for I *am* holy" (Lev 11.45) are interpreted by the sages of the Talmud in the following manner: "Just as I am holy, so are you holy. Just as I am separate, so you be separate."[19] The Pharisees considered themselves set apart from ordinary people and different from others (Lk 18.11). They made a special effort to observe ritual purity, guarded themselves against being defiled from touching anything unclean, and followed the strict observance of hygienic rules and the diet prescribed by the law of Moses. From this developed the code of laws of holiness on which the Pharisees constructed their piety.

---

[18]On the use of the words related to the root קָדֵשׁ (*qdš*—"to be holy") in the Old Testament, see G. Johannes Botterweck, Helmer Ringgren, and Heinz-Josef Fabry, eds., *Theological Dictionary of the Old Testament*, vol. 12, *pāsah—qûm*, trans. Douglas W. Stott (Grand Rapids, MI: Eerdmans, 2003), 521–543.

[19]*Sifra, Shemini* 12.3. Translation from: Jacob Neusner, *Sifra: An Analytical Translation*, vol. 2, *Sav, Shemini, Tazria, Negaim, Mesora, and Zabim* (Atlanta, GA: Scholars Press, 1988), 227.

The Pharisees were afraid most of all of being defiled—through touching something unclean, or through associating with people whom they considered unclean. Jesus, on the other hand, subverted the people of Israel's longstanding notion of uncleanness that had come down from the time of Moses; moreover, he did so consciously and consistently. In the Old Testament, the source of uncleanness was considered to be something external to a person, and a person was understood to be defiled if he or she touched something that was ritually unclean. Certain types of food were considered unclean: the list of these is contained in the book of Leviticus; if a person ate such food, he or she would be considered defiled.

Jesus, on the contrary, insisted that the cause for uncleanness must be sought not outside of a person, but inside a person. To the Pharisees Jesus said, "Woe unto you, scribes and Pharisees, hypocrites! For ye make clean the outside of the cup and of the platter, but within they are full of extortion and excess. . . . Woe unto you, scribes and Pharisees, hypocrites! For ye are like unto whitewashed sepulchers, which indeed appear beautiful outward, but within are full of dead men's bones, and of all uncleanness" (Mt 23.25, 27).

Can One Eat with Unwashed Hands?

Jesus' polemic with the Pharisees very often revolved around the idea of purity and holiness. Here is another characteristic episode:

> Then came together unto him the Pharisees, and certain of the scribes, who came from Jerusalem. And when they saw some of his disciples eat bread with defiled, that is to say, with unwashed, hands, they found fault. For the Pharisees, and all the Jews, except they wash their hands oft, eat not, holding the tradition of the elders. And when they come from the market, except they wash, they eat not. And many other things there be, which they have received to hold, such as the washing of cups, and pots, brazen vessels, and of tables. Then the Pharisees and scribes asked him, "Why walk not thy disciples according to the tradition of the elders, but eat bread with unwashed hands?" He answered and said unto them, "Well hath Isaiah prophesied of you hypocrites, as it is

written, 'This people honoureth me with their lips, but their heart is far from me. Howbeit in vain do they worship me, teaching for doctrines the commandments of men.'[20] For laying aside the commandment of God, ye hold the tradition of men, as the washing of pots and cups, and many other such like things ye do." And he said unto them, "Full well ye reject the commandment of God, that ye may keep your own tradition. For Moses said, 'Honour thy father and thy mother,'[21] and, 'Whoso curseth father or mother, let him die the death.'[22] But ye say, if a man shall say to his father or mother, 'It is Corban,'"—that is to say, a gift—"'by whatsoever thou mightest be profited by me,' he shall be free. And ye allow him to do nothing more for his father or his mother, making the word of God of no effect through your tradition, which ye have delivered. And many such things do ye." (Mk 7.1–13)

The washing of hands that is spoken of here was not only a hygienic requirement: in the first place, this custom of washing after visiting the market was motivated by the concern that one might have involuntarily come into contact with unclean people or unclean food. The washing of cups, pots, vessels, and tables was motivated by the same considerations. Instructions regarding this type of washing are contained in the Old Testament. In particular, in the book of Leviticus, it is prescribed that if a dead lizard, mole, or mouse falls into a vessel, one must put the vessel into water and leave it there until evening (Lev 11.32); a wooden vessel "that he who hath a discharge toucheth" also must be washed (Lev 15.12).

In the "tradition of the elders," a multitude of other prescriptions were added to the regulations of the law of Moses, transforming the religion of the Pharisees into the detailed, scrupulous observation of thousands of unwritten rules. At the same time, they found various loopholes that allowed them to avoid fulfilling the ordinances of the Mosaic law. Jesus gives one such example in his speech: when a son dedicated to God something that did not belong to himself, but something that he was supposed

---

[20]Is 29.13.
[21]Ex 20.12; Deut 5.16.
[22]Ex 21.17; Lev 20.9.

to have given to his parents, he considered himself free from any obligation to them.

"Whatever entereth a man from outside cannot defile him"

Jesus moves on from rebuking the Pharisees to instructing all the people. However, this instruction was not understood even by his disciples:

> And when he had called all the people unto him, he said unto them, "Hearken unto me every one of you, and understand. There is nothing from outside a man, that entering into him can defile him. But the things which come out of him, those are they that defile the man. If any man have ears to hear, let him hear." And when he was entered into the house from the people, his disciples asked him concerning the parable. And he saith unto them, "Are ye so without understanding also? Do ye not perceive, that whatever entereth a man from outside cannot defile him. Because it entereth not into his heart, but into the belly, and goeth out into the sewer, purging all foods?" And he said, "That which cometh out of the man, that defileth the man. For from within, out of the heart of men, proceed evil thoughts, adulteries, fornications, murders, thefts, covetousness, wickedness, deceit, lasciviousness, an evil eye, blasphemy, pride, foolishness. All these evil things come from within, and defile the man." (Mk 7.14–23)

In Matthew this same episode is presented in a condensed form (Mt 15.1–11). The words "goeth out into the sewer" (*eis ton aphedrōna ekporeuetai*)[23] are used to describe the natural process by which a body is purged. They show that Jesus disdained neither the human body nor its natural functions. He applied the term "uncleanness" not to the condition of the body, but to the condition of a person's soul, to that person's inner world, in which the source of every sin originates. It is sin that is uncleanness, and not illness or infection; it is not the sewer that is spiritually unclean, but the soul of a person, when it becomes like one.

---

[23]Other English translations similarly pass over the word for "sewer": other versions render this phrase as "is eliminated" (NKJV), "passes on" (RSV), or "is expelled" (ESV).—*Trans.*

Matthew adds a dialogue that is absent from Mark:

Then came his disciples, and said unto him, "Knowest thou that the
Pharisees were offended, after they heard this saying?" But he answered
and said, "Every plant, which my heavenly Father hath not planted, shall
be rooted up. Let them alone. They are blind leaders of the blind. And if
the blind lead the blind, both shall fall into the ditch." (Mt 15.12–14)

In Luke another episode is recorded, which corresponds in content but
not in the details. In his Gospel, Luke describes how "a certain Pharisee
asked [Jesus] to dine with him; and he went in, and sat down to dinner. And
when the Pharisee saw it, he marvelled that he had not first washed before
dinner." Jesus responds: "Now do ye Pharisees make clean the outside of
the cup and the platter, but your inward part is full of ravening and wickedness. Ye fools, did not he that made that which is outside make that which
is within also? But rather give alms of such things as ye have; and, behold,
all things are clean unto you" (Lk 11.37–41). And then he pronounces the
rebukes (Lk 11.42–54) that are close in content to what Jesus would say in
Jerusalem not long before his arrest, according to Matthew (Mt 23.2–28).

In opposition to the teaching of the Pharisees that holiness consisted
exclusively in observing external prescriptions (hygienic, dietary, and others), Jesus presents the teaching that holiness is a totality of inner qualities.
While being on the one hand deeply rooted in the Old Testament tradition, Jesus' instruction on the other hand essentially stood for a radical
break with the understanding of holiness that, on the basis of a distorted
interpretation of the Old Testament, took hold as the "tradition" of the
Pharisees and scribes. In the context of the Jewish tradition of his time as
expressed in the teaching of the Pharisees and scribes, Jesus' teaching was
revolutionary.

Can One Pluck Heads of Grain on the Sabbath?

The third episode relating to the initial stage of the conflict between Jesus and the Pharisees is also included in all three Synoptic Gospels. The fullest version of it is contained in Matthew:

> At that time Jesus went on the sabbath day through the grain; and his disciples were hungry, and began to pluck the ears of grain, and to eat. But when the Pharisees saw it, they said unto him, "Behold, thy disciples do that which is not lawful to do upon the sabbath day." But he said unto them, "Have ye not read what David did, when he was hungry, and they that were with him? How he entered into the house of God, and ate the showbread, which was not lawful for him to eat, neither for those who were with him, but only for the priests? Or have ye not read in the law, how on the sabbath days the priests in the temple profane the sabbath, and are blameless? But I say unto you, that in this place is one greater than the temple. But if ye had known what this meaneth, 'I desire mercy, and not sacrifice,' [Hos 6.6] ye would not have condemned the guiltless. For the Son of man is Lord even of the sabbath day. (Mt 12.1–8; cf. Mk 2.23–28; Lk 6.1–5)

This episode inaugurates the theme of the profanation of the Sabbath, which would recur in all four Gospels.[24]

The commandment to observe the Sabbath rest was one of the Ten Commandments of the law of Moses: "Remember the sabbath day, to keep it holy. Six days shalt thou labour, and do all thy work. But the seventh day is the sabbath of the Lord thy God; in it thou shalt not do any work" (Ex 20.8–10; cf. 31.13–17; Deut 5.12–15). In Israel this commandment, which is thrice repeated in the Pentateuch, was scrupulously observed. Over the centuries, the commandment became overgrown with various kinds of

---

[24]See John P. Meier, *A Marginal Jew: Rethinking the Historical Jesus*, vol. 4, *Law and Love*, Anchor Yale Bible Reference Library (New Haven, CT: Yale University Press, 2009), 235–341; Yong-Eui Yang, *Jesus and the Sabbath in Matthew's Gospel*, Journal for the Study of the New Testament Supplement series 139 (Sheffield: Sheffield Academic Press, 1997), 139–274; Phillip Sigal, *The Halakhah of Jesus of Nazareth According to the Gospel of Matthew*, Studies in Biblical Literature 18 (Atlanta, GA: Society of Biblical Literature, 2007), 145–186.

*The Disciples
Plucking Corn
on the Sabbath,*
engraving,
Gustave Doré,
1860s.

prescriptions relating to what one was allowed and not allowed to do on
the Sabbath. There were lists of things that were forbidden to be done
on the Sabbath, while at the same time different rabbis interpreted these
lists differently. There was the concept of a Sabbath day's journey (Acts
1.12), which referred to the maximum distance one could travel on the
Sabbath.

The Pharisees were perpetually condemning Jesus for profaning the
Sabbath. It was not to their liking that the disciples of Jesus, walking along
the road on the Sabbath, were plucking heads of grain and eating them.
It was not to their liking that, coming to the synagogue on Sabbath days,
Jesus performed miracles there (Mt 12.10–13; Mk 3.1–5; Lk 6.6–10; 14.1–6;
Jn 5.1–10). In the story of the healing of the woman who was bent over,
the ruler of the synagogue addresses the people with these words: "There
are six days in which men ought to work. In them therefore come and be
healed, and not on the sabbath day." At this, Jesus replies to him, "Thou

The Healing of the Man Born Blind, Vasily Khudoyarov, 1860s–1870s.

hypocrite, doth not each one of you on the sabbath loose his ox or his ass from the stall, and lead him away to watering? And ought not this woman, being a daughter of Abraham, whom Satan hath bound, lo, these eighteen years, be loosed from this bond on the sabbath day?" (Lk 13.14–16).

Jesus insisted that "it is lawful to do good on the sabbath days" (Mt 12.12). He maintained that "the sabbath was made for man, and not man for the sabbath" (Mk 2.27). Jesus' reaction to the Pharisees' demand that he refrain from healing on the Sabbath was emotional: this demand provoked his anger and sorrow (Mk 3.5). The Pharisees, too, reacted emotionally to Jesus' words and actions: his relaxed attitude to Sabbath norms led them into a rage (Lk 6.11).

Not all Pharisees reacted in the same negative way to the activity of Jesus that broke the Sabbath rest: sometimes, they were divided in their opinions. After Jesus healed the blind man on the Sabbath, "some of the Pharisees [said], 'This man is not of God, because he keepeth not the sabbath day.' Others said, 'How can a man that is a sinner do such miracles?' And there was a division among them" (Jn 9.16). However, Moses remained their main authority. Therefore, despite the obvious nature of the miracle that had taken place, they admonished the man who had been blind: "Thou art his disciple; but we are Moses' disciples. We know that God spake unto Moses: as for this fellow, we know not from whence he is" (Jn 9.28–29).

In the episode presented in the Synoptics, Jesus, responding to the Pharisees, refers to the story in 1 Samuel of how David asked the priest Ahimelech for bread, but the latter had nothing except the showbread (the bread of the presence): by giving David this bread, which was supposed to be eaten only by priests, Ahimelech broke the letter of the law (1 Sam 21.1–6). Jesus' words that "the priests in the temple profane the sabbath" most likely refer to the commandment regarding the Sabbath burnt offering (Num 28.9–10). In order to fulfill this commandment and bring two lambs for sacrifice, the priests had to break the Sabbath rest.[25]

Thus, from Jesus' point of view, in the law of Moses itself there were certain directives that were more important than others. He gives a similar argument in the dispute with the Jews recorded in the Gospel of John. There he refers to the custom of circumcising on the Sabbath: "Moses therefore gave unto you circumcision . . . and ye on the sabbath day circumcise a man. If a man on the sabbath day receive circumcision, that the law of Moses should not be broken, are ye angry at me, because I have made a man entirely whole on the sabbath day? Judge not according to the appearance, but judge righteous judgment" (Jn 7.22–24). The directive regarding circumcision, like the directive about offering the burnt sacrifice on the Sabbath, turns out to be higher than the commandment to rest on the Sabbath.

The dispute between Jesus and the Pharisees over interpreting the prescriptions of the law of Moses is reflected on the pages of all four Gospels, but it is more fully elaborated on by Matthew and John. A significant portion of the Sermon on the Mount is dedicated to the interpretation of the law (Mt 5.17–48). The last major rebuke that Jesus addressed to the Pharisees, which begins with the words, "The scribes and the Pharisees sit in Moses' seat" (Mt 23.2), is to a significant degree dedicated to the same theme.

---

[25]See Leon Morris, *The Gospel According to Matthew*, The Pillar New Testament Commentary (Grand Rapids, MI: Eerdmans; Leicester: Inter-Varsity Press, 1992), 302.

In his multiple dialogues with the Jews, which are given in the Gospel of John, Jesus returns again and again to the theme of the law of Moses, its significance, and its correct interpretation. John gives the following words of Jesus, among others: "Do not think that I will accuse you to the Father: there is one that accuseth you, Moses, in whom ye trust. For had ye believed Moses, ye would have believed me, for he wrote of me. But if ye believe not his writings, how shall ye believe my words?" (Jn 5.45–47).

These words, as well as many other things that Jesus said to the Pharisees, were a direct challenge to them. With each new episode and dialogue, their irritation increased.

* * *

The Jewish tradition did not take up Jesus' call to internal cleansing and, after his death and resurrection, continued to codify laws on the observance of ritual purity with even greater zeal. The Talmud, the Mishnah, and other monuments of rabbinical literature continued the development of a code of holiness in exactly the direction that Jesus sharply criticized.

Characteristic in this respect is the treatise of the Jewish philosopher and theologian of the second half of the twelfth century Maimonides (Moshe ben Maimon), *The Book of Holiness*,[26] which is the fifth volume of the fourteen-volume code of laws and prescriptions known under the general title *Mishneh Torah*.[27] Introducing *The Book of Holiness*, Maimonides writes: "I will include in it the Commandments Concerning Illicit Intercourse and the Commandments Concerning Forbidden Foods, for it is in these matters that the Omnipresent One has sanctified us and has separated us from the heathens."[28]

The treatise consists of three sections: laws on forbidden relations, laws on forbidden foods, and laws on the slaughtering of livestock. The first section includes thirty-seven commandments ("Not to have intercourse with one's mother," "Not to have intercourse with the wife of one's

---

[26]Hebrew *qədûšā*.

[27]Hebrew *mišnē tôrā*—literally, "Repetition of the Torah."

[28]Moses Maimonides, *The Code of Maimonides (Mishneh Torah)*, Bk. 5, *The Book of Holiness*, trans. Louis I. Rabinowitz and Philip Grossman, ed. Leon Nemoy, Yale Judaica Series 16 (New Haven, CT: Yale University Press, 1965), xix.

Statue of Maimonides
in Córdoba, Spain

father," "Not to cohabit with one's sister," "Not to lie with an animal," "Not to intermarry with heathens," etc.). In the second section there are twenty-eight commandments ("To examine the tokens of domesticated animals and wild beasts, in order to distinguish between clean and unclean," "Not to eat unclean domesticated animals or wild beasts," "Not to eat unclean birds," "Not to eat unclean fish," "Not to eat winged insects," etc.). The third section includes five commandments ("To eat meat only after šĕhitah [ritual slaughter] has been performed," "Not to perform šĕhitah on a dam and its young on the selfsame day," etc.).[29]

Each of the 70 commandments is interpreted with the help of 150 to 200 clarifying instructions, which contain detailed and graphic descriptions of possible ways to break these commandments, including various sexual perversions. At the same time, the presentation of many of these commandments is accompanied by a list of exceptional circumstances in which the commandments need not be observed. Here are only a few examples:

> There are other things which the Sages have forbidden, these prohibitions, although without root in the Torah, having been decreed by them in order to keep the people away from heathens. . . . If a heathen cooks figs, the rule is as follows: If they were sweet prior to cooking, they are permitted, but if they were bitter and became sweet through the cooking, they are forbidden. . . . Roasted lentils [cooked by a heathen], whether kneaded with water or with vinegar, are forbidden. Roasted wheat or barley, which is kneaded with water, is permitted. . . . In localities where the practice is to put wine into brine pickle, the latter is forbidden; but where wine is more expensive than brine pickle, it is permitted. . . . It is likewise forbidden to delay the normal evacuation

[29]Maimonides, *The Book of Holiness*, 3–4, 147–148, 257.

of one's large or small orifices, and he who does so is counted among those who make themselves abominable.[30]

Modern readers unfamiliar with this type of literature, which is difficult to understand for the public at large, often do not recognize the scale of the problem at all. They do not understand why Jesus, in rebuking the Pharisees, devoted such attention to awkward and peculiar customs, which hardly anyone remembers today (for example, the washing of cups, pots, vessels, and tables). Meanwhile, behind these customs stood an entire worldview, according to which true religion consisted of a person's ability to synchronize every single step with the sum of regulations known as the "tradition of the elders." Rabbis created rules for every situation in life—even down to how one was to answer the call of nature—and were convinced that observing these rules brought them closer to God.

It is this type of religiosity that Jesus criticized most sharply, accusing the Pharisees of "transgress[ing] the commandment of God" for the sake of their own tradition (Mt 15.3). And while in the cited treatise of Maimonides the "Laws Concerning Forbidden Foods" consists of more than a hundred pages, and forbidden foods are understood to be unclean foods that defile a person, Jesus, on the contrary, did not consider any food unclean at all, and through this resolved the topic of unclean foods for his followers once and for all.

In the book of Acts, the following incident is described: the apostle Peter wished to eat and, while the food was being prepared, he "fell into a trance" and saw a sheet, on which "were all manner of fourfooted beasts of the earth, and wild beasts, and creeping things, and fowls of the air." A voice from heaven said to him, "Rise, Peter; kill and eat." But Peter answered, "Not so, Lord; for I have never eaten any thing that is common or unclean." Then the voice proclaimed, "What God hath cleansed, call not thou common." This happened three times, after which the sheet went up to heaven (Acts 10.10–16).

This story is in full agreement with the worldview that Jesus brought to earth. At the same time, it testifies to the radical break of early Christianity

---

[30]Ibid., 250–255.

with the Jewish tradition. This break began with Jesus' preaching and continued in the Christian Church. The comparison of the monuments of
rabbinical literature, such as the abovementioned treatise of Maimonides,
to the New Testament and subsequent Christian literature shows how far
the Christian and Jewish traditions have diverged in their conception of
holiness. From the common root of the Old Testament, two different fruits
have emerged.

Attempts to reconcile these two understandings of holiness—the one
Jesus preached, and the one expressed by the scribes and Pharisees—cannot find success, in spite of the efforts of certain contemporary scholars to
present the conflicts between Jesus and his opponents as "family rows."[31]
Jesus' preaching in the synagogues met with complete rejection from the
religious leaders of the Jewish people (Lk 4.16–30), and this was entirely
expected. The very first generation of Christians had to decisively break
with the synagogue, because Jesus' teaching about perfection, which they
were striving to live out, did not fit in the narrow confines of the Jewish
tradition. As for the Jewish tradition itself, it continued along the same
trajectory on which it had been placed by Jesus' opponents—the scribes
and Pharisees of his time—and their followers.

---

[31]John Ashton, *Understanding the Fourth Gospel*, 2nd ed. (Oxford: Oxford University Press,
2007), 78–96.

Chapter 8

JESUS: HIS WAY OF LIFE AND CHARACTER TRAITS

T he Gospels are not full-fledged biographies of Jesus; they devote little attention to the everyday details of his life and to his character traits. Nevertheless, certain pieces of information scattered throughout the Gospel narratives allow us to put together a general picture of the kind of life Jesus led, and also to obtain some idea of the traits of his character.

This present chapter in no way claims to give a full portrait of Jesus. Such a portrait would emerge on the basis of the entire text of the Gospels; moreover, as we have said, each Gospel presents Jesus in its own way, examining his life and activity from its own characteristic perspective. We find the most information about the traits of Jesus' character in the story of the passion, which will be examined in the sixth volume of our study. It is in this story that Jesus is most fully revealed as a man, capable of being afraid, mourning, suffering, and experiencing physical pain and grievous spiritual torments.

In the present chapter we will only make a few sketches relating to Jesus' way of life and certain aspects of his personality. This is not a portrait, but "brushstrokes toward a portrait," meant to facilitate an understanding of the "historical Jesus" as he is presented on the pages of the Gospels.

1. Appearance

In the entire New Testament, there is not a single description of Jesus Christ's outward appearance, even though great significance was attached to this in classical literature.[1] Evidently, for the evangelists, Jesus' appearance was secondary in importance to his teaching and acts.[2]

However, as Christianity spread among the Gentiles, church writers began to wonder what Jesus looked like. The authors of the second and third centuries were of the opinion that "He was a man without comeliness,"[3] he "appeared without comeliness,"[4] and "had no form nor comeliness."[5] The idea that Jesus was unattractive is based on a literal reading of the prophecy of Isaiah: "he hath no form nor comeliness; and when we shall see him, there is no beauty that we should desire him. He is despised and rejected of men, a man of sorrows, and acquainted with grief, and we hid as it were our faces from him; he was despised, and we esteemed him not" (Is 53.2–3). Tertullian summed up the views of the early Christian authors regarding Jesus' appearance in his treatise, *On the Flesh of Christ*:

> Indeed it was from His words and actions only, from His teaching and miracles solely, that men, though amazed, owned Christ to be man. But if there had been in Him any new kind of flesh miraculously obtained . . . it would have been certainly well known. As the case stood, however, it was actually the ordinary condition of His earthly flesh which made all things else about Him wonderful, as when they said, "Whence

---

[1] In Greco-Roman culture the idea was widespread that there was an inextricable connection between a person's outward appearance, facial features, and physical build on the one hand, and that person's character on the other: the one could be discerned through the other. Even among the Qumran manuscripts, fragments of compositions about physiognomy have been found.

[2] In general, in the New Testament texts, descriptions of a person's appearance are rarely encountered and constitute the exception rather than the norm. Thus, for example, we are informed that Zacchaeus was short of stature (Lk 19.3), but only because this explains why he climbed the tree.

[3] Irenaeus of Lyons, *Against Heresies* 3.19.2 (*ANF* 1:449).

[4] Justin Martyr, *Dialogue with Trypho* 88 (*ANF* 1:244).

[5] Clement of Alexandria, *The Instructor* 3.1 (*ANF* 2:272).

Left: Christ,
Vasily Polenov,
1887.

Right: Christ,
Ilya Repin, 1884.

hath this man this wisdom and these mighty works?" [Cf. Mt 13.54.] Thus spake even they who despised His outward form. His body did not reach even to human beauty, to say nothing of heavenly glory. Had the prophets given us no information whatever concerning His ignoble appearance, His very sufferings and the very insult He endured bespeak it all. The sufferings attested His human flesh, the insult proved its abject condition.[6]

Later on, however, this idea was reconsidered, and already in the fourth century Jerome wrote that "the very splendor and majesty of his hidden divinity, which was even shining forth in his human face, was capable from the first glance of drawing those who looked toward it."[7] In the *Letter to the Emperor Theophilus*, attributed to John Damascene (eighth century), the appearance of Jesus is described thus: "of good stature, with meeting eyebrows, beautiful eyes, a prominent nose, curly hair, slightly bent, with a healthy complexion, black beard, His skin the colour of ripe corn like His mother's, long fingers, a melodious voice, pleasantly spoken, very gentle, calm, patient, forbearing."[8]

[6]Tertullian, *On the Flesh of Christ* 9.5–6 (*ANF* 3:530, modified).

[7]Jerome, *Commentary on the Gospel of Matthew* 1.9.9 (PL 26.56). Translation from: Jerome, *Commentary on Matthew*, trans. Thomas P. Scheck, The Fathers of the Church 117 (Washington, DC: Catholic University of America Press, 2008), 107.

[8](Pseudo-)Damascene, *Letter to the Emperor Theophilus* 3 (PG 95:349). The text does not belong to John of Damascus. Translation from: Joseph A. Munitiz, ed., *The Letter of the Three*

Jesus, mosaic, 11th c.

In the work of the late Byzantine author Nicephorus Callistus (fourteenth century) we find the following portrayal of Jesus:

> I shall describe the appearance of our Lord, as handed down to us from antiquity. He was very beautiful. His height was not less than seven spans. His hair was bright auburn, and not too thick, and was inclined to wave in soft curls. His eyebrows were black and arched, and His eyes seemed to shed from them a gentle golden light. They were very beautiful. His nose was prominent; His beard lovely but not very long.

He wore His hair, on the contrary, very long, where no scissors had ever touched it, nor any human hand, except that of His mother when she played with it in His childhood. He stooped a little, but His body was well formed. His complexion was that of the ripe wheat, and His face like His mother's, rather oval than round, with only a little red in it, but through it there shone dignity, intelligence of soul, gentleness, and a calmness of spirit never disturbed.[9]

In medieval Europe, the apocryphal *Letter of Lentulus*[10] received wide circulation. In it, the following is said about Jesus:

> ... a man of stature somewhat tall and comely, with a very reverend countenance, such as the beholders may both love and fear, his hair of the colour of a chestnut full ripe, and plain almost down to his ears, but from the ears downward somewhat curled, and more orient of colour waving about his shoulders. In the middest of his head goeth a seam or partition of his hair, after the manner of the Nazarites; his forehead

Patriarchs to Emperor Theophilus and Related Texts (Camberley, Surrey: Porphyrogenitus, 1997), 148.

[9]Nicephorus Callistus, *Ecclesiastical History* 1.40 (PG 145:748–749). Translation cited from quotation in Frank W. Gunsaulus, *The Man of Galilee: A Biographical Study of the Life of Christ* (Chicago, IL: Chas. B. Ayer Co., 1899), 171.

[10]This text became widely known as part of the popular *Vita Christi* (Life of Christ) written by the Carthusian Ludolph of Saxony (d. 1378).

very plain and smooth; his face without spot or wrinkle, beautified with a comely red; his nose and mouth so formed as nothing can be reprehended; his beard somewhat thick, agreeable in colour to the hair of his head not of any great length, but forked in the midst; of an innocent look; his eyes gray, clear, and quick. In reproving he is severe, in admonishing courteous, and fair-spoken, pleasant in speech mixed with gravity. It cannot be remembered that any have seen him laugh, but many have seen him weep: in proportion of his body well shaped and straight, his hands and arms very delectable to behold; in speaking, very temperate, modest, and wise. A man for his singular beauty surpassing the children of men.[11]

While the early Christian idea of the unattractive appearance of Jesus was based on a literal reading of the prophecy of Isaiah, the later ideas that Jesus possessed a beautiful and attractive appearance most likely drew upon the iconographic tradition.

This tradition itself, however, did not just stem from human fantasy. As we have pointed out elsewhere,[12] the emergence of iconographic depictions of the countenance of Jesus Christ in large numbers dates to the fifth and sixth centuries. It is to this period that the story of the discovery of the image of Jesus Christ "Not Made by Hands" belongs, which may be identified with the sheet known today as the Shroud of Turin.

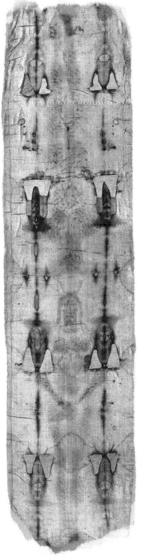

The Shroud of Turin

[11]Translation cited, with changes to capitalization only, from Pseudo-Lentulus, *Publius Lentulus his report to the Senate of Rome concerning Jesus Christ* (London, 1677), printed for Francis Smith at the Elephant and Castle near the Royal Exchange in Cornhil.

[12]See Metropolitan Hilarion Alfeyev, *Orthodox Christianity*, vol. 3, *The Architecture, Icons, and Music of the Orthodox Church*, trans. Andrei Tepper (Yonkers, NY: St Vladimir's Seminary Press, 2014), 127–134.

Left: Negative of the image on the Shroud of Turin

Right: The icon of the Savior "Not Made by Hands," icon, 12th c.

On the shroud is the imprint of the figure of a middle-aged man, about 170 centimeters (5 feet and 7 inches) tall, with a face oblong in shape, long hair parted in the middle, and a mustache and beard. This is how Jesus is depicted in the majority of canonical icons. The many traces of blood left on the shroud are evidence that it was wrapped around a person who had been subjected to flogging, and then crucified on a cross.

There is no unified opinion among scholars regarding how the image appeared on the shroud. Some think that it appeared as a result of the evaporation of vapor from the body of the dead man; others think that it was a consequence of radioactive emissions; yet others think that it appeared due to exposure to sunlight. Whatever the case may be, examinations of the shroud have shown that there is no trace of paint on it—but there were no other methods of creating pictorial images, other than with the help of pigments, in antiquity or in the Middle Ages. Therefore, the shroud, in any case, is not a depiction made by human hands.

The abovementioned textual testimonies about the appearance of Jesus are beyond the scope of the canonical text of the four Gospels, which are for us the main source of information about his life and teaching. As for the Shroud of Turin, if one accepts its authenticity, it becomes the central source of evidence for what Jesus looked like and what sufferings he underwent before his death. It is not incidental that those who believe in the authenticity of the shroud call it the "fifth Gospel."

2. Distances

Accords to the Gospels, Jesus and his disciples were almost constantly on the road. They went from city to city and from village to village, covering significant distances on foot. The expression "a day's journey," which is used in both the Old and New Testaments (Gen 30.36; Ex 3.18; 8.27; Num 10.33; Lk 2.44), refers to a distance of about twenty to forty kilometers (twelve to twenty-five miles); this distance could be longer or shorter based on a person's physical condition, height, and sex; the end point of the journey; and speed. In all likelihood, Jesus and his disciples traveled fairly quickly when they had to go from one city to another. Within a city or a village, naturally, they moved more slowly.

The distances between Galilean cities are not very substantial by modern standards. For example, the distance between Nazareth and Capernaum is only fifty kilometers (thirty-one miles): one could cover this distance at a brisk pace within one day.

More substantial was the distance between Galilee and Judea: depending on the point of departure and the destination, it could be from 100 to 200 or more kilometers (62 to 124 miles). The distance from Jerusalem to Nazareth today is 130 to 150 kilometers (81 to 93 miles). Taking into consideration road conditions in the first century, one can assume that in those times the journey from Jerusalem to Nazareth would take several days. With rest stops, it could take several weeks.

On certain days, at least, Jesus and his disciples had to cover distances beyond the standard length of "a day's journey." For example, on the day after his meeting with John the Forerunner on the banks of the Jordan, Jesus "wanted to go forth into Galilee" (Jn 1.43). He finds Philip, and Philip finds Nathanael, who was in Bethsaida of Galilee (Jn 1.43–44). The meeting of Jesus and Nathanael (Jn 1.47–51) takes place somewhere along the way from Judea to Galilee. On "the third day" Jesus, with several of his disciples, are already present at the wedding in Cana of Galilee (Jn 2.1), which stood 150 to 200 kilometers (93 to 124 miles) from the place where we presume the Forerunner was baptizing. The text does not indicate in relation to which event this day was the third: to the day of Jesus' last meeting with the Forerunner, or to the day his meeting with Nathanael took place. In the first case, Jesus would have had to have covered the distance from Bethabara to Cana within two incomplete days, which is not very realistic. In the second case, he would have had three full, or not quite four, days to cover this distance, which is realistic, but still assumes a long journey over the course of each day.

Jesus spent most of his time in Galilee. However the Gospel of John notes several of Jesus' journeys of Jesus to Jerusalem—on the feasts of Passover, Tabernacles, and the Restoration of the Temple. Besides Jerusalem, he occasionally also traveled to other cities and regions beyond the borders of Galilee. In particular, he visited Bethsaida, which was a part of the tetrarchy of Philip, but which was located so close to Galilee that it was treated as part of the latter.[13] Jesus visited the area beyond the Jordan (Mt 19.1; Mk 10.1), the region of Caesarea Philippi (Mt 16.13; Mk 8.27), and the "coasts of Tyre and Sidon" (Mt 15.21; cf. Mk 7.24).

At the same time, he went at least once from the coasts of Tyre and Sidon to the Sea of Galilee not directly, but through the Decapolis (Mk 7.31). Such a route seems to many scholars to be improbable (its trajectory is akin to journeying from New York to Washington, DC via Cleveland, although, of course, the distance was much smaller). However, Jesus was not at all obliged to choose the shortest path from one point to another. In the given instance, he could have set out on the long route in order to cover predominantly Gentile regions as he preached.[14]

The term "Decapolis" referred to the region east of the Jordan, where there were ten cities marked by the strong influence of Greek and Roman culture. One of these cities, Gadara, gave its name to the region of the Gadarenes (Mk 5.1; Lk 8.26, 36). In Matthew, this region is called the country of the Gergesenes (Mt 8.28).

---

[13]Mark A. Chancey, *The Myth of a Gentile Galilee*, Society for New Testament Studies Monograph Series 118 (Cambridge: Cambridge University Press, 2004), 177.

[14]Gerd Theissen, *The Gospels in Context: Social and Political History in the Synoptic Tradition*, trans. Linda M. Maloney (Minneapolis, MN: Fortress, 1991), 243–245.

As has already been said, Jesus occasionally was in Samaria, but only on the way from Galilee to Jerusalem and back.

In order to travel constantly on foot, including over long distances, one had to be in good physical condition. We have every reason to believe that both Jesus and his disciples were physically fit. In contrast to our contemporaries, most of whom have to participate in sports in order to maintain their health, the contemporaries of Jesus did not need to do so: their way of life itself was sufficiently healthy and athletic. The fresh air and simple food that most of the population of Palestine partook of also had a beneficial effect.

Jesus chose the way of life of an itinerant preacher. His words about how "foxes have holes, and the birds of the air have nests; but the Son of Man hath nowhere to lay his head" (Mt 8.20) can be understood as a generic reference to this way of life. But they can also be understood as informing us quite concretely that Jesus did not have a home—neither in Capernaum, where these words were pronounced, nor in any other place. Commenting on the account of how Jesus sent the disciples into the city to prepare the Passover meal in the Synoptics (Mt 26.17–19; Mk 14.12–16; Lk 22.7–13), John Chrysostom notes: "So even from this it is manifest, that He had no house, no place of sojourning."[15]

On the earth, the Son of God was homeless. When he was born, while he was yet an Infant, there was no place found for him at the inn (Lk 2.7). He was driven out from his hometown of Nazareth (Lk 4.29). Sometimes he would stay with his disciples—not only for "honoring them and making them more zealous,"[16] but more likely precisely because he had nowhere else to lay his head. This wandering, homeless way of life was for him a matter of conscious choice, and not simply a consequence of the confluence of circumstances.

It was the home of Peter in Capernaum that became a sort of staging post where Jesus would stop when returning to Capernaum from his journeys. There were at least four people living in this house: Peter, his wife, his mother-in-law, and his brother Andrew (Mk 1.29–30). It is possible that

---

[15]John Chrysostom, *Homilies on the Gospel of Matthew* 81.1 (*NPNF*[1] 10:485).
[16]Ibid., 27.1 (*NPNF*[1] 10:184).

other relatives were living there as well, such as Peter's parents or children (if he had any). As a rule, houses were not divided into rooms: all lived in one common room, in plain view of each other. Chrysostom says: "And yet consider of what sort were the houses of these fishermen; but for all that, He disdained not to enter into their mean huts."[17]

It should be noted that, according to the Gospel of John, Peter and Andrew were from Bethsaida (Jn 1.43). It is possible that they were originally from Bethsaida, while their home was located in Capernaum.

Travelling from city to city, Jesus made short stops to rest. In these instances, weary from the road, he could sit down and send the disciples into the city to buy food (Jn 4.6–8).

3. Diet

What did Jesus and his disciples eat? Their diet must have been extremely simple; the most common foodstuff formed its basis: bread, fish, water, wine. Bread and fish are mentioned multiple times in the Gospels as the primary food of Jesus' disciples: their very profession suggests that they mainly ate fish. At the Last Supper, Jesus gives the disciples bread and wine, and even after his resurrection he breaks bread with them (Lk 24.30) and partakes of a meal consisting of bread and fish (Jn 21.13).

However, the diet of Jesus and his disciples was evidently not always restricted to the most simple foodstuffs. Jesus accepted invitations to dinner from people in various social positions: this is mentioned more than once in the Gospels. We see him reclining in the home of the publican Matthew (Mk 2.15), in the home of Simon the leper (Mt 26.6–7; Mk 14.3), in the home of Simon the Pharisee (Lk 7.36–40), in the home of "one of the chief Pharisees" (Lk 14.1), and in the home of Lazarus (Jn 12.1–2). These dinner parties involved the presence of various kinds of dishes and a large number of guests. Concerning the meal in the home of Matthew Levi, the

---

[17]Ibid., 27.1 (*NPNF*[1] 10:184–185).

evangelist Luke makes it clear that the host made for Jesus "a great feast in his house, and there was a large company of tax collectors and others reclining at table with them" (Lk 5.29, ESV).

The verb "recline" (*katakeimai*), which is often used in the Gospels in the description of these meals, refers to the widespread custom in the Greco-Roman world of eating while half-reclined on special couches (or bedding) placed around a low dining table.

In his way of life, Jesus greatly differed from John the Baptist. While the latter lived in the desert and the people came to him, Jesus himself traveled to the cities and villages, preaching on the streets, in synagogues, and in private homes. While John was distinguished by his singular asceticism, to which the evangelists devote special attention (Mt 3.4; Mk 1.6), nothing similar is said of Jesus in the Gospels. Jesus himself contrasted his own way of life with that of the Baptist: "For John the Baptist came neither eating bread nor drinking wine, and ye say, 'He hath a demon.' The Son of Man is come eating and drinking, and ye say, 'Behold a gluttonous man, and a drunkard, a friend of publicans and sinners!'" (Lk 7.33–34).

The difference between the community of Jesus' disciples and that of John the Baptist's was that Jesus' disciples did not observe the longstanding Jewish tradition of fasting. Did Jesus himself observe it? And what was his attitude towards fasting?

As we recall, before going out to preach, Jesus fasted for forty days and forty nights (Mt 4.2): Matthew uses here the same phrasing that is used in the Old Testament concerning Moses. Luke simply says that over forty days Jesus "ate nothing" (Lk 4.2).

On the other hand, the disciples of John the Baptist and those of the Pharisees accused Jesus' disciples of not observing the fasts:

> The disciples of John and of the Pharisees were fasting. Then they came and said to Him, "Why do the disciples of John and of the Pharisees fast, but Your disciples do not fast?" And Jesus said to them, "Can the friends of the bridegroom fast while the bridegroom is with them? As long as they have the bridegroom with them they cannot fast. But the days will come when the bridegroom will be taken away from them,

The healing of the demon-possessed boy, miniature, 11th c.

and then they will fast in those days. No one sews a piece of unshrunk cloth on an old garment; or else the new piece pulls away from the old, and the tear is made worse. And no one puts new wine into old wineskins; or else the new wine bursts the wineskins, the wine is spilled, and the wineskins are ruined. But new wine must be put into new wineskins." (Mk 2.18–22, NKJV)

From this episode, which is also given in the other two Synoptics (Mt 9.14–17; Lk 5.33–39), it is only clear that Jesus' disciples did not fast: nothing is said about Jesus himself. John's disciples are perplexed because of the behavior of Jesus' disciples, and not that of Jesus himself.[18] In Jesus' answer (in Matthew this answer is given in a somewhat different form: "Can the children of the bridechamber mourn, as long as the bridegroom is with them?" [Mt 9.15]), Jesus also does not say anything about himself, but only about his disciples in the third person. We cannot exclude the possibility that his practice differed from that of his disciples, and that at least on certain days, when he withdrew from them, he fasted. However, this is nothing more than a guess, unsupported by any texts in the New

[18]Gary Yamasaki, *John the Baptist in Life and Death: Audience-Oriented Criticism of Matthew's Narrative*, Journal for the Study of the New Testament Supplement Series 167 (Sheffield: Sheffield Academic Press, 1998), 104.

Testament. From the Gospels we learn only that he would sometimes leave his disciples in order to spend time in solitary prayer.

Indirect evidence that Jesus' fasting practice could have differed from the practice of his disciples is found in the story of Jesus' healing of the demon-possessed boy. After the miracle took place, "the disciples [came] to Jesus apart, and said, 'Why could we not cast him out?' And Jesus said unto them, 'Because of your unbelief. For truly I say unto you, if ye have faith as a grain of mustard seed, ye shall say unto this mountain, "Remove hence to yonder place," and it shall remove. And nothing shall be impossible unto you. Howbeit this kind goeth not out but by prayer and fasting'" (Mt 17.19–21).[19] Jesus names unbelief as the main reason for the disciples' inability to cast out the demon. But he adds that the specific kind of demon is driven out only with the help of prayer and fasting.

Jesus' answer to the question of John's disciples contains two important points. The first relates to the period after his death: "when the bridegroom will be taken away from them." The second point is expressed in the images of the piece of new cloth sewn onto an old garment and of the new wine poured into old wineskins. This image relates not only to the Jewish practice of fasting: in a broad sense, it relates to the entire Jewish religious tradition, the most vigorous exponents of which were the scribes and Pharisees. Jesus' point can be interpreted in the following way: the wine of the New Testament cannot be poured into the wineskin of the Old Testament rules and regulations; the outward forms of piety stemming from the observation of the law of Moses are incapable of accommodating the spirit of Jesus' teaching, which is distinguished by its radical originality and requires new forms of religious practice.

The wineskins here refer to bags made of animal skin, in which one would store wine. We have multiple attestations in the Gospels that wine was a part of the diet of Jesus and his disciples. Besides the words cited above, where he himself speaks of this, the main piece of evidence for this

[19]Critical editions of the text omit the last verse (v.21). The corresponding passage in Mark contains these words (Mk 9.29), although critical editions omit "and fasting." The fuller form of the verse is used liturgically in the Orthodox Church (the Markan passage is read on the Sunday of St John Climacus in Great Lent, where the word "fasting" is significant, given the liturgical season).—*Ed.*

is the Last Supper, at which Jesus "took the cup, and when he had given thanks, he gave it to them, and they all drank of it. And he said unto them, 'This is my blood of the new testament, which is shed for many. Truly I say unto you, I will drink no more of the fruit of the vine, until that day that I drink it new in the kingdom of God'" (Mk 14.23–25; cf. Mt 26.27–29; Lk 22.17–18, 20). Wine—weak and usually diluted with water—was the main beverage in Palestine during the time of Jesus.

The speculation put forth at various times that Jesus observed a special diet or, for example, did not eat meat,[20] does not find any support in the Gospels. If Jesus did not eat meat, he would not have taken part in the Passover meal, at which the main dish was a lamb roasted over a fire with bitter herbs (Ex 12.5–8).

4. Celibacy

Jesus was not married. This is clear from the Gospel narratives, where among his relatives are mentioned his Mother, brothers, and sisters, but nothing is ever said about a wife or children. Any speculations that Jesus could have had a wife or children are not only rejected without fail by the Church, but also not taken seriously by the scholarly community.[21] If Jesus had been married and had had offspring, this would undoubtedly

---

[20]This opinion was probably held in antiquity by members of the sect of the Ebionites. See Epiphanius of Salamis, *Panarion* 30.15 (GCS 25:352–353). According to Epiphanius, the Ebionites did not eat meat, and he refers moreover to the example described in the *Travels* of the apostle Peter, an apocryphal text that was accepted as sacred by the Ebionites (according to Epiphanius, the Ebionites introduced a series of distortions to the apocryphal text as well).

[21]Such speculations are found, for example, in Dan Brown's novel, *The Da Vinci Code* (2003). In 2012, Professor Karen L. King of Harvard Divinity School announced the discovery of a text that was called "the Gospel of Jesus' wife" by the media. This was a small papyrus fragment, which is written in Coptic and supposedly dates to the fourth century, and which contains a sentence fragment: "Jesus said to them: My wife . . ." Later in the text it says: ". . . she is able to be my disciple." This fragment is supposedly part of an early apocryphal work (it demonstrates some similarity to the *Gospel of Thomas*). It is possible that it reflects the opinion of one of the sects that broke away from the Church in the second or third century. However, the fragment is too incomplete to allow us to judge the content of the text (for example, the full text could

have been mentioned in the Gospels, or in the Acts of the Apostles, or in other historical sources: a wife and children cannot simply disappear and go completely unnoticed.

Was Jesus' celibacy the result of a conscious choice? To this question he gives a fairly unambiguous answer in a discussion with his disciples. The starting point of the conversation was Jesus' words about marital infidelity. The disciples react with perplexity: "If the case of the man be so with his wife, it is not good to marry." Instead of developing the theme of the spousal relationship further, Jesus takes up the disciples' remark and says something that must have been greatly unexpected to them: "All cannot receive this saying, save those to whom it is given. For there are some eunuchs, which were so born from their mother's womb; and there are some eunuchs, which were made eunuchs by men; and there are eunuchs, which have made themselves eunuchs for the kingdom of heaven's sake. He that is able to receive it, let him receive it" (Mt 19.10–12).

The context of what Jesus says clearly demonstrates that he is speaking here about celibacy as a conscious choice, which he himself has made and which he is offering to those who are "able to receive it." More than once Jesus offers his listeners not one, but several moral options, which correspond to different levels of spiritual maturity and different degrees of readiness to respond to his call to perfection. The story of the rich young man is an example of this: one moral code is sufficient for having eternal life, and another, more radical code is offered for the attainment of perfection. Jesus did not demand from Zacchaeus complete renunciation of earthly riches, although he does consider this a sign of perfection. In the same way, he does not demand celibacy of his disciples, but speaks of celibacy as a particular way of life accessible only to those who are "able to receive it." He offers as the absolute moral ideal the way of life that he himself was able to receive.

Jesus' words about voluntary celibacy must have astonished his contemporaries and compatriots, as these words went against Old Testament

include the words, "My wife is the Church," or something along those lines). [Further investigation indicates the fragment is likely a forgery. See Ariel Sabar, "The Unbelievable Tale of Jesus's Wife," *The Atlantic*, July–August, 2016.—*Ed.*]

morality. In the Old Testament, the blessing of God was expressed first of all by his giving a man a good wife and many offspring. Having children was understood as the primary way for a man to achieve self-fulfillment and as the main calling of a woman. What did the covenant that God made with Abraham consist of? How was the special blessing that God gave to the progenitor of the Jewish nation made manifest? In God's promise to him to make of him a great nation (Gen 12.2; 17.2–7) and that his descendants would be as numerous as the grains of sand on the earth (Gen 13.16). And suddenly Jesus calls people to reject the very thing in which, according to the Holy Scriptures, their highest calling and meaning are expressed—the continuation of their family line. However, this call is by no means addressed to all, but only to those who wish to imitate Jesus in everything, including voluntary celibacy.

According to the teaching of the Church, Jesus was a virgin. In ascetic and monastic literature he is presented as the absolute ideal of virginity and chastity. Methodius of Olympus wrote about Christ in the third century: "He preserved the flesh which He had taken upon Him incorrupt in virginity. . . . the Word, when He was incarnate, became chief Virgin."[22] St Jerome wrote in the fourth century: "Christ Himself is a virgin; and His mother is also a virgin; yea, though she is His mother, she is a virgin still."[23] John Damascene wrote in the eighth century: "Christ Himself is the glory of virginity, who was not only-begotten of the Father without beginning or emission or connection, but also became man in our image, being made flesh for our sakes of the Virgin without [conjugal] connection, and manifesting in Himself the true and perfect virginity." At the same time he notes that Christ "did not enjoin [virginity] on us by law," that is, he did not make virginity compulsory for his followers, but "in actual fact He taught us that and gave us strength for it."[24]

Despite the obvious fact that Jesus was unmarried, he lacked any aversion toward marriage, familial relations, and things related to them. He did not refuse the invitation to the wedding feast (Jn 2.1–2), addressed

[22]Methodius of Olympus, *The Banquet of the Ten Virgins* 1.5 (*ANF* 6:313).
[23]Jerome, *Letters* 48.21 (*NPNF²* 6:78).
[24]John of Damascus, *An Exact Exposition of the Orthodox Faith* 4.24 (*NPNF²* 9:97b).

the topic of familial relations in his sermons (Mt 5.31–32), blessed children (Mt 19.13–15; Mk 10.13–16), and visited the homes of his disciples and followers (Mt 8.14–15; Lk 2.15; 19.6–17). At the same time he always emphasized that faithfulness to him and his mission was more important than any family and parental relationships (Mt 10.37; 19.27–29).

St John Chrysostom, mosaic, late 9th c.

Jesus' words concerning eunuchs for the sake of the kingdom of heaven were subsequently interpreted in various ways. According to Eusebius of Caesarea, Origen understood these words in a literal sense and castrated himself in his youth.[25] However, this piece of information is disputed by a range of modern scholars as being unreliable.[26] Origen himself[27] and subsequent Christian exegetes firmly opposed a literal understanding of Jesus' words about eunuchs for the sake of the kingdom of heaven. John Chrysostom, in particular, calls self-castration a transgression, a diabolical deed, and the deceit of Satan, since he understands Jesus' words about eunuchs for the sake of the kingdom of heaven in an exclusively spiritual sense—as praise of virginity and celibacy.[28]

In the early Christian Church, celibacy and virginity were highly regarded. The ideal of virginity was already preached in the apostolic era by Paul (1 Cor 7.1, 7, 25–26). Nevertheless, the other apostles, as far as we can tell, were married.

Concerning the marital status of the apostles, in the Gospels we have only the mention that Peter had a mother-in-law and, by extension, a wife. At the same time, the Gospels contain a dialogue between Jesus and Peter, in which the latter asks, "Behold, we have forsaken all, and followed thee;

[25]Eusebius of Caesarea, *Ecclesiastical History* 6.8.1–2 (*NPNF*[2] 1:254).

[26]An overview can be found in Bryan Litfin, "Origen," in *Shapers of Christian Orthodoxy: Engaging with Early and Medieval Theologians*, ed. Bradley G. Green (Downers Grove, IL: InterVarsity, 2010), 115.

[27]Origen, *Commentary on the Gospel of Matthew* 15.1–5 (PG 13:1253–1265).

[28]John Chrysostom, *Homilies on the Gospel of Matthew* 62.3 (*NPNF*[1] 10:384).

what shall we have therefore?" Jesus replies, "Everyone that hath forsaken houses, or brethren, or sisters, or father, or mother, or wife, or children, or lands, for my name's sake, shall receive a hundredfold, and shall inherit everlasting life" (Mt 19.27–29).

If we understand the words "forsaken all" and Jesus' reply literally, then it follows that the apostles left their families, including their wives and possibly their children, when they went to follow Jesus. This supposition, however, is refuted by the words of the apostle Paul, written around AD 56: "Have we not power to lead about a sister, a wife, as well as other apostles, and as the brethren of the Lord, and Cephas?" (1 Cor 9.5). Here it is clearly indicated that the apostles, including Peter, remained married two decades after Jesus' death and resurrection.

Nevertheless, celibacy, not without the influence of Paul, gained more and more adherents in the early Christian Church. In the second century, Justin Martyr testified that in his community "many, both men and women, who have been Christ's disciples from childhood, remain pure at the age of sixty or seventy years."[29]

Many church writers, including Methodius of Olympus, whom we cited earlier, composed treatises in defense of virginity. However, celibacy was never established as the norm, and the Church sharply argued against the sects and movements that propagandized the abhorrence of marriage. Around the year 340, the Council of Gangra issued an entire series of canons against those who practiced virginity based on an abhorrence of marriage. The first canon of this council reads: "If any one shall condemn marriage, or abominate and condemn a woman who is a believer and devout, and sleeps with her own husband, as though she could not enter the Kingdom [of heaven] let him be anathema."[30] The ninth canon says: "Whoever preserves virginity not on account of its beauty but because he abhors marriage, let him be anathema."[31] Finally, in the tenth canon we read: "If any one of those who are living a virgin life for the Lord's sake shall treat arrogantly the married, let

---

[29]Justin Martyr, *First Apology* 15 (*ANF* 1:167).
[30]*Canons of the Council of Gangra* 1 (*NPNF*² 14:92).
[31]Ibid., 9 (*NPNF*² 14:95).

him be anathema."[32] These canons appeared as the Church's response to the teaching of Eustathius, the bishop of Sebastia, who, according to the church historian Socrates Scholasticus, had "done many things repugnant to the ecclesiastical canons. For he had 'forbidden marriage,' and maintained that meats were to be abstained from: he even separated many from their wives."[33]

In rejecting the temptation of excessive asceticism while encouraging the practice of virginity for all who are "able to receive it," the Church strictly follows the teaching of Jesus. Celibacy never became and cannot become the norm for Christians. Nevertheless, in the community of Jesus' followers, beginning with the apostle Paul, there have always been persons able to "receive" such a way of life. Communities of Christians who voluntarily chose to not enter into marriage constituted the foundation of the monastic movement in the fourth century; from that time, this movement has played a significant role in the history of the Church. Up to the present day, in the Orthodox Church, all bishops are chosen from the ranks of celibates and monastics, while in the Latin rite of the Catholic tradition the requirement of celibacy extends to priests as well.

5. Character Traits

A close examination of Jesus' human traits is important not only from a historical point of view, but also from a theological perspective. Our starting position is the conviction that Jesus is God and that all his human traits are organically linked to his divine nature.

It is difficult—if not impossible—to paint a psychological portrait of Jesus, to put together an idea of the traits of his character and of the peculiarities of his human personality, on the basis of disparate mentions in

---

[32]Ibid., 10 (*NPNF*[2] 14:96).
[33]Socrates Scholasticus, *Ecclesiastical History* 2.43 (*NPNF*[2] 2:72).

the Gospels of his emotional experiences or of his reactions to the behavior of those around him. Many authors, both ancient and modern, have attempted to paint such a portrait and give a characterization of Jesus as a personality. Here are just a few examples:

> Our Instructor is like His Father God, whose son He is, sinless, blameless, and with a soul devoid of passion; God in the form of man, stainless, the minister of His Father's will. . . . He is to us a spotless image; to Him we are to try with all our might to assimilate our souls. He is wholly free from human passions; wherefore also He alone is judge, because He alone is sinless. As far, however, as we can, let us try to sin as little as possible.[34]

> [T]hough called "demoniac" and "madman," by men who had received from Him ten thousand benefits, and that not once or twice but many times, not only did He refrain from avenging Himself, but even ceased not to benefit them. To benefit, do I say? He laid down His life for them, and while being crucified spake in their behalf to His Father. This then let us also imitate, for to be a disciple of Christ, is the being gentle and kind.[35]

> In all those natures which were not purified until they had gone through struggles and violent disruption (think only of a Paul, an Augustin, and a Luther), the shadowy colours of this exist for ever, and something harsh, severe, and gloomy, clings to them all their lives; but of this in Jesus no trace is found. Jesus appears as a beautiful nature from the first, which had only to develop itself out of itself, to become more clearly conscious of itself, ever firmer in itself, but not to change and begin a new life.[36]

> Now in Jesus Christ. . . . [t]he image of God has entered our midst, in the form of our fallen life, in the likeness of sinful flesh. In the teaching and

---

[34]Clement of Alexandria, *The Instructor* 1.2 (*ANF* 2:209–210).

[35]John Chrysostom, *Homilies on the Gospel of John* 60.4 (*NPNF*[1] 14:219).

[36]David Friedrich Strauss, *The Life of Jesus for the People*, authorized trans., 2nd ed., vol. 1 (London: Williams and Norgate, 1879), 282–283. First published in German as *Das Leben Jesu* in 1835–1836.

Image of the Savior on the Sudarium, icon, 13th c.

acts of Christ, in his life and death, the image of God is revealed. . . . it is the image of one who enters a world of sin and death, who takes upon himself all the sorrows of humanity, who meekly bears God's wrath and judgment against sinners, and obeys his will with unswerving devotion in suffering and death, the Man born to poverty, the friend of publicans and sinners, the Man of sorrows, rejected of man and forsaken of God. Here is God made man, here is man in the new image of God.[37]

First of all, we are struck by the exceptional integrity and harmony of the personality and character of the Savior. . . . It is worth noting the astonishing, impeccable purity of his moral character, his ideal humility and meekness, his inexhaustible longsuffering, his indomitable courage, and the integral resoluteness of his religious will. . . . The character of Christ is comprehensive and universal, common to humanity, and is

[37]Dietrich Bonhoeffer, *The Cost of Discipleship*, 1st Touchstone ed. (New York, NY: Touchstone, 1995), 300–301. First published in German as *Nachfolge* in 1937.

the moral ideal for all times and all peoples. This character is unparalleled in the strength of its grace-filled influence on the historical life of humankind. Christ is the prototype and prefiguration of all that is perfect; the rays of his most perfect personality are reflected in the great saints, but all of these saints are like starts in comparison to the sun.[38]

The evangelists paint Christ as profoundly human. On His eyes were seen tears; He was seen to mourn, to be amazed, to rejoice, to embrace children, to admire flowers. His very speech breathes forbearance for the weaknesses of man, but He never slackened His requirements. He could speak with tender goodness and could be strict, even sharp. Occasionally bitter irony flickered in His words. . . . Usually mild and patient, Jesus was merciless to hypocrites; he expelled merchants from the temple, shamed Herod Antipas and lawyers, reproached His disciples for lack of faith. He was peaceful and constrained, but was sometimes seized by holy wrath. Nonetheless He was a stranger to internal discord. Christ always remained Himself. . . . Being in the thick of mortal life, it was as if at the same time He was in another world, in solitude with the Father. Those close to Him saw in Him a Man Who desired only one thing, "to do the will of Him Who sent [Him]."

Christ was far from morbid exaltation, from the frantic fanaticism characteristic of many zealots and founders of religions. An illuminating sobriety was one of the chief traits of His character. When He spoke about unusual things, when He called people to difficult deeds and bravery, He did it without false pathos and strain. He could converse simply with people at the well or at the holiday meal, and He could pronounce words that shook everyone—"I am the Bread of life." He spoke of trials and struggle, and He carried light everywhere, blessing and transforming life.[39]

---

[38]I. M. Andreyev, *Pravoslavno-khristianskaya apologetika. Kratkoe konspektivnoe izlozhenie kursa lektsiy, chitannykh v Svyato-Troitskoy dukhovnoy seminarii* [Orthodox-Christian apologetics. A summary of a course of lectures, presented in the Theological Seminary of the Holy Trinity, Jordanville, NY] (Jordanville, NY: Holy Trinity Monastery, 1965), 81.

[39]Alexander Men, *Son of Man*, trans. Samuel Brown (Torrance, CA: Oakwood Publications, 1998), 50–51.

Jesus was a very dynamic man, a man who valued life in all its dimensions. . . . Jesus is a rabbi who has the purity of spirit necessary to have a proper grasp of reality while maintaining the right distance from it. . . . His words often show that he has observed people and things; his observations are full of color, of exaggerated imagery, of paradoxes and insightful humor.[40]

Christ, mosaic in the Church of the Savior on Blood, Mikhail Nesterov, 1897.

We have intentionally selected quotations from the works of authors belonging to various periods and various cultures and worldviews: a church writer from third-century Alexandria, a fourth-century Church father from Antioch, a German rationalist theologian of the nineteenth century, an outstanding German Lutheran theologian and pastor who died in a Nazi concentration camp, Russian Orthodox apologists of the twentieth century—a layman and a priest, and a contemporary Catholic expert on the New Testament. Each of them reveals the image of Jesus in his own way, and each of the given characterizations contains its own grain of truth. While the early church writers emphasized Jesus' divine nature, his obedience to the will of the Father, and his sinlessness and passionlessness, humility and meekness, in modern times, the emphasis is shifted to those human qualities of his that bear witness to a harmonious personality, lacking any internal division whatsoever, a personality compelling and unique, living in full unity with God.

We will not comment here on these characterizations or try to paint our own psychological portrait of Jesus. We will only point out certain passages in the Gospels that allow readers to create such a portrait for themselves.

[40]Armand Puig i Tàrrech, *Jesus: A Biography*, 316–317.

Emotional Disposition

Was Jesus emotional? What do the Gospels tell us about his human character and his reactions to the behavior of those around him?

In the Synoptic Gospels, all mentions of Jesus' moods or emotions are connected either to accounts of miracles, or to the narrative of the passion. In the Gospel of John, Jesus also displays emotions either before performing a miracle (one clear example is the story of the raising of Lazarus), or in connection with the suffering and death that awaited him. However, in John's account of the passion of Christ, the emotional element is reduced to a minimum.[41]

The list of expressions referring to Jesus' emotional reactions to situations includes the following: "marveled" (Mt 8.10; 7.9), "was moved with compassion" (Mt 9.36; 14.14; Mk 6.34; Lk 7.13), "had compassion" (Mt 20.34; Mk 1.41), "sternly charged" (Mk 1.43), "looked round about on them with anger" (Mk 3.5), "sighed" (Mk 7.34), "sighed deeply" (Mk 8.12), "rejoiced in spirit" (Lk 10.21), "groaned in the spirit, and was troubled" (Jn 11.33), "wept" (Jn 11.35), "was troubled in spirit" (Jn 13.21). The verb "loved" (Mk 10.21, also Jn 11.5), when it expresses Jesus' attitude to specific people, also has an emotional overtone.

The evangelists' brief mentions of Jesus' emotional states are evidence that he was a living man who had access to the entire scale of human emotional experiences—from sorrow to joy, from anger to compassion. At the same time, as one scholar notes, "At precisely the point where Jesus' emotions appear to be the most human, they turn out to be paradoxically divine."[42]

Surprise

Jesus was capable of being surprised. This is demonstrated by Matthew and Luke's account of the healing of the centurion's servant. The words of

---

[41]See Stephen Voorwinde, *Jesus' Emotions in the Fourth Gospel: Human or Divine?*, Journal for the Study of the New Testament Supplement Series 284 (London, T&T Clark, 2005), 48–49, 82.

[42]Ibid., 64.

the centurion surprised Jesus (Mt 8.10; Lk 7.9). Surprise is the natural reaction of a person to something unexpected. While being God, Jesus preserved all his human capabilities; while possessing the power to raise the dead and heal diseases, including at a distance, Jesus was still surprised by the simple words of a person who had come to him with a request. While having the ability to penetrate into the thoughts of a person (Mt 9.4; 12.25; 16.7–8; Mk 2.8; Lk 5.22; 6.8; 9.47; 11.17; Jn 21.38), Jesus nevertheless did not anticipate everything that a person could say to him.

But surprise can be connected not only with positive impressions: there is also surprise that is connected with disappointment. Describing Jesus' visit to his home town and his interaction with its inhabitants, the evangelist notes that "he marveled because of their unbelief"—so much so that "he could there do no mighty work, save that he laid his hands upon a few sick folk, and healed them" (Mk 6.5–6).

Compassion and Sympathy

The feeling of compassion and sympathy was natural to Jesus. Matthew mentions how, "when [Jesus] saw the multitudes, he was moved with compassion on them, because they fainted, and were scattered abroad, as sheep having no shepherd" (Mt 9.36). In another instance, Jesus healed the sick when he "saw a great multitude, and was moved with compassion toward them" (Mt 14.14). Since he "had compassion on" two blind men, Jesus healed them (Mt 20.34). Jesus healed a leper, being "moved with compassion" (Mk 1.41). The miracle of the feeding of the four thousand with seven loaves and a few fishes is preceded by Jesus' words to his disciples: "I have compassion on the multitude, because they continue with me now three days, and have nothing to eat, and I will not send them away fasting, lest they faint in the way" (Mt 15.32).

Joy

There is the opinion that Jesus "always maintained a serious expression on his face," and that he "never smiled, but often wept."[43] This constantly repeated opinion is based on the words of John Chrysostom, who was discussing not laughter in general, but immoderate laughter:

> And this indeed one may often see Him do [i.e., weep], but nowhere laugh, nay, nor smile but a little; no one at least of the evangelists hath mentioned this. . . . And these things I say, not to suppress all laughter, but to take away dissipation of mind. For wherefore, I pray thee, art thou luxurious and dissolute, while thou art still liable to such heavy charges, and are to stand at a fearful judgment-seat, and to give a strict account of all that hath been done here?[44]

Indeed, Jesus' tears are mentioned in the Gospels, but never his laughter. However, *argumentum ex silentio*[45] cannot always serve as a reliable proof of some assertion or other. The Gospels do not contain a single story on whose basis one could suppose that Jesus ever laughed, but several episodes do testify that in his life there were moments when he rejoiced.

In particular, the Gospel of Luke tells of how the seventy disciples returned from the task that Jesus had sent them to carry out. The noun "joy" and the verb "rejoice" are used multiple times in this text, which we have cited before:

> And the seventy returned again with *joy*, saying, "Lord, even the demons are subject unto us through thy name." And he said unto them, "I beheld Satan as lightning fall from heaven. Behold, I give unto you power to tread on serpents and scorpions, and over all the power of the enemy, and nothing shall by any means hurt you. Notwithstanding in this *rejoice* not, that the spirits are subject unto you; but rather *rejoice*,

---

[43]Boris Gladkov, *Tolkovanie Evangeliya* [Commentary on the Gospels] (Sergiev Posad: Troitske-Sergieva Lavra, 2014), 218.

[44]John Chrysostom, *Homilies on the Gospel of Matthew* 6.8–9 (*NPNF*[1] 10:41).

[45]An argument from silence.

because your names are written in heaven." In that hour Jesus *rejoiced* in spirit . . . (Lk 10.17–21, emphasis added).

In this scene, Jesus' joy is a response to the joy of the returning disciples. We see how keenly Jesus is aware of his unity with his disciples, and how much he takes their joys and sorrows to heart. At the same time, at his conversation with the disciples, the Father is present, whom he addresses as if his presence is just as obvious to the other participants in the conversation. We see a similar situation in Jesus' final discourse with his disciples at the Last Supper. There, much would also be said about joy (Jn 16.19–23), and Jesus also interrupts the conversation with his disciples in order to raise up a prayer to the Father (Jn 17.1).

How did the evangelist find out that Jesus "rejoiced in spirit" when he heard about his disciples' success? There is only one way to know someone's mood: by the expression of that person's face, by his or her eyes, by a smile. The above account confirms not only that Jesus was capable of rejoicing, but also that this joy was noticeable to others.

A smile is, of course, not a laugh. We really have no evidence that Jesus ever laughed. But there is no report whatsoever that he "always maintained a serious expression on his face." Did he consider laughter a vice? At least once, in the Sermon on the Plain, he mentioned laughter as a reward: "Blessed are ye that weep now, for ye shall laugh" (Lk 6.21). On the other hand, in the same sermon, he said, "Woe unto you that laugh now! For ye shall mourn and weep" (Lk 6.25). The whole context of the sermon allows us to say that laughter as such was not the focus of Jesus' attention in the given sayings, and if in the second saying laughter is condemned, then it is not condemned in itself, but as one of the characteristic features of a life lived according to the laws of this world, along with wealth and satiety.

Sense of Humor

Did Jesus have a sense of humor? Of course—if by humor we mean not only humorous stories and jokes, but, primarily, a person's ability to notice comical aspects in other people or his surroundings. Jokes and humorous stories are not found in the Gospels: in this, the Gospels differ from many other literary works of the ancient world (including rabbinical literature, which is full of humorous stories and witticisms). As for the ability to notice the comical aspects in the reality around him, Jesus certainly possessed this ability. Here is a characteristic example:

> But unto what shall I liken this generation? It is like children sitting in the markets, and calling unto their fellows, and saying, "We have piped unto you, and ye have not danced. We have mourned unto you, and ye have not lamented." For John came neither eating nor drinking, and they say, "He hath a demon." The Son of Man came eating and drinking, and they say, "Behold a man gluttonous, and a winebibber, a friend of publicans and sinners." But wisdom is justified by her children. (Mt 11.16–19)

Here the entire situation is laced with subtle humor: the image of the children playing on the street, the way Jesus succinctly and dryly sums up the accusations of his opponents, and the proverb that concludes his retort. We do not know the tone in which it was pronounced—denunciatory or condescending; we do not know what the expression on Jesus' face was. But to deny that he had a sense of humor—in this case, even with a hint of satire—is impossible.

Here is one more exhortation, addressed to the disciples:

> Consider the ravens: for they neither sow nor reap; which neither have storehouse nor barn; and God feedeth them. How much more are ye better than the fowls? And which of you by taking thought can add to his stature one cubit? . . . Consider the lilies how they grow: they toil not, they spin not; and yet I say unto you, that Solomon in all his glory was not arrayed like one of these. (Lk 12.24–25, 27)

Here one can also hear hints of humor, at least in how Jesus speaks about obvious things: it is impossible to increase one's height by a special effort; lilies do not labor or spin; all the splendor of Solomon cannot be compared with a simple flower of the field.

One of the miracles performed by Jesus reminds one more of a joke than of the full-fledged accounts of miracles that fill all four Gospels. Matthew tells of how collectors of the temple tax come to Peter and ask him, "Doth not your master pay tribute?" (Mt 17.24). Peter gives a positive answer, but, judging by the rest of the story, he does not have the money and is expecting Jesus to do something. When they enter the house, Jesus asks him, "What thinkest thou, Simon? Of whom do the kings of the earth take custom or tribute? of their own children, or of strangers?" Peter answers, "Of strangers." Jesus says to him, "Then are the children free. Notwithstanding, lest we should offend them, go thou to the sea, and cast a hook, and take up the fish that first cometh up; and when thou hast opened his mouth, thou shalt find a piece of money. That take, and give unto them for me and thee" (Mt 17.24–27). What is this—a joke or a miracle? By the way, Matthew says nothing about whether this miracle actually took place. That is implied, but not made explicit.

Elements of humor are encountered in Jesus' parables. In particular, the protagonist of the parable of the unjust steward is a crook who suggests to his master's debtors that they doctor the receipts, reducing the amount of their debt by fifty or twenty percent. This grotesque figure is used to illustrate the idea that "the children of this world are in their generation wiser than the children of light" (Lk 16.1–8).

Jesus' rebuke of the Pharisees is not devoid of humor. Granted, here it is more appropriate to speak of bitter irony. Jesus speaks ironically about the Pharisees when he describes how they stand on street corners and pray so that others can notice them (Mt 6.5); how they "disfigure their faces, that they may appear unto men to fast" (Mt 6.16); how "all their works they do to be seen by men. They make broad their phylacteries, and enlarge the borders of their garments, and love the uppermost rooms at feasts, and the chief seats in the synagogues, and greetings in the markets, and to be called by men, 'Rabbi, Rabbi'" (Mt 23.5–7).[46]

Powers of Observation

As a man, Jesus was observant. He was able to notice things that were happening around him, and paid attention to the details of people's behavior.

---

[46] About Jesus' sense of humor, see also Puig i Tàrrech, *Jesus*, 316.

While he was a guest at the house of one of the rulers of the synagogue, Jesus noticed how those invited were choosing the most honored places. His exhortation is not devoid of humor:

> When thou art invited by any man to a wedding, sit not down in the highest place, lest a more honorable man than thou be invited by him, and he that invited thee and him come and say to thee, "Give this man place," and thou begin with shame to take the lowest room. But when thou art invited, go and sit down in the lowest room, that when he that invited thee cometh, he may say unto thee, "Friend, go up higher." Then shalt thou have honor in the presence of them that sit at dinner with thee. (Lk 14.8–10)

In the Temple of Jerusalem, Jesus sat opposite the treasury and saw how the people put money in it. The two coins placed in the treasury by the poor widow did not escape his notice (Mk 12.41–44; Lk 21.1–14).

Anger

Was Jesus capable of being angry? It seems that a positive answer is obvious from a whole series of accounts. The anger of Jesus was called forth by the Jews' constant reproaches for his breaking the Sabbath. In one such episode, when Jesus was visiting a synagogue, where among those present was a man with a paralyzed hand, people were watching him specifically to see if he would heal on the Sabbath. Knowing that people wanted to accuse him, he called the sick man into their midst and asked, "Is it lawful to do good on the sabbath days, or to do evil? To save life, or to kill?" Nobody answered. Then, "when he had looked round about on them with anger, being grieved for the hardness of their hearts, he saith unto the man, 'Stretch forth thine hand'" (Mk 3.4–5). He stretched out his hand—and it was healed. Here Jesus' anger is expressed in his look.

In the parallel narratives in Matthew and Luke (Mt 12.9–13; Lk 6.6–10) there is no mention of anger: it is possible that these two evangelists considered it inappropriate to apply the term "anger" to Jesus. Certain commentators also consider it inappropriate to speak of anger in relation to Jesus Christ, the Savior of the world:

> The words of the evangelist, "with anger," give some reason to suppose that Jesus became angry at the scribes and Pharisees. But was this the case? How was his anger expressed? The evangelist says that Jesus' anger was expressed only by a look; but he adds that in this look there was grief for the hardness of heart of the Pharisees and scribes. And can there possibly be anger where there is grief? These feelings do not go with each other; they are of different spirits. . . . At Jesus' conversation with the Pharisees and scribes, his disciples, of course, burned with anger at them; indeed, it was impossible for a normal person to look upon their obstinacy calmly. That is why the disciples, who were themselves looking on in anger at the enemies of their Teacher, and seeing the grieved, yet stern, face of Jesus, could take the stern expression on his face to be one of anger, thinking in a human way that even he could not help but be angry. This was their impression, this was their assumption; but Jesus' grief and the lack of any external manifestation of his anger compel us to acknowledge that in this case, as always, he was a stranger to this emotion, which was condemned by him.[47]

This interpretation is a typical example of how an entirely sincere and pious desire to imagine Jesus as being absolutely above reproach with respect to spiritual, moral matters, and absolutely uninvolved in any sort of human passion at all, compels the author to read into the lines of the Gospel narrative (or more precisely, between the lines) something that does not exist in them. The evangelist Mark speaks of Jesus' anger, which is expressed in his look. This is the testimony of an eyewitness, or information based on such a testimony. Everything else is an interpretation of this testimony. Some may think that the very concept of anger cannot be applied to the God-Man Christ, but, in any case, the author of one of the four canonical Gospels did not think that. If we wish to come close to the image of the "historical Jesus," the most reliable method is to keep as

---

[47]Gladkov, *Tolkovanie Evangeliya* [Commentary on the Gospels], 218. [English translation by present translator.—*Trans.*]

"Savior of the Fiery Eye,"
icon, 14th c.

close as possible to the text of the Gospels and not attempt to read between the lines something that contradicts what is said in the text.[48]

In all four Gospels we find the story of Jesus driving out traders from the Temple. Here is Mark's version:

> And they come to Jerusalem, and Jesus went into the temple, and began to cast out them that sold and bought in the temple, and overthrew the tables of the moneychangers, and the seats of them that sold doves, and would not suffer that any man should carry *any* vessel through the temple. And he taught, saying unto them, "Is it not written, 'My house shall be called by all nations the house of prayer?' [Is 56.7; Jer 7.11] but ye have made it a den of thieves." (Mk 11.15–17; cf. Mt 21.12–13; Lk 19.45–46)

Narrating a similar event, John notes: "And his disciples remembered that it was written, 'The zeal of thine house hath eaten me up'" (Jn 2.17). Here a text from the Psalter is applied to Jesus (Ps 68.10). In this case, the term "zeal" (also translated elsewhere as "jealousy") has a religious meaning, but in its emotional content it is close to the concept of anger. The scene itself is described such that it is difficult to imagine Jesus acting calmly and in cold blood: what is being described is more likely an outburst of anger motivated by deep spiritual perturbation.

---

[48]If it is necessary to look for an apology for Jesus' anger, this can be found in the teaching of the Church Fathers about righteous, controlled, and timely anger, and also about anger against the devil. See Gregory of Nazianzus, *Against Anger* (PG 37:813–851)—about righteous and controlled anger; John Chrysostom, *Homilies on the Gospel of Matthew* 16.9 (PG 57:248) (English translation: *NPNF*[1] 10:110)—about timely anger; Basil the Great, *Homily 10: Against Those Who Are Prone to Anger* (PG 31:368–369) (English translation in *Saint Basil: Ascetical Works*, by Basil the Great, trans. Monica Wagner, The Fathers of the Church 9 [Washington, DC: Catholic University of America Press, 1962], 447–462)—about anger against the devil.

Meekness and Humility

In Jesus, the ability to show anger and zeal is coupled with meekness and humility. He says about himself: "Come unto me, all ye that labour and are heavy laden, and I will give you rest. Take my yoke upon you, and learn of me; for I am meek and lowly in heart, and ye shall find rest unto your souls. For my yoke is easy, and my burden is light" (Mt 11.28–30). Isolated flashes of anger apparently did not destroy the deep inner peace that Jesus possessed at all times due to his being of one nature with God. This peace flowed out from him to those around him.

Humility (poverty of spirit) and meekness are the two human qualities with which the Beatitudes begin (Mt 5.3, 5). In them, just as in the Sermon on the Mount as a whole, Jesus paints a self-portrait. He does not simply declare the importance of some quality or other: he himself possesses these qualities. His humility and meekness were displayed in full strength in how he conducted himself in the last days and hours of his life: at the trial before the chief priests and Pilate, and at Golgotha.

Tears, Agitation, Grief, Sorrow

Jesus' tears are mentioned in the Gospel of Luke and the Gospel of John. Luke tells of how Jesus wept when he foretold the destruction of Jerusalem:

> And when he was come near, he beheld the city, and wept over it, saying, "If thou hadst known, even thou, at least in this thy day, the things which belong unto thy peace! But now they are hid from thine eyes. For the days shall come upon thee, that thine enemies shall cast a trench about thee, and compass thee round, and keep thee in on every side, and shall lay thee even with the ground, and thy children within thee, and they shall not leave in thee one stone upon another, because thou knewest not the time of thy visitation." (Lk 19.41–44)

In the story of the raising of Lazarus, as described by John, we see the whole range of Jesus' emotional experiences, which are noticeable to those around him:

Then when Mary was come where Jesus was, and saw him, she fell down at his feet, saying unto him, "Lord, if thou hadst been here, my brother would not have died." When Jesus therefore saw her weeping, and the Jews also weeping which came with her, he groaned in the spirit, and was troubled, and said, "Where have ye laid him?" They said unto him, "Lord, come and see." Jesus wept. Then said the Jews, "Behold how he loved him!" And some of them said, "Could not this man, who opened the eyes of the blind, have caused that even this man should not have died?" Jesus therefore again groaning in himself cometh to the grave. (Jn 11.32–38)

This is undoubtedly one of the most emotionally charged scenes from the entirety of the Gospels. In the variety of the emotional experiences recorded in it, it is comparable only to the Synoptics' accounts of Jesus' prayer in the garden of Gethsemane and of his crucifixion. We see how Jesus reacts to the weeping of others: he "groaned in the spirit, and was troubled" (*enebrimēsato tō pneumati kai etaraxen heauton*). We see what emotions he experiences when he is asked to go and see the tomb where Lazarus was laid: he "wept," and even those around him were surprised at the depth of his love for the dead man. Coming to the tomb, he "again [groaned] in himself," which was undoubtedly expressed in his face and eyes. The evangelists are usually very sparing in conveying emotions, both those of Jesus and also of other persons. However, in this case, John, who is likely the eyewitness of this scene, describes it vividly and in detail, paying particular attention to the emotional experiences peculiar to Jesus as a human being.

The verb "to trouble" (*tarassō*), which in the passive voice means "to be agitated," "to be upset," "to be in great perplexity," indicates a very intense state of emotional distress. This verb is used in the Gospel of John to convey Jesus' emotional state two more times.

Speaking with the Jews six days before his last Passover and foretelling his death, Jesus unexpectedly interrupts the conversation with the words: "Now is my soul troubled [*tetaraktai*]; and what shall I say? 'Father, save me from this hour'; but for this cause came I unto this hour. Father, glorify thy name." At this moment a voice resounds from heaven: "I have both glorified it, and will glorify it again" (Jn 12.27–28). Jesus does not conceal from his disciples or the people his fear in the face of death and his inner agitation. However, he overcomes it, turning to the Father in prayer and receiving encouragement from the Father.

In another instance, the expression "troubled in spirit" appears in the evangelist's narrative voice, when he records Jesus' prediction of Judas' betrayal: "When Jesus had thus said, he was troubled in spirit [*etarachthē tō pneumati*], and testified, and said, 'Truly, truly, I say unto you, that one of you shall betray me'" (Jn 13.21).

In this way, three times over the course of a comparatively short extract from the Fourth Gospel, in three chapters in a row—John 11, 12, and 13— the same word "troubled" appears, which indicates Jesus' emotional state in the last days before his arrest. John 14 begins with the word "troubled," this time used by Jesus to refer to his disciples: "Let not your heart be troubled [*tarassesthō*]" (Jn 14.1). While being deeply troubled himself, he calls his disciples not to be troubled, but to strengthen their hearts with faith in God and faith in him.

All three Synoptic Gospels describe the prayer in the garden of Gethsemane. According to their accounts, before his arrest, Jesus came to Gethsemane and left his disciples there, saying to them, "Sit ye here, while I go and pray over there." After this, taking Peter, John, and James with himself, he "began to be sorrowful and very heavy" (according to Mark and Luke, "to be exceedingly amazed, and to be very heavy"). He said to the three disciples with him: "My soul is exceeding sorrowful, even unto death; tarry ye here, and watch with me." Going away a short distance from them (according to Luke, a stone's throw away), Jesus prayed to the Father that, if it were possible, the cup of suffering should pass from him (Mt 26.36–42; Mk 14.32–39; Lk 22.39–42). As he was praying, "his sweat was as it were great drops of blood falling down to the ground" (Lk 22.44).

At this time, we will not be commenting in detail on this scene, which will be the subject of our particular examination in the sixth book of the series *Jesus Christ: His Life and Teaching* (dedicated to the death and resurrection of Jesus). We will only point out the whole range of words that the evangelists use to convey Jesus' emotional state before his arrest: sorrowful, heavy, amazed (i.e., in horror). His soul is "sorrowful, even unto death." He prays to the point of sweating blood.

This account is one of the Gospel texts that the Church used to refute the opinion of the Docetists—heretics who asserted that Jesus' sufferings were only apparent,[49] since, being the passionless God, he could not be subject to passion (the Greek word *pathos* means both "passion" and "suffering"). The idea of the illusory character of Christ's sufferings supposedly already appeared in the first generation of Christians: the realism with which John, in his Gospel, describes the human emotional experiences of Jesus can be connected with the polemic against this idea. All the major early Christian authors, including Ignatius of Antioch, Irenaeus of Lyons, Hippolytus of Rome, and Tertullian, pursued this polemic.

The main significance and thrust of the early Church's struggle against Docetism consisted in the defense of the reality and genuineness of the human nature of Jesus Christ. While recognizing that Jesus is God incarnate and confessing faith in his resurrection, at the same time, the early Church defended in every possible way the idea of Jesus as a real man, an idea that emerges from the Gospels. He was fully God, but at the same time remained fully human, and capable of experiencing human emotion.

As the author of Hebrews emphasizes, Jesus was like other people in every way, "yet without sin" (Heb 4.15). In human beings, the emotional element is often attended by sin or evil. For example, anger can come from irritation, malice, or dislike towards some person or other. Laughter can be sinful if it arises from a contemptuous or mocking attitude towards another person. Humor can be evil. Tears can come from offense, resentment, or hatred. Jealousy can be the result of egoism, the sinful desire of one person to possess another person as property.

In Jesus, none of these qualities bore a sinful overtone, but the absence of sin did not make his human essence inadequate. Sin is what is introduced

---

[49]The root of the word "Docetism" comes from the verb *dokeō*, which can mean "to appear."—*Ed.*

into a person's life by the action of the devil (Gen 3.1–7). In Jesus Christ, human nature is freed from slavery to sin (Jn 8.34–36), while remaining full-fledged human nature, with all its characteristic properties.

Love and Friendship

In the Gospels there are several mentions of people whom Jesus loved. We are not speaking of the love with which, as incarnate God, he loved all people, including his enemies. In these specific instances, we are speaking of human love, which singles out one person from among others.

We have seen that Mark, as he tells of Jesus' meeting with the rich young man, notes: "Jesus beholding him loved him" (Mk 10.21). This detail cannot be construed as anything but the manifestation of a human feeling that arose unexpectedly. Commentators speak in this case of fatherly love, comparing it with the feeling, described multiple times in the book of Genesis, that a father experiences towards his son (Gen 22.2; 25.28; 37.3; 44.20).[50] But with all the restraint of the book of Genesis in its description of human emotions, the verb used in the abovementioned instances, "love," refers to earthly, human love, expressed in deep feelings and emotional experiences.

In the Gospel of John, several people are mentioned whom Jesus loved. He "loved Martha, and her sister, and Lazarus" (Jn 11.5). Of Lazarus he said to his disciples: "Our friend Lazareth sleepeth" (Jn 11.11). Seeing Jesus' tears at Lazarus' tomb, the Jews said in surprise, "Behold how he loved him!" (Jn 11.36). Here, love comes across as a human feeling in relation to specific people, the members of a single family, while friendship comes across as something that connected Jesus with one of the members of this family.

In the same Gospel, as we have said, the disciple "whom Jesus loved" is mentioned multiple times (Jn 13.23; 19.26; 20.2; 21.7, 20). The word "loved" in this case indicates that Jesus singled out this disciple in a special way from among the twelve disciples: a clear expression of this is how he leaned

---

[50]Joel Marcus, *Mark: A New Translation and Commentary*, vol. 2, *Mark 8–16*, The Anchor Yale Bible 27A (New Haven, CT: Yale University Press, 2009), 722.

on Jesus' breast at the Last Supper, such that even Peter had to make a sign
to him to ask Jesus a question (Jn 13.23–24). Jesus distinguished Peter as
the most senior of the twelve, but, judging by the Fourth Gospel, he experienced a particular human affection for John.

It is possible that this had to do with John's young age. In that case, the
feeling that Jesus experienced towards him could be akin to the feeling of
a father towards his youngest son, in the way that this feeling is described
in the biblical story of Jacob and his twelve sons: from among them the
father singled out the youngest, to whom he was especially attached (Gen
42.4).

Jesus experienced human love and affection towards all his disciples.
This is especially apparent in the story of the passion. At the Last Supper,
Jesus, in washing the feet of his disciples, "having loved his own who were
in the world, he loved them unto the end" (Jn 13.1). In his final discourse
with his disciples, as it is recorded in the Gospel of John, he speaks plainly
and more than once to them about his love for them: "A new commandment I give unto you, that ye love one another, as I have loved you, that ye
also love one another" (Jn 13.34); "As the Father hath loved me, so have I
loved you; continue in my love" (Jn 15.9). Declaring his love to the disciples,
Jesus calls them his friends:

> This is my commandment, that ye love one another, as I have loved
> you. Greater love hath no man than this, that a man lay down his life
> for his friends. Ye are my friends, if ye do whatsoever I command you.
> Henceforth I call you not servants. For the servant knoweth not what
> his lord doeth. But I have called you friends; for all things that I have
> heard of my Father I have made known unto you. (Jn 15.12–15)

Immediately before his arrest, Jesus prays fervently to the Father about
his disciples. In the words of this prayer, his last will is expressed:

> I pray for them. I pray not for the world, but for those who thou hast
> given me, for they are thine. And all mine are thine, and thine are mine;
> and I am glorified in them. And now I am no more in the world, but
> these are in the world, and I come to thee. Holy Father, keep through

thine own name those whom thou hast given me, that they may be one, as we are. While I was with them in the world, I kept them in thy name: those that thou gavest me I have kept, and none of them is lost, but the son of perdition, that the scripture might be fulfilled. . . . Father, I will that they also, whom thou hast given me, be with me where I am; that they may behold my glory, which thou hast given me: for thou lovedst me before the foundation of the world. O righteous Father, the world hath not known thee, but I have known thee, and these have known that thou hast sent me. And I have declared unto them thy name, and will declare it: that the love wherewith thou hast loved me may be in them, and I in them. (Jn 17.9–12, 25–26)

These words are pronounced after Judas, one of the twelve, called here the "son of perdition," had already abandoned Jesus and gone to the chief priests and elders in order to betray him to them. However, Jesus does not exclude him from the number of his disciples and friends. When they meet in the garden of Gethsemane, to which Judas comes in the company of a detachment of soldiers, Jesus meets him with the words, "Friend, why hast thou come?" (Mt 26.50). For Jesus, this disciple remains his friend, even after the latter has betrayed him.

The deep human feelings that Jesus experienced in relation to those whom he loved are in harmony in him with the absolute and supernatural love that is not conditional upon the actions of the other person. This is the sacrificial and all-embracing love that leads him to the cross.

6. Peculiarities of Speech

A significant portion of the material of the Gospels consists of Jesus' direct speech: his preaching and parables, his instructions to the disciples, and his disputes with the Jews. Usually, when we read these texts, we pay particular attention to their meaning, and rarely consider their verbal structure, logic, poetry, and imagery.

Jesus' words have come down to us through two stages of translation. First spoken in Aramaic, they are preserved only in Greek translation, while we read them translated into our native language. No translation can fully reflect the richness and beauty of the original. Suffice it to say that poetry loses its rhythm and assonance in a literal, line-by-line translation; in other words, it turns into prose.

And yet Jesus' speech was deeply poetic. Attempts undertaken by scholars to reconstruct the Aramaic original show that he often rhymed two halves of a sentence (this is sometimes successfully preserved even in translation), for example: "Bless them that curse you, and pray for them which despitefully use you" (Lk 6.28). A hypothetical reconstruction of the Aramaic original of this sentence reads thus: *bārekūn lǝ-lāytêkon sallōn 'al rāḏǝpêkon*.[51] The formula "many are called, but few are chosen" (Mt 22.14) also contains a rhyme in reconstruction: *śaggī'īn zǝmīnīn zǝ 'ērīn bǝhīrīn*.[52] There are a fair number of examples of a similar nature. Jesus' speech was often aphoristic, and for aphorisms and proverbs, the use of rhymes is entirely typical.

[51]C. F. Burney, *The Poetry of Our Lord: An Examination of the Formal Elements of Hebrew Poetry in the Discourses of Jesus Christ* (Oxford: Clarendon, 1925), 169.

[52]Gustaf Dalman, *The Words of Jesus Considered in the Light of Post-Biblical Jewish Writings and the Aramaic Language*, trans. D. M. Kay (Edinburgh: T&T Clark, 1902), 119. Dalman proposed another reconstruction, which also rhymes, in his later work: Gustaf Dalman, *Jesus-Jeshua: Studies in the Gospels*, trans. Paul P. Levertoff (London: S.P.C.K., 1929), 228. Both of these reconstructions are oriented towards the traditional academic norm of reading the texts in the Galilean Aramaic dialect. They recreate the verbal structure and syntax of Jesus' speech, but not its sound. A phonetic reconstruction of the sentences in question would be in the following form: *bārekūn lilā'etêkon sallōn 'al rāḏepêkon; śaggī'īn zamīnīn za 'ērīn bahīrīn.*

No less typical for Jesus was the use of semantic and verbal parallelism, which is when a sentence is divided into two halves, with one half corresponding to the other in meaning and verbal structure. The formula "many are called, but few are chosen" is only one example of parallelism, based on the principle of contrast. Here are other examples: "He that is not with me is against me; and he that gathereth not with me scattereth abroad" (Mt 12.30); "And whosoever shall exalt himself shall be abased; and he that shall humble himself shall be exalted" (Mt 23.12; cf. Lk 14.11); "Whosoever shall seek to save his life shall lose it; and whosoever shall lose his life shall preserve it" (Lk 17.33). There are also not a few examples of parallelism based on the principle of comparison: "The servant is not greater than his lord, neither he that is sent greater than he that sent him" (Jn 13.16).

Jesus' speech has a particular rhythmic character, which is audible even after two stages of translation. For example: "Ask, and it shall be given you; seek, and ye shall find; knock, and it shall be opened unto you. For every one that asketh receiveth; and he that seeketh findeth; and to him that knocketh it shall be opened" (Mt 7.7–8). Here the first half of the sentence consists of three short formulas, each of which has the same structure, while the second half consists of three other formulas, which parallel the first set of formulas in meaning and which are identical to them in their verbal structure.

Jesus often used refrains consisting of one or a few words. The Sermon on the Mount begins with a series of Beatitudes, in which the word "Blessed" is used nine times at the beginning of each sentence (Mt 5.3–11). Further on, the refrain "Ye have heard that it was said. . . . But I say unto you" (Mt 5.21–44) is used six times. In the rebuke of the Pharisees, the formula "Woe unto you, scribes and Pharisees, hypocrites" (Mt 23.13) is pronounced seven times. In the Sermon on the Plain, four sentences beginning with the word "Blessed" are contrasted with three sentences beginning with the words "Woe unto you" (Lk 6.24–26).

Jesus used formulaic refrains in order to emphasize a sentence or idea, distinguishing it from the general context of the speech. At the beginning of a sentence, he might say: "Truly I say unto you" (in the Gospel of John,

"Truly, truly, I say unto you").[53] He might conclude a sermon with the formula, "He that hath ears to hear, let him hear."

An oft-used device is the repetition of words within a short extract or within one sentence: "If the world hate you, ye know that it hated me before it hated you. If ye were of the world, the world would love his own; but because ye are not of the world, but I have chosen you out of the world, therefore the world hateth you" (Jn 15.18–19); "Judge not, that ye be not judged. For with what judgment ye judge, ye shall be judged; and with what measure ye measure, it shall be measured to you again" (Mt 7.1–2).

Jesus had his own characteristic style of communicating with people. He rarely said what they expected to hear from him. In response to questions posed to him, he sometimes did not answer at all, while sometimes he would respond with a question. Often, the answer to the question would be Jesus' silence.[54]

People often asked Jesus questions on one level, but received an answer on another level. Many dialogues from the Gospel of John can serve as examples, especially the conversation with Nicodemus (Jn 3.1–21) and the conversation with the Samaritan woman (Jn 4.7–26), as well as the conversation with the Jews about the bread from heaven (Jn 6.24–65). These dialogues show a typical situation: the people conversing with Jesus are thinking in earthly, fleshly categories, while he, with each new answer or statement, is trying to lead them to a different, higher spiritual level of understanding and perception. This was by no means always successful. The conversation about the bread from heaven, as we recall, ended thus: "From that time many of his disciples went back, and walked no more with him" (Jn 6.66).

After asking Jesus a question, instead of getting a direct answer, interlocutors might have heard a whole series of images taken from daily life. They had to derive the implied answer themselves from these images. One

---

[53]What is translated into English as ""truly" is the Greek exclamation *amēn*, which obviously derives from the Aramaic original.

[54]For many examples from all four Gospels, see Eckhard J. Schnabel, "The Silence of Jesus: The Galilean Rabbi Who Was More Than a Prophet," in *Authenticating the Words of Jesus*, eds. Bruce Chilton and Craig A. Evans (Leiden: Brill, 1999), 204–220.

such example is Jesus' conversation with the disciples of John the Baptist, which is mentioned above (Mt 9.14–17; Mk 2.18–22; Lk 5.33–39).

Jesus' speech was distinguished by its own particular system of imagery. Images adopted from the natural world constantly appeared in his sermons. As he spent much time out in the fresh air, Jesus observed the life of nature. Sunsets and sunrises, mountains and fields, flowers and trees, animals and birds, fish and reptiles—none of these escaped his notice. Here are only a few examples:

> Behold the fowls of the air: for they sow not, neither do they reap, nor gather into barns. . . . Consider the lilies of the field, how they grow; they toil not, neither do they spin. (Mt 6.26, 28)

> The foxes have holes, and the birds of the air have nests. (Mt 8.20)

> What man shall there be among you, that shall have one sheep, and if it fall into a pit on the sabbath day, will he not lay hold of it, and lift it out? (Mt 12.11)

> The kingdom of heaven is like a grain of mustard seed, which a man took, and sowed in his field, which indeed is the least of all seeds. But when it is grown, it is the greatest among herbs, and becometh a tree, so that the birds of the air come and lodge in the branches thereof. (Mt 13.31–32)

> Again, the kingdom of heaven is like unto a net, that was cast into the sea, and gathered of every kind, which, when it was full, they drew to shore, and sat down, and gathered the good into vessels, but cast the bad away. (Mt 13.47–48)

> When it is evening, ye say, "It will be fair weather, for the sky is red." And in the morning, "It will be foul weather to day, for the sky is red and lowering." (Mt 16.2–3)

> If ye have faith as a grain of mustard seed, ye shall say unto this mountain, "Remove hence to yonder place, and it shall be removed." (Mt 17.20)

> If a son shall ask bread of any of you that is a father, will he give him a stone? Or if he ask a fish, will he for a fish give him a serpent? Or if he shall ask an egg, will he offer him a scorpion? (Lk 11.11–12)

> Say not ye, "There are yet four months, and then cometh harvest?" Behold, I say unto you, "Lift up your eyes, and look on the fields, for they are white already to harvest." (Jn 4.35)

Many images in Jesus' sermons and parables are adopted from city or village life, from domestic life, or from the world of trade and commerce:

> But unto what shall I liken this generation? It is like unto children sitting in the markets, and calling unto their fellows, and saying, "We have piped unto you, and ye have not danced; we have mourned unto you, and ye have not lamented." (Mt 11.16–17)

> The kingdom of heaven is like unto leaven, which a woman took, and hid in three measures of meal, till the whole was leavened. (Mt 13.33)

> Again, the kingdom of heaven is like unto treasure hid in a field, which, when a man hath found, he hideth, and for joy thereof goeth and selleth all that he hath, and buyeth that field.

> Again, the kingdom of heaven is like unto a merchant, seeking goodly pearls, who, when he had found one pearl of great price, went and sold all that he had, and bought it. (Mt 13.44–46)

The peculiarities of Jesus' speech have become the subject of many scholarly investigations. Thus, for example, one scholar examined Jesus' conversation with the Samaritan woman in light of the modern linguistic theory of speech acts and came to interesting conclusions concerning Jesus' style of speech as recorded in the Fourth Gospel.[55] Jesus used a rich spectrum of conversational devices, which made his speech dynamic, unusual, striking, persuasive, and memorable.

---

[55]J. Eugene Botha, *Jesus and the Samaritan Woman: A Speech Act Reading of John 4:1–42*, Supplements to Novum Testamentum 65 (Leiden: Brill, 1991), 188–200.

These devices, however, were not used deliberately or artificially, and were not the result of education, instruction, or training. They arose in Jesus' speech naturally when he expressed what he wanted to say using verbal formulas. The richness of the conversational devices used reflected the richness of the content of what Jesus was saying, and the richness of his own inner world.

Icon of the Savior "Not Made by Hands," icon, 19th c.

The most succinct evaluation of Jesus' speech was given by the officers who were sent by the Pharisees and chief priests to seize him. Without fulfilling their task, they returned to the Pharisees with the words: "No man ever spoke like this man" (Jn 7.46). This evaluation was given by people who did not expect to hear what they heard, and it was given, as can be seen, not so much on the basis of *what* Jesus said, as much as on the basis of *how* he said it.

A similar reaction can arise even two thousand years later in a person who takes up the Gospels for the first time and unexpectedly discovers in Jesus' words and speech such richness of meaning and content and such beauty in the embodiment of this content in verbal formulas, which cannot be explained by any scholarly theories and cannot be reduced to the sum of conversational devices or other external factors. The impression that Jesus' speech produced and continues to produce on millions of people is connected to the fact that his words were the words of God and of a man simultaneously.

* * *

In the person of Jesus we see a man who was able to rejoice and weep, be angry and have compassion, rebuke and comfort. He was capable of simple human friendship; he was uncompromising towards vice, but forbearing towards sinners; he hated pharisaical hypocrisy and sanctimoniousness, but did not refuse to recline at the same table with Pharisees. His reactions were often emotional and abrupt. Like other people, he experienced hunger and grew tired. He was a real man with all the qualities proper to a man, besides sin and everything connected with it.

In the person of Jesus, we have the only example in history of a man who possessed absolute perfection. Theologians speak of how his human nature was wholly divinized, that is, imbued with the divine presence, inseparably connected with the divine nature. At the same time, he possessed the qualities of a full-fledged human being, including a rich spectrum of feelings and emotional experiences.

The Christian ideal of holiness as the endeavor to imitate Christ does not assume complete freedom from human qualities at the highest levels of perfection. The idea of saints as people who are unable to or have forgotten how to cry and laugh, grieve and get angry, be surprised or be afraid, and the idea of passionlessness as apathy and the lack of all feeling—all this does not correspond to the highest ideal that Christianity possesses in the person of its divine founder. The ideal of struggle with sin does not assume freedom from emotion and from the condition of being human. It assumes that the usual feelings and emotions proper to a human being will be gradually freed from the element of passion and sinfulness, by the action of the grace of God; thanks to this, a person can approach the ideal revealed to all mankind in the person of Christ—the Son of Man and Son of God. It was in Christ himself that these feelings and emotions were freed from this element in the first place, by virtue of the inseparable unity of his human and divine natures.

CONCLUSION

I n 1971, the famous American preacher Billy Graham released a book entitled *The Jesus Generation*. In it he gave a multitude of examples testifying to the unflagging interest of his contemporaries in the person and teaching of Jesus Christ.[1]

In that same year, appearing before an audience of several thousands in Chicago, he mused aloud about the phenomenon to which he had dedicated his book. The musical *Godspell*, which was based on the parables in the Gospels, had only just been composed: it played in theaters all across America, and thousands of people were talking about Jesus. A year earlier, two Englishmen, the composer Andrew Lloyd Webber and the poet Tim Rice, had written the rock opera *Jesus Christ Superstar*, which quickly gained popularity. With characteristic passion, Billy Graham exclaimed:

> It's interesting to me that, in 1971, the plays, the books, the operas, the movies about Jesus—our generation cannot escape Jesus. And when *Good News for Modern Man* came out, a new translation of the New Testament by the American Bible Society, they sold twenty-five million copies. We cannot escape Jesus! I've never heard of an opera or a play being about Buddha, or Mohammed, or Gandhi. But our generation has become hung up on Jesus. Young people are talking about Jesus. He's the subject of conversation today on the campus, in the high schools, everywhere. Young people are discussing Jesus Christ, and they're asking the question, "Who is he?"[2]

---

[1] Billy Graham, *The Jesus Generation* (Grand Rapids, MI: Zondervan, 1971).
[2] Transcribed from Billy Graham, *Images of Christ*, Billy Graham Library Classics Collection (1971; Charlotte, NC: Billy Graham Evangelistic Association, 2007), DVD.

Jesus Christ Superstar (scene from the film)

During the time when atheist regimes held sway over all of Eastern Europe, Billy Graham traveled to countries in the Eastern Bloc, interacted with believers, and spoke in churches; and then, when he returned to America, he spoke to his compatriots of what he had seen. Already at that time, in the 1970s, he foretold that in the countries of Eastern Europe, including Russia, there would be a mighty religious revival, and that their peoples would return to their Christian roots. At the end of the 1980s he had the opportunity to see millions of people in Russia, Ukraine, Belarus, Moldavia, Poland, Romania, Bulgaria, Serbia, Georgia, Armenia, and other countries of the former Soviet Union and the Warsaw bloc accept faith in Jesus Christ.

Forty-six years have passed since Billy Graham delivered his famous speech in Chicago. Since then, two new generations have grown up. But can one possibly say that they are *not* Jesus generations? Can one possibly say that interest in the person and teaching of Jesus has flagged or decreased since then?

The author of these lines belongs to a generation that was not the Jesus generation. In the 1960s and 1970s, few in the Soviet Union knew or spoke of Jesus Christ: his name was mentioned only in specialized literature on "scientific atheism." Believers of various church communities lived isolated lives; the theme of religion practically did not exist in the public sphere; the name of Jesus was not mentioned in magazines or on television or in history textbooks. People knew about the Bible and the Gospels mainly from atheist literature, and about Christ mainly from Mikhail Bulgakov's novel *Master and Margarita*.

But the times changed, and at the end of the 1980s to the beginning of the 1990s the generation that was *not* the Jesus generation *became* the Jesus generation. Millions of people read through the Gospels, discovered Jesus as God and Savior for themselves, came to Church, and received baptism.

For nearly two thousand years now, the earth has resounded with the call that first sounded in the wilderness from the lips of John the Forerunner and then became the leitmotif of the preaching of Jesus Christ: "Repent, for the kingdom of heaven is at hand" (Mt 4.17). Hundreds of millions of people in various corners of the world are responding to this call. Over two billion inhabitants of our planet consider themselves followers of Jesus, belonging to various Christian confessions, and each day the global community of Jesus' disciples increases by tens of thousands of new members.

Sixteen centuries have passed since the Gospels became the most-read book on earth. Translated into more than two thousand languages, it maintains this status to this day.

Christianity began from something that by human standards can be called a complete failure. The tragic death of Jesus, as it appeared then to many, erased all hope for the success of the movement that he started. And nevertheless it was this movement that became the most successful missionary project in the entire history of humankind. Over the course of two thousand years, the persistent growth in the number of Christians continues, even if today Christianity is facing the competition of other large-scale missionary projects.

In the West, many call our age "post-Christian." People speak of the decay of Christian civilization, of the decrease in the number of the faithful, of the fall in the number of priestly and monastic vocations, and of the closing of churches and monasteries.

In order to be convinced that we in no way live in a post-Christian age, it is sufficient to visit one of the Orthodox countries, in which a large-scale revival of religious life continues that began more than a quarter of a

Holy Rus',
Mikhail
Nesterov,
1901–1906.

century ago. In the Russian Orthodox Church alone, within a quarter of a century, there have been more than twenty-five thousand churches either built or reconstructed from ruins: this means that a thousand churches were opened each year, or three churches a day. More than eight hundred monasteries were opened, which have been filled with monks and nuns, mostly young ones. After a seven-decade-long interruption, more than fifty seminaries and religious schools have been established or resumed activity; theological institutes and universities have appeared; in secular universities, schools and departments of theology have been opened.

This upsurge in religious life in the territory of a former atheist empire, unexpected by many and unprecedented in scale, cannot be explained by natural or sociopolitical factors alone. It has uncovered a powerful source of spiritual energy, which Christianity bears in itself and which is supernatural. This source stems not from Christian moral or social teaching, and not from divine services or theological studies. It has a single origin—the person of the God-Man Jesus Christ, who continues to act in historical space and time, which he unexpectedly invaded two thousand years ago.

Like a spring, which can be compressed and decompressed, historical Christianity in different ages and in different places has experienced periods of persecution and periods of external prosperity; it has become, correspondingly, a "little flock" (Lk 12.32) at times—a small community of those persecuted and rejected—and, at other times, has become an army of many millions of good soldiers for Christ (2 Tim 2.3). But external success must never lead to triumphalism, just as an apparent lack of success must not become a cause for discouragement or despair.

Beginning from what seemed to be complete failure, Christianity, in the person of its divine founder, has in the final reckoning prevailed in such a victory over the evil and falsehood of this world that there is no other analogue to it in history. It has compelled millions of people to reexamine their ideas about God, the world, and themselves. By his intrusion into history, the incarnate God has changed its trajectory once and for all. Even if the victory that he has achieved is recognized and acknowledged not by all and not in all places, even if many do not notice it—just as two thousand years ago many did not notice that God had come into the world—this victory has absolute and lasting value. The unflagging interest in Christianity and in the person of its founder testifies to this.

The strength of Christianity stems from the fact that, having once come to earth, Christ has not left it to go elsewhere: in the body he ascended to heaven, to the Father, but in spirit he remained with his followers on earth (Mt 28.20). The Church that he founded continues to be the place of his living presence, and millions of people are convinced of this in their personal experience.

The post-Christian age will come only after the second coming of Jesus Christ. As long as the history of mankind continues on earth, Christ will continue to act in this history. His divine countenance will always attract people, and generation after generation will become Jesus generations.

ABBREVIATIONS

ANF *The Ante-Nicene Fathers*. Edited by Alexander Roberts and James Donaldson. Buffalo, 1885–1887. 10 vols. Repr., Peabody, MA: Hendrickson, 1994.

NPNF¹ *The Nicene and Post-Nicene Fathers*, Series 1. Edited by Philip Schaff. New York, 1886–1889. 14 vols. Repr., Peabody, MA: Hendrickson, 1994.

NPNF² *The Nicene and Post-Nicene Fathers*, Series 2. Edited by Philip Schaff and Henry Wace. New York, 1890. 14 vols. Repr., Peabody, MA: Hendrickson, 1994.

GCS Die griechischen christlichen Schriftsteller der ersten Jahrhunderte. Leipzig; Berlin. 1897–

PG Patrologia Graeca. Edited by J.-P. Migne. 162 vols. Paris, 1857–1886.

PL Patrologia Latina. Edited by J.-P. Migne. 217 vols. Paris, 1844–1864.

PPS Popular Patristics Series. Crestwood, NY [Yonkers, NY]: St Vladimir's Seminary Press, 1996–

SC Sources Chrétiennes. Paris: Les Éditions du Cerf. 1942–

BIBLIOGRAPHY

1. The Old and New Testaments

The Holy Bible: King James Version. Standard text ed. Cambridge: Cambridge University Press, 1995.

Aland, Kurt. *Synopsis Quattor Evangeliorum: Locis parallelis evangeliorum apocryphorum et partum adhibitis.* 13th rev. ed. Stuttgart: Deutsche Bibelgesellschaft, 1988.

Biblia Hebraica Stuttgartensia. Edited by Rudolf Kittel, Wilhelm Rudolph, and Hans Peter Rüber, et al. 4th ed. Stuttgart: Deutsche Bibelgesellschaft, 1977.

Novum Testamentum Graece. 28th rev. ed. Stuttgart: Deutsche Bibelgesellschaft, 2012.

Septuaginta: id est, Vetus Testamentum graece iuxta LXX interpretes. Edited by Alfred Rahlfs. Editio minor. Stuttgart: Deutsche Bibelgesellschaft, 1979.

2. Works of the Fathers and Teachers of the Church

Amphilochius of Iconium. *De recta fide* [On the true faith]. In *Amphilochii Iconiensis Opera*, Corpus Christianorum Series Graeca 3, 309–319. Turnhout: Brepols, 1978.

Augustine of Hippo. *Against the Epistle of Manichæus.* NPNF[1] 4:125–150.

_____. *Confessions.* PL 32:659–868.

_____. *Sermons.* NPNF[1] 6:245–545.

_____. *The Harmony of the Gospels.* NPNF[1] 6:65–236.

_____. *The Works of Saint Augustine: A Translation for the 21st Century.* Translated by Edmund Hill. Edited by John E. Rotelle. Pt. 3, vol. 3, *Sermons on the New Testament, 51–94.* Brooklyn, NY: New City Press, 1991.

Basil the Great. *Homily on Psalm 28.* PG 29:279–306.

_____. *Letters.* NPNF[2] 8:109–327.

_____. *On the Holy Spirit.* Translated by Stephen Hildebrand. Popular Patristics Series 42. Yonkers, NY: St Vladimir's Seminary Press, 2011.

————. *Saint Basil: Ascetical Works.* Translated by Monica Wagner. The Fathers of the Church 9. Washington, DC: Catholic University of America Press, 1962.

————. *Saint Basil: Exegetic Homilies.* Translated by Agnes Clare Way. The Fathers of the Church 46. Washington, DC: Catholic University of America Press, 1963.

Clement of Alexandria. *The Instructor. ANF* 2:207–298.

Clement of Rome (Pseudo-). *Recognitions.* PG 1:1157–1474.

Cyril of Alexandria. *Commentary on the Gospel of Matthew* [=Fragment 219]. In *Matthäus-Kommentare aus der griechischen Kirche; aus Katenenhandschriften gesammelt und hrsg,* edited by Joseph Reuss, Texte und Untersuchungen zur Geschichte der altchristlichen Literatur Bd. 61, 226. Berlin: Akademie-Verlag, 1957.

————. *Commentary on the Gospel of Matthew* 29 [=Fragment 29]. In *Matthew 1–13,* Ancient Christian Commentary on Scripture New Testament 1a, edited by Manlio Simonetti, 53. Downers Grove, IL: InterVarsity, 2001.

Cyril of Jerusalem. *Lectures on the Christian Sacraments.* Translated by Maxwell E. Johnson. Popular Patristics Series 57. Yonkers, NY: St Vladimir's Seminary Press, 2017.

Epiphanius of Salamis. *Panarion.* In *Ancoratus und Panarion.* 3 Bd. Die Griechischen christlichen Schriftsteller der ersten drei Jahrhunderte Bd. 25, 31, 37. Leipzig: J. C. Hinrichs, 1915–1933.

Gregory of Nazianzus. *Against Anger.* PG 37:813–851.

————. *Festal Orations.* Translated by Nonna Verna Harrison. Popular Patristics Series 36. Crestwood, NY: St Vladimir's Seminary Press, 2008.

————. *On God and Christ: The Five Theological Orations and Two Letters to Cledonius.* Translated by Frederick Williams and Lionel Wickham. Popular Patristics Series 23. Crestwood, NY: St Vladimir's Seminary Press, 2002.

————. *Orations. NPNF*[2] 7:184–434.

Gregory of Nyssa. *On the Baptism of Christ. NPNF*[2] 5:518–524.

————. *The Great Catechism. NPNF*[2] 5:471–509.

Ignatius of Antioch. *The Letters.* Translated by Alistair Stewart. Popular Patristics Series 49. Yonkers, NY: St Vladimir's Seminary Press, 2013.

Irenaeus of Lyons. *Against Heresies. ANF* 1:315–567.

Jerome. *Commentary on Matthew*. Translated by Thomas P. Scheck. The Fathers of the Church 117. Washington, DC: The Catholic University of America Press, 2008.

————. *Letters*. NPNF² 6:1–295.

————. *The Homilies of Saint Jerome*. Vol. 2, *Homilies 60–96*. Translated by Marie Liguori Ewald. The Fathers of the Church 57. Washington, DC: The Catholic University of America Press, 1966.

John Chrysostom. *Homilies on Romans*. PG 60:583–680.

————. *Homilies on the Gospel of John*. NPNF¹ 14:1–334.

————. *Homilies on the Gospel of Matthew*. NPNF¹ 10.

————. *Homily on the Nativity of Our Savior*. PG 49:351–362.

————. *On the Incomprehensible Nature of God*. Translated by Paul W. Harkins. The Fathers of the Church 72. Washington, DC: Catholic University of America Press, 1982.

John of Damascus. *An Exact Exposition of the Orthodox Faith*. NPNF² 9:1b–101b.

————. *De Haeresibus* [Heresies]. In *Die Schriften des Johannes von Damaskos*, vol. 4, *Liber de Haeresibus. Opera Polemica*, edited by Bonifatius Kotter, Patristische Texte und Studien 22, 19–67. Berlin: Walter de Gruyter, 1981.

————. *Second Homily on the Dormition*. In *On the Dormition of Mary: Early Patristic Homilies*, translated by Brian E. Daley, Popular Patristics Series 18, 231–240. Crestwood, NY: St Vladimir's Seminary Press, 1998.

————. *Writings*. Translated by Frederic H. Chase, Jr. The Fathers of the Church 37. Washington, DC: The Catholic University of America Press, 1958.

Justin Martyr. *Dialogue with Trypho*. ANF 1:194–270.

————. *First Apology*. ANF 1:163–187.

Maximus the Confessor. *Maximus Confessor: Selected Writings*. Translated by George C. Berthold. Classics of Western Spirituality. New York, NY: Paulist Press, 1985.

————. *St. Maximus the Confessor's Questions and Doubts*. Translated by Despina D. Prassas. DeKalb, IL: Northern Illinois University Press, 2010.

————. *Two Hundred Chapters on Theology and the Incarnate Economy of the Son of God*. Translated by Luis Joshua Salés. Popular Patristics Series 53. Yonkers, NY: St Vladimir's Seminary Press, 2015.

Methodius of Olympus. *The Banquet of the Ten Virgins*. ANF 6:309–355.

Origen. *Commentary on the Gospel of Matthew* 1, 2, 7, 10–15. PG 13:829–1800.

_____. *Commentary on the Gospel of Matthew* 10–11. SC 162.

_____. *Commentary on the Gospel on Matthew* [fragments]. GCS 38, 40, 41/1 and 41/2.

_____. *Contra Celsum*. SC 132, 136, 147, 150, and 227.

_____. *Homilies on Luke; Fragments on Luke*. Translated by Joseph T. Lienhard. The Fathers of the Church 94. Washington, DC: The Catholic University of America Press, 1996.

_____. *On First Principles*. ANF 4:239–384.

_____. *The Philocalia of Origen*. Translated by George Lewis. Edinburgh: T&T Clark, 1911.

Pseudo-Damascene. *Letter to Emperor Theophilus on the Holy and Venerated Icons*. In *The Letter of the Three Patriarchs to Emperor Theophilus and Related Texts*, edited by Joseph A. Munitiz, 142–203. Camberley, Surrey: Porphyrogenitus, 1997.

Rufinus Aquileia. *Introduction to the Translation of Clement of Rome's "Recognitions."* PG 1:1205–1208.

Sayings of the Desert Fathers. PG 65:71–441.

Symeon the New Theologian. *On the Mystical Life: The Ethical Discourses*. Translated by Alexander Golitzin. 3 vols. Crestwood, NY: St. Vladimir's Seminary Press, 1995–1997.

Tertullian. *On the Flesh of Christ*. ANF 3:521–543.

Theodoret of Cyrus. *Commentaries on the Prophets*. Vol. 3, *Commentary on the Twelve Prophets*. Translated by Robert Charles Hill. Brookline, MA: Holy Cross Orthodox Press, 2006.

Theophylact of Ochrid. *Explanation of the Gospel of Luke*. PG 123:683–1126.

_____. *Explanation of the Gospel of Matthew*. PG 123:243–486.

_____. *The Explanation by Blessed Theophylact of the Holy Gospel According to St. Luke*. Vol. 3 of *Blessed Theophylact's Explanation of the New Testament*. Translated by Christopher Stade. House Springs, MO: Chrysostom Press, 1997.

3. Other Sources

Al-Qurān Al-hakīm [Holy Qur'an]. Translated by M. H. Shakir. 2nd U.S. ed. Elmhurst, NY: Tahrike Tarsile Qur'an, 1983.

Bulgakov, Mikhail. *The Master and Margarita*. Translated by Michael Glenny. New York, NY: Harper & Row, 1967.

Canons of the Council of Gangra. NPNF² 14:87–101.

Cureton, William, trans. and ed. *Spicilegium Syriacum: Containing Remains of Bardeson, Meliton, Ambrose and Mara bar Serapion.* London: Francis and John Rivington, 1855.

Dostoyevsky, Fyodor. *The Grand Inquisitor: With Related Chapters from "The Brothers Karamazov."* Translated by Constance Garnett. Edited by Charles B. Guignon. Indianapolis, IN: Hackett, 1993.

Eusebius of Caesarea. *Ecclesiastical History.* Translated by Kirsopp Lake and J. E. L. Oulton. 2 vols. Loeb Classical Library. Cambridge: Harvard University Press, 1926–1932.

_____. *The History of the Church from Christ to Constantine.* Translated by G. A. Williamson. Harmondsworth: Penguin Books, 1989.

The Festal Menaion. Translated by Mother Mary and Archimandrite Kallistos Ware. South Canaan, PA: St. Tikhon's Seminary Press, 1998.

Josephus, Flavius. *Josephus.* 9 vols. Translated by Henry St. J. Thackeray, Ralph Marcus, and L. H. Feldman. Loeb Classical Library. Cambridge, MA: Harvard University Press, 1926–1965.

_____. *The Works of Flavius Josephus.* Translated by William Whiston. Auburn and Buffalo, NY: John E. Beardsley, 1895.

The Lenten Triodion. Translated by Mother Mary and Archimandrite Kallistos Ware. South Canaan, PA: St. Tikhon's Seminary Press, 2002.

Luther, Martin. *Preface to the German Translation of the New Testament (1522).* In *The Protestant Reformation*, edited by Hans J. Hillerbrand, Harper Torchbooks TB 1342, 37–42. New York, NY: Harper & Row, 1968.

Macrobius. *Saturnalia.* Edited by Robert A. Kaster. 3 vols. Loeb Classical Library 510–512. Cambridge, MA: Harvard University Press, 2011.

Maimonides, Moses. *The Code of Maimonides (Mishneh Torah).* Bk. 5, *The Book of Holiness.* Translated by Louis I. Rabinowitz and Philip Grossman. Edited by Leon Nemoy. Yale Judaica Series 16. New Haven, CT: Yale University Press, 1965.

The Nicene Creed. NPNF² 14:3.

Nicephorus Callistus. *Ecclesiastical History.* PG 145 and 146.

Pedanius Dioscorides of Anazarbos. *Pedanii Dioscuridis Anazarbei de materia medica libri quinque.* Edited by Max Wellmann. 5 vols. Berlin: Weidmann, 1906–1914.

Philo of Alexandria. *The Works of Philo: Complete and Unabridged.* Translated by C. D. Yonge. Updated ed. Peabody, MA: Hendrickson, 1993.

Protevangelium of James. ANF 8:361–367.

Pseudo-Lentulus. *Publius Lentulus his report to the Senate of Rome concerning Jesus Christ.* London, 1677.

Pushkin, Alexander. *Ruslan and Liudmila.* Translated by Walter Arndt. Ann Arbor, MI: Ardis, 1974.

Socrates Scholasticus. *Ecclesiastical History. NPNF²* 2:1–178.

Tacitus. *Tacitus.* Translated by Maurice Hutton, William Peterson, Clifford H. Moore, and John Jackson. Revised by R. M. Ogilvie, E. H. Warmington, and Michael Winterbottom. 5 vols. Loeb Classical Library 35, 111, 249, 312, 322. Cambridge, MA: Harvard University Press, 1996–1999. Originally published 1914–1937.

4. Cited Literature

Aicher, Georg. *Kamel und Nadelöhr: eine kritisch-exegetische Studie über Mt 19,24 und parallelen.* Neutestamentliche Abhandlungen Bd. 1 heft. 5. Münster: Aschendorff, 1908.

Aland, Kurt. *Kurzgefasste Liste der griechischen Handschriften des Neuen Testaments.* Arbeiten zur neutestamentlichen Textforschung Bd. 1. Berlin: Walter de Gruyter, 1994.

Albright, W. F., and C. S. Mann. *Matthew: Introduction, Translation, and Notes.* Anchor Bible 26. Garden City, NY: Doubleday, 1971.

Alekseyev, A. A. *Tekstologiya Novogo Zaveta i izdanie Nestle-Alanda* [Textual Criticism of the New Testament and the Nestle-Aland edition]. St Petersburg: Dmitriy Bulanin, 2012.

Alexander, Loveday. "Luke's Preface in the Context of Greek Preface-Writing." In *The Composition of Luke's Gospel: Selected Studies from* Novum Testamentum, edited by David E. Orton, 90–116. Leiden: Brill, 1999.

_____. *The Preface to Luke's Gospel: Literary Convention and Social Context in Luke 1.1–4 and Acts 1.1.* Society for New Testament Studies Monograph Series 78. Cambridge: Cambridge University Press, 2005.

Alfeyev, Metropolitan Hilarion. *Christ the Conqueror of Hell: The Descent into Hades from an Orthodox Perspective.* Crestwood, NY: St Vladimir's Seminary Press, 2009.

_____. *Orthodox Christianity*. Vol. 2, *Doctrine and Teaching of the Orthodox Church*. Translated by Andrew Smith. Yonkers, NY: St Vladimir's Seminary Press, 2012.

_____. *Orthodox Christianity*. Vol. 3, *The Architecture, Icons, and Music of the Orthodox Church*. Translated by Andrei Tepper. Yonkers, NY: St Vladimir's Seminary Press, 2014.

_____. *Orthodox Christianity*. Vol. 4, *The Worship and Liturgical Life of the Orthodox Church*. Translated by Andrei Tepper. Yonkers, NY: St Vladimir's Seminary Press, 2016.

_____. *Orthodox Christianity*. Vol. 5. Translated by Nathan Williams. Yonkers, NY: St Vladimir's Seminary Press, forthcoming.

_____. *Svyashchennaya tayna Tserkvi* [The Holy Mystery of the Church]. St Petersburg: Aleteiya, 2002.

Andreyev, I. M. *Pravoslavno-khristianskaya apologetika. Kratkoe konspektivnoe izlozhenie kursa lektsiy, chitannykh v Svyato-Troitskoy dukhovnoy seminarii* [Orthodox-Christian apologetics. A summary of a course of lectures, presented in the Theological Seminary of the Holy Trinity, Jordanville, NY]. Jordanville, NY: Holy Trinity Monastery, 1965.

Anthony (Bloom), [Metropolitan]. *Vo imya Ottsa i Syna i Svyatogo Dukha: Propovedi* [In the name of the Father and the Son and the Holy Spirit: Sermons]. Klin: Khristianskaya zhizn', 2001.

Ashton, John. *Understanding the Fourth Gospel*. 2nd ed. Oxford: Oxford University Press, 2007.

Augstein, Rudolf. *Jesus Menschensohn*. Munich: C. Bertelsmann, 1972.

Aune, David E. *The New Testament in Its Literary Environment*. Library of Early Christianity 8. Philadelphia, PA: The Westminster Press, 1987.

Barrett, C. K. *The Holy Spirit and the Gospel Tradition*. London: S.P.C.K., 1947.

Barton, Stephen C. *Discipleship and Family Ties in Mark and Matthew*. Society for New Testament Studies Monograph Series 80. Cambridge: Cambridge University Press, 1994.

Bauckham, Richard. "For Whom Were the Gospels Written?" In *The Gospels for All Christians: Rethinking the Gospel Audiences*, edited by Richard Bauckham, 9–48. Grand Rapids, MI: Eerdmans, 1998.

_____. *Gospel Women: Studies of the Named Women in the Gospels*. Grand Rapids, MI: Eerdmans, 2002.

_____. *Jesus and the Eyewitnesses: The Gospels as Eyewitness Testimony.* Grand Rapids, MI: Eerdmans, 2006.

_____. *The Testimony of the Beloved Disciple: Narrative, History, and Theology in the Gospel of John.* Grand Rapids, MI: Baker Academic, 2007.

Benedict XVI, [Pope]. *Jesus of Nazareth: From the Baptism in the Jordan to the Transfiguration.* Translated by Adrian J. Walker. New York, NY: Doubleday, 2007.

Bieler, Ludwig. *Theios anēr, das Bild des "göttlichen Menschen" in Spätantike und Frühchristentum.* 2 vols. Vienna: O. Höfels, 1935–1936.

Blackburn, Barry. *Theios Anēr and the Marcan Miracle Traditions: A Critique of the* Theios Anēr *Concept as an Interpretative Background of the Miracle Traditions Used by Mark.* Wissenschaftliche Untersuchungen zum Neuen Testament II 40. Tübingen, J. C. B. Mohr, 1991.

Blomberg, Craig L. *Jesus and the Gospels: An Introduction and Survey.* 2nd ed. Nashville, TN: B&H Academic, 2009.

Bonhoeffer, Dietrich. *The Cost of Discipleship.* 1st Touchstone ed. New York, NY: Touchstone, 1995.

Borchert, Gerald L. *Jesus of Nazareth: Background, Witnesses, and Significance.* Macon, GA: Mercer University Press, 2011.

Borg, Marcus J., and John Dominic Crossan, *The First Christmas: What the Gospels Really Teach About Jesus's Birth.* New York, NY: HarperOne, 2007.

Botha, J. Eugene. *Jesus and the Samaritan Woman: A Speech Act Reading of John 4:1–42.* Supplements to Novum Testamentum 65. Leiden: Brill, 1991.

Botterweck, G. Johannes, Helmer Ringgren, and Heinz-Josef Fabry, eds. *Theological Dictionary of the Old Testament.* Vol. 12, *pāsah—qûm.* Translated by Douglas W. Stott. Grand Rapids, MI: Eerdmans, 2003.

Bowman, Robert M. and J. Ed Komoszewski. *Putting Jesus in His Place: The Case for the Deity of Christ.* Grand Rapids, MI: Kregel Publications, 2007.

Boxall, Ian. "Luke's Nativity Story: A Narrative Reading." In *New Perspectives on the Nativity,* edited by Jeremy Corley, 23–36. London: T&T Clark, 2009.

Breck, John. *The Shape of Biblical Language: Chiasmus in the Scriptures and Beyond.* Crestwood, NY: St Vladimir's Seminary Press, 1994.

Brown, Jeannine K. *The Disciples in Narrative Perspective: The Portrayal and Function of the Matthean Disciples.* Academia Biblica 9. Leiden: Brill, 2002.

Brown, Raymond E. *An Introduction to the Gospel of John.* New Haven, CT: Yale University Press, 2003.

_____. *An Introduction to the New Testament*. New Haven, CT: Yale University Press, 1997.

_____. *Jesus, God and Man: Modern Biblical Reflections*. Milwaukee, WI: Bruce, 1967.

_____. *The Birth of the Messiah: A Commentary on the Infancy Narratives in the Gospels of Matthew and Luke*. Updated ed. Anchor Bible Reference Library. New York, NY: Doubleday, 1999.

_____. *The Gospel according to John (I–XII)*. Anchor Bible 29. Garden City, NY: Doubleday, 1966.

Bultmann, Rudolf. *Existence and Faith: Shorter Writings of Rudolf Bultmann*. Translated and edited by Schubert M. Ogden. New York, NY: Meridian Books, 1960.

_____. *The History of the Synoptic Tradition*. Translated by John Marsh. Oxford: Blackwell, 1963.

Burney, C. F. *The Poetry of Our Lord. An Examination of the Formal Elements of Hebrew Poetry in the Discourses of Jesus Christ*. Oxford: Clarendon, 1925.

Burridge, Richard A. *Four Gospels, One Jesus?: A Symbolic Reading*. 2nd ed. Grand Rapids, MI: Eerdmans, 2005.

Cadbury, Henry J. *The Style and Literary Method of Luke*. Cambridge, MA: Harvard University Press, 1920.

Carruth, Shawn, and Albrecht Garsky. *Q 11:2b–4*. Documenta Q. Leuven: Peeters, 1996.

Carter, Warren. *Matthew: Storyteller, Interpreter, Evangelist*. Peabody, MA: Hendrickson, 2004.

Casey, Maurice. *Jesus of Nazareth: An Independent Historian's Account of His Life and Teaching*. London: T&T Clark, 2010.

_____. *The Solution to the 'Son of Man' Problem*. The Library of New Testament Studies 343. London: T&T Clark, 2007.

Chancey, Mark A. *The Myth of a Gentile Galilee*. Society for New Testament Studies Monograph Series 118. Cambridge: Cambridge University Press, 2004.

Childs, Hal. *The Myth of the Historical Jesus and the Evolution of Consciousness*. Atlanta, GA: Society of Biblical Literature, 2000.

Conzelmann, Hans. *The Theology of St. Luke*. Translated by Geoffrey Buswell. New York, NY: Harper & Row, 1961.

Cook, Michael L. *Christology as Narrative Quest*. Collegeville, MN: Liturgical Press, 1997.

Crossan, John Dominic. *Jesus: A Revolutionary Biography.* San Francisco, CA: HarperSanFrancisco, 1994.

_____. *The Historical Jesus: The Life of a Mediterranean Jewish Peasant.* San Francisco, CA: HarperSanFrancisco, 1991.

Crouzel, Henri. *Origen.* Translated by A. S. Worrall. Edinburgh: T&T Clark, 1989.

Cullman, Oscar. *Prayer in the New Testament: With Answers from the New Testament to Today's Questions.* London: SCM Press, 1994.

_____. *The Christology of the New Testament.* Translated by Shirley C. Guthrie and Charles A. M. Hall. 2nd English ed. London: SCM Press, 1963.

Culy, Martin M., Mikeal C. Parsons, and Joshua J. Stigall. *Luke: A Handbook on the Greek Text.* Waco, TX: Baylor University Press, 2010.

Dalman, Gustaf. *Jesus-Jeshua: Studies in the Gospels.* Translated by Paul P. Levertoff. London: S.P.C.K., 1929.

_____. *The Words of Jesus Considered in the Light of Post-Biblical Jewish Writings and the Aramaic Language.* Translated by D. M. Kay. Edinburgh: T&T Clark, 1902.

Davies, Stevan L. *Jesus the Healer: Possession, Trance, and the Origins of Christianity.* New York, NY: Continuum, 1995.

Davies, W. D. *The Setting of the Sermon on the Mount.* Cambridge: Cambridge University Press, 1964.

Deutsch, Celia. *Hidden Wisdom and the Easy Yoke: Wisdom, Torah and Discipleship in Matthew 11.25–30.* Sheffield: JSOT Press, 1987.

Dibelius, Martin. *From Tradition to Gospel.* Translated by Bertram Lee Woolf. New York, NY: Scribner, 1935.

Dix, Gregory. *The Shape of the Liturgy.* New ed. London: Continuum, 2005.

Dodd, C. H. *The Parables of the Kingdom.* Rev. ed. New York, NY: Scribner, 1961.

Dodson, Derek S. *Reading Dreams: An Audience-Critical Approach to the Dreams in the Gospel of Matthew.* The Library of New Testament Studies Series. New York, NY: T&T Clark International, 2009.

Dunn, James. *A New Perspective on Jesus: What the Quest for the Historical Jesus Missed.* Grand Rapids, MI: Baker Academic, 2005.

Edwards, James R. *The Hebrew Gospel and the Development of the Synoptic Tradition.* Grand Rapids, MI: Eerdmans, 2009.

Ehrman, Bart D. *How Jesus Became God: The Exaltation of a Jewish Preacher from Galilee.* New York, NY: HarperCollins, 2014.

_____. *Jesus: Apocalyptic Prophet of the New Millenium.* Oxford: Oxford University Press, 1999.

Evans, Craig A. *Fabricating Jesus: How Modern Scholars Distort the Gospels.* Downers Grove, IL: IVP Books, 2006.

Farmer, William R. *The Synoptic Problem: A Critical Analysis.* Dillsboro, NC: Western North Carolina Press, 1976.

Farrer, Austin M. "On Dispensing with Q." In *Studies in the Gospels: Essays in Memory of R. H. Lightfoot,* edited by D. E. Nineham, 55–88. Oxford: Blackwell, 1955.

_____. *A Study in St. Mark.* Westminster: Dacre, 1951.

_____. *St. Matthew and St. Mark.* Westminster: Dacre, 1954.

Ferrari d'Occhieppo, Konradin. *Der Stern von Bethlehem: in astronomischer Sicht: Legende oder Tatsache?* (Giessen: Brunnen, 1991).

Finegan, Jack. *Handbook of Biblical Chronology: Principles of Time Reckoning in the Ancient World and Problems of Chronology in the Bible.* Rev. ed. Peabody, MA: Hendrickson, 1998.

Fitzmyer, Joseph A. *The Gospel According to Luke: Introduction, Translation, and Notes.* 2 vols. Anchor Bible 28 and 28a. Garden City, NY: Doubleday, 1981–1985.

Fotheringham, John Knight. "The Evidence of Astronomy and Technical Chronology for the Date of the Crucifixion." *Journal of Theological Studies* 35 (April 1934): 146–162.

France, R. T. *The Gospel of Mark: A Commentary on the Greek Text.* Grand Rapids, MI: Paternoster Press, 2002.

_____. *The Gospel of Matthew.* Grand Rapids, MI: Eerdmans, 2007.

Freed, Edwin D. *The Stories of Jesus' Birth: A Critical Introduction.* Biblical Seminar 72. Sheffield: Sheffield Academic Press, 2001.

Freyne, Sean. *Galilee and Gospel: Collected Essays.* Boston, MA: Brill, 2000.

Funk, Robert W., ed. *The Acts of Jesus: The Search for the Authentic Deeds of Jesus.* San Francisco, CA: HarperSanFrancisco, 1998.

Gale, Aaron M. *Redefining Ancient Borders: The Jewish Scribal Framework of Matthew's Gospel.* New York, NY: T&T Clark, 2005.

Garrett, Susan R. *The Temptations of Jesus in Mark's Gospel.* Grand Rapids, MI: 1998.

Gibson, Jeffrey B. *The Temptations of Jesus in Early Christianity.* London: T&T Clark International, 1995.

Gladkov, Boris. *Tolkovanie Evangeliya* [Commentary on the Gospels]. Sergiev Posad: Troitske-Sergieva Lavra, 2014.

Gnilka, Joachim. *Das Evangelium nach Markus.* Vol. 1, *Mk 1–8,26.* Evangelisch-Katholischer Kommentar zum Neuen Testament II/1. Zürich: Benziger; Neukirchen-Vluyn: Neukirchener, 1978.

Goulder, Michael D. *Luke, A New Paradigm,* 2 vols. Sheffield: JSOT, 1989.

Graham, Billy. *Images of Christ.* Billy Graham Library Classics Collection. 1971; Charlotte, NC: Billy Graham Evangelistic Association, 2007. DVD.

_____. *The Jesus Generation.* Grand Rapids, MI: Zondervan, 1971.

Green, Joel B. *The Gospel of Luke.* New International Commentary on the New Testament. Grand Rapids, MI: Eerdmans, 1997.

Green, Joel B., Scot McKnight, and I. Howard Marshall, eds. *Dictionary of Jesus and the Gospels: A Compendium of Contemporary Biblical Scholarship.* Downers Grove, IL: InterVarsity, 1992.

Grinchenko, O. S., and V. L. O. "Iuda, brat Gospoden'" [Judas, the brother of the Lord]. In *Pravoslavnaya Entsiklopediya* [The Orthodox Encyclopedia], vol. 28, 380–387. Moscow: Tserkovno-nauchnyy tsentr "Pravoslavnaya Entsiklopediya," 2012.

Gundry, Robert H. *Matthew: A Commentary on His Handbook for a Mixed Church under Persecution.* 2nd ed. Grand Rapids, MI: Eerdmans, 1994.

Hahn, Ferdinand. *The Titles of Jesus in Christology: Their History in Early Christianity.* Translated by Harold Knight and George Ogg. London: Lutterworth, 1969.

Hannan, Margaret. *The Nature and Demands of the Sovereign Rule of God in the Gospel of Matthew.* London: T&T Clark, 2006.

Head, Peter M. *Christology and the Synoptic Problem: An Argument for Markan Priority.* Society for New Testament Studies Monograph Series 94. Cambridge: Cambridge University Press, 1997.

Hebrew Union College Jewish Institute of Religion. "Comprehensive Aramaic Lexicon Project." http://cal1.cn.huc.edu/.

Hengel, Martin. *Saint Peter: The Underestimated Apostle.* Translated by Thomas Trapp. Grand Rapids, MI: Eerdmans, 2010.

_____. *The Charismatic Leader and His Followers.* Translated by James D. G. Greig. Edited by John Riches. Edinburgh: T&T Clark, 1981.

Hobart, William Kirk. *The Medical Language of St. Luke.* Dublin, 1882.

Hoehner, Harold W. *Chronological Aspects of the Life of Christ*. Grand Rapids, MI: Zondervan, 1977.

Incigneri, Brian J. *The Gospel to the Romans: The Setting and Rhetoric of Mark's Gospel*. Leiden: Brill, 2003.

Jastrow, Marcus. *A Dictionary of the Targumim, the Talmud Babli and Yerushalmi, and the Midrashic Literature*. London: Luzac, 1903.

Jeremias, Joachim. *Jerusalem in the Time of Jesus*. Translated by F. H. Cave and C. H. Cave. London: SCM Press, 1991.

_____. *New Testament Theology: The Proclamation of Jesus*. New York, NY: Scribner, 1971.

Johnson, Luke Timothy. *The Writings of the New Testament: An Interpretation*. 3rd ed. Minneapolis, MN: Fortress, 2010.

Jung, Chang-Wook. *The Original Language of the Lukan Infancy Narrative*. London: T&T Clark International, 2004.

Karavidopoulos, Iōannēs. *Eisagogē stēn Kuinē Diathēkō* [Introduction to the New Testament]. Thessaloniki: Ekdoseis P. Pournara, 2007.

Kartashev, Anton V. *Vetkhozavetnaya bibleyskaya kritika* [Old Testament biblical criticism]. Paris, 1947.

Kasper, Walter. *Jesus the Christ* Translated by V. Green. New York, NY: Paulist Press, 1976.

Keener, Craig S. *The Gospel of John: A Commentary*. 2 vols. Peabody, MA: Hendrickson, 2010.

_____. *The Gospel of Matthew: A Socio-Rhetorical Commentary*. Grand Rapids, MI: Eerdmans, 2009.

_____. *The Historical Jesus of the Gospels*. Grand Rapids, MI: Eerdmans, 2009.

Kelber, Werner H. *The Oral and the Written Gospel: The Hermeneutics of Speaking and Writing in the Synoptic Tradition, Mark, Paul, and Q*. Philadelphia, PA: Fortress, 1983.

Kilpatrick, George Dunbar. *The Origins of the Gospel According to St. Matthew*. Oxford: Clarendon, 1946.

Kirill (Gundyaev), [Patriarch]. *Slovo pastyrya. Bog i chelovek. Istoriya spaseniya* [The pastor's word. God and man. The history of salvation]. Moscow: Izdatel'skiy sovet Russkoy pravoslavnoy tserkvi, 2004.

Kloppenborg, John S. *Excavating Q: The History and Setting of the Sayings Gospel*. Minneapolis, MN: Fortress, 2000.

_____. Q, *The Earliest Gospel: An Introduction to the Original Stories and Sayings of Jesus.* Louisville, KY: Westminster John Knox, 2008.

Koehler, Ludwig, and Walter Baumgartner. *Hebräisches und Aramäisches Lexikon zum Alten Testament.* 5 Lfg. and Supplementband. Leiden: Brill, 1967–1996.

Kwong, Ivan Shing Chung. *The Word Order of the Gospel of Luke: Its Foregrounded Messages.* Library of New Testament Studies 298. London: T&T Clark, 2005.

Lane, William L. *The Gospel According to Mark: The English Text with Introduction, Exposition, and Notes.* New International Commentary on the New Testament 2. Grand Rapids, MI: Eerdmans, 1974.

Lebedev, A. P. *Brat'ya Gospodni: Issledovaniya po istorii drevney Tserkvi* [The Brothers of the Lord: Studies in the history of the early Church]. 2nd ed. St. Petersburg: Izdatel'stvo Olega Abyshko, 2010.

Lee, David. *Luke's Stories of Jesus: Theological Reading of Gospel Narrative and the Legacy of Hans Frei.* Journal for the Study of the New Testament Supplement Series 185. Sheffield: Sheffield Academic Press, 1999.

Leisegang, Hans. "Der Gottmensch als Archetypus." In *Aus der Welt der Urbilder: Sonderband für C. G. Jung zum fünfundsiebzigsten Geburtstag, 26 Juli 1950,* edited by Olga Fröbe-Kapteyn, Eranos Jahrbuch 18, 9–45. Zürich: Rhein-Verlag, 1950.

Léon-Dufour, Xavier, ed. *Dictionary of Biblical Theology.* Translated under the direction of P. Joseph Cahill. Revised and translated by E. M. Stewart. 2nd ed. London: G. Chapman, 1988.

Leske, Adrian. "Jesus as a Ναζωραῖος." In *Resourcing New Testament Studies: Literary, Historical, and Theological Essays in Honor of David L. Dungan,* edited by Allan J. McNicol, David B. Peabody, and J. Samuel Subramanian, 69–81. New York, NY: T&T Clark International, 2009.

Linnemann, Eta. *Biblical Criticism on Trial: How Scientific is "Scientific Theology"?* Translated by Robert Yarbrough. Grand Rapids, MI: Kregel, 1998.

Litfin, Bryan. "Origen." In *Shapers of Christian Orthodoxy: Engaging with Early and Medieval Theologians,* edited by Bradley G. Green, 108–152. Downers Grove, IL: InterVarsity, 2010.

Luz, Ulrich. *Das Evangelium nach Matthaus.* Bd. 1. Zurich: Benziger, 1985.

_____. *Studies in Matthew.* Translated by Rosemary Selle. Grand Rapids, MI: Eerdmans, 2005.

MacArthur, John F. *Matthew 1–7*. The MacArthur New Testament Commentary. Chicago, IL: Moody Bible Institute, 1985.

Mack, Burton L. *The Lost Gospel: The Book of Q & Christian Origins*. San Francisco, CA: HarperSanFrancisco, 1993.

Maluf, Leonard J. "Zechariah's 'Benedictus' (Luke 1:68–79): A New Look at a Familiar Text." In *New Perspectives on the Nativity*, edited by Jeremy Corley, 47–66. New York, NY: T&T Clark, 2009.

Manson, William. *Jesus the Messiah*. London: Hodder and Stoughton, 1943.

Marcus, Joel. *Mark: A New Translation with Introduction and Commentary*. New York, NY: Doubleday, 1999.

_____. *Mark: A New Translation and Commentary*. Vol. 2, *Mark 8–16*. The Anchor Yale Bible 27A. New Haven, CT: Yale University Press, 2009.

_____. *The Way of the Lord: Christological Exegesis of the Old Testament in the Gospel of Mark*. Louisville, KY: Westminster / John Knox Press, 1992.

Mauser, Ulrich. *Christ in the Wilderness: The Wilderness Theme in the Second Gospel and Its Basis in the Biblical Tradition*. Studies in Biblical Theology First Series 39. Eugene, OR: Wipf & Stock, 2009. First published 1963 by SCM Press.

McDonnell, Kilian. *The Baptism of Jesus in the Jordan: The Trinitarian and Cosmic Order of Salvation*. Collegeville, MN: Liturgical Press, 1996.

McGrath, Alister E. *Reformation Thought: An Introduction*. 4th ed. Oxford: Wiley-Blackwell, 2012.

Meier, John P. *A Marginal Jew: Rethinking the Historical Jesus*. Vol. 1, *The Roots of the Problem and the Person*. New York, NY: Doubleday, 1991.

_____. *A Marginal Jew: Rethinking the Historical Jesus*. Vol. 2, *Mentor, Message, and Miracles*. New York, NY: Doubleday, 1994.

_____. *A Marginal Jew: Rethinking the Historical Jesus*. Vol. 3, *Companions and Competitors*. Anchor Bible Reference Library. New York, NY: Doubleday, 2001.

_____. *A Marginal Jew: Rethinking the Historical Jesus*. Vol. 4, *Law and Love*. Anchor Yale Bible Reference Library. New Haven, CT: Yale University Press, 2009.

_____. *Matthew*. Collegeville, MN: Liturgical Press, 1980.

_____. *The Vision of Matthew: Christ, Church, and Morality in the First Gospel*. Eugene, OR: Wipf & Stock, 2004.

Men, Alexander. *Son of Man*. Translated by Samuel Brown. Torrance, CA: Oakwood Publications, 1998.

Metzger, Bruce M. *A Textual Commentary on the Greek New Testament: A Companion Volume to the United Bible Societies' Greek New Testament*. 3rd ed. Stuttgart: Deutsche Bibelgesellschaft, 1971.

_____. *The Canon of the New Testament: Its Origin, Development, and Significance*. Oxford: Clarendon, 1987.

_____. *The New Testament: Its Background, Growth, and Content*. 2nd ed. Nashville, TN: Abingdon Press, 1983.

Metzger, Bruce M., and Ehrman, Bart D. *The Text of the New Testament: Its Transmission, Corruption, and Restoration*. Oxford: Oxford University Press, 2005.

Meyendorff, John. *Vvedenie v svyatootecheskoye bogoslovie: konspekty lektsiy* [Introduction to patristic theology: lecture notes]. Translated by Larissa Volokhonskaya. Klin: Khristianskaya zhizn', 2001.

Morris, Leon. *The Gospel According to Matthew*. The Pillar New Testament Commentary. Grand Rapids, MI: Eerdmans; Leicester: Inter-Varsity Press, 1992.

Mowinckel, Sigmund. *He That Cometh: The Messiah Concept in the Old Testament and Later Judaism*. Translated by G. W. Anderson. Grand Rapids, MI: Eerdmans, 2005.

Murphy-O'Connor, Jerome. *The Holy Land: An Oxford Archaeological Guide from Earliest Times to 1700*. 5th ed. Oxford: Oxford University Press, 2008.

Nebol'sin, A. S. "Brat'ya Gospodni [The Brothers of the Lord]." In *Pravoslavnaya entsiklopediya* [The Orthodox Encyclopedia], vol. 6, 213–215. Moscow: Tserkovno-nauchnyy tsentr "Pravoslavnaya Entsiklopediya," 2003.

Neusner, Jacob. *Sifra: An Analytical Translation*. Vol. 2, *Sav, Shemini, Tazria, Negaim, Mesora, and Zabim*. Atlanta, GA: Scholars Press, 1988.

Nolland, John. *The Gospel of Matthew: A Commentary on the Greek Text*. The New International Greek Testament Commentary. Grand Rapids, MI: Eerdmans, 2005.

Orton, David E. *The Understanding Scribe*. Sheffield: JSOT Press, 1989.

Painter, John. *Just James: The Brother of Jesus in History and Tradition*. Edinburgh: T&T Clark, 1997.

Parker, Richard A., and Waldo H. Dibberstein. *Babylonian Chronology 626 B.C.–A.D. 45*. Studies in Ancient Oriental Civilization 24. Chicago, IL: University of Chicago Press, 1942.

Peabody, David B., Lamar Cope, and Allan J. McNicol, eds. *One Gospel from Two: Mark's Use of Matthew and Luke: A Demonstration by the Research Team of the International Institute for Renewal of Gospel Studies.* Harrisburg, PA: Trinity Press International, 2002.

Pentiuc, Eugen J. *Long-Suffering Love: A Commentary on Hosea with Patristic Annotations.* Brookline, MA: Holy Cross Orthodox Press, 2002.

Perrin, Norman. *The Kingdom of God in the Teaching of Jesus.* Philadelphia, PA: Westminster Press, 1963.

Peterson, Dwight N. *The Origins of Mark: The Markan Community in Current Debate.* Leiden: Brill, 2000.

Pines, Shlomo. *An Arabic Version of the Testimonium Flavianum and its Implications.* Jerusalem: The Israel Academy of Sciences and Humanities, 1971.

Plummer, Alfred. *A Critical and Exegetical Commentary on the Gospel According to St. Luke.* International Critical Commentary 28. New York, NY: Charles Scribner's Sons, 1896.

Pokorný, Petr, and Ulrich Heckel. *Einleitung in das Neue Testament: seine Literatur und Theologie im Überblick.* Tübingen: Mohr Siebeck, 2007.

Ponomarev, A. V. "Kviriniy" [Quirinius]. In *Pravoslavnaya entsiklopedia* [The Orthodox Encyclopedia], vol. 32, 299–302. Moscow: Tserkovno-nauchnyy tsentr "Pravoslavnaya Entsiklopediya," 2013.

Price, Robert M. *The Incredible Shrinking Son of Man: How Reliable is the Gospel Tradition?* Amherst, NY: Prometheus Books, 2003.

Pudussery, Paul S. "Discipleship, A Call to Suffering and Glory: An Exegetico-Theological Study of Mk 8,27–9,1; 13,9–13 and 13,24–27." Ph.D. diss., Pontifical Urban University, Rome, 1987. 18.

Puig i Tàrrech, Armand. *Jesus: A Biography.* Waco, TX: Baylor University Press, 2011.

Reicke, Bo. "Synoptic Prophecies on the Destruction of Jerusalem." In *Studies in the New Testament and Early Christian Literature: Essays in Honor of Allen P. Wikgren,* edited by David Edward Aune, 121–134. Leiden: Brill, 1972.

Reinhartz, Adele. *Caiaphas the High Priest.* Studies on Personalities of the New Testament. Edited by Moody D. Smith. Minneapolis, MN: Fortress Press, 2013.

Richardson, Alan. *The Miracle-Stories of the Gospels.* London: SCM Press, 1941.

Robinson, John A. T. *The Priority of John.* Edited by J. F. Coakley. London: SCM Press, 1985.

Roskam, H. N. *The Purpose of the Gospel of Mark in Its Historical and Social Context.* Leiden: Brill, 2004.

Rowe, C. Kavin. *Early Narrative Christology: The Lord in the Gospel of Luke.* Grand Rapids, MI: Baker Academic, 2006.

Sanders, E. P. *The Historical Figure of Jesus.* London: Penguin Press, 1993.

Scheide, William Hinsdale. *The Virgin Birth: A Proposal as to the Source of a Gospel Tradition.* Princeton, NJ: Princeton Theological Seminary, 1995.

Schlatter, Adolf von. *Der Evangelist Matthäus: seine Sprache, seine Ziel, seine Selbstständigkeit.* Stuttgart: Calwer Verlag, 1929.

Schnabel, Eckhard J. "The Silence of Jesus: The Galilean Rabbi Who Was More Than a Prophet." In *Authenticating the Words of Jesus,* edited by Bruce Chilton and Craig A. Evans, 203–257. Leiden: Brill, 1999.

Schnackenburg, Rudolf. *Jesus in the Gospels: A Biblical Christology.* Translated by O. C. Dean. Louisville, KY: Westminster John Knox Press, 1995.

———. *The Gospel of Matthew.* Translated by Robert R. Barr. Grand Rapids, MI: Eerdmans, 2002.

Schönborn, Christoph. *God Sent His Son: A Contemporary Christology.* Translated by Henry Taylor. San Francisco, CA: Ignatius Press, 2010.

Schulthess, Friedrich. *Lexicon Syropalaestinum.* Berlin: G. Reimer, 1903.

Schürer, Emil. *The History of the Jewish People in the Age of Jesus Christ (175 B.C.– A.D. 135).* Revised and edited by Geza Vermes, Fergus Millar, and Matthew Black. Rev. English ed. 3 vols. in 4 pts. Edinburgh: T&T Clark, 1973–1987.

Sergiy (Spasskiy), [Archbishop]. *Polny mesyatseslov Vostoka* [The complete Menaion of the East]. 3 vols. Moscow: Pravoslavnyy palomnik, 1997.

Shargunov, Aleksandr. *Evangelie dnya* [The Gospel of the day]. 2nd ed. 2 vols. Moscow: Izdatel'stvo Sretenskogo monastyrya, 2010.

Sigal, Phillip. *The Halakhah of Jesus of Nazareth According to the Gospel of Matthew,* Studies in Biblical Literature 18. Atlanta, GA: Society of Biblical Literature, 2007.

Sloyan, Gerard S. *The Crucifixion of Jesus: History, Myth, Faith.* Minneapolis, MN: Fortress Press, 1995.

Smith, R. Payne. *Thesaurus Syriacus.* 2 vols. Oxford: Clarendon, 1879–1901.

Soares Prabhu, George M. *The Formula Quotations in the Infancy Narrative of Matthew.* Analecta Biblica 63. Rome: Biblical Institute Press, 1976.

Sokoloff, Michael. *A Dictionary of Jewish Babylonian Aramaic of the Talmudic and Geonic Periods*. Dictionaries of Talmud, Midrash and Targum 3. Ramat-Gan: Bar Ilan University Press, 2002.

_____. *A Dictionary of Jewish Palestinian Aramaic of the Byzantine Period*. Dictionaries of Talmud, Midrash and Targum 2. Ramat-Gan: Bar Ilan University Press, 1990.

Spencer, Patrick E. *Rhetorical Texture and Narrative Trajectories of the Lukan Galilean Ministry Speeches: Hermeneutical Appropriation by Authorial Readers of Luke-Acts*. London: T&T Clark, 2007.

Stanton, Graham N. *Jesus of Nazareth in New Testament Preaching*. Society for New Testament Studies Monograph Series 27. London: Cambridge University Press, 1974.

_____. *A Gospel for a New People: Studies in Matthew*. Edinburgh: T&T Clark, 1992.

Stendahl, Krister. *The School of St. Matthew and Its Use of the Old Testament*. Uppsala: C. W. K. Gleerup, 1954.

Strauss, David Friedrich. *The Life of Jesus for the People*. Authorized trans. 2nd ed. 2 vols. London: Williams and Norgate, 1879.

Streeter, Burnett Hillman. *The Four Gospels: A Study in Origins: Treating of the Manuscript Tradition, Sources, Authorship, and Dates*. London: Macmillan, 1964.

Tannehill, Robert C. *Luke*. Nashville, TN: Abingdon, 1996.

Taylor, Vincent. *The Formation of the Gospel Tradition: Eight Lectures*. 2nd ed. London: Macmillan, 1935.

Telford, W. R. *The Theology of the Gospel of Mark*. New Testament Theology. Cambridge: Cambridge University Press, 1999.

Theissen, Gerd. *The Gospels in Context: Social and Political History in the Synoptic Tradition*. Translated by Linda M. Maloney. Minneapolis, MN: Fortress, 1991.

Thompson, Michael B. "The Holy Internet: Communication Between Churches in the First Christian Generation." In *The Gospels for All Christians: Rethinking the Gospel Audiences*, edited by Richard Bauckham, 49–70. Grand Rapids, MI: Eerdmans, 1998.

Thompson, William G. *Matthew's Advice to a Divided Community: Mt. 17:22–18:35*. Rome: Biblical Institute Press, 1970.

Tkachenko, A. A. "Evangelie. Strukturno-tematicheskaya kompozitsiya Evangeliy. Zhanr i literaturnye formy. Proiskhozhdenie i istochniki Evangeliy" [The Gospels. The structural and thematic composition of the Gospels. Genre and literary forms. Origin and sources of the Gospels]. In *Pravoslavnaya entsiklopediya* [The Orthodox Encyclopedia], vol. 16, 646–680. Moscow: Tserkovno-nauchnyy tsentr "Pravoslavnaya Entsiklopediya," 2007.

Trubetskoy, S. N. *Uchenie o Logose v ego istorii* [The doctrine of the Logos in its history]. Moscow: Izdatel'stvo ACT, 2000.

Tuckett, Christopher M. *Q and the History of Early Christianity: Studies on Q.* Edinburgh, T&T Clark, 1996.

Turner, C. H. "Markan Usage: Notes, Critical and Exegetical on the Second Gospel." In *The Language and Style of the Gospel of Mark: An Edition of C. H. Turner's "Notes on Markan Usage" Together with Other Comparable Studies,* edited by J. K. Elliott, 3–146. Leiden: Brill, 1993.

Turner, David L. *Matthew.* Baker Exegetical Commentary on the New Testament. Grand Rapids, MI: Baker Academic, 2008.

Tyson, Joseph B., and Thomas R. W. Longstaff. *Synoptic Abstract.* The Computer Bible 15. Wooster, OH: Biblical Research Associates, 1978.

Vermes, Géza. *The Authentic Gospel of Jesus.* London: Penguin, 2004.

_____. *The Changing Faces of Jesus.* London: Penguin, 2001.

Viviano, Benedict T. *Matthew and His World: The Gospel of the Open Jewish Christians.* Fribourg: Academic Press, 2007.

_____. *What Are They Saying About Q?* New York, NY: Paulist Press, 2013.

Voorwinde, Stephen. *Jesus' Emotions in the Fourth Gospel: Human or Divine?* Journal for the Study of the New Testament Supplement Series 284. London, T&T Clark, 2005.

Vorster, Willem S. *Speaking of Jesus: Essays on Biblical Language, Gospel Narrative and the Historical Jesus.* Edited by J. Eugene Botha. Supplements to Novum testamentum 92. Leiden: Brill, 1999.

Weinreich, Otto. "Antikes Gottmenschentum," *Neue Jahrbuücher für Wissenschaft und Jugendbildung* 2 (1926): 633–651.

Wenham, John. *Redating Matthew, Mark and Luke: A Fresh Assault on the Synoptic Problem.* Downers Grove, IL: InterVarsity, 1992.

Wink, Walter. *John the Baptist in the Gospel Tradition.* Society for New Testament Studies Monograph Series 7. London: Cambridge University Press, 1968.

Wortley, John, trans. *Give Me a Word: The Alphabetical Sayings of the Desert Fathers*. Popular Patristics Series 52. Yonkers, NY: St Vladimir's Seminary Press, 2014.

Wright, N. T. *Jesus and the Victory of God*, Christian Origins and the Question of God 2. Minneapolis, MN: Fortress, 1996.

_____. *Judas and the Gospel of Jesus: Have We Missed the Truth about Christianity?* Grand Rapids, MI: Baker Books, 2006.

_____. *What Saint Paul Really Said: Was Paul of Tarsus the Real Founder of Christianity?* Grand Rapids, MI: Eerdmans, 1997.

Yamaguchi, Satoko. *Mary and Martha: Women in the World of Jesus*. Maryknoll, NY: Orbis Books, 2002.

Yamasaki, Gary. *John the Baptist in Life and Death: Audience-Oriented Criticism of Matthew's Narrative*. Journal for the Study of the New Testament Supplement Series 167. Sheffield: Sheffield Academic Press, 1998.

Yang, Yong-Eui. *Jesus and the Sabbath in Matthew's Gospel*. Journal for the Study of the New Testament Supplement series 139. Sheffield: Sheffield Academic Press, 1997.

Yanovskaya, Lidiya. *Tvorcheskiy put' Mikhaila Bulgakova* [The creative career of Mikhail Bulgakov]. Moscow: Sov. Pisatel', 1983.